GEORGE BERKELEY

GEORGE BERKELEY

A Study of
His Life and Philosophy

BY

JOHN WILD

NEW YORK
RUSSELL & RUSSELL · INC
1962

PREFACE

THE pages which follow are a study of Berkeley based upon all the evidence available for an understanding of his life and thought. In form as well as content it has grown out of an attempt to meet the demands of a suggestion made by Berkeley himself. "I could wish," he wrote his friend Johnson in 1730, "that all the things I have published on these philosophical subjects were read in the order wherein I have published them, to take in the design and connexion of them, and a second time with a critical eye, adding your own thought and observation upon every part as you went along." In the case of Berkeley there can be no rigid separation of the individual treatises from the character of their author. Any account of his intellectual development without some understanding of his life must remain as hopelessly artificial as any account of his life without some understanding of his philosophy. The "design and connexion" of his works is the man himself.

Berkeley has long been regarded as a difficult author. The fertility of his ideas from youth onwards, his intense absorption in the technical minutiae of particular problems, and finally the severe criticism to which he constantly subjected himself, have stood in the way of a conclusive understanding. Actually, he has been regarded in the tradition of "history" as an immature Hume, an untimely "Platonist," or a confused mixture of the two. Even though it may be impossible to accept these all too simple classifications as finally adequate, Berkeley's commentators owe a great debt to the painstaking researches of the late Campbell Fraser, who added the weight of his authority to this tradition, but who also first discerned the importance of the *Siris* as the final expression of that *philosophia prima* for which Berkeley's earlier writings only paved the way. Fraser, however, never pursued this discernment to the point of placing the separate works in their original "order" and of thus comprehending them as phases of a single development. His *Life and Letters* (1871), the standard biography of Berkeley, was unfortunately written before the discovery of the Percival letters, and the work in which Fraser later gave a summary of these all-important letters (*Berkeley*, 1881) was restricted to the limits of a short sketch.

In preparing the present study I have fortunately been able to make use of all the available manuscript material both in this country and abroad. I am particularly grateful to Mr. A. A. Luce for placing at my disposal the detailed results of his recent researches and discoveries of manuscript remains, letters, and other Berkeleiana. The three unpublished sermons printed in the Appendix were found among the Chapman manuscripts in the British Museum. They are included in the present volume because of their importance in understanding the nature and course of Berkeley's intellectual development. The almost universal neglect of the sermons by previous commentators must be attributed to that *horror theologiae* which has for the last century seriously impeded historical study both in Europe and in America.

I wish to take this opportunity of expressing my thanks to Professor F. H. Anderson of the University of Toronto for his helpful criticism of the manuscript, and to my wife for her constant assistance. To the Guggenheim Foundation, through whose aid I was enabled to investigate the European manuscript material, to the American Council of Learned Societies and the Harvard Department of Philosophy, which have made possible the publication of this volume, and finally to the Harvard University Press for its generous cooperation, I owe a heavy debt of gratitude.

CAMBRIDGE, MASSACHUSETTS,
    January 2, 1936.

CONTENTS

PART I

THE REVELATION OF THE CONCRETE

PART II

CONCRETE AND ABSTRACT REASON. THE EARLY SYSTEM

PART III

SCEPTICISM AND FAITH. THE EMERGENCE OF THE PRACTICAL

BIBLIOGRAPHICAL NOTE

All references to Berkeley's works in the text, unless otherwise specified, are to *The Works of George Berkeley* in four volumes, edited by A. C. Fraser, Oxford, 1901 (F. i, ii, iii, iv). The following abbreviations also will be generally employed.

P.O.	*Passive Obedience*, F. iv, pp. 101 ff.
G. Ess.	*Essays in the Guardian*, F. iv, pp. 139 ff.
J.J................	*A Letter to Sir John James, Bart. on the Differences between the Roman and Anglican Churches*, F. iv, pp. 521 ff.
N.T.V.	*An Essay towards a New Theory of Vision*, F. i, pp. 277 ff.
N.T.V.V.	*The Theory of Vision, or Visual Language Vindicated and Explained*
Pr.	*A Treatise concerning the Principles of Human Knowledge, Part I*, F. i, pp. 233 ff.
Pr. Int.	*Author's Introduction to the Principles of Human Knowledge*, F. i, pp. 237 ff.
Pr. Ms.	*Rough Draft of the Introduction*, F. iii, pp. 357 ff.
3 D. (also 1D., 2D., 3D.)	*Three Dialogues between Hylas and Philonous*, F. i, pp. 373 ff.
D.M.	*De Motu*, F. i, pp. 501 ff.
Alc.	*Alciphron or the Minute Philosopher in Seven Dialogues*, F. ii, pp. 31 ff.
An.	*The Analyst or a Discourse Addressed to an Infidel Mathematician*, F. iii, pp. 17 ff.
S.	*Siris, a Chain of Philosophical Reflections and Inquiries concerning the Virtues of Tar-Water*, F. iii, pp. 141 ff.
C.B.J. or J.	*Berkeley's Commonplace Book*, ed. by G. A. Johnston, London, Faber & Faber, 1930
C.B.H. or H.	*Philosophisches Tagebuch*, ed. by Hecht, Leipzig, Meiner, 1926

Unless otherwise stated, Berkeley's letters to Percival refer to Rand, *The Correspondence of George Berkeley and Sir John Percival*, Cambridge, 1914; and his letters to Prior, to Fraser, *Life and Letters of George Berkeley*, Oxford, 1871 (Life).

PART I

THE REVELATION OF THE CONCRETE

"It seems to me that will and understanding — volitions and ideas — cannot be severed, that either cannot be possibly without the other." (J. 825.) "The *concrete* of the Will and Understanding I must call Mind." (J. 725.)

CHAPTER I

THE NEW PHILOSOPHY

GEORGE BERKELEY was born March 12, 1684 at Kilkrin near Thomastown in Ireland. Of pure English descent on his father's side,[1] he was always a loyal subject of the King. He occasionally refers to himself as an Irishman,[2] but never as a "native Irishman."[3] There was a connection with the English family of Berkeley, but a reference in 1713 to Lord Berkeley of Stratton as simply "a Lord of my name"[4] proves that this was remote.[5] His grandfather expended a large fortune in the service of King Charles I, remitted large sums of money to Charles II, and in return (as Berkeley's daughter-in-law, Eliza Berkeley, records) was made "collector of the port of ————," which occasioned the old gentleman's leaving his malediction on any descendant of his who should ever in any way assist any tyrant."[6]

On the 17th of July, 1696, he was entered at Kilkenny School, and placed in the second class, a sign of unusual precocity. Aside from this fact, very little is known concerning his boyhood. It is certain, however, that he possessed from the first an active and sceptical turn of mind. "I was distrustful at eight years old," reads one of the memoranda in the *Commonplace Book*, "and consequently by nature disposed for . . . new doctrines."[7] This restlessness of mind and disposition remained a fundamental trait throughout the course of his development,

[1] Through his mother, he was related to the family of General Wolfe, the conqueror of Quebec. Cf. Monck Berkeley, *Poems*, p. ccclxxiii, note.

[2] J., 938 and 939, and *Word to the Wise*, F. iv, p. 545, "my countrymen."

[3] Cf. Cave of *Dunmore*, F. iv, p. 80, Qu. 91 and 92, and *Word to the Wise*, F. iv, p. 549.

[4] Letter to Percival, May 7, 1713.

[5] His daughter-in-law quotes Swift as introducing Berkeley to the Earl in the following words: "My Lord, here is a fine young gentleman of your family. I can assure your Lordship it is a much greater honour to *you* to be related to him, than it is to him to be related to you." The

always interesting but not overly accurate Mary Granville — Mrs. Delany — states that Berkeley was a "cadet of the family of Earl Berkeley." *Autobiography and Correspondence of Mary Granville*, vol. I, p. 319, note. See also Monck Berkeley, *Poems*, p. clxxix.

[6] George Monck Berkeley, *Poems*, Preface (by Eliza Berkeley), p. ccclxxii, note. This preface is full of valuable biographical material. The book itself is very rare, most of the original edition having been lost in the fire which destroyed the Nichols printing house early in the 19th century. There is one copy in the British Museum.

[7] J., 275.

leading him constantly into conflict with established opinions. So strong did this tendency become in his youth that he sometimes found it necessary while at college to admonish himself privately. "N.B.," he writes at one point in his diary, "to rein in ye satyrical nature." [8] That this "satyrical nature" brought him into opposition with ideas of the most unimpeachable authority is indicated by his further warnings "to confute the mathematicians with the utmost civility & respect, not to stile them Nihilarians, &c.," [9] and "to use utmost caution not to give the least handle of offence to the Church or Church-men." [10]

We must not suppose, however, that Berkeley's scepticism led him, as is so often the case, only to the point of questioning the views of others. His "distrust" was from the first too intense to be utilized as a convenient cloak for dogmatism. The critical spirit which hindered him from readily accepting the beliefs of others also discouraged any comforting confidence in himself. His youthful diary is full of caustic self-criticism. "I am young, I am an upstart, I am a pretender, I am vain," he writes,[11] "but one thing I know I am not guilty of, . . . I do not adhere to any opinion because it is an old one, a received one, . . . or one that I have spent much time in the study and cultivation of."

This readiness to doubt himself perhaps explains why his tendency to disagreement did not prevent his forming many friendships which led him to a further appreciation of the dangers of absorption in a private dogmatism. There is apt to be a grain of truth even in an "erroneous" position which it is essential to recognize and explain. Hence, as Berkeley writes, "he that would bring another to his opinion must seem to harmonize with him at first, and humour him in his own way of thinking," [12] a habit which has occasionally led to misunderstandings.[13]

The tendency to turn his scepticism against himself as well as others led Berkeley in his earliest youth not only to recognize the necessity of respect for the opinions of those with whom he disagreed, but also for truths possibly altogether out of his reach. "For my part," he says, "I think it is . . . irrational to

[8] J., 643.
[9] J., 642.
[10] J., 727. Mr. G. A. Johnston regards this as evidence of a "deliberate decision not to annoy the Church, in order to avoid the possibility of prejudice to his own

chance of advancement." *Development of Berkeley's Philosophy*, p. 332.
[11] J., 464.
[12] Brit. Mus. Add. Ms. 39304. Cf. F. i, p. 92.
[13] As in the N. T. V., where Berkeley

pretend to dispute at, cavil, and ridicule holy mysteries, — i.e. propositions about things that are altogether above our knowledge." [14] It was this same dissatisfaction with the limitations of theory, no doubt, that led him at first to seek instruction from the immediate and seemingly unquestionable "facts" of concrete experience. Here also, as well as perhaps in the mysteries, was a field apparently free from the endless uncertainties of speculation. Popular tradition has insisted upon regarding Berkeley as a "vague" and "romantic" dreamer, and it has been alleged that he was given to the reading of fairy-tales and to fantastic imaginings. One biographer, Duncombe, actually convinced himself of the truth of the prevalent belief which had worked its way into book-sellers' catalogues, that Berkeley was the author of the *Adventures of Signor Gaudentio di Lucca*, a popular romance of the time.[15] Only after the express statement of members of the family that not one of them had even read the work did he publicly retract this view.[16] All the available evidence points to a directly opposite tendency in Berkeley's character. His wife, in fact, definitely stated that he always strongly disliked the reading of romances.[17] One anecdote recounted of his early youth, while it may be partly fanciful, at least testifies to his desire for immediate first-hand experience. After witnessing an execution, he returned home, wondering what "pains and symptoms a malefactor felt upon such an occasion." Consequently he made his friend Contarini string him up to the ceiling, and the experiment did not terminate until he became unconscious. When "brought around," he said, "Bless my heart, Contarini, you have quite ruffled my band." Contarini declined his turn.[18]

There are, however, many less dubious indications of that singularly concrete turn of mind which led him to question all theoretical prejudices and prepossessions. It is manifest in the intense curiosity with which, as a fourteen year old boy, he explored the pillars and passages of the Cave of Dunmore,[19]

---

speaks throughout in terms of the "vulgar error" that tangible objects "exist without the mind." Cf. Pr., sec. 44.

[14] J., 732.

[15] *Biog. Brit.* Cf. *Retrospective Review*, vol. 4, p. 332, and *Notes and Queries*, vol. II, pp. 327–328. See *Bibliography*.

[16] *Biog. Brit.*, vol. III, Corr. and Add., p. 252.

[17] "It is not true . . . that Dr. Berkeley was much addicted to the reading of romances. On the contrary, he did very strongly and at all times, dislike them, regarding them as no better than fooleries." *Ibid*.

[18] Annual Register, 1763. "Memoirs of the late Dr. Berkeley, Bishop of Cloyne," p. 2.

[19] Molyneux Papers, Trinity College Ms. Also cf. F. iv, p. 78.

in the pains he took on his Italian tour in clambering over mountains and creeping into caverns to investigate their natural
history, and finally in the daring which led him to view an eruption of Vesuvius at first hand, a feat that almost cost him his
life. "I scarce remember to have discoursed with him," says
his friend, Thomas Blackwell, "on that Art, liberal or mechanic,
of which he knew not more than the ordinary practitioners.
With the widest views he descended into a minute detail, and
begrudged neither Pains nor Expence for the means of information. . . . I have known him sit for hours in Forges and
Founderies to inspect their successive operations." [20]

TRINITY COLLEGE

Berkeley entered Trinity College March 21, 1700 at the age
of sixteen years. "Here he soon began to be looked upon as the
greatest genius, or the greatest dunce, in the whole university;
those also who were slightly acquainted with him, took him for
a fool, but those who shared his most intimate friendship looked
upon him as a prodigy of learning and good nature." [21] He
seems at once to have given evidence of intellectual brilliancy,
since he was made a scholar of the House in 1702. In 1704 he
received the bachelor's degree, and the master's degree in 1707,
while on June 9 of the same year he was admitted to a fellowship, after an examination passed with great distinction. He
was tutor in the College from 1707 to 1724, though after 1712
in name only. He became sub-lecturer in 1710, junior dean in
1710 and 1711, and in 1712 (when only twenty-eight years of
age) junior Greek lecturer.

The Trinity College of Berkeley's day was physically just
recovering from the difficulties of the revolution, during which
the halls were used as barracks by James I. Several new buildings were under construction. But the spirit of the new century was not content to express itself only in the formal lines
of its "classic" architecture. The "new ideas" of Descartes
and Malebranche, Locke and Newton, were also gaining headway against the traditional scholastic compendia, and the study
of pure physics and mathematics had been introduced into the
curriculum. Many minds were being excited by the successful
application of the new mathematics of such "moderns" as

[20] Thomas Blackwell, *Memoirs of the*
Court of Augustus, vol. 2, p. 277.   [21] Annual Register, 1763.

Galileo, Kepler, Copernicus, Newton, and Descartes. Soon after his entrance into the College, Berkeley plunged with great enthusiasm into the study of mathematics under the guidance of his tutor, the Reverend John Hall.[22] "By his exhortations," Berkeley says, "I was excited to the delightful study of mathematics."[23] This discipline was the object of his first deep intellectual interest, to which he devoted himself at intervals throughout his life. The earliest researches resulted in two mathematical treatises, published anonymously in Latin in 1707, but written at least two years earlier.[24] While they possess little intrinsic value, they show ingenuity, and are of significance in relation to his later development, since this early enthusiasm soon gave way to a more distinctly critical attitude toward "the science."[25]

The extent of this early interest in mathematics has not been sufficiently recognized. He writes with particular eloquence concerning algebra. "Through all these [the arts and sciences]," he says, "is diffused the wonderful power of algebra. It is styled by all, the great, the wonderful art, the highest pinnacle of human knowledge, the kernel and key of all mathematics; and, by some, the foundation of all sciences."[26] Newton is referred to as the most eminent man in the world.[27] The really noteworthy feature of these juvenile studies, however, is the attempt to define and state the basic principles of arithmetical reasoning, which the author believed had been neglected. "Most students in mathematics," he writes, "whilst they carefully and successfully master the demonstrations of theorems of inferior utility leave untouched the principles and reasonings of arithmetical operations, though these last are of such efficacy and value, that they give the most important aid, not only to

[22] Hall, the Vice Provost of the College, was not, however, primarily a mathematician. That his guidance was external and hortatory rather than specific and technical is indicated by the following passage from "A Defence of Free-Thinking in Mathematics," F. iii, p. 72: "And, as I never had a master in Mathematics, so I fairly followed the dictates of my own mind in examining and censuring the authors I read upon that subject, with the same freedom that I used upon any other; taking nothing upon trust, and believing that no writer was infallible."

[23] *Arithmetica*, F. iv, pp. 6–7.

[24] "Proinde e re tyronum futurum ratus, si haec mea qualiacunque in lucem emitterem, ea postquam, si minus omnia, pleraque certe per integrum fere triennium in scriniis delituerint, publici juris tacio." *Arithmetica*, Praefatio, F. iv, p. 5.

[25] C. B. J., 389–391 *et passim*.

[26] "Quippe per hasce omnes diffunditur mirifica algebrae vis. Eadem apud omnes ars magna, mirabilis, supremus cognitionis humanae apex, universae matheseos nucleus et clavis, imo apud nonneminem scientiarum omnium fundamentum audit." *Arithm.*, F. iv, p. 60.

[27] Cf. *Arithm.*, F. iv, p. 48.

other branches of mathematics, but to the interests of men of all denominations." [28] In mathematical proofs Berkeley at last found precise answers to his questionings. He was deeply impressed by "the clear light of demonstration . . . wherefore," he says, "I am anxious that all votaries of mathematics should apply their minds to master the reasons and grounds of the rules of arithmetic." [29] While it cannot be maintained that these early treatises were profound, the general quest after the logical foundations of mathematics which they inaugurated certainly bore fruit. They finally made Berkeley realize how uncertain these foundations were and, after the discovery of his new principle, led to his early treatise *Of Infinites*, and to its later and profounder sequel, the *Analyst*, in which he maintains the necessity of an intelligible logical basis for the new *Calculus* as well as for mathematics itself.

During this period of uncritical enthusiasm Berkeley considers algebra as much more than a sign system, primarily of use in abbreviating and organizing vast ranges of knowledge into a convenient and workable form, though this is one of its essential uses. He accordingly suggests certain changes in mathematical symbolism which should be of value in the direction of symbolic efficiency, notably in the case of the signs for algebraic roots. But he speaks also with deep appreciation of the immediate aesthetic pleasure attending the manipulation of mathematical signs, and praises especially the absolute certainty of mathematical conclusions. He even expatiates upon the profound moral effect of mathematical studies, which "abstract the mind from the senses, sharpen and confirm the talents." [30] We shall attempt to trace Berkeley's mathematical views in detail in later chapters. It must suffice here merely to point out that in the course of his examination of the "reasons and grounds" of mathematics, particularly after the discovery of his "new principle" in 1707, he gained an insight into the "ab-

---

[28] ". . . hinc fit ut plerique mathesi operam navantes, dum bene multorum minoris usus theorematum demonstrationes studiose evolvunt, interea operationum arithmeticarum, quarum ea est vis et praestantia, ut non modo caeteris disciplinis mathematicis, verum etiam hominum cuiuscunque demum sortis usibus commodissime famulentur, principia ac rationes intactas praetereant." (*Arithm.*, Praefatio, F. iv, p. 5.)

[29] ". . . in clara demonstrationum luce. . . . Quamobrem omnes matheseos candidati ad regularum arithmeticae rationes ac fundamenta percipiendum animos adjungant, summopere velim et exoptem." *Arithm.*, Praefatio, F. iv, p. 6.

[30] ". . . quod mentem a sensibus abstrahant, ingeniumque acuant et figant." *Arithm.*, F. iv, p. 61.

stract" character of the science, which resulted in a considerable mitigation of his original enthusiasm. This significant development of thought can be traced in the course of the *Commonplace Book*, and in the short treatise, *Of Infinites*, written only two or three years after the *Miscellanea Mathematica*.

Such transitions were typical of Berkeley's development at Trinity College. He absorbed all the elements of the "new philosophy" with the greatest enthusiasm. He mastered them, not, however, in an uncritical, passive way, but maintaining his early "distrust." In the case of Locke, for instance, while there can be no question of his determining influence, the whole *Commonplace Book* is a standing proof of the continuous cross-fire of question and criticism to which the master was subjected by the pupil. As Berkeley himself puts it, "Such was the candour of this man that I persuade myself, were he alive, he would not be offended that I differ from him: seeing that even in so doing I follow his advice, viz., to use my own judgment, see with my own eyes, & not with another's." [31] He absorbed every aspect of the "new philosophy" without becoming a disciple, whether in agreement or disagreement, for even when opposing the new tendencies he did not attack Locke as a schoolman, nor Newton as a Cartesian, but preferred rather to forge his own weapons.

There was another phase of the contemporary fermentation brought forth by the scientific philosophy which must also have influenced Berkeley during his student days. This was the Deist controversy. Newton's *Principia* had appeared in 1687, Locke's *Essay* in 1690, and Toland's *Christianity Not Mysterious* in 1696. The result was a wave of liberalism and so-called rationalism in religion which caused a veritable furore. Toland's treatise was burned by the hangman in Dublin, censured by the Irish Parliament, and denounced from every pulpit. Balfour reports the comment of an Irish peer "as to his church" that "once he heard something there about his Saviour, Jesus Christ, but now all the discourse was about one John Toland." [32]

The universities, of course, took part in the strife, which Berkeley could not have altogether escaped, although there are no direct references to it in the *Commonplace Book*.[33] His nature

[31] C. B. J., 700.

[32] Biographical Introduction to the *Works* of Berkeley, ed. George Sampson, London, Bell, 1897.

[33] There is no reference to Toland in the C. B., but only a few short remarks concerning Epicureanism and Hobbism, and against "idolatry, whether of images or of gold, &c., that blinds the greatest part of the world, as well as of that shame-

was characterized by a certain religious seriousness combined with the critical tendency to which he himself refers as a general "distrust" of established opinions, but at this time these two phases of his personality were not integrated into any comprehensive system. Rather, they lay side by side as two superficially harmonized but opposed aspects of his thought. On the one hand, in matters of "Revelation," he says, "an humble implicit faith becomes us," [34] and yet he speaks disparagingly of "Scripture and possibility" as "the *onely* proofs with Malbranch." [35] He talks ambitiously of the "great articles of religion," [36] which are at regular intervals "proved with the clearest and most immediate evidence," [37] and then forgotten. Certain statements, nevertheless, show a genuine depth of religious feeling. "After all," he says in the *Principles*,[38] "what deserves the first place in our studies is the consideration of God and our Duty; which to promote, as it was the main drift and design of my labours, so shall I esteem them altogether useless and ineffectual if, by what I have said, I cannot inspire my readers with a pious sense of the presence of God." Berkeley seems to have had, however, on the whole, little difficulty in restricting his religious feelings to a proper and altogether subordinate station. One cannot read his early works without realizing that he is throughout this period essentially a Deist.

He speaks, as we have seen, with typical Deistic enthusiasm of mathematics and the mathematical method, and almost worships Newton. He takes great pains to show how all the truths of science may be reconciled with his principles. "Experimental philosophers," he says, "have nothing whereat to be offended in me." [39] His mind is dominated by a complete confidence in the power of "reason" to deal adequately with all issues. In this he was a confirmed adherent of the "new Philosophy," which was winning so many impressive triumphs. Thus, his *Principles*, as the title informs us, is to be an argument in which "the grounds of scepticism, atheism and irreligion" are to be

---

ful immorality that turns us into beasts." Cf. C. B. J., 407, also J., 17. Berkeley did not himself enter specifically into the Deist controversy, until his visit to London in 1713 when he read Collins' *Discourse*, and saw something of the Freethinkers' Clubs. Mr. G. A. Johnston's statement that "in the Commonplace Book the free-thinkers come in for much criticism" (*Development*, p. 328) is not

justified, and the argument that in his religious position Berkeley "had an eye" to "the main chance" (*Development*, p. 332 ff.), therefore loses its force.

[34] J., 732.
[35] J., 697.
[36] Three Dialogues, F. i, p. 478.
[37] *Ibid.*
[38] Sec. 156, F. i, p. 347.
[39] C. B. J., 402.

rationally "inquired into." It has not apparently occurred to him that one may be led into scepticism on other than strictly rational "grounds." The "design" of his *Three Dialogues*, as expressed in the title, is "plainly to demonstrate . . . the incorporeal nature of the Soul, and the Immediate Providence of a Deity in opposition to Sceptics and Atheists."

The silence of the *Commonplace Book* with respect to the Deist controversy, therefore, must be construed as meaning that Berkeley was himself at one with "the freethinkers," at least in his rationalism. He quickly discovered, however, what he came to call the "abstractness" of the mathematical method, and attempted to develop in its place a new, concrete logic which was to lead him eventually far beyond the limits of his early position. His youthful philosophical diary (the *Commonplace Book*) contains occasional instances of this method in actual operation, and hence yields us fragmentary glimpses, so to speak, of the "future" course of Berkeley's thought, and the strange regions that were to be revealed to him. In the earliest period of his life, however, the deeper forces of his personality remained latent, except for occasional outbursts to which he himself seemed almost oblivious. We must think of him at Trinity College as turning in relief from his mediaeval textbooks to plunge (with most of the other youthful spirits of the time) into the study of mathematics and the "new philosophy." That the inherent "distrust" which we have noted as a predominant trait in his character finally carried him beyond the "new," as it now carried him beyond the old, is an essential feature of his later development.

THE PHILOSOPHICAL SOCIETIES

Berkeley's earliest formative period as an undergraduate in Trinity College was followed by five or six years of extraordinary intellectual activity, during which he published his most famous works, and developed most of the original ideas historically associated with his name. We are able to follow the inception and growth of these ideas with unusual accuracy, owing to the survival of the *Commonplace Book*, a private diary which he kept during the years 1707 and 1708, and which now exists in the form of two note-books (A and B) bound together in a small quarto volume.[40] As a result of the painstaking re-

[40] Brit. Mus. Add. Ms. 39305. It is unfortunate that it is not possible to refer throughout the text to the most recent English edition of the C. B. by G. A.

search of Theodor Lorenz it has now been established that these note-books were bound in the wrong order and that the memoranda of B were as a matter of fact written before those of A. The present volume also contains two sets of statutes for discussion societies, a draft of a part of the Appendix to the *Miscellanea Mathematica* (1707), formulae for combinations in the *De Ludo Algebraico*, the description of the Cave of Dunmore published by Fraser, seven axioms and two problems of the *De Motu*, and a portion of a sermon. The fragments of the *De Motu* indicate that Berkeley had the volume with him during his second trip to Italy. It was probably at this time that the second part of the *Principles* was lost, and the bad condition of the manuscript, many pages of which seem to be water-marked, leads to the conjecture that these pages may have been carried with the lost papers, but happily saved through some accident. In view of the researches of Lorenz and Erdmann, the following explanation of the manuscript and its relation to the statutes is most probable.

Soon after receiving his degree in 1704, Berkeley seems to have played the leading part in the formation of a society to promote investigations in the "new philosophy" of Newton, Locke, and Malebranche. The first manuscript volume of the *Commonplace Book* contains the rules and statutes of this society, which was to meet every Thursday at five P.M. The existence of a "Keeper of the Rarities" seems to point to some experimental activity, but the primary purpose was to discuss, under the leadership of a certain member, subjects selected at previous meetings. The statutes are written in Berkeley's own handwriting,[41] and in the margin there is a note by him which reads,

Johnston, the only edition, save the confused version of Fraser, which is available to the English reader. Mr. Johnston's edition is regrettably inaccurate. A list of the more serious errors is given by R. I. Aaron in *Mind*, N.S., vol. XL, no. 160, pp. 455 ff. The German edition of Andreas Hecht (Berkeley: *Philosophisches Tagebuch, übersetzt, eingeleitet, und mit Anmerkungen* von A. Hecht, Leipzig, Meiner, 1926), which follows strictly the original numbering established by Lorenz and Erdmann (Erdmann, *Berkeley's Philosophie im Lichte seines wissenschaftlichen Tagebuchs*, Berlin, 1919) must be regarded at present as the standard edition, since it is

the only version which is approximately accurate. References in the text will refer both to Johnston (J) and Hecht (H). The Johnston edition is usable, if allowance is made for the corrections noted by Aaron.

[41] Fraser maintained that the statutes were *not* in Berkeley's hand. Certainly the writing is markedly different from that which follows in most of the *Commonplace Book*. I am inclined, however, to agree with A. A. Luce, *Hermathena*, vol. XXII, 1932, p. 7, that the statutes *are* written by Berkeley in his formal or "company" hand. This also seems to be the view of Hone and Rossi, *Bishop Berkeley*, p. 258.

"Agreed to Jan. 10, 1705," (new style, Jan. 21, 1706), probably the date of the first meeting. At this meeting, Berkeley apparently agreed to read a description of the cave of Dunmore,[42] which he had explored (purely for his diversion) "almost seven years before." In the Trinity College manuscript of this paper, which is not printed by Fraser, it is quite clear that he is addressing a gathering of the society, and there are several apologies for the unscientific character of the pleasure excursion described. The paper is remarkable, however, for the curiosity and courage shown by a fourteen year old boy in making such an expedition, as well as the almost romantic feeling for the awesomeness and grandeur of nature which it manifests.

The second series of statutes is dated almost a year later, December 7, 1706, and bears a more definitely philosophical character. It is indeed specifically stated that the purpose of this society is "to discourse on some part of the new philosophy," and the statutes are directly preceded by twenty-five subjects, or theses for discussion, in Berkeley's handwriting.[43] These themes are for the most part closely connected with Locke's philosophy, but they are aspects of this philosophy in which it is obvious that Berkeley would be particularly interested, and many of them imply criticisms which are clearly his own.[44] It is, of course, possible that these theses represent subjects which were actually discussed by the first society. The examination of the manuscript itself, however, indicates that they belong rather with the second set of statutes, and that they were probably written by Berkeley late in 1706 as projected topics for discussion during the ensuing year. This is also indicated by the more specifically philosophical character of the second set of statutes. Nothing is known concerning the membership of the two societies, nor the regularity of the meetings. Erdmann is inclined to be sceptical of the importance of the first, and suggests that the somewhat strict and elaborate rules brought an early end to this, as to so many other youthful enterprises.[45] S. P. Johnson, on the other hand, takes a more enthusiastic view, speaks of "a successful session," a widening "of their lines for the following year," and even suggests that the society may have been the nucleus which led to the revival

---

[42] This is suggested by the date "Jan. 10, 1705," which occurs in the Trinity College version. Cf. also F. iii, p. 409.

[43] G. A. Johnston in his edition of the *Commonplace Book* gives twenty-four.

[44] J., XXI, XXIII, XXIV.

[45] Erdmann, pp. 25–26.

of the Dublin Philosophical Society in 1707.[46] Fraser, it may be added, in general follows this opinion.[47]

Although it must be admitted that the Dunmore address was found among the Molyneux papers, and that Berkeley certainly was a close friend and tutor of Samuel Molyneux, who played a very active role in the revival of the Dublin Society, it is nevertheless clear that Johnson's statements go beyond the evidence. There is no way of knowing whether the first society was successful or not, and the history of the second, aside from the agreement to the charter and the suggested topics, is certainly a blank. Perhaps the most probable conjecture is that the membership in the two societies remained very largely the same, that in effect they are one and the same society, but that during the first year the interest of the leading members, or member, shifted in a more specifically philosophical direction which, together with the stringency and inflexibility of the first set of rules, necessitated a revision of the charter. The fact that Berkeley probably suggested the topics for the second society, and that he read the address at the inaugural meeting of the first is conclusive evidence that he was the leading spirit of the group. It is tempting to suppose, in view of his relation to Molyneux and the finding of the Dunmore address in the Molyneux papers, that the society was really connected with the revival of the Dublin Society, but in the light of the present evidence, this must remain conjectural. The societies may have involved only a few casual meetings, and the second may have died immediately after its birth.

However this may be, it is certain that the notices and memoranda which fill the body of the *Commonplace Book*, and which follow the second set of statutes, are Berkeley's own, and it is probable that they were written some time after the acceptance of the statutes in 1707, perhaps after the disintegration of the second society, when it became clear that the statute book could have no more official use. The entries are in his handwriting, and bear the peculiar imprint of his interests and method of thought. Furthermore, it is quite impossible to believe, as Fraser has suggested, that these memoranda have anything to do with the procedure of the second society. They are clearly intended only for private perusal, and must not, therefore, be confused with the twenty-five theses. The last page of the manuscript bears the date " 1708 August," and one

[46] *Hermathena*, vol. XI, 1901.   [47] App. E., F. iii, p. 409.

note [48] refers to an edition of Locke's Letters published in 1708, so that at least the last third and probably more was written in this year.[49]

The Trinity College manuscripts show that the first actual draft of the *Principles* was begun November 15, 1708, a fact hitherto neglected by commentators,[50] which probably sets a limit to the period actually occupied by the writing of the *Commonplace Book*. The succeeding six years, at any rate, are accounted for, and it is at least unlikely that the thread of the discussion would be resumed after so long an interval. Berkeley's youthful diary, therefore, was apparently composed between December 7, 1706 and September or October, 1708, probably at intermittent stages throughout the whole of this period, though it is possible that some of the entries were written quite late, during his Italian travels (1716-1720).[51] The chart on the following page shows the established dates, and the probable time sequence of these events.

The theses indicate that early in 1706 Berkeley was saturated with the philosophy of Locke, but well advanced in his own criticism of Locke's point of view and in the development, through such criticism, of his own thought.[52] We are, in fact,

---

[48] J., 721.

[49] Mr. R. I. Aaron, who first discovered the date of this edition (*Mind*, N. S. vol. XL, no. 160, p. 439) goes so far as to attribute the discovery of the New Principle to a hypothetical reading by Berkeley of Locke's *Examination of P. Malebranche*, published in 1706. I cannot agree with this opinion for the following reasons: (1) There is no further reference on Berkeley's part to this essay. (2) Berkeley does refer in the C. B. to Malebranche's *Recherche*, without mentioning Locke's criticism, or making the same points himself, as Mr. Aaron admits. (3) The queries with the statutes of December, 1706 were probably written before Berkeley read Locke's Posthumous Works (published in 1706) containing the *Examination of P. Malebranche*, and while these queries are obviously comments on the *Essay* they (particularly II, XXI, and XXIV) clearly show, in my opinion, that Berkeley was already well advanced in his own position as a result of his reading of the *Essay*, before he came in contact with the later work.

[50] In Fraser's edition, iii, p. 358, these all-important dates are omitted.

[51] The notes for the *De Motu* show that he had the volume with him on his Italian tour. If most of note-book A was written at this time we have an explanation of the great divergence between B and A. The summary at the end of B (903-953) written in July or August, 1708, when Berkeley was starting to write the Introduction to his *Treatise* would then constitute the end of the early *Commonplace Book*. The chief evidence against this view is the date, August 28, 1708, which appears on the last page of A, although it is of course not *necessary* to suppose that the present order of the notations in A corresponds to the temporal order in which they were written. Also the leaf bearing August 28, 1708 may have been misplaced.

[52] Mr. R. I. Aaron has questioned this, *op. cit.*, p. 444. I must call attention, however, to the close correspondence between thesis II and C. B. J., 106, between XXI and C. B. J., 52, as well as the sharp distinction between will and idea

here brought face to face with the origin and early growth of a new philosophic idea. In an intimate manner, intended only for his own use, Berkeley notes points that deserve to be remembered, applies his leading conceptions to new territory,

1706, Jan. 10, Statutes	Foundation of first Society; intensive study of Locke, Newton, Malebranche, and Descartes. *
1706, Dec. 7, Statutes	The Philosophical Society. Locke statutes; Criticism of Locke.
1707	First notations of *Commonplace Book*; Discovery of "New Principle."
1707, end of.	Dublin Society; first half of *Commonplace Book* (Note-book B).
1708	Locke letters published (after Jan. 2, probably spring or summer), p. 64 Ms., C. B. 721 (J.). Last third of C. B.†
1708, Aug. 28.	The Adventure of the (Shirt?), p. 95 Ms., C. B. 901 (J.).
1708, Nov. 15 to Dec. 18.	First draft of Introduction to the *Principles*.

* The mention of *Mr.* Newton (C. B., 327) who was knighted April, 1705, must be attributed to carelessness.

† I am indebted to Mr. R. I. Aaron for the establishment of this date, *Mind*, N.S. vol. XL, no. 160, October, 1931.

follows hints here and there, starts down bypaths, returns again, and generally expands his "new principle," as he called it, first in the direction of scientific experimental application, and later in the direction of metaphysics. In short, in a way which is almost unique in the history of philosophy, we are enabled to watch, at first hand, the play of ideas in the mind of a philosopher, freed from all the formal restrictions and hesitations incident to the publication and finished formulation of a "point of view." When properly understood and interpreted, the importance of this work for the comprehension of Berkeley's early thought can hardly be exaggerated. The situation confronting an interpreter, however, is a somewhat difficult one, requiring preliminary discussion.

so prominent in the whole of the C. B., and finally between XXIV and J., 178 and 179. These theses seem to indicate beyond question that Berkeley was well advanced in the development of his own new position at the very beginning of the year 1707, and that this development was stimulated chiefly by his reading of Locke's *Essay*.

The Commonplace Book and the Treatise

It is, of course, impossible to consider the *Commonplace Book* as a finished work, and to analyze and quote isolated sections as representing Berkeley's "views," as many writers have done. In a private note-book of this sort, a writer is bound to consider "views" with which he does not in the least agree, and to try out experimentally many intellectual pathways which almost at once are seen to lead nowhere. The diary must be considered as a whole, or not at all. If we examine it as separate, numbered sections it becomes, as we should expect, a mass of "contradictions." The only reasonable method of interpretation is to examine the book broadly as well as in detail, in the attempt to discover general tendencies of thought. What are the leading concepts? Do the "contradictions" tend in any one direction? This is the type of question we may hope to find answered, especially in view of Lorenz's establishment of the correct original order of the two note-books in the sequence B–A.[53] Only in view of the results of his painstaking and remarkably

[53] There is one respect, however, in which I must differ from Lorenz's results, which have been followed in general by all subsequent investigators save Hone and Rossi, who regard the matter as indecisive, on the basis of the external evidence. I cannot agree with this opinion, for as Lorenz pointed out, when the internal evidence is taken into consideration, the reasons for the priority of note-book B become quite inescapable. Indeed, the whole following discussion may be regarded as an attempt to justify Lorenz's view that in the order B (J., 1–395) and A (396–902), the C. B. as a whole comes to make sense, and the growth of Berkeley's thought becomes intelligible. (Cf. *Archiv. f. G. d. Phil.*, vol. XVIII, p. 551.)

On the basis of this internal evidence, however, which led Lorenz (*loc. cit.*) to his important discovery, I am forced to disagree with him concerning the entries (J.) 903–953 (Fraser, pp. 89–92) which are contained in note-book B, but which are placed by him (followed by Erdmann, Johnston, Rossi, and Hecht) after A at the very end of the entries, on the ground that these entries contain a sort of summing-up of salient points, and refer definitely to the *Principles*, published in 1710. Since, however, all the entries in the C. B. refer equally to the *Treatise*, and there is no cogent reason why Berkeley should not have made a summing-up at the end of note-book B, where they actually stand, as well as at the end of A, I cannot consider these points as convincing. Furthermore, the notations in question, from the standpoint of the growth of Berkeley's thought, are clearly retrograde and belong, with the other comments of B to an early stage of his thought, before the development of his conception of "Concrete Spirit," which falls in A. Their tone is thoroughly Lockian (907–908, 912, 915, 921). Prop. 913 also certainly precedes the concrete *esse percipi* principle, and the *active* view of perception so prominent in A, and the mathematical tone of 925–945 clearly belongs to B. I have, therefore, no hesitation in following the "natural" order, and in reading 903–953 (J) as they come in the manuscript after 395 (J), a context into which, I may add, they fit in an organic fashion, not only from the external standpoint of the manuscript which shows *no* break, but internally as well.

successful researches is it possible with any confidence to trace the growth and direction of Berkeley's thought during this critical time.

The *Commonplace Book* was written during a creative period when Berkeley was actually thinking out his ideas as they first came to him. The immediately succeeding published works, particularly the *New Theory of Vision* and the *Principles*, are, for the most part, only elaborations of suggestions originally developed in the diary. The traditional interpretation of Berkeley is largely based on the *Principles*. But not the least important fact revealed by the *Commonplace Book* is that this work is only a fragment, the first part or book of a larger "treatise" which, as projected, was to include three parts, the first concerning ideas and sensual experience, the second, and presumably the most important, concerning the will and morality, and the third consisting of a criticism of natural philosophy or science, in the light of the new system. The second part, later lost, was actually written by Berkeley. The *De Motu* and the *Analyst* probably include the most important ideas destined for the third.

The "introduction" is specifically mentioned at an early point,[54] and after this, frequent allusions to other parts of the work are scattered through the text. We must suppose, therefore, that in 1707 Berkeley conceived the plan of a systematic "treatise" consisting of a preface, introduction, and three books to embody the principles of his new philosophy. Most of the annotations of the *Commonplace Book* were allotted their approximate positions in this treatise by marginal letters which were clearly written in Berkeley's handwriting, at the same time as the annotations themselves. The key to these marginal letters, which is also written in Berkeley's hand, is, therefore, an outline of the proposed work. It runs as follows: Pref. (Preface), I (Introduction), M (Matter), P (Primary and Secondary Qualities), E (Existence), T (Time), S (Soul-Spirit), G (God), Mo (Moral Philosophy), N (Natural Philosophy). As originally projected, Part I, or Book I, was to include M, P, E, and probably T; Book II, S, G, and Mo; and Book III, N.

There can be no doubt that this "Treatise" is the whole, of which the published *Treatise concerning the Principles of Human Knowledge* is only a fragment. As to the Preface, the remarks of the *Commonplace Book* largely concern Berkeley's relation to Locke and the necessity of recognizing obligations to his predecessor.[55] This was omitted in the printed Preface to the *Principles* perhaps for the reason that by this time Berkeley felt his own position to be so distinct from that of Locke that no statement was really necessary. When we come to the Introduction we find such a marked similarity between the proposals of the *Commonplace Book* and the Introduction to the published *Principles* that there can be no question at all as to their relation. This similarity is verified even by isolated details.[56] In writing the published version of the Introduction, Berkeley, although his views had certainly developed in the interim, followed very closely the suggestions of the early diary.

When we pass to the remaining parts, the correspondence with the published text of the *Principles* becomes more obscure. There are, however, striking similarities.[57] We gather from the marginal headings that the first Book, as projected in the diary, was to include the discussion of matter, primary and secondary qualities, and existence; problems, that is, connected with sense qualities or ideas. If we turn to the *Principles*, we find, only a dozen pages from the end, the following statement: "Having despatched what we intended to say concerning the knowledge of *ideas* the method we proposed leads us in the next place to treat of *spirits*."[58] The published *Principles* thus follows in general the scheme outlined in the *Commonplace Book*. It is, however, only a fragment of the proposed treatise, as is made clear

[55] J., 689.

[56] For example, Berkeley says, "Even to speak somewhat favorably of the Schoolmen, and shew that they who blame them for jargon are not free of it themselves. Introd." (J., 728. Cf. Pr. Int., sec. 17.) Furthermore, "A man of slow parts may overtake truth, &c. Introd. Even my shortsightedness might perhaps be aiding to me in this matter — 'twill make me bring the object nearer to my thoughts . . ." (J., 755). The corresponding passage in the Introduction of the *Principles*, sec. 5, runs as follows: ". . . he who is shortsighted will be obliged to draw the object nearer, and may, perhaps by a close and narrow survey, discern that which had escaped far better eyes." The other references to the Introduction in the *Commonplace Book* concern the two main topics of the published introduction, i.e. words (J., 714, 729,

749), and the theory of abstraction (J., 397, 699, 838).

[57] For example, Berkeley proposes "to begin the first Book not with mention of sensation and reflection, but instead of sensation to use perception or thought in general" (J., 576). The connection of this passage with the famous first section of the *Principles*, which classifies all "the objects of human knowledge," is apparent. This much disputed passage becomes quite unambiguous when interpreted in the light of the *Commonplace Book*. To avoid all misunderstanding it should be altered to read as follows: "It is evident to any one who takes a survey of the *objects of human knowledge*, that they are either *ideas* actually imprinted on the senses; or *ideas* formed by help of memory and imagination; or else lastly, *objects* such as are perceived by attending to the passions and operations of the mind."

[58] Pr., sec. 135.

in the first edition, which carries Part I on the title page.
Berkeley also refers to other parts in his letters. What we have
in the main body of the published *Principles* is, therefore, Part I
of the projected treatise dealing with *ideas*. What does the diary
tell us concerning the other parts?

There are two passages referring to Part II, of which the first
is the more important.[59] It runs as follows: "The two great
Principles of Morality — the Being of a God & the Freedom of
Man. Those to be handled in the beginning of the Second
Book." That this Part was in Berkeley's estimation the most
important division of his philosophy is indicated in the last
section of the *Principles*, which was probably constructed originally as an introduction to Part II, and which reads as follows:
"after all, what deserves the first place in our studies is, the consideration of God and our Duty; . . . ." The other passage [60]
concerns the reason for using the word *idea* rather than *thing*.
This reason, Berkeley says, "I shall give in the Second Book."
If we turn to the last part of the *Principles*, which probably
represents a short sketch of the ideas worked out in Part II, and
which unfortunately represents all that we possess of this essential Part, so far as the published writings are concerned, we find
a reason at least indicated. Active spirit is sharply distinguished
from the passive idea,[61] and Berkeley specifically warns against
what he would have considered the fallacy of Hume and others
of inferring that there is no active spirit because "they could
not find they had any idea of it." [62] Berkeley opposes this position, declaring that the terms soul, spirit, and substance "do
mean or signify a real thing. . . ." [63] It is necessary to reserve
the word *thing* for the general meaning, which comprises both
active and passive beings, and to employ the word *idea* for sensory things alone.

All this, we must imagine, would have been made clearer in
the second Part, which Berkeley actually finished, but unfortunately lost on his Italian travels. From the nature of the last
sections of the *Principles*,[64] we must infer that the headings S,
G, Mo, or Soul, God, and Moral Philosophy, all of which concern the *active* side of existence, were to be treated in this important second Part. If we ask ourselves why Berkeley allowed
his philosophy to be brought before the world in such a fragmen-

59 J., 511.
60 J., 819.
61 Pr., secs. 136–138.
62 Sec. 137.
63 Sec. 139.
64 Secs. 135–156.

tary form, we can only refer to his letter to Johnson where he says that the distaste for rewriting a whole treatise, and lack of time, made it impossible for him to complete his work.[65] We must also remember that in the *Three Dialogues* the gap is at least partially filled, since the last two dialogues deal with religious matters, although in a popular and unsystematic form, and that Berkeley's moral philosophy is outlined, with respect at least to a certain critical problem, in the *Passive Obedience*.

There is only one note in the *Commonplace Book* which discusses Book III.[66] This concerns the "prejudice" that "we think we see an empty space, which I shall demonstrate to be false in the third Book." At the conclusion of his short discussion of infinitesimals in the *Principles*, Berkeley says, "But this will be more clearly made out hereafter.[67] That this allusion refers to the coming Part III is made almost certain by the fact that this passage was omitted in the second edition, after Berkeley realized that it would be impossible for him to complete the original project, and that the *Principles*, Part I, must stand alone. It is also clear that the reference in the *Analyst*[68] which refers to the "hints" of "twenty-five years ago," from which he was "diverted by other occupations," refers to those portions of the *Principles* where infinitesimals are cursorily discussed (1710-1735). We must conclude, therefore, that in general, secs. 101-134 of the *Principles* which deal with problems of natural science[69] are no more than anticipations of what Berkeley originally planned to treat at full length in Part III, which was not worked out until much later in the separate treatises *De Motu* and *Analyst*.

It must be emphasized once more that the core of this treatise, Part II, on the will, was lost, and that Berkeley, amid the manifold distractions of his active life, never had the opportunity to rewrite it. If we are ever to discover some further trace of the content of this essential Part, we must look for it in the *Commonplace Book*. There is, moreover, good reason for believing that such a search will not be in vain. Many of the later notes deal with the will, and the relation of the will to ideas or objects. This is, indeed, the central problem of the later portions of the

[65] Berkeley to Johnson, November 25, 1729. (Fraser dates this letter June 25, 1729, vol. II, p. 14.) Cf. Samuel Johnson, *His Career and Writings*, ed. Schneider, New York, 1929, vol. II, pp. 270 ff.

[66] J., 589.
[67] Sec. 132.
[68] Sec. 50.
[69] "N." in C. B.

diary. It is impossible to account for the presence of fragments connected with the *De Motu* without supposing that the volume accompanied Berkeley on his Italian travels, during which he wrote the second Part of the *Principles*. It is probable, therefore, that he referred to the later note-book A in composing the most essential portion of his "Treatise." It is even possible, as we have suggested, that sections of note-book A were actually written at this late date, in which case it would supersede all the other early work.[70] In any case, the *Commonplace Book* presents us with an intimate record of Berkeley's thought during a long period of formulation when, in and through a criticism of the standard authors of the day, especially Locke, he was tentatively finding his way. To chart the course which he followed through this maze of contemporary doctrine is an essential prerequisite for the understanding of his published works. The notes are, of course, fragmentary and inchoate, since they cover a wide range of topics. This very lack of order, however, is to some extent an advantage, since where the separate memoranda are not actually brought together in stated propositions, or where they are brought together in "contradictory" ways, it is nevertheless sometimes possible to discern the tendency of Berkeley's thought, which is often of much more importance than his stated "views."

[70] The early works would then follow the suggestive order: *Note-book B, New Theory of Vision, Principles, Three Dialogues, Guardian Essays,* and finally *Note-book A,* which is certainly favored by internal evidence.

CHAPTER II

THE COMMONPLACE BOOK

In spite of its fragmentary and occasional character, Berkeley's *Commonplace Book*, when read in the original order established by Lorenz, betrays a marked unity of thought. Most of the notations are consciously connected with one underlying conception or "principle," and all of the strictly philosophical comments may be traced to this source. Berkeley refers to this "principle" on the first page of the *Commonplace Book* [1] as "the immaterial hypothesis," and defines it as follows: "Nothing properly but persons, i.e. conscious things, do exist. All other things are not so much existences as manners of ye existence of persons." [2] It is interesting to note the increasing degree of certainty with which Berkeley refers to this conception. At first it is "the immaterial hypothesis." [3] Then it is "my doctrine." [4] Later it is an "obvious tho' amazing truth." [5] Finally it is referred to fairly consistently as "the Principle." [6] Berkeley, therefore, came to regard his principle as a truth which must become evident to any unprejudiced mind taking the trouble to examine the facts of experience. [7] Thus, he says, "Ignorance in some sort requisite in ye person that should disaver the Principle." [8]

Several passages show that Berkeley is very anxious to guard his new conception against the accusation of scepticism, which he felt from the first was apt to be urged against it. He says, for example, "There is a reality: there are things: there is a *rerum natura*." [9] He does not, therefore, mean to deny the reality of the external world, but only to assert its necessary relation to a superior factor held to be present in all experience. Hence, "the reverse of ye Principle introduced scepticism," [10] for, since all that we know or experience contains an "active" factor, a reality independent of consciousness can never in any way be known or experienced.

---

[1] J., 19.
[2] J., 24.
[3] J., 19.
[4] J., 199.
[5] J., 287.

[6] J., 293; cf. J., 314, 398, 407, 923.
[7] Cf. J., 287.
[8] J., 293.
[9] J., 316.
[10] J., 315; cf. 407.

The principle is not specifically mentioned until the nineteenth notation, but is implied in the fifth and thirteenth. It is very possible that the primary thought came to him as a result of reflection upon the nature of time with which these earliest notations are concerned.[11] Three of the theses, which Berkeley worked out as suggestions for discussion in the second philosophical society, refer to time,[12] and both the distinction between time or duration and its "measure,"[13] as well as the doctrine of the relativity of perceptual time,[14] which, for Berkeley, was identified with duration or actual existence,[15] are familiar to the reader of the *Essay*. The earliest formulations of the "new principle" might easily have been suggested by a careful reading of Locke's chapter on the *Idea of Duration*.[16] Time, in its actual conscious passage, differs from individual to individual and varies even in the same individual in different moods. But all our experience is necessarily in time. Therefore, "duration not distinguish'd from existence"[17] which is consequently relative and mind-dependent. Some such train of thought may very well have led up to the first definite formulation of the new principle.[18] The theses, particularly, show that even before the beginning of the *Commonplace Book*, Berkeley had progressed very far towards his new point of view through a careful reading and criticism of the *Essay*. In one thesis, indeed,[19] he specifically mentions five doctrines of Locke, the contradictories of which are prominent in the diary itself. In any case, it is certain that the principle, which underlies the whole structure of the *Commonplace Book* and provides Berkeley with his new point of departure, originated either late in 1706 or early in 1707, shortly after the second set of statutes, as a result of meditation upon Locke's *Essay*.

There has been much discussion concerning the relation between the "new principle" and the logic of abstraction. Erdmann particularly has taken the position that Berkeley's theory of abstraction was only a later and secondary theory devised *ad hoc* for the defense of his "spiritism" or "immaterialism," which is regarded by most of the German investigators as a "basic religious intuition."[20] When Berkeley's

[11] Cf. J., 16.
[12] J., XI, XIV, XXII.
[13] J., 10.   [14] J., 9.
[15] J., 5.
[16] *Essay*, II, 14.

[17] J., 5.
[18] J., 19 and 24.
[19] XXII.
[20] See especially Erdmann, *Berkeleys Phil. im Lichte . . .*, pp. 47 ff.

philosophical development, however, is regarded as a whole, it becomes manifest that this view is quite incorrect. As we hope to show in detail, Berkeley's fundamental insight was an insight into the connectedness of things, not an obstinate tendency to regard everything as inhering in disembodied ghosts. His hatred of abstraction led him constantly to see "wholes" where common sense saw only disjoined fragments. The famous *esse percipi* principle is simply a particular application of his concrete logic, or what he came to call his "mental" mode of "reasoning." The self and the world are not separate entities, lying side by side, but are intimately conjoined in a whole, without which either would be unthinkable. This, as the later development of Berkeley's thought, in the *Dialogues* and in the *Siris*, shows, is the true meaning of the "new principle." Against the argument of Erdmann and Lorenz that the "principle" is actually stated *before* the doctrine of abstraction, it must be replied: first, that the principle is itself an *application* of the doctrine of abstraction to the relation between the self and the world; second, that several of the theses written before the *Commonplace Book* also involve the principle of abstraction;[21] and third, that the earliest notations on time,[22] immediately preceding the first statement of the "new principle," concern the real inseparability of time from existence[23] and must also be regarded as applications of the new "concrete" logic. The world is not a heap of mechanical elements externally related to one another, but a system, the parts of which are essentially related, and the sharp lines drawn between "things" by common sense are artificial and unreal. Back of this artificial dismembered world of language and ordinary discourse, lies the world as it really is. This is the essential meaning of Berkeley's "new principle." The "spiritism" or "psychologism" in which it was first expressed is only a temporary crystallization of his new method which inevitably passed beyond this first subjectivistic formulation.

METHODOLOGY

Nothing in the *Commonplace Book* is more striking than the development of Berkeley's theory of demonstration, and more particularly the change in attitude toward mathematics which this involved. Berkeley's earliest published treatises, which we

[21] Especially J., IV, V, IX.   [22] J., 1–16.   [23] J., 5.

have good reason to believe were completed in 1705 or 1706, when the *Commonplace Book* was just begun, manifest, as we have observed, the greatest enthusiasm for mathematics and the mathematical method. This attitude is reflected in the earlier portions of the *Commonplace Book*. Mathematics, for example, has an important advantage over ethics and metaphysics in that its fundamental definitions do not encounter prejudice and are willingly agreed to by all men.[24] It is possible to demonstrate metaphysics and ethics in the mathematical manner.[25] Berkeley's enthusiasm, therefore, carries him even farther than the mathematical ethics suggested by Locke,[26] although, as he says, "Metaphysics is not so capable to be demonstrated in a geometrical way, because men see clearer and have not so many prejudices in ethiques."[27] Berkeley, however, did not long maintain this pan-mathematical point of view, and it is most interesting to follow in the *Commonplace Book* the process of self-criticism which finally led him more precisely to define and restrict the field of mathematical demonstration. This process is naturally somewhat confused, and there are lapses and false starts. It is nevertheless possible, in considering the *Commonplace Book* as a whole, not only to discern the direction of Berkeley's thought, but to discover several of its more important consequences.

The earliest methodological notations concern the inadequacy of language to express thought, and this sense of the deficiency of words remains a fundamental strand throughout the pattern of the book, being closely connected with the origin of the theory of abstraction.[28] This theory, indeed, was not fully and distinctly stated until 1708 in the first draft of the *Principles* (Introduction), but is clearly based on the linguistic criticism worked out in the memoranda of the *Commonplace Book*. Berkeley points out that we are in the habit of expressing insensible things in terms of metaphors drawn from the sensory realm,[29] and, as the *Commonplace Book* proceeds, he comes to place more and more emphasis on the philosophic difficulties resulting from this preoccupation with the sensory. Thus he observes that we know and experience many things for which we have no proper vocabulary.[30] Directly after remarking upon the metaphysical character of language, he says, "The grand

[24] J., 164.   [25] J., 165.   [28] Cf. J., 569, 566, 560.
[26] *Essay*, IV, iii, 18–20.   [29] J., 178.
[27] J., 248.   [30] J., 182 and 232.

mistake is that we think we have *ideas* of the operations of our minds." [31] The deceptiveness of language is, therefore, due to the fact that it seems to ignore the pure activity which for Berkeley was at this time a fundamental element in experience. This fact leads him to state that his "chief" purpose is to lay aside the "veil" of words, and return to the given facts of experience. "The chief thing I do or pretend to do is onely to remove the mist or veil of words." [32] This conception recurs again and again.[33] As long as we confine ourselves to the observation or intuition of experienced facts we cannot be mistaken. "To view the deformity of error we need only undress it." [34] Fallacies and mistakes occur only when we become confused in our symbol systems and imagine meanings for symbols which never really existed at all, or when "in long deductions made by signs" there may be "slips of memory." [35] Truth is the natural product of experience and intuition. Error is something that arises from an artificially abstract use of symbols.

Berkeley accordingly insists that even mathematical signs must be given some empirically verifiable *meaning* or idea.[36] He is nevertheless dominated by the mathematical ideal of knowledge, speaking constantly of demonstration in general, and more particularly of the demonstration of his doctrine. Thus he says, "I shall demonstrate all my doctrines," [37] and also, "Newton begs his principles; I demonstrate mine." [38] He does not think that certainty is confined to mathematics, but, following Locke, proposes to apply the mathematical method to ethics and to metaphysics. Even theology is subject to demonstration, ". . . for though the principles may be founded on Faith, yet this hinders not but that legitimate demonstrations might be built thereon; provided still that we define the words we use, and never go beyond our ideas. . . ." [39] There is nothing

[31] J., 179.
[32] J., 651.
[33] Cf. J., 497, 708.
[34] J., 750.
[35] J., 705.
[36] Not necessarily a *sensuous* meaning. The word *idea* is at first used vaguely to refer to significance in general. In J., 424 Berkeley defines *idea*, for example, as the "immediate object of thought." It is only toward the middle of the *Commonplace Book* that he gives this word the limited signification which it thenceforth

bears in his doctrine. Thus, in J., 492 he says, "Whether it were not better *not* to call the operations of the mind ideas, confining this term to things sensible?" In the passages where he discards infinitesimals and abstract ideas because they have no ideas or meanings, he is using the word in the general rather than in the specific or Humian sense as, for example, in J., 647–648.
[37] J., 592.
[38] J., 403.
[39] J., 590.

incompatible between "experience" and the mathematical method. We accept our basic propositions from an empirical source, and then proceed to demonstrate mathematical conclusions from them. Towards the end of the *Commonplace Book*, however, a most significant movement of thought occurs, in which the mathematical method is sharply sundered from the intuitions of experience.

This development is preceded by two preparatory phases, one connected with mathematics, and one with ethics. Early in the *Commonplace Book*, spurred on by his criticism of the doctrine of infinitesimals as empirically meaningless, he catches himself up brusquely, "What shall I say?" he asks himself, "Dare I pronounce the admired ἀκρίβεια mathematica, that darling of the age, a trifle?"[40] For a long period Berkeley evidently turned this revolutionary idea over in his mind. In two interesting propositions he compares the schoolmen with the mathematicians.[41] "The Schoolmen," he says, "have noble subjects, but handle them ill. The Mathematicians have trifling subjects, but reason admirably about them . . ."; [42] and again: "If we admire the method & acuteness of the Mathematicians, the length, the subtilty, the exactness of their Demonstrations, we must nevertheless be forced to grant that they are for the most part about trifling subjects, and perhaps mean nothing at all." [43] Though he is reluctant to pursue this criticism to its ultimate conclusion, the impetus of his thought led him on implacably. As he tested one mathematical proposition after another by his concrete test, it became evident to him that they had no actual application or meaning. What was left was mere symbolism. It was not that Berkeley ever came to doubt mathematical propositions. The result of his reflections was rather to deprive them of relevancy to the intuited experience which for him was the only reality. He never questioned that the sort of circle the mathematicians talk about cannot be squared. What he questioned was the applicability of this circle to the actual world. The experienced circle *can* be squared. Similarly, the experienced square has an *experienced* diagonal which consists of a certain number of minima, and therefore the experienced diagonal is commensurable with its sides, unless we are prepared to deny the theory of *minima* or thresholds. This position of Berkeley is not as absurd as has often been supposed. It is one thing to deny mathematics and another to deny its relevancy to empirical reality. What is the connection of the necessary judgments of mathematics with experience? Berkeley neither denied the fact that there were necessary judgments, nor that they were valid in some sense. What interested him from the very first was their application or meaning and what he finally affirmed was their essentially analytic or tautologous character.

The other line of thought which led him to this important conclusion was his criticism of Locke's doctrine of mathematical morality. According to this theory, "To demonstrate morality it seemed one need only make a dictionary of words, and see which included which." [44] The succeeding notation,[45] however, shows that this is not in the least Berkeley's own point of view.[46] This essential proposition runs as follows: "Locke's instances of demonstration in morality are, according to his own rule, trifling propositions." Berkeley is undoubtedly referring to Locke's famous distinction between real and trifling propositions [47] which we know attracted Berkeley's attention, for, shortly after, he makes the following memorandum, "Locke of trifling propositions. (Bk. 4 c. 8) Mem. Well to observe and con over that chapter." [48] Soon after his first criticism of mathematical morality [49] he reopens the question: "N.B. To consider well wt is meant by that wch Locke saith concerning Algebra — that it supplies intermediate ideas. Also to think of a method affording the same use in morals &c. that this doth in mathematiques."[50] The next proposition begins his essential criticism. "*Homo* is not proved to be *vivens* by means of any intermediate idea. I don't fully agree with Locke in wt he says concerning sagacity in finding out intermediate ideas in matter capable of demonstration & the use thereof; as if that were the onely means of improving and enlarging demonstrative knowledge." [51]

The reason for this disagreement is developed in the exceedingly important series [52] where, in a condensed form, Berkeley states his new conception of mathematics and lays the foundations for his own peculiar philosophic method. He begins with the concept of the solitary man, which he finds a most useful device to carry him back to the immediate facts of experience.

---

[44] J., 702; cf. 717.
[45] J., 703.
[46] As Mr. G. A. Johnston has supposed. See "The Influence of Mathematical Conceptions on Berkeley's Philosophy," *Mind*, N. S., XXV, 1916.

[47] Book IV, Chap. VIII.
[48] J., 784.
[49] J., 703.
[50] J., 709.
[51] J., 710.
[52] J., 739-753.

If such a man were taught to speak, the *words* would serve him only as mnemonic devices to record and rearrange his ideas.[53] In the primary *experience* of such a man, however, there would be no identical elements, and hence "there are no identical *mental* propositions."[54] It is useless, therefore, to search for intermediate terms which may eventually prove two experiences identical.[55] Such demonstrations, and the abstract identities involved in them, can be only verbal. Two *words* may be identical, as defined to stand for the same reality. Certainty, says Berkeley, seems to be a matter of mere words and definitions.[56] But in a marginal comment, which represents his final criticism of this view, he says, "This seems wrong. Certainty, real certainty, is of sensible ideas."[57] "I may be certain without affirmation or negation."

There are, in other words, two sorts of certainty — the verbal certainty which arises from the arbitrary definition of words and their substitution one for another in identical or analytic propositions, and the very different sort of certainty which involves concrete reality and is synthetic, since it relates different, non-identical elements together. Berkeley leaves us in no doubt as to which he himself considers the more important, at least for philosophy.[58] The mathematical certainty involving two identities is tautologous and obvious. "The reason why we can demonstrate so well about signs is, that they are perfectly arbitrary & in our power — made at pleasure."[59] It is no wonder that we may go on making definitions *ad infinitum*, and deducing consequences from them, according to certain rules. The sign world is at our disposal. This may be interesting and essential for certain purposes, but it is "trifling." The much discussed, traditional *aeternae veritates* thus "vanish,"[60] for they are tautologies resulting from arbitrary definitions subject to our will. They are all hypothetical. *If* we agree to define so and so as such and such, then all manner of so-called eternal truths must follow. The philosopher, however, is more interested in "mental propositions" which are not mere identities, like the *cogito* of Descartes,[61] but which relate together different facts

[53] J., 739.
[54] J., 740; my italics.
[55] J., 741.   [56] J., 743.
[57] J., 744.
[58] Cf. J., 753.
[59] J., 745.   [60] J., 748.
[61] J., 751; cf. 743, and Locke, *Essay*,

Book IV, Chap. V, where "mental propositions" are defined as those "wherein the ideas in our understandings are without the use of words put together, or separated," and contrasted with "verbal propositions" which "are words . . . put together or separated."

and, therefore, tell us something. "Knowledge, or certainty, or perception of agreement of ideas — as to identity and diversity, and real existence, vanisheth; of relation becometh merely nominal; of coexistence, remaineth."[62] All "real knowledge" is knowledge of "coexistence," which Locke had discarded as being relatively unimportant. Mathematical knowledge of relation, or agreement of ideas, is merely verbal and dependent on the will, while the knowledge of existent entities without the mind is again only verbal, for such entities are only verbal abstractions. The only real *knowledge* which remains is knowledge of coexistence.

This does not, however, imply that mathematics is to be discarded. It is altogether a matter of signs and definitions, but it is, nevertheless, "useful,"[63] and it is even possible to conceive of a "mixt" mathematical science of ethics.[64] Given that certain things are right, it may be very "useful" to deduce all the identical propositions which follow from these. The result of this important line of thought is a complete departure from the prevailing tendency which attempted to make mathematics the model of all valid thought. There are other perfectly valid modes of reasoning. "Certainly it is not impossible but a man may arrive at the knowledge of all real truth as well without as with signs, had he a memory and imagination most strong and capacious. Therefore *reasoning* & science doth not altogether depend upon words or names."[65] Berkeley does not doubt that the method of philosophy is synthetic rather than mathematical, and, so far as it is concerned, he gives up his previous ideal of a mathematical metaphysics and theology. "I must not pretend to promise much of demonstration. I must cancell all passages that look like that sort of pride, that raising of expectation in my readers."[66] The contrast between this and the mathematical enthusiasm of the earlier portions of the *Commonplace Book* and the *Miscellanea Mathematica* is striking.

Berkeley, in the later portions of the *Commonplace Book* and in the *Principles*, places a certain science of signs at the base of mathematics.[67] This science involves the primary rules of symbolic manipulation, and is entirely analytic or "trifling" in character. Geometry, however, is to be "reckon'd among the mixt mathematics," being "an application" of the abstracted

[62] J., 752.
[63] J., 865.
[64] J., 783, 865 and P. O., sec. 53.

[65] J., 895; my italics.
[66] J., 870.
[67] J., 780 and 781.

pure nominal mathematics "to points."[68] Berkeley, therefore, would not admit with Kant that arithmetic involved any intuitive process, though he would agree with him in associating geometry with the intuition of space. But the ultimate effect of his critique of mathematics was the same as that of Kant, namely the development of a concrete sort of logic to deal, not merely with verbal abstractions and arbitrary definitions, but to move among the concrete contents of experience. The logic of mathematics is not the logic of actuality, and therefore cannot be the logic of philosophical "reasoning." "*Reasoning* there may be about things or ideas, or actions; but demonstration can be only verbal. . . ."[69]

Berkeley's attempt to work out a concrete or "mental" mode of reasoning leads him to take issue with a tendency of thought which was peculiarly characteristic of the time — the disparagement of sense qualities as an insignificant and unreliable source of knowledge. Indeed, he often seems perilously close to the point of identifying the concrete with the sensory, though his doctrine of the ineffable, "transcendental" character of the self finally saves him from this danger. For Descartes, sense was notoriously confused and inadequate, and the same was, of course, true of Malebranche and Spinoza. Even Locke, though his position is somewhat obscure, in the end remains true to the mathematical ideal, and "sensitive knowledge," which is sharply distinguished from relational knowledge, since it is only probable, is placed on a distinctly lower level. Through the whole of the *Commonplace Book*, there are numerous passages which directly oppose this tendency to dismiss the senses. He says, for example: "Foolish in men to dispise the senses. If it were not for them the mind could have no knowledge, no thought at all."[70] And yet, as he clearly indicates in the rest of this passage, he does not mean that sense is the source but rather the condition of knowledge. "All . . . of introversion, meditation, contemplation, and spiritual acts, as if these could be exerted before we had ideas from without by the senses, manifestly absurd."[71] Without sense our reasoning is empty and verbal. ". . . We must have ideas or else we cannot think."[72] Geometry is an example which he constantly refers to. Without the space which we actually intuit, geometry becomes a

[68] J., 783.
[69] J., 816; my italics.
[70] J., 544; cf. 806.

[71] J., 544.
[72] J., 552.

set of symbols manipulated according to arbitrary rule. Thus, "Sense rather than reason or demonstration ought to be employed about lines and figures, these being things sensible. . . ." [73] Geometry that attempts to be purely rational really ceases to be geometry.[74] The attempt to make "pure intellect" by itself the judge of geometrical questions ends in destroying the question. "Say you, pure intellect must be judge. I reply that lines and triangles are not operations of the mind." [75] This is why Berkeley attempted in the *Commonplace Book*, without denying the traditional geometry, to lay the foundations for a sensory geometry which should be truly *applicable* and not a mere set of symbols with arbitrary meanings.

This insistence on "concreteness" was doubtless a most wholesome reaction to the prevailing abstract "intellectualism" of the day. There are certain respects, however, in which his very antagonism to an abstract intellectualism led him astray. The first and most dangerous of these was his marked tendency to identify the "concrete" with the "empirical," or what is sensorily *given* in experience. This passive or descriptive attitude really lies back of the "spiritism" or "psychologism" we have already noted in his early thinking. What is not "given" to some sense or "intuitive" faculty is not real, and is, therefore, attributed to obstinate verbalism. In spite of many warnings to the effect that the self *cannot* be made into an *object* or "thing," it is nevertheless viewed as the "object" of a *peculiar* "intuitive" faculty. This oscillation between the objective, empirical self conceived by an abstract logic and a truly "transcendental" principle developed through his new synthetic method is characteristic of Berkeley's early thought. He is never *quite* clear as to just *which* he means by the ambiguous term "self," though there can be no question as to the predominance of the abstract, spiritistic trend in the earlier portions of the *Commonplace Book*.

In the later portions, however, his concrete logic begins to dissolve away the fixed abstraction of the "self" about which his earlier reflections had crystallized, and leads him, in a development which is prophetic of the course later to be taken in the three *Dialogues* and finally in the *Siris*, to a new, transcendental level of thought. Before examining this first conquest of the new non-mathematical method, however, we must pause to con-

---

[73] J., 465.   [74] J., 512.   [75] J., 536.

sider the spiritistic theory of ideas, which, on the whole, dominates the earlier note-book (B) and comes to a final expression
in the published *Principles of Human Knowledge*.

BOOK I. PHILOSOPHY OF IDEAS (SUBJECTIVISM)

The passages in the *Commonplace Book* marked M, P, and E
(Matter, Primary and Secondary Qualities, and Existence) were
later elaborated and published in a finished form in the work
entitled *A Treatise Concerning the Principles of Human Knowledge*. All the conceptions developed in the main body of this
work are contained in germ in the earlier portions of the *Commonplace Book*. These conceptions fit together systematically
into a position conveniently indicated by the term subjectivism,
which is the first stable thought structure into which his new
concrete method crystallized, and with which Berkeley's name
has been since associated. We must now devote our attention
to an examination of this position as it is clearly suggested in the
earliest fragmentary notations of his intellectual diary.

"Nothing properly but persons, i.e. conscious things, do
exist. All other things are not so much existences as manners of
ye existence of persons," [76] and "'tis wondrous to contemplate
ye world empty'd of all intelligences." [77] This, as we have seen,
is the original form in which Berkeley stated his new principle.
It dominates the early sections of the *Commonplace Book*, and
traces of it are evident even in the later portions. What it represents, as we have already observed, is the application of Berkeley's new synthetic mode of reasoning to what are ordinarily
called "objects without the mind." Such objects, as Berkeley
soon discovered, are not absolutely or abstractly independent,
but relative to a "conscious thing" perceiving them. They "are
not so much existences as manners of ye existence of persons,"
in other words, "ideas." They are dependent upon the "conscious thing" in the sense that without it they would not be
what they are. The world of the fly is not our world,[78] and even
in the case of separate persons we must suppose that the worlds
of "ideas" which they perceive are, in fact, distinct. We may
classify what we perceive in various ways. There are primary
qualities, secondary qualities, spatial extensions, and temporal
successions, but it remains true that all objects whatsoever are
objects to a "conscious thing," and hence ideas. The first note-

[76] C. B. J., 24.   [77] J., 23.   [78] C. B. J., 48.

book (B) of the *Commonplace Book*, as well as the main body of the *Principles*, is devoted to the task of carrying out this formulation of Locke's "new way of ideas" with a rigid consistency which would seem to lead to a thoroughgoing solipsism.

The single self turns out to be the "bearer" of all time and existence. If we ask ourselves what really lies at the basis of this theory which has impressed certain minds as irrefutable, there can be only one answer. The "bearer" of the world is the individual, finite "person," or what Berkeley calls the "conscious thing." In his earlier works, he says very little more about this fundamental concept, but simply rests his case upon an "intuition," which he apparently thinks can be verified by any conscious being capable of introspection. The individual self is the "active" element in experience, and there is "no active power but the Will." [79] This "will" is an ubiquitous feature of our experience, which it is impossible convincingly to question. It is, in fact, the inescapable center, about which all our ideas revolve, for what is there that happens to us that cannot in the end be fitted into our lives as phases of our biographies? The will itself is simply "given," through an intuition so inescapable that "we cannot possibly conceive any active power but the Will." [80]

Berkeley's familiar subjectivism, according to which the ideas which we immediately or directly perceive "are" things themselves, is, of course, a consequence of this intuitive doctrine. If I intuit myself as a private individual center of consciousness, there seems no escape from the psychologistic conclusion that everything in the universe is a phase of my experience, since what could be meant by the universe of someone else must forever remain a meaningless verbalism to "me." Solipsism would, in fact, seem to be the only rigidly consistent conclusion derivable from this doctrine.

Berkeley, however, in the first half of the *Commonplace Book* feels no compelling drift in this direction. He follows Locke in believing that the principle of causation offers an impregnable refuge from the logic of the situation. Certain of my "ideas," it is true, those I call "imaginary," are within the control of "my" will, but other ideas, which I call real, are not similarly within my control. They are rather forced upon me by some "external" cause, since they are impressed upon me against my

---

[79] C. B. J., 133.   [80] J., 157.

will. Instead of supposing a world of "primary qualities" external to me, however, Berkeley differs from Locke, during this phase of his thought, in substituting for the "physical" universe the conception of an active agent, which he thinks it is fitting to describe as "God," since He acts in a "regular" way, and is clearly more "powerful" than ourselves. "The cause of all natural things," he says, "is onely God. . . . This Doctrine gives a most suitable idea of the Divinity." [81] We are not to imagine that there are sensations in this causal being, but only "powers" to cause sensations in us. This is the one respect in which Berkeley's early theory seems to possess an advantage over what is commonly accepted as the view of Locke. Material substance is inert. It is, therefore, "of great use to religion to take extension out of our idea of God, & put a power in its place." [82] There is an external world "independent" of us, just as in Locke's theory, but this is a world of active "powers" rather than inert, extended substances, possessing the primary qualities, for the primary qualities are just as clearly ideas as the secondary. "Nothing . . . without," says Berkeley, "corresponds to our primary ideas but powers." [83]

The crudity of this early view, which is, nevertheless, defended with great ingenuity in the *Principles*, was recognized by Berkeley himself at an early date, as is shown by the fundamental transformation of the doctrine in the latter portions of the *Commonplace Book*, and the *Third Dialogue* between Hylas and Philonous. Indeed, almost all of the fundamental criticisms Berkeley aimed with such deadly precision against Locke, apply with equal force against his own causal spiritism. How can the conception of transcendental, causal "powers" be reconciled with his own attack upon representationism, especially when he makes it apply specifically to Locke's "real and nominal essences"? [84] Does not the "causal theory" involve the same futile doubling of the world, against which he constantly urges such forcible objections? [85] How can a passive idea in the mind resemble an "active" cause without the mind? [86] With what right, indeed, of any sort do we apply the concept of causation beyond the world of our experience, since "there are no causes (properly speaking) but spiritual," [87] and the only direct and trustworthy knowledge of "spirits" is gained from ourselves?

[81] J., 430.
[82] J., 308.
[83] J., 41.

[84] J., 541.
[85] Cf. J., 309 and 897.

[86] Cf. J., 862.
[87] J., 862.

What enables us to make the transempirical leap from "ourselves" to God, especially in view of the fact that the *Commonplace Book* does not seem to admit any essential connection even between the causes and effects we actually experience? How much more tenuous must this connection then become, when one of the links is beyond all experience whatsoever? Is not Berkeley definitely undermining the force of his causal argument, when he refers to the axiom that "the effect is contained in the cause" as "an axiom I do not understand or believe to be true." [88]

These are a few of the more apparent objections which eventually led Berkeley completely to abandon the early spiritism he developed under the influence of Locke, and defended so ingeniously in the *Principles*. In the first half of the *Commonplace Book*, it is accepted as almost a truism, and even identified with the new logical principle. We know ourselves by an undeniable intuition to be "active" spirits, impressed from without by various real "ideas" or objects. For all "sorts" of sensations or "collections of thoughts" there are corresponding "collections of powers" in God.[89] He sends our sensations to us in regular clusters or "sorts," and for every such cluster there is a separate causal principle in Him. Our minds are also active principles, and in so far as they are able to interpret the sensory sequences, may arrive at some conception of the causal agencies producing them, but all degrees of interpretation and misinterpretation are possible. Every advance in the understanding of nature, every discovery of a natural law or "sort," is a step in the direction of understanding God. "Every sensation of mine, which happens in consequence of the general known laws of nature, & is from without, i.e. independent of my will, demonstrates the being of a God. . . ." [90] This is, of course, the conception which he sometimes indicated by the image of the "universal" or "divine language of nature,"[91] though it does not occur in the *Commonplace Book* itself, and is of no special importance in the development of Berkeley's underlying thought.[92]

[88] J., 793.

[89] J., 290.

[90] J., 850.

[91] In the *New Theory of Vision*, sec. 147, and the *Principles*, F. i, p. 317 *et passim*.

[92] Bergson, *Rev. de Meta. et de Morale*, 19, 1911, has maintained that Berkeley's fundamental "intuition" is embedded in this simile. "Il me semble que Berkeley aperçoit la matière comme une mince pellicule transparente située entre l'homme et Dieu," p. 819. The evidence of the *Commonplace Book* does not support the view that Berkeley's thought was based upon any such "intuition."

This early Lockian conception, which we shall refer to as spiritism or psychologism, since it is based upon a supposed direct "intuition" of the self as an independent will or "thinking thing," is summarized in a concise formula near the middle of the *Commonplace Book*. "Existence," he says, "is *percipi*, or *percipere* (or *velle*, i.e. *agere*). . . ." [93] All reality may be divided into two separate types. On the one hand, there are the "active" substances, which will carry on other activities, and perceive. They are thinking "things," capable of existing in their own right, not dependent upon anything outside themselves. Their *esse* is hence *percipere* or *velle* or *agere*. On the other hand, there are the passive, dependent objects or ideas perceived by these thinking substances. They are not similarly independent and self-existent. They cannot simply be what they are in themselves, but are rather relative in nature. Their essences extend beyond themselves, and their *esse* is *percipi*. Without an active "will" to perceive them, they could not be. But the "conscious things," or persons, can exist in abstract isolation from all objects. They can will, therefore, without willing anything, and can perceive without perceiving anything, though it is absurd to think of the existence of an idea existing without its being perceived. It is the independence or priority of the "active," finite will which, on the basis of an incontrovertible intuition, is supposed to exist in utter independence, that underlies the thought of the early *Commonplace Book* and Berkeley's whole philosophy of ideas. Objects are dependent, and hence only ideas, but the self is an independent substance. The *esse* of all objects is *percipi*, but "the will wills." We shall henceforth refer to this position as spiritism or subjectivism. It dominates the early *Commonplace Book* and the *Principles*, although the concrete logic, which, as we have seen, is the fundamental methodological basis of Berkeley's reflections, leads him, even in these works, to insights with which this plausible "position" cannot be reconciled. His concrete method of "reasoning" finally led him far beyond this abstract spiritism of his youth, which he really abandoned at the age of twenty-eight. We must now turn to the important movement of thought through which this step was hesitantly accomplished in the later notebook (A) of the *Commonplace Book*.

93 J., 426.

Book II. The Dialectic of the Self

The sections in the *Commonplace Book* marked S (Soul-Spirit), G (God), and Mo (Moral Philosophy) occur for the most part in the later note-book (A) which Berkeley presumably carried with him on his Italian travels when he was preparing the second part of the *Principles*. It is not surprising, therefore, that the notations of this book betray a grasp immeasurably profounder than the earlier entries. Whether these later entries of note-book A were written in 1707 as is usually supposed, or, as is at least possible, in 1715 or 1716,[94] they reveal a most essential development of Berkeley's thought from the crude spiritism of note-book B.[95]

There are still traces of the spiritistic position. At one point, Berkeley even says: ". . . I know with an intuitive knowledge the existence of other things as well as my own soul." [96] But the hesitant scepticism, evinced at one or two points in the earlier *Commonplace Book*, concerning the basic "intuition" of the self, on which the whole position rests, is now deeply intensified.[97] Passage after passage expresses doubt as to whether the activity of the soul may be made the object or idea of any faculty whatsoever. Objections are raised against Locke's definition of power as a "simple idea." [98] Somewhat further we find the remarkably strong statement that "it seems improper to make the word person stand for an idea, or to make ourselves Ideas. . . ." [99] The activity of the self can never be the object of any sense, or of any intuition no matter how "peculiar," since as soon as we sense or intuit it, it becomes an object or idea, and hence not the self at all. There are many notations in which Berkeley impresses upon himself the fact that the soul must be known in a fashion entirely different from that in which we know ideas or objects. All our ordinary categories of thought, such as existence, are directed outwardly to ideas or objects, but if we attempt to apply these objective categories uncritically to the self, essential distortions inevitably arise. This scepticism finally developed such an irresistible logical

---

[94] Because of the water-marks marring the lower part of note-book A (J. 396-902), the predominance of interest in the "Self," the subject of which Part II of the *Principles* was to be devoted, and most important of all, the notations referring to the *De Motu*, written at the end of his second Italian tour in 1720.

[95] J., 1-395 and 903-953.

[96] J., 568.

[97] Cf. J., 239.

[98] J., 460.   [99] J., 527.

force that Berkeley says near the end of the book, "The Will is *purus actus*, or rather pure spirit, not imaginable, not sensible, not intelligible, in no wise the object of the understanding, no wise perceivable."[100] The soul, or will, is no object of any sort, since it is the very act (*purus actus*) through which we know such objects. It is at the same time the most ubiquitous and the most elusive element in our experience. Not only is Berkeley now not in a position to make the self the bearer of all experience, but his early exaggeration of subjectivity leads him to the point of doubting whether there is any such thing. It is only his newly discovered logic of "reasoning," which saves him from this predicament, and the process through which this consequence is avoided is so essential that we must trace it in detail.

Spiritism or psychologism was correct, as far as it went. The trouble was that it was based altogether on a consideration of the objective side of consciousness. The self, or will, had been simply assumed or postulated as an "intuited datum." Once having started to reflect seriously or to "reason" upon the nature of the self, it is not long before Berkeley discovers that its logical position is precisely similar to that of "passive" or dependent objects. What he now discovers is that the self or soul is relative in exactly the same sense. There is no object (*esse*) without perception (*percipi*). But it is equally true that there is no activity without some object. As Berkeley remarks: "Certainly if there were no sensible ideas there could be no soul, no perception, remembrance, love, fear, &c; no faculty could be exerted."[101] Nevertheless, as he declares in the immediately following passage: "The soul is the Will . . . and . . . is distinct from ideas."[102] The more he is forced to think of these two aspects of experience as distinct, the more he is forced to think them together, and the more he pursues this line of thought the more distinct they become. Berkeley returns again and again to this puzzling situation, and the development of thought to which it leads is unquestionably the most interesting feature of the later sections of the *Commonplace Book*.

The first, and what we may call the more uncritical portion of the *Commonplace Book*, consists of secs. 1–469 and 901–953. It contains the doctrines which we have already considered. Experience may be analyzed into two distinct factors, the passive reception of ideas, or what Berkeley consistently calls

[100] J., 840; cf. 718.   [101] J., 479.   [102] J., 480.

"understanding," and the active will. Thus " . . . the mind"
is "the active thing wch I call 'I,' 'myself' — yt seems to be
distinct from the understanding. . . ."[103] Perception is nothing
but the "passive recognition of ideas"[104] and is, therefore,
equivalent to understanding. It is not until about the middle
of the *Commonplace Book* in note-book A[105] that Berkeley begins to reflect seriously upon the relation between these two
disparate functions. The "soul" is not an independent entity,
but necessarily *requires* objects.[106] This reflection inaugurates a
new development in his thought. Perception and will, existence
and *percipere*, ideas and mind necessarily belong together.

The first important result of this synthetic tendency is the discovery of a new and more general function — "thought in general." This is identified with the word "perception," which
consequently ceases to be merely the passive "reception" of
ideas, but now comes to include something active in its nature.
It is, therefore, important "To begin the First Book not with
mention of sensation and reflection, but instead of sensation to
use perception or thought in general."[107] Berkeley is at this
stage so impressed by the unity of consciousness that in the next
section he says: "I defy any man to imagine or conceive perception without an idea, or an idea without perception."[108] Ideas
are *not* altogether passive, but include an element of activity
(perception) in their very nature. Furthermore, this union is of
such an essential character that it is impossible to conceive
action, or what Berkeley has hitherto termed soul, without idea
or sensory content. "The very existence of ideas, constitutes
the Soul,"[109] and, "Consciousness, perception, existence of
ideas, seem to be all one."[110]

These passages, together with those immediately following,
have been interpreted as implying a Humian reduction of the
mind to a series of sense impressions. Professor Fraser, for example, suggests that Berkeley means, "like Hume afterwards,
that ideas or phenomena constitute the ego, so that I am only
the transitory conscious state of each moment."[111] Such an
interpretation, however, is possible only if certain passages[112]
are completely isolated from their context, and the movement

[103] J., 379.
[104] J., 311.
[105] J., 479; H., 465.
[106] J., 479.
[107] H., 560; J., 576; cf. *Principles*, sec. 1.
[108] H., 561; J., 577.
[109] H., 567; J., 583.
[110] H., 568; J., 584.
[111] F. i, p. 27, note 2.
[112] Such as H., 569; J., 585.

of Berkeley's thought is ignored. What he really means is not that the mind does not exist, but that what we call the "mind" is essentially united with its objects in a higher or larger unity. Thus he does not say: "What find you . . . besides several perceptions," but "Wt find you . . . besides several perceptions *or thoughts.*" [113] The word "perception" now includes the element of activity in its meaning, so that without it, idea or object is an abstraction. Mind, *by itself*, however, is also a verbal reification. What we *really* mean by this word is not isolated activity, but activity united with a content. ". . . Take away perceptions and you take away the mind. Put the perceptions and you put the mind." [114] The action of perceiving, and the thing or object perceived, are phases of a greater whole, neither one of which can have any *actual* meaning when isolated from the other. "Wherein does the perception of white differ from white mem." [115] Berkeley is simply making another telling application of his doctrine of abstraction. It is absurd to think of the mind as one of its own objects, but equally absurd to think of all objects as psychologically "subjective." What experience reveals to us is a *larger* whole of which object and mind, idea and perception are abstracted phases. To isolate and reify the objective phase is the basic fallacy of materialism. "The distinguishing betwixt an idea and perception of the idea has been one great cause of imagining material substances." [116]

Spiritism is simply the opposed fallacy. There can be little doubt that in this movement of thought we have the key to explain Berkeley's preference for the later formula "*esse est percipi,*" a formula conveying a much clearer conception of the essential relation which holds thought or perception and its object together. The order of words in this formula is accidental, for it is also true that *percipi est esse.* Each term enters into the meaning of the other in such a way that, though distinct, nevertheless, as aspects of an inseparable whole, extending beyond either, the two are identical. "The understanding taken for a faculty is not really distinct from ye will. This allowed hereafter." [117]

That this identity of thought and object, however, does not preclude their essential difference when abstracted, and that

[113] H., 569; J., 585; my italics.
[114] H., 570; J., 586.
[115] H., 575; J., 591. Johnston reads *men* for *mem.*

[116] H., 599; J., 615.
[117] H., 607; J., 623–624.

it is also necessary to make this abstraction, is proved by the following sections of the *Commonplace Book*, which are full of passages emphasizing even more acutely than before the uniqueness of the will. Thus, "The grand cause of perplexity and darkness in treating of the Will is that we imagine it to be an object of thought: (to speak with the vulgar) we think we may perceive, contemplate, and view it like any of our ideas; whereas, in truth, 'tis no idea, nor is there any idea of it. 'Tis *toto coelo* different from the Understanding, i.e. from all our ideas. . . ." [118] He even goes so far as to say that so different is action from idea that it is contradictory to think of an "idea of a volition," [119] and he often maintains in a manner reminiscent of earlier passages in note-book B the two-fold character of reality: "Things are two-fold — active or inactive. The existence of active things is to act; of inactive to be perceived." [120] Yet, in spite of this basic opposition, Berkeley is now continually forced, in attempting to do justice to the concrete reality confronting him, to bring the two together. "There is," for example, "somewhat active in most perceptions, i.e. such as ensue upon our volitions . . .," [121] and, a little further, "Distinct from or without perception there is no volition; therefore neither is there existence without perception." [122] The will is quite distinct from the objects of experience and pervades them in a unique sort of way, but nevertheless without them it would not be what we mean by will. The two together enter into each other to constitute a concrete or essential whole which is more than either. "The concrete of the Will & understanding I must call mind. . . ." [123]

Berkeley, it is true, still speaks at times as though it were the will or active element, the "me" which binds the different objects of experience into a self-identical unity, and organizes the separate ideas into a world. The drift of his thought, however, remains clear. Action without an object cannot be exerted, and is, therefore, unthinkable. "Pure intellect I understand not." [124] This is why we find him approving the axiom of the schoolmen that "Nihil est in intellectu quod non prius fuit in sensu," [125] not meaning the absurdity of denying the intellect, but rather the absolute emptiness of an intellect with

---

[118] H., 634, J., 652; cf. H., 649; J., 666; H., 651; J., 669.
[119] H., 655; J., 673.
[120] H., 665; J., 684.
[121] H., 664; J., 683; cf. J., 845.

[122] H., 666; J., 685.
[123] H., 796; J., 725.
[124] H., 770; J., 822.
[125] H., 770; J., 792.

no object. Pure passivity, however, is equally absurd. Apart from perception, which is now clearly classified with imagination as something active, there is no existence. The pure object, passively received by consciousness, is just as much an artificial abstraction as the pure activity apart from any object. "The existence of anything imaginable is nothing different from imagination or perception." [126] "Perception" or "understanding" is no longer viewed as a purely passive reception or "recognition." "Understanding is in some sort an action." [127] It makes no difference at which side of the opposition we begin. If we start with pure, passive perception, we find it is an incomplete abstraction which leads us to the "concrete" unity, and if we start, on the other hand, with the pure activity, this likewise, when submitted to Berkeley's logic of "reasoning," turns into an empty abstraction, pushing us on to the same goal. "It seems to me that will and understanding — volitions and ideas — cannot be severed, that either cannot be possibly without the other." [128] This is the final statement of his new position. Mind and object mutually imply each other, and enter into each other in such a way that neither can possibly be without the other.

Berkeley refers to the "concrete" unity of will and ideas or understanding as "Spirit," and the traditional faculties so tortuously composed and decomposed by Locke are abstractions which smack of the linguistic laboratory. "I must not [129] mention the understanding as a faculty or part of the mind. I must include understanding and will &c. in the word Spirit — by which I mean all that is active." [130] The extent to which this represents a critical advance from the "subjectivism" or "spiritism" of note-book B is apparent. "The Spirit, or Mind, is neither a volition nor an idea." [131] The latter are no more than aspects of a larger unity which, *as* separate entities, are nothing at all, since they cannot exist except as phases of the whole which enters into them and makes them one with itself. "I must not say the Will & Understanding are all one, but that they are both abstract ideas, i.e. none at all — they not being even *ratione* different from the Spirit *qua* faculties, or active." [132] The unity of spirit is not an abstract identity but an identity in which difference is preserved. The mind, while it is one with

---

[126] H., 782; J., 804.
[127] H., 811; J., 833.
[128] H., 829; J., 853.
[129] Johnston omits this all-important *not*.

[130] H., 836; J., 860.
[131] H., 837; J., 861.
[132] H., 859; J., 883.

its objects and enters into them, is nevertheless distinct from them. "Bodies exist without the mind i.e. are not the mind, but *distinct* from it. This I allow, the mind being altogether different therefrom." [133] To explain his meaning further Berkeley uses the example of imagination: "If a man with his eyes shut imagines to himself the sun & firmament, you will not say *he* or *his mind* is the sun, or extended, tho' neither sun nor firmament be without the mind." [134]

This insight into the mutual dependence of subject (*percipere*) and object (*esse*) in the concrete perception (*percipi*) of spirit is the veritable climax of the *Commonplace Book*. In order to appreciate its importance for Berkeley's later development it would be necessary to give a résumé of his later works. We must be content, at this stage, to point out one essential consequence which Berkeley does explicitly recognize in the *Commonplace Book* itself. As a result of his spiritism, he had been forced to assert the constant annihilation and re-creation of objects, correlated with the fluctuations of individual attention. When I close my eyes, the objects surrounding me disappear or vanish into nothingness so far as I am concerned. From the standpoint of spiritism this is equivalent to annihilation. Even the self, when we cease to "intuit" it, passes out of existence. Berkeley, therefore, is forced to the conclusion that "Men die, or are in [a] state of annihilation oft in a day," [135] and agrees with Locke's common-sense assertion that "the mind thinks not always."

The new insight into the concrete unity of spirit, however, enables Berkeley to transcend the crudity of such a plausible position. It is no more possible to think of the non-being of the self independently of objects or ideas than the being of the self. We can no more think of the self as being annihilated in abstract isolation from the world than we can think of the annihilation of a sense object in isolation from a perceiver. To assert that *anything* is annihilated is to assert that something else exists. *My* being asleep would have no meaning were it not possible for me to think of events in the interval. Thought must grasp the passage from unconsciousness to consciousness and remain immune to it, or the transition itself would be meaningless. The non-being of *my* thought is not absolute non-being, or I could not even refer to *my* being asleep, and when I awake I should have to begin immediately from my *last* waking moment,

[133] H., 851; J., 875.   [134] H., 873; J., 898.   [135] J., 84.

with no awareness of the interval. Such "intervals" would be "nothing." [136] This, however, is not the case. I can perfectly well think of myself as asleep, or unconscious, or dead. But the *I* which thinks this is not the finite self *I* know. There is an underlying *continuity* binding both my conscious states, and my unconscious states together, and making up a world into which I as well as other finite objects enter and from which *they* depart.

The negation of *my* consciousness, or of any other finite thing is not absolute non-being or annihilation, but merely the assertion of something else. Even if I pass beyond all consciousness whatsoever to the negation of everything finite, I arrive not at what is ordinarily called non-being, but at absolute metaphysical nothingness, which is pure thought, or pure "Spirit" itself. "To say the mind exists without thinking is a contradiction, nonsense, nothing." [137] Pure existence, as well as pure non-existence, are both thoughts, though not *my* thought nor *your* thought. It is meaningless to think of mind without such existence, or of existence without mind, although it is exceedingly easy to think of vast intervals in which neither I nor any other finite object exists, by the simple procedure of thinking of something else. It is, however, impossible to escape from thought itself. Berkeley, consequently, now finds himself in agreement with Descartes as against Locke with regard to the proposition that "the mind always and constantly thinks," [138] although "the mind" *here* referred to is neither my mind nor any finite mind whatsoever, but "Spirit." Berkeley was doubtless unaware of all the implications of this startling discovery. It was not until the *Dialogues* of 1713 that he clearly recognized the sort of transcendentalism it implies,[139] and not until much later in the *Analyst* [140] and the *Siris* that it took full possession of his thought. But the fragmentary dialectic of the *Commonplace Book* itself is enough to show the direction in which his concrete logic was impelling him.

This dialectic movement which culminates in the concept of the "concrete" unity of spirit is the crowning feature of the *Commonplace Book*, and it underlies the whole of Berkeley's philosophy, for it is presupposed in the condensed and abbreviated formula "*esse est precipi*," in which he summed up the

---

[136] J., 596.
[137] J., 661; cf. 660.
[138] J., 660.

[139] Cf., however, Pr., sec. 118.
[140] An. query 49, F. iii, p. 58.

burden of his early reflections, though it did not achieve a fully conscious expression until the Platonism of the third *Dialogue* and the final metaphysics of the *Siris*. As so often happens, however, when philosophers attempt to summarize the "results" of their reflections, the actual movement of their thought, which is really the valuable thing, is lost. We may imagine that, had Berkeley published the second part of his treatise, we should have had a better idea of this critical development through which he first hesitantly and falteringly forced himself to the level of "pure Spirit" which is neither subject nor object but necessarily prior to both. Many years of arduous and painful reflection were necessary before his thought was able to move with any confidence in this realm which is only vaguely glimpsed in the early works. What mars these works is the continued confusion of pure "Spirit" with that "spiritism" or "psychologism" which, while it reduces the external objects to appearances in space and time, nevertheless uncritically accepts the "self" or "will" naively as presented. The individual "will," however, is also in time, and must itself, therefore, as "active," or as "will," be reduced to the rank of an appearance. The whole world of experience, indeed, including the self with which it is so intimately united, must be regarded as dependent upon a truly transcendent principle, neither subject nor object but rather that concrete "idea" of which both "will" and understanding are abstract elements.[141] It is only in the final phases of his thought that Berkeley, with the aid of Plato and Plotinus, really reaches this ultimate height of the pure idea. The path by which he advanced from his earlier psychologism to such a conclusion will constantly occupy us in the following chapters.

BOOK III. APPLICATIONS OF THE NEW PRINCIPLE IN NATURAL SCIENCE

Whatever we may think of Berkeley's criticism of the mathematical rationalism of his day, it cannot be denied that his attempt to penetrate through the veil of language to concrete reality led him to extremely influential discoveries in several fields of scientific study. It is interesting to observe that the germs of all these contributions are to be found in the *Commonplace Book* — for the most part under the heading N (Natural Philosophy). Berkeley originally intended to work out these

[141] J., 883.

suggestions in the third Book of the "Treatise," but his thought soon developed them far beyond the limits of his original "system" and they were accordingly published separately as the *New Theory of Vision*, the *De Motu*, and the *Analyst*. The detailed exposition of these points must, therefore, be postponed to later chapters.[142] We must here comment only on the light which the *Commonplace Book* throws upon their genesis, and their connection with the new concrete logic.

The *New Theory of Vision* was published in 1709, only a few years after the *Commonplace Book* was completed, and the latter is full of references to the problem of visual perception. Many detailed points developed in the published work, such as the first solution of the inverted image problem, are already worked out in the early diary. The distinction between sight and touch, so prominent in the new theory, was apparently arrived at very early in his reflections. The space which we *see* is not to be identified with the space that we touch. At first the connection between these two types of sensation is attributed to arbitrary association, there being "no necessary connection" [143] between the immediate object of vision and the depth or solidity which constitutes the third dimension of space. This is doubtless the dominant conception implied by the notations dealing with vision, which are for the most part contained in note-book B, and therefore belong to the earliest stage of Berkeley's reflections.

A pure idea or sensation, however, is a meaningless abstraction. This, as we have seen, is the outcome of Berkeley's new concrete method as expressed in the formula *esse est percipi*. It is possible to discern the influence of this synthetic mode of thought even in the first comments upon vision. Thus he says, "wt I see is onely variety of colours and light. Wt I feel is hard or soft, hot or cold, rough or smooth, &c." [144] Space, in other words, is not a sensation at all. "Extension seems to be perceived by the eye, as thought by the ear." [145] Space, while it cannot be dissociated from a sensory factor, essentially involves an "active," interpretative element. We perceive spatial relations not as mere data "but by reasoning." [146] The extension of objects, therefore, is not so much the result of an arbitrary association of disparate sensations, as of their rational correlation. The first radical distinction between the space of sight

---

142 Chaps. IV, X, XIV.   144 J., 235.   146 J., 210.
143 J., 201.   145 J., 225.

and the space of touch is thus leading Berkeley to the recognition of the fact that space is not a sensation at all.

The theory of sensory minima, which is also prominent in the earlier note-book, is corrected by a similar synthetic tendency. In all fields of sensation there is a minimum beyond which we cannot pass. Thus, " . . . there [is] no one idea diminishable *ad infinitum*." [147] Every sensory "given" must consist of such minimal units, beyond which it is impossible to pass. Furthermore, the concrete "given" must consist of a finite or numerable number of such minima, for "Points tho' never so many, may be numbered. . . . Also if by infinite idea you mean an *idea* too great to be comprehended or perceived all at once, you must excuse me. I think such an infinite is no less than a contradiction." [148] What we perceive in the concrete are finite clusters of minima, related in various ways by the mind. Thus, while the mathematically defined circle may not be squared, "Any visible circle possibly perceivable of any man may be squar'd . . .," [149] since a square may be constructed which will contain the same number of minima as the circle, and the difference between the two, since it cannot be perceived, is non-existent *in the concrete*. "I say the invisibles are nothings, cannot exist, include a contradiction." [150]

At first this seems to involve the most radical disintegration of experience into discrete given "sensa." Almost at once, however, we find Berkeley correcting this tendency not so much by the introduction of an external principle of unity, as by simply allowing the distinction to work itself out. The minimum, through its very meaning, necessarily involves a concrete whole of which it is the minimum. Hence Berkeley concludes that each person's spatial minimum, together with his field of space, is identical with that of every other. "Your M. V. (minimum visibile) is suppose, less than mine. Let a third person have perfect ideas of both our M. V. His idea of my M. V. contains his idea of yours & somewhat more. Therefore, 'tis made up of parts; therefore his idea of my M. V. is not perfect or just, which divests the hypothesis." [151] It is easy to see from this how Berkeley's concrete method, even at this early stage, is gaining headway against his spiritism. It is absurd to speak in spiritistic terms of *my* space as distinguished from *your* space, since such a plurality of private spaces is simply not what we mean

[147] J., 75.
[148] H., 461; J., 475.
[149] H., 251; J., 259.
[150] H., 449; J., 463.
[151] J., 281.

by space. We must postpone the fuller discussion of this important conception to a later chapter,[152] taking occasion at this point only to note Berkeley's denial of extension as a pure sensation and his suggestion that space is a universal rational interpretation of sensation, as a most important though hesitant development of the new concrete logic.

It remains for us to consider briefly Berkeley's criticism of the "Modern Analysis," or infinitesimal calculus, which was also initiated during this period.[153] Pure mathematics, Berkeley now held, is the science of symbolism—the study of the analytic relations obtaining between signs which we have arbitrarily defined. Such definitions lose all value if they are not clear and distinct. Geometry, on the other hand, or "mix't mathematics,"[154] involves the application of such an analytic procedure to certain objects or "ideas." The conception of the infinitesimal that Berkeley found in the exposition of such continental mathematicians as De l'Hospital, however,[155] seemed neither clear and distinct, nor in any sense empirical. The infinitesimal is certainly not an object or idea,[156] and yet the many confused and inconsistent definitions given by the mathematicians lack the precision and clarity necessary in the field of pure mathematics.

At no time in his career did Berkeley ever dispute the utility of pure mathematics, nor did he question the practical value of the new analysis. In the early treatise *Of Infinites*, indeed, he expressly states that the method *may*, doubtless, be developed *a priori* without the confused concept of infinitesimals, as Newton himself had stated. The pure, analytic method is necessary and important in its place, but this is a restricted one, since the objects of mathematics are artificial abstractions rather than concrete realities. It is for this reason that the method of mathematics cannot be the method of philosophy, whose function is rather to explain this *real* world than to deduce analytic systems of propositions from arbitrary premises. As for geometry, it is the application of this method to extension, and, as such, it cannot afford to ignore these facts, for it is an applied

---

[152] Chap. IV.
[153] Cf. the Treatise *Of Infinites*, F. iii, p. 410, written after 1705, and J., 324–480, with which this Treatise is clearly correlated.
[154] J., 783.

[155] The *Analyse des infiniment petits* by the Marquis de l'Hospital appeared in 1696. It is referred to in *Of Infinites*, F., III, p. 411.
[156] J., 411–418.

science. It is, therefore, a "folly of the mathematicians in not judging of sensations by their senses." [157]

Mathematical knowledge by itself is "trifling," "symbolic," or analytic. Berkeley was led by his acute realization of this fact to search for a new logic or "way of reasoning" which should be adequate to the "concrete" world of "reality," and yet also remain necessary or rational without being merely tautologous or "trifling" in character. While much of his reflection, particularly his handling of the relation between the self and the world which led to the *esse percipi* formula, as seen from a later and more fully conscious standpoint, does, as a matter of fact, exemplify such a "concrete" logic, Berkeley himself did not succeed in formulating its principles, and his new method of "reasoning" is, in the *Commonplace Book*, often confused with empirical association. The overcoming of this early "empiricism," which he took over uncritically from Locke and the "scientific" atmosphere of his day, through his gradual realization of the significance of concrete logic is unquestionably the dominant feature of his mature development.

This development is already clearly indicated in the *Commonplace Book*. Even the "spiritism" which dominates the earlier note-book is an advance beyond Locke, since it involves the consistent destruction of Locke's hypostatized material substances. It is true that Berkeley at first set equally artificial *spiritual* substances in their place. But the ultimate conquest of his concrete logic (the "new principle") over this position is assured by the critical reflections of the later note-book (A). In this essential movement of thought Berkeley comes to realize that spiritual substance (the thinking thing) is just as illegitimate an abstraction as the material substance of Locke. Both subject and object are phases of a reality more actual and concrete than either, the concrete unity of spirit. Berkeley's reflections at this point rise to a level beyond materialism, spiritism, or any other *ism*, the level of pure thought, or what he was later to call the "idea." His attempts to explore this realm are at first tentative and feeble. We cannot expect his progress to be a steady, triumphal march. There will be many false starts and lapses into that spiritism which, as it was the first systematic position into which his reflections crystallized, continued to exert a powerful influence upon his mind. The early history of

[157] H., 369; J., 382.

Berkeley's thought which we are now about to trace is the history of a struggle in which, with the aid of his new synthetic mode of "reasoning," he gradually shakes himself free from subjectivism. Before turning to this history, however, we must at least briefly consider the "influences" which played a significant role in this development. These influences are primarily two, that of Locke, whose thought determined the outlines of the spiritistic philosophy dominating his youth, and that of Plato, who, more than any other philosopher, guided his concrete logic on its later course, after the collapse of his early system.

CHAPTER III

BERKELEY AND HIS PREDECESSORS

ALTHOUGH the *Commonplace Book* is a remarkably independent document, the sense in which Berkeley's early thought developed in and through a close study of preceding authors is made manifest on almost every page. There is one writer in particular with whom the diary is almost continually preoccupied. Without an understanding of their relation to the doctrines formulated in Locke's *Essay*, most of the notations remain altogether obscure. It is clear that during the interval in which he was using the first note-book (B), Berkeley was actually reading the *Essay*. Not only is the vocabulary of the first diary taken over bodily from this source, but the doctrine of spiritism which dominates the earlier pages is itself a form of Lockianism. Even the new synthetic or "mental" mode of reasoning, which is certainly the most important as it is the most original idea of the *Commonplace Book*, was obviously suggested to Berkeley by Locke's distinction between "mental" and "verbal" propositions in Chapter V of Book IV of the *Essay*, and the distinction between "real" and "trifling" knowledge in Chapter VIII of Book IV. Berkeley's development and application of this method, however, as we have seen, led him, in the second notebook (A), far beyond his youthful "spiritism" into realms of thought entirely strange to the earnest literalism of his predecessor. Before following Berkeley's synthetic method further into these profounder realms, however, we shall pause at this point to consider more precisely the relation between Berkeley's new mode of thought or "principle" and that of the philosophical writers he was reading at the time of its first formulation. The source of all understanding is contrast.

LOCKE

All the main doctrinal features of the spiritism which dominates the early *Commonplace Book* and the published *Principles* are taken over bodily from Locke. This spiritism, as we have seen, is based upon a supposed, immediate sense of "power" or causal efficacy in something called "ourselves." The source of this conception is obviously to be found in the *Essay*. In his famous chapter on "Power," for example, Locke says: "The idea of the *beginning* of motion we have only from reflection on what passes in ourselves." [1] "Power," or agency, is something which we simply intuit, or "find in ourselves." [2] The word "spirit," in fact, is used constantly in the *Essay* to refer to the substantial being, which is capable of "thinking, understanding, willing, knowing, and . . . beginning motion." [3] Locke, moreover, divides these various capacities into the two general faculties, "Will" and "Understanding," [4] which are first made familiar to the reader of the *Commonplace Book* as the "active" and "passive" faculties of the mind. The conception of God as the "first" or ultimate cause is also a Lockian conception, and Berkeley only followed his predecessor in thinking of Him as the chief member, or "head," of the society of spirits. "God" and "spirits" are constantly joined together in the *Essay* as essentially analogous to one another, as, for example, in Book II, where "for the clearest idea of *active* power" we are referred "to the consideration of God and spirits." [5]

The spiritism of the early *Commonplace Book* and the *Principles*, therefore, is really a modified form of Lockianism. Berkeley simply removed the vague, material substance or "supposed I know not what," [6] hovering in Locke's mind between God and His attendant choir of spirits. This, however, as has often been pointed out, was a step for which Locke himself had somewhat more than paved the way. "We are as far from the idea of the substance of body," he says in one place, "as if we knew nothing at all." [7] The difference between this position, which is reiterated throughout the *Essay*, and the famous "immaterialism" of the *Principles* is exceedingly tenuous. Berkeley, of course, simply pointed out the consequence that primary and secondary qualities must be placed on strictly the same level as ideas "in" some spirit, since it is impossible consistently to consider any "ideas" as the copies of spatial entities subsisting "outside" spirits in a material world. Such ideas are rather the direct effects of the omnipresent, "causal" activity of God, acting on the subordinate "selves," and inducing different "worlds" of ideas in them. This position is not

[1] Ess., II, xxi, 4.
[2] Ess., II, xxi, 5.
[3] Ess., II, xxiii, 15.
[4] Ess., II, xxi, 5.
[5] Ess., II, xxi, 2.
[6] Ess., II, xxiii, 15.
[7] Ess., II, xxiii, 16.

exactly Locke. It is Locke shorn of a vast amount of hesitation, irrelevancy, and downright inconsistency. But there is not a single "alteration" that Locke did not himself clearly suggest, and what remains, viz. a great hierarchy of spirits with God as the King or head spirit, is only Locke reduced to bare essentials. It is extremely misleading to think of this as Berkeley's philosophy. All the important features of his intellectual history are associated not with the fact that he once held this view, but that he transcended it. The criticism to which he at once subjected it is clearly discernible, as we have seen, in the later portions of the *Commonplace Book*.

We shall not need to describe again the development of the new concrete logic of synthesis which is the beginning of all that is distinctively original in Berkeley. It will suffice simply to note the importance of the negative role played by the *Essay* in this development. Locke's thinking, which seems to have impressed many of his countrymen as an extraordinarily accurate and adequate account of concrete experience, struck Berkeley as a mass of abstract verbalism. The *Essay* seemed full of tedious reiterations and circumlocutions. Locke talks endlessly of "powers," "cohesions," and "faculties" of this, that, and the other. "Putting together the ideas of so-and-so . . . we have the idea of so-and-so" is the structure of a typical Lockian sentence. Berkeley was repelled by the downright wordiness of this style. "Locke's great oversight," he exclaims, "seems to be that he did not begin with his third book" on language.[8] The second and fourth books of the *Essay* seem to have been written with no regard for the warnings against verbalism contained in the third. "Certainly the 2^d & 4th books don't agree with wt he says in ye 3^d."[9] Berkeley also objects strenuously to the assertion of the *Essay* that truth concerns the "joining and separating of signs."[10] This seemed to him a typical example of Locke's mistaken exaggeration of the importance of language in thinking. The author of the *Essay* should have stood by his statement that "all knowledge [is] only about ideas," and left the signs out of it.[11] Had he done so, he would have qualified his excessive reverence for the symbolic certainties of abstract mathematics. These "certainties" as Berkeley came to recognize are, in Locke's own phrase, "trifling" or analytic in character. "Locke's instances of demonstration in morality are, ac-

[8] H., 710; J., 729.
[9] J., 729.
[10] H., 544; J., 559.
[11] H., 511; J., 526.

cording to his own rule, trifling propositions." [12] Manipulating our symbols according to certain rules, we think we have "demonstrated" something about the true natures of things, when, as a matter of fact, we have simply discovered something about the arbitrary definitions we have ourselves concocted. Berkeley felt that the substitution of words for concrete objects was the greatest defect of the *Essay*,[13] and this instructive example of the ever present danger of "abstraction" played an important role in the formulation of his new method.

The supreme instance of such verbalism Berkeley found in Locke's famous description of a "general triangle." One of the later notes reads: "Mem. To bring the killing blow at the last, e.g. in the matter of abstraction to bring Locke's general triangle in the last." [14] This "general idea of a triangle" is, in Locke's own words, "something imperfect, that cannot exist; an idea wherein some parts of several different and inconsistent ideas are put together." [15] But why talk about "something imperfect that cannot exist"? After reading Locke's laborious discussions of modes, relations, and substances compounded, "framed," and "put together" in all sorts of preposterous ways, Berkeley resolved, above all else, to "be upon his guard against the fallacy of words." [16] He is not interested in the "general idea of a triangle" which "cannot exist" but rather the universal which not only can but does hold true. He is not interested in the mathematics of symbols, but in the mathematics of things, not in the logic of symbols but in the logic of reality. This fundamental insight into the abstractness of Locke's thought underlies all the further detailed criticisms of the doctrine of the *Essay* which are to be found in Berkeley's early writings.

Locke's spiritism is really based upon a supposed immediate intuition of self-activity. We have already noticed the scepticism concerning this intuition which creeps into the notations of the later diary. The knowing self cannot be identified with the self that is known. This fundamental criticism seems to have vaguely suggested itself to Berkeley's mind during what must have been almost his first reading of Locke. Thus, in one of the "theses" written early in 1706, Berkeley says, "Power not perceived by sense." [17] This scepticism becomes so pronounced towards the end of the *Commonplace Book* that, as we

---

[12] H., 684; J., 703; cf. H., 762; J., 784.
[13] J., 560, 601, 645, and 647.
[14] H., 680; J., 699.

[15] Ess., IV, vii, 9.
[16] J., 708.
[17] J., XXI.

have noted, he even questions at certain points whether the knowing self can be known at all. It is, in any case, absurd to think of it as the "given" object of a faculty or intuition. No such object or perception "can be the image of, or like unto that which is altogether active." [18] Berkeley came to believe that it was possible to trace many of Locke's more serious difficulties to this confusion of the active, knowing self with one of its own objects. Such objects may be connected together by the relation of causality, so that it is appropriate to speak of one as "determining" the other. But it is absurd to think of the thought which employs this concept as being itself determined. Causality itself is not a cause. To treat the activity of thought as a passive object is an example of that "grand cause of perplexity and darkness in treating of the Will . . . that we imagine it to be an object of thought." [19] Much of Locke's laborious discussion of the "freedom of the will" in his chapter on power is, therefore, based upon a misunderstanding. "'Tis an absurd question wch Locke puts, whether man may be free to will." [20] To ask such a question is already to answer it, for the conception of will or action already means freedom as distinguished from the passive, determined ideas or objects. Thus, "to ask whether a man can will either side is an absurd question, for the word *can* presupposes volition." [21] To ask such a question is to ask whether the activity of thought is really the activity of thought, or only one of its own objects. It is in fact like asking whether black is black, or white, since the action of the mind is "*toto coelo*" different "from all our ideas." [22]

Although the movement of Berkeley's thought is obscured by his continued adherence to the ambiguous term "Will" to describe the essential activity which opposes the whole world of perceived or intuited objects, the direction in which he is being taken becomes clear in certain pungent comments which he makes from time to time in the later note-book. Instead of following Locke, for example, in hypostatizing the activities of the mind into distinct faculties or independent entities, he sees that such faculties are already objects, and, therefore, presuppose an underlying activity of thought determining them. "It seems to me," he says, "that will and understanding — volitions and ideas — cannot be severed, that either cannot be possibly without the other." [23] The underlying activity of thought which is

[18] J., 718.
[19] J., 652.
[20] J., 891.
[21] J., 625; cf. 635–636.
[22] J., 652.
[23] J., 853.

presupposed by *both* these concepts is not Locke's abstract faculty of thought or *judicium*. This is a mere abstraction. Thus Berkeley says "Locke to Limborch &c. talk of *judicium intellectus* preceding the volition: I think *judicium* includes volition." [24]

In the midst of much confusion and hesitation one can nevertheless in the later diary discern a subtle transformation of Locke's spiritism. The hypostatized self is not the carrier for the whole world, but rather this self, together with all other objects, is relative to an underlying field of meaning without which it would not be intelligible. The union of the world of existence with this field of meaning is what Berkeley really means by the unity of "spirit," which, as we have seen, is the crowning conception of his early thought. According to this view, there is no need of thinking of the world as being constantly annihilated in a day, as he had first supposed, for, while *my* thought comes into existence and passes away, thought itself is eternal. Existence, and even absolute nothingness, are still forms of intelligibility, and hence, in this sense, thought. "Locke," therefore, "seems to be mistaken wn he says thought is not essential to the mind." [25] Berkeley agrees rather with Descartes that "there are innate ideas, i.e. ideas created with us." [26] From this point, Berkeley can no longer be viewed as a thoroughgoing spiritist or Lockian. The new concrete or "mental" mode of thought gradually took him far beyond the point of view of the writer who had first suggested it to his mind. While his early writings, as we shall see, are marred by many lapses into the early common-sense position, he gradually freed himself from it and passed on into those "transcendental" realms through which his concrete logic was destined to lead him.

DESCARTES

Both the *Discourse on Method* and the *Meditations* are specifically cited in the *Commonplace Book*, and Berkeley's comments show that he became thoroughly acquainted with these works during the later part of his formative period (probably during 1707 or 1708, when he was already well advanced in his criticism of spiritism). While it is doubtless true, as we have indicated, that there are certain aspects of the Cartesian rationalism with

[24] H., 736; J., 756.   [25] J., 659.   [26] J., 658.

which he found himself in essential agreement, the dualism of physical and psychical substance in which it had apparently crystallized could now prove no more satisfactory to his newly discovered sense for the concrete than the spiritism of Locke. The later diary is consequently filled with objections and criticisms of the Cartesian point of view.

Most of these objections, as we should expect, are based upon the fundamental opposition between Berkeley's concrete method and the mathematical or analytic method, which Descartes had attempted to apply to all fields of knowledge. This method begins by analyzing the concrete reality surrounding it into various phases or aspects, which it then proceeds to 'hypostatize' into separate, self-existent entities or substances. Since these are neither justifiable nor truly "self-evident," but absolutely essential for the later development of the method, the analyst seeks to justify them by speaking of them as if they were "self-evident" or simply "given" with unquestionable certainty to any mind. Once possessing these artificial substances, the analyst then proceeds to divide them further, looking at them now this way, now that way, but always continuing to reify the results of his dichotomies into further entities, for which he invents various names and definitions. Since all these names fall within a field determined by the nature of the first artificially isolated entity, it is also possible to discover equivalences between the definitions which are in fact essentially tautologies, though the symbols involved may be quite different. Berkeley, as we have seen, while he recognized that this sort of symbolic reflection had its place, was convinced that it was not appropriate for the purposes of philosophy, or any other discipline seriously attempting to describe the natures of things as they are, rather than the natures of the symbol systems in terms of which they may be described. Instead of losing himself, therefore, in a maze of artificial verbalism Berkeley determined at the very beginning of his philosophical career to direct his attention not to reality as it is described but as it *is*. The inevitable result of this determination was a profound dissatisfaction with Descartes' mathematical procedure.

"'Cogito ergo sum,'" he says, "Tautology. No mental proposition answering thereto." [27] There are two ways of looking at this proposition, which asserts a connection between thought and being. We may either hold that thought and

---

[27] J., 751.

being are different things, in which case the proposition is synthetic or "mental" in character, and possesses a legitimate meaning. In this case, however, the proposition loses its "self-evidence" and is no longer mathematically compelling. This, therefore, is not the Cartesian sense. For Descartes, the synthetic connection of thought and being is already presupposed or "given" as innate or self-evident. The "sum" is *already* really contained in the "cogito." Hence the predicate is simply another symbol for what is meant by the subject. There is no movement of thought or meaning, but only a movement of symbols. "Cogito" and "sum" are only different ways of referring to the same given thing. It is, therefore, mathematically certain that thought implies being. "Cogito ergo sum." But the mathematical certainty or "proof" is purchased only through the loss of significance. The proposition ceases to be meaningful or "mental" in character, and sinks to the level of tautology. What yields a spurious plausibility to the Cartesian argument is its suggestive wavering between the analytic and the synthetic points of view. This oscillation is, however, purely accidental, and the argument itself is unable to reveal any essential relation between the two.

The main features of Berkeley's attack on the universal applicability of the mathematical method are already familiar. We need only point out that it lies at the basis of all of his objections to Descartes. The only necessity which the analytic mentality seems capable of recognizing is the impure or arbitrary necessity of symbolic equivalence or "tautology." The various "primitive assumptions," therefore, or "self-evident" truths, which the method requires as starting points, remain isolated, independent "substances," lying side by side in a chaotic, irrational mixture. Hence, another "primitive postulate" or self-evident truth is required. Some purely arbitrary, capricious principle such as "human nature," or "pre-established harmony," or "God" is therefore assumed in order to hold the various, separate pieces together in a "world," since the fragments, as independent substances, are obviously incapable by themselves of fitting into any order.

For Descartes, accordingly, the relation between mind and body is conceived as some sort of "interaction" through the mediation of the pineal gland, or simply as a mystery to be felt rather than understood. His analytic method, indeed, could lead to no other result. Spiritual substance is one "clear and distinct idea," and material substance another. Berkeley is as ruthless in rejecting this "system" as in attacking the corresponding set of abstractions in Locke. Thus, in his *Guardian Essays* of 1713, he ridicules the "pineal gland." "Ask ... a Cartesian," he exclaims in the *Commonplace Book*, "why he supposes this vast structure, this compages of bodies? He shall be at a stand; he'll not have one word to say." [28] In such an analytic "system," all moves with impressive, tautological necessity, until one penetrates to the primitive assumptions, or "self-evident principles," upon which the whole edifice rests. Then, one is suddenly plunged into confusion and perplexity. *Why* suppose a separate, isolated world of material substances? There is only one possible answer. It is a "self-evident" truth — or "datum."

Instead of verbalizing or hypostatizing the material aspects of experience as an independent, self-existent "world," Berkeley tended rather to view the various sense qualities as phases of a more inclusive whole, without which, indeed, they themselves would not be what they are. "I differ from the Cartesians," he says, "in that I make extension, colour, &c. to exist really in bodies independent of our mind." [29] Bodies are related to "us" precisely as being external to our bodies in space, or "independent." To think of them as being independent of *meaning*, however, is to indulge in what is not even nonsense. The various qualities do not inhere in a mysterious "substance," existing without significance. This, Berkeley correctly diagnoses as the ultimate source of epistemological scepticism. The qualities are just where we see them to be. ". . . The pain is *in* my finger &c. according to my Doctrine." [30] Berkeley, therefore, believes Newton right as against Descartes "in assigning colours to the rays of light." [31] Colourless light is again perhaps a "useful," but nevertheless an artificial abstraction, which, if taken too seriously, must lead to scepticism.

It is, therefore, no wonder that Berkeley says, "I agree in nothing with the Cartesians as to ye existence of Bodies & Qualities." [32] These hypostatized material "entities" are only artificial constructions of the rationalist, which do not exist in the world as it *really* is. This does not mean, however, as we

[28] H., 463; J., 477; cf. *Siris*, sec. 304: "As for those absolute magnitudes and figures which certain Cartesians and other moderns suppose to be in things; that must seem a vain supposition, to whoever considers, it is supported by no argument of reason, and no experiment of sense."

[29] H., 791; J., 813.
[30] J., 441.   [31] J., 452.
[32] J., 421.

have seen, that Berkeley accepts the opposed hypostatization of the independent, isolated self. This "self" can no more exist as a "substance" than its "opposite" matter. The self and material objects are *both* in the world, as we know them to be. They are both, in other words, phases of a certain "concrete" reality extending beyond them — the unity of spirit. Berkeley's true originality consisted not in formulating a new theory to replace an older theory, but rather in perceiving that many of the difficulties of Descartes, as well as of Locke, arose not from any doctrine whatsoever, but from an abstract way of thought.

Spinoza

Berkeley apparently read Spinoza soon after Descartes in 1707 or 1708, and in several notes towards the end of the *Commonplace Book* he refers to both the *Epistles* and the *Ethics*. In certain essential respects Berkeley's thought was moving in definitely Spinozistic lines, and one or two comments show that he himself was to some extent aware of this fact. In Spinoza's *Ethics*, Berkeley found a criticism of the abstractions ordinarily termed "universals" which was in fundamental agreement with his own attack on "abstract general ideas." It is not surprising, therefore, to find him commenting on Spinoza's account of the origin of these abstract images (*termini transcendentales*), so commonly confused with genuine universals.[33] Spinoza states almost in Berkeley's own language that genuine or true universals cannot be obtained from the mutilation of particulars, or, as he puts it, "from individual things, represented by the senses to us in a mutilated and confused manner." [34] It is indeed impossible to believe that Berkeley, at this impressionable period of his life, was altogether uninfluenced by Spinoza's distinction between *termini transcendentales*, which are only mutilated, particular images, and the *notiones communes* which are "adequate ideas," [35] and therefore active, since, "in so far as [our mind] has adequate ideas, it necessarily acts." [36]

We have already commented upon Berkeley's view of the "active" character of thought,[37] and we cannot escape the con-

[33] J., 838. Berkeley here refers specifically to Eth., Pt. II, 40, schol. 1.
[34] Eth., II, 40, schol. 2.
[35] Eth., II, 40, schol. 2.
[36] Eth., III, 1.
[37] "Judicium includes volition." J., 756.

clusion that he received considerable encouragement at this time from the *Ethics*, in pursuing further the development of his concrete logic. This surmise is further substantiated by the significant fact that Berkeley later [38] came to employ the Spinozistic term "notion" to refer to the true, "active" universals, as distinguished from the "passive," mutilated particulars with which they are usually confused.[39] Spinoza's realization of the danger of confusing artificial, logical constructions with reality, and his polemic against the false, abstract "entities," which lead us to "confuse universals with individuals, and the entities of reason and abstractions with realities,"[40] are precisely parallel to Berkeley's sense of the artificiality of Locke's strange world of "essences," "complex modes," and "capacities," and his polemic against "abstract general ideas."

There are, moreover, other similarities in specific points of doctrine. It is most tempting, for example, to imagine a Spinozistic "influence" in Berkeley's distinction between two sorts of infinity, that of "extension consisting of innumerable parts," and that of the sphere which "has no end." [41] We have also commented upon Berkeley's identification of will and understanding. Such superficial points of resemblance, however, must be regarded as arising primarily from the underlying similarity of method. When we penetrate below the surface, we find that the thought of both Berkeley and Spinoza is determined by an attempt to avoid the artificial distinctions of ordinary, abstract thought. The process by means of which we separate aspects of reality from their contexts and reify them into artificial "entities" seemed to both thinkers the source of most of the basic misapprehensions of common-sense or *imaginatio*.

What really underlies the thought of both Berkeley and his great predecessor, therefore, is an attack upon the common employment of the category of substance, and a persistent attempt to think reality together as it really is, rather than in

[38] First tentatively in the *Three Dialogues*, and then consistently in the second edition of the *Principles* of 1734.

[39] Sergeant also uses the term "notion," but as there is only one short reference to him in the *Commonplace Book* on an irrelevant topic, and, as it is clear from the *Alciphron* that Berkeley was reading Spinoza at the time when he consistently adopted this terminology (1734), it seems far more probable, in connection with the evidence of the *Commonplace Book*, that Berkeley had in mind the "notiones communes" of Spinoza rather than the notions of Sergeant. Cf. pp. 77–80.

[40] Eth., II, 49, schol.

[41] H., 461; J., 475; cf. Spin., Epistle 12.

the artificial "lumps" of ordinary discourse. These "lumps" have the advantage of being conveniently clear and distinct, but they are unfortunately false. The objects which vulgar discourse dignifies by the term "thing" are, for Spinoza, modes, and for Berkeley phases or "considerations." It is also remarkable that it was his synthetic logic which led Berkeley, as it had led Spinoza, to the conclusion that there is, in the end, only one true substance or cause. Berkeley says, "Spinoza . . . will have God to be 'omnium rerum causa immanens,' and to countenance this produces that of St. Paul, 'in Him we live,' &c. Now this of St. Paul may be explained by my doctrine as well as Spinoza's, or Locke's, or Hobbs's, or Raphson's, &c." [42] The early thought of Berkeley, as is quite evident from the third of the *Dialogues between Hylas and Philonous*, does, as a matter of fact, terminate in just such an absolute whole or "infinite mind of God," [43] as the all-inclusive Absolute, which Spinoza similarly apotheosized. "The dependence of all things on God," says Berkeley, is "manifest." [44] Spinoza was, of course, a "disreputable author," and a youth of twenty-two or twenty-three could not fail to be influenced by such an "accepted" tradition. It is not surprising, therefore, to find him, at the beginning of his discussion, grouping Spinoza with "Epicurus" and "Hobbs" as "a declared enemy of religion." [45] But the further development of his earlier thought makes it quite clear that the debt he owed his great predecessor was by no means negligible.

Berkeley's concrete logic, however, could not stop with that absolute whole of all being in which Spinoza's thought finally crystallized. His criticism of this conception, and his passage to a philosophic view quite distinct from it, is, indeed, as we shall see, the dominant feature of Berkeley's later development. While both Berkeley and Spinoza persistently attempted to develop a mode of reflection that should transcend the artificial "entities" of common sense, there is a most significant difference between the concrete logic of Berkeley and the "*scientia intuitiva*" of Spinoza. "Intuition" is the apprehension of something already given or finished and contemplated from the outside, whereas Berkeley's concrete method embodies a "movement," [46] which makes it rather a species of dialectic than contemplation. Berkeley's later development,

---

[42] J., 839.   [44] 3D., F. i, p. 473.   [46] Cf. "transition" in the *Siris*.
[43] 3D., F. i, p. 453.   [45] J., 836.

therefore, includes a "practical" moment, entirely missing in the mystical intellectualism of Book V of the *Ethics*. That is why, in Berkeley's more mature writings, his antipathy to Spinoza assumes an intensity which is really justified by the essential character of his own thought. Certain of the comments of the *Commonplace Book*, indeed, vaguely indicate the nature of this fundamental divergence.

The criticism of the mathematical method, which we have traced, could not fail to bring Berkeley into collision with the mathematical form which Spinoza apparently considered as adequate to express his fundamental intuition of the connectedness or relatedness of all things. He consequently objects to the Spinozistic axiom "ex nihilo nihil fit," as being a tautology having no "positive signification," [47] and views all such *veritates aeternae* as being arbitrary definitions rather than truths. "Wt becomes of the aeternae veritates?" he asks himself. "They vanish!" [48] They "vanish" as mere redundancies, expressing "trifling" facts concerning the nature of our symbol systems rather than significant truths concerning reality.

It also seemed to Berkeley, even at this early period, that Spinoza had only imperfectly and incompletely carried out the implications of his synthetic "intuition." Hence, he comments, "Dico quod extensio non concipitur in se et per se, contra quam dicit Spinoza." [49] One of the most evident "results," as it seemed to him, of a truly concrete way of thought must be the abandonment of the ordinary hypostatization of an independent, spatial world conceived *in se*. Spinoza's attempt to escape this difficulty by regarding space as only an "attribute," and hence *not* strictly conceived *in se*, seemed to him a contradictory and, therefore, inadequate solution. He accordingly takes exception to the whole doctrine of attributes as unclear. [50]

At a later point in his development, after his concrete logic had carried him beyond the speculative absolute of the third dialogue, his antipathy to Spinoza is much more pronounced. In the *Alciphron* he criticizes Spinoza for "undermining religion under the pretence of vindicating and explaining it," and more particularly for attempting to demonstrate it "as one may demonstrate anything." [51] Concrete reason is certainly something more than mathematical reason, something more even

[47] J., 843.
[48] J., 748; cf. 843.
[49] J., 856; cf. Epist. II ad Oldenburgium.
[50] J., 857.
[51] Alc., VII, p. 362.

than what is commonly called "reason." The "practical" reflections to which this logic led ultimately demand a "submission in points above our knowledge." [52] The mystical absorption in the whole of being, on the other hand, in which Spinoza's thought seemed to terminate appeared to him as identical with the opinion "that men are mere machines impelled by fatal necessity," [53] and to arise from an imperfect realization of the fact that "reason," even taken in the broadest sense, must, in the end, pass beyond itself.

The detailed consideration of this further development of Berkeley's concrete logic, however, will be postponed to later chapters. We must be content here with the bald assertion that his synthetic method finally led him away from the contemplative mysticism of Spinoza towards a manner of thought which, as is increasingly evident, can be identified only with that of "Plato, Aristotle, and Socrates," the "authority" of whom, for Spinoza, as he himself admits, held "not much weight." [54]

PLATO AND PLATONISM

Berkeley's relation to Plato opens up a question which is as confused as it is important. The usual view that Berkeley's early position is altogether dominated by "the spirit of empiricism" [55] and that the "intellectualism" of the *Siris* represents a tissue of senile inconsistencies [56] is not borne out by a careful consideration of the textual evidence. What this evidence shows is rather a very gradual process in which, as if carried by an irresistible inner impetus, he brings himself more and more under the spell of the Platonic tradition. Nothing, indeed, is more essential for an understanding of Berkeley's "development" than this growth in his understanding of the

[52] Alc., VI, p. 313.
[53] Alc., VII, p. 362.
[54] Epist. 56, Boxel.
[55] Erdmann, *Berkeley's Philosophie*, p. 37.
[56] Cf. Mabbott, "The Place of God in Berkeley's Philosophy," *J. of Phil. Studies*, vol. VI, no. 21, January, 1931, who asserts that: "In the Siris we find a new world. Its Platonic mysticism, its toleration of forms and influences, its reverent agnosticism, its dependence upon the Timaeus and Proclus, are poles apart from the Berkeley of the other works. It

is true that Divine Ideas are important in Siris. . . . There is nothing Berkeleyan about them. To attempt to unite the hints and gropings of Siris into some kind of dusky Christian Platonism, and then to regard the result as characteristic of Berkeley, would be like making the Catholic faith the central belief of Voltaire on the strength of his reputed death-bed conversion. Catholicism and Voltaire make as strong bed-fellows as Siris and Berkeley" (p. 27). This is the ordinary view. Cf. also Hone and Rossi, *Bishop Berkeley*, chap. XII.

meaning and importance of Platonism, though it has been hitherto rather strangely neglected by commentators. There was no stage in Berkeley's intellectual career when he was not familiar with at least certain of the Platonic Dialogues, though his comprehension and appreciation of their significance developed hand-in-hand with the deepening of his thought. We must, in fact, think of Berkeley himself as a passage or movement — the passage from Locke to Plato.

Berkeley was appointed "Junior Greek Lecturer" at Trinity College in 1712, certainly implying at least a vague acquaintance with Plato for some years, a fact that is actually verified by several specific references in the early works. Thus, in 1707 he refers to Plato as a representative *par excellence* of the "subtil & scholastique strain." [57] Two years later, however, in a letter of October 21, 1709, he recommends the *Crito* to his friend Percival, and in another of December 27, 1709, he speaks enthusiastically of the *Phaedo*. In 1710, after writing the *Principles*, he penned a most interesting letter, in answer to Lady Percival, who had wished to question him concerning the relation between his views, as expressed in the *Principles*, and the "Mosaic Creation." In this letter he says: "I do not deny the existence of any of those sensible things which Moses says were created by God. They existed from all eternity in the Divine Intellect, and then became perceptible (i.e. were created) in the same manner and order as is described in Genesis." [58] It is impossible to miss the connection between this unmistakably Platonic conception and the note of the *Commonplace Book* written in 1707, wherein he says, "My doctrine excellently corresponds with the Creation. I suppose no matter, no stars, sun, &c. to have existed before." [59] This is also correlated with the general conception of the Divine Nature, which, as expressed in the *Commonplace Book*, is not only eternal, [60] but contains "in" it "the properties of all things," [61] though not as passive ideas. [62] In the *Passive Obedience* of 1712, which partially fills the gap left by Part Two of the *Principles*, there is one specific reference to Plato's *Seventh Epistle*, [63] and the essential role played in this treatise by "the *eternal rules of Reason*," [64] which may be demonstrated by "the deductions of reason," [65] is hard to reconcile

[57] J., 310.
[58] September 6, 1710.
[59] J., 351.
[60] J., 3.
[61] J., 824.

[62] J., 686.
[63] F. iv, p. 130.
[64] P. O., sec. 12.
[65] P. O., sec. 4.

with the traditional view of the young Berkeley as an iconoclastic "empiricist."

It is true, as we have pointed out in connection with the
Commonplace Book, that Berkeley did rebel against the prevailing intellectualism of the day. "Vain," he cries, "is the *distinction* 'twixt the Intellectual and Material world." [66] But at
no point is this equivalent to a "denial" of the "intellectual
world," — the usual interpretation made by those who insist
on viewing Berkeley as a "boyish" Hume. The problem with
which Berkeley was really wrestling was the hardly un-Platonic
problem of somehow thinking the "sensual" and "intellectual"
worlds together as *one*. The emphasis on the "concrete" rather
than the "abstract," which motivates all of Berkeley's writings,
is not *essentially* an emphasis on the "sensual" rather than the
"intellectual." Indeed, the truth of the matter is that Berkeley's attempt to brush aside words and abstractions, in order to
penetrate through the "veil" of language to the "real," led him
on inevitably to the "intellectual," the "world of ideas," or as
he preferred to call them in the *Dialogues*, "archetypes."
Berkeley was forced by his love of the real, complete, or truly
"empirical" to the non-empirical, the "archetypes," and the
"transcendental."

Berkeley has been interpreted by two generations of his-
torians who have seen in him only an immature Hume. This
interpretation has been aided by the fact that the most "scientific," though by no means the most adequate, presentation of
his position, the *Principles*, as it has come to be called, is only a
fragment dealing with the sensory world, which does not even
pretend to treat of "God and the Self" (as first projected), and
consequently never arrives at metaphysics. This unfortunate
hiatus in Berkeley's published writings is partially rectified by
the *Dialogues*, written probably in 1711 or 1712, without a
thorough consideration of which, any attempt to do justice to
Berkeley's early thought is random speculation. In this work,
which is still seriously marred by his early causal "spiritism,"
the Platonism inherent in his position from the very first
comes clearly to light. The world of temporal existence absolutely requires the "intelligible world" for its completion, since
"I do by an act of reason, necessarily infer the existence of a
God, and of all created things in the mind of God." [67] But,
though "God knows or hath ideas . . . His ideas are not con-

⁶⁶ J., 543; italics not in text.   ⁶⁷ 3D., F. i, p. 448.

veyed to Him by sense." [68] There are, therefore, two orders: the complete order, "the archetypal and eternal," which "existed from everlasting in the mind of God"; [69] and "the ectypal or natural state of things," which "was created in time." [70] It must be admitted that the archetypal theory is not fully worked out, as is only to be expected in a "popular" work such as the *Dialogues*. But there is enough, particularly in the third Dialogue, to show how thoroughly Berkeley's mind was steeped in the Platonic tradition. It is idle to speculate as to just what particular channel actually brought him this Platonic influence. In a letter of November 27, 1710, he disavows any connection with Malebranche or Norris, but was certainly acquainted with the works of both, and he could not very well have escaped contact with the schoolmen, though his references to them in the *Commonplace Book*, following the fashion of the age, are almost wholly derogatory, and he mentions only one (Scaliger) by name. [71] There is no need, however, for speculating as to such secondary channels, since, as we have already pointed out, he became directly acquainted while at Trinity College with certain Dialogues, as well as the *Epistles*, in the original. The Platonic impulse was certainly present in Berkeley's thought from the very first, and, as we shall hope to establish, his philosophical development is largely an unfolding of this original germ.

There are several references to Plato in the *Guardian Essays* of 1713, the most important of which are a long translation of a section of the *Gorgias*, [72] and a reference to the account of the philosophic life in the *Theaetetus*. [73] By this time Berkeley was, therefore, acquainted with the *Crito*, *Phaedo*, *Gorgias*, *Theaetetus*, and *Epistles*, and probably with most of the other dialogues. In the *De Motu* of 1720 he refers to the *Timaeus*. [74] Platonism furthermore did not desert him in his period of scepticism, for there are references in the *Alciphron* to the *Gorgias*, [75] the *Protagoras*, [76] the *Io*, [77] the *Philebus*, [78] the *Symposium*, [79] and the *Phaedrus*. [80] These references reflect the "practical" interest

[68] 3D., F. i, p. 459.
[69] 3D., F. i, p. 475.
[70] *Ibid.*
[71] J., 393.
[72] Essay II, *Natural Grounds to Expect a Future State*, F. iv, p. 145.
[73] F. iv, p. 171.
[74] D. M., sec. 32.

[75] Alc., VI, pp. 270–271; II, p. 90.
[76] Alc., II, p. 101; V, p.213; VI, p. 269; and VII, p. 368.
[77] Alc., VI, p. 262.
[78] Alc., II, p. 96.
[79] Alc., III, p. 132.
[80] Alc., VI, pp. 269 and 343.

which was dominant in this period of his life, and deal exclusively with the religious and moral implications of Platonism. We must also regard the emphatic introduction of the term "notion" to stand for the sort of knowledge hitherto associated with the causal "acts" or "operations" of the finite self, which occurred at this time,[81] as a definitely though incompletely Platonic step. The self which holds the separate parts of the world together is no longer identified with the finite individual, but rather with a noetic self which "relates" opposed fragments together into a universal system.

Berkeley did not, however, come to realize in full the epistemological and metaphysical implications of Platonism until the very end of his life. We must postpone a detailed account of these implications, as Berkeley then came to see them, chiefly through the eyes of Plotinus, to a later chapter.[82] Here it must suffice to indicate that the *Siris*, Berkeley's only metaphysical treatise, ends with an attempt to give some account of the realm of "notions" or "Divine Ideas" which lie at the source of all knowledge and reality, and which are, indeed, required by the world of sense as a necessary completion. Experience is thus seen to lead essentially, *not* "causally," beyond experience, just as knowledge leads beyond knowledge, sense beyond sense to reason, and man beyond man to God. The "notions" underlying all knowledge are no longer conceived as temporal "acts" of the finite self or "will" but as "ideas" of the "intelligible world," transcendental forms of meaning.

The development of Berkeley's thought is, therefore, the reverse of Plato's. Berkeley started with sense, and fought his way up to an intuition of the transcendental, whereas Plato, beginning with an insight into the nature of the transcendental, wrestled "to save the appearances." Both, furthermore, attempted at the end of their lives to crystallize their reflections in a half-mythical, intuitive picture of the cosmos as a whole, and both have been accused of radical inconsistency in making this attempt. The parallel between the *Siris* and the *Timaeus* strikes the eye almost at first glance. Both works seek to bring together the world of sense and the world of reason; both are cosmological, centering about the world of nature, and the attempt to work out a defensible meaning or interpretation of this world; and both find themselves most readily able to accom-

---

[81] 2nd ed. of Pr., 1734, but cf. *Dialogues*, F. i, p. 448.   [82] Chap. XVI.

plish this in terms of a "divine tradition" transmitted from the ancient past. The distinctively Christian conception of creation from nothing, however, enabled Berkeley to escape at least certain of the difficulties connected with the traditional Greek conception of matter, and the God of the *Siris* is, therefore, something more than an artificer. But Berkeley himself refers to the *Timaeus* in connection with his conception of space as an incomplete or spurious type of reasoning, and the general atmosphere of this last treatise is as unmistakably Platonic in character as is its climax.

Perhaps the most truly Platonic aspect of Berkeley's thought, however, is to be found in the synthetic or "mental mode of reasoning," which he applied sporadically in his early works, but which later led him on to the conception of a "*philosophia prima*" neither hypothetical nor "analytic" in character, but "a certain transcendental science superior to and more extensive than mathematics" [83] dealing with "the first causes of things" [84] and their essences. The final development of this method is to be found in the subtle "transitions" and thought movements of the *Siris*. It is hard to escape from the conclusion that here we have in a modern guise, stated in terms of a different language, but as a result of the same compelling stream of thought, Plato's conception of dialectic.

THE CAMBRIDGE PLATONISTS

Since it is quite clear that Berkeley does, as a matter of fact, belong to the Platonic tradition, his relation to the most famous representatives of this tradition in his own country becomes a subject worthy of careful attention. When Berkeley's thought is viewed as a whole, several marked similarities to the philosophy of the Cambridge school are apparent. There is, for example, the common dependence upon the insight of Plotinus, which became characteristic of both. There also seems to be, at first glance, a marked likeness between the "romantic" view of nature found in Berkeley's *Siris*, and the various opinions which have led critics to label Henry More, at least, as an "extravagant author," though this would hardly apply to his great predecessor Cudworth. Most of the Cambridge Platonists, however, would certainly be in sympathy with Berkeley's final attempt to interpret the world of nature as "alive and in

[83] An., Qu. 49. [84] D. M., secs. 71 and 72.

motion," as well as with his conception of sense as a language suggesting basic meanings or interpretations innate in the mind.[85] Berkeley's profound sympathy with Christianity would also seem to afford us a link binding him to his Platonic predecessors. This would seem to extend even to the underlying rationalism, in the light of which both apparently felt that it was necessary to adjust and interpret the traditional dogmas. Thus, the *Siris* seems clearly Platonic, in the Cambridge sense, in its tendency to identify Christianity with an "universal light," though Berkeley speaks rather of an "universal tradition," and was no longer satisfied with such terms as "natural light," or "natural reason." [86] Nevertheless, there does seem to be a definite point of union in the attempt of the *Siris* to bridge the chasm between faith and reason, and to maintain that there is at least a basis for the dogmas of the Church in the "revelation" of reason itself. The fact, however, that Berkeley both at the beginning [87] of his career and at the end of the *Siris* [88] felt himself in profound opposition to the Cambridge thinkers must lead us to search further than these somewhat superficial points of resemblance.

Such a search will reveal, I think, certain reasons which altogether justify Berkeley's feeling of antipathy, or at least render it quite impossible to think of him as, in any precise sense, a belated member of the Cambridge tradition. There is, for instance, as we have already suggested, a most fundamental difference between the two types of "rationalism." This difference is indicated by the ease with which the Cambridge doctrine was turned into deism or "natural light" philosophy by such writers as Locke and Shaftesbury.[89] According to Whichcote, "Whatsoever there is *Good Reason* for the Doing of is Warranted of God." [90] It is, therefore, God who must ac-

---

[85] Cf. *Siris*, secs. 309 ff., and sermon, "*Thy Will be Done* . . .," Luce, *Hermathena*, XXII, p. 30. These passages make it clear that Berkeley finally accepted the doctrine of "innate ideas" in a form which would certainly be acceptable to these thinkers.

[86] In his final draft of the sermon, *Thy Will be Done* . . ., for example, he scratched out all instances of these phrases, which never occur without qualification in his later writings. Cf. *Siris*, sec. 360.

[87] See J., 308.

[88] "Cudworth," secs. 251, 255, 352.

[89] Concerning the influence of the "Cambridge Latitudinarians" on Locke during his early student days see Fox Bourne, *Life of Locke*, I, p. 77; Von Hertling, *John Locke u. die Schule von Cambridge*; Gibson, *Locke's Theory of Knowledge*, pp. 236–241; and also Powicke, *Cambridge Platonists*, pp. 200 ff. For Shaftesbury see Powicke, *op. cit.*, p. 198.

[90] *Aphorisms, Moral and Religious*, Salter, ed., London, 1753. Cf. also no. 37, "We cannot put a greater abuse upon

commodate Himself to our reason, rather than our reason which must ultimately pass beyond its abstract nature and accommodate itself to the transcendent. As a result of this deistic rationalism, we find the Cambridge Platonists subscribing wholeheartedly and almost without exception to the abstract mathematical ideal of knowledge, and showering their contemporaries with treatises purporting to bring other branches of knowledge up to the ideal level of certainty achieved by mathematics, the field of ethics being particularly favored in this respect.[91] We have already noted the critical process through which Berkeley freed himself from the analytic shackles of the mathematical ideal, and his substitution of the principle of completeness or concreteness for that of abstract identity. This distinguishes him fundamentally from the various members of the Cambridge school, whose mathematico-logical rationalism led them to condemn altogether the world of sense or to see in it only a "confused" or "fuddled" reason.[92] Speaking specifically of Cudworth in this connection Berkeley says that ". . . the whole series of things in this visible world, which we call the Course of Nature, is so wisely managed and carried on that the most improved *human* reason cannot thoroughly comprehend even the least particle thereof; so far is it from seeming to be produced by fuddled or confounded reason." [93] Nothing could more clearly reveal the basic distinction between the non-psychological rationalism in which Berkeley's thinking terminated and the mathematical idealism of his predecessors. What seems absolutely muddled and confused from the mathematical point of view is, in reality, in the highest degree clear and orderly, and what is clear and certain to *human* reason may be in the highest degree confused or even "trivial" to God. While Berkeley still distinguishes between sense and reason in the *Siris*, the distinction loses its mathematical sharpness, for there is a continuity between the two. "The lowest is

God than to say He is *obscure*," and no. 76, "to go against *Reason* is to go against God"; also nos. 572, 633, 646, 705, and 877.

[91] Cf. More's *Enchiridion Ethicum*, London, 1711, p. 24: "Depromam igitur ex hac penu Principia quaedam immediate vera nulliusque indiga probationis, sed in quae omnis fere Ratio Moralis (quemadmodum Demonstrationes Mathematicae in *communes suas* sententias) per-

spicue facileque resolvitur." Also, Cudworth's *Treatise on Immutable Morality*.

[92] See Cudworth, *Intellectual System*, Bk. I, ch. III, Dissertatio De Natura Genitrice: "Natura vero ratio est mersa in materiam et confusa ac veluti corpore ebria." Ed. London, 1773.

[93] *Siris*, sec. 255; italics in text. Berkeley thus objects to a co-eternal matter limiting God, as implied by Cudworth's conception of "plastic nature."

joined to the highest." Berkeley also objects very strongly to Cudworth's leniency to materialistic hypotheses which "intelligibly solve the corporeal phenomena. . . ." [94] Against this concession Berkeley asserts roundly that "it will be found not to solve any phenomenon at all," [95] since the concept of matter on which they are based is an artificial abstraction, a word which attempts to eliminate all consideration of the relations without which it could not be. [96]

Berkeley is constantly quarreling with the abstract distinctions of the understanding which seem to lose sight of the identity without which the difference would lose all meaning. Thus, Cudworth asks if it must not be admitted that "the First Hypostasis or Person in the Platonic Trinity (if not the Christian also) is ἄνους or ἄλογος, senseless and irrational, and altogether void of mind or understanding?" [97] To this Berkeley replies that "the maintaining a distinction of priority between τὸ Ἔν and Νοῦς doth not infer that the one ever existed without the other." Indeed, Νοῦς is only Νοῦς over against τὸ Ἔν. It could not be what it is "without the other." [98] Therefore, "it follows, that the Father, or τὸ Ἔν may, in a certain sense, be said to be ἄνους without Atheism, or without destroying the notion of a Deity; any more than it would destroy the notion of a human soul, if we should conceive a distinction between self and intellect, or intellect and life." [99] The very making of such a distinction would presuppose and indeed intensify the larger unity or identity on the ground of which alone our distinction gains any meaning or validity. Such dialectical considerations, altogether foreign to the thought of the Cambridge school, were an inevitable consequence of the concrete method which Berkeley developed as a result of his early criticism of mathematics.

The abstract rationalism of the Cambridge Platonists not only forced them, as we have seen, into Arianism, but the charge of Arminianism, frequently brought against them, was certainly not without justification. Obeying the eternal principles of reason is the sum and substance of religion. There is

---

[94] *Intellectual System*, Bk. I, 1, 45.

[95] *Siris*, sec. 251.

[96] *Ibid.*

[97] *Intell. System*, Bk. I, IV, 36, p. 894, ed. 1773.

[98] *Siris*, sec. 352. Revelation, therefore, is no mere abstract historic event.

Its timeless *meaning* (Νοῦς) is essential to it.

[99] *Ibid.* While Berkeley disagreed with Cudworth's abstract logic, he was often able to put to good use the latter's really vast erudition. Cf. *Siris*, sec. 363.

nothing beyond these rules, for even God Himself is bound by them. "The Judge," says Whichcote, "is nothing but the Law speaking." [100] Such moralism kept forcing the Cambridge logicians to the heresy of self-salvation. "The righteousness of faith," writes Smith, "is that powerful attractive which . . . draws down the virtues of heaven into the souls of men." [101] After his first mathematical enthusiasm, Berkeley opposed this type of abstract moralism even more vigorously than the abstract unitarianism of Cudworth. There could be no question of God's adapting Himself to the ways of man. The sum and substance of all morality and religion was rather the coincidence of man with "the Will of God." [102] Morality was nothing without religion, and *human* reason could not exist except as against the divine.[103] Indeed, the notion of a "human" reason is a self-stultifying concept, since we must in the first place presuppose reason itself to arrive at the concept of humanity. Berkeley was, therefore, able to preserve his orthodox Augustinian position without having to fall back on "dark doctrine" and mysticism. On the other hand there was no anthropomorphizing of the Deity, no attribution to Him of a "perfection" too evidently betraying its all too human origin, no sentimentalizing of the Divine Goodness into what "must needs be good as good can be." [104] Berkeley never questioned the primary Augustinian tenet that God is from beginning to end the initiating Agent in the process of salvation. This Berkeley realized consistently from the *Passive Obedience* to his last Sermon.[105] He must, therefore, have been somewhat sickened by the confidence with which certain of the Cambridge mathematical divines deduced attributes of the divine nature, and the pathetic obstinacy with which they clung to the principles of their mathematically demonstrated morality. Berkeley understood that it was possible in this mortal state to catch only a few "glimpses" here and there of "divine things," [106]

[100] *Aphorisms*, 319.

[101] Smith, John, *Select Discourses*, Cambridge, 1673, ff. 142–143; cf. Whichcote, "There is nothing Desperate in the state of *Good Men*," *Aphorisms*, 200; and also "He will save every one that can be saved," *ibid.*, 439.

[102] Sermon, Luce, *Hermathena*, XXII, p. 38 *et passim*.

[103] *Siris*, sec. 360.

[104] "The Religious represent God to themselves as Amiable; the Superstitious represent God to themselves as Formidable," Whichcote, *Aphorisms*, 947. Cf. also "The State of Religion lies in a good Mind, and a good Life," *ibid.*, 835; and "Goodness is the *proper* Notion of God," *ibid.*, 787.

[105] *Sermon*, Luce, *Hermathena*, XXII, p. 40.

[106] *Siris*, sec. 367.

and that there must be many "moral" matters which transcend the mathematical understanding. But this irrationalism was not something held apart from everything else in a separate compartment, something *sui generis* with a rationale and method of its own, like that of Henry More, who used his all too "human" logic as far as it would go, and then straightway jumped to ghosts and mystic formulae. For Berkeley, the irrational became far too essential to be expressed in any such convenient mysticism. Indeed, without the irrational, the rational would cease to be rational. He maintained that the two belong together in one and the same universe. There is a certain transcendent "necessity" hovering over all "things," though not the mechanical necessity of the free-thinkers, which is so unmistakably the reverse side of their own abstract "freedom." The moral "resignation" to which the recognition of this necessity leads, however, is not a resignation to fate, but to the "Will of God." [107]

Berkeley's concrete logic does not fail him altogether even in contemplating the question of the relation of God to the world. He condemns equally the abstract Sabellianism of those who maintain so "logically" that God is transcendent and hence above and beyond the world, having nothing whatsoever to do with its finite temporality and sin, at least after the creation, and the abstract pantheism of those who follow Henry More (i.e. Newton and Locke) in identifying God with space. He is "everywhere about us and within us," [108] and yet so infinitely beyond that no human reason may ever hope to comprehend Him, immanent as the λόγος, transcendent as τὸ Ἕν. It makes no difference "whether we prescind Unity from essence and Intellect; since metaphysical distinctions of the divine attributes do not in reality divide them; or whether we consider the universal system of things as One; since the union, connexion, and order of its members do manifestly infer a mind or intellect to be cause thereof." [109] There is no difficulty, therefore, in seeing why the "greatest" of the ancient philosophers "held a Trinity in the Godhead," and why this doctrine is not only the heart of religion, but the essence of the life of reason itself.

We have now indicated the two major influences which moulded Berkeley's thought, the descriptive, empirical influence of Locke upon his early reflections, and the rationalistic,

[107] Sermon, Luce, *Hermathena*, XXII, p. 34.

[108] F., iv, p. 168.

[109] *Siris*, sec. 353.

"dialectical" influence of Plato, which continued to become more and more prominent as his thought matured. In the *Commonplace Book* "Platonism" is associated with the "lofty strain," [110] with "flourish" and extravagance of imagination. But as his mind advanced in depth and grasp, he outgrew this Lockian prejudice, and was constantly forced by the inner logic of his own position closer and closer to Plato. That this development was not in the least an unconscious one is evidenced by his reiterated statements to the effect that Plato was his "favorite author." Mrs. Berkeley, indeed, mentions "Plato and Hooker" as "two of his principal favorites," [111] and his great admiration for "his favorite Plato" is attested on many sides, even by those who discount this aspect of his thought.[112] After impartially viewing the evidence, it is impossible to deny that, whatever our own feeling concerning the justification of the process may be, Berkeley himself grew out of Locke into Platonism. This is in fact, as we shall see, the determining undercurrent of his philosophic development.

This Platonism was not passively received or accepted. Berkeley had to win it for himself by an intense process of self-criticism that caused him, even in the *Commonplace Book*, to abandon many of the leading tenets of the Lockian spiritism which was his point of departure, and led him finally to the obscure Platonic insights he attempted to express in the *Siris*. We turn now to a closer study of this development as it manifests itself in Berkeley's published writings, though we shall also (as we proceed) seek to clarify the biographic context which is often of value in interpreting those successive works in which he sought, sometimes with only partial success, to express the course of his reflections.

NOTE ON JOHN SERGEANT

There is one reference in the *Commonplace Book* to John Sergeant and his "solid philosophy," obviously meaning his "*Solid Philosophy asserted Against the Fancies of the Ideists*," printed in London in 1697. The complete lack of enthusiasm and even interest, however, manifested in Berkeley's comment [113] makes it very unlikely that any decisive "influence" came to him from this source. Certainly the brief memorandum indicates no careful study of Sergeant's works, dealing

---

[110] J., 310.
[111] *Biog. Brit.*, III, Add. & Corr., p. 258.
[112] Cf. Hone and Rossi, *Bishop Berkeley*, etc., p. 220.
[113] J., 852.

as it does with a point concerning Berkeley's *New Theory of Vision*, and not with any major tenet of Sergeant's system. Indeed, there is no evidence that Berkeley had ever studied Sergeant. The one reference, however, calls for a further consideration of the possible impression that such a study might have made on Berkeley at the time of the *Commonplace Book*.[114]

Sergeant criticizes Locke because of the subjectivism and scepticism which he feels must result from his position. Instead, however, of attacking the *causal* theory of perception in general, as Berkeley finally did, and thus preparing the way for an effective transcendence of the theory of "representative perception," Sergeant himself falls into the very same difficulties for which he so acutely criticizes Locke.[115] His attack, therefore, really comes to nothing more, in the end, than the substitution of one "causal" theory for another. He demolishes the theory of "knowledge through ideas or phantasms," because to know the picture as a picture we must first know the thing,[116] and then proceeds to elaborate a theory of emanations "sent out from bodies," which "imprint the very Body itself . . . on that material part which is the Seat of Knowledge," [117] a theory, we must add, which differs from Locke's only in its more daring dogmatism. Sergeant never decisively takes the step upon which all of Berkeley's speculations are really based, of substituting the principle of continuity or completeness for the common-sense view of causal "efflux" or influence, though certain of his remarks on the notion of "substance" as the "whole" of which the attributes are merely aspects, or the "Thing" itself "as *diversely considered*," [118] certainly lead in this direction, and may have been noted by Berkeley, though there is no direct evidence to this effect.[119]

Berkeley's "concrete" logic finally enabled him to maintain the incompleteness and hence the unreality of the perceived world without adopting the notion of an unperceived "cause" lying back of it, while Sergeant never got rid of the causal view. This is what is really involved in Berkeley's criticism of the "solid philosophy" according to which we must "*see* solids." Sergeant, in order to justify his common-sense realism, is forced to maintain dogmatically that the whole object is directly given to us through the "effluvia" which bring the essence of the object, including its solidity, to the mind. Thus the object we perceive both is and is not the *real* object. Berkeley is able

---

[114] Certain "similarities" between Berkeley's views and those of Sergeant have been emphasized by Mr. G. A. Johnston in his *Development of Berkeley's Phil.*, pp. 61 ff. and 162 ff.

[115] In connection with his "Aristotelian" doctrine of "effluvia."

[116] Sergeant, *Solid Phil.*, pp. 340 ff.

[117] Sergeant, *op. cit.*, Prelim. Disc. 4.

[118] Sergeant, *op. cit.*, p. 97; cf. p. 320.

[119] Cf., however, Berkeley's use of the word *consider* in C. B., J., 263, 330, 734, though all of these occur before the specific reference to Sergeant in J., 852. The ultimate source of this usage is doubtless Aquinas, *S. Theol.* I. q. 85. a. I ad I: Et hoc est abstrahere universale a particulari vel speciem intelligibilem a phan-

to reconcile this contradiction through his logic of completeness, according to which the object we perceive is real so far as it goes, but since what we perceive inevitably relates itself to all sorts of things we do *not* perceive (in this case "solidity"), what we perceive, if taken abstractly by itself, is to this extent unreal, though what it requires for its completion is not something "causal," and therefore lying back of experience in a "noumenal" hinterland, but something presupposed by it, or, in Berkeley's language, "without which it could not be."

It is true that Sergeant distinguishes sharply between sense images and "notions," and speaks of "Archetypes" in "the Divine Mind," but it is not necessary to conjure up such a source as Sergeant for these features of Berkeley's system, ingrained as they were in the intellectual tradition upon which he was first nurtured. So far as Berkeley's employment of the word "notion" in a sense closely similar to that of Sergeant is concerned,[120] it must be admitted that such a borrowing is conceivable. But when we remember that Berkeley did not begin to use the word "notion" consistently in this sense until 1734 [121] and that the only evidence that he read Sergeant at all is the one cursory comment written at least twenty-five years before, the suggestion loses force. If we must seek an authority for this usage Spinoza's "notiones communes" [122] seems a far more plausible "source," since the *Alciphron* (1732) shows that he was reading Spinoza at this period of his life.

Berkeley and Sergeant exemplify very different modes of thought and the superficial similarity of doctrinal points, in their common antipathy to Locke, does not justify any attempt to go beyond the slight evidence afforded by the *Commonplace Book* in order to prove any "influence" of the latter on the former. Sergeant represents what he conceived to be "the true Aristotelian doctrine," [123] defending the "clear way" of mathematics as the only method of escape from "those deviations from truth and disagreements among philosophers in their tenets and conclusions which we find in the world," [124] while Berkeley, as we have noted, starting out with a similar enthusiasm for analysis, soon discovered this mathematico-logical beacon to be an *ignis fatuus*. Sergeant sharply distinguished between the concrete world of individuals and the abstract thought of the "Understanding." But, instead of attempting to discover a new logic which might do justice to reality, he took the far easier course of the intellectualist, holding, that is, to his abstract logic, but inventing a special "world"

---

tasmatibus, considerare scilicet naturam speciei absque consideratione individualium principiorum, quae per phantasmata repraesentantur.

[120] A point stressed by Mr. G. A. Johnston, *Development of Berkeley's Phil.*, pp. 162 ff.

[121] He does, however, employ the word "notion" in this connection in the *Dialogues* of 1713; cf. F. i, p. 448.

[122] Eth. II, 40, schol.

[123] *Op. cit.*, p. 329.

[124] Sergeant, *The Method to Science*, preface, London, 1696.

or "realm" to justify or exemplify it. This Berkeley would never do. For this, indeed, he was too much of an "empiricist." He utterly lacked the defiance of the "rationalist," who can say "this is logic; therefore the world must be so, and if not, so much the worse for the world!" Berkeley as an idealist was far too "realistic" to indulge in such anthropomorphic exuberance. For him there was an "independent actuality" to which logic must conform, the world in the concrete, as it *is*. If logic does not conform, so much the worse for it. There is only one "real" world.

PART II

CONCRETE AND ABSTRACT REASON.
THE EARLY SYSTEM

"God has dealt more bountifully with the sons of men than to give them a strong desire for that knowledge which he had placed quite out of their reach." (*Principles*, Int., sec. 3.)

CONCRETE AND ABSTRACT REASON.
THE EARLY SYSTEM

The first period of Berkeley's intellectual life was one of intense activity in which he worked out the fundamental principles guiding him in his later thought. As we have tried to show, it is possible by a careful study of the *Commonplace Book* to anticipate, to some degree, the course which these later reflections were destined to take. In actually developing his early intuitions, however, Berkeley is forced to cope with problems hitherto only half glimpsed, to eliminate contradictions hitherto only half perceived, and in many ways to qualify and "clarify" his doctrine. This is, on the whole, a gain. But the very elimination of contradictions in the consistent solution of a certain problem may involve a blindness to other essential factors only temporarily forced below the surface. It is safe to assert that in spite of, and partly because of its many contradictions and its vague, half-formulated character, the *Commonplace Book* gives us a far more adequate view of Berkeley *as a whole* than any one or any two of his published works with the exception of the *Siris*. It is only when they are taken together that these later works offer us a picture which may truly transcend and fulfill the ideal Berkeley so vaguely and yet so suggestively outlined in the *Commonplace Book*. In the study of his published writings, therefore, one by one, we must be prepared, especially at first, for what may seem to be reactions and reversions, although if we bear in mind the concrete ideal of his earliest thought we shall be able to appreciate the sense in which each work does fulfill a part at least of the early sketch, as well as the sense in which it is, if taken by itself alone, only a tendency or phase.

The first period, to which we shall now turn, is a particularly fertile one from the standpoint of written publications. It is, however, only an abstract aspect of Berkeley's thought that is given expression, and we must count it a great misfortune that these youthful works alone have gained the serious attention of the general as well as the philosophical public. During this period Berkeley was for the most part living in Dublin as a resident Tutor of Trinity College. His interest is ostensibly to combat the "atheism" associated with the new mechanical world-view, by means of his new logic. But he is not fully conscious of the deeper implications of his method, and constantly confuses it with the "logic" of his opponents. An essentially deistic confidence in "reason" is, indeed, the prevailing tone of his writings, which are seemingly oblivious to the critical ambiguities hidden under this disarming cloak. He offers "proofs" for the existence of God and His "immateriality," [1] as well as a demonstration following "the most rigid laws of reasoning" for "the comfortable expectation of Immortality," [2] and is confident that it will be possible "to convince sceptics and Infidels" [3] by using their own weapons against them. As such traces of "rationalism" would lead us to expect, there are many concepts which are accepted on authority, without appreciating the fundamental modification they must undergo if brought into serious relation with the "concrete." This is particularly true of the concept of "causation" which is uncritically or dogmatically employed throughout this period. In the most mature of the early works, however, the *Three Dialogues*, he begins to become conscious of the profounder implications of his new method, and initiates that turning to Plato which is so conspicuously its final outcome. His attack on materialism directs him primarily to the field of epistemology in the *New Theory of Vision*, the *Treatise Concerning the Principles of Human Knowledge*, and, above all, the *Three Dialogues between Hylas and Philonous*. But the field of moral and religious philosophy is not altogether neglected, as is indicated by the *Passive Obedience*, the several sermons delivered at Trinity College, and the *Guardian Essays*, a brief consideration of which will conclude our study of this first productive period in Berkeley's development.

[1] Pr., pref.
[2] 3D., pref., F. i, p. 377.
[3] 3D., pref., F. i, p. 377.

CHAPTER IV

THE APPEAL TO THE CONCRETE
(NEW THEORY OF VISION)

THE *New Theory of Vision* was not published until 1709, though, as we have seen, its germinal ideas may be traced to the earliest parts of the *Commonplace Book*. It will not be surprising, therefore, if we discover that many of these ideas, when compared with Berkeley's more mature thought, seem unformed. The permanent significance of the new theory lies in its attempt to penetrate through the abstractions of common sense to concrete, visual experience as it really is, to understand what happens when "the mind simply sees," as Berkeley puts it, though, as he becomes increasingly aware of the enormous difficulty of the task, he realizes the inadequacy and "abstractness" of certain features of his first formulation.

THE PROBLEM

If we ask ourselves why it was that Berkeley chose first to confront the public with the discussion of such a detailed problem rather than with the presentation of his general position, we shall be led to certain considerations which will throw much light on this difficult, and from the standpoint of Berkeley's development, "primitive" work. In the first place, he no doubt realized from conversation with his friends how strange and paradoxical these new views must appear to his contemporaries, especially in the form in which he was first forced to state them. Berkeley's early career was, indeed, dominated by a losing struggle against the dead weight of "common sense" which has always rendered metaphysical speculation so difficult in Anglo-Saxon countries, and he was, of course, aware of the sort of opposition any "new principle" must arouse even in "enlightened circles." [1] His early "habit of humouring an opponent" may have led him to see the wisdom of attempting first to capture an outpost before storming the citadel of the very principles of human knowledge. We know also that he himself had a strong "practical" interest. As he specifically states in the

[1] Cf. letter of Percival, November 27, 1710.

Commonplace Book: "my end is not to deliver Metaphysiques altogether in a general scholastic way, but in some measure to accommodate them to the sciences, and shew how they may be useful in Optiques, Geometry, etc." [2] This interest must be attributed not so much to the influence of the "new experimental philosophy" as to the profound sense of the "concrete" which we have already noted as the most outstanding feature of the *Commonplace Book*. Metaphysics, as he saw it, was never an "abstract" study moving exclusively in a separate "ether" of its own, but something also working in "natural knowledge," bringing it to higher consciousness of its relations to other fields not usually considered as "appropriate" to it, and thus rendering it not only theoretically, but even technically, more fruitful. It was partly in order to demonstrate this "technical" fruitfulness of "metaphysics" when applied to a restricted "scientific" field that Berkeley undertook the detailed investigation of visual perception which constitutes so large a portion of the early *Commonplace Book*, and which was finally completed as the *New Theory of Vision*.

But it is not necessary to elaborate further such extraneous reasons to explain Berkeley's genuine interest in the various problems connected with spatial perception. The faculty of sight seems to present us with a world of *independent* objects existing *outside* us in space, while Berkeley's new logic, as we have seen, involves the assertion of the *interdependence* of all objects in the concrete unity of Spirit. If, however, as Newton supposed, there is a huge objective, spatial "box," in which we ourselves, as well as other objects, are simply "located," the concrete unity of Spirit becomes a subordinate and altogether subjective matter, involving only an unimportant aspect of the great, physical system which constitutes the universe *as it really is*. To state the problem crudely, — is the mind in space, or is space in the mind? Are we to accept the mathematico-mechanical logic of the atheists and mathematicians as adequately applying to the actual world, or the "concrete" logic of the *Commonplace Book*? Is the newly discovered mechanical universe of the Renaissance an aspect of spirit, or is spirit an insignificant aspect of physical nature? We are, of course, left in no doubt by the *Commonplace Book* as to the assuredness with which Berkeley held the former view. Thus he says: "I wonder how men cannot see a truth so obvious, as that extension cannot

[2] J., 215.

exist without a thinking substance." [3] Nowhere, in fact, does Berkeley's new logic of concreteness, according to which all things must be seen together, come into more striking conflict with ordinary opinion than in the process of visual perception which is naively supposed on all sides to present us with objects entirely separate and distinct from us, as well as from one another. It is, therefore, apparent that in order to convince an unsympathetic audience of the bare plausibility of his doctrine it was first necessary to break down this prejudice of an abstract, independent world of space. This is the inner, systematic necessity which forced Berkeley to develop a new theory of vision and to present it to the public in 1709.

The "Concrete" as the Immediate

Berkeley begins his discussion by an appeal to "immediate experience," that is, experience in its pristine purity, before it is veiled by the cloak of language and the hackneyed interpretations that rule our daily life. For example, in section 12 he says: "I appeal to anyone's experience, whether, upon sight of an object he computes its distance by the bigness of the angle made by the meeting of the two optic axes. . . . Everyone is himself the best judge of what he perceives and what not." And in section 43 he states further: "I appeal to any man's experience, whether the visible extension of any object do not appear as near to him as the colour of that object." The reader must "not stick in this or that phrase or manner of expression but . . . laying aside the words as much as possible consider the bare notions themselves." [4]

Such appeals are of constant occurrence in the *New Theory of Vision*. Berkeley apparently feels that if we could only achieve "an entire deliverance from the deception of words" [5] and simply "contemplate" experience as "given," we should be at once confronted with the world as it is in its concrete entirety, though he has no illusions as to the difficulties of such a task. Thus he "scarce dares" to promise himself "an entire deliverance" from the deception of words, "so difficult a thing it is to dissolve a union so early begun, and confirmed by so long a habit, as that betwixt words and ideas." [6] The universal "immediate experience" which Berkeley wishes to describe is hence

---

[3] J., 279. Cf. J., 18, 34.
[4] N. T. V., sec. 120.
[5] Pr. Ms., F. iii, p. 381.
[6] *Ibid.*

not to be identified with the world of common sense, though it cannot be denied that at several points he himself did, as a matter of fact, confuse the two.

It became evident later in Berkeley's career that the attempt to discover an uninterpreted "datum" is doomed, since to speak of a datum as uninterpreted is to interpret it; the *concept* of "datum" itself is not *given*. The purely phenomenal, descriptive attitude toward experience was, in Berkeley's case at least, more of negative than of positive importance. The "return" to the immediate enabled him to sweep the slate *clean* of past "predilections and prejudices," and to start again from new foundations. It is easy to understand, however, why, after Berkeley's youth, he gave up the exclusive emphasis on the descriptive approach which we find in the *New Theory of Vision* and the *De Motu*, for the concepts we use in describing the "given" are not themselves given. The attempt to ignore the *a priori* leads not to its elimination, which is strictly impossible, but simply to the passive acceptance of common sense as the *a priori*. This is why we find Berkeley, at the conclusion of his early "productive" period, forced to a theory of ideas or archetypes. Without such a set of stable or "eternal" concepts any attempt to find a solid basis for philosophy is certain to fail, for meaning or intelligibility, the "logos" itself, is prior to what is "given."

It cannot, therefore, be denied that the tendency of Berkeley's early works to attribute philosophic disagreement and obscurity to the "veil of language" was, as he himself came to perceive (in the *Siris*), somewhat naive, since to tear aside one veil is inevitably to substitute another. In the *New Theory of Vision*, however, as we shall be forced to remark more than once, Berkeley's tendency to take the observational attitude, to identify the "concrete" with the "given," led him into just what he so persistently warned against, the reiteration of a common-sense or accepted (given) prejudice. The idea that all philosophic problems are to be solved by the continuous employment of a mysterious category such as that of the "given," and the passive "observation" of what floats past the "eye of consciousness," is an easy and mechanical conception, very similar to such abstractions as "the materialistic conception of history," and the view which would attribute "the development of modern science" to such events as the invention of the telescope or microscope. The statement, for example, addressed by Berkeley to the reader in the author's introduction to the *Principles* that "I do not see how he can be led into error by considering his own naked undisguised ideas," [7] if taken seriously, can be interpreted only as an encouragement to intellectual sloth. Fortunately, even in the *New Theory of Vision*, where this attitude is more prominent than elsewhere, Berkeley does not, as he of course *cannot*, interpret it strictly. Indeed, the burden of the *New Theory of Vision* is devoted to the elaboration of the point that what *seems* to be immediately given in visual experience is *really* not given at all, but ultimately emanates from another source. It is true that in the *New Theory of Vision*, as in the *Principles*, this other source was first conceived after the passive "empirical" analogy. But in the end, as we shall be able to show, Berkeley was forced to go beyond the "given" to account for this source.[8] Experience leads us necessarily beyond experience. The given is not itself given, and the "concrete" is not in the least to be identified with the empirical. This is the *result* of Berkeley's early experiments with phenomenalism.

THE VULGAR ERROR

Despite the conception of the concrete unity of Spirit, which is the culminating insight of the *Commonplace Book*, and despite the fact that he must have been fully convinced of that organic unity in which every aspect of experience, including the spatial, must find its place, we find Berkeley in the *New Theory of Vision* speaking of tangibly extended objects as being "external" [9] or "without the mind." [10] He himself was fully aware of this "vulgar error," as he called it in his *Treatise Concerning the Principles of Human Knowledge*, published a year later in 1710. Here he says [11] that the supposition that "tangible objects" are, in a certain sense, "without the mind" was not necessary

[7] F. i, p. 256.

[8] I cannot, therefore, agree with Hecht, who says, *Berkeleys Lehre*, p. 29: "Wahrscheinlich haben aber beide, Abstractionslehre wie Immaterialismus, ihre Wurzeln in einer Gegenstandslehre, die es sich zum Ziele gesetzt hatte, die Natur des ursprünglich gegebenen festzuhalten." This is an example of the sort of interpretation which arises from too exclusive an attention to certain works and a consequent failure to grasp the whole. When the attempt is made to understand Berkeley's development, to understand the *Commonplace Book* as well as the *Principles*, the *Siris* as well as the *New Theory of Vision*, I think it becomes evident that Berkeley's Immaterialism, as well as his early "phenomenalism," are, as a matter of fact, *applications* of his new "concrete logic" of abstraction.

[9] N. T. V., F. i, p. 166.

[10] N. T. V., sec. 94, p. 174.

[11] Sec. 44, p. 280.

"for establishing the notion therein laid down," but was only assumed "because it was beside my purpose to examine and refute it in a discourse concerning Vision." We must pause for a moment to examine the reasons lying back of this strange lapse in terminology which, as we shall be forced to point out, not only confuses the reader, but is also associated with certain ambiguities which mar the argument of the *New Theory of Vision* itself.

In the first place, it is impossible to deny a certain weight to the excuse offered in the *Principles* that Berkeley was not here attempting to develop his whole philosophy, but only to show how it could be made "usefull in optiques." [12] But this hardly accounts for the extreme to which he goes in speaking of tangible objects as "external," when a word such as "real" would have placated common sense without compromising his own view. This applies also to the excuse suggested by Berkeley's tendency to "humour an opponent," and "to correct men's mistakes without altering their language," [13] which must also be granted a certain weight. There are other features of the *New Theory of Vision*, however, which lead us to suppose that during the writing of this treatise Berkeley was not only "humouring" his opponent but himself as well in certain "vulgar" fallacies quite inconsistent with his new approach. This is readily understandable in the light of the fact, already noted, that the ideas expanded in the *New Theory of Vision* belong to the very beginning of his reflections, before the consequences of his concrete logic had fully developed, so that it is reasonable to suppose that even later it might be natural for him to fall back upon the original and inadequate forms in which the argument had first taken shape. It is not surprising, moreover, that Berkeley should generally adopt common-sense and slipshod attitudes concerning the object of "touch," since as we shall point out, this concept contains in its shadowy depths all the other weaknesses and ambiguities which detract so much from that ultimate sense of conviction which the new theory might otherwise convey. While it is true that the *New Theory of Vision Vindicated*, published in 1733, constitutes a much maturer formulation and corrects many of the blunders of the earlier statement, nevertheless it cannot be said to succeed in clarifying the most serious ambiguities hovering over the mysterious word "touch." Thus, although the *New Theory of*

[12] J., 215.   [13] J., 189.

Vision Vindicated does not speak of tangible objects as being "without the mind," it certainly does not completely realize Berkeley's intention of avoiding the abstractions of "Anatomy" and "Geometry," and of explaining *in the concrete* "how the mind of man simply sees," or of understanding "the true nature of vision, considered as a faculty of the soul." [14] Berkeley's lapses into the abstractions of physiology are much more prominent, however, in the earlier statement of his view, where they constitute a grave defect in a treatise attempting to describe vision in the concrete — an even more serious extension of the vulgar error, since on this point there can be no question of consciously "humouring an opponent."

For example, we find Berkeley identifying an actual visual experience, "the appearance upper," with certain physiological events "painted lower on the retina," both of which "are the same thing." [15] Such physiological "explanations" cannot be uncritically accepted in this way from the "concrete" point of view, since the physiological events are only phases of experience, and cannot be used to "explain" other phases which are, as a matter of fact, phenomenally on the same level. [16] The essential features, however, of Berkeley's *New Theory of Vision* do not in the least depend on any such physiological considerations, and in the *New Theory of Vision Vindicated*, written in 1733, as we have observed, he takes at least *some* pains to correct these erroneous abstractions. Thus in speaking of "the inverted pictures on the retina" [17] he says they are only "supposed" to be the proper objects of sight, and points out in so many words that the "tangible images on the retina" are not "the proper immediate objects of sight," and are, therefore, irrelevant to his purpose. [18]

It is to be regretted that so little attention has been paid to Berkeley's *New Theory of Vision Vindicated*, for in this treatise he constantly corrects at least the more extreme forms of the

[14] N. T. V. V., sec. 43, p. 399.

[15] N. T. V., sec. 63, p. 157. Cf. N. T. V., sec. 88, p. 171.

[16] Kemp Smith has observed this inconsistency and even gone so far as to state that Berkeley's whole position can be arrived at only through such physiological considerations which, after the position has been arrived at, are then unceremoniously set aside. While such a criticism may apply to the N. T. V., considered in isolation from Berkeley's strictly philosophical works, it cannot apply to his fully self-conscious position, which is always developed, as in the *Principles*, through a description of the concrete field of consciousness with no such reference to physiology or anatomy. *Commentary to Kant's Critique*, p. 588.

[17] Sec. 49, p. 402.

[18] Sec. 50, p. 402.

"vulgar error," and states his theory in a generally more mature and consistent form. Particularly in one important passage he makes it clear that he is proceeding, as in his philosophy as a whole, from the basis of a description of the concrete content of consciousness, and sharply distinguishes this standpoint from the more limited point of view of the sciences, which restrict themselves to separate *realms* of experience, and do not consider the relation of the object to the subject, or allocate themselves in the field of experience as a whole. "To consider particles as moving in certain lines, rays of light as refracted, or reflected or crossing, or including angles, is quite another thing and appertaineth to Geometry. To account for the sense of vision by the mechanism of the eye is a third thing which appertaineth to anatomy and experiments. These two latter speculations are of use in practice, to assist the defects and remedy the distempers of sight, agreeably to the natural laws contained in this mundane system. But the former theory [how the mind of man simply sees] is that which makes us understand the true nature of vision, considered as a faculty of the soul." [19] It was by putting aside mechanical and physiological presuppositions and penetrating to concrete consciousness, including its suggested fringes and backgrounds, that Berkeley achieved his new results. What is the whole conscious context of visual perception? This is the question which he really asks himself, though it cannot be denied that his answer at many points falls back into the ruts of common-sense abstraction. It is, nevertheless, to this answer that we must now direct our attention.

The New Theory of Vision

Berkeley begins his discussion with an assumption regarding which he finds all parties in agreement, — namely, that distance from the eye, or depth, is not perceived directly by vision. This assumption, resting as it does, at least in part, on physiological grounds, is not adequately discussed,[20] and the later treatise of 1733 does not proceed in this way. The "proper" or "concrete" objects of sight are light and colour, and the three-dimensional spatial relations, which obtain between these ideas, cannot emanate from visual perception alone. Berkeley bases this partly on introspective grounds, partly on the hypothetical case of a blind man who suddenly recovers his sight (verified

[19] N. T. V. V., sec. 43, p. 399.   [20] Sec. 2.

by Cheselden), and finally, and most tellingly, on the fact that the visual magnitude of objects is not what we mean by the "actual" size of an object,— the moon for example. The visual size or magnitude may vary, while the "actual" size and position remain the same. This, of course, implies that visual objects have *some* size, though not the *actual* size. What we mean by the *actual* size, distance, and situation of objects is not something that is directly given in the experience of seeing. What we immediately see is a varying field of light and colour. How then do we arrive at the perception of permanent or actual space?

Berkeley finds the prevailing theory to be that we judge the true external position of objects by a certain "natural geometry" of the eyes. When an object is close, the two optic axes make an angle which is greater than when the object is at a distance. And even with one eye, an object which is seen by more diverging rays is judged closer. Berkeley disposes of this mechanism on introspective grounds. We are not in the least aware of such rays and angles. He shows, furthermore, that this sort of explanation is unable to cope with certain visual phenomena, especially visual hallucination. Spatial perception involves a *judgment* [21] not based on visual phenomena alone. Nor can it be based on any such geometrical computations concerning angles and rays. What then is the source of this judgment?

Berkeley now turns to another field of experience, the field of touch. In this field objects are given more permanently and reliably. The visual image of the chair may run through a whole gamut of changes; the chair that I feel remains constant.[22] A long distance may appear no longer than an inch so far as pure vision is concerned, but when I come to walk the distance I cannot be deceived.[23] Indeed, an ocular illusion may be defined as a visual appearance that cannot be later verified by touch, and Berkeley, therefore, seems to conclude that real objective, permanent space is "tangible" space. He let the matter rest at this point so far as his *New Theory of Vision* is concerned, and never fully described the process through which

---

[21] "Suggestion" is the word which is employed most frequently in the earlier treatise. In sec. 65 of the N. T. V. V., p. 408, however, Berkeley speaks of "our judgments or apprehensions either of the greatness or distance of an object." Cf. sec. 69; also sec. 66, p. 409.

[22] Cf., however, Pr., secs. 9, 10, 11.

[23] But cf. 1D.

space is achieved by means of "touch." This view, however, is most questionable on Berkeley's own grounds, for does he not himself show later that touch sensations are also variable and relative?[24] In the experience of touching or grasping an object it is true that we gain an immediate sense of its resistance, but this is very far from what we mean by space. Space is no more a series of sensations of hardness and softness [25] than it is a series of colors or lights. If he had only addressed himself to as careful an examination of the sense of touch as he gave to the sense of sight, he would have been able to correct the main faults of his new theory, and might have come much more rapidly to the position to which the intrinsic logic of his thought as a whole was surely driving him.

In the *New Theory of Vision*, however, he devoted almost all of his effort to the description of the mechanism of *transfer* through which visual lights and colours become spatialized, rather than to the analysis of spatial perception itself. This is to be attributed to the fact that the *New Theory of Vision*, like the other early works, is a polemic treatise, and it was on this point of transfer that Berkeley felt himself most definitely opposed to the traditional point of view, which held to the conception of a certain "natural geometry," by means of which we are supposed to compute the distance and magnitude of objects directly and necessarily on the basis of the given, visual appearances. Not only does he deny such computation on introspective grounds, but he takes great pains to show how it is inadequate for the explanation of visual hallucinations. Our perception of space involves inference and "reasoning." [26] This is the position to which he finally turns, in spite of the more careless statements concerning "touch" which have with some justification been interpreted as the crudest sort of sensationalism. But spatial judgment is a type of reasoning which moves in the sensations, connecting them in a certain order, and not an abstract sort of reasoning which may move in a realm by itself, isolated from experience. This is the essential difference between Berkeley and his opponents. Space is neither a pure sensation [27] nor a purely rational concept [28] or operation of the mind. As a rule by which we order our sensations, it involves both datum and interpretation. This attempt to balance the empirical and "intellectual" factors involved in spatial per-

---

[24] I D., F. i, pp. 399–402 *et passim.*
[25] N. T. V., sec. 103.
[26] J., 210.
[27] J., 292, 723.
[28] J., 536.

ception is responsible for many misconceptions of Berkeley's view. Independently of all experience we should never originally arrive at the conception of space, for this order is incompletely *suggested* to us by experience itself, not by any purely "rational" necessity. And yet, though he is more ambiguous on this point, space is not merely a "simple idea." It is more than a sensation. Thus, in his discussion of vision, he first shows that space is not given directly as a visual sensation, but rather, in so far as it is seen, is an interpretation ultimately emanating from another source, described vaguely in the *New Theory of Vision* as "touch."

The task is made easier for him through the fact that it was already admitted that distance from the eye — "outness" — is not directly given in vision. Berkeley further has no difficulty in showing that the immediately given visual extension is not what we mean by the actual extension of an object, since an object which is *actually* very large may be given in vision as something very small indeed, and *vice versa*. He then devotes a great deal of effort to discussing the mechanism through which the actual magnitudes, derived, as he claims, from or rather *through* tactual experience, are suggested. Thus, actual or "tactual" distance is *suggested* by: (1) binocular accommodation; (2) confusion or strain, indicating nearness to the eye; (3) number, size, and kind of object, as in the case of the moon, which is judged by various extraneous reasons of this sort to be very large, although its visual appearance is quite small. These visual signs have no necessary connection with the actual distances they signify, but are learned on the basis of experience, and become so "blended" with the visual signs that we come to say that we actually see the distance, though this is no more the case than that we hear the meaning of a spoken word. The interpretation thus enters into the experience itself so that we actually *see* what is not strictly there as a "datum."

This sort of process is also involved in the visual perception of actual magnitude, which is given only in the same sense as distance. Berkeley here takes sharp issue with the accepted tradition, which maintained that the perception of magnitude is secondary, being computed geometrically on the basis of the actual distance. Berkeley maintains, on the contrary, that actual magnitude can be suggested *as* directly as distance, and by exactly analogous signs. These signs are: (1) visible magnitude, larger magnitude, in the absence of other factors, indicating greater actual magnitude; (2) confusion indicating small actual magnitude; (3) vigor and faintness of the image, faintness generally indicating distance, and therefore large size; (4) the number and situation of intervening objects, objects placed higher on the field of vision generally suggesting greater magnitude, at least until the line of the horizon is reached.[29] All this is directed to the one goal of showing that spatial relations are not directly "given" through sight alone, but through an interpretation ultimately derived from another realm, though the nature of this ultimate derivation is left quite indistinct. So far as the *New Theory of Vision* is concerned, Berkeley leaves the question as to the real nature of space unanswered, nor is he even quite clear as to the extent to which space is, or is not, directly given in vision, wavering uncertainly with respect to what he calls "visual magnitude." This uncertainty, however, is not without significance, as we shall see, in the development of his theory of space.[30]

The essential features of Berkeley's *New Theory of Vision* come to light most clearly in his peculiarly interesting discussions of concrete problems and the solutions he was led to find for them by his new theory, since his mind generally needed some such definite center around which to crystallize its speculations. Furthermore, the *Commonplace Book* shows that his *New Theory of Vision* developed from the start in the closest relation with these problems. Thus the question concerning the larger apparent magnitude of the horizontal moon appears at the beginning of the *Commonplace Book* in connection with his earliest meditations on vision.[31] His ultimate explanation of this phenomenon involves two factors: first, the greater faintness of the horizontal moon, directly suggesting greater size, and secondly the peculiar isolated position of the vertical moon. In this isolated position there are no intervening objects which ordinarily lead us to infer great magnitude. These being absent, the isolated vertical moon is judged smaller.[32] The spatial interpretation derived from another source enters into the appearance itself making it larger or smaller.

Another problem which occupied Berkeley from the beginning was the problem of the inverted image which is mentioned early in the *Commonplace Book*. "Why," he asks, do "we see

[29] N. T. V. V., sec. 55.

[30] This inconsistency has been noted by all of Berkeley's best critics from the first, but particularly by Bailey, *A Review of Berkeley's Theory of Vision.*
[31] J., 127, 142.   [32] N. T. V., p. 162.

things erect when painted inverted?" [33] Berkeley's answer to this question carried him far into the implications of his theory, even beyond its first stated limits. Suppose, for example, that I see a man standing erect. According to the physiological theory, the image on the retina is inverted. But how and for whom is the image inverted? Berkeley distinguishes between the immediate experience and the explanation of the experience. This explanation is made from a position external to that of experience itself. We place the individual in question, together with his retina, in an artificial, abstract space, and try to include his experiences as a part of such a space. We then say that *his* image is upside-down in *our* space. Berkeley's reply is that the individual in question with his experience cannot possibly be reduced to such a part of another space. His experiences are organized by him into a space of his own which is a *whole* (or nothing), into which *all* external experiences fit. This space is an absolute whole, and must be such a whole to be space. The antinomy results from trying to turn such an absolute whole into a part. When I see an erect man, the erectness is not a mere sensation or image "given" to me. It is a system or order fitting into a larger system. What I mean is that by "turning the eye up and down" I am directed "to make a suitable judgment of the situation of objects." [34] If I move my head upward, I see the head or the upper part of the man's body. If I turn my head down I see the feet. These results are furthermore correlated with the results I obtain through touch by moving my hand over the object. Space is not any one image or impression, but a system into which all ideas must be fitted. The erectness of the man is a "judgment," through which I place the object in this system, *as a whole*. When, however, I think of the image in another person's eye as being inverted I am thinking not of his system, or the *one* system, but of two abstract systems, one of which attempts to include the other as a part of itself. The antinomy thus arises, and *I* cannot see how *he* can see the object as erect. But I have torn this one experience from its context, which is here precisely the matter at issue, for space consists in the constant "connection" or relation of *all* objects to this context. Science makes a necessary abstraction from this system, and tries to reify certain incomplete experiences (retinal image, etc.), which already presuppose the spatial whole, into another external system of its own. In doing

[33] J., 128.   [34] N. T. V., sec. 98, p. 176.

so it may discover "useful" truths, but it falls into antinomies, such as that of the inverted image, which can only be ultimately explained by a philosophical discipline adhering closely to the realities of pure consciousness and hence viewing vision in its proper setting as a "faculty of the soul."

This necessity of viewing space as a whole, in spite of the "subjectivism" or "spiritism" which mars Berkeley's analysis, becomes even clearer in the case of another difficulty which occupied him from the first pages of the *Commonplace Book* and is worthy of the closest attention. This is the question of the visible minimum. A conscious experience cannot be infinitely divided. There is a last element or threshold beyond which we cannot perceive. The visual field for Berkeley consisted of a set of such points, and from the very first [35] he was forced to the seemingly paradoxical position that the "minimum visible is exactly equal in all beings whatsoever that are endowed with the visive faculty." [36] But it will be asked, must it not be supposed that the *minimum visibile* of a mite, for example, is less than that of a man, and that men differ in sharpness of sight? Berkeley replies with a decisive negative, "for, suppose it otherwise, and that the *minimum visibile* of a mite, for instance, be less than the *minimum visibile* of a man; the latter therefore may, by detraction of some part, be made equal to the former. It doth, therefore, consist of parts, which is inconsistent with the notion of a *minimum visibile* or point." [37]

This is a beautiful example of the sharpness and consequence with which Berkeley pushed his theory of abstraction. Perceived space is always a whole, and every part of it must be seen in relation to this whole, though he had unfortunately not yet realized the fatal effect of such "concrete" considerations upon his "spiritism." When seen in relation to *the* whole a *minimum visibile as a minimum* must be the same for every conscious being,— for when this one experience is torn from its context and placed in another "sharper" consciousness which analyzes it into parts it is no longer a minimum, or what it was to the "duller" consciousness. To enter into another field of spatial consciousness it is necessary to enter into it as a whole or not at all. Without the constant realization of the necessity of this essential relation to space itself, any such absolute comparison must remain an abstraction. Thus Berkeley comes to

---

[35] J., 281.   [36] N. T. V., sec. 80, p. 168.   [37] N. T. V., sec. 80.

realize that consciousness cannot be supposed to consist of a mass of sensory minima side by side. The minimum is a minimum only in relation to the whole.

Berkeley drew several important consequences from this insight. Whether I am in my chamber, or out of doors, or looking through a microscope, "I see just as many visible points." [38] The difference lies in the interpretation or "the secondary and mediate objects of vision." [39] These interpretations, being acts or relations, may be identical even in different individuals, though the immediate given sensory matter may be variable. He is thus very far from deriving a solipsistic conclusion from this analysis of spatial perception, and takes issue with Malebranche for maintaining that, strictly speaking, we can never be sure that we are seeing what another sees,— for the interpretation or relations, *which may be identical*, enter into the given ὕλη, and actually merge with it as something that I see. The field of consciousness is not like an automatic camera, for it can *make allowances* for the differences of position and the peculiarities of its private point of view, determining its judgments by *the* space which is one and the same for all. This is, in fact, probably one of the most compelling reasons which led Berkeley later to abandon his early solipsistic "spiritism."

In the solution of such specific problems Berkeley is led to make useful applications of his concrete logic and to show that metaphysics is really "of use in optiques." The antinomy of the inverted image arises from the reification of an abstraction. It is impossible to say that a man is upside-down until we further state *with reference to what* he is inverted. This frame of reference must then further be related to other frames beyond it, and so forth. If we simply stop the process at any one level, and reify *it* as *space*, we fall into difficulty, for there will then be "other" spaces with conflicting claims. Space is not an objective "thing," which exists like a lump of lead or a box, but a system of relations,[40] the very meaning of which lies in its completeness. A partial space "included" in "another" space is *really* not space at all. The minute we have begun to speak of *space* we have thereby expressed our intention to deal with *all* of space and not a part, since a part can be a part only by being part of the whole. And yet if we ever attempt to view any *given* space as complete, it thereby ceases to be complete, and

---

[38] N. T. V., sec. 82.   [39] *Ibid.*   [40] N. T. V., sec. 116.

becomes an abstraction leading to antinomies. It is the essence of space to be complete only in its incompleteness, to be a whole of fragmentary parts, to be sure, but fragmentary only by necessary reference to the whole. Space, therefore, can be one only as an active, non-mechanical system which is constantly *present* in all of its parts, though without them it cannot be, and any attempt to fix it or circumscribe it is bound to lead to "mighty difficulty" and confusion.[41]

All this lies implicit in Berkeley's discussion of the inverted image and the visual minimum, though his solipsistic spiritism often led him to stop with "my space" or "his space" as natural or logical resting points, and thus prevented the fuller development of the idea. As he himself was to discover, however, in the *Siris*, such a development is necessary. The same logic which compels me to pass from one object to another until I have related all the objects in *my* space to what is beyond or outside them, must also lead me to relate my space with other spaces outside my space. Beyond "my space" and "his space," necessarily presupposed by *both* of them, is *Space*. Not only does this apply to "my space" and "his space," but, as Berkeley so acutely perceived in his discussion of the retinal image, also to *all* physiological or physical "explanations" of spatial perception. *Any* such explanation must, to begin with, presuppose the *whole* of space as consciously perceived, a fact which is, of course, fatal to any form of interactionism or parallelism or, indeed, the whole conception of such a thing as a "mind-body problem."[42] This is the meaning of Berkeley's rejection of physiology in his treatment of the inverted image.

The same sort of dialectic is involved, as we have seen, in the minimum argument. A minimum cannot be a minimum *for me* or a minimum *for you* if it is to be a true minimum, since the minimum is not an abstract, self-existent *thing* which can be set aside and compared with others. It is a relation involving all the other spatial elements which enter into it, and *without which it would not be a minimum*. Any specific minimum presupposes, therefore, the relation of minimality which "is exactly equal in all beings whatsoever that are endowed with the visive faculty."[43] It is no use to say that a mite, for example, must have a smaller minimum than mine, since what is *smaller than a minimum* is an absurdity. The existence of two

[41] N. T. V., sec. 88.
[42] Cf. 2D., F. i, pp. 421, 422.
[43] N. T. V., sec. 80, p. 168.

different worlds such as the mite's world and mine presuppose a system of relations absolutely identical in both. Thus, in the case of the *minimum visibile*, "No exquisite formation of the eye, no peculiar sharpness of sight, can make it less in one creature than in another; for it not being distinguishable into parts, nor in any wise consisting of them, it must necessarily be the same to all." [44] The smallest is absolutely and universally the smallest. These solutions of definite problems represent the culmination of the new theory, and the inevitable drift of Berkeley's concrete logic to a theory of *a priori* archetypes "exactly equal in all beings whatsoever" [45] is clearly discernible, though it is hindered from explicit development by the obstinate spiritism which clings to his early reflections and which he does not consciously begin to shake off until the *Three Dialogues* of 1713.

THE "TREND" OF THE NEW THEORY

The most significant feature of Berkeley as a thinker is the self-criticism running through all his writings, leading to that growth of doctrine which is so annoying to a type of interpretation which cannot rest satisfied until it has reached a "consistent" system, but so illuminating to one which is willing to take the pains necessary for the comprehension of a *tendency* or *direction* of thought. If the *New Theory of Vision* is compared with later statements in other works, and especially the *New Theory of Vision Vindicated*, such a trend in Berkeley's theory of spatial perception becomes discernible. Before passing critical judgment on his view, therefore, it is only fair to pause for a moment to examine the direction in which his thought was moving. It will become evident from such a study that, in certain vital respects, Berkeley has passed beyond, and therefore judged himself.

Perhaps the most striking "inconsistency" in Berkeley's theory of vision concerns his doctrine of "visual magnitude," and it has been seized upon by most of his commentators as indicating obscurity and indecision. [46] A careful comparison of the passages, however, will, I believe, show that the change is in a definite direction, so that the "indecision" represents a most essential movement of thought, rather than a "mere"

---

[44] *Ibid.*
[45] *Ibid.*

[46] Especially Bailey, *A Review of Berkeley's Theory of Vision*, London, 1842.

contradiction. In the early parts of the *New Theory of Vision* Berkeley speaks very often of the "visible magnitude" of an object,[47] and, indeed, he even offers this as one of the criteria by means of which we infer the real or actual magnitude. He refers, for example, to the "visible magnitude" as being variable,[48] and mentions the "distance" between visible points.[49] He speaks of "visible figure"[50] and the relative "posture" or position of visual objects.[51] Throughout this line of argument he seems to suppose that there is a visual, *two*-dimensional space which is directly perceived in sight, but that this space is not the *real* space, but a space needing correction and interpretation on the basis of the more reliable data of "touch."

There are, however, clear traces in the *New Theory of Vision* of a more radical position which becomes emphatic at the close of the discourse. Thus he speaks of "colours" as "the proper and immediate object of sight,"[52] and says, "I know very well that in a strict sense, I see nothing but light and colours, with their several shades and variations."[53] Berkeley goes so far in this direction that he even denies that the "planeness" of a picture is "perceived immediately by vision."[54] A plane is something which is obtained only by abstracting from solidarity. It cannot, therefore, be said that we really see a plane any more than a solid. "What we strictly see are not solids, nor yet planes variously coloured — they are only diversity of colours."[55] Berkeley would doubtless admit that unextended colour was an abstraction which could never actually exist,[56] and, indeed, there are places, as in the Introduction to the *Treatise Concerning the Principles of Human Knowledge*,[57] where it is definitely asserted that colour "without extension" is "not possible," but nevertheless in succeeding discussions of his theory of vision he seems to be tending ever more clearly in the direction of separating the spatial interpretation from the visual datum. Thus in an addition to the second edition of a year later, he says, "what we immediately and properly see are only lights and colours in sundry situations and shades"[58] and furthermore in the *New Theory of Vision Vindicated* we find Berkeley even more sharply stating his position that extension is *in no sense* imme-

---

[47] Sec. 59, p. 154; cf. sec. 74, p. 163.
[48] Sec. 61, p. 155; cf. sec. 79, p. 167.
[49] Sec. 112, p. 182.
[50] Sec. 45, p. 148.
[51] Sec. 114, p. 183.
[52] Sec. 43.

[53] Sec. 130; cf. sec. 156, p. 204.
[54] Sec. 157, p. 204.
[55] Sec. 158, p. 204.
[56] J., 123.
[57] Sec. 7, p. 240.
[58] N. T. V., sec. 77.

diately perceived. Thus he says, "What we immediately and properly perceive by sight is its primary object — light and colours," [59] and a little further, "the proper, immediate object of vision is light in all its modes and variations. . . ." [60] It is still true, however, that he speaks of visual quantity and the "magnitude" of the visual image,[61] and occasionally admits a "situation" of visual objects with respect to each other, though he tries to maintain, with no great degree of success, that this purely visual situation is quite distinct from that gained through the "spatial" sense of touch.

On the basis of this evidence I think it is fair to conclude that Berkeley's reflections led him to attribute less and less importance to the immediate "given" element in vision, so far as space is concerned. Space, that is, becomes, for him, less and less a sensation, and more and more an intellectual "construction," entwined with the original datum which, in itself, considered abstractly, is not spatial at all. Thus if we restrict our attention to Berkeley's discussion of visual perception, which is, after all, the chief object of inquiry in the *New Theory of Vision*, we find that he becomes less and less of an "empiricist" as his argument proceeds. Less and less, that is, comes to be attributed to the visual data which are only "lights and shades," and more and more to the construct or "interpretation" which constitutes the specifically *spatial* element. The interpretation of Berkeley as a primitive empiricist finds its justification, however, in the obstinate tenacity with which he continues to assert that space is somehow miraculously "given" in the "sense" of "touch." The *New Theory of Vision*, of course, is extremely vague as to just *how*. If Berkeley had written a treatise on the *New Theory of Touch*, must he not have come to a conclusion analogous to that which he so painfully but certainly arrived at in the *New Theory of Vision*, that space is not touched any more than seen, as a datum, but is, in fact, an interpretation coming from another source, and so on through the whole gamut of the senses? [62] Only then could he really be

---

[59] Sec. 42.

[60] Sec. 44; thus eliminating "situation" as an immediate object of sight.

[61] N. T. V. V., secs. 54, 55, p. 404.

[62] Thus, as Abbott urges, there is no legitimate reason, in the end, why Berkeley should suppose that space is not *as directly* given in sight as it is in touch.

The point, however, missed by Abbott, is that, on the basis of Berkeley's analysis, in the end, space is not "given" at all. See T. K. Abbott, M.A., *Sight and Touch: an attempt to disprove the Received (or Berkeleian) Theory of Vision*, Ch. 3, London, 1864.

said to have substantiated his conclusion that we see not with the physical eye but with a "faculty of the soul." [63] What, after all, does Berkeley mean by "touch"? Do his actual statements show any growth in the direction of an increased stress upon the interpretative rather than the immediate sensory factor? I think that a careful examination of the various works will again show such a "trend," rather than a mass of meaningless "inconsistencies."

In the first place, the *New Theory of Vision* makes it fairly clear, in spite of its vagueness, that Berkeley is far from naively asserting that we feel space with our hands. Thus he says, "that which I see is only a variety of light and colours," not space, and then, "that which I feel is hard or soft, hot or cold, rough or smooth,"— even more evidently not space.[64] Now, while Berkeley was anything but clear on the point, we cannot without further effort accuse him of asserting that space is a mere set of sensations of "hot" and "cold" and "hard" and "soft," when he denies, almost in the same breath, that space has anything to do with "light" and "colour" as sensations. One significant point must be granted him at once. Even in the *New Theory of Vision* he makes it clear that by "touch" he includes the "motion" of our bodies, "which is perceivable by touch." [65] May we not suppose, therefore, that, in his early writings, a "kinesthetic" theory of the nature of spatial perception was hovering over Berkeley's thought? The *Principles* and the treatise *De Motu* seem to verify this conjecture, for there are several passages which definitely associate space with "the parts of our body," and "the free power of moving our members unchecked by any obstacle." [66] Since, however, in both treatises Berkeley is even more emphatic on the point that motion necessarily presupposes space,[67] we cannot suppose that this "kinesthetic" theory, associated as it is with Berkeley's spiritism, is anything more than a passing phase in the development of his thought.

To discover the germ of what finally proved to be the decisive strand in his theory of spatial perception we must rather go

[63] N. T. V. V., sec. 43.
[64] Sec. 103, p. 178.
[65] Sec. 45, p. 149.
[66] Nihilominus si rem attento animo recolamus, constabit primo concipi spatium relativum partibus nostri corporis definitum: 2. movendi membra potestatem liberrimam nullo obstaculo retusam: et praeter haec duo nihil. D. M., sec. 55, p. 521; cf. sec. 58; cf. Pr., secs. 116, 117.
[67] Motus autem sine spatio concipi non potest, D. M., sec. 55; cf. sec. 58: motum nullum intelligi posse sine determinatione aliqua seu directione . . . ; and also Pr., secs. 10, 11.

back to the use of the word "judgment" in the *New Theory of Vision*, already noted. Here, for example, he gives a short preliminary statement of his theory as follows: "that the estimate we make of the distance of objects considerably remote is rather an *act of judgment* grounded on experience than of sense." [68] He says also that "the *judgment* we make of the distance of an object viewed with both eyes is entirely the result of experience,"[69] and furthermore that "this confused appearance of the object doth therefore seem to be the medium whereby *the mind judges* of distance." [70] If we remember the course of reflection which led to the "concrete" unity of Spirit, the *esse est percipi*, which is the crowning conception of the *Commonplace Book*, we cannot fail to perceive how far Berkeley is from an extreme empiricism, though it cannot be denied that his terminology is often so careless as to lend considerable plausibility to such an interpretation. After reading the *Commonplace Book* in any critical fashion it is impossible to believe that he could use the word "experience" in a purely "empirical" sense, without including in it that activity of the mind which, as we have noted at so many points, is a necessary element intertwined as part of the essential meaning of datum or "idea." "Wherein," for example, he asks, "does white differ from the perception of white?" [71] It is impossible to believe that a man who had been led by his logic of abstraction to ask such questions, and to give such answers to them as he gives on almost every page of the later *Commonplace Book*, could, in the next year, write about "touch" as though it were a pure, abstract or unapprehended datum. When Berkeley, therefore, writes of distance as "perceivable by touch" [72] he cannot be supposed to mean that space is nothing but a tactual sensation. He is not maintaining a primitive form of the associative theory of spatial perception, as he has been sometimes interpreted. The very closeness and essentiality of the synthetic union binding together datum and apprehension, "understanding" and "Will," "*esse*" and "*percipi*" encouraged the carelessness of terminology which has led to such misunderstandings. It must be granted, however, that Berkeley was at first far from clear as to the precise role played by these two factors in the apprehension of space, and his later development shows that he changed his mind concerning their relative importance.

---

[68] Sec. 3; my italics.
[69] Sec. 20.
[70] Sec. 22; cf. secs. 24, etc.
[71] J., 591.   [72] N. T. V., sec. 45.

What seems to have led him first to realize the more crucial role of construction or interpretation in spatial perception was a reflection upon the nature of geometry, which so obviously demands concepts such as *point*, that go beyond the direct evidence of the senses, though there is something unmistakably empirical about them. Thus in his second letter (B) to Leclerc, written about 1710, he speaks of "imagination" in this connection, and of its creative "forming" of ideas "after the pattern of things perceived by touch." [73] The point, line, and angle of geometry are thus mental constructions. They contain a certain sensory content, but they may be ordered, and organized, and completed in the imagination to constitute the pure objects of geometry. [74]

This tendency towards a more precise statement of the relative roles played by apprehension and datum in spatial perception, undoubtedly associated with an increased appreciation of the significance of the former, is clearly evidenced by the *New Theory of Vision Vindicated* of 1734. Here he makes it clear that "judgments and inferences" are made "by the understanding," [75] and that it is "the mind or soul of man" which "simply sees." [76] There is one essential passage especially in which the whole past course of his reflections comes to a focus. "Those immediate objects," he says, "whose *mutual respect and order* come to be expressed by terms relative to tangible place, being connected with the real objects of touch, what we say and *judge*

---

[73] Nimirum figura, angulus, linea, punctum, quae mente contemplatur Geometria, etsi ipsa sub sensum non cadant, tamen ad tactum referuntur, unde originem aliquo modo habent, quum per operationem mentis formentur ad speciem idearum tactui primitus impressarium." Letter to Leclerc (B), *Archiv*, vol. XVII, p. 163.

[74] Such constructions are, however, limited by the structure of experience, if they are to be *real* or applicable, and hence cannot proceed below the empirical threshold. Thus an infinitely divisible space is impossible to *imagine* as (cf. Pr., sec. 125) "existing." Berkeley does not deny the possibility of conceiving infinite divisibility. What he denies is the applicability of any such process to experience. *Real*, perceived space is finite. The infinitely divisible space of geometry is thus a pure construct which is distinct from

the space which confronts us in real or imaginary experience. In so far, however, as Berkeley's speculations led him to view space as a principle of order, rather than as a given object, the relevance of many of his empirical arguments against infinite divisibility, such as Pr., secs. 125 ff., may be questioned; for a principle, as he himself pointed out, is something inherently universal which inevitably takes us beyond its particular exemplifications. Thus from the *laws of nature* we can infer objects *not* immediately given in experience, such as the revolution of the earth. Why not similarly with the order of space? Berkeley would doubtless reply that this experience *can* at least be given, since it fits with the general structure of perception, whereas an infinitesimal below the conscious threshold is impossible in this sense.

[75] Sec. 42.

[76] Sec. 43; cf. sec. 48.

of the one, we say and *judge* of the other, transferring our *thought or apprehension* from the signs to the things signified."[77] Space or "place" is, therefore, something "thought" or "apprehended," and involves not so much the sensations themselves as their "mutual respect and order." It is a system of "judgments" *transferred* or applied from the impressions of one sense to another, which remains itself identical.

Once having made this crucial step,[78] it is clear that the original treatise was quite correct in maintaining that space is not directly perceived by the eye. There is no longer any necessity of demonstrating that it is transferred to vision from "touch" or any other sense whatsoever, for it is now clear that space is not apprehended as a sense datum at all, but is itself a form of apprehension, a way of ordering sensations, a "faculty" belonging to the "mind or soul," rather than to the eye or any aspect of the physical organism which rather presupposes it, since to have any such thing as an organism or physical process of any sort, we must already have space.[79] Hence in the *Siris* there is no longer any discussion of the unique relation between space and touch or of the transfer of spatial perception from one to the other, since space is perceived no more directly by the one than by the other. Berkeley sees at last that there is no reason for associating space with a particular sense, for space is perceived with the eye of the soul. It is the "mutual respect and order" in which the mind organizes its sensations. And yet it is not a pure thought or category. Not only is it not "perceived by any sense," but it cannot be "proved by any reason."[80] It is rather something which hovers between the two, requiring sense and yet not itself sensory, nor yet pure reason, but rather "the result of λογισμὸς νόθος, or spurious reasoning, and a kind of waking dream."[81] In the light of this development we must now pause for a brief critical comment on Berkeley's first essay into the field of the concrete sciences.

CRITICAL COMMENT

In spite of the immanent criticism which runs through Berkeley's later statements, even after he has been given the benefit of every doubt, it cannot be denied that his theory of vision is

[77] Sec. 48, p. 401; my italics.
[78] Cf. the theory of minima.
[79] D. M., secs. 55 and 58.

[80] *Siris*, sec. 271, p. 254.
[81] *Siris*, sec. 318, p. 278.

subject to serious objection. The lack of any adequate determination of the meaning of "touch" plunges his whole theory,
as we have seen, into a thick mist of obscurity which is dissi-
pated only in the *Siris* by the abandonment of the concept.
That the ambiguity hovering over this Protean term was not
merely external but one which had the most serious consequences for his own reflections is shown by his abortive attempts in
the *De Motu* and the *New Theory of Vision Vindicated* to derive
space from the "motions and situations of the head."[82] This
"kinesthetic theory" which was to have such a "Bainful" influence in the early nineteenth century upon those psychologists
who attempted to derive space from the "association" of ideas
or sensations, particularly the sensations attending motion, is
rendered immediately absurd by the simple reflection made by
Berkeley himself, as a result of his logic of abstraction, that no
motion is in any way conceivable without a determination or
direction,[83] and that motion, therefore, clearly presupposes
space.[84] This is indeed the rock on which all such "empirical"
attempts to "derive" space from "experience" are invariably
shattered. They all presuppose the whole of space in some
vague uncriticized term such as "motion," and then proceed to
"derive" it from this, plus other empirical catch-words such as
"kinesthesia," "local sign," etc., as a magician draws forth wonders from a mysterious hat. It cannot be denied that Berkeley's
doctrine at several points gives considerable encouragement to
such attempts. He was, however, as we have seen, too critical
in his reflections to be permanently lured by their superficial
plausibility. The real significance of this phase of Berkeley's
new theory lies in its final, *complete* abandonment in the *Siris*.
Here he came to see at last, though, it must be admitted, only
in a vague and intuitive manner, the implications really lying
implicit in his theory all the while. Space is no cluster of kinesthetic sensations suggested by visual ideas, but rather a
"mutual respect and order," a method of organizing ideas, a
relation between them, not an idea or cluster of ideas at all, but
a form of "reasoning."

In connection with the sensationalistic or passively descriptive tendency of his earliest thought we must note again his
confusion concerning "visual magnitude," and his tendency to
speak at certain points as if two dimensions of space were di-

---

[82] N. T. V. V., sec. 47, p. 401.   sine determinatione aliqua seu directione.
[83] . . . motum nullum intelligi posse   D. M., sec. 58.   [84] D. M., sec. 55.

rectly given in vision while the third is later added as a result of a totally different type of experience. This completely unwarranted destruction of the unity of space was also destined to fall before the irresistible criticism of his concrete logic, just as his early abstract statement in the *Commonplace Book* that "length breadth and solidity" are "three severall ideas" [85] is later corrected by his perception that it is a "fault" to believe that "length without breadth does exist." [86] It was, therefore, inevitable that the abstraction, attempted in the *New Theory of Vision*, of "depth" from the other dimensions of space, should be later corrected by his explicit recognition of the unity of space in the *Siris*, a union implicitly indicated, at least, in the remarkable discussion of the visible minimum and the inverted image in the *New Theory of Vision* itself.

The concrete truth that there is no colour without extension [87] only emphasizes the equally important truth apprehended so clearly in the later writings [88] that extension or space is itself *not* colour or any pure, sensory "datum" at all. We must also view the abstract distinction between "sight" and "touch," which is so stressed in Berkeley's early presentation of the *New Theory of Vision*, as a distinctly primitive tendency running counter to the concrete logic, which we have already noted as the dominant undercurrent of the *Commonplace Book*, and which finally emerges to explicit completion in the *Siris*. It was perhaps necessary for Berkeley to tear the world to pieces first in order to see it later as a whole. But the abstraction of depth from the other dimensions of space, of colour from extension, and sight from touch, so prominent in the early versions of the *New Theory of Vision*, only prepares the way for that realization of their necessary union which so definitely characterizes the later writings.

It is, doubtless, for this reason that the *New Theory of Vision*, in the generalized form of "the universal Language of Nature," [89] is so prominent throughout the period of Berkeley's scepticism and irrationalism before it is essentially abandoned in the *Siris*. In the *Alciphron*, for example, this language is sustained by a "Will" which binds the different sensory elements together only by means of an "arbitrary" connection, like that which Berkeley first maintained to be the link between the data of

[85] J., 107.
[86] J., 355; cf. 385, 485.
[87] J., 86, and Pr., sec. 99.
[88] N. T. V. V. and *Siris*.
[89] Cf. N. T. V., sec. 147.

vision and the "space" apprehended through "touch." [90]
Naturally blind faith alone is capable of apprehending the
dictates of such a "will." Berkeley's final transcendence of
this consequence of his "spiritism" in the *Siris*, where he at last
"glimpses" the necessity of the "divine ideas" which hold the
world together in a perfect chain or system, was to no small degree correlated with the course of reflection which we have just
followed. This train of reasoning, dictated by the irresistible
proddings of his concrete logic, led him to see that unextended
colour is as illegitimate an abstraction as colourless extension,[91]
and that to separate depth from the other dimensions of space
is as artificial as to separate length from breadth.[92] Thus in the
Principles he calls it a paradox to suppose that "extension may
be abstracted from all other sensible qualities," and declares
flatly "where the extension is, there is the colour too." [93] The
chief significance of Berkeley's new theory of vision, therefore,
lies in his later abandonment of what at first seemed to him to
be the most crucial features of it, but which were, in the light of
his own implicit logic, indefensible.

Starting out with the aim of penetrating through the veil of
language to the "given" reality, which needs only to be observed
passively to be understood, he ends with a theory of "ideal"
space, something "not perceived by any sense," but implicit in
the nature of experience. Space is neither seen nor touched nor
sensed in any way. It is the "order" in which all sensations
are placed, and hence prior to them. It is the common element
in all sensation, that which makes it possible to refer to sense in
general, and yet which is not itself a sensation but λογισμὸς νόθος.
We must now, however, turn to other aspects of the passage of
thought in which Berkeley was gradually forced to deepen and
Platonize his early phenomenalism. The course of reflection we
have just traced—in which *my* space, as a mere datum, came to
be the order of all sense, one and identical for all intelligences,
or, as he himself says, "exactly equal for all beings whatsoever"—played a most important role in this development.

[90] N. T. V., sec. 62, p. 156 *et passim*.   [92] Cf. J., 485.
[91] Cf. Pr., sec. 10; also J., 123.   [93] Sec. 99.

CHAPTER V

THE CONCRETE VERSUS THE ABSTRACT
(THE TREATISE CONCERNING THE PRINCIPLES OF
HUMAN KNOWLEDGE)

THE *New Theory of Vision*, as we have seen, is to be viewed as
a specific application of the new method to a practical problem
of general interest. It is a mere prelude destined only to prepare the way for that complete exposition of his principles in
the work to which Berkeley referred throughout the *Commonplace Book* as "the Treatise." He must have finished the final
writing of the *New Theory of Vision* during the first part of 1708,
for in the period from October to December of 1708, we find him
devoting all his time to the preparation of the first draft of the
introduction to the larger work.[1] The care which Berkeley took
with this first draft [2] shows that he now clearly perceived the
fundamental importance of his new "concrete" logic in the
development of all his views. That he had long before recognized the general significance of the theory of abstraction is
evidenced by the short polemic against abstract ideas contained
in sections 122 to 125 of the *New Theory of Vision*, a polemic
which is rather extraneous to the immediate context, and which,
as we have noted, is even inconsistent with certain of the stringent distinctions made in that treatise. It is this methodological polemic, now recognized as the very cornerstone of his position, which Berkeley next proceeded to develop from this first
draft, as well as from the preceding notations of the *Commonplace Book*, marked "Int."

Berkeley's dissatisfaction with the display of technical vir-
tuosity manifested in the *New Theory of Vision* is revealed by a
letter to his friend Percival explaining the haste with which he
had published the first part of his *Treatise*. He could not rest,
he says, until he had related his discussion of a specific problem
to the basic *principles* of human knowledge. His *New Theory of
Vision* must be corrected by placing it in its moral and metaphysical setting.

---

[1] Trinity Coll. Ms., marginal notations.   [2] F. iii, pp. 357-383.

There still remains [he declares] one objection with regard to the usefulness of that book [the *New Theory of Vision*], but in a little time I hope to
make what is there laid down appear subservient to the ends of morality and
religion in a treatise I have now in the press, the design of which is to demonstrate the existence and attributes of God, the immortality of the Soul, the
reconciliation of God's foreknowledge with the freedom of men, and by showing the emptiness and falseness of several parts of the speculative sciences, to
reduce men to the study of religion and things useful. How far my endeavor
will prove successful, and whether I have been all this time in a dream or no,
time will manifest.[3]

That the *Treatise* was, as a matter of fact, intended from the
first to correct the abstractness of the *New Theory of Vision* is
further manifested by the dedication to the Earl of Pembroke
in which he speaks of his "design to promote Useful Knowledge
and Religion in the world," and in the Preface, where he asks
for the attention especially of "those who are tainted with Scepticism, or want a demonstration of the existence and immateriality of God, or the natural immortality of the Soul."

The *Treatise* was thus finally written with the end of developing new "arguments" for God and immortality by means of
the logic of abstraction, which, Berkeley had now come to see
clearly, lay at the base of his new discoveries. This "Deistic"
goal, which he sets up before himself so definitely, offers a considerable contrast to the tone of the *Commonplace Book* in which
he simply follows the path of his new logic wherever it leads him.
His desire to "convince sceptics and atheists" of at least the
fundamental truths of "natural religion" led him in the published *Principles*, as we shall see, to certain premature conclusions and arguments which later turned out to be quite irreconcilable with the inner momentum of his thought. It must also
be borne in mind, in reading the *Principles*, that, as is indicated
by the original title (from which Part I was later removed),
it is only a fragment, the Part I mentioned by the *Commonplace Book*. The second part, as we have already observed, was
to deal with ethical matters, and probably "the reconciliation
of God's foreknowledge with the freedom of men." [4] It was
actually written but later lost on Berkeley's Italian travels. The
third part, dealing with "the emptiness and falseness of the
several parts of the speculative sciences" [5] is outlined in the last
sections of the published *Principles*. Several references in the
original text [6] show, however, that this discussion is only a pre-

[3] Percival letter, March 1, 1709–10.   [5] *Ibid.*
[4] *Ibid.*   [6] Secs. 125, 131, 132.

liminary sketch. There is reason to believe that the *De Motu* and the *Analyst* subsequently supplied this lack. But the published *Treatise concerning the Principles of Human Knowledge*, as we have it, is only a fragment, Part I of the projected *Treatise* of the *Commonplace Book*, which consciously limits itself to an application of the new logic to the world of sense or "ideas," and to an attempt to show that such an application leads to new "proofs" for the fundamental tenets of "natural religion," the existence of God, and the immortality of the soul. We must not be surprised, therefore, to find an emphasis on various "religious" phases of Berkeley's teaching which may seem to take us far beyond the strict implications of his new method, and it is, on the whole, quite impossible to view the published *Principles* as expressing his "system" in any adequate way, though, if considered in its context, it may provide us with considerable light.

PART I OF THE "TREATISE"

The published *Principles* begins with a long introduction in which Berkeley presents his reasons for dispensing with what he calls "abstract general ideas," and in the course of which he works out his conception of a concrete logic which will do justice to things as they *are*. This methodological introduction is undoubtedly the most important part of the *Principles*, since in it Berkeley consciously recognizes that such a logic underlies his whole thought structure, and for the first time devotes to its exposition a thoroughgoing discussion.

The main body of the *Principles* consists of various applications of this method, though there are points, particularly those that deal with the religious implications of his view, where he wanders off into a theory which we have already referred to as "causal metaphysics." This has very little to do with his underlying logic and is indeed, in certain respects, as we shall seek to show, definitely in conflict with it. Sections 1 to 25 of the *Treatise*, however, stick closely to the point, proving very acutely, time after time, that many concepts such as "motion," "number," "thing," etc., to which common sense clings tenaciously as independent, self-existent entities, are *really*, "inseparably united" with other distinct entities from which they are "not, even in thought, capable of being abstracted" as real or existent in themselves.[7]

7 Pr., sec. 10.

Berkeley first shows that the objects we perceive as external and independent are "combined, blended, or (if one may so speak) concreted together" [8] not only with one another, but in the unity of Spirit, so that they "cannot exist otherwise than in a mind perceiving them." [9] He does not in the least mean that esse *is* percipi in the sense of being abstractly or symbolically identical with it, as a mathematical sign may be defined to be *absolutely* identical in meaning with that of another sign. This is not at all Berkeley's intention. As he reiterates time and again, perceiving is altogether opposed to the thing perceived,— in his language one is active and the other passive. They are contrary poles, but by this very contrariety they are so intimately and essentially united that there is a "contradiction" or repugnancy [10] in the common-sense or abstract manner of conceiving these "objects of perception" as having "an existence independent of and without the mind." [11] Thus in section 5 he specifically states that he does *not* mean by abstraction "the conceiving separately such objects as it is possible may really exist or be actually perceived asunder," such as the trunk of a body without the limbs. In the case of the *esse* and the *percipi* we have something quite different, — a relation existing between two quite distinct and even opposed entities such that "it is impossible for me to see or feel anything without an actual sensation of that thing." [12] The "anything" and the "sensation of it" are opposite poles of a single whole which binds them together in such a way that either *without the other* becomes devoid of significance.

Berkeley points out that the primary qualities are just as evidently involved in this concrete unity of Spirit as the secondary qualities, so that the one as well as the other are "dependent beings; which subsist not by themselves, but are supported by, or exist in, minds. . . ." [13] To single out the primary qualities from this essential context and to think of them as enjoying some sort of *independent* existence of their own is to fall into empty verbalism. Berkeley then turns to the concept of matter or material substance and employs his logic of abstraction to show that, here again, the notion of an "independent substance without the mind" is only a verbal reification. Matter is nothing "existent" or "actual" without its context to oppose it, —

[8] Pr., sec. 99.
[9] Pr., sec. 3.
[10] Pr., sec. 56.

[11] *Ibid.*
[12] Pr., sec. 5.
[13] Pr., sec. 89.

nothing, that is, but a word with the meaning of independence, self-existence, or substance misapplied. Indeed, the first twenty-five sections of the *Principles* may be regarded as an exercise in the employment of the category of substance that common sense so constantly misuses and misunderstands in applying to aspects or phases which, however, "subsist *not* by themselves." [14] There is no genuine "substance" except one, — the concrete unity of Spirit. All other substances, the "things" and "matter" of ordinary realism, are only spurious substances which have no "existence" in reality "without" or independent of the mind. This is the meaning of Berkeley's polemic against the materialism of common sense.

He is quite clear at some points in guarding against the misunderstanding that "within the mind" means *spatially* within, or even "inherence." "Being in the mind" is an altogether unique relationship holding between objects or "ideas," and that "whereby they are perceived." [15] And yet in sections 25 to 35 we find Berkeley himself falling into a type of argument which is guilty of this very confusion, and is all the more inexcusable in view of his many warnings. This is the well-known "causal" argument, which we have already traced in the first origins of his reflections as they appeared in the *Commonplace Book.* It was only after a long and arduous process of self-criticism that he was able to rid himself of the last remnants of this common-sense mode of meditation, unquestionably the "blind spot" of his early thought. Hence, although he is quite clear when following his concrete logic that "Spirit is one simple, undivided, active being," which "as it perceives ideas is called the understanding, and as it produces or otherwise operates about them is called the "will," [16] nevertheless, after very acutely attacking the fallacy of abstracting the object or idea from the concrete unity of Spirit, he himself falls into the opposed and exactly equivalent fallacy of abstracting "spirit" as the "active side of consciousness," and of hypostatizing it into a self-existent substance or "soul," although, as he observes with great cogency in section 139, the very "existence" of "soul or spirit" as "active" consists in "perceiving ideas." [17]

[14] Pr., sec. 89. Husserl, who has, in general, understood the English "empiricists" more adequately than most commentators, defines abstraction in exactly Berkeley's sense as follows: "Ein unselbständiges Wesen heisst ein Abstrak-tum, ein absolut selbständiges ein Konkretum." *Ideen*, p. 29.

[15] Pr., sec. 2.

[16] Pr., sec. 27.

[17] Cf. C. B. J., 586, 623.

The self, active will, or "I" thus comes to be an isolated substance in which the ideas or objects inhere as modes, a mistake against which he specifically warns the reader in section 49. Berkeley is then, as a consequence, led straight to a subjectivism or solipsism which is the obverse of that same scepticism he apprehended so acutely as the inevitable implication of the *materialistic* abstraction. Once we hypostatize a mere phase or aspect of experience into a self-existent entity or substance, it becomes a hopelessly isolated island to which it is possible to penetrate only by relations which are "external," or not relations at all. Berkeley, in his early thought, with unrivalled perspicacity, points out the disastrous consequences of such abstraction in the case of the *object* or "matter," only to fall into the very same error, almost in the next breath, with respect to the mind or *subject*. What is a mind or subject in abstraction from all "ideas" or objects, isolated from the "world" to which it is, as he himself so convincingly shows, essentially related? "Pure (or abstract) intellect I understand not," he says roundly at the end of the *Commonplace Book*.[18] "Take away perceptions," he says in another pregnant notation, "and you take away the mind."[19] And yet in spite of this almost obvious consequence of his concrete logic, we find him in the *Principles*, as also in the *Commonplace Book*, hypostatizing or reifying the "self" into a self-existent substance, or, in other words, committing in sections 25 to 35 the very same fallacy against which he has so pointedly inveighed in sections 1 to 25.

Hence follows the reduction of the world as an appearance to *me*, or to the isolated abstracted soul, and the reconstruction of the world again through that uncritical employment of the concept of causation which has led generation after generation of critics to dismiss Berkeley's view as really solipsism in a thin disguise. The world is *mine*, but, following Locke, "the ideas imprinted on my senses are not the creatures of *my* will." There is, therefore, "some other Will or Spirit that produces them."[20] Here it is apparent that "other" means not the concrete "other" or "without" of his previous argument, but an absolute or abstract "other," an other or "outside," which it is difficult to believe Berkeley is not conceiving or imagining, in so far as he succeeds in imagining it at all, in *spatial* terms, in spite of the definite warning he gives against this very fallacy. The correction of common sense proceeds rigidly and cogently up to

[18] C. B. J., 822.   [19] C. B. J., 586.   [20] Pr., sec. 29.

the point of the self. Then the new logic is abandoned, and ordinary common-sense categories take its place. Just as his opponents, the materialists, abstracted the objective pole of spirit and "froze" it into a self-subsistent carrier for the rest of the world, so now Berkeley takes the opposite, subjective pole and "freezes" it into a self-subsistent soul. Spiritism or subjectivism now confronts materialism as its reverse side. Both are thus a result of the very same process of abstraction. One is the complement of the other, or rather the inverse of the other. Spiritism, that is, is nothing but a materializing, substantializing, or hypostatizing of the soul or self. The only excuse that can be made for Berkeley in falling into his own trap is the excuse that many of the Deistic principles which he was at this period of his life so interested in proving, principles such as "the natural immortality of the soul" and the "existence and immateriality (or in other words the *materiality*) of God," obviously rest upon such a process of abstraction from the concrete unity of spirit. It was easy for him to fall back, in this respect, upon a common sense, which seemed to bear out his religious arguments, though it conflicted most radically with the impulse of his new "concrete" method. The influence of Locke was also probably of great importance in this uncritical use of the category of cause,[21] by means of which the concrete unity of spirit, after being torn to pieces into a set of isolated abstract spirits, was then reconstructed by the divine and gratuitous intervention of Providence.

In sections 34 to 85 Berkeley discusses twelve objections to his view. Certain of these, such as numbers 6, 7, and 11, involve the sort of popular objection with which he had to contend during most of his life, and in answer to which he was always ready to take the most extraordinary measures in adapting his position to the level of that of the "fair and ingenuous reader."[22] In answer to such common-sense criticism Berkeley's general reply was that "we ought to think with the learned, and speak with the vulgar,"[23] though it is somewhat difficult to reconcile this with the great weight he at other points attaches to the snares and deceits of language. On the whole, it is quite unfortunate that he found it necessary to go so far in humouring his opponent, common sense, and attempting to reassure him, as he did throughout most of the early works, that there was

---

[21] Cf. *Essay*, Bk. II, 21; IV, 10 *et passim*.

[22] Pr., sec. 52.

[23] Pr., sec. 51.

nothing of serious moment between them.[24] That this was not the case later became quite evident. His view is, in the end, very different from that of common sense, which is a mass of abstractions and reified verbalisms, and therefore the very antithesis of the concrete mode of thought which was from the start the goal at least of his own reflections.

Certain of the objections are, however, of more importance. Number 1, for instance, concerns the distinction between illusion and reality. Against the criticism that his position turns the world into mere appearance, he replies that the order in which most of the "impressions" appear to one constitutes the *rerum natura*, and what is real as opposed to the chimerical. But is it not possible to experience a systematic delusion? Berkeley's opponent might well be pardoned for hesitating in the query as to whether a dream which should last throughout the period of one individual's life would be any the less a dream, *orderly* though it might be. The one really crucial question which Berkeley never asks himself is, what conceivable right may be adduced for passing into the objective, or universal world, once one has locked oneself up by an abstract logic in the close confines of an *individual* self?

It must be stressed, however, that the solipsistic, egocentric predicament in which Berkeley's causal spiritism ends is by no means a result of his concrete logic, but rather of the naive, common-sense abstraction into which he relapses at the critical concept of the self. Once this point is regarded as a self-existent entity or substance rather than as one pole of the subject-object antithesis, solipsism is the inevitable consequence, and he must ask himself questions like that of objection 4, which queries whether "things are every moment annihilated and created anew."[25] Much as we may admire the clever *tu quoques* and question-begging maxims which Berkeley develops on such occasions, we can never rest *quite* satisfied with the final answer he gives in section 48 that the lost world *may* still be saved, "since there *may* be some other spirit that perceives them though we do not." He is himself responsible for the devious and unplausible "possibilities," and "probabilities," and hypothetical conjectures which have befogged the discussions of "idealism" in the English philosophical tradition. Indeed, the whole unfortunate idea that "idealism" somehow in the end boils down to "solipsism" must be traced back to Berkeley's

[24] Pr., secs. 51, 91 *et passim*.   [25] Pr., sec. 45.

uncritical and inconsistent acceptance of Locke's causal metaphysics.

Sections 86 to 100 of the *Principles* are devoted quite convincingly to the task of showing how the illicit abstraction lying at the base of materialism is responsible for epistemological scepticism, since once we have supposed "real things" to subsist abstractly "without the mind" it is utterly impossible to conceive how the mind can get outside of itself to know them, though Berkeley, strangely enough, does not perceive that his own theory of spiritism lands him in exactly the same dilemma, since once we have supposed the mind to subsist abstractly in itself, or apart from other entities "without," it is equally impossible to conceive how these outer things may ever penetrate beyond themselves into the island of the abstract self. Sections 100 to 134 contain a sketch of the consequences of the new theory in natural science, later developed in the *De Motu* and the *Analyst*, and sections 134 to 156 constitute a very brief and inadequate introduction to Part II of the *Treatise*, dealing with God, the Self, and problems of moral philosophy.

Such is, in résumé, the fragmentary and inconclusive form in which Berkeley's new theory was first presented to his contemporaries. It is hardly surprising that it was received by them with some misgivings,[26] since it is, indeed, at war with itself. The *esse est percipi* leads inevitably to a *percipi est esse*, which consequence, however, Berkeley obstinately refuses to draw. He substitutes in its place an abstract *percipi est percipi* which makes solipsism unavoidable. The sort of logic which leads to the view that an object without a subject is inconceivable cannot rest at peace with the assertion that the subject, nevertheless, is perfectly conceivable with no object whatsoever. What is an "act" of perception which perceives nothing, or an "act of will" which wills nothing? Are these not the very same sort of abstractions which Berkeley discards so acutely in discussing matter? Such are the objections which prevented Berkeley's hard-headed countrymen from yielding to his spiritistic paradoxes.

The final outcome of Berkeley's spiritism must be reserved, however, for a later chapter, and we shall now direct our attention to what must be considered, both from its inherent profundity as well as from the nature of Berkeley's later development, as the basic kernel of the *Principles*. The various specific

---

[26] Percival letter, Aug. 26, 1710.

applications of the new, concrete logic are already familiar to the reader of the *Commonplace Book*, as is the Lockian metaphysics of cause, which blurs the later portions of the work. What, however, really distinguishes the *Principles*, what really represents an advance, is the polemic against abstract general ideas in the introduction. It is to this methodological core that we must now turn, making use of such supplementary material as the very significant correspondence with Leclerc, which took place just after the writing of the *Principles*, and especially the preliminary draft of this introduction made in 1708. We shall then pass to a brief consideration of the view of universals implied by this polemic, as well as to its later development in Berkeley's system. It is in this application of the concrete logic to the problem of universals that the chief significance of the *Principles* really lies.

"Pure Thought." The Letters to Leclerc

Berkeley's *New Theory of Vision* seems to have aroused little response from his countrymen beyond the rugged, though none too subtle "refutation" of Dr. Johnson. On the Continent, however, Berkeley found a reader who was able to give him criticism which was intelligent as well as understanding. One of the most widely read periodicals of the day was the *Bibliothèque Choisie* (Amsterdam), edited by Jean Leclerc. Volume 22, 1711, contained an adequate summary of the *New Theory of Vision*, written by Leclerc. This led Berkeley, shortly afterwards, to send him a copy of the *Principles* and a letter in Latin earnestly asking for criticism of the first part of his *Treatise*, "so that with this finished . . . I may proceed to deduce the various consequences, and prepare myself for the construction of the second part." [27] The summary of the *New Theory of Vision* included several footnotes, containing Leclerc's objections to the new theory, and in the later letter Berkeley points out "a few errors" in the summary and answers the objections. Although the *New Theory of Vision* contained only a short, and seemingly irrelevant, discussion of "abstract general ideas," Leclerc perceived quite clearly that Berkeley's whole thesis does, as a matter of fact, rest upon this theory of abstraction,

---

[27] Letter A to Leclerc. This letter, together with a later (B), was first discovered by Lorenz, who published them both in *Archiv für Gesch. der Phil.*, vol. XVII, p. 159.

and in his remarks he attempts to justify what Berkeley denies, and what, moreover, lay at the core of traditional rationalism, the conception of "pure thought." Leclerc in his footnotes defends this conception of a "pure" or abstract reasoning with respect to the innovations of the *New Theory of Vision*, and especially with respect to Berkeley's early "concrete" view of geometry as based on finite, perceived minima. He states very clearly the traditional conception of geometry, and asserts quite sharply that the points, lines, and angles constituting its objects have nothing whatsoever to do with sense or imagination, but are pure intellectual constructs. He presents, in other words, the extreme, opposed to the early, descriptive, sensualistic view of the *Commonplace Book*.[28] Berkeley's later view of space, as we have attempted to show, in the last chapter, is an attempt to synthesize these two extremes.

His direct reply to Leclerc, however, in letter B, while it deals specifically with geometry, is most essential for the understanding of his general theory of abstraction. "By no means," he says, "could I construct the abstract idea of a triangle or of any other figure." Neither by imagination nor by "pure intellect" is this possible, since when I imagine a triangle, the whole sensory and spatial context hovers over it, and it is not, therefore, abstract, while if I attempt abstractly to "conceive" a "pure" triangle without this context, I am left with a mere word. Of course, I may consciously ignore this context. As Berkeley says, "I can very well turn my mind to motion itself and mean this" alone, for example.[29] But the point is that by *consciously* "ignoring" the essential context I am thereby admitting it. By turning "my mind *to* motion" I am turning my mind *away* from other aspects such as spatiality and thingness, which I thus implicitly recognize as *really* bound up essentially with it. But the power of language enables us artificially to isolate such properties, and thus *unconsciously* to ignore the indispensable context. This is what Berkeley means by abstraction in the vicious sense,[30] as opposed to the concrete or conscious sort of

---

[28] Cf. C. B. J., 270–273 *et passim*.

[29] Tertio, illud praeteria animadvertendum est quod aliud sit attendere solummodo ad unam qualitatem, aliud eius ideam exclusa omni alia re aut qualitate in animo formare; e.g. possum ego in motuum natura et legibus inquirendis animum tantum ad ipsum motum praecipue advertere atque intendere, nego tamen illius ideam efformare nisi simul mente comprehendatur etiam res mota. (Leclerc B, *Archiv für Gesch. der Phil.*, vol. XVII, p. 163.)

[30] ideam efformare.

abstraction which he calls "considering." [31] I may make up a word for extension which shall simply mean extension by itself without its context. But I cannot think of it as *existing*. I cannot "imagine" it or construct it as it actually is. In Berkeley's words, I cannot "form an idea of it" [32] without its context, "since it is impossible and repugnant by any force of mind to disjoin the ideas. . . ." This distinction between conscious and unconscious abstraction, between what Berkeley calls "abstracting" and "considering," and to which he refers most clearly in his interesting correspondence with Leclerc, is of great importance in understanding his new logic, or what he refers to in the *Commonplace Book* as his new mode of "reasoning," as distinguished from the "pure thought" of the traditional rationalism. This pure thought, Berkeley insisted, was characterized at many points by unconscious or irresponsible abstraction from essential contexts, and was hence artificial or verbal rather than real or concrete. [33]

Two Misconceptions of Berkeley's Polemic

The extraordinary difficulty of the whole question of "universals" and the subtlety of the distinctions Berkeley is forced to make in his introduction have led to certain misapprehensions of his doctrine, which is so important, concerning, as it does, his basic method, that we must pause for a moment in the attempt to clarify the confusions on which these misunderstandings may be seen, with a little care, to rest. It must be stressed, in the first place, to the last point of emphasis that at no time in his career did Berkeley ever really identify what he called "abstract general ideas" with universals in general, though the carelessness in terminology, arising to some extent from the critique itself, does, in certain cases, give warrant to such a misunderstanding. Isolated passages may be quoted from the

[31] attendere solummodo ad unam qualitatem.
[32] *Loc. cit.*
[33] Berkeley's letter reached Leclerc, for in a later number of the *Bibliothèque Choisie*, vol. XXVI, p. 458, 1713, he corrected the mistakes in his earlier review of the N. T. V. But, so far as is known, he never answered Berkeley directly, nor did he review the *Principles*, though in vol. XXIII, p. 235, it is included in the list of books to be discussed, and on p. 464 he promises to deal with it in another volume. Leclerc, unlike Berkeley, was not at home in the heat of contemporary controversy. He preferred, as Lorenz divines, to survey the conflict from his serene editorial heights, and award the fruits of ultimate victory. Berkeley was too young and comparatively unknown, at this time, to win recognition from such a source. So the *Principles* remained uncriticized.

Commonplace Book in which Berkeley seems to deny universals altogether.[34] When the work is read as a whole, however, and some regard is paid to his underlying thought rather than to the symbolic form in which it is couched, it becomes quite clear that what he is attacking is not universals in general but only "abstract general ideas," something, it must be added, altogether different, at least in his own eyes. Thus the *Commonplace Book*, at several points, speaks of the "sorts "[35] and is interested in showing that "the mind makes the sorts."[36] In the *Commonplace Book*, therefore, it is fairly manifest that Berkeley is attacking not universals in general, but only "abstract general ideas."[37] The first draft of the *Principles* by no means denies "the universal element in knowledge," but gives a quite lengthy account of how "a word becomes general by being made the sign . . . of many particular ideas."[38] Such ideas "are said to be of the same sort" and between them "there is some likeness,"[39] although Berkeley maintains, as in the *Commonplace Book*, that "these sorts are not determined and set out by nature as was thought by most philosophers."[40] Rather they are the work of mind.[41] So far as his published *Principles* was concerned he was careful to say in the published introduction,

---

[34] For example J., 397, where he says, "no general ideas." This terminological carelessness is frequent in the *Commonplace Book*. Cf. J., 597. Johnston in his edition of the C. B. quite generally gives "abstract general idea" for "abstract idea," as in 499, 676. Even though this is probably the correct rendition of Berkeley's *meaning*, the text is, of course, no place for such interpretation. See Aaron, R. I.: *Mind*, vol. XL, no. 160.

[35] J., 296.

[36] J., 298.

[37] Single passages may be quoted from the early draft of the *Principles*, however, written in 1708, which do not seem to fit this view. Thus Berkeley speaks (F. iii, 359) of "abstract ideas or general conceptions of things" as if they were equivalent. But his explanation shows clearly that what he is referring to is "abstract ideas" *as* he finds "these terms explained by the best and clearest writers" (Pr. Ms., F. iii, p. 360), and in the same paragraph he uses the term "Abstract General Ideas." Johnston, *Develop-*

ment of Berkeley's Phil., p. 119, says, "In this rough draft . . . Berkeley denied entirely the universal element in knowledge." And furthermore, "his criticism is perfectly general, and is directed against "genera, species, universal notions, all which amount to the same thing" (119). The full sentence or rather phrase of Berkeley's manuscript in which the passage referred to by Johnston occurs runs as follows: "by abstract idea, genera, species, universal notions, all which amount to the same thing, *as I find these terms explained by the best and clearest writers.* . . ." This only shows, therefore, the extreme danger of quoting a dozen words from a sentence composed of sixty or seventy. Indeed, in the very next paragraph, he gives a lengthy description of the process of abstraction as understood by Locke and mediaeval philosophy.

[38] Pr. Ms., F. iii, p. 364.

[39] Pr. Ms., F. iii, p. 365, par. 2.

[40] Pr. Ms., F. i, pp. 365–366.

[41] J., 298.

". . . it is to be noted that I do not deny absolutely there are general ideas, but only that there are any *abstract general ideas*." [42]

There is another misunderstanding to which comments by Professor Fraser have given rise. He noted the fact that Berkeley omitted certain sections in the third edition of *Alciphron* VII,[43] dealing with abstraction, and suggests that "this polemic against Locke is therefore one of verbal confusion. In later life he probably saw this, as he saw deeper into the whole question involved. This is suggested by the omission of the argument against abstract ideas, given in earlier editions of the Alciphron. . . ." [44] Whether Berkeley's polemic is a matter of "verbal confusion" must be further discussed, but the idea that he ever retracted his polemic must be emphatically rejected, for he repeats it in other sections of the *Alciphron* which never were removed. Thus, Alciphron asks, "Will you not allow then that the mind can abstract?"[45] Euphranor replies that things which can really exist asunder can be conceived asunder, "but it will not thence follow that the mind can frame abstract general ideas, which appear to be impossible." Berkeley then proceeds to repeat the arguments of the *De Motu* against the idea of "force abstracted from body, motion, and outward sensible effects." [46] Furthermore, in the *Siris* (1744),[47] when expounding his doctrine of Platonic ideas or archetypes, he declares that they are not "figments of the mind, nor mere mixed modes, nor yet abstract ideas in the modern sense. . . ." We must suppose, therefore, that the omission of the three sections in the last edition of the *Alciphron* was motivated by purely stylistic reasons and has no particular doctrinal significance.[48] The subject of the discussion at this point is Faith, and it is quite easy to understand why he should have later decided that the discussion of abstraction was irrelevant. What settles the point, however, is that in 1752 Berkeley allowed the *De Motu* to be republished in his *Miscellany*, and this treatise is based from beginning to end on the doctrine of abstraction, containing an almost constant criticism of "the abstract and subtle and quintessential things," such as *pure* motion, *pure* space, and *pure* force, as well as

---

[42] Sec. 12.
[43] Pp. 323-326.
[44] Preface to *Principles*, F. i, p. 219.
[45] Alc., F. ii, p. 328.
[46] Alc., F. ii, pp. 329-331.

[47] Sec. 335, F. iii, p. 285.
[48] The indefensibleness of Fraser's view has also been pointed out by Joussain, *Philosophie de Berkeley*, chap. I, Paris, 1920.

warnings to "abstain as much as possible from abstract and general notions." [49] We must, therefore, conclude that the doctrine of abstraction, which plays a fundamental role in practically all of Berkeley's philosophical speculations, was maintained by him throughout the period of his life, and was never in any sense withdrawn. We may now proceed to discuss the doctrine itself. What does Berkeley mean by an abstract general idea, and what is the nature of his criticism?

THE POLEMIC AGAINST ABSTRACT GENERAL IDEAS

By Abstract Idea, Genera, Species, Universal Notions [says Berkeley in the early draft of the *Principles*], all which amount to the same thing, as I find these terms explained by the best and clearest writers, we are to understand Ideas which equally represent the Particulars of any sort, & are made by the Mind, which, observing that the Individuals of each kind agree in some things and differ in others, takes out and singles from the rest, that which is common to all, making thereof one Abstract General Idea: which contains all those Ideas wherein the particulars of that kind agree, separated from & exclusive of all those other concomitant Ideas, whereby they are distinguished one from another. To this abstract idea thus framed the Mind gives a general name & lays it up & uses it as a standard whereby to judge what Particulars are & what are not to be accounted of that sort; those only which contain every part of the general Idea having a right to be admitted into that Sort & called by that name.[50]

It will be noted that there are two steps in this process: first the comparison of several particulars and the apprehension of an agreement or similarity between them; and second the *"framing"* of an *idea* of this similar property *"exclusive of"* all the rest. It is clear from the first that Berkeley's polemic is directed against the second element of this process. He never dreamed of denying that particular entities could be compared and found similar to each other. What he denied was that it was possible for the mind to *isolate* this similarity and *"frame"* for itself an "idea" of this property distinct from all the rest. Furthermore, the universal is not a separate "idea" or object at all, and cannot be "given" as such objects are, for these are always concrete and particular, though they must, of course, involve universal aspects. Thus in the rough draft of the introduction to the *Principles* he says: "I cannot by any effort of Thought *Frame* to myself an Idea of Man that shall have nothing par-

---

[49] Caeterum sanior philosophandi ratio videtur ab notionibus abstractis et generalibus (si modo notiones dici debent quae intelligi nequeunt) quantum fieri potest abstinuisse. D. M., sec. 23.
[50] F. iii, p. 360.

ticular in it," [51] and in the *Principles*, "I deny . . . that I can *frame* a general notion, by abstracting from particulars in the manner aforesaid. . . ." [52] Berkeley never questioned that particular concrete things exist before us, nor that they possess a general significance.[53] Is there, however, another realm of existent entities consisting of the abstract or separate, universal properties of things as entities? This separate and distinct realm of universal entities is what he denied, for the universal, like the self, is not a thing or entity at all. Particular entities which are similar to each other exist, but the similarity is in the things and cannot be severed from them. There is no separate actual realm of universals — there are only concrete things bearing significance. Why did Berkeley so strenuously deny the justification of reifying *the* significance into a substantial field existing in its own right? Why are not universals *things* or *objects*?

The first argument Berkeley brings against the possibility of such a process of abstraction is that it must inevitably end, if strictly and consistently carried out, in *nothing* rather than in a universal.[54] He uses the example "man." What can we really mean by the abstract idea of man distinct from particulars or distinct from *all* the properties which distinguish *men* from one another? Such a man cannot be yellow, since *some* men are not yellow, or white, or red, etc. He thus cannot possess any one colour, nor any combination of colours, nor all colours together, since there are certainly particular men who will not fit into any of these classifications. What if we say such a being simply possesses colour in the abstract? Here Berkeley demurs. What can you possibly mean by "colour" in this sense, colour, that is, defined by the *negation* of all particular colours or combinations of colours? This colour, he insists, is simply a word. And so on with respect to the other "properties" of the abstract man. This man could possess neither eyes, nor ears, nor arms, nor legs, since in each case certain men can be found who lack these traits. Thus, as Berkeley says, "it must needs make an odd and frightful Figure of a man without all these." [55] The end

[51] F. iii, p. 362.
[52] Pr. Int., sec. 10. Cf. Pr. Int., F. i, p. 249, in regard to Locke's triangle: ". . . This will never prove that he can *frame* an abstract, general . . . *idea* of a triangle."
[53] " . . . Things, names, or notions being in their own nature *particular* are rendered *universal*." Pr. Int., sec. 15, p. 247.
[54] Pr. Ms., F. iii, 361; cf. Pr. Int., sec. 9.
[55] Pr. Ms., F. iii, p. 360, note 5.

of this mutilating process "is just nothing." [56] A true universal cannot possibly be derived from such a disintegration. The universal is something *per se*, — it is distinct from the particulars and yet it is *in* the particular, and if, in our attempt to define the universal, we try to "abstract from all particularity" we only succeed in leaving behind all reality whatsoever. The universal can never be derived from the progressive mutilation of particulars, for abstracted *from* them, in isolation, it is nothing. Rather it exists *in* the particulars and must always be thought together with them, though it is not, of course, a particular thing nor indeed any *thing* at all.

This becomes quite clear in Berkeley's discussion of the well-known Lockian triangle. [57] The most important phase of this discussion concerns the use of the word "the." What he is really objecting to is "*the* general idea of a triangle which is . . . neither oblique, nor rectangle, neither equilateral, equicrural, nor scalenon; but all and none of these at once," and which a man is supposed to "have the faculty of framing in his mind." [58] "The" indicates independence, self-sufficiency, substance. And it is "the" abstract triangle which he is attacking, not universality as such. If we continue to subtract particular characters from our "conception," *the* "triangle" will not be a triangle at all, but "just nothing." The minute, however, we arrive at anything which can be appropriately prefixed by the word "the," we have substantiality. What Berkeley is so positively and acutely asserting is the inseparable, indispensable *connection* between universality and particularity, such that the one without the other becomes entirely meaningless, or "just nothing."

That this is quite different from denying universality becomes immediately evident in the following sections, [59] where he makes it clear that his *point* is granted if in all cases the word "any" or "all" is substituted for "the." Thus, he says, universal propositions in geometry are possible in so far as I discover what is true of "any" triangle, "not because I demonstrated the proposition of *the* abstract idea of a triangle." [60] Nor does he advocate the elimination of the useful word "the" from language. One may "consider" a figure as triangular. "So far he may abstract." [61] It is only the hypostatization, the "theifi-

[56] Pr. Ms., F. iii, p. 361.
[57] Pr. Int., p. 246.
[58] Pr. Int., sec. 13.
[59] 15, 16.
[60] Pr. Int., sec. 16.
[61] Sec. 16.

cation" of *the*, to which Berkeley is objecting. Abstraction which is *conscious*, which recognizes itself as abstraction, as a phase or aspect, is justifiable, and, of course, indispensable. Universality is always a "phase." Suppose all concrete reality in the universe be obliterated! Berkeley's opponents would then assert something else, the abstract realm of universals, remains. For Berkeley, nothing would remain, for universals exist in particulars and cannot be abstracted from them and hypostatized into self-sufficient, subsistent entities.

This is, of course, only a typical example of the sort of reflection to which Berkeley was led by his "concrete" method of reasoning to which we have called attention in our discussion of the *Commonplace Book*. By this method of "reasoning" he was brought constantly to see wholes in experience, the aspects of which are altogether distinct, and yet bound together in an inseparable totality. Universality and particularity are bound together in just such a way, so that neither can exist without the other, although the universal is not particular, and not an entity at all, nor is the particular in itself universal. But this is only one peculiarly important and striking application of his method. Thus, for example, he says in the *De Motu*,[62] "too great an abstraction or division of things really inseparable causes perplexity as to the nature of motion," since "indeed it is impossible to conceive velocity without time or space." [63] We have already noted how the powers and acts of the mind are bound together in concrete experience in such a way that one cannot exist without the other,[64] and how the objects of sense consist of ideas which are "combined, blended, or (if one may so speak) concreted together." [65] The actual world of experience is, for Berkeley, full of such concretions, the most important example of such a relation being, of course, that between the object and the mind which is of such a character that "either cannot be possible without the other."[66] This is the true meaning of the *esse est percipi* principle. The real objects which actually confront us are "concretions," and the task of philosophy is to think reality. It is too often forgotten that abstract and concrete are correlative terms and that Berkeley's denial of abstraction follows from his primary assertion of the concreteness of reality. Hence in connection with abstraction

[62] Sec. 47.
[63] *Analyst*, F. iii, p. 48.
[64] Pr., sec. 143, p. 338.
[65] Pr., sec. 99, p. 313.
[66] C. B. H., 829; J., 853.

Berkeley always brings up the question of existence. In *Alciphron* VII,[67] for example, he asks, ". . . can a colour, or triangle such as you describe their abstract general ideas really *exist?*" And in the introduction to the *Principles* he says, "It is agreed on all hands that the qualities or modes of things do never really *exist* each of them apart by itself, and separated from all others, but are mixed, as it were, and blended together, several in the same object." [68] Berkeley's polemic is based on the assertion that this blending is of an inseparable character, so that the abstract products of analysis are artificial and unreal, and, as *separate existences*, only words.

Legitimate Abstraction (Considering)

Never, however, did Berkeley deny that all abstraction was impossible or unnecessary. This he makes clear not only in his correspondence with Leclerc, but at many points in his published works. Thus in Dialogue I Philonous says, "I acknowledge, Hylas, it is not difficult to form general propositions and reasonings about those qualities without mentioning any other; and in this sense to *consider* or treat of them abstractedly. But, how doth it follow that, because I can pronounce the word *motion* by itself I can form the idea of it in my mind exclusive of body?" [69] It is thus possible to *consider* phases of such a concrete whole and to form words to represent such phases, although it is impossible to "form an idea" of them. The act of consideration is thus a negative rather than a positive process. I may artificially eliminate certain irrelevant aspects of a concrete experience, but I cannot think of what is left as an existent entity or "idea." Its implicative aspects are hovering in the background. Thus, I may consider colour without extension, but I cannot regard colour by itself as an *existent* object. I may simply for the time being forget about extension, but it is really there as a phase of colour, as the forgetting or ignoring of it shows. The scholastic [70] word *consider* was used consistently by Berkeley in this sense. Thus in the *Commonplace Book* he says, "A great difference between *considering* length without breadth, & having an *idea* of, or *imagining* length without breadth," [71] which is further explained as follows: "The mind,

[67] 1st ed., F. ii, p. 325.
[68] Sec. 7, F. i, p. 240; my italics.
[69] F. i, p. 403.

[70] Cf. Aquinas, *S. Theol.*, I q. 85a. I ad. I, and Sergeant, *Solid Phil.*, pp. 97, 320.   [71] J., 263.

'tis true, can consider one thing without another; but then, considered asunder, they make not two ideas. But together can make but one." [72] Such a legitimate abstraction or consideration does not, therefore, obscure the primary truth that the elements we have singled out are different aspects of a *single* whole, but only emphasizes it. This sort of abstraction was always admitted by Berkeley. Thus he says in the *Principles*, "And here it must be acknowledged that a man may *consider* a figure merely as triangular; without attending to the particular qualities of the angles, or relations of the sides. *So far he may abstract*. But this will never prove that he can frame an abstract general, ... *idea* of a triangle. In like manner we may consider Peter so far forth as man, or so far forth as animal, without framing the forementioned abstract idea, either of man or of animal; inasmuch as all that is perceived is not considered." [73] In other words, universals as *phases* or *aspects* of particular, concrete realities (*so far forth*) may and indeed must be *considered*. But it must never be forgotten that they are only such phases or aspects, for in our very forgetting we are forced to remember. [74] Berkeley realizes that abstraction is necessary. We cannot in science especially regard the object in its concrete entirety, but must restrict ourselves to aspects. It must not be *forgotten*, however, that it is only an aspect which we are regarding or considering, and we must not attempt to reify such aspects into separate *objects* or things as if they had an independent existence. There is only one variety of independent existence, the concrete reality, which always involves *both* universality and particularity. Such reification is particularly dangerous in philosophy, since it is peculiarly the business of philosophy to think reality as a whole, or as it *is*. [75] Even in philosophy it is, of course, necessary to *consider* phases or aspects. But it is possible to be conscious of this fact, and never to hypostatize our *considerations* into a supposedly separate

[72] J., 330; cf. C. B. J., 734.
[73] 2nd ed., F. i, sec. 16, p. 249.
[74] Cf. 1D., F. i, p. 404. This sense of abstraction must be distinguished from the sense in which Berkeley asserts it is possible to abstract and conceive and imagine parts of external or *additive* wholes which *can* be so perceived. "... I own myself able to abstract in one sense, as when I consider some particular parts

of qualities separated from others, with which, though they are united in some object, yet it is possible they may really exist without them." Pr. Int., sec. 10, p. 242. Cf. Pr., sec. 5, p. 260, and Alc., VII, 328.
[75] "'Tis on the discovering of the nature & meaning and import of existence that I chiefly insist." C. B. H., 479; J., 493.

and distinct realm of existence or subsistence. No thought which does this can be considered genuinely philosophical.

LANGUAGE AS THE BASIS OF ILLEGITIMATE ABSTRACTION

Berkeley was quite clear on the point that this universal tendency is bound up with language.[76] Thus, in the early draft of the *Principles* he says, "I find it also declared in express terms that General Truths can never be well made known and are very seldom apprehended but as conceived and expressed in words. All which doth plainly set forth the inseparable connexion and mutual dependence that is thought to be between words and Abstract Ideas." [77] We have already noted in the *Commonplace Book* Berkeley's assertion of the communicative or symbolic function of language. Words employed in this way are symbols which must stand for realities in concrete experience. If such a meaning cannot be found, then the word is meaningless jargon.

I do not deny that they [words] are necessary for communication, and so making me know the ideas that are in the Mind of another. But when any Truth whether about general or particular ideas is once made known to me by words so that I rightly apprehend the ideas contained in it, I see no manner of reason, why I may not omit the words, and yet retain as full and clear a conception of the ideas themselves, as I had while they were clothed with words, words being so far as I can see, of use only for recording and communicating, but not absolutely apprehending ideas.[78]

Yet it is a mistake to suppose that every word must have an idea attached to it, in the sense of a "passive" object of perception, though this is the more obvious type of meaning. The other active element in our immediate experience may also become the meaning of a symbol. "Besides, the communicating of ideas marked by words is not the chief and only end of language, as is commonly supposed. There are other ends, as the raising of some passion, the exciting to or deterring from an action, the putting the mind in some particular disposition. . . ." [79] Meanings may be active as well as passive. We may use symbols directly to influence the behavior of another as in exhortation, or indirectly as standing for certain operations or procedures. Thus, ". . . for instance, the algebraic mark, which denotes the

---

[76] "I come now to consider the *source* of this prevailing notion, and that seems to me to be *language*." Pr. Int., sec. 18, p. 250.

[77] Pr. Ms., 18, F. iii, p. 371.

[78] *Op. cit.* pp. 371–372.

[79] Pr. Int., sec. 20, p. 251.

root of a negative square, hath its use in logistic operations, although it be impossible to form an idea of any such quantity," [80] and the symbol "force" in physics is of the same character, for ". . . I do not find that I have or can have any such idea." [81] This offered Berkeley a means of explaining the "origin" of abstract ideas.

The self and its actions are opaque. What confronts us in consciousness is always an object, and the action of mind is so constantly present that we become as oblivious to it as to the atmosphere in which we live. Hence our ineradicable tendency to "illustrate spiritual things by corporeal." Thus, "we speak of spirits in a figurative style, expressing the operations of the mind by allusions and terms borrowed from sensible things. . . ." [82] Everywhere we tend to objectify our thought and find some sensory reality to which we can cling. This is also true in the case of language. We insist with Locke that "every noun substantive stands for a distinct idea that may be separated from all others; which hath occasioned infinite mistakes." [83] Thus, for example, when we find a word like "force" we at once attempt to find some objective embodiment in experience, which has occasioned "no small controversies . . . about the notions or definitions of these terms," [84] since, of course, no such objectification can be found. Not discovering any such particular embodiment, the theory arose that these words must stand for abstract general ideas, "for when men were indubitably conscious to themselves that many words they used did not denote any particular ideas, lest they should be thought altogether insignificant, they were of necessity driven into the opinion that they stood for general ones." [85] Hence the origin of "abstract general ideas" as *substances*. The natural and understandable absorption of men in the "external" world of ideas gives rise to an inveterate tendency to objectify everything, not only "acts" of the mind which are not objects or things at all, but universals as well.

Once embedded in men's minds, the conception of abstract ideas has led them also to coin all sorts of verbal definitions and verbal combinations for which no concrete meaning of *any sort* can be discovered either in idea or action. Encouraged, however, by the doctrine that nevertheless some substantial ab-

[80] Alc., VII, F. ii, p. 344.
[81] Alc., VII, p. 329.
[82] Alc., VII, p. 343.

[83] Pr., sec. 116, p. 323.
[84] Alc., VII, p. 330.
[85] Pr. Ms., F. iii, p. 378.

stract meaning for all words must exist, they have proceeded unabashed, until they have become involved in "that fine and subtle net of abstract ideas, which has so miserably perplexed and entangled the minds of men. . . ." [86] Such men consequently live in a verbal universe of their own construction. No concrete meanings of any sort can be discovered for their symbols, which thus become reified into distinct things with supposed independent existence. There is nothing there, however, but the word. The fallacy of abstraction is thus ultimately verbalism. Language, instead of exercising its proper mediative function, becomes an end in itself, and men think themselves to be studying the laws of nature when, in fact, they are absorbed and lost in their own grammar and syntax. It is no wonder that Berkeley ends his polemic against abstraction by cautioning himself to get clear of all controversies purely verbal, though we may find his many optimistic assertions to the effect that it is only necessary to "draw the curtain of words" to be freed altogether from their "embarrass and delusion" and to "behold the fairest tree of knowledge" [87] somewhat extravagant. Here, he is clearly straining the point. It was only in his Lockian youth that he was able to think of the quest for truth in any such simple fashion as the "drawing aside of a curtain." What he was struggling against in his polemic against abstraction was no mere "veil of language," but the far more opaque veil of common-sense reflection, which builds for itself a thick wall of abstraction isolating it from reality. This struggle is not made easier by the sublime obstinacy with which common sense thinks of its poverty-stricken abstractions as, in truth, the concrete, and of the true concrete, which, of course, seems faint and obscure, as seen through this wall, as the abstractest of the abstract. But the fact that the object of Berkeley's endeavors was not only a new language but a new *logic*, — that most subtly difficult of all things to understand, since it involves the very faculty of understanding itself, — a new method or mode of reasoning, *this* fact became perfectly clear to him only in his latest reflections.

THE MEANING OF BERKELEY'S POLEMIC

The first draft of the introduction to the *Principles*, written in 1708, makes it clearer even than the published version that Berkeley's own theory of universals grew out of a criticism of

[86] Pr. Int., sec. 22, pp. 253–254.   [87] Pr. Int., F. i, p. 255.

the doctrine of the *Essay*. According to this doctrine it is impossible to have a word for every single existent thing. Hence the origin of "general ideas," which, through the process of abstraction, come to refer to many particulars. As Locke himself says,[88] in a passage quoted in the rough draft of the introduction to the *Principles*:

> It is not enough for the perfection of language that sounds can be made signs of ideas, unless those signs can be so made use of as to comprehend several particular things: for the multiplication of words would have perplex'd their use, had every particular thing need of a distinct name to be signified by. To remedy this inconvenience Language had yet a farther improvement in the use of general terms whereby one word was made to mark a number of particular existences which advantageous use of sounds was obtained only by the difference of the Ideas they were made signs of, those names becoming general which are made to stand for general ideas, and those remaining particular where the Ideas they are used for are particular.[89]

There are thus, according to Locke, two ways of referring to reality, the direct way in which we signify by a proper name, for example, a real existent thing, and an indirect way in which we signify this same reality through the agency of abstract general ideas, which for Locke are given a vague sort of status, half real and half unreal. His position is, therefore, close to that traditionally known as "conceptualism," for he is constantly emphasizing that universals are somehow "in the mind," whatever that may mean, and yet that they have, to some extent, a justifiable claim to reality. Berkeley, as a result of his critique of the process of abstraction, finds such an independent "subsistent" realm of universals, either "in the mind" or "outside the mind," unnecessary. In his view there can be only *one* world, and if there are any such things as universals they must be in, or rather *with*, this same world, united with the particulars, or not at all. He asks, therefore, why we may not refer directly to many particulars, to *all* or *any* (not to *the*) without first having to become involved in the opaque medium of "abstract general ideas." "I would fain know," he says, "why a word may not be made to comprehend a great number of particular things in its signification without the *interposition* of a general idea. Is it not possible to give the name colour to black, white & red without first having made that strange and to me incomprehensible Idea of colour in abstract . . . which shall have nothing particular in it?"[90]

---

[88] Bk. III, 1, 3 of the *Essay*.   [90] Pr. Ms., sec. 9, F. iii, p. 365; my
[89] F. iii, p. 364.   italics.

Berkeley was never a "nominalist" at any period of his thought. He never dreamed of denying that things may be meaningfully referred to as "alike." Thus, for example, he points out in the rough draft of the introduction to the *Principles* that a word may be "made the Sign of a great number of particular ideas, between which there is some likeness, & which are said to be of the same sort." [91] But the "likeness" is in the things themselves and inseparable from them, not in a separate, abstract realm of subsistence either without the mind or in it. Hence he rejects both the realism and the "conceptualism" of Locke, whose vague inconsistency, however, he recognizes by connecting him with nominalism as well. Thus in a crucial passage of the first draft of the introduction he says: "Every one's experience may convince him that . . . General Names do not stand either for Universal Natures distinct from our conceptions as was held by the Peripatetics & Generality of Schoolmen, nor yet for Universal Notions or Ideas as is the opinion of that sort of Schoolmen called Nominals & of the Author of the Essay." [92] Berkeley, therefore, is neither realist, nominalist, nor conceptualist, as these terms are traditionally understood, though his position is derived from a criticism of the last, as found in Locke's somewhat rambling disquisitions. He wishes to separate himself from Locke in two respects. On the one hand he desires to distinguish the universal far more sharply from the particular "thing" than Locke. Hence, as he asserts, it is impossible to refer to the universal as a "thing" or "idea" at all. Universals are *sui generis*. And yet, on the other hand, he wishes to maintain a far closer union between them than Locke, who saw the two simply as juxtaposed in an experience which "contained" them both as "elements." Berkeley, as opposed to this, argued an *essential* relation between them. They are dependent in their very *meaning*, one on the other.

These two opposed and yet interlocking movements of thought constitute Berkeley's early theory of universals. On the one hand there is no such thing as *the* universal, *the* abstract triangle, or *the* abstract colour red, existing or subsisting as objects or *things* in a "realm" of their own. All this is the result of the inveterate and vicious tendency to regard as independent substances what are, in fact, only dependent phases or aspects of a larger whole. There is no such thing as *the* uni-

---

[91] Pr. Ms., F. iii, p. 365. [92] Pr. Ms., F. iii, pp. 365 366, note 10.

versal triangle, though it is perfectly appropriate, and indeed absolutely essential,[93] to refer to *all* triangles, or *any* triangle. Universals pervade experience. They are valid *of* it, but they do not themselves exist as separate substances. This is why Berkeley asserts that "*The* aeternae veritates vanish," [94] though he is in no sense whatsoever a nominalist. *The* "aeternae veritates," existing in sublime and abstract isolation above, beyond, or underneath the real world "vanish." *Above, beyond,* and *under* are all "ideas" in *this* world, so that what is beyond in *this* sense is not beyond at all, but is this world over again. Transcendence is never to be attained through the hypostatization of dependent aspects.

And yet, while universals must not be regarded as things, while they must in no sense be confused with particular objects, there is another sense, though a quite different one, in which they must be so confused. Universality is opposed to particular *existence* in space and time, but nevertheless it is altogether dependent upon such *existence*. Were it not for such particular existence universality would altogether disappear. This is the meaning of Berkeley's subtle examination of the process of abstraction, through which universality or identity is somehow achieved by the *annihilation* of difference. Annihilate all the particular differences between blue and red and yellow, and so forth, and what remains is not the abstract universal, but nothing. It is only some faint though inconsistent trace of particularity still allowed to hover over the abstract universal we think we obtain through such a process of extermination that enables us to give it any meaning at all. If the extermination is *really* carried out, if we are *really* consistent in destroying the particulars, then the universals also vanish. Universality without particularity is *nothing*. Identity or "likeness" without *difference* is a meaningless abstraction.

Admitting the entire justification of Berkeley's criticism of the abstract universal and the profundity and subtlety of the results yielded by his "concrete" method of reasoning, nevertheless, it must be granted that his own doctrine, at least so far as the *Principles* is concerned, leaves much to be desired in explicitness. Granting that the universal is no thing nor entity, and that we cannot think of it in spatial or temporal terms

[93] "It is, I know, a point much insisted on, that all knowledge and demonstration are about universal notions, *to which I* *fully agree.*" Pr. Int., F. i, sec. 15, p. 247; my italics.

[94] C. B. J., 748; my italics.

as *existing*, nor even as *existing* in some other abstract sense, though what such a sense would be remains a mystery, this does not tell us how we are to think of it. Granting that *the* universals, or universalities as separate entities are mere *linguistic* constructs to some extent unavoidable, but nevertheless hideously artificial, and that in laboriously discussing *them* we are more often analyzing grammar than saying anything of the remotest relevance to reality, granting all this, nevertheless, we have yet to learn what a "concrete" universal *is*. Something which pervades reality, something which is not a particular existent, but is nevertheless bound up with it so essentially that to destroy the one means to destroy the other, — this is about as far as the polemic of the *Principles* takes us. Yet there are hints of a more positive doctrine, though in briefly attempting to indicate them it will be necessary to refer to Berkeley's later writings, where his conception is more adequately treated.

The only hint which he gives in his published *Principles* of a more definite position is to be found in the introduction, section 15, page 247, where he says, "universality so far as I can comprehend, not consisting in the absolute positive nature or conception of anything, but in the *relation* [my italics] it bears to the particulars signified or represented by it, by virtue whereof it is that things, names, or notions being in their own nature particular, are rendered universal." [95] The universal is, accordingly, a "relation." Why is it that Berkeley should choose *this* particular term to describe the essence of universality when he himself in the *Commonplace Book* states specifically that "The obscure ambiguous term *relation* . . . which is said to be the largest field of knowledge, confounds us, deceives us"? [96]   If we bear in mind the context of this passage from the *Commonplace Book* I think it will not be difficult to discern the reason. Relation is not a *thing* at all. It cannot even be said to exist, but is rather, if it is any*thing* (which it is not), an "act of mind." [97] This is why the term is "obscure" and "ambiguous," — because we so inveterately attempt to make an existent thing or entity out of it. But this very source of obscurity, this unfitness of the term for ordinary discourse, constitutes its precise fitness for Berkeley's meaning. The universal *also* is not a thing or entity. It does not *exist* as do particular things.

---

[95] Cf. Pr. Int., pp. 244-245.
[96] C. B. J., 746.

[97] "The sorts are the work of the mind," C. B. J., 296.

Rather it pervades them, as true relations pervade their terms. Furthermore, a relation with no terms to relate is obviously in the same position as the abstract universal, isolated from its particulars. Both reduce to nothing, or even less than nothing, for nothing, after all, has meaning. It is not difficult, therefore, to see why Berkeley, in the *Principles*, began to think of universals as *relations*, utterly distinct from their terms but nevertheless essentially dependent upon them.

That this represents a permanent tendency in Berkeley's thought is evidenced by many passages in the later works, as in *Alciphron* VII, for example, where he says, "these relations (or proportions of things) are not abstract general ideas, being founded in particular things, and not making of themselves distinct ideas to the mind, exclusive of the particular ideas. . . ." [98] In the second edition of the *Principles* (1734), in speaking of the unique sort of knowledge we seem to possess of our minds, he says, "We may be said to have some knowledge or *notion* of our own minds, of spirits, and active beings; whereof in a strict sense we have not *ideas*. In like manner, we know and have a *notion* of relations between things or ideas." [99] Universals are, therefore, *relations* distinct from the existent particulars from which they can be derived by no sort of abstraction or progressive mutilation. They must be viewed rather as binding the particulars together, holding them in a union from which neither the one nor the other in their entirety can ever be isolated. Such is Berkeley's first view. In his early thought, it is true, he tended mistakenly to conceive of these relations as "acts of mind," meaning acts of *my* mind or *your* mind, arbitrary acts of "Spirit." Notional knowledge or universal knowledge thus becomes personal or biographic knowledge, and is confused with the existent particular *me*, or *you*, or *God*, *acting* in space or time. It was not until the final period of his reflections that Berkeley actually overcame this error, against which he himself warned so convincingly, both in the *Commonplace Book* and in the *Treatise* itself. The difficulty, however, is not by any means a simple one, since as he himself came to see, it involves the extraordinary and mysterious idea of the subject that can become an object and yet still remain a subject, of a "One" which is both "Intellect and Life." [100]

[98] P. 341.
[99] Pr., sec. 89, p. 307, 2nd ed. Cf.
3D, F i, p. 448, written in 1713.

[100] *Siris*, sec. 362.

This final phase of his doctrine, however, was rendered possible only by the abandonment of his solipsistic spiritism, and his substitution for the finite "my" mind of the early works "the" mind of the *Siris*.[101] The ultimate relational forms, through which *the* world (not many personal worlds) is at last seen to be held together, are not finite acts in time, but timeless archetypes in *the* mind of God. But it required many years of absorption in the profounder depths of the history of philosophy, as well as ceaseless self-criticism and abnegation, before Berkeley was able to feel his way gropingly to that vague and transempirical level from which he was at last able to "seize some imperfect glimpses of the Divine Ideas." [102] The first steps of this development, however, are clearly discernible in the *Three Dialogues between Hylas and Philonous*, written three years later and certainly the most profound of his early works. Here it is that his thought is first deeply touched by that Platonism which was later, with the assistance of his concrete logic, to eradicate all traces of spiritism (materialism), and to effect in it such a generally fundamental and truly philosophical transformation. Before directing our attention, however, to this work with its introduction of the all-important conception of "archetypes," we must first complete our understanding of Berkeley's early "spiritism" by an examination of the rationalistic, or even Deistic, ethical and religious philosophy with which it was intimately associated.

[101] *Siris*, secs. 294–295, p. 265.   [102] *Siris*, sec. 337, p. 286.

CHAPTER VI

ABSTRACT ETHICS AND RELIGION

IN THE period from 1705 to 1713, during which Berkeley was a student and officer of Trinity College, his reflections seemed to carry him to well-defined and "consistent" conclusions. It is true that the method of abstraction was later destined to lead him far beyond his early "discoveries." But, throughout this period, he proceeds, confident in the assurance that he is following only "the plain dictates" of "the light of reason." It is this "reason" which leads him to view the world as a "society of spirits" with God as their leader, each spirit carrying a separate and distinct world of his own locked up in himself, and communicating not only with other spirits but with God as well, by means of the divinely instituted "language of nature," the physical universe, or rather that particular aspect of the physical universe with which each finite "soul" is familiar.

We have already noted the remarkable fact that there is no reference to Toland or the other Deists in Berkeley's early writings, though the controversy they had aroused was waging on all sides with fierce intensity. We cannot avoid concluding, from his strange silence on the subject, as well as from the direct evidence of his early sermons, that his disagreement with these heterodox authors was at this time not as marked as it might have been. The two most prominent orthodox leaders of Dublin were Peter Brown, Provost of Trinity College,[1] who published an attack on Toland's *Christianity Not Mysterious* shortly before Berkeley's entrance into the College, and William King, the sharp-tongued Archbishop of Dublin whose *Origin of Evil* was published in 1702. In opposition to the "rationalistic" free-thinkers, King and later Brown both maintained that God was "beyond" human knowledge, and King went so far as to deny "the attributes," maintaining that neither goodness, wisdom, nor knowledge could appropriately be applied to God.

Berkeley's early opinion of King and the sayings of his caustic tongue are perhaps indicated in a remark concerning them

[1] Brown in his *Analogy* (1733) attacked Berkeley's *Alciphron*, but Berkeley did not consider his remarks worthy of reply. Johnson letter, April 4, 1734, F. *Life*, p. 221.

recorded by his daughter-in-law: "The noticing them," she says, "would be like preserving a dirty fly in amber." [2] Another anecdote of this period, also recounted by his daughter-in-law, however, inadvertently indicates that later in life at least Berkeley's opposition to the bold orthodoxy and still bolder wit of the great archbishop was by no means as pronounced as the female members of his family would have us suppose.

This old monster (King) and Bishop Berkeley, then Fellow of Dublin College, a *little* known in the learned world, were both at dinner in Dublin at the house of an Earl, whose title the Editor does not at present recollect, but who had a beautiful Lady and a house full of remarkably fine children. During the time of dinner, half a score of servants in waiting, this *purpled* brute said, "Whenever I see a parcel of fine children, I *always* look round the table to see which of the footmen is the father of them." With these words he threw his *devilish* eyes around the room. The Lay Peer must have been in a faint not to have ordered his domestics to drag the spiritual one nine times through the kennel, and the Lady must have been either an *angel* or a *fool* not instantly to have risen from table. They, however, contented themselves with never admitting his Grace within their doors any more. The late Dr. Berkeley used frequently to relate this and two or three other stories, in order, as he used to say to Mr. Berkeley [George Berkeley, Jr.], "to call your mother out." To be sure, Mrs. Berkeley used to *storm nobly* on these occasions to the great diversion of her amiable husband, who used to ask, "What would *she* have done had she been Lady ——?" [3]

Berkeley's youthful Deism led him at this time to oppose King's sceptical assertions that reason can yield us only the being of God. In a letter to Percival of March 1, 1709, he says:

I do not see how it is possible to demonstrate the *being* of God: there being no argument I know of for his existence which does not prove him at the same time to be an understanding, wise and benevolent Being, in the strict, literal and proper meaning of those words. [4]

In a more mature stage of his reflections he criticizes this same doctrine as not sceptical enough, but he is now disappointed in the irrationalism of the orthodox. They have erred in yielding "reason" to their enemies. The "finiteness of our mind" is only an "excuse" [5] to cover intellectual sloth. "Reason" is fully competent, as he distinctly asserts in the preface of the *Principles*, to "prove" God, the "natural immortality" of the soul, and all the truths necessary to religion. This Deistic motif is clearly discernible in the *Treatise*, which confidently asserts that the Lord conceals Himself only "from the eyes of the sen-

[2] Berkeley, *Poems*, p. ccxxvii.
[3] *Ibid.*, p. ccxxvii.
[4] My italics. Cf. also Alc., pp. 188–189.
[5] C. B. J., 363–364.

sual and lazy, who will not be at the least expense of thought," [6] and that "stupid neglect" alone is responsible for "atheism." [7] Deism is even more clearly manifest in the early sermon of 1708 on "The Revelation of Immortality," [8] in the slightly later sermon on the text "Let your Zeal be according to Knowledge," probably delivered in Trinity College Chapel as a "commonplace," [9] and in the treatise on *Passive Obedience* of 1712, all of which more specifically concern religious topics. Berkeley also maintained at the end of his life that "reason" was a pathway to religion or even identical with religion, and that it was, as a matter of fact, only the abstract logician who, by reducing "reason" to tautology, required "faith." But during this period of his youth, he was still unaware of the basic ambiguity concealed in the word. His eagerness to defend the competency of *human* reason to "demonstrate" God and immortality in the Deistic fashion must be referred to that confused and pious Arminianism which, as we have seen in connection with his theory of knowledge, led him to attempt to make "man the measure of all things." It is to a fuller consideration of this youthful and enthusiastic "humanism" that we must now turn.

Among Berkeley's friends during this period were Prior, Samuel Madden,[10] Palliser,[11] Dering,[12] and Conterini, the good uncle of Goldsmith. Three are especially worthy of comment. The first is Samuel Molyneux, the son of the "ingenious gentleman" of Locke's *Essay*, who was Berkeley's friend and student at Trinity College. He was deeply interested in optics and astronomy, and later introduced Berkeley to the Princess, afterwards Queen, Caroline.[13] The second is St. George Ashe, Bishop of Clogher, at whose suggestion a branch of the *Society for the Propagation of the Gospel in Foreign Parts* was established at Dublin, and whose missionary zeal brought Berkeley, as a senior Freshman, into contact with the activities of the society,

---

[6] Pr., sec. 151.

[7] Pr., sec. 155; cf. sec. 63.

[8] F. iv, 87.

[9] Cf. Luce, *Hermathena*, vol. XXII, 1932, p. 16.

[10] Madden is mentioned in C. B. J., 574, as a friend with whom he had discussed certain ethical matters. He also says in this connection that "I am glad the people I converse with are not all richer, wiser, &c. than I." Madden, however, later edited the *Querist*, and looked after its publication. Prior, March 5, 1737.

[11] William Palliser, the son of the Archbishop of Cashel, to whom Berkeley's *Arithmetica* is dedicated, and who seems to have possessed kindred mathematical interests. (See dedication, F. iv, 3.)

[12] C. B. J., 129, 207.

[13] This statement is made by Stock but is unsubstantiated by other biographical sources.

especially in America.[14] The third is Lord Percival, whom
Berkeley probably met through the Derings, relatives of the
former residing in Dublin. He became a lifelong friend and
correspondent, though unfortunately Lord Percival's various
attainments did not include philosophical proficiency. The
early letters to him, however, are not without theoretical interest, particularly in regard to political issues, for Berkeley
was not so wrapped up in his spiritistic philosophy as to be
oblivious to the political excitements of the time.

The costly battle of Malplaquet had caused great resentment
against the French war, and new life had been infused into the
Tory party during the unpopular trial and impeachment of Dr.
Sacheverell for preaching non-resistance and passive obedience
in St. Paul's. The fever of political unrest, of course, touched
Ireland. "The said Dr.," Berkeley writes, "is entirely the subject of discourse, and everyone is engaged either for or against
him." [15] Berkeley himself, however, seems to have held aloof
from the conflict, though, on the whole, his political sentiments
were then and continued to be on the Tory side. Nevertheless,
he found aspects of either case to criticize. He speaks of one of
the Whig pamphlets as "writ with an affectation of more wit
than in truth it really has," and yet he cannot agree with Hig-
den, one of the Tory pamphleteers, who "seems to be against all
resistance whatsoever to the king de facto," by which "it appears his principles do not favour the late Revolution." [16]
"After all," he says, "we are forced to place the right of kings in
the consent and acquiescence of the people: whence it follows,
that whoever has the crown in possession, and the people or
their representatives, i.e. Lords and Commons concurring with
him, the same is rightful king." [17] Berkeley was no Jacobite.
He never doubted that it was the duty of all Englishmen to pay
allegiance to the existing government, and yet his constant interest in the subject shows that the issue was a living one to
him. His intense thought on this troublesome question led him
to work out a political and ethical philosophy which transcended both sides, and took him far beyond contemporary
issues. That his earliest emotional sympathies, however, were
with the Tory cause is clearly proved by the final passage of an

[14] Cf. H. Vere White, *Bishop Berkeley
as a Missionary*, Office of the Irish Auxiliary of the Society for the Propagation of
the Gospel in Foreign Parts, Dublin, 1900.

[15] Percival letter, March 1, 1709–10.
[16] Percival letter, October 21, 1709.
[17] *Ibid.*

earlier letter to Percival. "The other night," he says, "Archdeacon Percival, Dan Dering, and myself were drinking your and Dr. Sacheverell's healths at your brother's." [18] We must think of Berkeley during his Trinity College days as a very moderate Tory.[19] These political reflections were crystallized in three discourses delivered in Trinity College Chapel at this time, and published in the year 1712 as the *Discourse on Passive Obedience*.[20]

MATHEMATICAL MORALITY (THE PASSIVE OBEDIENCE)

This treatise deserves serious attention, since the opinion has become current that for some reason, presumably because he lived in the eighteenth century, Berkeley must be regarded as a utilitarian. Both Leslie Stephen [21] and Fraser [22] have supported this opinion. Such a label, however, does not do justice to Berkeley's position. According to this position God has the universal interest of mankind in view when He frames the laws of nature, but these laws work for the interest of mankind, because it is rational for them to do so; they are not rational because they work for the interest of mankind. Reason rather than utility is the supreme principle. "Nothing is a law merely because it conduceth to the public good, but because it is decreed by the will of God." [23] It is, of course, rational that the universe should be a system, and that the laws should work for our interest. "But, though it afterwards come to pass that they accidentally fail of that end, or even promote the contrary; they are nevertheless binding." [24]

It is also clear that any definition of goodness as pleasurable consciousness is far from Berkeley's meaning. "Nothing in a natural state can entitle one man more than another to the favour of God, except only moral goodness," which consists "in a conformity to the laws of God." [25] When Berkeley speaks of a moral universe he does not mean a universe in which the maximum amount of pleasurable units are accumulated, but a

[18] March 1, 1709–10.
[19] Cf. Percival letter, September 6, 1710.
[20] According to Stock the *Discourse* was published to counteract the "false accounts" of three discourses delivered in Trinity College Chapel. *Passive Obedience* was, of course, associated with Jacobitism.
[21] *Dictionary of National Biography*, vol. IV.
[22] *Works*, ii, p. 107, 1871 ed.
[23] P. O., sec. 31, F. iv, p. 121.
[24] *Ibid.* [25] P.O., sec. 7, F. iv, p. 106.

universe in which the moral freebooter is shipwrecked on the immutable rock of the moral law. We cannot entrust our ethical judgments to any such vague and hesitant guide as "moral sense" or "conscience." Too often such words confuse themselves with subjective aversions or physical habits. "We must not be directed . . . by any emotions in our blood and spirits, but by the dictates of sober and impartial reason." [26]

If we must find a label for Berkeley's early position we shall have to apply that of the school which has been traditionally most opposed to the utilitarian way of thought. It is God's place to think of the consequences. We may be sure that He has done so, for this is eminently reasonable, but "in the ordinary moral actions of our lives . . . our practice must always be shaped immediately by the rule." [27] By the criterion of this rule we shall be judged, and it is our duty to follow it even to death. We may well believe that many of the ideas originally intended for the second part of the *Principles* found their way into this rationalistic discourse,[28] which is nothing but a further development of "spiritism." The universe is a great society speaking a language of color, sound, and touch, instituted and maintained by a divine architect. By *reason* we may know something of its universal order and structure, and the rules through which we may play our respective parts. To submit ourselves to God's will, thus revealed, is goodness.

Berkeley is quite clear that there is a fundamental difference between a natural law and a moral law. "We ought to distinguish," he says, "between a twofold signification of the terms *law of nature*; which words do either denote a rule or precept for the direction of the voluntary actions of reasonable agents; and in that sense they imply a duty: or else they are used to signify any general rule which we observe to obtain in the works of nature, independent of the wills of men; in which sense no duty is implied." [29] The prescriptive law which directs the actions of a free, rational agent is thus distinguished from a law which merely describes phenomena. The former may be broken, since the rational agent is free, while a natural phenomenon is inert and cannot help itself. Nevertheless, both orders have been

[26] P. O., sec. 21, p. 115.
[27] P. O., sec. 31, p. 121.
[28] There is a close connection between several of the ethical notations of the C. B. and passages in the *Passive Obe-*dience, — for example beteeen C. B. J., 865, where "definition" is said to be of peculiar ethical importance, and P. O., sec. 32, F. i, pp. 121, 122.
[29] P. O., sec. 33, pp. 122, 123.

established as "laws of nature," eternal, immutable, knowable, and instituted by God.[30]

There is an element in our nature for which we have no responsibility. Our body, with its physical demands and instincts, is subject to certain "laws of nature" such as the tendency towards self-preservation. But these natural tendencies do not constitute duties.[31] As natural organisms we simply move and behave like other phenomena, and it is absurd to speak of the rightness or wrongness of such motions. Everything in a state of nature is equally good and equally bad. "Nothing in a natural state can entitle one man more than another to the favour of God except only moral goodness," which consists "in a conformity to the laws of God." [32] As free agents, however, we become aware of certain prescriptive principles which we may either obey or not obey and which are essentially opposed to our animal nature. We are moral only in so far as we obey them, thus ourselves creating and entering into the moral system or harmony through our own action. This sharply dualistic ethics is clearly formulated in the *Passive Obedience*, and dominated Berkeley's early thought. Morality is identified with rationality. There are certain prescriptive principles or "laws of nature" which every thinking being may discover to be valid. Moral worth consists solely in the conformity of our actions with such principles.

It is easy to see from these youthful, rationalistic predilections why Locke's idea of a mathematical morality should appeal to Berkeley, why he toys with the idea in the earlier portions of the *Commonplace Book*,[33] and why in the *Passive Obedience* (1712) he compares moral rules with "propositions in geometry" and reserves for them "the same immutable universal truth," [34] though he admits that something more than mathematics is necessary to *apply* the rule. Such is also the case, however, in geometry, for "there must be a triangle, and you must use your senses to know this before there is room for applying your mathematical rule." [35] Doubtless Berkeley was thinking of this in the *Commonplace Book* when he said, "morality may be

---

[30] This parallelism between the laws of nature and the laws of morality is a prominent feature of Berkeley's early metaphysics. Cf. H. W. Orange, "Berkeley as a Moral Philosopher," *Mind*, 1890, vol. XV, p. 514.

[31] P. O., sec. 35, p. 123.
[32] P. O., sec. 7, p. 106.
[33] Cf. C. B. J., 348, 694, 248.
[34] P. O., sec. 53, p. 133; cf. C. B. J., 467.
[35] P. O., sec. 53, p. 134.

demonstrated as mixt Mathematics." [36] After 1713, however, this mathematical view is never again mentioned by Berkeley, and while we have already discussed certain reasons for his abandoning it, we must return again to a consideration of this important phase of his thought, in which he attempts to carry out Locke's suggestion of an ethics based upon *rules* as clear and certain as those of mathematics.

These rules, Berkeley now insists, are necessary and recognizable as such by all rational agents. Difficulties arise only from taking a too limited or "narrow" view. Thus, for example, though a person may be in sincere doubt as to the benefits of loyalty to the state in a certain instance, he cannot be in doubt as to the general advantages derived from loyalty throughout the course of history, for upon loyalty rests that order and stability which is the basic requirement for all goods realized in social and individual life. The *Passive Obedience*, therefore, begins with an attempt to attain the broadest, most universal perspective, free from the bias of peculiar interests. From such "an equal and enlarged view of things, it is not possible there should be so great, if any, disagreement at all amongst candid rational inquirers after truth." [37] In other words, we must first achieve the pure and universal standpoint of "reason" itself, uninfluenced by any extraneous circumstance. It is impossible to derive moral principles from "natural inscriptions on the mind," "from the authority of learned men," "from the consent of nations," or, indeed, from anything but "the deductions of reason" itself.[38]

It is true that Berkeley proceeds to deduce the various moral laws from the nature of God, who must will the good of all His "creatures," since He is "a being of infinite goodness." [39] This at first seems to imply the ultimate supremacy of an arational factor lying "back of" reason. A closer examination of the argument, however, reveals that such is not the case. In the first place, God's will is deduced. Its existence "is a truth evident by the light of nature." [40] In the second place, Berkeley insists throughout the *Passive Obedience* upon the "eternal" character of the laws of nature and reason. Such laws, he says, "are termed *eternal rules of reason* because they necessarily result

[36] J., 768.
[37] P. O., sec. 29, p. 120.
[38] P. O., sec. 4, p. 104.

[39] P. O., sec. 7, p. 106.
[40] P. O., sec. 6, p. 105.

from the nature of things, and may be demonstrated by the infallible deductions of reason." [41] Since these laws are eternal we must suppose them to be binding upon God as well as man. God willed the good in order to be rational. He was not rational in order to be good. The deduction of the good from the rational, however, while it is assumed by the *Passive Obedience*, is never actually accomplished, and we must regard the impossibility of doing so as constituting one of the essential reasons for Berkeley's later abandonment of moral Deism. In the *Passive Obedience* he is a strict rationalist accepting the ontological argument, in so far as God's existence is made a consequence of His rationality.

Since God as a rational being must will the welfare or happiness of His creatures, it is at once possible to deduce certain general utilitarian principles as means to this end. Truth, righteousness, and chastity, for example, are justified as moral principles, because they have "a necessary connection with . . . universal well-being." [42] It is imperative that such principles be obeyed universally and with the most rigid exactitude in order that they should adequately achieve their end. If moral decisions are left to the private judgment of each individual, Berkeley insists that the most horrible confusion must result. When we start from the peculiar situation confronting us the alternative sets of consequences are too complex. But if we enlarge our perspective and become "distant spectators" [43] of the whole frame of things, then we may see that there are certain general laws such as loyalty to the forces which sustain order in the community, which, if observed by all, must tend to the welfare of the whole. These laws are willed by God and thus become moral principles,[44] since "he that willeth the end doth will the necessary means conducive to that end." [45] They provide the objective standard on the basis of which we may determine the morality or immorality of *any* action, and Berkeley is quite clear that they must be obeyed no matter how serious or terrible the consequences may be in any particular case. "No private interest, no love of friends, no regard to the public good, should make us depart from them," [46] and "he who squares his actions by this rule can never do amiss, though thereby he should bring himself to poverty, death or disgrace: no, though he should in-

[41] P. O., sec. 12, p. 108.

[42] P. O., sec. 15, p. 111.

[43] P. O., sec. 28, p. 119.

[44] P. O., sec. 31, p. 121.

[45] P. O., sec. 11, p. 108.

[46] P. O., sec. 13, p. 109.

volve his family, his friends, his country, in all those evils which are accounted the greatest and most insupportable to human nature." [47]

Never has the ethics of principle been stated more uncompromisingly. It is true that the principles are justified on general utilitarian grounds, but these utilitarian grounds are justified by God's will, and God's will is justified by His reason. Berkeley leaves us in no doubt that the whole system of divine Providence, which involves the universal well-being of all men, is demonstrable by reason. At no point does he maintain that it is necessary to accept God's will simply as God's will. Indeed, he says, at the very beginning of his treatise: "I intend not to build on the authority of Holy Scripture, but altogether on the Principles of Reason common to all mankind." The existence of God as a perfect "omniscient" being is a truth "evident by the light of nature," which alone is sufficient to justify the rationality of the basic utilitarian principle. This principle is the supreme law of nature, from which the others are deduced, but it derives its validity from the "natural light." God Himself is a moral being subject to the eternal laws of nature, and willing the utilitarian principle in accordance with them. Berkeley does not show how this principle is to be deduced from the rational. But the possibility of doing so is clearly implied by his position, which is that of theological rigorism or rationalism rather than that of "theological utilitarianism." The universal welfare is not moral simply because God willed it. He willed it because it was rational.

Berkeley attempted to mitigate the intemperance and even fanaticism of this doctrine by distinguishing between negative and positive precepts. The basis of this distinction, as he explains,[48] lies in the fact that "either through the difficulty or number of moral actions, or their inconsistence with each other, it is not possible for one man to perform several of them at the same time; whereas it is plainly consistent and possible that any man should at the same time abstain from all manner of positive actions whatsoever." In other words, Berkeley admits that "positive duties" may conflict. That is, my duty of obeying the ordering power in the community may conflict with my duty of telling the truth. If we phrase the duties negatively, however, we do not fall into this difficulty, for no matter how complicated the moral situation, it will always be possible for a man *not* to disobey the government, and therefore at least to avoid the violation of any negative precept. It is to be doubted if such a change in phraseology would prove of much assistance to a person in a moral dilemma, for if it is immoral to neglect one duty at the expense of another, it is certainly much more so to neglect both. If morality may be reduced to a set of negative precepts, then a rock is moral.

This is typical of the sort of difficulty into which Berkeley falls as a result of his mechanical rationalism. Doing nothing can never be a duty. Berkeley admits of all duties that "those which enjoin the doing of an action allow room for human prudence and discretion in the execution of them," [49] and with this admission he also implies that all duties are subject to limitation. The fact that it is possible to phrase them negatively cannot alter the situation. "Thou shalt tell the truth" and "Thou shalt not lie" are at least *morally* equivalent, and one cannot *morally* conform to them by ceasing to act. Berkeley is confusing reason with its dead deposits, and the tangle of literalisms which results is baffling even to his youthful ingenuity.

The motive back of this unfortunate distinction, of course, is the attempt to save the objectivity of morality. If morality is to be "rational," there must be universal principles which are always valid without exception. Berkeley saw that beyond the bare form of rationality there seems to be no such principle. The moment this bare form becomes crystallized into any strictly defined set of duties, difficulties arise. Not only does reality confront us with unforeseen situations with respect to which our formulations become confused and contradictory, but there is something mechanical, and therefore absurd, about a person who insists upon adhering blindly to a given formula. Indeed, can we not say that there is something profoundly irrational about such conduct, for reason is certainly more than any of its formulations? Nevertheless, if rationality is something which can never be stated, is it not really irrational? Berkeley, during his youth, felt this objection to be unanswerable. The essence of morality is rationality. If so, we must be able to state what rationality means in the form of certain valid, moral principles with definite content. No positive principle of this sort can be laid down as valid without exception. So Berkeley ingeniously suggests negative principles. If we cannot say that

[49] *Ibid.*

it is always moral to tell the strict truth, we can at least maintain that it is always wrong to lie. If the duty of truthfulness conflicts with the duty of humanity we may remain true to the letter of the law by obeying neither. That is, by making the law negative in form, we may make it universally valid. But, in this case, we have destroyed morality, since moral situations offer no middle way out. For a human being amorality is equivalent to immorality.

Berkeley's youthful suggestion thus offers no real solution. A moral command, though it may be phrased negatively, always represents something positive to be done, and such commands, as he admits, can never be laid down as universally valid without exception. This is, indeed, clearly indicated by his elaborate discussion of the duty of passive obedience, or the command that "Thou shalt not resist the Supreme Power," as phrased negatively and thus universally, whereof "the least breach hath the inherent stain of moral turpitude." [50] Not only does Berkeley finally have to admit certain "limitations and restrictions in order to a distinct definition of the duty," [51] but also the possibility of "controversies" concerning "the seat of the Supreme Power." [52]

Even when we have achieved a "distinct definition of the duty," the question of *applying* it still remains. In an important passage, added in the third edition of 1713, Berkeley insists upon the parallelism of morality, in this respect, with mathematics. "Multiply the height by half the base" is an eternal principle which is universally valid for the measurement of a triangle. Given a triangle, it must come under this formula. But "there must be a triangle and you must use your senses to know this, before there is room for applying your mathematical rule." [53] Morality is thus to be demonstrated only as "mixt mathematics." [54] The *application* of the principles involves sensory intuition. A government must be present before we may obey it. But in time of revolution this is, of course, precisely the point at issue, and the mathematical moralist during such a period must adopt the essentially amoral, and therefore essentially immoral, position of doing nothing until the situation clarifies itself, — until he finds a triangle. Thus again a formal, negative morality is purchased only through a state of quietism,

---

[50] P. O., sec. 15, p. 111.

[51] P. O., sec. 54; cf. sec. 32 with regard to "killing."

[52] P. O., sec. 54, p. 134.

[53] P. O., sec. 53, p. 134.

[54] J., 768.

which purports to be neither moral nor immoral, but is really the latter.

One cannot carefully read Berkeley's ingenious arguments for absolute non-resistance without becoming convinced of the grave weaknesses of his position. Indeed, it is somewhat obscure why his friends should have had difficulty in persuading the government that this treatise could never be used in behalf of Jacobitism. His position, like that of Hobbes, with which it has close similarities, cannot be logically used in favour of any party, save of that which happens to be in control. And even here the position, as argued on purely rational grounds, is subject to such qualifications that it is hard to see how it could ever be objected to by anyone, "except" as purporting to give an adequate description of a distinct moral duty.

It is not difficult to understand why this is the last we hear of a "mathematical morality," and why, after this ambitious beginning, Berkeley definitely abandoned the attempt to deduce a rational set of moral formulae which should be applied as "mixt mathematics." Not only does the question of application loom up so large in this field that uncertainty of the *mixture* destroys the certainty of the mathematics, but the mathematical propositions themselves involve definitions which are subject to the most damaging qualifications and limitations. Just what do we mean by obedience, for example? In the case of the command "*Thou shalt not kill*" Berkeley admits that the word "*murder*" must be substituted in order to take care of the case of the soldier. But once this sort of admission is made we are lost in a tangle of confused, particular cases, each of which must be argued on its own merits. Is murder in self-defence, for example, to be called murder? Similar questions must, of course, arise with respect to obedience. Does our duty of absolute passive obedience require submission to "usurpers or even madmen"? Berkeley is forced to admit a qualification in this respect,[55] though he insists that this is not so much "limiting the duty as defining it."[56] The difficulties, however, of arriving at a definition which can do justice to the infinite variety of the concrete are insuperable, as his own discussion very clearly shows. No matter how we limit or safeguard our formula, the exception will arise. The mathematical moralist, who sticks to his formula come what may, becomes in the end not only fanatical but absurd and irrational. It is not necessary to turn to

[55] P. O., sec. 52, p. 133.   [56] *Ibid.*

"experience" to become aware of the inadequacy of such casuistic recipes. Can it not always be left to reason itself to show their dogmatism and irrationality? How is their specifically moral content justified? This leads us to the fundamental weakness of Berkeley's position — the missing demonstration of the utilitarian principle.

We have shown that he presents this principle as a basic law of nature from which he deduces the rest. But we look in vain for its demonstration. God wills the universal welfare of mankind. But why — on what rational grounds? Because He is good. Why is He good? Because He is perfect, and a perfect being must will the good. But why is it rational to be perfect? It may be maintained that rationality ultimately involves perfect rationality, but perfect rationality does not necessarily involve perfect morality. To say that the most reasonable being is also good is a synthetic or "instructive" proposition. Rationality, for Berkeley at this time, meant formal consistency.[57] But goodness is intrinsically something more. The force of his criticism of mathematical morality as being trifling or analytic,[58] and its application to his own doctrine as outlined in the *Passive Obedience* is now clear. Moral propositions are synthetic, and cannot be deduced from the formal principles of "reason." If we start with the rationality of God, we shall never be able to show why He must be morally good. No inherent contradiction would have arisen had He willed evilly, or had He willed nothing at all. This is the most glaring weakness in Berkeley's early moral system. The deduction of the good from the rational is assumed, but nowhere accomplished, and God's willing of the universal welfare of humanity confronts us as a blind, irrational act. Such a situation can only be met, either by recognizing the irrational element in morality, or by developing a new and broader definition of rationality, that is, by conceiving it as something other than mathematical consistency or lack of contradiction.

Both these movements did, as a matter of fact, take place in Berkeley's later thought. Instead of attempting to "deduce" the good from the rational, the *Siris* proceeds in the opposite fashion, setting up value not only as the supreme principle, but the supreme explanatory principle, though "explanation" or "reason" is consequently conceived as non-mathematical or synthetic in character. This "derationalizing" of reason is cor-

---

[57] Cf. Pr. Int., secs. 2, 3.   [58] Cf. chap. II.

related with a very different attitude toward moral questions. Instead of the belligerent confidence of his youth which hoped to enchain the concrete reality with a set of abstract principles, we find a "resignation" to that same reality. No longer does he advocate the ruthless "subjection of our passions to the immutable decrees of reason," [59] but rather a "harmony" which shall "include the gratification of all our faculties." [60] The "benevolence" or charity which in his youth seemed to him "more dangerous than other passions," [61] and therefore to be "restrained and kept under," lest it "betray us into as great enormities as any other unbridled lust," is now conceived as an attribute of God, "there being no one perfection or attribute of the Deity more glorious or spiritual than the most diffused and active benevolence." [62] The infectious enthusiasm which believed that "the greater part, if not all, of those difficulties which have hitherto amused philosophers, and blocked up the way to knowledge, are entirely owing to ourselves," [63] is now replaced by an extreme tentativeness which holds that "though our light be dim, and our situation bad, yet if the best use be made of both, perhaps something may be seen." [64] To trace the various pathways by which this movement of thought advanced is the task now confronting us, though we must first pause for a moment to glance at the religious form in which his early rationalism crystallized.

"Reason" in Religion (The Early Sermons)

In comparing the *Passive Obedience* with the two sermons which have survived from this period, and with the "religious" passages of his more philosophical works, it becomes evident that Berkeley's early attitude towards religion was characterized by a "rationalism" no less rigid than that which marks his ethical philosophy. Thus, in his introduction to the *Principles*, he takes the position that the various obscurities and seeming contradictions which characterize religious and philosophical discussion are due to mistakes which may be cleared up by more accurate observation and careful reasoning. "God has

---

[59] P. O., sec. 38, p. 125.
[60] John Wild, "An Unpublished Sermon of Bishop Berkeley. With a Foreword," *Phil. Rev.*, vol. XL, no. 6, 1931, p. 535. This sermon is dated 1751.

[61] P. O., sec. 13, p. 109.
[62] Wild, *op. cit.*, p. 530.
[63] Pr. Int., sec. 3.
[64] *Siris*, sec. 263.

dealt . . . more bountifully with the sons of men . . . than to give
them a strong desire for that knowledge which he had placed
quite out of their reach." [65] This attitude is clearly revealed
in the *Commonplace Book.* Here he not only maintains that it
is possible through rational argument to become "certain" of
God's existence, but he inveighs sharply against the "excuse"
offered for our ignorance in religious matters which is based
upon "the finiteness of our mind." [66] The loss of the "excuse,"
he states further, may be damaging to the doctrine of transubstantiation, but not to that of the Trinity,[67] seeming to
imply that the latter dogma may be justified on purely "rational" grounds. Furthermore, he declares in so many words
that his "doctrine," according to which God is pure, spiritual
action, yields "a most suitable idea of the Divinity." [68] God is
"the cause of all natural things," [69] and there is "but one volition acknowledged to be God." [70] Such a definition, based upon
the notion of causation, he maintains, is "much clearer than
that of Descartes and Spinoza." [71]

This confident attitude comes to light in all of Berkeley's
early sermons, where he constantly emphasizes that "Knowledge is the lamp of the soul that guides its faculties to proper
objects and regulates their respective operations," [72] and that
it is possible "by the unassisted force of reason" to "demonstrate" the main articles of religion, such as immortality.[73] If
we then ask what is the function of religion as an institution, we
find Berkeley with the ready and "plausible" Deistic answer.
By far the "greatest part of mankind" lack "the extraordinary
parts and application," the "leisure or abilities" to discover for
themselves the fundamental religious truths "by the unassisted
force of reason." [74] Supernatural means, such as "miracles"
and revelation, therefore, are necessary to bring about "conviction" only in the masses. One who has the leisure and ability
to think may "necessarily infer the existence of God — by an
act of reason," and may prove "with the clearest and most immediate evidence" the "incorruptibility of the soul."

The Berkeley of the *Principles* and the early sermons is a
typical mouthpiece of the Enlightenment. He finds himself,

[65] Pr. Int., sec. 3.
[66] C. B. J., 364.
[67] C. B. J., 363.
[68] J., 430.
[69] *Ibid.*
[70] J., 725; cf. 842, 850.

[71] J., 857.
[72] Sermon: "Let Your Zeal Be According to Knowledge," Luce, *Hermathena*, vol. XXII, p. 16.
[73] *The Revelation of Life and Immortality*, F. iv, p. 87.   [74] *Ibid.*

therefore, in agreement with those who were later to become his great enemies, the Deists, and is hardly aware of the forces in his personality which were later to lead him into opposition to them. "Reason" is enough to confound sceptics and infidels. It is enough to prove the "great articles of religion," [75] and thus essentially to satisfy the religious consciousness. By removing "the long ambages of words" and the subtle misconceptions that have dogged the footsteps of philosophy we may arrive directly and necessarily at the spiritual view of reality which is the basis of religion. The historic Church and ritual are necessary for the masses, but add nothing essential to genuine religious insight.

This favorite conception of the Enlightenment, of an esoteric religion for the few and an exoteric religion for the many, was supplemented by another tendency constituting the burden of his sermon on the text "Let thy Zeal be According to Knowledge," the very title of which makes manifest its Deistic character. What Berkeley stresses above all else in this juvenile "commonplace" is "good works," which, as "the most necessary condition of our Salvation," "justly lays claim to the highest degree of our zeal." [76] We need no further proof of the Arminianism into which his rationalism was driving him when we read that, as revealed by "the universal voice of Reason," every man "shall be rewarded according to his works," [77] and that "Faith" claims only "the next degree of our zeal." [78] This sermon is also characterized by typical Tolandian warnings against the "early notions" accidentally derived from "country, friends, and persons whom they esteem," [79] Chubbsian sneers at "the poor ignorant papist," muttering "what he does not understand," [80] and all the familiar armoury of the very free-thinkers against whom he was later to wage a relentless war.

When we piece together the fragments of this picture, the universal religion of the superior few, a God who allows Himself to be "demonstrated" and expressed in mathematical clarity as the "wise," the "good," and "perfect," who wills the "happiness" of His creatures, and who is finally forced to judge men by their "works," the picture becomes the familiar one so tediously and humourlessly repeated in the "free-thinking" articles which flooded the libraries and publications of the early eight-

[75] D. 3, F. i, p. 478.
[76] Luce, *Hermathena*, vol. XXII, p. 23.
[77] Luce, *op. cit.*, p. 23.
[78] Luce, *op. cit.*, p. 24.
[79] Luce, *op. cit.*, p. 21.
[80] Luce, *op. cit.*, p. 27.

eenth century.[81] Berkeley's early treatises are all, in fact, dominated by the same spirit of confidence in "reason" which guided the speculations of the free-thinkers themselves. When we realize finally that he himself put forth his *Three Dialogues* as an outline of "the principles of natural religion," [82] we cannot avoid concluding that the reigning atmosphere of Deistic discussion in Dublin during his student days had no small influence in determining the course of his early speculations.

We must not forget, however, that he was even at this time distinguished from the free-thinkers by a most sincere and intense feeling for religion, and there are several passages in the *Commonplace Book* which point out the unique importance of faith.[83] But his faith was one thing and his reason another, and while he *assumed* or *supposed* a harmony between the two, this harmony was an external "synthesis," not arising from the intrinsic nature of either. It is also apparent that he thought of the "harmony" in a one-sided fashion, that is, of faith as harmonizing with reason, rather than of reason with faith. In the *Commonplace Book*, for example, his whole effort is directed towards showing the "rationality" of the scriptural view, and its essential agreement with his own. Thus he says: "there is nothing in Scripture that can possibly be wrested to make against me . . .," [84] and curtly disposes of Malebranche's "Scripture" proof for the existence of matter without even a discussion.[85] There is no necessity for resting the religious case on such questionable authority. Rather it is a "truth," which "glares so strongly on the mind" that it is only "by an aversion of thought, a wilful shutting of the eyes" that we may "escape seeing it." [86]

At no point does this early "rationalism" stand in a more striking contrast to Berkeley's maturer thought than in his treatment of the problem of immortality. In the *Commonplace Book* it is one of the "interests of religion" firmly guaranteed by

---

[81] Cf. for example the following article signed "Socrates" in *Gent. Mag.*, 1732, II, p. 1107: ". . . by free-thinking we are able to prove there is a Being infinitely Wise, Good, and Powerful, at the Head of Affairs in the Universe; who being absolutely perfect, and having no self-interest, could have no Views in making the World but to communicate Happiness to all his Creatures. . . . By Free-Thinking we may discover the eternal Differences of Things in Nature, the natural standard of action, and the reason of our duty. . . ." How closely this approaches the early point of view of the *Passive Obedience* it is hardly necessary to remark.

[82] Preface, F. i, p. 377.
[83] Cf. J., 590, 732.
[84] J., 289.
[85] J., 697.
[86] Pr., sec. 154, F. i, p. 346.

the new principle. As a consequence of his fundamental distinction between the active will and the passive ideas he states that "the Soul, taken for the Will is immortal, incorruptible." [87] This is the doctrine to which he refers later, in the *Principles*, as that of the "natural immortality of the soul." [88] The spiritual activity which perceives the dissolution of external bodies is not itself dissoluble, — the consciousness which divides is not itself divisible. Thus "the motions, changes, decays, and dissolutions which we hourly see befal natural bodies . . . cannot possibly affect an active, simple, uncompounded substance." [89]

As his introductions to the *Principles* and the *Three Dialogues* clearly show, this "proof" of the doctrine of immortality gave him no small satisfaction. In his early sermon on the *Revelation of Life and Immortality*, before he had convinced himself of the proof, he coldly calculates the "odds," and concludes that "the hazard, though never so small and uncertain of a good so ineffably, so inconceivably great ought to be more valued and sought after than the greatest assurance we can have of any sublunary good." [90] During the remainder of his early thought, however, he directs all his efforts towards a proof which, as we have seen, is very little more than the traditional argument based upon the distinction between the soul as a simple, indivisible entity and the world of extended objects, which are all compounds and thus subject to dissolution. Berkeley introduced the element of epistemological dependence into this contrast. If the very being of objects is their being perceived, then the coming and going of objects cannot be supposed to affect the perceiving consciousness, since the very going of the objects necessarily implies the permanence of the consciousness for which they disappear. This is why he is so confident that the "comfortable expectation of immortality" must result from "a close and methodical application of thought." [91]

As Berkeley himself points out, however, this "proof" is far from adequate, since it does not show that the soul "is absolutely incapable of annihilation," but only that "it is not liable to be broken or dissolved by the ordinary laws of nature or motion." [92] The notion of a simple soul substance is really foreign to his thought, as his general polemic against the doctrine of substance clearly reveals. The soul, for him, is really the

[87] J., 826.
[88] Pr., sec. 141, F. i, pp. 336–337.
[89] *Ibid.*

[90] *Rev. of Life and Imm.*, F. iv, p. 90.
[91] 3 D., Pref., F. i, p. 377.
[92] Pr., sec. 141, F. i, pp. 336–337.

"will," the "activity" which knows and perceives ideas. While it is true that the "activity" is to be placed on a different level from that of the ideas, — simply to show that the will cannot be destroyed by the same processes which destroy external objects does not mean that it cannot be destroyed by *any* process. This, Berkeley himself clearly realizes and states. The proof is, therefore, hardly a proof. Furthermore, the dependence of the ideas upon the act of perceiving would seem to imply a similar dependence of the perceiving upon the objects of perception. What is an act of perception without anything to perceive? What is an act of will without anything to will? Berkeley's many attempts temporarily to escape this implication of his own theory of abstraction were unsuccessful. It may be impossible to conceive of an object without a subject, but it seems equally impossible to conceive of a subject without an object. We have already noted the process in the *Commonplace Book* through which he came to the conclusion that "experience" is a concrete unity from which both the pure self and the pure object were, as a matter of fact, illicit abstractions. In spite of the attempt to ignore this implication in the sermons and the *Treatise*, we find him putting less and less stress on the purely subjective side of his doctrine. Thus in the *Three Dialogues* he hardly mentions the "proof," after referring to it rather grandiosely in the preface, and in the *Alciphron* he abandons all attempts to "prove" immortality, and the doctrine of the "natural immortality of the soul" is dropped altogether from his writings.

The Arminianism of Berkeley's early thought reached its climax in the anthropomorphic and utterly unorthodox conception of God in which his "causal" metaphysics culminated. We have already noted his insistence, as against his ecclesiastical superiors (with whom he was, however, soon to find himself in essential agreement), that God, if He is to be known at all, must be known as "understanding, wise, and benevolent"; [93] and in the *Principles* he proves, to his own satisfaction, that a spirit "infinitely wise, good, and powerful" is "sufficient to explain" all the appearances of nature.[94] Unfortunately, however, something much less impressive is "sufficient," since Berkeley's "causal" argument for God, even admitting it to be valid, can only justify some other *spirit* analogous to *me*. The strength of the "causal" argument is, therefore, really a grave weakness, since it leads only to an exaggerated man. "God" is derived simply from the sense of resistance running through experience. By far the greater part of my ideas come to me "independent of my Will," [95] and, therefore, as Locke argued, they must come from some other, active source, since it is an eternal "axiom" that "every idea has a cause, i.e. is produced by a Will." [96] Such a "God" is only a power "distinct from us," and "on whom we depend." [97] He is an active being like ourselves, who caused the world [98] and maintains it by an arbitrary fiat of His "will."

Such an argument is, however, subject to at least two grave objections. In the first place, it involves the gratuitous transposition of the active causation we "feel" in ourselves to an object which is beyond us, and hence unknowable. In order to justify this, Berkeley was later forced to maintain the existence of a certain peculiar rational inference, [99] which can give us transcendental knowledge. But then, as Hume and others have pointed out, Berkeley's polemic against matter loses its force. If we may "rationally infer" the existence of a spirit outside ourselves, why may we not with equal cogency argue the existence of material objects outside ourselves? Causation is, as a natural consequence of Berkeley's own reflections, an immanent principle which loses its meaning when placed in a field beyond experience. This becomes peculiarly apparent in connection with his theory that God is a timeless being. [100] What meaning can we give to the idea of causal action abstracted from all connection with time? The attribution of causation to a transcendent being beyond experience is entirely unjustified on the grounds of his own philosophy. Is not the sense of dependence and passivity itself only another idea or set of ideas? Its *esse* therefore is *percipi*. It leads necessarily to a mind perceiving it, by no means to a transcendental cause.

In the second place, as we have observed, the analogical argument, even if it were valid, could not prove what Berkeley wants it to. Philonous has to admit in the *Third Dialogue*, when pressed, that his knowledge of God is based upon his knowledge of himself. But he himself is a finite limited being, and the causal analogy could, therefore, never justify the only sort of

[95] C. B. H., 827; J., 850.
[96] J., 843.
[97] J., 41.
[98] C. B. H., 820; J., 842. Cf. H., 300; J., 308.
[99] N. T. V. V., sec. 42.

[100] Letter, Berkeley to Samuel Johnson, March 24, 1730. See H. and C. Schneider, *Samuel Johnson, President of King's College; His career and writings,* New York, 1929, vol. II, p. 282.

God capable of justifying anything like religion — "a Being of transcendent and unlimited perfections" whose nature "is incomprehensible to finite spirits." [101] The analogy with the self, which underlies the whole "causal" argument, however, can by no means prove God, but only another, finite limited being, perhaps *more* powerful and *more* active. We must conclude that Berkeley, in adopting Locke's epistemological form of the cosmological argument, while winning a certain superficial plausibility, paid a very serious and even impossible price by giving up all pretensions to logical rigour. The traditional cosmological argument, even in its most popular form, at least employs the concept of a first cause which is on an entirely different level from that of ordinary causes. Berkeley's argument, as presented in the *Principles*, however, does not even reach this point. It passes merely to "another" cause to which the attribution of the various religious predicates becomes unusually gratuitous. It is not surprising to discover, therefore, that the force of Berkeley's own reflection led him, a little later, in the *Three Dialogues* to abandon this argument.

He attempts at various points, it is true, to bolster up this very ineffectual "proof" by references to teleology and design. Thus, in the *Principles*, it is "from the constant uniform method of our sensations" that we "collect the goodness and wisdom of the Spirit who excites them in our minds. . . ." [102] The constant connections which we observe in our experience, he tells us, must justify the belief in the wisdom and goodness of their cause. But this uniformity is by no means a necessary one. There is no intrinsic reason why water should run down rather than up. Such connections, therefore, are arbitrary, like the connections between linguistic symbols and the meanings that they signify. But surely if the connections themselves are arbitrary, much more arbitrary is the connection with their "beneficent" cause. Such a "leap" into the unknown not only closes its eyes to the dysteleological features of experience, but even at best justifies only a beneficent or perhaps many beneficent beings like ourselves, not by any means a God who is "omniscient and omnipotent."

It is not surprising, therefore, to find Berkeley, at the end of the *Principles*, introducing a mystical note into the argument, [103] maintaining that we actually "see" God. This starts out as

[101] 3 D., F. i, p. 475.
[102] F. i, p. 297.
[103] Pr., sec. 150, F. i, pp. 342–343.

a rational argument, "which lies so near and obvious to the mind," that the general failure to recognize it "is a sad instance of the stupidity and inattention of men." [104] We do, of course, "see" other persons, but what we actually perceive is "only certain sensations or ideas excited in our own minds." [105] "Hence it is plain we do not see a man, if by *man* is meant that which lives, moves, perceives, and thinks as we do." So Berkeley concludes that "after the same manner we see God," [106] or rather do *not* see God, for the whole force of this argument really lies in its *tu quoque* character. How we see or know other minds is a mystery, since we do not really see them, but only infer their existence. Hence we should swallow the even greater mystery involved in the knowing of God. By first landing us in solipsism, which he here recognizes as the logical outcome of his spiritism, Berkeley then points out that if we are fools enough to believe in the world and other minds, we may as well believe in God as well. But it is a simple matter to evade this grotesque *tour de force* by perceiving what Berkeley himself for the first time perceived in the *Three Dialogues*, — the total indefensibility of the causal subjectivism on which it is primarily based. He could not hope to find a satisfactory or even intelligible interpretation of religion until he had worked his way out of the Lockian "spiritism" which so hampered his early reflections.

SPIRITISTIC RATIONALISM

Berkeley's early ethics and theology not only shed a great deal of light on his philosophy of "spiritism," but also on the abstract or analytic mode of thinking which originally led him to the formulation of such a position. This analytic logic proceeded only by chopping up into fragments whatever came into contact with it, fragments so utterly distinct that the only sort of connection which could then be asserted of them would be, in Berkeley's words, "arbitrary." Thus, the result of his first meditations on the nature of time and space led him, as we have seen, to a temporary position which ignored the continuity of experience. The world, as Berkeley first analyzed it, was a set of isolated atoms or "minima," as he called them, possessing no inherent connection, but requiring the "arbitrary fiat" of an

---

[104] Pr., sec. 149, F. i, p. 342.   [106] *Ibid.*, pp. 341–342.
[105] Pr., sec. 148, F. i, 341.

external principle to bring them together. It is no wonder, therefore, that his system, if it can be called a system at all, culminates in the view of reality as a "set" or "society" of entirely separate "spirits," with an exaggerated spirit or Deity "at their head," who, with a relentless arbitrariness, thrusts "sets" of separate ideas upon them, one by one. It has often been supposed by critics that Berkeley's religious faith is responsible for this extraordinary point of view, that he proceeded "rationally" and "logically" until all of a sudden, "because he was a Bishop," his "religious" prejudices got the better of him, and he solved all difficulties with a *deus ex machina*.

Nothing could be more irrelevant than this easy criticism, which is based upon a perfect network of misunderstandings. Not only was Berkeley not a bishop when he elaborated this point of view, as a result of his reading Locke, but there is the strongest evidence, as we have attempted to show, that he was, himself, proceeding along definitely Deistic lines, with perfect confidence in "reason," and in utter opposition to the introduction of irrational or superrational principles ("the excuse"). It is precisely "reason," or "analytic" logic which ruthlessly and inevitably led him, just as it later led Hume, to the irrational. It matters not whether the arbitrary, external factor be called "God" or "human nature." Once we have split the world to pieces in a set of analytic fragments, nothing but mystery and faith can ever bind them together again. This is a necessary consequence of any type of "rationalism" which attempts to follow the mathematical ideal of certainty (i.e. tautology), and thus paralyzes itself from the outset by making it impossible to move from one point to another, to "relate," to "associate," to "create," to "set up a *first* premiss." If reason is to be deductive (tautological), as Berkeley first supposed, there is absolutely no escape from an irrational God. This sort of reason leads irresistibly to "faith," to "mystery," to "imagination," to "human nature," "to assumption," to "postulation," or any of the other popular names by which "He" has come to be known in more recent times. Far from being only a gratuitous, ecclesiastical supposition, Berkeley's God, as he clearly saw, is an absolutely "rational" necessity. Without it, his world would be a set of totally unrelated fragments, not even fragments, since really to be fragments they must be fragments of *some* whole. Analytic logic requires alogic, for it must have *something* to analyze, which it cannot furnish by itself. Deductive "reason" requires the *irrational*, or it will never gain a premiss from which to deduce. Hence, Berkeley's early system of spiritism, inspired by Locke and the deductive ideal of mathematics, consistently culminated in the mysterious, ineffable, and *arbitrary* will of God, on the one hand, and the analytic "set," or society, of separate, solipsistic "spirits" on the other.

This is why Berkeley's early thought betrays such a jumpy and erratic character. He will begin at a certain point, develop it "logically," and then all of a sudden leap "arbitrarily" to another, from *the* self to *other* selves, from the idea of sight to the idea of touch, from man to God. The passage from his chaotic world of isolated souls to "universal laws of nature" which shall hold for all creatures is likewise such an arbitrary and inconsistent jump, although it is perfectly consistent with his method of abstract consistency (tautology), and, indeed, dictated by it. There must be universal, moral principles, or the world of spirits will dissolve away into an anarchy which is not even anarchy, since anarchy or chaos can be defined only with reference to order. Hence the *Passive Obedience*.

But once having "leaped" to the abstract universal, his stringent deductive method will not allow him to advance. He must consequently leap once more to the good. It is reasonable for God to will the good! But there is no demonstration, no deduction of this critical step. Indeed, such a demonstration is strictly impossible, since it is the very nature of deduction not to be a *step* at all, but a *mere* deduction (i.e. tautology). That the rational is the good is thus another leap, another "postulate." God wills the good. But what kind of good? The good in general, the abstract universal good, a good which is the good of nobody in particular, not *my* good, nor *your* good, nor *anybody's* good, but a good which is common to all these, or, in other words, abstract *from* all. It is no wonder that this good turns out to be nothing at all rather than good, and that Berkeley finds himself, in the end, arguing for "doing nothing," in order to preserve the "universality" of his good, which is obviously compromised by *any* extraneous element of particularity. Doing good, therefore, turns out to be doing nothing at all, and Berkeley's *Passive Obedience*, as we might expect from the title, culminates in that passivity which means no more than the acceptance of things as they are, and thus the final destruction of morality. In spite of this series of "irrational leaps,"

Berkeley's ethical philosophy leaves him exactly where he started.

His religious philosophy shows the same characteristics. Here, also, we have the same succession of "irrational leaps, from myself to other selves, from man to God, and then from God to man, and the same sense of final futility, inasmuch as we have never *really* moved from our starting point. This starting point was unfortunately selected, or arbitrarily "postulated," to begin with, as the finite particular self. After deductively unfolding himself in various ways, he then passes "by analogy" to other selves, which, however, are not really "other" at all, but only *himself* over again. In so far as they are justified, that is, by his argument of "analogy," they are like himself. The same applies to God, who is really an exaggerated self, subject to the universal laws of nature. He is therefore a "moral" being, forced by the "laws of nature" to reward man's "works," a finite mechanism, contrived *ad hoc*, to satisfy a mathematical ideal of abstract justice. The extent to which this truly monstrous solipsism is dictated by an abstract, "deductive" logic is clear. Starting with man as a postulate, Berkeley arrives, after a series of intricate though "trifling" deductions, at *man* in exaggerated proportions, a man who is only all the more obviously human through the assumption of this new role of Deity. Later, Berkeley found it not surprising that certain "rationalists" had selected "elephants" as "the most religious animals" in place of man! [107]

Before he could arrive at a more adequate ethics and theology it was necessary for him to complete the process of logical criticism we have noted as an undercurrent in the *Commonplace Book* and the *Treatise*. This criticism of abstract logic ended by crushing out all traces of his spiritistic metaphysics, and finally led him to philosophic and religious insights undreamed of in his early youth. This first process of criticism reaches its climax in the next and most important treatise of Berkeley's youth, *The Three Dialogues between Hylas and Philonous*. This treatise is a strange medley of spiritism and Platonism, of religion and Deism, of Arminianism and Christianity, the key to which is to be found only in the growing dissatisfaction of Berkeley himself with the results of his abstract logic, and his somewhat groping

[107] Alc., VI, 297.

efforts to develop that other "concrete" mode of "reasoning" which he had vaguely anticipated in the *Commonplace Book* as a logic which should not merely express the vagaries of human syntax, but should do justice to things *as they really are*. To this treatise, which represents the high point of Berkeley's early reflections, the culmination of his spiritism, as well as of the early criticism he had never completely ceased to oppose against it, we must now turn for further light.

CHAPTER VII

THE CONQUEST OF THE CONCRETE (THE THREE DIALOGUES BETWEEN HYLAS AND PHILONOUS)

THE chorus of abuse with which Berkeley's *Treatise* was received by his hard-headed contemporaries is described vividly in a letter written from London, dated August 26, 1710, by Berkeley's friend Percival, soon after the publication of Part One. He says:

A physician of my acquaintance undertook to describe your person, and argued you must needs be mad, and that you ought to take remedies. A Bishop pitied you that a desire and vanity of starting something new should put you on such an undertaking, and when I justified you in that part of your character, and added the other deserving qualities you have, he said he could not tell what to think of you. Another told me an ingenious man ought not to be discouraged from exercising his wit, and said Erasmus was not the worse thought of for writing in praise of folly, but that you are not gone so far as a gentleman in town who asserts not only that there is no such thing as matter but that we have no being at all.

Even those who made some slight effort to read the *Principles* and to grasp its meaning insisted from their vantage point of common sense that these speculations carried them into the thinnest ether of abstraction. In his letter of October 30, 1710, Percival writes that Berkeley is classified by the more intelligent with such enthusiastic writers as Malebranche and Norris as a fine-spun metaphysician, whose labours could be "of little use to mankind for their abstruseness." This inevitable misunderstanding of his efforts to think concretely was naturally a source of irritation to Berkeley, who answers:

As to what is said of ranking me with Father Malebranche and Mr. Norris, whose writings are thought too fine spun to be of any use to mankind, I have this to answer: that I think the notions I embrace are not in the least coincident with, or agreeing with theirs, but indeed plainly inconsistent with them in the main points, insomuch that I know few writers whom I take myself at bottom to differ more from than them. Finespun Metaphysics are what I on all occasions declare against, and if anyone shall shew me anything of that sort in my "Treatise" I will willingly correct it. [1]

---

[1] November 27, 1710.

Berkeley's annoyance with his critics is, in fact, much more easily understood than the somewhat tiresome attempt to "humour his opponent" and talk down to his "fair and sanguine" reader, which mars much of his early writing, and which leads him even here to speak slightingly of Malebranche and that "fine-spun" metaphysics towards which, as we shall see, his own reflections were already inexorably carrying him. A "concrete" that is non-abstract is itself an abstraction, as Berkeley himself was beginning to perceive, and in the end his logic forced him into thought-patterns certainly as "fine-spun" as those of the author of the *Recherche*.

Through Percival, Berkeley arranged to have copies of his *Treatise* sent to Clarke, probably the reigning theologian of the day, and William Whiston, one of his popular and well-known followers. A friend even went so far as to assure Dr. Clarke that one letter would satisfy Berkeley, but Dr. Clarke would not at this time be drawn into debate, though Percival reports he "thought your principles you go on are false." [2] As for Whiston, he professed himself unable to cope with these new arguments, but, as usual, echoed Dr. Clarke's sentiments in proclaiming that his "first principles were wrong." [3] Nowhere in England could Berkeley even gain a hearing, to say nothing of an understanding criticism of his views, and the unfortunate effect upon his philosophical development of the ingrained Anglo-Saxon dislike of "enthusiasm," "speculation," or, in other words, concrete thought, can hardly be exaggerated. [4] Percival was willing, as a patron, to take every sort of trouble in protecting his friend, but philosophy itself was, from his own point of view, a clever accomplishment rather than an occupation to be taken with any degree of seriousness. The only real intellectual aid he was able to give was the transmission of a question which occurred to his wife in reading the last sections of the published *Principles*, where Berkeley discusses the "religious" and scriptural import of his philosophy. Lady Percival wondered what became of "the Mosaic account of the creation" in Berkeley's system.

---

[2] Percival letter, December 28, 1710.

[3] "Whiston relates that he recommended the task of confuting it [the *Principles*] to Dr. Clark, being unequal to it himself." *Gent. Mag.*, death notice, 1753, p. 51.

[4] Berkeley was unusually sensitive to criticism, as his *Commonplace Book* shows, and was always ready to meet objections, no matter how crude or even grotesquely "sensible" they might be. This chivalrous tendency, as Lord Balfour has remarked in his biographical notice (*Berkeley's Works*, Sampson edition, vol. I, 1895), prevented him at many points from developing his own position.

This question penetrated to a fundamental weakness of his *Treatise* in a most discerning fashion, and Berkeley's reply shows the extent to which he was immediately led to an important systematic transformation.

I beg you will inform Her Ladyship that I do not deny the existence of any of those sensible things which Moses says were created by God: they existed from all eternity in the Divine Intellect, and then became perceptible (i.e. were created) in the same manner and order as is described in Genesis. For I take creation to belong to things only as they respect finite spirits, there being nothing new to God. Hence it follows that the act of creation consists in God's willing that those things should be perceptible to other spirits which before were known only to Himself. Now both reason and scripture assure us there are other spirits (as angels of different orders, etc.) besides man, who, 'tis possible might have perceived this visible world according as it was successively exhibited to their view before man's creation. Besides, for to agree with the Mosaic account of the creation it is sufficient if we suppose that a man, in case he was then created and existing at the time of the chaos, might have perceived all things formed out of it in the very order set down in Scripture which is no ways repugnant to our principles.[5]

The doctrine of "things" existing "from all eternity in the Divine Intellect" is certainly a development beyond the somewhat simple metaphysics of the *Principles*, according to which God is "the great Creator" or "Omnipotent Spirit" who can "produce everything by a mere *fiat*. . . ."[6] This is, indeed, the first statement of that theory of eternal "archetypes" which, in the *Three Dialogues*, makes Berkeley's philosophy 'theocentric" or "aprioristic," rather than anthropocentric and solipsistic. It is no wonder, therefore, that he decided to interrupt his work on the second part of the *Principles* in order to develop the essential theory of archetypes and to reformulate his whole system in this "new light."[7] Hence, it is a great mistake to think of the *Three Dialogues* as only a popularized elucidation of the *Principles*,[8] though the attempt to answer "plausible Objections" was, no doubt, the preponderant motive leading to Berkeley's selection, for the first time, of the dialogue form as his method of exposition.

The *Dialogues* represent a very significant advance beyond the position of the *Principles*, a genuine "new light." Not only

---

[5] September 6, 1710.
[6] Pr., sec. 152.
[7] "But before I proceed to publish the Second Part [of the *Principles*] I thought it requisite to treat more clearly and fully of certain Principles laid down in the First, and to place them in a new light." Pref. to 3 D., F. i, p. 376; cf. the discussion of "the Mosaic account of the Creation," 3D., pp. 471–472.
[8] Fraser in F. i, p. 357.

does he now explicitly adopt a "Platonic" doctrine of eternal archetypes in the Divine Mind, but his reasons for doing so clearly involve a serious modification of his early spiritism towards a position more in keeping with his concrete logic, which time after time leads him on, almost against his will, to surprising conclusions quite out of line with the solipsistic metaphysics of cause he had accepted while under the influence of Locke. In addition to the patient attempts of Philonous to put his thoughts in such a way as not to offend the susceptibilities of "the good Hylas," there is another subtler and far more interesting dialogue between Berkeley the spiritist and Berkeley the concrete thinker, who is undermining many of his most cherished tenets by a somewhat wavering, but none the less insistent, application of his new logic of abstraction. The ascendancy of this logic is by no means complete. Berkeley is often abashed by his own results, and falls now and then into spiritistic lapses all the more extreme because of the difficulties that he himself has now learned to see in them. But these attempts to persuade himself of his own view become more and more unconvincing until, especially in the third dialogue, spiritism is forced by the inherent logic of the situation to beat an ignominious retreat on all fronts before the encroachments of a quite different way of thought. It is like the infiltration of a new atmosphere which is there even before the author is aware of it. Berkeley seems constantly to pull himself up short, to pause in amazement at the results towards which he is being led, to return to the point from which he started, only to find that this too has meanwhile imperceptibly altered, and is no longer what it was.

The *Three Dialogues between Hylas and Philonous* are unquestionably the most profound of all Berkeley's early treatises. In them alone is to be discerned in vague outline the position towards which his new logic was irresistibly impelling him, a position quite different from the causal metaphysics of the earlier works. It is rather difficult, indeed, to define the new situation as a " position " at all, since what it really represents is the abandonment of all fixed "positions" whatsoever, particularly the "position" of the substantial self or "soul" that had constituted the stable (solipsistic) foundation upon which he had built his whole early, causal system. The self is now seen as "dependent." This is the real meaning of the *Dialogues*. The self, as well as the world, is an abstraction. Hence the note of scepticism and irrationalism on which the discussion ends, and to which it gave rise in his personal development. Nothing can be accepted as a solid basis. Everything is dependent upon something else. Everything is both true and false. Everything is "appearance," and yet absolutely real. Reason ends in a hopeless, endless attempt to say something without saying something more. The only refuge to be found is "faith." This is the final result of the implicit criticism of spiritism which makes the *Dialogues*, without doubt, the most mature and interesting of Berkeley's early writings.

SPIRITISM

Berkeley's early spiritism rests on the supposed "intuition" of an unique, "active" factor which he identified with the individual, finite self, the "me." This "self" or "spirit," he maintains, is known "intuitively" by a simple "reflex act,"[9] and he often refers to it as a "thing," though he sometimes attempts to qualify this, as in the *Three Dialogues*, by pointing out that he is using the concept in the sense of "a spiritual substance or support of ideas," but meaning only "that a spirit knows and perceives ideas."[10] Nevertheless, he speaks of it, especially in connection with his "proof" for "the natural immortality of the soul," in traditional terms as a "simple, uncompounded substance,"[11] though the extent to which his own reflections were leading him, even at an early date, to a quite different conception, is indicated by his frequent assertions (so prominent in the *Commonplace Book*) that the self is "unknowable," as, for example, in the *Principles*, where he says that "the nature of Spirit, or that which acts . . . cannot be of itself perceived, but only by the effects which it produceth." Instead, however, of standing by this conception of the self as indirectly implied by its "effects," Berkeley, throughout the *Principles*, clings to the more "plausible" view that the self is "something"[12] known by a direct "intuition" to which he later gave the term "notion."[13]

This conception of an unique soul entity, intuitively known as carrying the objective world somehow inside itself,[14] runs through all Berkeley's early thought, and he seems totally un-

[9] 3D., F. i, p. 448.
[10] *Ibid.*, p. 451.
[11] Pr., sec. 141.
[12] Pr., sec. 27.
[13] Fraser conveys the impression that the introduction of this term, in 1734, represented a crucial change in Berkeley's position. "Idealess meaning," however, is a prominent concept throughout the *Commonplace Book*, and Fraser's interpretation of section 1 of the *Principles* is untenable. Cf. his note 3, F. i, p. 272.
[14] Pr., sec. 3.

aware, throughout this period, that it is this illicit abstraction which is really responsible for the solipsism from which he tries so vainly to extricate himself.[15] His first definitions of the "self," which succeed in throwing light on this extraordinarily hazy concept only by opposing it to the passive ideas or objects of the perceived world, unconsciously indicate the unjustifiable character of such an abstraction. The principal contrast lies in the "passive" character of "ideas" as distinguished from the self, which, as Berkeley asserts dogmatically, i.e. "intuitively," in the early treatises, is "active," or "that which perceives ideas, and wills and reasons," and hence is itself "neither an idea, nor like an idea." [16] Berkeley is so struck at times by the absolute "difference" between "spirits" and "ideas" that he occasionally asserts that they have nothing whatsoever in common. "*Spirits* and *ideas*," he says in the *Principles*, "are things so wholly different, that when we say 'they exist,' 'they are known,' or the like, these words must not be thought to signify anything common to both natures. There is nothing alike or common in them." [17]

If this is true it is somewhat difficult to see how they may both be referred to as "things," or as "they," or how, indeed, "*they*" may be "compared" at all, or even said to be "different." Certainly it is absurd to think of spirits, if they are so altogether different, as being particular, human individuals, I and you and he, for these distinct individuals, even if they are not supposed to exist in space, nevertheless can hardly be supposed to exist apart from time. What, indeed, can possibly be meant by "*me*," as a peculiar individual, if "I" am not supposed to exist in a spatial locus within a certain span of time? But then I become an object, like other "ideas" making up the spatio-temporal world. No matter how peculiar the "intuition" or "notion" may be with which I come to know the self or spirit, it must be known, in so far as it is known at all, as an object in time, for my acts, to occur at all, must occur as elements in the succession, which, as Berkeley says, constitutes time. If known directly or "intuited" in any sense the self becomes *myself*, an object among other objects in space and time, an element in the objective world, not the transcendent carrier of all experience. But if not known directly, if in some sense inferred as the transcendental consciousness, then it becomes the carrier of *me*, as well as of all the other objects in the world, and loses individuality and distinctness. This is the underlying dilemma of Berkeley's early writings, which so unsuccessfully but persistently attempt to combine both empirical and transcendental self into a logical monstrosity, known indirectly "only by the effects," and yet also "intuitively" by "notions." Berkeley, in other words, does not see that in singling out a portion of the world, the individual *me*, and reifying it into a self-existent substance, he is doing exactly the same sort of thing for which he so effectively criticizes the materialists.

It is this materialism of the spirit, of course, tha creates the wholly artificial and insoluble problem of "other selves." Once the individual self has been isolated from its essential context and hypostatized into a separate substance, it becomes impossible to conceive how we may "know" other selves equally isolated or hypostatized. Thus, as Berkeley says, "The knowledge I have of other spirits is not immediate as is the knowledge of my ideas; but depending on the intervention of ideas, by me referred to agents or spirits distinct from myself, as effects." [18] In other words, I can have no "knowledge" of other spirits, but only of my own ideas. Interpreting these, however, I may jump to the inference that other spirits do exist. But what justifies this inference? Berkeley never succeeds in offering any justification that will bear the slightest critical strain. Once I have absolutized the self into the bearer of the world, there is no escape from its dominion, for it is the bearer of the whole world, and all "outsideness," no matter how far "outside" it is projected, still falls inside the original "within." The popular "argument" based on the experience of "resistance" or "what is against my will," by which Berkeley seeks to extricate himself, breaks down completely; for, as he himself points out in the *Commonplace Book*,[19] all my ideas as ideas or objects are equally against my will or "outside." But I have agreed to call everything outside inside, and now, much as I may regret having taken this position there is no "consistent" way of abandoning it. All feelings of resistance, as well as all conceptions of transcendent "outsides," are placed *within* the magic solipsistic circle, and there can be no consistent escape.

We have already noted in the last chapter Berkeley's unfortunate attempt to make the very absurdity of this situation prove God. While admitting, on the one hand, the inherent solipsism

[18] Pr., p. 339.   [19] C. B. J., 817.

of his position, that "it is plain we do not see a man, if by *man* is meant that which lives, moves, perceives, and thinks as we do: but only such a certain collection of ideas, as directs us to think there is a distinct principle of thought and motion, like to ourselves, accompanying and represented by it," [20] Berkeley, nevertheless, proceeds to conclude that "after the same manner we see God." What his whole argument really proves, however, is the exact opposite, and solipsism cannot be supposed to further very effectively "the case" for God, even in the minds of Berkeley's common-sense audience. Because "we" may have committed an error full of contradictions is hardly an adequate reason for demanding that "we" commit a worse one. As generations of critics have pointed out, if we can accept the unutterable mystery of a great spirit who produces all our ideas "from without," why not accept the whole, abstract, material world? Why not hypostatize the sun and moon and stars and set them "outside" to swim in a noumenal ether, "causing" in us the appropriate sensations? The point is that causation *per se*, whether it be material or spiritual causation, if lifted into such a transempirical atmosphere becomes meaningless. As Berkeley himself says, do I not through my very conception relate what I am thinking about, whatever it may be, whether noumenal God or noumenal sun, to the system of consciousness, so that the concept of anything, God, or sun, outside or independent of conception includes "a contradiction," or, as he phrases it, "conceiving" the "unconceived." [21] Something conceived as substantial, independent, and external is *ipso facto* related to consciousness, and hence, through this very fact, unsubstantial, dependent, and internal, though, of course, not internal to *my* consciousness, since I am myself internal to this system. The trouble with Berkeley's spiritistic "position" lies in his identification of the system of consciousness with *my* consciousness, or an individual consciousness which is clearly an abstraction from the system to which the "transcendental argument" does, as a matter of fact, apply. Berkeley's early spiritism is thus dominated by an extraordinary ambiguity hovering over the term "I," which, part of the time, stands for the transcendental unity of consciousness, including in one system not only all empirical objects but all empirical selves as well, and, part of the time, for the empirical self only, which moves in time and space, as a restricted individual, bound up in the most intimate way with other objects in the world. Once having hypostatized this phase of experience and turned it into a substantial carrier for the rest of the world, Berkeley is lost in a finite solipsism from which there is no consistent escape.

All discussion of a causal deity or causal not-self forcing sensations on me against my will, as water is forced back into a spout, all this is the most obvious sort of violation of the very concrete (synthetic) kind of reasoning by means of which Berkeley was able to justify the transcendental solipsism he so thoughtlessly identified with solipsism. How can the most re-sistant sensation conceivable, if it is *my* sensation, justify the in-ference to something not a sensation at all, but beyond my ex-perience altogether? And even were there such a thing, how could it, as a transcendent being not in time, be the "cause" of ideas bound up with other elements in a temporal succession? It is as utterly impossible to derive God causally from *my* world as to derive my world causally from God. Causation, however we choose to define it, has meaning only with respect to events in time, and when isolated from the rest of experience becomes a word. And furthermore, as we attempted to show in the last chapter, even if the causal argument for God were in any way justified, it would be of no use to "religion," for, as Berkeley himself says, on such a subjective basis, "all the notion I have of God is obtained by reflecting on my own soul, heightening its powers. . . ." [22] Hence, the solipsistic argument, even if valid, would not lead to God at all, but to a "heightened" man. It was only in his Deistic youth, before he had even remotely begun to glimpse the true meaning of religious experience and that abso-luteness without which God ceases to be even Jupiter or Vishnu, that Berkeley could have devised such an "argument."

This array of dialectical and causal arguments, of concrete and abstract, of Deism and Christianity, can be discerned in an unstable but recognizable equilibrium as a dominant note in Berkeley's early writings, from the *Commonplace Book* to the *Treatise concerning the Principles of Human Knowledge*, and to it, following Berkeley's example, we have attached the label "spiritism." It did not definitely disintegrate until the third dialogue between Hylas and Philonous, though as we have sought to show, the new concrete logic had already developed certain results incompatible with it, such as the view, so clearly arrived at in the *Commonplace Book*, that experience constitutes

[22] 3D., F. i, p. 448.

a whole of which both will and understanding, subject and object, are nothing but abstract aspects neither of which "can be without the other." The inconsistency of this conclusion with Berkeley's persistent hypostatization of the individual self is manifest. His "concrete" logic was bound, in the end, irresistably to crush the abstract hypostatizations from which his spiritism had been pieced together. It is only in the *Three Dialogues*, however, that the issue becomes clear, and not really until the third dialogue that Berkeley himself consciously abandons his spiritistic position in its most vital respect, and surrenders the independent, substantial soul or self. It is to the immanent self-criticism which constitutes the chief importance of these dialogues, as well as to its surprising results, that we must now turn our attention.

THE CRITIQUE OF SPIRITISM

There are three basic theses on which Berkeley's system of spiritism rests. First and most important of all is the empirical or phenomenalistic attitude we have seen to be so deeply embedded in his conception of objects or ideas as "passive," a view which he especially emphasizes in his many unfortunate attempts to convince the "vulgar" that there is nothing out of the ordinary in his concrete type of thought. Such thought, however, as we have seen, if taken seriously, means the abandonment of common sense. But so long as Berkeley himself held to the common-sense conception of reality as something that could be directly or immediately "given" through some sort of "passive" presentation, he could never transcend his spiritism, for it is exactly this tendency that led him to confuse the transcendental self with the empirical, or, in other words, to think of the organizing principles presupposed by [23] the sensory world as being themselves "intuited" or "given." Forced from one such "given" stronghold in the field of sensory phenomena, Berkeley seeks to placate common sense by another even more vicious abstraction, — the self as a "given" entity or thing. As long as he continued to regard reality as "frozen" into substances which simply have to be "taken" as they "are," his thought, like that of common sense, was forced to fall from one hopeless abstraction into another.

[23] Or known "only by the effects" of. Pr., sec. 27.

We must, therefore, look for some criticism of this phenome-nalistic attitude, if any permanent transcendence of spiritism or materialism is to be won. Indeed, there can be no question of thinking "concretely" until such "independent" entities have first been melted away by criticism. But once the impossibility of merely "accepting," granting, supposing, postulating any fixed points as "given" is really comprehended, the exclusion of such reified concepts as "causation" and the empirical "I" or "self," which lie at the basis of Berkeley's spiritistic position, follow at once. We must look in the *Three Dialogues* first of all, therefore, for any possible traces of the abandonment of the common-sense view that what is real is somehow "given," or presented, or "impressed" upon us, as Berkeley says, "against our will." Until this type of fixed concept is eliminated, thought cannot hope to transcend common sense. If such a general melt-ing of abstractions does actually take place, we must not then be surprised, in the second place, at the collapse of the whole causal position, according to which real objects are impressed upon "the mind" from some sort of "outside" source, and finally, in the third place, and most important of all, at the abandon-ment of the fixed "I" or "self," which, in Berkeley's spiritistic thought, is reified into an abstract carrier for the rest of the world.

PHENOMENALISM

We do not have far to look to find evidence for Berkeley's realization that his new, concrete logic cannot be reconciled with a "fixed" reality impressed upon us somehow from without, but must, on the contrary, lead to a complete disillusionment with regard to the abstraction of anything such as fixed sensa or "data" of any kind. Indeed, this point is clearly called to our attention more than once in each of the *Three Dialogues*. In the first, for example, we find Berkeley developing and sharpening the insight of the *Principles* which had revealed that the various data of sense were not existing in abstract isolation, as common sense supposes, but were in reality so "concreted and blended" together that it was meaningless to conceive them asunder. Not only is this seen to be true of the primary and secondary qualities, so that it is impossible without thinking of extension to think of colour meaningfully, but he now shows that there are other qualities of value (pleasure and pain) which also permeate experience, and without which "sense-data" cease to be what, in actuality at least, they manifestly are.

This, of course, is nothing more than an extension of the argument of the *Principles*, though a most important one. When we turn to the other type of argument by which Berkeley had justified his *esse percipi* principle, the argument from relativity, we find a more significant development. In the *Principles* it is mentioned only in section 14 as proving the "subjectivity" of the primary as well as of the secondary qualities, just as "sweetness," for example, is not "anything settled and determinate," because "*the thing* remaining unaltered, the sweetness is changed into bitter, as in case of a fever or otherwise vitiated palate." [24] The argument is here stated only in a restricted form and not by any means pushed to a final conclusion. There is a "thing" which remains absolute, unaltered, and "given," over against the changing and relative sweetness. There must be some sort of given datum, or constant "thing" over against which properties or qualities may be *seen* to be changing. But the argument from relativity in the first dialogue does not pause so easily satisfied. After considering the variation or relativity of colour perception, Berkeley does not conclude that some colours may be seen to change over against a certain one which remains constant, but that "*All* colours are equally apparent." [25]

There is, therefore, no absolute given "thing" which can consitute a norm or frame of reference, as common-sense reflection supposes. When we look through a microscope, for example, we do not by any means perceive an object which is more real than what we ordinarily perceive "crudely" with our "unaided" vision, though it may be something more useful for certain purposes. No matter how fine our instruments may be there are always finer ones, and there is not, nor can there be, an absolutely fine or perfect instrument. All given data whatsoever are by nature relative. An absolute "datum" is a strict impossibility. By its very nature as a datum, through its essential meaning, it is relative. The truth, therefore, can never be found in any such existent datum, but only in the connection of such data. "The more a man knows of the connection of ideas the more he is said to know of the nature of things." [26] There is no "one single, unchanged, unperceivable, real Nature." [27] The absolute, the truth, that is, does not lie beyond the relative in a perfect exist-

---

[24] Pr., sec. 14; my italics.
[25] F. i, p. 395; cf. 396; my italics.
[26] 3D., F. i, p. 464.
[27] *Ibid.*

ent realm of its own, but in the relative, as well as beyond the relative, in its connections and relations. By itself, in abstraction, as datum, or sensum, a perceived "thing" is relative or incomplete. It is only by comparing, by contrasting, by passing beyond each such fixed abstraction that we may discover what it really is. Nothing is only "given," for even to realize that a thing is "given," we must pass beyond its givenness, and place it in a larger context of meaning; we must see it in its relations or connections with something not itself, not given. This is, of course, the death of common sense, or abstract logic. And time after time we find Berkeley in the *Three Dialogues* applying his concrete "reasoning" to the favourite fixations of common sense, no one of which can long endure the strain without soon losing its rigidity and melting away into relativity, having in itself no meaning whatsoever.

A beautiful example of this is afforded at the beginning of the second dialogue by Berkeley's examination of that favorite abstraction of physiology and common-sense thought, according to which

it is supposed the soul makes her residence in some part of the brain, from which the nerves take their rise, and are thence extended to all parts of the body; and that outward objects, by the different impressions they make on the organs of sense, communicate certain vibrative motions to the nerves; and these being filled with spirits propagate them to the brain or seat of the soul, which, according to the various impressions or traces thereby made in the brain, is variously affected with ideas.[28]

Berkeley, who was temporarily unaware that he was at the same time destroying his own "causal" view, forthwith proceeds to annihilate this position by showing that "the brain," thus "supposed" to exist in splendid isolation in an absolute world of its own, "outside" or "beyond" that of sense, loses all meaning, and cannot sensibly be referred to as a "brain," unless considered in "connection" with other "sensible ideas"[29] which are "perceivable." What would a "brain" be that is not situated somewhere in space as part of an organism, also situated in space, with an environment, and what would the whole world in space, which is thus necessarily presupposed by a brain, be if it were not "perceived," and thus related to a whole of consciousness extending beyond itself? Before we can, therefore, with any meaning at all, speak of a "brain," we must already have presup-

[28] 2D., F. i, p. 421.   [29] *Ibid.*

posed the whole sensory universe of ideas or objects which this "brain" is "supposed" to explain. Thus Berkeley asks, in a bewilderment which is inescapable, how it may be "reasonable to suppose that one idea or thing existing in the mind occasions all other ideas"?[30] When common sense attempts to escape the difficulty by asserting that it is not talking about this brain, but another brain, existing "outside" the whole sensory world, "causing" the subjective brain, it is obvious we have before us again, in an only slightly different form, the very fallacy of illegitimate hypostatization, to which Berkeley attached his expressive word "abstraction."

This image, this cause, this copy of the actual brain is not a thing at all. There is, indeed, not the slightest sense in discussing *it*, for *it* is not an entity, a theory, or even a point of view. It is something much more fundamental than any of these. To oppose to it another theory is simply to become further entangled. This other brain, this double, this noumenal "somewhat" is not a philosophy, not a point of view, not an epistemology at all, but a logic. It is nothing but the hypostatized form of separateness, or externality, or self-identity, which common-sense logic gives its objects. The point at issue here is not a theory, or system, as Berkeley so acutely perceived, but a *method*. The "other" brain, the double, the archetype, is obviously the same real brain over again, only set in a fixed and rigid form, categorized, tagged, and labelled by the abstract, logicizing mind. Winning its concepts, in the first place, by contrasted effects and connections, this mind then isolates its results in the form of an absolute, self-subsistent entity or cause, independent of the relations or connections without which it could not have been conceived as real. The "other world," therefore, of Locke, the "intelligible world," is not another world at all, but another logic, based upon the uncritical and unconscious application of the categories of identity, causation, and substance. The various doctrines known as epistemological realism, which range all the way from common sense to "Platonism," rest upon an abstract abuse of these categories, particularly the category of substance.

But with common-sense or "realistic" epistemology, in its various sorts and degrees of abstraction, goes Berkeley's own spiritism as well. It is no better to abstract and reify a causal act than a material object. The view that somehow separate selves or spirits can be isolated from their contexts into self-

[30] *Ibid.*

existent, causal entities lying back of, or underneath, or alongside of the one actual world is just as absurd as "realism," or
rather the one type of "realism," spiritual realism, is just as
vicious and commits the same sort of error as physical or material realism. Berkeley's common-sense spiritism corrected one
abstraction only to fall into another of the very same sort. This
is why his early subjectivism or solipsism is so much more convincing to common sense, and so much more familiar than other
more genuine forms of idealism, because the ordinary abstraction of the "self," already familiar to common sense, is preserved intact; that is, the rigidity of the common-sense world is
only partially weakened. But, in the end, this "frozen" substance can no more resist the melting effect of the concrete logic
than "matter." Neither, in fact, can be referred to meaningfully
without referring beyond itself.

But Berkeley does not come to recognize this fact until the
second dialogue, where, for the first time, he seriously concerns
himself with the conception of "nature."[31] For his abstract, spiritistic view, indeed, there can be no such thing as "nature," but
rather thousands and millions of separate "natures," since each
"spirit" carries one of his own "within" him. Thus in the *Principles*, when answering his own question concerning the "sun,
moon, and stars . . . houses, rivers, mountains, trees, stones,
nay even . . . our own bodies," and what may become of them,
whether, that is, they are "but so many chimeras and illusions,"
Berkeley reassures us that "whatever *we* see, feel, hear, or any-
wise conceive or understand, remains as secure as ever, and is as
real as ever,"[32] provided it is "strong, orderly, and coherent."[33]
This proves too much. How reassuring is it to know that the
body I perceive occupying its place in the order of nature is real,
when other "spirits" perceive different bodies fitting into a different order? Must I not then be supposed to possess fifty or
sixty different bodies all of which, as fitting into different orders
or systems, are real? And is not the same true of the whole of
nature? How, indeed, can I speak of "the" order of nature,
when the fundamental conception of spiritism necessitates hundreds, thousands, millions of "isolated natures" each locked
up in a separate consciousness. Once having made this abstraction it is useless to maintain that the "order" or "pattern" is one and the same in separate consciousnesses. It is

---

[31] *Ibid.*, pp. 422-425.
[32] Pr., sec. 34; my italics.
[33] Pr., sec. 33.

just as difficult for me to jump out of my mind into that of another to discover what his "order" is as to discover what his
"private sensations" are. There are, unfortunately, systematic
delusions, and just because my sensations happen to fit into an
order, it is unwarranted dogmatism for me to assume or postulate that this same order must apply to all experiences in the
minds of all spirits. The only possible answer to such a position,
as Berkeley saw, is a logical answer, which disallows the validity
of the original abstraction. If everything were mine, I should
never, assuredly, become conscious of this fact, for an *I*, to have
any meaning or sense, must refer beyond itself to a *you*. The
world, as I perceive it, necessitates not solipsism, but the world
as it really is. Without the absolute, the relative loses all meaning and ceases to be relative. The very distinctness of the isolated spirits is a relation binding them inextricably one to the
other.   Berkeley's concrete method of reasoning must necessarily lead to a world which is basically united.

Hence, we find him speaking throughout the dialogues of "the
world," "nature," and at the beginning of the second dialogue,
in an important passage, he refers to "the natural beauties of
the earth," in a way hitherto rendered impossible by his abstract
spiritism.   He speaks of "The motion and situation of the
planets," of "the laws of nature," of "the whole system im-
mense, beautiful, glorious beyond expression," [34] because, having at last seriously abandoned the abstract logic of common
sense, he is able to see, by his "concrete" method of reasoning,
how all things, even the things which are not things at all, are
"linked in a mutual dependence and intercourse with each
other," [35] so that, instead of many separate worlds, it is now
clear that by their very separateness is "displayed" the "energy
of an all-perfect Mind," [36] not many minds, but one mind, one
world, one system — not my mind nor your mind, that is, as
before, but the infinite mind of God, as Berkeley now, throughout the second and third dialogues, refers to that system of systems, that consciousness of consciousnesses, any abstraction
from which becomes *ipso facto* a bond of intimate union. It is
the necessity of this system, of "the infinite Mind," [37] which
makes scepticism "extravagantly absurd," [38] not the necessity
of *me* or *you*, or any other finite element or point, for all such

[34] 2D., F. i, p. 423.   [37] 2D., F. i, p. 424.
[35] *Ibid.*   [38] *Ibid.*
[36] *Ibid.*

finite centers presuppose this system, without which they could not conceivably or meaningfully *be*.

That this is not merely a "creative" interpretation, but that Berkeley himself was actually forced through such a movement of thought by his concrete logic is evidenced by the third dialogue,[39] where, for the first time, he puts to himself the vital difficulty of his spiritism. "The *same* idea," he says, "which is in my mind cannot be in yours, or in any other mind. Doth it not therefore follow . . . that no two can see the same thing? And is not this highly absurd?"[40] The following passage is in many ways the turning point of Berkeley's early thought, representing as it does the definite abandonment of the spiritistic position, for he cannot deny the point of this objection. To assert that when thirty people are sitting in a room there is no sense in which they are all sitting in one room, rather than thirty, is sheer nonsense, made even more obviously absurd by the solipsistic paradox as to how the same single and distinct I can nevertheless be thirty. If we take our original solipsism or spiritism seriously, if each I is absolutely different and distinct from the others, then we shall not have thirty in the original room but 900, since each distinct I-atom will perceive thirty distinct selves (admitting that he can perceive something other than himself, which is, of course, impossible), and there will be a different and distinct set of thirty selves in each perceiving solipsistic center. Nor is this all, since part of each self is his perception of the others. Hence, from our absolute (though impossible) position as an "objective" observer, we must admit, in leaping from one mind to another (which is impossible), that each self in perceiving each other, perceives not only that other, but the thirty distinct selves which *he* perceives, and so forth, so that finally we shall have to increase the tally to 27,000, and so forth.

The way out of the dilemma is not obvious. So deep does this seemingly simple objection cut that Berkeley is forced, in order to answer it, to abandon his spiritism altogether, and to introduce a system of eternal "archetypes," existing not as objects exist for us, but "in that Mind which," as he now maintains in opposition to his former view, "comprehends all things."[41] It is true that Berkeley himself, at the time, does not realize the full importance of his concessions. Thus, at one point he insists that

39 F. i, pp. 466–468.   41 *Ibid.*, p. 468.
40 3D., F. i, p. 466.

"the dispute is about a word." [42] Nevertheless the burden of his remarks is clear. There must be a "uniformness" in "what was perceived," and there must be a "diversity," [43] and one without the other is impossible or "abstracted," that is, meaningless. It is, therefore, possible for "men" to "dispute about identity and diversity, without any real [concrete] difference in their thoughts," [44] for certain minds may concentrate on some abstracted logical aspect and other minds on another, without being aware of the fact that either alone, or "abstracted" by itself, is strictly nonsense. Thus, while not denying the fact that a perceived object includes differences, Berkeley now has to admit that a perceived thing also has a moment of identity, and that "the ends of identity" must be "served." [45] In other words, his spiritistic philosophy was an illicit abstraction which singled out the differences without the identity. But if there were no sense in which *the object* is identical, one and the same, it would be senseless and strictly meaningless to speak of different perceptions of this object or differences in it, just as pure identity isolated from all difference is "an abstracted [impossible] idea of identity." The very meaning, therefore, of different perceptions or views of an object involves the notion of one identical object, and the notion or meaning of separate and distinct spirits necessarily presupposes "archetypes" in "that Mind which comprehends all things." [46] It is, consequently, after this point impossible to conceive of Berkeley as a sensualist or phenomenalist, since phenomena, if there are such things, as Berkeley never doubted, by their very meaning, necessitate identical archetypes other than themselves, without which, indeed, they, as phenomena, can possess no meaning. Nor, furthermore, is it possible to think of him as a spiritist, since separate and distinct spirits, if they exist, presuppose an absolute or "infinite" mind which comprehends all things.

It is difficult to appreciate the significance of this introduction of "archetypes" for Berkeley's further reflections, a significance which only very gradually became clear in his own mind. But this much, at any rate, is obvious. The *rapport* with common sense is definitely broken. No longer, after the *Dialogues*, can Berkeley legitimately claim or constantly seek that squaring of his notions with those of "the good Hylas" which mars not only the *Principles* but, at many points, the *Dialogues* themselves,

[42] *Ibid.*, p. 467.
[43] *Ibid.*
[44] 3D., F. i, p. 468.
[45] *Ibid.*
[46] *Ibid.*

and even stands in the way of a proper comprehension of the true meaning of what he is saying. That the force of his own speculations has at last destroyed this faith in "vulgar" discernment, however, is evidenced by a passage at the end of the third dialogue which, in spite of its mildness, affords a definite contrast to the many appeals "to the plain common sense of mankind," and to "a mind not yet debauched by learning," [47] which so frequently dulled the edge of his earlier conclusions. Truth is not the exclusive possession of "philosophers." But neither does it lie in the hands of everyone possessing eyes and ears. It is rather, as Berkeley now cautiously admits, "shared between the vulgar and the philosophers: the former being of opinion, that *those things they immediately perceive are the real things*; and the latter, that *the things immediately perceived are ideas, which exist only in the mind.*" [48]

The common-sense position that the "given" things are real is only a half-truth or, by itself, in abstraction, a falsity, for the things we perceive constitute only "a relative or hypothetical existence." [49] They require for their completion, to be what they are ("hypothetical" appearances), archetypes in the divine mind which truly exist, or rather, in the common-sense acceptation of this word, do not properly exist at all, for the existence of such archetypes is not "ectypal or natural," but "archetypal and eternal." [50] Existence, in other words, to have any meaning as existence, presupposes the non-existent, as the temporal presupposes the eternal, the ectypal presupposes the archetypal, and man presupposes God. Common sense, therefore, requires philosophy, as the abstract, "realistic" logic of common sense requires a concrete logic to complete its meaning. This abandonment of common sense and its abstract logic, of "givenness," "phenomenalism," "immediate intuition," "data," "sense-data," and the remaining host of abstractions in which it seeks to disguise itself as philosophy, through the discovery of an "eternal" field of significance, presupposed by the former, is the result of the *Three Dialogues between Hylas and Philonous*. With the abandonment of common-sense phenomenalism goes spiritistic realism, together with the other "entities" which "vulgar" thought reifies into substances, though so deeply grained had this abstraction become in Berkeley's own reflections that his realization of the negative consequences of his thought is waver-

[47] Pr., sec. 123.
[48] 3D., F. i, p. 484.
[49] Ibid., p. 474.
[50] Ibid., p. 475.

ing, though nevertheless clearly discernible in the later portions of the *Dialogues*.

"Causal" Perception

All this is only a development of that criticism of the ordinary employment of the category of substance which we have noted in our discussion of the *Principles*. Ordinary things are not things or substances at all, but dependent upon something else, "ideas in a mind." At first, Berkeley conceived this "something" upon which all things are dependent as the individual active self. The importance of the *Three Dialogues*, however, lies in their establishment of the fact that this self is also dependent, that the category of "action" or "causation" is subject to the same illegitimate sort of application as the category of substance. To think of the ordinary things of experience as being caused by an active self outside them destroys the abstract self-subsistence of the original things, but it unfortunately leaves us, in the end, with the same sort of hypostatized "entity" on our hands. But the point of Berkeley's criticism, which is logical or methodological in nature, and, therefore, penetrates deeper than any "argument," is that no ordinary existent entity whatsoever is abstractly independent, or, in other words, that through its independence it thereby becomes dependent. Is there any evidence in the *Three Dialogues* that Berkeley actually applied this destructive criticism to his own doctrine of "causal" perception?

Such evidence, as we should expect, is wavering and hesitant, but a careful reading of the *Dialogues* reveals that it is nevertheless present. This is most evident in his discussion of "divine," that is, actual perception in the third dialogue.[51] Berkeley first repeats his primitive, "causal" argument for God.[52] But it soon becomes clear, through the employment of his concrete method of reasoning, that the early notion of God as force or "power"[53] is entirely inadequate, for, though "from the effects I see produced, I conclude there are actions,"[54] nevertheless, action by itself is an abstraction, so that from "actions" I must conclude "volitions," and "because there are volitions, there must be a *will*."[55] Action, in other words, presupposes volition, and volition presupposes one single, identical will. Nor is this

[51] F. i, pp. 457–459.
[52] *Ibid.*, p. 457.
[53] C. B. J., 430; J., 850.

[54] F. i, p. 457.
[55] *Ibid.*, p. 458.

all, for will itself is an illegitimate abstraction. What is a will with nothing to will? [56] The will must have an object, and an object requires or presupposes a world of objects with a faculty to perceive them or an understanding (*esse percipi*). "But will and understanding constitute in the strictest sense a mind or spirit," [57] and "the powerful cause, therefore, of my ideas," not being a powerful cause at all, "is in strict propriety of speech a *Spirit*." [58] God is, therefore, not the powerful "cause" of our sensations, forcing them into our minds, but "a Pure Spirit, disengaged from all such sympathy or natural ties." [59] Yet "God knows or understands all things . . . even every sort of painful sensation," [60] but "no corporeal motions are attended with the sensations of pain or pleasure in His mind." [61] In other words, actual perception, as it *is*, in God, is not causal, for God cannot be supposed to perceive things as impressed from without in the naive, common-sense fashion, for "outside" can have no meaning when applied to Him.

Berkeley is not aware, at the time, that this reflection also destroys his causal view with respect to man, for he says explicitly that "*We* are chained to a body: that is to say, *our* perceptions are connected with corporeal motions," and, "by the law of our nature, *we* are affected upon every alteration in the nervous parts of *our* sensible body." [62] But here again he is confusing the transcendental with the empirical self. What "we" is he here talking about? If he means the empirical self that is perceived in space and time, not the self that actually (as God) perceives, this, as he himself proceeds to point out in the same sentence, "is nothing but a complexion of such qualities or ideas as have no existence distinct from being perceived by a mind"; so that, as Berkeley himself concludes, "this connection of sensations [the 'causal' connection] with corporeal motions means no more than a correspondence in the order of nature, between two sets of ideas. . . ." [63] In other words, the "causal" sort of perception is not actual perception at all, but an empirical connection between sets of ideas or perceived objects, all of which presuppose the actual (divine) sort of perception that is in no sense causal. The spatio-temporal self does not, therefore, perceive at all, but rather is perceived. True, actual perception is in no

[56] Cf. C. B. J., 479.
[57] F. i, p. 458; cf. C. B. J., 860-861.
[58] F. i, p. 458.
[59] Ibid., p. 459.
[60] Ibid., p. 458.
[61] Ibid., p. 459.
[62] Ibid; my italics.
[63] Ibid.

sense "passive" or "causal." Indeed, it cannot even be supposed to "occur" in time, being, rather, "archetypal" and
"eternal."

But is not this all read into Berkeley from a later point of
view? Is there any real evidence that he himself was consciously
forced into the transcendental (non-causal) by the logic of the
"human" situation itself, independent of all reference to a
"divine" and hence "impossible" ideal? Such evidence is to be
found in the well-known discussion of the "tulip," [64] which has
been the occasion of so much disagreement among Berkeley's in-
terpreters. Indeed, it cannot be said that he was himself altogether clear on the meaning of this all-important discussion, in
which he seems forced against his will into a conclusion quite at
odds with his cherished "spiritism" or "activistic realism."
But the burden of his thought is clear when seen in the setting of
the treatise as a whole. According to the doctrine of spiritism,
every "object," such as a tulip, must have two phases or aspects
inseparably intertwined one with the other, but nevertheless
analyzable into two elements, "the one an action of the mind,
the other not." [65] Furthermore, "this action cannot exist in, or
belong to, any unthinking thing," [66] but rather to "a thinking
being" or spirit,[67] for only finite selves are active. But if the
active, thinking "thing" can be isolated in this fashion, it follows, as Berkeley is forced to admit, that the "passive" side of
experience can be identified and reified in the very same way,
and we have matter and the whole common-sense position on
our hands again. Thus Philonous has to concede, as a consequence of his spiritism, that "whatever more there is [beyond
the self-subsistent, active side of the tulip] as that I perceive
such a particular smell, or any smell at all — this is independent
of my will, and therein I am altogether [abstractly] passive." [68]
But what then of the *esse percipi* principle, according to which
there can be no such independent or "altogether passive"
matter? This situation is indeed so serious that the discussion
has to be gently removed from the hands of "the good Hylas"
and handed over to the more competent Philonous, who goes
over the points again one by one.[69] "Seeing," that is, the spiritistic action, "consists," obviously enough, "in opening and turning the eyes." But "opening and turning the eyes" is "without

[64] 1D., F. i, pp. 406-408.   [67] 1D., F. i, p. 408.
[65] *Ibid.*, p. 406.   [68] *Ibid.*, p. 407.
[66] *Ibid.*   [69] *Ibid.*.

doubt" not "*seeing.*" [70] The empirical self, the I or you or he, the individual in space and time is, then, not the self which "sees," and perceives light and colours, but only another object, — a reified abstraction, a spiritual matter, hypostatized through the very same sort of process as that which generated the matter of the materialist.

As Philonous then proceeds to show with ruthless consequence, the isolation of such a spiritual element is nothing but the reverse form of materialism. If, for example, in the case of the tulip, the "turning of the eyes" or the "drawing the air through my nose" is abstracted into a distinct spiritual (i.e. material) entity, then the whole new principle must be abandoned, as Philonous clearly sees, since "the very perception of light and colours," the actual perception, becomes an isolated object, "altogether passive" or objective, just as the action is "altogether" or abstractly subjective. For "doth it not follow . . . that the perception of light and colours, including no action in it, may exist in an unperceiving substance?" [71] In other words, if we reify spirit, there is no means of avoiding the reification of matter, and vice versa. To escape one, we cannot merely flee to the other, but must avoid the reification of either and realize, once and for all, that they both result from an analysis, the products of which can be given *meaning* only over against each other, not as "independent" substances. "Light and colours, tastes, sounds, etc. are . . . all equally . . . sensations in the soul;" neither in my soul nor your soul nor any finite soul, but in *the* soul, though "you may indeed call them *external objects*, and give them in words what subsistence you please." [72] But such "subsistence" is pure verbalism. One is then ceasing to think really or concretely. Philonous, it is true, then hands the argument over to Hylas, who in summing it up [73] in his own (common-sense) way, as usual, completely misses the point, and misinterprets the whole discussion as applying only to one side of the relation, the objective side; but it is quite clear to Philonous, as to the alert reader, that the argument, if it eliminates one, also eliminates the other. Berkeley has finally forced himself to the recognition of the fact that the I or self which truly perceives is not the perceived self located in space and time, not the self who turns up his eyes and draws in air through his nose,[74] not the

[70] *Ibid.*
[71] *Ibid.*
[72] *Ibid.*, p. 408, my italics.

[73] F. i, p. 408.
[74] *Ibid.*, p. 407.

self who is causally "affected" by "external" objects, but another self altogether, the self whose action cannot be perceived or "given," and with respect to which it is meaningless to refer to an "outside."

SPIRITISM VERSUS SPIRIT

Nevertheless, it will be urged, this also is interpretation of a too obviously "creative" sort. Where is there evidence to show that Berkeley ceased to be Berkeleian, and actually shifted his philosophic center from an empirical to a transcendental self? Such evidence is not lacking. It comes to light most manifestly perhaps in an important passage in the third dialogue,[75] where Berkeley develops a "proof" for the existence of God, proceeding on altogether different lines from the earlier "causal" proof. In the *Principles*, for example, God is derived from the fact that "the ideas imprinted on them [my senses] are not creatures of *my* will," so that "there is therefore some other Will or Spirit that produces them." [76] He also adds that "the constant regularity, order, and concatenation of natural things" show us that "the aforesaid Spirit" is "One, Eternal, Infinitely Wise, Good, and Perfect," [77] though, as we have pointed out, how natural "effects" which are variable, fleeting, and always imperfect can prove by Berkeley's argument a cause which is "One, Eternal, . . . and Perfect" is anything but clear. It is true that, in answer to the objection that on his principles "things are every moment annihilated and created anew," [78] he replies that this does not follow, "since there *may* be some other spirit that perceives them though we do not." [79] But this is a casual suggestion which, in the *Principles*, is not brought into connection with the existence of God.

In the third dialogue, however, we find the discontinuity of experience used in an entirely different fashion, by an entirely different sort of logic, to prove "necessarily" a continuity, not only that there "may" be another mind perceiving things when I am annihilated or unconscious, but that there "must" be such a mind. Otherwise I could by no means *significantly* refer to my annihilation. In other words, if I were the whole world, or if the whole world were contained in me, as in the theory of spiritism, there would then be no sense in referring to my annihilation,

---

[75] 3D., F. i, pp. 446-450.
[76] Pr., sec. 29.
[77] Pr., sec. 146.

[78] Pr., sec. 45.
[79] Pr., sec. 48; my italics.

since I should already have been annihilated by being turned into all things, into being itself, or "*something in general,* which being interpreted proves *nothing.*" [80] This is the result of a thought which can be traced back to the *Commonplace Book,* where Berkeley says, "In sleep and trances the mind *exists not,*" [81] or, as he continues in the next notation, to speak of abstract existence with no concrete content at all is "nonsense, nothing." [82] Hence Berkeley, in the light of his early spiritism, concluded that "the mind," meaning my mind, "always and constantly thinks," [83] since to speak of the mind simply as existing without existing as anything in particular (thinking), is the same as to say that it does not exist, and to deny an essence which is already absolutely non-existent is to assert pure being. "The mind," as everything in general, "always and constantly thinks," since to deny something which is not something at all, but an abstract essence, still leaves us with just what we had before, an abstract essence, — being or nothing.

Berkeley does not abandon his earlier position in the third dialogue. But he now sees the absurdity of applying this sort of argument to the finite self, the *me* or *you.* For the first time, he clearly and consciously recognizes the distinction between the empirical, perceived self, the finite *me* or spirit, and the transcendental or perceiving self, a distinction which means the collapse of the abstract substance which he had made the carrier of all experience, and the foundation of his whole "society of spirits" philosophy. "When I deny sensible things an existence out of the mind," he now explicitly states for the first time, "I do not mean my mind in particular, but *all minds.*" Also, he continues, "it is plain they have an existence exterior to *my* mind; since I find *them* by experience to be *independent* of it." [84] In other words, in direct contradiction to his early spiritistic position, Berkeley now asserts the "independence" and "externality" of perceived objects, for the minute I think of myself at all, I must necessarily think of something independent and external to me, or I am thinking only of "something in general" which proves "nothing at all." [85] He recognizes explicitly that the previously asserted dependence of all external independent objects on the self involves an equally necessary and intimate dependence of the self upon objects which are external and inde-

[80] 2D., F. i, p. 437.
[81] C. B. J., 660.
[82] C. B. J., 661.
[83] C. B. J., 660.
[84] 3D., F. i, p. 446; my italics.
[85] *Ibid.,* p. 437.

pendent of it. The one cannot be significantly asserted without the other. Nowhere in the world of given existence is there any fixed resting point. To single out the finite self or spirit as the absolute is to fall into the same obvious error as that of the materialists. All things that can possibly be "given," whether ideas or spirits, are relative. "All is apparent," or dependent, the hitherto absolutized individual self as well as the whole realm of perceived, "independent" objects. They become independent only by becoming independent *of* something.

It is, however, a mistake to suppose that we have reached an absolute in the concept of "dependency." To isolate or reify this term into an absolute, — to assert that all things are finite and dependent would be as grave a fallacy as to isolate or reify the concept of "independence" after the manner of the "realistic" materialist or spiritist. Dependency itself is dependent. If all things were dependent, the statement would lose its significance, or rather in making the significant assertion that all things are dependent, we necessarily refer obliquely to independence, though not the independence of any thing, nor the independence of an entity that can in any way be given or conceived, except in its inconceivability. We refer to something which can be asserted only through the negation of absolutely everything, and particularly of everything associated with what I call myself. As Berkeley now puts it, "from my own *being*, and from the *dependency* I find in *myself* and *my* ideas, I do by an act of *reason*, *necessarily* infer the existence [i.e. the non-existence] of God." [86] By my very "being," which is finite, limited, spatiotemporal in its essence, I "necessarily . . . infer . . . God," the infinite, the unlimited, the non-spatial, and non-temporal. I cannot significantly refer to myself as I know I am, and must be, a finite, temporal "being," carrying the germs of dissolution ("dependency",) in my essence, without necessarily meaning or implying that on which I am dependent. How can I refer to the self, without thinking of it as an active being, i.e., as acting in time? And how can I think of myself in time without thinking of "before my birth" and "my annihilation"? [87] But "the same is true with regard to all other finite created spirits." [88] I must, therefore, think of the end of all finite existence, the end of all existence, the end of ending, the end of time. Hence, as Berkeley puts the matter "it necessarily follows there is an

---

[86] *Ibid.*, p. 448; my italics.   [88] *Ibid.*
[87] *Ibid.*, p. 447.

omnipresent eternal Mind, which knows and comprehends all things." [89]

This represents the crisis of Berkeley's early reflections, involving as it so obviously does the abandonment of his spiritistic position. From this point on, there can be no more discussion of "spiritual substances," which are obverse reflections of "material substances," of a solipsism which denies itself in its own assertion, of an independent self, which cannot possibly become independent without becoming independent of something, and thus losing its independence, and finally of a causal Deity which, as a "highest spirit," becomes indissolubly and irrevocably entwined with the lowest. The "concrete" logic has turned back upon its maker and destroyed the position for the sake of which it was developed. Indeed, it has destroyed all fixed "positions" whatsoever, for what "position" or "theory" is there which does not contain in it the indelible imprint of its finite manufacture, and thus, by its very "being," lead to its destruction? There is no fixed point, no position which is really stable, nothing whatsoever which is not a false abstraction. This is the result of the "concrete" logic as it finally manifests itself not only in the dialogues between Philonous and the "good Hylas," but in the other dialogues Berkeley carries on with himself, which end so unexpectedly not only in the refutation of all the opinions of the "good Hylas" but in the refutation of all the opinions of the "good Philonous," and of Berkeley as well, for all is opinion, position, abstraction, even the concrete logic itself, which, after consuming all else, must itself die away.

THE RESULT

What then is the result of these dialogues?

There is no result save a tension, a movement, carrying our thought always beyond itself, and destroying every fixed "result" that comes in its way. Starting with the wholly independent matter of the materialists, the basic, underlying, self-existent stuff of which the universe is composed, Berkeley shows that, as thus absolutized, it loses its meaning. A matter with no form, a substance with no accidents, an object with no subject, but to which the subject itself is reduced, is not matter at all, not a self-existent stuff, but the purest of pure form, metaphysi-

[89] *Ibid.*

cal nothingness, abstraction. It matters not what form this phantom of absoluteness takes, whether it masquerades as a "matter" underlying all existence, as pure being, abstract possibility, or pure causation. Wherever we find the notion of fixation, rigid isolation, anything in its naked, undeveloped, material state, the result is the same,— nothingness. Matter is no more than the form, the essence, the core, the immediate, the given, the undeveloped; nothing, that is, which can be conceived without reference to development, relation, mediation, opposition, if it is to be conceived at all.

It matters not how we think of our starting point. The same fate hovers over us. If we attempt to begin, as the materialist, with the "brain," we find ourselves defeated at the beginning, or rather before we begin, since, with the brain, we have already supposed the rest of the "organism," the whole of space, and a "mind" to perceive. In abstraction from this, the brain is no brain, for "the brain . . . you speak of, being a sensible thing, exists only in the mind." [90] But, you may say, the brain I am talking about is not any actually perceived brain, but a perceivable brain, a pure possibility, since "the existence of a sensible thing consists in being perceivable, but not in being actually perceived." [91] Hence, matter is abstract, hypostatized, absolute possibility, "subsisting" in isolation. But do I mean actual possibility, or a purely possible possibility, which is, therefore, not really possibility? *Actual* possibility, however, loses its self-subsistence in mediation. It ceases to be matter alone, and becomes enformed. As Berkeley so pointedly asks, "what is perceivable but an idea? And can an idea exist without being actually perceived?" [92] The more we hypostatize possibility, the more truly and actually it becomes possibility, and hence the less hypostatized.

One may object: the brain I am talking about is not even a possibility. It is pure matter, not an object, since this requires a subject, not a substratum since this itself requires a substratum, not a substance since this requires accidents, but mere "*entitiness*," "something in general." This last climax in "independence," "being" in its purity, what absolutely and entirely is — this is pure dependence, pure subjectivity, what entirely is not, for "lastly, *something in general*, . . . being interpreted proves *nothing*. So Matter comes to nothing." [93] Thus hypostatization,

[90] 2D., F. i, p. 421.   [92] *Ibid.*
[91] 3D., F. i, p. 451.   [93] 2D., F. i, p. 437; Berkeley's italics.

reification, isolation, immediacy, "stuff" and "givenness," turn out to be pure thought, pure form, and come to nothing. Berkeley had realized this, at least vaguely, before. The uniqueness of the *Three Dialogues* consists in their application of the concrete logic to Berkeley's own hypostatizations, to his own absolute, the empirical self, and in the consequent revelation that this last refuge must also be washed away by the "concrete" method. The self itself is "dependent" in its independence, objective in the very absoluteness of its subjectivity. Berkeley admits, therefore, that the *actus purus*, or self-causation, is also another "given" hypostatization, matter again, with a different name. All "things," material as well as spiritual, are not "things" at all, but only phases, aspects, finite modes. "The same is true with regard to all other finite created spirits," [94] and all "things" whatsoever have only "a relative existence." [95] But even relativity cannot be hypostatized into an absolute; the non-absolute is no more an absolute than the absolute itself. Existence which is "relative" requires non-existing eternal "archetypes" in "that Mind which comprehends all things." [96] The different "hypothetical" [97] objects, which alone exist, require such eternal "archetypes" to serve "the ends of identity," for without permanence there can be no flux, and without identity there can be no difference. But these absolute archetypes are not existent "things," for they do not exist in time, but are rather "eternal." They are not things, but rather those "archetypes" or forms of identity, which are presupposed by "relative existence." Nevertheless, they must not be hypostatized, even as forms. They are not self-substantial identities, for such identity would be only an "abstracted idea of identity." [98] Identity isolated, separated from all difference, all "hypothetical existence," becomes pure isolation, or abstraction, — in other words, pure diversity. Identity has meaning only as against diversity; the archetypes can be eternal only as against change; and God is God only as against man. Thus the absolute, which is presupposed by the relative, itself presupposes the relative. The shifting things of this world themselves become archetypes for the archetypes, and man as man becomes God. Nowhere is there any fixed point; nowhere is there any rest; only an infinite circle of relations, an endless network of categories and concepts, a ceaseless fire consuming itself.

94 3D., F. i, p. 447.   96 *Ibid.*, p. 468.   98 *Ibid.*, p. 468.
95 *Ibid.*, p. 472.   97 *Ibid.*, p. 474.

From such reflections there can be only one "result." This "result" is nothing more nor less than scepticism, that pure scepticism for which everything is relative, and which is consequently forced beyond everything, most of all itself. But what is beyond pure scepticism, beyond the pure, self-identical form of thought of which it is constituted? Is it the all-inclusive whole, that "mind which comprehends all things," and which, therefore *ipso facto*, becomes dependent upon them? Surely this intellectual absolute is not beyond, nor does it therefore provide a genuine escape, since it passes beyond only by remaining within, and escapes only by becoming itself imprisoned. Such rationalism can never break the chain of absolute self-identity or consistency which it forges by eternally contradicting itself, just as the abstract logic of consistency never ceases to fall into contradiction. From this there can be no surcease. As long as we think, there can be no surcease from the forms of thought and the absolute forms of logic, "the eternal archetypes in the Mind" which "comprehends all things," but only by being dependent on them. Such an absolute is no absolute at all, but a network of relations, a monotonous mechanizing of the non-mechanical, an endless dependence on something that is itself dependent.

There is no escape in the field of thought. Its concepts are all abstractions, and its absolute the pure form of relation in disguise, a transcendent that is at the same time immanent, and thus not transcendent, a God who is at the same time earth and air, and man. It is not surprising, therefore, to find Berkeley, after completing those exhausting and disillusioning exercises in logic in which his dialogues culminate, forced beyond thought altogether, towards another absolute. "God," he says, towards the end of his third and last dialogue, "is a being of transcendent and unlimited perfections: His nature, therefore, is incomprehensible." [99] Thus ended Berkeley's prolonged endeavours to "prove" God, that enthusiastic Deism through which he was "to convince Sceptics and Infidels by reason," [100] and to arrive at "the sublime notion of *a* God from a close and methodical application of thought." [101] What "reason" gave him was not God at all, nor even *a* God, but reason itself, or the absolute, something without beginning or end. "*God* is a Being of transcendent and unlimited perfections: *His* nature, therefore, is incomprehensible."

---

[99] *Ibid.*, p. 475.   [100] Pref., F. i, p. 377.   [101] *Ibid.*; my italics.

On a late December day at the end of the year 1713, breaking off his connections with the College, leaving logic and its absolute far behind him, Berkeley set out for London with his dialogues in his pocket, to seek a different sort of "proof" in the book of the world.

CHAPTER VIII

BEYOND THE ABSOLUTE

THE *Three Dialogues between Hylas and Philonous* represent a crisis in Berkeley's reflections. The concrete logic has at last jeopardized spiritism as well as materialism. Not only is he compelled to admit the "dependency" of all "external" appearances upon eternal forms or "archetypes," but the "dependency" of the finite mind or spirit as well. Just as the hard and fast "objects" of common sense are only "fleeting" appearances, dependent in their very difference and temporality upon identical and eternal archetypes, so is the hard and fast "self," the "I" of common sense, in its difference and temporality, in all that makes it "firm" and "objective," dependent upon something to perceive it. The finite consciousness, in so far as it is perceived or known, requires a deeper consciousness to perceive or know it, and so on, until we arrive at a consciousness of consciousnesses, a system of systems, or as Berkeley phrases it, "that Mind which comprehends all things." [1]

There must be such a consciousness, if there are finite selves. There must be identity, if there is difference, eternity if there is time, and God if there is man. It is no wonder, therefore, that Berkeley was deceived for the moment into offering this as a new demonstration of the Deity. And, indeed, its vast superiority over his earlier "causal" and "teleological" arguments cannot be denied. There is no question that the new proof did prove something, and there is in fact only one consideration perhaps capable of turning the balance against it. That is God Himself. Would a God whom man could "prove" be God? Would an absolute which is itself relative to the relative be an absolute? Would an *a priori* to which the *a posteriori* is itself prior be really *a priori*? Can we miss the irony, only half-concealed, in all discussions of an "absolute position," an "absolute point of view," an absolute which is itself caught in the network of the relative, a God who is Himself dependent on man, who is proved, comprehended, and otherwise disposed of, — who is uncritically referred to as "who"? Such an absolute is not and

[1] 3D., F. i, p. 468.

cannot be *the* absolute. Such a beyond is beyond only by being within.

It is no wonder, therefore, that Berkeley is pushed by his concrete logic beyond logic altogether, beyond the whole network of relations to the unrelated, beyond conception to the unconceived, beyond the whole field of the theoretical and its absolute to the practical, beyond the absolute to God. This shifting of axis from the intellectual to the practical was by its nature something more than a theoretical alteration. It affected not only what he had called his philosophy and what he had called his religion, but his "outward" life and habits as well. Thus, while his *Guardian Essays* show us that he was by no means philosophically inactive during the following period in his life, these writings, by their very occasional and polemic nature, are in definite contrast with the earlier, more systematic treatises. Instead of attempting to elaborate a complete or final philosophical system he is now content, by essays of a more or less casual character, to correct at various points that "poverty of imagination and narrowness of *soul*" [2] which mar our ordinary "manner of reasoning," and thus by a certain theoretical incompleteness to suggest an even more essential completeness of spirit. In connection with this intensification of self-consciousness Berkeley unquestionably underwent what is sometimes called a "religious" experience, although in his case at least, this was not distinguishable from the sudden realization of the fact that contemplation of the universe is not the universe, that lives to be perceived must first be lived by someone, and that value is more than truth. In accordance with this sudden realization that thought is after all only "thought," and that a pathway stretches not only before his reflections but before *him*, Berkeley, probably for the first time, decides definitely upon a career, and leaving his academic retreats plunges into the turmoil of "the world."

LIFE IN LONDON. THE ANNUS MIRABILIS

Nothing in Berkeley's extraordinary life is more remarkable than his first conquest of London. He came as an obscure, Irish tutor, known only to a few for his strange subjective ideas and a suspicious tinge of Jacobitism. In less than a year's time

[2] G. Ess., F. iv, p. 146; my italics.

he emerged as an intimate friend of the leading literary men of
the day and the author of a philosophy which was the talk of the
town, having converted such men as Addison, Smalridge, the
Dean of Christ Church, and, temporarily, even Arbuthnot. As
early as May, Percival says he hears "that your opinion has
gained ground among the learned; that Mr. Addison is come
over to you; and now what seemed shocking at first is become so
familiar that others envy you the discovery and make it their
own."[3]

Berkeley possessed an unusually engaging personality. He
seems to have made no enemies, and to have moved with equal
ease among the representatives of all parties and in all circles of
society. He was doubtless already acquainted with Lord Pembroke, the founder of the Irish Royal Society, to whom he had
dedicated his *Treatise*, and he at once became a frequent guest
at Wilton, the Earl's estate. Richard Dalton, a close friend
who later accompanied Berkeley to America, is reported to have
said of these visits, "when the Bishop was a young man, soon
after his first arrival in England, frequently visiting at Lord
Pembroke's after several weeks sejour there he was always
obliged to use some *innocent* strategem to leave Wilton; so exceedingly did Lord Pembroke and the ladies of the family delight in his learned, refined, improving, entertaining conversation."[4]

These numerous friendships and social engagements kept him
so busy in 1713 that with the exception of his *Guardian* articles
he had no time for writing, and it is no wonder that Berkeley
comments to Percival on the kindness of his friends, "which
lightens my expence, and makes it easier living here than I expected."[5] At the table of his namesake, Lord Berkeley of
Stratton, to whom he was introduced in April by Swift,[6] and to
whom he dedicated his *Three Dialogues*, he must have been a
regular guest, for he says, "There is here a Lord of my name, a
man of letters and a very worthy man, from whom I have received great civilities; I dine two or three times a week at his
table, and there are several other places where I am invited."[7]
Among these latter he may have been thinking of the Van Hom-

[3] Percival letter, May 14, 1713.
[4] *Gent. Mag.*, vol. LXVII, 1797, p. 455.
[5] Percival letter, May 7, 1713.
[6] See Monck Berkeley, *Poems*, p. ccclxxxi, and also Swift's *Journal*, April 12, 171? Another version of the introduction is given by G. M. Berkeley, *Literary Relics*, p. liv: "My Lord, here is a relation of your Lordship's who is good for something; and that, as times go, is saying a great deal."
[7] Percival letter, May 7, 1713.

righ's and the dinner party where he met Vanessa, though at the time this made no particular impression on him.

It must not be supposed that Berkeley spent all his time with such noble relatives and patrons, for he soon came to number among his personal friends the leading literary lights of the day, Gay, Steele, Addison, Swift, Pope, and Arbuthnot. The statement of Atterbury, to whom he was introduced by Swift and who remained a close friend, is of course well known: "So much understanding, so much knowledge, so much innocence, and such humility, I did not think had been the portion of any but angels, till I saw this gentleman." [8] It is impossible to attribute Berkeley's success merely to verbal grace or favourable appearance. More than this was necessary to gain the enduring interest of Swift. More than "innocence and humility" were necessary to draw forth the unqualified admiration of Pope, and more than "knowledge" or even "understanding" to win the friendship of the warm-hearted Steele, and the genial Dr. Arbuthnot. It was extraordinarily fortunate that Berkeley came to London during the most brilliant months of that *Annus Mirabilis*, 1713, for in less than a year amity had turned to bitterness, the political equilibrium had been destroyed, Swift was in exile, and most of the Tory chiefs were in prison. During this short though intense period of intercourse with minds as active as his own, Berkeley absorbed many influences and, in collaboration with his friends, even began to promote a plan for a National Academy to improve the English language and to stimulate an interest in national history. This scheme, however, which had the support of Swift, Bolingbroke, and others, fell through at the death of Queen Anne and the collapse of the Tory government.[9]

Even were we without the testimony of his writings, we should be forced by the impression made upon such a circle to acknowledge that Berkeley possessed to a unique degree, in addition to his penetrating logic and, as we must now add, his religious feeling, that open sesame, that queen of the eighteenth century graces, that *Clavis Universalis* to the hearts and souls of men — wit. Steele seems to have been the first of the many prominent persons with whom he became acquainted at this time. He owed this not to any personal introduction but to his

[8] *Gent. Mag.*, vol. XLVII, 1777, p. 13.
[9] *Annual Register*, 1763, p. 2. Berkeley also speaks of it in *An Essay Towards*

Preventing the Ruin of Great Britain, F. iv, p. 333.

work alone. Someone had given Steele a copy of the *Principles*, and he became so interested that he took steps through his printer to meet the author. "For my part," writes Berkeley, "I should reckon it a sufficient recompense of my pains in writing it, that it gave me some share in the friendship of so worthy a man." [10] In spite of the fact that Steele "heard" he was a Tory, he "dined frequently" at the house in Bloomsbury Square. "His wit, natural good sense, generous sentiments, and enterprising genius," writes Berkeley at the time, "with a peculiar delicacy and easiness of writing, seem those qualities which distinguish Mr. Steele." [11] We are told, however, that he never "thought highly of the learning" of his new acquaintance.[12] He apparently encouraged his impetuous friend to continue writing,[13] and Steele took Berkeley into his confidence with regard to the long-projected *Guardian*, and sought his aid in the new venture.[14] "You will soon hear," says the latter on March 7, "of Mr. Steele under the character of the *Guardian*." Just one week later, in the third number of the new journal, appeared the first of Berkeley's fourteen contributions, in which he was enabled to wage war upon those whom he had at last come to perceive were his proper enemies — the apostles of "narrow" or abstract reason, and of abstract virtue "for its own sake," — as it was understood from the start that he was "to defend some branch of Christianity against the free-thinkers of the age." [15] Berkeley "had a guinea and a dinner with Steele for every paper which he contributed." [16] The papers themselves must have served to gain a wider audience for his ideas, and the association with Steele was peculiarly important in bringing him into contact with other prominent men of the day.

Berkeley met Addison, however, through Swift. "This morning," he writes to Percival on March 27, "I breakfasted with Mr. Addison at Dr Swift's lodging." He refers to his host as at this time "one of the best natured and agreeable men in the world." He also speaks in this letter about the keen interest in Addison's forthcoming play, and was himself present in the author's box on the April evening when *Cato* was first performed. It was received with the greatest applause by "the

10 Percival letter, February 23, 1713.
11 Percival letter, March 27, 1713.
12 *Biog. Brit.*, Addenda & Corrigenda, vol. III.

13 Percival letter, February 23, 1713.
14 Wrangham, *British Plutarch*, London, 1816, vol. VI, p. 74.
15 *Ibid.*   16 *Ibid.*

fullest audience that ever was known," [17] but we have Pope's testimony to the effect that the "author sweated behind the scenes with concern to find the applause proceeded more from the hand than the head." The author was too well-known to be judged on purely aesthetic grounds, and both Whigs and Tories were anxious to claim this last production as their own. It naturally had a long run — almost too long, in fact, for a month later Berkeley writes that Mrs. Oldfield, Cato's daughter, had a midwife stationed behind the scenes, and that she couldn't "hold out much longer." [18]

Berkeley was already too much of a philosopher to have extreme party opinions, and he seems to have moved with as much ease and pleasure among the Whigs as among the Tories for whom, however, he felt more political sympathy. In May he speaks of dining with the Whigs at Dr. Garth's. Concerning Addison, Berkeley says that with respect to speculative studies he excelled "any of the wits that I know." [19] The two apparently conversed at frequent intervals concerning philosophical and religious subjects, and during one such conversation Addison informed his young friend of the heterodox views of the astronomer Halley and their openly destructive effects. [20]

It was Swift who actually "recommended" Berkeley to Dr. Arbuthnot, [21] the Queen's physician, the author of the "Art of Political Lying" and the "John Bull" tracts, and the genius of the Scriblerus Club. But it was, of course, impossible to be a friend to Swift and Pope and Steele without knowing him. Berkeley dined with him the evening of April 16, [22] and continued to speak with characteristic enthusiasm of his mathematical and philosophical attainments. He was evidently kind enough to read the manuscript of the *Dialogues*, as yet unpublished, and is mentioned by the author as the first "proselyte" made by this work. [23] Like many of his friends, Berkeley found Arbuthnot's conversation and criticism enormously stimulating. In a letter of August 7 he says that to the non-existence of matter Arbuthnot can find no objection, but that he does not agree on "the necessity of the laws of nature." Arbuthnot, as a physician, was probably not a willing recipient of the view that

[17] Percival letter, April 16, 1713.
[18] Percival letter, May 7, 1713.
[19] Percival letter, March 27, 1713.
[20] "He [Addison] assured me that the infidelity of a certain noted mathematician, still living, was one principal reason assigned by a witty man of those times for his being an infidel." F. iii, p. 66. This "witty man" may have been Garth.
[21] Swift, *Journal*, April 12, 1713.
[22] Percival letter, April 16, 1713.
[23] *Ibid.*

the physical organism is nothing but an abstracted nexus of sense impressions, but as a man of wit he was apparently forced by the weight of the argument. Berkeley's newly conceived absolute, however, and the distinction between the ectypal and the archetypal [24] may have been too metaphysical for the genial doctor, as a year later in a letter to Swift he hardly speaks as a proselyte to the new doctrine.[25] "Poor philosopher Berkeley," he says, "has now the *idea* of health, which was very hard to produce in him, for he had an *idea* of a strange fever upon him, so strange that it was very hard to destroy it by introducing a contrary one." Yet he certainly remained a close friend, since in 1717 Berkeley wrote for him an account of his daring observations of the eruption of Vesuvius, which was published later, probably at his instigation, by the Royal Society. [26] Berkeley's first judgment of him is probably not far from the truth, in spite of its enthusiasm: "He is . . . in great esteem with the whole Court. Nor is he less valuable for his learning, being a great philosopher, and reckoned among the first mathematicians of the age. Besides which he has likewise the character of very uncommon virtue and probity." [27]

Berkeley met Pope at Steele's house late in February or early in March.[28] Duncombe states that it was Swift who brought about the introduction, but the letter to Percival, which describes the first meeting with Swift "two nights before," implies an acquaintance with Pope already fairly intimate. "I had last night," says Berkeley,[29] "a very ingenious new poem upon Windsor Forest given me by the author Mr. Pope. This gentleman is a Papist, but a man of excellent wit and learning. . . ." He must have come to know Pope fairly well in the following months, for he writes to him regularly during his Italian travels.

Although Steele provided Berkeley with a popular audience, Arbuthnot read and criticized his ideas, and Pope showered upon him the fruits of literary intimacy, it was Swift who took a practical interest in the young philosopher and at once employed his waning power to give him material assistance in making his career. On Berkeley's side we may well imagine

[24] 3D., F. i, p. 475.
[25] Percival also writes July 18, 1713: "I hear Dr. Swift has said you have not made a convert of Dr. Arbuthnot."
[26] Cf. *Gent. Mag.*, XX, 1750, pp. 161-162.
[27] Percival letter, April 16, 1713.

[28] This is the conjecture of the editors of Pope's letters, Elwin & Courthope, London, 1886, which, in view of the Percival letters, seems more probable than Duncombe's suggestion.
[29] March 7, 1713.

that, at this crisis in his own life, the elemental passions which Swift may have erred at times in mistaking for reasons certainly seemed to him refreshing in comparison with the external polish of Pope and the formalized moralism of Addison. At any rate, this was the beginning of a lasting friendship in which each was able to render service to the other. Swift, on his part, not only introduced his young protégé to many important people in London society, including his noble relative, Lord Berkeley of Stratton, but also procured him his first official ecclesiastical position as chaplain to Lord Peterborough, the new ambassador to Sicily, and probably also a much more "considerable offer," [30] which Berkeley decided for some reason to refuse, perhaps because he preferred the stimulation of foreign travel. In any case, this is certainly the most interesting of Berkeley's friendships and the most intriguing to the imagination, for by several peculiar accidents of fate their paths crossed and recrossed, and though his lips were sealed by friendship, Berkeley probably came into possession of most of the keys required for an understanding of the inner motives of his enigmatic benefactor.

Many erroneous statements have been made concerning Berkeley's meeting with Swift. It is quite certain from the Percival letters, however, that they met "by chance at my Lord Pembroke's" [31] on March 5, about two months after Berkeley's arrival in London. A few weeks later Berkeley was breakfasting at the house in Bury Street and speaking of his host with the greatest enthusiasm. "If I were not afraid of disobliging my Lady and Mrs Parker," he writes to Percival, "I should tell you that I think him one of the best natured and agreeable men in the world." [32]

Swift's *Journal* contains three notations concerning Berkeley The first shows the extent to which Swift, in one month's time, was impressed by Berkeley's candid personality and philosophic genius. "I went to court today," he says early in April, "on purpose to present Mr Berkeley, one of your fellows of Dublin College, to Lord Berkeley of Stratton. That Mr Berkeley is a very ingenious man, and a great philosopher, and I have mentioned him to all the ministers, and given them some of his writings." [33] His generosity is all the more remarkable in that this was a time of stress for Swift himself, his own future being undecided, and his spirits depressed by his unpleasant pros-

[30] Percival to Grafton, May 28, 1716.
[31] Berkeley to Percival, March 7, 1713.
[32] Percival letter, March 27, 1713.
[33] April 12, 1713.

pects and the seeming ingratitude of the ministry. One evening he speaks of discussing the relative advantages, or rather disadvantages, of St. Patrick's and the Prebendary of Windsor with Lady Masham. That he sometimes found relief in Berkeley's company is revealed by a later notation of April 21: "I dined at an alehouse with Parnell and Berkeley; for I am not in humour to go among the ministers, though Lord Dartmouth invited me to dine with him today, and Lord Treasurer was to be there. I said I would if I were out of suspense." Swift's "suspense" gave way only to gloom and bitterness. But his efforts in Berkeley's behalf were successful, as, in October, the latter left for France and Sicily as chaplain to Lord Peterborough.

THE GUARDIAN

While Berkeley entered whole-heartedly into the life of the town and made many lasting friendships with the great wits of the day, there were certain aspects of this life which, as he came to know it better, shocked and depressed him. Although he must have been fascinated by the smoothness and subtlety of Pope's wit, he could not fail to notice its shallowness. While he found in Addison a certain sympathy with his new feeling for the inescapable realities of the inner life, there was a formalism about Addison's moralistic recommendations which must have repelled him. And while in the truly savage materialism of Swift, perhaps more than anyone else, he found some sort of response to the intense fermentation which was proceeding in his own mind, nevertheless there was a coarseness and narrowness which must have made this most profound and philosophical of his acquaintances seem incomprehensible and even at times repulsive to him. There was an emptiness back of the glitter of the "literary" atmosphere. There was brightness, cleverness, and wit, but what had a man like Pope to say? Berkeley could not have failed to discern the intellectual insensitiveness amounting almost to irresponsibility that was later to furnish such an exquisite polish to the platitudes of the *Essay on Man*. The rationalism of the age which prided itself on having understood all things and having banished mystery from the universe had nothing now left but to pick "the dunces" to pieces with a destructive brilliance that has never been excelled. Samuel Clarke, the reigning theologian of the day, whom he may have heard at St. James', seemed more interested in defending and interpreting Newton than Christ, and even Swift appeared to preserve his orthodoxy only by ceasing to think about it altogether, except as a source of annuities. There was, as it seemed to Berkeley, a lack of speculative imagination, an absorption in the surfaces of things, a laxity in thought as well as life, which intensified the despair that had already taken possession of his mind.

The visit to London, however, at last enabled him to concentrate this vague fermentation upon its proper object, for Berkeley was not long in perceiving the connection between the superficiality of the age and his own past philosophic failures. The cynicism and materialism he saw about him, as well as the materialism he had now come to see in himself and his own "spiritism," had a common root in the abstract "rationalism" which, having destroyed all other values, now lay over the intellectual landscape like a cloud, dulling other eyes as well as his own to the deeper and vaster prospects of existence. He was, indeed, presented with a most apt and concrete bit of evidence for the demoralizing effects of this abstract faith in "reason" almost immediately after his arrival in the town. This was the appearance of a pamphlet on "Free-Thinking" by one of the heterodox lights of the day, Anthony Collins. More than any other single event it helped him to crystallize his growing dissatisfaction with the whole structure and method of his past speculations, and led him to the first formulation of an entirely new attitude which arose as much from the impetus of his own thought and the crisis at which it had arrived as from the external crisis afforded by his sudden plunge into the brilliant world of the *Annus Mirabilis*.

Collins' *Discourse* [34] was published in January, 1713, and made a great stir. Berkeley refers to it in the first letter written to Percival after arriving in the metropolis. "There is lately published," he says, "a very bold and pernicious book entitled a *'Discourse on Free Thinking.'*" [35] The fact that Collins had been a friend and correspondent of Locke made Berkeley only more clearly conscious of the chasm between his new attitude and the liberalistic tendencies of his past thought. He therefore gladly embraced the opportunity, afforded by his acquaintance with Steele, of combating this abstract rationalism, which he

[34] Anthony Collins: *A Discourse of Free-Thinking, Occasion'd by the Rise and Growth of a Sect Call'd Free-Thinkers,* London, 1713.
[35] Percival letter, January 26, 1713.

now came to see lay at the root not only of the imaginative sterility of the day, but of many difficulties and even errors in his own past reflections. In preparation for the first *Guardian* essay, which he decided to devote to Collins' *Discourse*, he made it a point to frequent the free-thinker's clubs and to listen to their discussions. Later he told his friend Johnson how "On one of these occasions he heard Collins declare that he had found a demonstration against the being of a God." [36]

Collins' book embodies an unusually strong statement of the Deistic case. It begins with a plea for rationalism, or what he calls independent or "free thought." The only way to make men see truly is to allow them to see freely,[37] for reason is like sight. If we argue that to think freely means to run the risk of falling into error, and that, therefore, we should submit to authority, we are thereby contradicting ourselves, since it requires thought to appreciate this argument.[38] Even the *Society for the Propagation of the Gospel* is based upon free-thinking, for how else could its missionaries approach the heathen than by asking them to think freely? And yet the priests, and organized religion in general, are really a great conspiracy to reduce us to intellectual slavery and thrust mysterious and absurd dogmas down our throats. This is inconsistent with knowledge. "Thus before the Restoration of Learning, when Men were subject to the Impositions of Priests, a prodigious Ignorance prevail'd." [39] Yet if we will only open our eyes we shall see that the priests, in spite of their clever machinations, have never been able to unite.[40] Archbishop King, for example, believes that God is so far beyond and above us that we cannot attach to Him any human attribute. The Archbishop of Canterbury, on the other hand, maintains with equal certainty that God is just and good and true, and that the essence of religion is the imitation of God. Then there is a parade of the different interpretations of such dogmas as the Trinity.[41] And "If any good Christian happens to reason better than ordinary, they presently charge him with Atheism, Deism or Socinianism: as if good Sense and Orthodoxy could not subsist together." [42] In part three of the *Discourse* there is a great muster of names and quotations to

[36] Johnson, *Autobiog.*, Schneider, *Samuel Johnson*, vol. I, p. 26.
[37] Collins, *Discourse*, p. 17.
[38] *Ibid.*, p. 26.
[39] *Ibid.*, p. 8.
[40] *Ibid.*, pp. 47 ff.

[41] *Ibid.*, pp. 65 ff.
[42] *Ibid.*, p. 85. It must be noted that he himself (p. 101) admits that free thought will create an inevitable diversity of opinion which is not socially deleterious.

show that practically all of the great men of history from Socrates to Chillingworth were "free thinkers." Jesus, for example, was a "free thinker" and an enemy of the priests, because he appealed to the reason of all men. Aristotle was a "free thinker," because he had to flee from Athens for attacking religion. Solomon "would have been calumniated as an Atheist, unless he had recommended himself to the priests by the building of Churches." [43] Cicero was a sceptic who had no belief in immortality. A marked antagonism to the whole doctrine of immortality is apparent throughout the book.[44] Collins does not dare to come out in print as an atheist, and he even admits a demonstration of God's existence.[45] But this God is a "Spinozistic Being" who is "destitute of all parts and Passions," who receives no comfort from our worship, and who cannot blame us if we do our best.[46]

Berkeley's new sense of the relativity of reason, as well as his own experiences in the city, led him to realize at once that he was dealing with a popular movement rather than a philosophy, a matter of mood rather than pure argument. But he was now most eager to do what he could to fight the spirit of the age, and addressed himself in his essays with considerable skill to the task of refuting not only "points," but shrugs and sneers as well. Though he could not help losing his temper now and then, he adopted, on the whole, a tone of urbane banter with respect to "these sages of iniquity" who are themselves "only speculatively wicked." [47] As to the harangues against priests and their machinations, Berkeley sometimes allows himself to be angry, as in *Essay I*, but usually adopts the wiser course of ridicule, as in the case of his visit to *The Pineal Gland of a Free-Thinker*,[48] in whose mind he at first discerns a "great castle" surrounded by "the bones of men" and "garrisoned by certain men in black of gigantick size, and most terrible forms," which, upon closer inspection, however, "shrunk into a few innocent clergymen." He has little trouble in revealing the feebleness of Collins' pretensions to scholarship,[49] but attempts rather to suggest indirectly the poverty-stricken character of the "humanistic" perspective of Collins and his followers than to argue with them point for point.

[43] *Ibid.*, p. 150.
[44] Cf. *ibid.*, p. 66, for example.
[45] *Ibid.*, p. 8.
[46] *Ibid.*, p. 34.

[47] G. Ess., F. iv, p. 141.
[48] *Ibid.*, IV.
[49] *Ibid.*, I.

What seems to have most impressed Berkeley at this time
was the inhumanism of "humanism," the impossibility of
becoming humanly self-conscious without somehow gaining a
sense of what is beyond the human. Page after page bears
testimony to the constant attempt to gain a truly objective, a
more than merely human, perspective. Thus he affects a certain
condescension towards his "fellow creatures," labouring "in a
toilsome and absurd pursuit of trifles," [50] and betrays for the
first time that almost romantic feeling for "nature" which was
henceforth to become so characteristic of his writings. "Fair
weather is the joy of my soul; about noon I behold a blue sky
with rapture, and receive great consolation from the rosy dashes
of light which adorn the clouds of the morning and evening.
When I am lost among green trees, I do not envy a great man
with a great crowd at his levee. And I often lay aside thoughts
of going to an opera that I may enjoy the silent pleasure of
walking by moonlight, or viewing the stars sparkle in their azure
ground; which I look upon as part of my possessions." [51]

In this state of mind, it was only natural that he should accept the invitation of his friend Smalridge [52] to visit Oxford,
and he spent the summer months rambling about through the
country. The contrast afforded by this relatively quiet retreat,
after the intense though rather meaningless bustle of the town,
left an impression upon Berkeley which remained until the end
of his life. Thirty years later he wrote to his friend James:
"Oh, that you had a farm of a hundred acres near Oxford.
What a pleasure it would be to improve and embellish the face
of nature, to lead the life of a patriarch rather than a friar, a
modern cloistered friar." [53] This impression became even more
than an impression, and formulated itself finally into a cherished dream, sustaining him in many of his later grapplings
with the world. It certainly guided his hand in drawing the
plans of "Seminary," "Houses," and "Cypress Walk" for his
College of St. Paul's, and became so alluring to him during his
episcopal duties in Ireland at the end of his life that, though he

---

[50] *Ibid.*, V, F. iv, p. 158.

[51] *Ibid.* Cf. the eloquent passage on
the order of nature at the beginning of the
second dialogue, F. i, pp. 422 ff.

[52] Swift, in his letter to Carteret
(Spence, *Anecdotes*, pp. 252–254), speaks
of Berkeley's first visit to London and
alludes to Smalridge: "he [Berkeley] be-

came the founder of a sect there called the
Immaterialists by the force of a very
curious book upon that subject. Dr.
Smalridge and many other eminent persons were his proselytes."

[53] *Letter to Sir John James*, Anderson
ed., p. 30, F. iv, p. 534.

could not live among those "gentlemen at Oxford who made divine things their study, and proposed to wean themselves from what is called the world," [54] he nevertheless could and did propose to die there.

It is impossible to refrain from connecting this sudden distaste for "what is called the world" with the same crisis which, as we have noted, first drew him away from his academic haunts into the world. One who had become convinced of the emptiness and vanity of human thought could hardly be permanently soothed by the boisterous excitement of an all too human "life." It is not, therefore, surprising to find Berkeley, after his short and brilliant encounter with "the world," writing his friend Percival from his new academic retreat in the following words: "I have been now about one month in this town and think it to be the most delightful place I have ever seen."[55] And in August he says again: "The more I think on it, the more I am persuaded that my happiness will not consist in riches and advancement. If I could prosecute my studies in health and tranquillity, that would make me as happy as I expect to be in this life." [56]

While "nature" offered Berkeley a temporary relief from the petty foibles and intrigues of men ("spirits"), and from that rationalism in which "they" are so unmistakably expressed, it provided his troubled mind with no permanent content. After all, what is nature but another human or spiritistic conception, or "idea"? In speaking of the vastness of astronomical space he observes that though "these ideas wonderfully dilate and expand the mind," they become insignificant when compared with spiritual truth that takes us beyond "ideas" altogether. "Astronomy," he says, "opens the mind, and alters our judgment, with regard to the magnitude of extended beings [ideas]; but Christianity produceth an universal greatness of soul." [57] It is to the end of suggesting so far as possible such an "universal greatness of *soul*" that Berkeley devoted his efforts in the *Guardian Essays*, the last of which were written during his sojourn in Oxford, and to which we must now turn for more detailed comment.

[54] *Ibid.*, p. 24. Cf. F. iv, p. 530.
[55] July 19, 1713.
[56] Percival letter, August 7, 1713.
[57] G. Ess., F. iv, p. 172.

"NARROWNESS" OF SOUL

Berkeley refers on almost every page to the "narrowness" of the humanistic or rationalistic perspective of the "free-thinkers." Thus when he had "repaired to the Grecian coffee-house" where he found one of the most eminent of the sect, having entered into his Pineal Gland and discovered the "seat of the Understanding," expecting "to find there a comprehensive knowledge of all things human and divine," he was astonished to observe on the contrary that the place was "narrower than ordinary." And descending "a story lower into the imagination," which was "larger indeed, but cold and comfortless," he discovered "Prejudice in the figure of a woman standing in the corner, with her eyes close shut, and her forefingers stuck in her ears," and "many words, in a confused order, but spoken with great emphasis, issued from her mouth." [58] Berkeley had learned to his own cost that nothing could be quite so dogmatic as that "cold" rationality which masquerades as the entire lack of all dogmatism. Had he not discovered in his own case that many of the truths which had seemed so certain, reasonable, and universally self-evident were, as a matter of fact, nothing but popular prejudices, and that their "universality" was nothing but the false universality of a generally accepted dogma? What was reason itself on the lips of a man like Pope but the echo of a popular fashion? The free-thinkers, in dogmatically attaching themselves to one "abstract" faculty of the soul at the expense of all else, became "men of short views and mean souls." [59] As Berkeley had now learned, through his own mistakes, and through the irresistible impetus of his concrete logic: what is understanding itself, if absolutized into a self-existent entity exclusive of its essential context? Not only the imagination, therefore, but also the "Understanding" of the free-thinker, the very faculty he believes himself to be so exclusively emphasizing, "wants to be opened and enlarged" [60] in order to be really an understanding.

It is not surprising that Berkeley, therefore, devotes the whole of one of his most impressive essays to the "narrowness of Freethinkers," [61] in which he attempts indirectly to suggest "the nobler sentiments" and "greater views" which must "stir the

---

[58] *Ibid.*, p. 151.   [60] *Ibid.*, p. 152.
[59] *Ibid.*, p. 175.   [61] *Ibid.*, p. 169.

soul . . .[62] when the whole capacity of her nature is branched out into new faculties."[63] These new or other than rational faculties are required by reason itself, for reason, if it were made all-inclusive, would then cease to be reason. They must lead the soul to "more sublime and remote objects,"[64] extending "beyond the light of nature," for if there were no such "beyond," would not the polemic of the free-thinkers against the super-rational lose its force? There is no sense in arguing a "case" for what is already everything.

In none of these essays does Berkeley argue against either "reason," or "the light of nature," or the "truths" revealed by this dry light. He never puts himself in the position of an advocate or a defendant, for this would be to enter the lists as the proponent of one abstraction over against another, and would thus stand in the way of those "general views"[65] which are "too big for the grasp of a human intellect,"[66] and in connection with which he quotes the sublime passage on the philosophic life from the *Theaetetus*.[67] There is now no question of an easy agreement with the point of view of "common sense," for "philosophers judge of most things very differently from the vulgar."[68] The thoughts of the vulgar, like the "thoughts of a free-thinker," are "employed on certain minute particularities"[69] or abstractions quite opposed to that "largeness of mind" or concreteness necessary for a "true judgment of things."[70]

Berkeley is not pleading for any particular attitude or point of view against others, but rather for something entirely different, something opposed to any attitude or point of view, — that to which all attitudes and points of view are relative. Thus, in walking through St. Paul's "the other day" and meditating upon the "just, plain, and majestic architecture,"[71] he suddenly "beheld a fly upon one of the pillars," and "it straightway came into my head, that this same fly was a Free-thinker." His "prospect was confined to a little part of one of the stones of a single pillar," small inequalities in the surface of which "in the view of the insect seemed so many deformed rocks and precipices," since he missed completely the "joint beauty of the

---

[62] *Ibid.*, pp. 172, 173.
[63] *Ibid.*, p. 173.
[64] *Ibid.*, p. 172.
[65] *Ibid.*, p. 170.
[66] *Ibid.*, p. 171.

[67] *Ibid.*
[68] *Ibid.*, pp. 170–171.
[69] *Ibid.*, p. 170.
[70] *Ibid.*
[71] *Ibid.*

whole." Berkeley does not, therefore, "take sides." There is a sense in which the "views" of the rationalists cannot certainly be denied all truth. But for "every view" there is an opposed "view," and rationalism would lose its meaning were there not an opposed and equally abstract irrationalism. Berkeley, in his essays, does not deny the rational nor does he deny the irrational; or, rather, he denies both to an equal degree. This is the language of scepticism, a scepticism revealed in his many statements to the effect that the "immensities" are "too big for the grasp of a human intellect." [72] This is a scepticism, however, too devastating and complete, too self-conscious and consistent to be rooted in anything other than the absolute itself, — something far different from the relative absolute of the rationalist, which omits the irrational fringe hovering over all as well as each of its conceptions.

FÉNELON'S DEMONSTRATION

We have noted how Berkeley's concrete logic led him beyond materialism, beyond his own spiritism, and, in the last dialogue, finally beyond all other "isms" to a position which, in so far as it can be justifiably referred to as a "position" at all, must be identified with absolute scepticism, or in other words, absolutism. It is not surprising, however, in view of the character of the "concrete" logic, that it should, in the end, carry him beyond even this last sceptical stronghold of reason, beyond all "isms" whatsoever, beyond reason itself into a new horizon or level of existence, beyond absolutism to the absolute. This movement is discernible in the *Guardian Essays*.

The network of relations in which Berkeley's early rationalism terminates is a system of concepts, each of which gains meaning by standing over against other concepts from which it can separate itself only by being first joined. Thinking can progress only by dividing what is already united, or uniting what is already divided. This is the outcome of Berkeley's "concrete" logic. But this applies to the concrete logic itself and the "complete" network of relations, or "whole," in which it seems to terminate. This absolute "whole," which "reconciles" all contradictions, is itself in contradiction with the contradictions it reconciles and without which it could not be.

Nor does it improve matters to think of this absolute as a *whole*, since is not a whole relative to its parts? At no point is thought able to arrive at anything truly substantial. What is any substance without accidents? Nor is it any use to say that substantiality is to be found in the process of struggling for it, in passing from one accident to another, in all the accidents taken together, as if by taking enough mice we could somehow make a man. A hundred, a thousand, a million accidents are still accidents. It is, indeed, true to say that unless we somehow conceived of substantiality as an ideal, we could never dismiss everything as accidental. But we conceive it only as not conceiving it (as an ideal). The absolute of thought, no matter how absolute we make it, can be defined only as what is more than itself, what contains its other (what it does not contain) in itself. But this merely makes the contradiction inherent in the absolutely non-contradictory, the relativity of the absolute, the incompleteness of what is wholly complete, all the more clear. For what contains its other, no matter to how great a degree, contains it only by not containing it, and remains contradictory and incomplete. Thought by its very nature thinks or contains reality only by not containing it, or not being it, and must remain to the end a contradiction. The absolute must remain beyond it. Thought may become absolute only by recognizing that it is throughout only thought, and concrete logic can become truly concrete only by passing beyond itself, and realizing that it too is an abstraction. This is the essence of Berkeley's crisis.

We commonly state the matter in another fashion. Concepts, we say, strive to become true, but they do so only at the cost of relating themselves to what is false, since what is perfectly or completely true would cease to be truth, or would pass beyond truth altogether. There is, in other words, a germ of error involved in the contrast-effect which constitutes the essence of truth. We often think of the matter in a pictorial fashion which, in spite of its crudity, involves the same criticism of truth as an abstract or exclusive ideal that Berkeley suggests in his eleventh essay, entitled "Happiness Obstructed by Free-Thinkers." Thought, as we picture it to ourselves, is a contemplation *of* reality, something which must conform to, or coincide with, something beyond itself. But suppose the coincidence to be perfect identity. The picture would be destroyed. Thought would no longer be a representation or contemplation *of* something beyond it, or outside it, but the thing itself. There would, therefore, no longer be any contemplation, or theorizing (θεωρία), or intuition, and it would hence be impossible any longer to speak of truth since all possiblity of error would have been eliminated. This is the meaning of Berkeley's statement that "liberty [free thought] and truth are not in themselves desirable, but only as they relate to a further end." [73] Truth is by its very nature incomplete or relative, in a state of "dependency" upon error. Were all error eliminated, were we to coincide ultimately with reality rather than to contemplate it from without, truth, as an ideal, would lose all meaning. Truth, in other words, is not itself "desirable," but only as a means to "a farther end," the destruction of truth, or perfect oneness with reality, i.e., the absolute elimination of error. Thinking or contemplation has meaning only in the context of something which lies beyond it, and it is, therefore, impossible to regard the relative absolute of reason as a final resting point. The absolute, if and exactly when it becomes really absolute, ceases to be rational, or in any respect relative. Beyond the absolute of reason, of contemplation, of θεωρία, which is only a relative absolute, there is *the* absolute, uncontaminated by any relativity or contradiction. There can be no doubt that in this crisis of his thought, Berkeley himself was making that passage from the theoretical to the practical which is always of such fatal consequence for meditative minds, and which, if and when it does occur, is something that must always be lived as well as thought.

This reference to an absolute beyond the whole intricate field or network of relations which constitutes the world of reason is unmistakable in the *Essays.* "The mind of man" must be transformed, "must be raised to a higher pitch" [74] in order to comprehend rather than merely to contemplate this passage, a passage so critical and fundamental that it is something "which we cannot directly understand." [75] It may be understood only by negation — by first setting up such positive constructions and then eliminating them, by reason rather than understanding, by dialectic rather than deduction, by religion rather than philosophy. Berkeley now refers to God not as the mind which knows all things, not as the light of reason, but, following the language of his great predecessor in the discovery of practical philosophy, as "the Father of lights," the source of

[73] *Ibid.*, p. 177.   [74] *Ibid.*, p. 184.   [75] *Ibid.*, p. 185.

knowledge rather than knowledge itself, and hence beyond truth, since "His greatness is unsearchable" and "we know Him not." [76] We know Him not, for He is beyond all knowledge as its source and condition — the inescapable context without which reason cannot be reason, the absolute who can be neither known nor intuited, but only lived and apprehended (rather than comprehended) from within.

"The existence of a God is so far from being a thing that wants to be proved, that I think it is the only thing of which we are certain." [77] Here speaks the man who only a year before had planned confidently to offer the world "a plain demonstration of the Immediate Providence of an all-seeing God, and the natural immortality of the soul." [78] Nothing is perhaps more revelatory of the nature of the crisis through which Berkeley passed in the year 1713 than the eighth essay,[79] at the beginning of which occurs this surprisingly arational statement. There is now no need to prove God, for a God that could be proved would not be God at all. The best, and indeed the only, proof for God is the apprehension of the utter impossibility of such a proof. To see the sort of proof which Berkeley now has in mind, one needs only to glance at his free rendition of Fénelon's prayer, or "Fénelon's Demonstration" as he calls it.[80]

God is not a vague objective "He," referred to in the third person, but an intimate "Thou," not a "Being" who may be externally contemplated, but a force or spirit who "cannot be known directly" but only lived. "Thou . . . art the eternal fountain of light and beauty," [81] not the light and beauty itself, as he had formerly maintained in connection with his teleological proof. "Thou, who art the life of all that truly live, those can never fail to find Thee who seek for Thee within themselves," [82] not in the "effects of nature," where he had previously directed those who sought evidence for a "Wise Good and Perfect Spirit." [83] The "exact harmony and correspondence of the whole" [84] to which he had there pointed as "evincing" the "Author of Nature" is now viewed "as a Veil which

[76] *Ibid.*, p. 182.
[77] *Ibid.*, p. 166.
[78] 3D., Pref.
[79] *Fénelon's Demonstration.*
[80] This prayer is a free translation of the *Prière à Dieu* at the end of the first part of his *Démonstration de l'Existence de Dieu*, nouvelle ed. Chatelain, 1731, Tome

I, p. 175. Cf. *Biog. Brit.*, Add. and Corr., III, p. 258; also *Gent. Mag.*, vol. L, 1780, p. 125.
[81] P. 168.
[82] *Ibid.*
[83] Pr., F. i, p. 340.
[84] *Ibid.*

hides Thee from our eyes." [85] Indeed, to gain a sense of this presence it is necessary to transcend completely, even to reverse, all the ordinary judgments of common sense, for, "Wretches that we are, we consider shadows as realities, and truth as a phantom," and "That which is nothing is all to us, and that which is all appears to us nothing." [86] It is hard to believe that this is the same man who, in his *Treatise,* referred so contemptuously to those "paradoxes which have such a direct repugnancy to the plain common sense of mankind," [87] and railed against "fine spun metaphysics."

The contrast is even more intense when we remember the former position of the finite "spirit," or "self," which was the foundation upon which Berkeley built his whole early system of spiritism, and which even afforded him an image or likeness of God,[88] since "all the notion I have of God is obtained by reflecting on my own soul." [89] The sort of crisis through which Berkeley was passing could be given no more vigorous expression than the remarkable and very free rendition of Fénelon, in which Berkeley cries:

Thou and only Thou, appearest in everything. When I consider Thee, O Lord, *I* am swallowed up and lost in contemplation of Thee. Everything besides Thee, even my own existence, vanishes and disappears in the contemplation of Thee. *I* am lost to myself and fall into *nothing* when I think on Thee. The man who does not taste Thee has a relish of nothing. *His* being is vain, and his life but a dream.[90]

So much for spiritism. So much for rationalism, and indeed all "isms" whatsoever, for "everything . . ., even my own existence, vanishes and disappears." God is proved not through my existence, nor through the existence of anything, but rather through the relativity, the dependence, the nothingness of everything, objects, subjects, the world of sense, the concepts of reason, and the rational, relative absolute upon which all such reasoning rests. God is not such an absolute, but *the* absolute, and He is proved not by the self, but by its annihilation, not through the adequacy of any deductions or demonstrations, but through their inadequacy, not through thought, not through contemplation, but through life.

---

[85] G. Ess., F. iv, p. 168.
[86] *Ibid.*, p. 169.
[87] Pr., F. i, p. 327.

[88] 3D., F. i, p. 448.
[89] *Ibid.*
[90] G. Ess., F. iv, p. 169; my italics.

LIFE

In accordance with this new sense of the practical, we find Berkeley already beginning to qualify the rigid, mathematical, ethical doctrine he had offered to the world only a year before. Reason, it is true, is still considered the "more noble" part of the soul,[91] or "the human part," as distinguished from the passions "common to us with brutes." [92] But morality leads us beyond the "human" altogether, and something more than human reason is required by the soul in its struggle with evil, for a human soul, if "it were not aided from heaven by religion would almost universally be vanquished." Human reason is no longer "the great spring and source of moral actions," [93] but "the main duty," now placed "above all others, is charity." [94] And charity is no longer recommended on the ground of utility or any purely rational *ground* whatsoever, but "because it is agreeable to the intention of the Author of our being," [95] not the "Author of Nature" who figured so prominently in the *Treatise*.

Just as reason must be transfigured by that sense of the irrational which determines it to be reason, so also education must be more than the study of "certain minute particulars which are valuable for no other reason but because they are despised and forgotten by the rest of mankind." [96] Education must be made practical, though what is truly practical is precisely that which, judged from the common-sense point of view, is impractical, for the university is a monastery, a "blessed retreat" remote from the world, where men enjoy "the sweets of solitude, and yet converse with the greatest *Genii* that have appeared in every age." [97] Common sense takes certain desires or interests for granted, and regards as "practical" whatever conduces to the realization of these fixed or "abstract" ends. Education, however, as Berkeley now comes to see, consists precisely in breaking down such inner rigidities, in initiating a fermentation which, far from leaving the soul intact, as it was before, enters into its very core and transforms all its desires and interests, "opening the imagination," developing "reason," and lifting the soul "in the ascent of life." [98]

[91] *Ibid.*, p. 179.
[92] *Ibid.*
[93] *Ibid.*, p. 188.
[94] *Ibid.*, p. 189.
[95] *Ibid.*

[96] *Ibid.*, p. 174.
[97] *Thoughts on Public Schools and Universities*, G. Ess., F. iv, p. 164.
[98] *Ibid.*, p. 163.

In this eminently Platonic conception, even the tripartite form of the Platonic psychology is preserved, for "in the scale of pleasure," writes Berkeley,[99] "the lowest are sensual delights, which are succeeded by the more enlarged views and gay portraitures of a lively imagination; and these give way to the sublimer pleasures of reason, which discover the causes and designs, the frame, connection, and symmetry of things, and fill the mind with the contemplation of intellectual beauty, order, and truth." In youth, the mind is fascinated by the novelty and luster of sensuous objects,[100] and some, indeed, "from a want of knowing other pursuits" never advance beyond this inner childhood. Education, however, is the process in which we come to "live," or in which our higher faculties unfold through imagination and reason, until finally the soul, becoming conscious of itself as this unfolding, and grasping the dynamic principle of its own being, wastes itself away "tortured with an extreme innate desire of that perfection which it despairs to obtain."[101] Reason itself is only a midpoint, a subtle link between the human and that nothingness beyond the human, a phase or aspect of life. Hence "the mind of man must be raised to a higher pitch," beyond reason to life, and beyond life to death.

DEATH

The crisis which threatened Berkeley's speculations at this time and which lifted them to another plane was based primarily upon a new self-consciousness, a sudden sense of the vital background that underlies all speculation and *obliquely* yields it its proper meaning as speculation (*speculum*). This consciousness of "the gradual opening of the imagination" and the "unfolding," or "ascent of life," as the larger practical setting within which all "rational" speculation must take place, inevitably "kindles a new fire in the soul," [102] for it leads on by a new and more disquieting dialectic to an absolute in whom "I am lost to myself and fall into nothing," [103] a final nothingness in which "everything . . . vanishes and disappears." [104] It is only an abstract or inadequately conscious type of reflection that can think of life without thinking of death. Three of

[99] *Ibid.*, p. 164.
[100] *Ibid.*, p. 163.
[101] G. Ess., F. iv, p. 184.

[102] *Ibid.*, p. 159.
[103] *Ibid.*, p. 169.
[104] *Ibid.*

Berkeley's *Guardian* essays are entirely devoted to this subject alone, but the thought of death hovered over all the writings of this period and it was this which, it is not difficult to see, really constituted the crisis through which he was passing.

There are clear traces of his former rationalistic view of "immortality," as in the sixth essay, where he speaks of the necessity of "regards beyond the grave" for "the bulk of mankind." [105] Except for a few passages of this sort, however, it is clear that the whole tone of his feeling has altered, especially in the last essay, which he devoted specifically to this topic.[106] "Immortality" is no longer an external problem, as it appeared to the free-thinkers, a theory to be weighed in the balance and proved or disproved or judged questionable according to the categories of "reason." It is rather something concerning life itself, or the very consciousness out of which all such categories grow, and thus too important to be proved, or disproved, or even dealt with in any such way. Rather it is a "question" not a problem, a question which he *himself* faces. There is no further talk of a "natural immortality," or any sort of doctrine, "following" from rational "presuppositions." Rather it belongs to the more intimate sphere presupposed by all such presuppositions. He speaks of it as "a new fire in the soul," [107] an "appetite," [108] a "sense," [109] and a "belief . . . supernaturally revealed," [110] for it is constituted only by that supernature brooding over all things natural, that irrational attending all things rational, and that "nothing" in which "I am swallowed up and lost." [111] The lack of it cannot be repaired, therefore, by any "rational" or "natural" argument, nor by the observation of any "natural" fact, for it cuts much deeper than these. It belongs to a different plane of existence, and the failure to grasp it proceeds from an abstraction, an unconsciousness so profound that it may only be described as "a poverty of imagination," or more adequately as a "narrowness of soul," [112] of a soul, that is, which has not yet "unfolded" to a final breaking point, nor yet developed a sense of life.

Berkeley, therefore, begins his last essay on this subject with a consideration not of the beginning, but of the ending of

[105] *Ibid.*, p. 161.
[106] *Christian Ideas of a Future State,* G. Ess., F. iv, p. 183.
[107] G. Ess., F. iv, p. 159.
[108] *Ibid.*, p. 144.
[109] *Ibid.*, p. 145.
[110] *Ibid.*, p. 146.
[111] *Ibid.*, p. 169.
[112] *Ibid.*, p. 146.

"reason and understanding," which though it "placeth us above the brute part of the creation, doth also subject our minds to greater and more manifold disquiets." [113] The unfolding or "ascent of the soul" ends, as it begins, with "disquiet." "Immortality" is such a disquiet, the final disquiet, a "torture" [114] which can never be appeased save only in the mystery of its infinite anguish. It is the "sense" of that "nothing" into which "everything vanishes and disappears," or finally of that "eye of infinite wisdom" [115] judging every finite action and "beholding the very soul, the naked soul." [116]

[113] *Ibid.*, p. 183.
[114] *Ibid.*, p. 184.

[115] *Ibid.*, p. 158.
[116] *Ibid.*, p. 145.

PART III

SCEPTICISM AND FAITH.
THE EMERGENCE OF THE PRACTICAL

"To consider the ways of men, one would think them never to die."
Rhode Island Sermon. (F. iv, p. 386.)

SCEPTICISM AND FAITH. THE EMERGENCE
OF THE PRACTICAL

DURING the period we have just considered Berkeley was occupied with his first elaboration of the logical principles suggested in the *Commonplace Book*. In this first development of his thought he was guided by a strong faith in "reason" and a general sympathy with the Deistic currents of contemporary thought. While he began with an appeal to the concrete, which he temporarily confused with the empirically given, and while his concrete logic at many points led him beyond the results of such thinking, he was, until the *Three Dialogues*, largely unconscious of this conflict, and confused his new logic with the method of the rationalists. Like them, he thought of himself as building theories and eventually erecting a "system" which should refute scepticism, clear up obscurities impeding the advance of human "knowledge," and generally justify the ways of God to man by means of the "light of nature," just as Newton had "explained" the workings of the physical universe by means of a fixed, mechanical "system."

Although there are a few specific points, it is true, on which Berkeley finds himself bound to disagree with the new mechanical science, as, for example, fluxions, he never thinks of generally questioning its results, and views his own work as a broader application of the same method. Thus he declares in the *Commonplace Book* that "We can prove Newton's propositions more accurately, more easily, & upon truer principles than himself." [1] He was, therefore, actuated by the same basic motive as the Deists, and it is most significant that he does not directly attack them until the crisis of the third dialogue and the *Guardian Essays*, though the Deistic controversy was raging in Dublin throughout the whole of this period. Indeed, as we have seen, while Berkeley nowhere specifically advocates Deism in so many words, he does, nevertheless, radically oppose the more traditional, orthodox irrationalism of his superior, Brown, and of King. Leading a secluded life within the confines of Trinity College, he shared the widespread enthusiasm engendered by the "New Philosophy," and endeavoured through his

[1] C. B. H., 901; J., 927.

new method to lead it to further conquests in the explanation, by purely "rational" principles, of the phenomena of vision, the paradoxes of the new mathematics, and the "articles" of religion. The strangely irrational consequences to which his new method really led him, however, brought him to the crisis we have attempted to trace in the last two chapters.

This crisis is followed by a remarkable change in tone, which is discernible in every phase of Berkeley's life. In contrast to the preceding period, he now emerges as the defender of a definitely irrational faith, and hence comes into violent and persistent collision with Deism. In place of the marked sympathy with the results and methods of "science" so clearly observable in the early writings, he now recognizes more adequately the destructive import of his concrete method, and consequently undertakes a detailed logical examination of scientific procedure both in natural science and mathematics. In his writings he betrays a profound scepticism concerning what was commonly called "reason," and turns from contemplation to "action." There is a polemic note in all of his publications that is lacking in the earlier treatises, which he had dedicated more to the exposition of new principles for their own sake than to the criticism of theoretical and ultimately practical errors. In turning to this period of Berkeley's life, it is as if we were shifting to a different key, or passing from one level of existence to an entirely different plane, the plane of the practical as opposed to the theoretical, of "life" as opposed to reason, and of religion as opposed to philosophy.

CHAPTER IX

PRACTICAL PHILOSOPHY

BERKELEY returned from his long visit to Oxford toward the end of August. In September, Lord Peterborough must have decided to offer him, on the basis of Swift's recommendation, the position as chaplain in his embassy to the King of Sicily. Foreign travel was then so expensive that it was impossible for one in Berkeley's circumstances to go abroad except as the member of an embassy or as a tutor. Locke had obtained his early foreign experience in the former manner, Hobbes in the latter. Berkeley was fortunate enough to be able relatively early in life to take advantage of both methods. In October he received a license permitting him to absent himself from the College, and on the fifteenth he left London for France.

One of the other members of the embassy was named Oglethorpe, and it has been suggested that he was the future general whose Georgia colony later flourished on the ruins of Berkeley's Bermuda project, but he was probably a brother.[1] In Paris, Berkeley was shown the sights of the city by the Abbé d'Aubigne, who apparently knew Malebranche, for on November 24, 1713, he writes Percival: "today he is to introduce me to Father Malebranche." It is not certain whether the visit ever took place, as Berkeley says nothing more in this connection. The fantastic story, told by Stock and elaborated by De Quincey and others, that Berkeley's visit was responsible for Malebranche's death is unquestionably false, as this event did not occur until two years later, at which time Berkeley was in England. Nevertheless, it is quite possible, as his remark to Percival shows, that he did see Malebranche in 1713, though none of the extant letters speaks further of such a meeting. A personal conversation may have convinced him that he was not really so far from the position of the great philosopher-priest as he had once imagined,[2] although there can be no question that his feeling of divergence, so marked in the references of the *Commonplace Book* as well as the *Treatise* and the *Three Dialogues*, was grounded on a very real contrast not only in the

---

[1] Bruce, *Life of Oglethorpe.*   [2] Percival letter, November 27, 1710.

speculative "results" of the two thinkers but in the underlying method generating these results. That the nature of this contrast became clearer to Berkeley is manifest from the more profound and more methodological character of his later criticism in the third edition of the *Dialogues* (1734).[3] Indeed, the relation between Berkeley and his great French contemporary throws so much light on Berkeley's thought and the "practical" phase of it which was at this time dominant, and which may have been rendered even more dominant by actual contact with the most eminent living representative of the Cartesian rationalistic tradition, that we must pause to consider it in further detail.

BERKELEY AND MALEBRANCHE

The *Commonplace Book* indicates that Berkeley possessed a thorough knowledge of Malebranche's masterpiece, the *Recherche de la Vérité*, and the many detailed similarities of doctrine show the considerable extent to which he was influenced by his early reading of this justly famous work. Thus, almost all of his arguments concerning the relativity of the sensory qualities, such as the "tepid water" argument of the first dialogue, can be found in Malebranche. Furthermore, Malebranche, like Berkeley, made no distinction between the primary and secondary qualities, maintaining that all sensory qualities are equally subjective. Malebranche also chose sight for particular consideration as the "noblest" sense, and his resulting theory of vision, according to which distance is not perceived directly but at least in part indirectly from sensory signs, could not have failed to influence Berkeley. Moreover both philosophers maintained that the self was not known through sensation, or "idea," but through another avenue which Berkeley finally called notional knowledge, and Malebranche the "sentiment intérieure." At first sight, this parallelism seems to be maintained even when we compare the broader aspects of the two systems, since Malebranche certainly possessed an intense feeling for religion which not only coloured many detailed features of his thought, but determined the actual course of his life, and must in many ways have exemplified the very ideals which were becoming dominant in Berkeley's own life at the time of his visit to Paris.

---

[3] Though in *Alciphron*, 1732 (F. ii, p. 174), he merely restates the early "common-sense" objections of the *Principles*.

In spite of these points of similarity, however, Berkeley had felt from the first that his whole approach was opposed to that of Malebranche, a feeling which is apparent in the *Commonplace Book*, and which he never lost. Thus, in the *Principles* he criticizes "occasionalism" as "extravagant" and "incomprehensible." [4] In the second dialogue, he supplements this rather unphilosophical criticism by the more specific objections that the "action" of the self and of "God" cannot be known as an "idea" or object, and that in Malebranche's view "the material world" serves "no purpose." [5] It is not until the third edition of the *Dialogues* in 1734 that Berkeley definitely comes to base his criticism on a difference in method. In spite of the religious feeling, which he now shares with Malebranche, and his agreement "that in God we live and move and have our being," [6] he perceives that there is a fundamental difference between them with respect to logic. Malebranche "builds on the most abstract general ideas," and remains, notwithstanding his deep religious feeling, a rationalist or intellectualist. It is this fundamental difference in method which justified Berkeley's sense of opposition, and which underlay the many more detailed criticisms of Malebranche's conceptions scattered through his writings, to which we must now at least briefly refer.

Perhaps the most remarkable similarity between Berkeley and Malebranche concerns their theories of vision. Malebranche points out in one of his chapters on vision that our judgments of visual distance are so confused that it is often necessary for us to verify them by means of touch. [7] As Berkeley twice refers to this same chapter in the *Commonplace Book* [8] it is impossible to avoid the conclusion that it influenced him in connection with the exaggerated importance assigned to touch in his *New Theory of Vision*. [9] Malebranche speaks also of certain "natural" judgments by means of which we correct the confused impressions of sense so that we see the further corners of a cube presented in perspective, for example, as large as the nearer corners. [10] These "natural judgments," he says, are like other

---

[4] Pr., secs. 70, 71, 148.
[5] 3D., F. i, pp. 426–427.
[6] *Ibid.*, p. 427.
[7] "Nous avons même de la peine à juger avec quelque certitude du rapport qui se trouve entre deux corps qui sont tout proche de nous; il les faut prendre entre nos mains et les tenir l'un contre l'autre pour les comparer. . . ." *Oeuvres de Malebranche*, 2 v., Paris, 1853, Deuxième Série, *Recherche de la Vérité*, Book I, ch. 6, p. 55.
[8] C. B. J., 264, 266.
[9] Cf. Ch. IV.
[10] *Op. cit.*, p. 57.

and more correct sensations excited in us by the author of nature, and his language reminds one strongly of Berkeley's "sudden judgments" by which distances are "suggested" to us, and even of the "divine language of nature" in which the *New Theory of Vision* culminates.[11] These similarities are so striking that one writer has even suggested that Berkeley's new theory is completely unoriginal.[12] A careful comparison of the two theories, however, shows that such is not the case.

In the first place, the underlying purpose of Malebranche's whole discussion of vision is to demonstrate the unreliability of sensory knowledge. Sight is chosen as the "noblest" of the senses, and used as a crucial example. If this sense can be shown to be deceptive, the inaccuracy of the rest will follow.[13] Such an attack on the veracity of the senses, and the resulting contrast between sensual and purely intellectual knowledge of the external world, was foreign to the deeper currents of Berkeley's thought. Thus, in the *Three Dialogues* he says of Malebranche: "he maintains that we are deceived by our senses, and know not the real natures or the true forms and figures of extended beings; of all which I hold the direct contrary." [14] For Berkeley the isolation of the intellectual from the sensory in this way, and its hypostatization into an independent "external world," was one of the most common and most dangerous examples of artificial abstraction, or misuse of the category of substance. Furthermore, this intellectualistic conception of the external world led Malebranche, as it had led Descartes, to think of visual knowledge in a mathematical way, and to speak of a "natural geometry" of the eye.[15] Berkeley denied, from the beginning, the relevance of rays and angles to the concrete facts of vision, and he is rightly given the credit for being the first to study vision "phenomenologically" rather than on the basis of some abstract theory of how vision must be. He did not deny the importance of geometry. This would be absurd, of course, for our judgments may be correlated with geometrical facts and relations.

---

[11] "Cependent ce qui n'est en nous que sensation, pouvant être considéré par rapport à l'auteur de la nature qui l'excite en nous comme une espèce de jugement, je parle quelquefois des sensations comme de jugements naturels. . . ." Bk. I, ch. 7, p. 57.

[12] Mahaffy, *Descartes*, p. 150. He is thinking of Descartes rather than of Malebranche. Malebranche, however,

follows Descartes' *Dioptrique* very closely.

[13] "Ainsi il suffira de ruiner l'autorité que les yeux ont sur la raison pour nous détromper et pour nous porter à une défiance générale de tous nos sens." Ch. 6, p. 44.

[14] 2D. (3rd ed.), F. i, p. 427.

[15] *Dioptrique*, Disc. VI, *Oeuvres* (Adam), VI, p. 137.

What he denied was the reduction of visual perception to the abstractions either of geometry or physiology, and what he strove for was a description of the concrete whole of consciousness, of which these "realms" are only artificially reified aspects. Such an attempt to describe concrete consciousness was quite alien to Malebranche, for whom the conscious visual perception was a mass of confused subjective impressions, themselves regarded as the causal "results" of true and absolute things revealed by reason (abstraction).

Malebranche held that distance was directly perceived, although the diagram which he constructed and which is printed at the beginning of chapter nine of the *Recherche de la Vérité*, if pushed to its logical consequences, seems enough to prove the truth of Berkeley's conclusion that distance is rather a "construction" than a datum. Malebranche, however, after showing that our judgments of rectilinear distance are inevitably inaccurate, lets the matter drop.[16] His point of view is, nevertheless, closer to Berkeley's than that of Descartes, since he laid less stress on "the natural geometry of the eye," and mentioned five other indirect methods of judging distance, which, in the main, agree with those of Berkeley.[17] Malebranche even goes so far as to identify the indirect method of intervening objects as the principal means of judging distance,[18] and followed Descartes in explaining the increased apparent magnitude of the horizontal moon through this principle.[19] Berkeley's explanation of this phenomenon, on the other hand, stressed the factor of faintness resulting from atmospheric interference, and the general association of spatial magnitude with horizontal rather than vertical distances.[20]

---

[16] *Op. cit.*, p. 65.

[17] The methods Berkeley recognizes are: 1. intervening objects; 2. binocular accommodation; 3. confusion when an object approaches very close to the eye; 4. faintness indicating distance; 5. monocular accommodation; 6. size and kind of object (past experience); 7. apparent magnitude. Malebranche recognizes besides the natural geometry, which he seems to confuse with binocular accommodation (p. 65): 1. monocular accommodation; 2. apparent magnitude; 3. past experience; 4. confusion and faintness, indicating distance; 5. and principally, intervening objects. The difference with respect to confusion is explained

by the fact that Berkeley was thinking of the confusion arising from objects extremely close to the eye, while the indistinctness of distant objects, which Malebranche called confusion, was termed *faintness* by Berkeley. The only essential difference between the two positions is Berkeley's sharp denial of the natural geometry and his consequent isolation of binocular accommodation as a separate method not to be confused with the natural geometry.

[18] *Ibid.*, p. 69.

[19] *Ibid.*, pp. 70–71. Cf. Descartes, *Dioptrique*, Disc. VI, *Oeuvres* (Adam), VI, p. 145.

[20] N. T. V., secs. 68–73.

The fundamental opposition between the two theories, however, is connected with Berkeley's sense for the concrete realities of experience, and his unwillingness to abandon these for the sake of remote geometrical and physiological theories. Thus Malebranche's discussions of the vast number of inconceivable worlds which may be involved in a drop of water,[21] and the elaborate discussions of brain traces and animal spirits which fill Book III of the *Recherche de la Vérité* seemed inconclusive as well as dull. It is not so easy to separate the rational from the empirical, with which it is fused and interfused. One cannot simply abandon experience as inaccurate, and then theorize the world into existence. This is the true meaning of the criticisms of Malebranche's theory of vision in the *Commonplace Book*.

At the beginning of chapter six, Malebranche describes the physiology of the eye and, in connection with his natural geometry, shows how the lens acts as a natural glass, necessarily altering the appearance of the object as it changes in figure, in distance from the retina, and from the other lens.[22] Hence it follows that one can never be sure that two men see objects in the same way, since it cannot be doubted that the configuration of the ocular organs is at least slightly different.[23] Berkeley objects strenuously to this undue extension of the field of physiology,[24] which ignores the conscious judgment that is always present, interpreting and correcting our sensations. Conscious vision cannot be compared with an automatic camera, because conscious vision constantly corrects itself, something that no camera can do. Not only do we correct our mistakes, but these corrections actually enter into what we see,[25] so that it is never really possible, after the facile manner of Malebranche, to separate the inadequate, "confused," sensory content from the exclusively intellectual (abstract) truth. If sense is confused, intellect is also confused, and if intellect is clear what we see also will be clear. It will thus be possible for two men with exceedingly different sensory organs to make allowances for these differences,

---

[21] Ch. 6.

[22] ". . . nous devons considérer que nos propres yeux ne sont en effet que des lunettes naturelles; que leurs humeurs font le même effet que les verres dans les lunettes; et que, selon la situation qu'ils gardent entre eux, et selon la figure du *cristallin* et de son éloignement de la *rétine*, nous voyons les objets différemment." Bk. I, ch. 6, p. 49.

[23] "De sorte qu'on ne peut pas assurer qu'il y ait deux hommes dans le monde qui les voient précisément de la même grandeur, ou composés de semblables parties, puisqu'on ne peut pas assurer que leurs yeux soient tout à fait semblables." *Ibid.*

[24] C. B. J., 264, 266.

[25] Cf. Berkeley's explanation of the horizontal moon phenomenon.

and not only this, but actually to see the same thing in the same space, for what we see is not merely an ineffable sense impression, but something, — an interpretation as well. Hence we find the pregnant notation in the *Commonplace Book* [26] written during the early development of the *New Theory of Vision*: "Malebranche out in asserting we cannot possibly know whether there are two men in the world that see a thing of the same bigness. V. L I c. 6."

We have already referred to Berkeley's criticism of what seemed to him Malebranche's arbitrary separation and hypostatization of the primary qualities, together with certain mathematical relations, into an isolated, "real" world. His criticism of this position, together with the ultimate scepticism it implies, runs through the whole *Commonplace Book*, and is repeated again in the third edition of the *Three Dialogues* published in 1734, so that we must suppose it to be a most fundamental element in his opposition to Malebranche's system. The development of this objection, as revealed in the *Commonplace Book*, is of great interest. Berkeley's first notation concerns the ontological distinction between colour and extension. Why should colour not be in bodies as much as extension? [27] Shortly after this, he sees the sceptical implications of Malebranche's theory of matter in their full meaning. If matter is to be wholly external to consciousness how can we know the spatial "proportions" of things? [28] It is a high tribute to Berkeley's youthful perspicacity that he was able to see that it was an abstract, hypostatizing, and "externalizing" logic, which inevitably brought the Cartesian "demon" of scepticism in its train. [29] Later, he comments on the weakness of Malebranche's "proofs" for the existence of matter, and though his short criticism [30] does not reveal a very thoroughgoing understanding of the Cartesian point of view, [31]

[26] J., 266.
[27] C. B. J., 274.
[28] C. B. J., 278.
[29] Malebranche's account of the "demon" is Cartesian to the last detail. Thus he says no demon whatsoever could convince us of immediate intuitive truths such as simple mathematical propositions. It is only where memory comes into play that the demon may fool us. P. 618.
[30] C. B. J., 697.
[31] Berkeley, for example, mentions "Scripture" as one of Malebranche's proofs. This is hardly fair. Malebranche

directly follows Descartes in basing his belief in matter on God's perfection and His consequent inability to deceive. Thus he says: "De ce principe que Dieu n'est point trompeur, on pourrait aussi conclure que nous avons effectivement un corps auquel nous sommes units d'une façon particulière, et que nous sommes environnés de plusieurs autres." Bk. VI, ch. 6, p. 620. Furthermore, the existence of God and His perfection do not rest upon the authority of revelation but are, according to Malebranche, subject to strict rational proof. "Il est évident que

no one can read Malebranche's discussion of this question [32] without realizing the weakness of the "causal" position which does at last lead him to offer as a real "reason" what Berkeley calls "our great propension to think so."[33] In the next notation,[34] however, Berkeley checks his sceptical doubts concerning Malebranche's matter. "On second thoughts," he says, "I am on t'other extream. I am certain of that which Malbranch seems to doubt of, viz. the existence of bodies." Malebranche's matter is a figment of the philosophic imagination, an abstraction, a word. It is absurd to doubt the existence of external bodies, — and this is the only sense in which it is appropriate to use the word "matter."[35] After playing abstraction against abstraction, therefore, he comes back, as always, to the concrete whole of experience of which all such external worlds are only phases.

Malebranche disagrees with Descartes concerning our knowledge of the self. While we know it more distinctly than we know our own and surrounding bodies, our knowledge of it is far less perfect than our knowledge of them.[36] This is because we do not know the soul by idea but only *a posteriori* and by a certain "interior sentiment." If we possessed the "idea" which God has of our soul we should have *a priori* the knowledge of all the sensory modifications of which we are capable.[37] This eminently rationalistic conception of the soul was very repugnant to Berkeley. The soul and its acts were for him something totally different from a geometrical figure whose properties could be de-

---

la certitude de la foi dépend aussi de ce principe qu'il y a un Dieu qui n'est point capable de nous tromper. Car l'existence d'un Dieu et l'infaillibilité de l'autorité divine sont plutôt des connaissances naturelles et des notions communes à des esprits capables d'une sérieuse attention, que des articles de foi. . . ." P. 620. G. A. Johnston has followed Berkeley in attributing the appeal to scriptural authority to Malebranche and thus making his view of the existence of matter weaker than it really was. Berkeley nowhere gives any criticism of Malebranche's direct proof of God.

[32] Bk. IV, pt. ii, ch. 6.

[33] ". . . mais c'est qu'il n'est pas nécessaire d'examiner d'abord par de grandes réflexions une chose dont personne ne doute, et qui ne sert pas de beaucoup à la connaissance de la physique considérée comme une véritable science." Bk. VI, pt. ii, p. 624.   [34] C. B. J., 698.

[35] Also cf. C. B. J., 812.

[36] "On peut conclure de ce que nous venons de dire qu'encore que nous connaissions plus distinctement l'existence de notre âme que l'existence de notre corps et de ceux qui nous environnent, cependant nous n'avons pas une connaissance aussi parfaite de la nature de l'âme que de la nature des corps. . . ." Bk. III, pt. ii. ch. 7, p. 306.

[37] "Mais si nous voyions en Dieu l'idée qui répond à notre âme, nous connaîtrions en même temps ou nous pourrions connaître toutes les propriétés dont elle est capable; comme nous connaissons ou nous pouvons connaître toutes les propriétés dont l'étendue est capable, parce que nous connaissons l'étendue par son idée." *Ibid.*

duced in such a way. While he also first thought of the self in "causal" terms, he always maintained that to know the "soul" required an unique sort of knowledge. You cannot know the soul by algebra or geometry. This is the emphatic and reiterated burden of the *Commonplace Book*. We cannot, therefore, be surprised at Berkeley's strong dissent from Malebranche's divine mathematics of the soul: "Absurd," he writes, "that men should know the soul by idea — ideas being inert, thoughtless. Hence Malbranch confuted." [38] This divergence naturally became more extreme as Berkeley gave up his early spiritism, and substituted the more profound view suggested in the doctrine of the later *Commonplace Book* that the self cannot be "known" at all. Thus, he could by no means rest satisfied with the "sentiment intérieure" through which we are supposed by Malebranche to know the soul.[39] How is it to be distinguished from idea or sensation? This point becomes particularly decisive when one finds that according to Malebranche not only the soul but also its modifications are known in this way.[40] For Berkeley, even as a spiritist, there were only subjects or objects and nothing hovering in between. Thus he says: [41] "De Vries will have it that we know the mind as we do hunger not by idea but sensation *conscientia*. So will Malbranch. This a vain distinction." It is not only vain but deceptive, since it rests primarily on a confusion between the self and its objects, a confusion of which Berkeley, as we have seen, finally became conscious. The real self is quite distinct from its modifications, and, indeed, we have seen how Berkeley always felt the category of substance to be entirely inadequate in understanding the self. To Malebranche's analytic understanding, however, the self was simply one among many objects. It was not known in the same clear manner as other objects, it is true, but Malebranche looked on this as an unfortunate limitation of the human mind. For God, it is only another object, like a triangle, whose properties may be deduced. From Berkeley's point of view this was to miss the significance of the self, first as an active subject, demanding an unique non-mathematical, noetic method, and finally as an ubiquitous factor involved in all experience, and in no sense whatsoever an "object" or "idea."

---

[38] C. B. J., 239. Cf. 3D., F. i, p. 426.
[39] *Recherche*, p. 307.
[40] ". . . on ne connaît ni l'âme ni ses modifications par des idées, mais seule- ment par des sentiments, et que tels sentiments de plaisir par exemple, de douleur de chaleur, etc." P. 307.
[41] C. B. J., 900.

The difference becomes even more acute when we approach the problem of freedom, which is, perhaps, the chief systematic difficulty in Malebranche's whole philosophy. It is true that Malebranche in various places asserts the freedom of the self. Thus, he says that our knowledge of the soul is sufficient to prove its immortality and liberty.[42] But it is unfortunately very difficult to see how his occasionalistic premises make any human freedom possible. This becomes particularly evident in Book VI, part two, where Malebranche denies any active agency not only to bodies but to souls as well.[43] Causal connections to be truly causal must be necessary. This leads to a thoroughly Humian result, for there is no really necessary connection, for example, between my willing to move my arm and the movement itself, nor between any two "objects" taken in abstract isolation from one another.[44] Hume's atomistic (abstract) sensationalism and Malebranche's extreme (abstract) rationalism thus lead to the same result.[45] Our will is only an occasional cause. It precedes the supposed effect but is not its real cause.[46] Only the infinite will of an infinitely perfect being may be a necessary and therefore true cause.[47] Finite beings cannot even move their own limbs. For to do so it would be necessary to understand the manipulation of the blood stream, the nerve currents, and the best anatomist would be at the same time the best athlete.[48]

Berkeley, as might be expected, took sharp issue with this outcome of Malebranche's rationalistic teaching. "We move our legs ourselves," he says in the *Commonplace Book*. "'Tis we that will their movement. Herein I differ from Malbranch." [49] It is true that Malebranche, in desperation, finally places human freedom among the transcendent mysteries of religion which, together with the Trinity, is to be believed rather than under-

---

[42] "Encore que nous n'ayons pas une entière connaissance de notre âme, celle que nous en avons par conscience ou sentiment intérieur suffit pour en démontrer l'immortalité, la spiritualité, la liberté et quelques autres attributs qu'il est nécessaire que nous sachions." P. 307.

[43] Thus he says: "Mais non seulement les corps ne peuvent être causes véritables de quoi que ce soit, les esprits les plus nobles sont dans une semblable impuissance." Bk. VI, pt. ii, p. 574.

[44] "Mais quand on examine l'idée que l'on a de tous les esprits finis, on ne voit point de liaison nécessaire entre leur volonté et le mouvement de quelque corps que ce soit; on voit au contraire qu'il n'y en a point et qu'il n'y en peut avoir." P. 573.

[45] Can it be accidental that even the same examples are employed by Hume?

[46] ". . . on ne doit pas s'imaginer que ce qui précède un effet en soit la véritable cause." P. 578.

[47] "Il n'y a donc que Dieu qui soit véritable cause et qui ait véritablement la puissance de mouvoir les corps." P. 576.

[48] P. 575.   [49] C. B. J., 553.

stood.[50] But this classification must have seemed to Berkeley to arise more from peculiar systematic exigencies than from any logic intrinsic in the situation itself. When Malebranche follows out the strict implications of his thought, the finite will is powerless and inert. Indeed, it is lost in the Godhead, for God is not only the cause of bodily motion, but also the source of all knowledge and of all voluntary action in subordinate spirits.[51] The fundamental voluntary urge in all men is directed by a necessary law towards the good or towards Himself.[52] Even when we sin we are striving toward the good in a confused way.[53] Sin is a reality, but Malebranche naturally has difficulties in explaining its possibility on the basis of such presuppositions. Thus he is not sure that it is a power,[54] and in the end it is God who vitalizes all things, and only God who thinks and acts.[55]

While Berkeley, at first, in consequence of his own similarly "causal" position, had to confront the same difficulty, he was never willing to sacrifice the concrete facts of moral experience for the sake of systematic (abstract) consistency. He never rationalized his conception of causality into a tautological necessity. Causal activity was always something creative for him and beyond the purely mathematical understanding. Thus, at first he believed that his fundamental distinction between the realm of objective fact and subjective action provided him with a means of reconciling God with human freedom, though, as we have seen, this distinction ultimately took him altogether beyond the "causal" position. Confronted with the same fundamental "mystery" which "causation," "action," or synthesis must possess for the analytic (abstract) understanding, Malebranche denied all "finite" causation whatsoever, and escaped, as all "rationalists" must escape, by means of an utterly (abstract) irrational principle, — the "will of God." It is this "infinite," incomprehensible will which alone is capable of holding the disunited elements of the world together. Berkeley was

[50] "En effet la raison humaine ne nous fait point comprendre qu'il y ait un Dieu en trois personnes, que le corps de Jésus-Christ soit réellement dans l'eucharistie, et comment il se peut faire que l'homme soit libre, quoique Dieu sache de toute éternité tout ce que l'homme fera." P. 265.

[51] "Ils ne peuvent rien connaître si Dieu ne les éclaire. Ils ne peuvent rien sentir si Dieu ne les modifie." P. 574.

[52] "Ce ne sont pas eux qui se meuvent vers le bien en général, c'est Dieu qui les meut." P. 575.

[53] P. 575.

[54] "Mais je ne sais si cela se peut appeler puissance." P. 574.

[55] "Corps, esprits, pures intelligences, tout cela ne peut rien. C'est celui qui a fait les esprits qui les éclaire et qui les agite. . . . Enfin c'est l'auteur de notre être qui exécute nos volontés." P. 578.

238 GEORGE BERKELEY

acute enough to see, though at first only vaguely, that the difficulty was logical, and while in his early spiritism he was himself guilty of attempting to escape by erecting an extraordinary "causal" or synthetic concept (the "infinite" or God) to "solve" all such disconcerting problems, he did perceive, at last, that such a *deus ex machina*, required by rationalism as a sort of waste-basket for everything "irrational," was no solution, and that the only escape was a new logic.

This difference leads us to a central point of view from which we can most readily discern the essential divergences of the two systems. Malebranche is essentially a rationalistic and contemplative philosopher, while Berkeley was becoming, both personally and logically, a voluntarist. For Malebranche, the contemplative ascetic, knowledge is impressed upon us from without by the divine will acting in our minds. We must free ourselves from the influences of sense and train our wills to submit to the divine illumination. We might be led to suppose that the essence of the universe is this constant omnipresent activity of God. But such is not the case. Before God could create the world, or act, He must first have had an idea.[56] The eternal ideas of all created things and all spirits thus lie in God as in a place.[57] For Berkeley God is never a place, — He is, even as a spirit, pure creative action, or will rather than idea. Ideas are in no sense prior to His will. The understanding that is necessary for conscious action is, of course, present in Him, or rather contained in the very notion of His will, for understanding and will are one.[58] When we turn to "man," we find that the same holds good. Knowledge is in no sense a passive contemplation, but rather an action of the mind. The divine light, or λόγος, is not something which impresses us from the outside as a stamp impresses wax, but something that lives and moves in us.

The original features of Berkeley's philosophy all arise from his attempt to work out this active, dynamic conception of knowledge, which finally culminated in a synthetic logic. This "causal" sort of logic often enables Berkeley to mediate between the sharp cleavages and distinctions in which Malebranche's thought so often terminates. Malebranche's world is

---

[56] "...il est absolument nécessaire que Dieu ait en lui-même les idées de tous les êtres qu'il a créés, puisqu'autrement il n'aurait pas pu les produire." Bk. III, p. 295.

[57] "Dieu est le monde intelligible ou le lieu des esprits, de même que le monde matériel est le lieu des corps...." Bk. III, p. 303.

[58] C. B. J., 866.

formally unified, it is true. All things are in God. But what a
medley this unity is! In the first place, there is God's intellect,
or ideas, which are distinguished from and prior to His will.
There is the world of corporeal objects, which was constructed
by God, but which, after being created, was essentially (abstractly) "external" to Him. Then, there are the finite spirits,
which are so sharply sundered from their own and other bodies
that no sort of interaction may ever occur between them, and in
whom the confused sense-impressions are separated from the
abstract thought. The new, active knowledge which Berkeley,
in his period of irrationalism, came to call "notional" enabled
him, in many cases, to transcend these dualisms. Thus intellect
and will are one.[59] God is not "external" to the natural world,
but, even as a spirit, is rather the living force which moves in it,
giving sense and meaning to its passive symbols, and making it a
divine language full of life and motion, transmitting a sense of
meaning and purpose to finite creatures. Furthermore, during
Berkeley's spiritistic phase, while the self is for him distinct
from its objects in a manner even more striking than for Malebranche, it nevertheless moves through them as an organizing
principle, and is bound together with them in such a way that
one cannot exist without the other. One may say that even the
unity of all things in God is simply another sharp mathematical
position, an "abstracted" identity, which exists alongside of
the obvious diversity and independence of things with which it
can never really be reconciled. On the one hand, the world is a
unity. On the other, it is a diversity of independent units. For
Malebranche's mathematical mind this is an insoluble mystery,
simply to be believed.

Nowhere does Berkeley's attempt to think causally or "actively" contrast more sharply with the analytic method than in
his treatment of the relation between knowledge and faith. For
Malebranche, the two are distinguished, and stand side by side
as two opposed methods of knowing, for what is a contradiction
to reason can be held by faith. For Berkeley also the two were
opposed, but not in such a way as to be ultimately (abstractly)
irreconcilable. Thus, like Berkeley, Malebranche held that faith
and reason offered parallel ways to truth,[60] but, for him, faith
was something definitely transcendent and non-rational, and
any synthesis of the two was unthinkable. Any attempt, for ex-

[59] *Ibid.*   [60] *Recherche*, p. 688.

ample, to reconcile human freedom with God's foreknowledge, or to explain the mystery of the Trinity was *a priori* doomed to failure.[61] Such mysteries are in a realm "above" and totally (abstractly) "distinct" from the realm of reason.

Although Berkeley started, as we have seen, from such a typically *Aufklärung* position, the effect of his wrestling with these problems, as shown in the *Siris*, was to bring the two realms together in the development of a form of knowledge which is not merely knowledge, in the accepted *Aufklärung* sense, nor yet merely faith. This makes it possible for him to find philosophical significance even in the "mysterious" doctrine of the Trinity. Berkeley finally felt most intensely the truth of Malebranche's own statement that God desires to be loved by an intellectual love rather than by blind instinct,[62] but, unlike Malebranche, he came to feel that this demanded a serious philosophical consideration even of the most intimate and sacred mysteries of religion. He did not feel that the dignity or integrity of the religious mysteries was in any sense destroyed in this process, for in the *Siris*, at least, it is not so much that religion is reduced to the level of the mathematical understanding as that mathematical understanding is lifted to the level of religion. As Berkeley finally came to perceive, understanding and mystery are not abstractly opposed categories. The realization of mystery is a necessary form of understanding, something that Malebranche would not admit. Thus, in the third book of the *Recherche*, he classifies the tenets of religion, distinguishing those that are understandable and provable from those that are incomprehensible. The "doctrines" of the immortality of the soul, original sin, and the necessity of grace can be proved by reason as well as tradition,[63] but human freedom, transubstantiation, and the Trinity, as the most sacred mysteries, cannot be established on the basis of human logic.[64] But is not the ultimate

---

[61] "On peut dire au contraire que les objections que l'on forme contre les principaux articles de notre foi, et principalement contre le mystère de la Trinité, sont si fortes qu'il n'est pas possible d'en donner des solutions claires évidentes, et qui ne choquent en rien notre faible raison, parce qu'en effet ces mystères sont incompréhensibles." Bk. III, ch. 2, p. 265.

[62] "Dieu veut en être aimé d'un amour de choix, plutôt que d'un amour distinct et d'un amour indélibéré, semblable à celui par lequel on aime les choses sensibles." Bk. III, ch. 4, p. 276.

[63] *Ibid.*, p. 266.

[64] "Mais on voit au contraire tous les jours qu'ils prennent occasion de la faiblesse des raisonnements de quelques scolastiques pour tourner en raillerie les mystères les plus sacrés de notre religion, qui dans la vérité ne sont point établis sur toutes ces raisons et explications humaines, mais seulement sur l'autorité de la parole de Dieu écrite ou non écrite, c'est à dire

supremacy of reason contained in the very nature of such a sharp classification? How can religion be dismembered into the perfectly demonstrable part and the mysterious part? This procedure, indeed, pays lip-service to the irrational. It recognizes its existence, classifies it, and then passes on oblivious.

Berkeley, on the other hand, could not thus "conveniently" ignore the irrational. He had to wrestle with it, trying to "reconcile" the freedom of man with God's foreknowledge, and trying to find "significance" in the doctrine of the Trinity. The result was that his reason was enriched through this contact with the irrational, and became at last in the *Siris* something far different from the mathematical understanding of the *Aufklärung*. He could not isolate the irrational as a certain fixed territory which could be tagged and then avoided. His concrete logic led him to see that things are too complexly interwoven to escape the difficulty in such a simple manner. While, for example, he distinguished the universal element from the sensory element in experience, he recognized at the same time that the two were bound together in such a way that universals deprived of all sensory content are empty and verbal. The abstract universals of Malebranche are not only bereft of all sensory content but of all connection with mind as well, so that they float on high in a pure and abstract ether of their own. This is the vicious, otherworldly sort of "Platonism" which even Malebranche wishes to eschew, for he repeats time and again that the eternal universals are *in* God. Nevertheless, neither he nor his English disciple Norris ever proves this fact. It is not organic to their thought, which in the end comes much nearer to demonstrating that God is in the universals than that the universals are in God. Berkeley felt acutely the inadequacy of a God who was no more than a receptacle for mathematics. Thus he says: "Malbranch does not prove that the figures and extensions exist not when they are not perceived. Consequently he does not prove, nor can it be prov'd on his principles, that the sorts are the work of the mind, and only in the mind." [65] This is why the eternal verities must "vanish." [66] They must vanish, that is, as abstractions.

Such, then, are the issues which Berkeley might have discussed with his great French contemporary if he actually met him at Paris in 1713. It would, of course, be absurd, in the light

transmise jusqu'à nous par la voie de la   [65] C. B. J., 296.
tradition." Bk. III, ch. 2, p. 265.   [66] C. B. J., 748.

of the evidence of the *Commonplace Book*, to deny Malebranche's influence on Berkeley's earlier reflections. In the explanation of evil which he offers at the end of the published
Principles, for example, and in his emphasis on the interest of
God (reason) in the whole system of reality rather than single
parts, in the *Passive Obedience*, as well as at other points, he definitely adopted thoughts which Malebranche had made peculiarly his own. Also in his use of the principle that God's wisdom
demands that He proceed through the simplest methods,[67] he is
following his French predecessor, though Berkeley used this
very principle with good effect in his criticism of the occasionalistic view of matter.[68]

But, as his thought advanced, the underlying methodological
difference between the two thinkers manifested itself more
clearly. While Berkeley undoubtedly learned a great deal from
Malebranche's theory of vision, the way in which the latter used
the abstractions of geometry and physiology to "explain" other
aspects of visual experience makes the similarity between the
two theories only a superficial one. Perhaps the most obviously
unsatisfactory result of Malebranche's abstract way of thought
was his theory of a "material" world existing in independence
from both "God" and the world of spirits. Not only did Berkeley's concrete, "irrational" logic break down this fixed and un-
yielding matter existing at the back of the world, but, as we
have noticed, it finally attacked the equally fixed and abstract
spiritual substance of the Cartesians as well. Malebranche recognized the inevitable difficulty which the concept of cause or
spiritual action must afford all abstract rationalism, since it is,
in its very nature, synthetic rather than analytic, and never can
become what is ordinarily termed an "object." It must consequently either be denied altogether (Hume) or thrown into a
"convenient" (systematic) pigeon-hole, the course chosen by
Malebranche. His solution was to reify this insoluble problem
into a mysterious, self-existent "Will of God." This will,
through its "infinite" rationality (i.e. irrationality), is the
necessary cause of all things, though for human (abstract)
reason the causing of one thing by another, the union of two
opposed or different things, must always remain incomprehensible. For an infinite reason, however, such differences resolve

---

[67] *Passive Obedience*.

[68] 3 D., F. i, pp. 431–434, and Pr.,
F. i, pp. 296–297. Cf., however, *Recherche*,
Bk. VI, p. 576, "Dieu n'a pas besoin d'instruments pour agir, il suffit qu'il veuille
afin qu'une chose soit."

into identities or "necessary" tautologies. Malebranche, like Berkeley himself in his youth, first destroyed all the connections of things by his abstract, rationalistic logic, and then conferred the impossible task of restoring them upon the "infinite" will of God, — thus "establishing" religion as a necessary repository for the residuum created by a first mistake. His thought is, therefore, never complete (concrete), but only a "reason" condemned to permanent partiality. The Cartesian "demon" dances over the fragments of this dismembered universe, and "blind" faith in the "premises" is the necessary counterpoise to the beautiful consistency of Malebranche's mathematical deductions.

Berkeley could not permanently rest content with any such equivocal solution, — the preservation of an utterly necessary (tautological) reason at the expense of an equally necessary unreason, the preservation of knowledge at the expense of faith, and of mathematical certainty at the expense of the Cartesian "demon." He himself started from such a position, but instead of continuing as before by jumbling all the difficulties together into one huge paradox, he preferred thinking through his paradoxes as he went along, irrationalizing or de-logicizing his abstract method itself in order to see if the humanity of his thought might be made a little less "human," and the thought perhaps a little less obviously "thought." This is the fundamental difference between them, a difference which may well have come to light in any conversation occurring in 1713, as Berkeley was at this time clearly aware of the revolutionary implications of his new, concrete mode of thinking, and the irrational realms into which it was irresistably pushing him. In February, Berkeley left Paris and the rationalistic visions of his great contemporary, and turned his thoughts to Italy.

PRACTICAL PHILOSOPHY

Berkeley was impressed by the impoverished condition of France. "I could assure you," he writes Percival, "that the French nation is so impoverished and dispeopled by the war, that we need not entertain any apprehensions of having a Pretender imposed upon us by their power. I speak this of my own knowledge, having passed through the heart of France, and been an eye-witness of its misery." [69] The ambassadorial party,

[69] Percival letter, February 19, 1714.

which counted nine nations among its members, crossed the
Alps in the heart of winter, and reached Leghorn in the middle
of February. That Berkeley's new feeling for the beauties of
nature was stimulated by this first passage of the Alps is apparent in a letter to his friend Pope, which recommends the glories
of Italy in general, and prescribes in particular mountain travel
as a literary necessity. "To enable a man to describe rocks and
precipices," he says, "it is absolutely necessary that he pass the
Alps." [70] He also expatiates in the same letter on the "Rape of
the Lock," which he had just read for the first time in finished
form, speaking enthusiastically of "those images, allusions, and
inexplicable beauties which you raise so surprisingly and at the
same time so naturally out of a trifle."

Peterborough left Leghorn alone and incognito, abandoning
his followers to while away the winter as best they could in their
somewhat uninteresting surroundings. "There are 2000 clergy
in the town," writes Berkeley, "and not one man of letters
worth knowing." In one of the Franciscan libraries, indeed,
they even showed him their "English" books, which turned out
to be Hebrew. Berkeley did, however, find a friend in Basil
Kennett, the author of *Roman Antiquities*, who was at that time
in charge of a chapel which the English residents had been
permitted to build at the special request of Queen Anne. Here
Berkeley preached two sermons.

The first of these, entitled "The Mission of Christ," was
preached on Palm Sunday, 1714. It reveals the extent to which
Berkeley's new feeling for the practical had transformed and
deepened his appreciation of the meaning of religion. It is true
that he starts by admitting that the natural light of "reason"
may give us "some sense of a Providence and of Religion," [71]
but he then proceeds to show in the main body of the text how
altogether inadequate this light is by itself, and how the message
of religion concerns all "mankind," [72] rather than merely those
lacking "leisure or abilities" and requiring "miracles" for their
conviction, as he had so plausibly and so Deistically maintained
in his youthful sermon on "The Revelation of Life and Immortality" in 1708. [73] The whole tone is now completely undeistic
in character, and shows that Berkeley is speaking not as a
spectator, reviewing various "theories" of religion, but as a

---

[70] Pope's *Works*, vol. IX, ed. Elwin
and Courthope, London, 1886.
[71] F. iv, p. 194.

[72] *Ibid.*, p. 193.
[73] *Ibid.*, p. 87.

participator trying to formulate something actually felt and lived not only by others but by himself. "Let us bethink ourselves," he says, "that in a few days the healthiest and bravest of us all shall lie mingled with the common dust." [74]   It is this sense of the "few days," speculatively, Deistically so trivial, that has lifted a new horizon of existence, lived existence, into the focus of his reflections, and relativized and subordinated all his past thought. A new logic is necessary to deal with those theoretically insignificant "situations" which we "ourselves" have to face. It is life as it has to be lived with which Berkeley is now grappling, not the "problem" of life. And it is not surprising, therefore, that the problematic in which he finds himself moving is that out of which his earliest reflections grew, the problematic of time. It is death which has cast its light (i.e. its shadow) over Berkeley's thought, not the abstract essence of death, but the unique, inescapable presence of *his* death. It is this light which has now revealed to him a new level of concreteness and bestowed upon his sermons their more vital tone.

He shows, however, the not wholly unbeneficent effects of his previous philosophical training in his grasp of the "practical" issue, for he wastes no time arguing the moral depravity of man, but proceeds at once to the heart of the matter, his metaphysical depravity. It is the hopelessly evanescent, temporal quality of finite existence that constitutes "the miserable forlorn condition of all mankind," [75] and that "estrangement from God" which, in spite of the "natural light" and all the other pitiful "endowments" of our nature, makes us all the more "by nature ignorant and brutish" and condemns us irrevocably to "the slavery of sin and death." [76] Thus "we cannot live without sinning," for to live is to be finite, to take the place of something else, to be chained in a network of inescapable relations, oppositions, and contradictions, "and the unavoidable reward of sin [i.e. life] is death." [77] To speak of a rational "escape" from such a metaphysical situation merely adds to the bitterness of our imprisonment, for any conceivable "escape," to say nothing of the "rational" escape, only entangles us further in the web of relativity. "By nature we are vessels of wrath, polluted with" a "corruption" which is essential, "unavoidable," and "original." This corruption most certainly enters into the knowing

[74] *Ibid.*, p. 204.
[75] *Ibid.*, p. 198.
[76] *Ibid.*, p. 199.
[77] *Ibid.*, p. 198.

faculty, which, as a phase of finite existence, is itself cursed with
relativity, "the shadow of death," and is capable of leading us,
therefore, only into further "darkness" and "ignorance." [78]
From this night there can be no conceivable escape. If there is
an inconceivable one, we may only "believe" in it,[79] nor "must
it be thought that the faith here required is an empty, notional
belief," [80] or just another sort of theory, since by passing to the
absolute we must, among other things, abandon the realm of
theory, not only for the unknown, but for the unknowable. In
the midst of the absolute nothingness, which is not even nothingness, that surrounds us, we must, therefore, accept, if we are
to accept anything, a hope that is a "hope" only through its
hopelessness. Such a "hope" is not to be attended with any enthusiastic rejoicing, nor with any sort of Deistic satisfaction, but
"with fear and trembling." [81]   In taking this "step," we are
leaving all "hope" far behind us. "Faith" must be a faith in
nothing, for what is there in which we may have faith? It will be
a faith "that sanctifies the heart," for what else can it sanctify?
It "shews itself in the fruits of the Spirit," [82] for in what else can
it show its fruits?

There can be no salvation through legal rites or ceremonial
observances,[83] since they only involve us further in that maze of
relativity from which there is no escape save through what may
"perfect or regenerate the soul." [84] What else may be regener-
ated? In contrast to his previous rationalistic position, Berkeley
now asserts that it is "in vain to expect salvation by the works
of the Law," [85] since human nature is too essentially corrupt "to
perform a perfect unsinning obedience" even "to it," and, in
fact, there is no "salvation" at all, but only a "faith," which, in
contrast to his earlier recommendations, cannot be "without
zeal or fervour," [86] in view "of our littleness" and the absolute
"majesty of . . . God." [87] Even were we able to fulfill the most
stringent of such rational regulations as those prescribed by the
"light of reason," we should, nevertheless, be far from the goal.

This becomes particularly manifest in the second sermon,
preached in the English chapel, on the subject of Christian
charity. The metaphysical "sin" in which we find ourselves

[78] *Ibid.*, p. 195.
[79] *Ibid.*, p. 201.
[80] *Ibid.*
[81] *Ibid.*, p. 201.
[82] *Ibid.*
[83] *Ibid.*, p. 196.

[84] *Ibid.*
[85] *Ibid.*, p. 197.
[86] *Ibid.*, p. 202. Cf. the sermon "Let
thy Zeal be according to Knowledge,"
Ch. VI.
[87] *Ibid.*

requires a metaphysical salvation. We cannot hope to extricate ourselves by any finite act or type of act, by the performance of this rather than that, by the fulfillment of any law, no matter how severe. Such a law will in the end be determined and therefore conquered by what it opposes, since in dissolving that, and thereby fulfilling itself, it will only dissolve itself. Salvation can be achieved by neither the fulfillment nor lack of fulfillment of any law, neither by evolution nor by revolution, since the most basic and destructive revolution conceivable would still leave us where we were. "Though you could speak with the tongues of men and angels, though you had the gift of prophecy and understood all mysteries and all knowledge, and though you had all faith so that you could remove mountains . . .," you are still "nothing." [88] All such changes no matter how extreme or violent leave us metaphysically where we were. "All knowledge" will not help, for "all knowledge" is relative, or, as we say, "about" something lying beyond ourselves, while "salvation" concerns "ourselves." No sort of "change" can assist us, for it is finiteness, relativity, or "change" that is the root of evil. Destroy everything, and you are still what you were, — "you are nothing," [89] and "the state of such persons [all persons] is desperate." [90] "They cannot hope for salvation," except through a revolution far more destructive and profound.

"Charity is the principal duty . . . without which all other pretensions to purity of faith or sanctity of life avail nothing at all." [91] It is in *caritas* that Berkeley finds the only truly metaphysical answer to that question which he has at last come to realize is the result of serious and unromantic reflection on the human state. Only through *caritas* is there any hope of effecting a revolution or change of state which can really change our state, since it overturns all things by leaving them just as they are, and conquers by opposing nothing. It rejects by accepting, and thus rejects absolutely, since in obeying the command that we should love one another,[92] we love not only our neighbour but what is not our neighbour, or, in other words, we love him not as our neighbour, but as an image of that One in whom and through whom we may pass beyond appearances, and, transcending the temporal and spatial barriers that separate all things, love him as "ourselves," as nothing. So "above all things, put on charity,

[88] *Ibid.*, p. 208.
[89] *Ibid.*
[90] *Ibid.*, p. 217.
[91] *Ibid.*, p. 211.
[92] *Ibid.*, p. 205.

which is the bond of perfectness"[93] and, therefore, the only possible gesture of defiance, the only paradox which is truly paradox (παρὰ δόξαν).

Through his concrete logic, which has led him past the whole network of relations or appearances in which our reason weaves its variegated patterns, Berkeley is brought into the realm of practical existence that possesses a metaphysics and a dialectic of its own. One of the first results of this chain of reflections, and one of the most obvious, is the change in his evaluation of charity, or *caritas*, which was in the *Passive Obedience* only one among several virtues enjoined by the law of reason, but which now comes to occupy an utterly unique position because of its absolute or dialectic character.

ADVICE TO TORIES

Stock tells an amusing anecdote [94] of one of Berkeley's experiences as a foreigner during his long stay in Leghorn. While sitting in the anteroom of the chapel one day, he was surprised by the sudden entrance of a number of priests, who made a complete circuit of the room muttering together a religious chant. As the representative of a foreign creed, Berkeley was alarmed lest he himself and his ministrations were being cursed or exorcised in some mysterious manner. The incantations, however, proved to be only the prevailing mode of rat extermination.

Peterborough returned from the South in the spring of 1714, but Berkeley felt the various restraints of his official position somewhat irksome, and in July took his leave of the rather quixotic ambassador, returning immediately to London by way of Paris, only a month before the death of the Queen.[95] Swift had just been sent to his unwelcome Irish exile. Other friends, however, were in the city, and he enjoyed further literary and philosophical discussions with Arbuthnot, Addison, and Pope. Several months later he wrote to Percival that the "troublesome times" made study infrequent.[96] He was in London at the time of the sudden death of the Queen, and witnessed at first hand the coming of the Hanovers, as well as the crash of the great Tory edifice which Bolingbroke had so brilliantly built and adorned. He was not at all well, and in July, 1715, was forced to retire into Gloucestershire for a two or three weeks' rest. Dur-

[93] *Ibid.*, p. 218.
[94] *Memoirs.*

[95] Percival letter, July 13, 1714.
[96] Percival letter, November 17, 1715.

ing this period of leisure he read Pope's *Homer* and paid his sensitive friend a most welcome compliment with regard to the relative merits of his translation and that of Addison's protégé Mr. Tickell.[97] "Some days ago," he writes, "three or four gentlemen and myself, exerting that right which all readers pretend to over authors, sate in judgment upon the two new translations of the first Iliad. Without partiality to my countrymen I assure you, they all gave the preference where it was due, being unanimously of opinion, that yours was equally just to the sense with Mr Tickell's, and without comparison more easy, more poetical, and more sublime." [98]

Berkeley's general sympathy with Tory principles only exaggerated his dismay at the revolutionary measures involved in the espousal by the party leaders of the Stuart cause; and, in this time of stress directed by his new sense of the futility of earthly revolutions, he remained steadfastly loyal to the government, and condemned the rebellion in the strongest terms. "If this news prove true, and the Tories openly engage in the attempt," he writes, "I shall think them guilty of as barefaced perjury and dishonesty as ever could be imputed to any set of men." [99] So intense were his feelings on this subject that he himself entered the arena and wrote a political treatise directed to "The Tories Who Have Taken The Oaths" abjuring them to refrain from all "illegal measures." [100] This treatise is definitely addressed to churchmen and those interested in the survival of Christianity. Such people were, like Berkeley himself, naturally in sympathy with the Tory party. They had, however, sworn oaths to support the government. The pamphlet purports to show that no considerations of personal sympathy or private advantage can justify the breaking of such oaths. Indeed, many features of this essay testify to the new importance which "practical" considerations were coming to possess in Berkeley's eyes. Thus, while it is only those who "will not be at pains to inquire into the merits of the Cause," who will judge the Church by the external behaviour of its votaries, Berkeley, nevertheless, maintains that what "gives any Church or Religion the Advantage

---

[97] This rivalry had led to the final rift between Pope and Addison.

[98] Pope, *Works*, vol. IX, ed. Elwin and Courthope, p. 3 (July 7, 1715).

[99] Percival letter, August 18, 1715.

[100] This anonymous treatise is entitled *Advice to the Tories who have taken the Oaths*. London, printed by R. Baldwin, and sold by R. Burleigh in Amen-Corner, 1715. Berkeley was first identified, from the evidence of the Percival letters, as its author by Th. Lorenz, who printed the text in *Arch. f. Gesch. der Phil.*, XIV, Heft iii, April, 1901, p. 312.

above Others, is the Influence it hath upon the Lives of its Professors."

There are several interesting passages in which Berkeley's Tory sentiments come to light. "I have neither so ill an opinion of you," he says, "nor so good a one of your Adversaries as to believe every Thing which they report to your Disadvantage." What he insists on is the "plain duty" of all to follow the oaths, and obey the legally constituted government. This may be rationally apprehended as a binding obligation since, "if Oaths are no longer to be esteemed sacred, what sufficient Restraint can be found for the irregular Inclinations of Men?" The objection is raised that if men had always been faithful to their oaths the Revolution could not have occurred. Berkeley replies, however, that "When the person ceaseth to be Sovereign, the Allegiance ceaseth to be due to him, and the Oath of course to bind. In the judgment of most Men this was the Case at the Revolution." It would be interesting to know what Berkeley might have replied if pressed further. How about the actual initiator of the Revolution? It is difficult to see how the motives of such an instigator could have been justified on Berkeley's principles. Like Hobbes, he could consistently pay allegiance to a revolution only after it was a *fait accompli*. This is the philosophy of a political spectator rather than a participator, and such was Berkeley's essential position. Our duty is to fit into the established scheme of things, not because it is in any way justifiable, but because the results of any "rebellion" are even less so. He remains aloof from the whole political turmoil as from the political universe, advising his Tory friends in the Church not to bother about the government so long as it is established, but to follow their "plain duty." Only thus, he was convinced, could they best serve those higher values to which their lives were dedicated, surely not by further jeopardizing them for the sake of violent measures, futile in the very degree of their violence.

It is interesting to follow Berkeley's comments on the stormy course of events. Walking through St. James Park one evening, he overheard a rebel whispering of "hereditary right" to a sentinel.[101] He comments on the apparent incompetency of the government and the ministers, and the "cheerful insolent behaviour of the Jacobites."[102] On November 3, after visiting with a high Tory friend, he says: "Things are altered . . . now," for he is "in

---

[101] Percival letter, September 8, 1715.   [102] Percival letter, September 22, 1715.

low spirits." A short time later he is reassured by Peterborough, now returned to London, who had from the first been sceptical of the Revolution. On November 17, he rejoices over the rebel defeat at Preston and the coming of what he hoped might be more quiet times. "I would much rather correspond with you," he finally writes to Percival, "on the beauties of the Latin authors than on the subject of news."

Berkeley was now thirty years old, and in spite of his powerful friends had, as yet, no stable position, beyond his very unremunerative connection with the College. It was most natural for him, therefore, to seek something more advantageous. In May, 1716, his friends had evidently been able to do something in his behalf, for he writes Percival that he soon expects to take "Charles Carr's living of St Paul's in Dublin," which was worth only one hundred a year, but was "consistent" with his Fellowship. Berkeley's association with the Tory cry of "Passive Obedience" proved, however, too much of a handicap.[103] Percival wrote to the Duke of Grafton, mentioning his recent pamphlet as a proof of loyalty. But it was of no avail. The Lords Justices in Ireland "made a strong representation against him," [104] and "one Tirrel" gained the living. So Berkeley had to abandon his hopes of a quiet niche where he might pursue his studies with some degree of comfort. During the summer he was offered the position of tutor to the son of Ashe, the Bishop of Clogher, whom he had known previously in Dublin, and with whom he was now much better acquainted, possibly through Swift, their mutual friend. According to G. M. Berkeley, his grandson, he was informed at this time by Ashe of the marriage of Swift and "Stella," and there is even a rumour that he himself persuaded Swift to take this step,[105] which cannot be regarded as impossible, since Berkeley was undoubtedly in Dublin at this time on the most intimate terms of friendship with both Swift and the Bishop of Clogher. Eliza Berkeley, indeed, goes so far as to assert as her "belief" that "both Dean Swift and Mrs. Johnson were actually the children of Sir William Temple, and the heavy tidings arrived not until the day on which the indissoluble knot

---

[103] According to Stock, it was owing to this that in spite of the favourable impression Berkeley had made on the Prince and Princess of Wales, to whom he was presented in 1716 by Molyneux, Lord Galway and the Lords Justices blocked his ecclesiastical preferment. Cf. Dering to Percival, June 1, 1716.

[104] Dering to Percival, June 1, 1716.

[105] Brit. Qu. Rev., "The Works of Berkeley," by G. N. Wright, vol. XXVI, 1857, p. 75.

was tied." [106] This, at least, affords some additional support for the view that Swift and Stella were in fact married. As other possibilities seemed closed to him, Berkeley decided to accept the offer of the Bishop of Clogher, and, in the fall, set off with young Ashe for a second and more extensive European tour.

[106] The passage from Monck Berkeley, Preface, runs as follows: ". . . the Editor *firmly* believes from what she learned from Dr Berkeley's very old beloved friend, Dean Delany — that both Dean Swift and Mrs Johnson were actually the children of Sir William Temple, and the heavy tidings arrived not until the day on which the indissoluble knot was tied." There is, of course, no support for this assertion beyond the information she may have possessed as Berkeley's daughter-in-law and Delany's friend. See also B. Rand: *Berkeley's American Sojourn*, p. 8, and Marguerite Hersey: *New Light on the Evidence for Swift's Marriage*, Publications of the Modern Language Association of America, vol. XLII, March, 1927, pp. 157–161.

CHAPTER X

THE CRITIQUE OF NATURAL SCIENCE (DE MOTU)

FROM the absolutistic or sceptical standpoint, to which Berkeley has now pushed his reflections, it seems apparent that no fixed "position" or "view," such as "the common sense" of any period, can be substantially justified. These fixed "positions" must, in the end, turn out to be only relative phases or fragments, which depend for their meaning upon other phases or fragments lying beyond them, until the theoretical whole or system of systems is reached. But this system or whole, as a system, is relative to its parts or fragments. Scepticism would itself be impossible were there not something of which to be sceptical. Hence this speculative scepticism must at last destroy itself and lead to a new and deeper scepticism, based upon another absolute, from which the realm of reason or theory may be seen as a whole. The last act of reason, so to speak, is to become conscious of itself from a deeper standpoint that cannot, therefore, be considered as "rational." From this truly absolute standpoint, it is apparent that reason itself is relativized and its substantiality jeopardized.

It is manifest that such scepticism (absolutism) cannot tolerate rigidly fixed systems. All such systems, even the most complete and subtle, if asserted as finally true, must appear as unwarranted dogmatism, even the speculative assertion of this theory as a theory. It is not surprising, therefore, that we no longer find Berkeley attempting, as in his youth, to work out the consequences of a "new principle," or indeed of any principle whatsoever, since all such principles are, in the end, doomed to relativity and "dependency." In place of rationalism we now find irrationalism, in place of affirmation negation, in place of dogmatism criticism. There is no conceivable means of arriving directly at the absolute. Any absolute that could be intelligibly stated as a theory would at once cease to be absolute. The absolute is to be arrived at indirectly, not merely by affirmation, but by negation as well. In our situation, it is possible for us to gain a sense of the absolute only through the "dependency" or destruction of all else. Only through the negation or criticism of the finite can we penetrate indirectly, obliquely, dialectically to the absolute. Hence Berkeley, in this practical phase of his life, in so far as he devoted himself to theoretical matters at all, devotes himself to the criticism of "accepted" (i.e. dogmatic) views. First, in the case of "Science," which had at this time become solidified into a system almost as inflexible as that of common sense itself, later in the case of the almost equally fixed or plausible formulations of the Deists, and finally in the case of the new mathematics, Berkeley applies his concrete logic to break down in one way or another the rigid thought-structures to which his contemporaries had become so dogmatically and even fanatically attached. It is to the first of these attempts to criticize or relativize certain fundamental "scientific" concepts of the day, which he published as a Latin treatise, the *De Motu*, during his second and more extended tour of the Continent, that we must now turn our attention.

The Grand Tour

Bishop Ashe's son was in bad health, and, since his own illness of a year before, Berkeley was not too robust. It was thought that Ashe might find relief in the climate of southern Italy; so Berkeley crossed Mt. Cenis for the second time in the winter of 1716, and arrived at Rome early in January. Here he began a diary which he kept regularly during the Italian tour. Certain parts, however, were unfortunately lost en route, together with the second part of the *Principles*, evidently completed on the trip. The surviving fragments, although they are somewhat full of population statistics and therapeutic remedies, nevertheless do present an interesting picture of Berkeley's intimate occupations and interests during the period.

Berkeley had some feeling for music, but his imagination took particular delight in the forms of architecture and sculpture, most of all in the play of colour which painting adds to the play of form. "I am a judge of painting," he says, "though not of music." [1] He is "never weary" of viewing the Pantheon, and admires the Circus of Caracalla,[2] but of the great Jesuit churches remarks only that "they seem to show a greater respect to Ignatius Loyola than to our blessed Saviour, the church of the former being much the greater and finer of the two." [3] His en-

---

[1] Percival letter, March 1, 1717.　　　[3] *Ibid.*, p. 234.
[2] Journal, F. iv, p. 246.

thusiasm is all for the ancient forms, whose cool aloofness seemed, perhaps, to offer him a refuge from the "modern" doubt and confusion in which he had become so inextricably entangled. "Gothic" is a term of disparagement.[4] He prefers the Villa Borghese to St. Peter's, and revels in the sensuous graces of Correggio and Raphael. Titian especially calls forth his admiration. Many of his portraits, he says, "seemed to breathe." [5] Berkeley finds very little to approve in contemporary Rome. He is annoyed at not being able to visit an ancient military tower "because it is hemmed up in a convent of nuns,"[6] amused at the costly entertainment given by Prince Barberini to the apostate Queen of Sweden,[7] and bored by the Italian theatre.[8] He remarks upon the survival of many ancient customs and rites in the Roman religion, such as the decorations of their churches "somewhat like lectisterniums," [9] but is far from shocked. "After all it may be said that the greater part of the ceremonies and customs borrowed from the heathens are harmless. . . . Modern Rome hath inventions of her own worse than the old, and withal hath *enchéri* upon the old." [10] He seems to have found far more to his taste in the remains of the days of Trajan than in the life of his own time.

In early spring Berkeley took his charge to Naples, and on April 6 wrote an enthusiastic letter to Percival. "The air of this happy part of the world," he says, "is soft and delightful beyond conception, being perfumed with myrtle shrubs and orange groves, that are everywhere scattered throughout the country; . . . the heat tempered to a just warmth by refreshing breezes from the sea." [11] He quotes with approval Horace's "Nullus in orbe sinus Baiis praelucet amoenis." The two travellers then went further south into "the most remote and unknown parts of Italy." [12] On this journey, always eager for curious and exceptional details, he heard accounts of the tarantula and the mad dancing fevers induced by its bite. He seems to have spent some time investigating these accounts, attempting to observe the animals themselves [13] and various persons professing the symptoms, often, as he was assured by a doctor, for lewd purposes.[14] His habits of exact observation had not

[4] *Ibid.*, p. 245.
[5] *Ibid.*, p. 233.
[6] *Ibid.*, p. 242.
[7] *Ibid.*, p. 236.
[8] *Ibid.*, p. 245.
[9] *Ibid.*, p. 305.
[10] *Ibid.*, p. 307.
[11] Percival letter, April 6, 1717.
[12] Percival letter, June 18, 1717.
[13] F. iv, p. 258.
[14] *Ibid.*, p. 268.

been relaxed by philosophical study, for his journal is full of other queer pieces of information and records of little things that caught his fancy, such as the flies that shone in the moon-light near Mt. Sarki.[15] There are also many notes of landscape scenes, and many exact measurements of the proportions of buildings, temples, and columns. The result of this detailed architectural study was a further intensification of his love for the noble form and grace of the ancients. "The old Romans," he says, "were inferior to the Greeks, and . . . the moderns fall infinitely short of both in the grandeur and simplicity of taste." [16]

Berkeley was not impressed by the intellectual culture of the monasteries, many of which he visited, and which abounded in "miracles, indulgences, and reliques numberless." [17] In one of them, which possessed a large scholastic library, he found, indeed, that the expressions Whig and Tory were not altogether unknown, and one of the "most knowing fathers" asked "whether Ireland were a large town." [18] That the conversations were not always on this level, however, is proved by the record of a meeting with the guardian of a Franciscan convent and another friar, during which "Thomas and Scotus" were dis-cussed in Latin.[19] It would be interesting to know more about this conversation. We can well imagine his taking the part of Scotus and his more voluntaristic rationalism against the Thomists, but he was still too much the child of his age to enter deeply at this time into these older forms of dispute.

Berkeley seems to have been particularly impressed by the ancient city of Lecce (Aletium). In a letter to Percival he says: "perhaps it may be new to you to hear that the most beautiful city in Italy lies in a remote corner of the heel. Lecce is the most luxuriant in all ornaments of architecture of any town that I have seen." [20] He found the church and convent of the Jesuits "wonderfully grand," [21] and observed a peculiarly rich variety of embellishments in the town. "Nothing in my travels," he ex-claims, "[is] more amazing than the infinite profusion of alto-relievo, and that so well done: there is not surely the like rich architecture in the world." [22] It was not only the "simplicity" of the ancient architectural styles that impressed him. He pre-

---

[15] *Ibid.*, p. 251.
[16] Percival letter, June 28, 1718.
[17] F. iv, p. 282.
[18] *Ibid.*, p. 274.

[19] *Ibid.*, p. 268.
[20] Percival letter, June 18, 1717.
[21] F. iv, p. 265.
[22] *Ibid.*, p. 266.

ferred simplicity, but he did not object to profusion if it conveyed a sense of completeness.[23]

He returned to Naples in June and "found Vesuvius in a
terrible fit."[24] He had climbed the mountain on his former visit
in April and observed the crater "filled with red-hot liquid
matter, like that in the furnace of a glass-house, which raged
and wrought as the waves of the sea."[25] But now an actual
eruption took place, and Berkeley, with the intense curiosity
which we have already noted as an essential ingredient of his
character, resolved to observe it at close range. The story of his
first-hand observations is best told in the words of his own vivid
description, which he sent to Arbuthnot, and which was later
published by the Royal Society.

Three or four of us got into a boat, and were set ashore at *Torre del Greco*,
a town situate at the foot of Vesuvius to the Southwest, whence we rode four
or five miles before we came to the burning river, which was about midnight.
The roaring of the volcano grew exceeding loud and horrible as we approached.
I observed a mixture of colours in the cloud over the crater, green, yellow,
red, and blue; there was likewise a ruddy dismal light in the air over that tract
of land where the burning river flowed; ashes continually showered on us all
the way from the sea-coast: all which circumstances, set off and augmented by
the horror and silence of the night, made a scene the most uncommon and
astonishing I ever saw which grew still more extraordinary as we came nearer
the stream. Imagine a vast torrent of liquid fire rolling from the top down
the side of the mountain and with irresistible fury bearing down and consuming vines, olives, fig-trees, houses; in a word, everything that stood in its way.

In this adventure, Berkeley walked so far ahead of his com-
panions along the river of fire that he was "obliged to retire in
great haste," surprised by the sulphurous stream and almost
suffocated.[26]

Berkeley's new-found feeling for the moods of nature also
comes to light in connection with a visit, soon after the eruption, to the island of Ischia (or Inarime) in the Bay of Naples,
which he describes in a letter to Pope of October 22, 1717.

The Island Inarime is an epitome of the whole earth, containing within the
compass of eighteen miles a wonderful variety of hills, vales, ragged rocks,
fruitful plains, and barren mountains, all thrown together in a most romantic

---

[23] Cf. *Alciphron*, pp. 136 ff., where he
criticizes the modern architects, who "in
their bold sallies seem to act without aim
or design; to be governed by no idea, no
reason, or principle of art, but pure
caprice, joined with a thorough contempt

of that noble simplicity of the ancients,
without which there can be no unity,
gracefulness or grandeur in their works."
[24] Percival letter, June 18, 1717.
[25] F. iv, p. 286.
[26] *Ibid.*, pp. 287–288.

confusion. The air is in the hottest season constantly refreshed by cool breezes from the sea. . . . The hills are the greater part covered to the top with vines, some with chestnut groves and others with thickets of myrtle and lentiscus. The fields in the Northern side are divided by hedge-rows of myrtle. Several fountains and rivulets add to the beauty of this landscape, which is likewise set off by the variety of some barren spots and naked rocks. But that which crowns the scene is a large mountain rising out of the middle of the island, (once a terrible volcano, by the ancients called Mons Epomeus). Its lower parts are adorned with vines and other fruits; the middle affords pasture to flocks of goats and sheep; and the top is a sandy pointed rock from which you have the finest prospect in the world, surveying at one view, besides several pleasant islands lying at your feet, a tract of Italy about three hundred miles in length, from the promontory of Antium to the Cape of Palinurus.

His ward, young Ashe, was an invalid and, as we have said, Berkeley's own health was causing him considerable worry. This explains the interest which he took in the mineral baths of Ischia. He even goes so far as to give a list of the different waters and their respective curative powers.[27] The two travellers did not, however, linger in the South, but went on to Rome in the early part of July. There they learned the news of the Bishop of Clogher's death, and young Ashe returned home. But Berkeley, whose leave of absence had been once more prolonged in 1717, stayed on. He must have remained in Rome the rest of the summer, for in November, 1718, he writes Percival from there that the city is swarming with followers of the Pretender and that it is an "uneasy place for men of different principles." It was for this reason that he went north. Not much is known of his activities there during the next year, but in July, 1720, he writes Percival about certain medals and busts that the latter had commissioned him to buy. Lord Pembroke had also asked him to purchase a number of books.[28] He probably performed many errands of this nature in the company of such congenial friends as Smibert, the painter, whom he met at this time.[29] What leisure he had he devoted to certain scientific matters connected with the third part of the *Principles*. These thoughts finally crystallized in the treatise *De Motu*, which he submitted to the French Academy, in competition for a prize offered for the best essay on this subject. In this work Berkeley now embodied in a critical form most of the ideas he had originally intended to include in Part III of the *Treatise*.[30]

[27] *Ibid.*, p. 309.
[28] Percival letter, July 28, 1718.
[29] Updike, *Hist. Narr.*, p. 523.
[30] According to his letter to Samuel

Johnson, November 25, 1729, Berkeley finished during his Italian travels, and then lost, the important Part II of the *Treatise*. Samuel Johnson: His Career

The Relativity of Science

The most significant feature of the *De Motu* is its tone. Hitherto Berkeley's attitude towards science or "natural philosophy" had been, on the whole, sympathetic. As a result of his early confusion of the concrete with the phenomenal, he thought of natural science as a study of sensory "facts," or things as they really are. He was, therefore, at first, most anxious to show how harmoniously his own speculations fitted with the results of such empirical study, "to accommodate them to the sciences." [31] Thus, in the *Commonplace Book*,[31a] while he admits that it will be most difficult to reconcile his position with that of "Moralists" and "Divines," he excepts "Natural Philosophers," maintaining that "Experimental philosophers have nothing whereat to be offended in me," since, through their experiments, they discover "facts," which cannot be questioned.

Berkeley has now perceived, however, to his own cost, that there is unfortunately nothing that cannot be questioned, nothing that is permanent and substantial, least of all the fleeting sense-data on which scientific observations are based, and which, as he has come to realize, are not at all "concrete," but, as a matter of fact, possess only "a *relative* or *hypothetical exist-ence.*" [32] The data of sense, far from being trustworthy and self-existent "facts," are incomplete and "dependent." Do they not require, even to be data, a mind or a perceiving consciousness *to* which they must be given? Furthermore, are they not, by their temporal and perpetually variegated character, dependent in their meaning upon "eternal" and "identical" archetypes? Are they not all obviously dependent from the first, in their very independence and factuality, on what is meant by a fact? The idea that thought or theory must, therefore, follow photographically the outlines of what is "given" to it is indefensible, for "givenness" must be given to the given from another source, and factuality itself presupposes a complex theoretical structure to begin with. In other words, there are no such things as facts (substances) which require no interpretation whatsoever, but which simply or purely "are," for pure being, "*something in general* . . . proves

and Writings, ed. H. and C. Schneider, Columbia University Press, 1929, vol. II, p. 270.

[31] C. B. J., 215.
[31a] J., 402.
[32] 3D., F. i, p. 474.

nothing." [33] A fact to be a fact requires something more, in the first place, factuality (not a fact), and in the second place, a system or conceptual fringe to give this concept meaning. There is no way of escaping meaning. The most rigid sensory datum must possess it, and all meaning or interpretation whatsoever can be questioned. Hence it is not surprising to find that Berkeley's attitude toward science has considerably altered, as a result of the painful logical exercises carried out in the *Principles* and the *Three Dialogues*. His tone is now no longer that of dogmatic acceptance but of criticism, for there is nothing that is uninterpreted or meaningless. Science is for him no longer a mere photographing of given facts, but an interpretation, depending upon certain basic concepts or categories, and these are subject to question. Much of this criticism he had anticipated, it is true, in the course of his examination of natural philosophy in the *Principles*.[34] But there is, now, a most important difference in Berkeley's understanding of the results gained through the application of his concrete logic to this field.

It will be unnecessary to refer in any further detail to Berkeley's criticism of the category of substance, which is presupposed throughout the *De Motu*, as throughout all of his later writings. Indeed, as we have seen, his whole "concrete" logic must be viewed as, in the end, an attack upon the common-sense employment of this category. The things around us, which we commonly regard as independent, are not really "things" at all, but only aspects or phases of other things, which are also only aspects, and so forth. It is not that these are dependent upon some one finite super-thing called the self or soul, for this is itself only another result of the illegitimate employment of the category of substance. Nowhere in the field of finite existence can we discover anything that is not relative or "dependent" in its nature. The rigid form of independence or self-identity, which ordinary reflection gives its objects, can, therefore, be viewed as expressing only a certain ultimately unjustifiable neglect of other phases or fringes of these objects which are arbitrarily excluded from consideration by such a logic. When we think of the brain, for example, as a "thing," and attempt to explain other phenomena by means of it, we are making what Berkeley called an illicit abstraction; for the brain itself, in so far as it has any meaning, is not such an

<hr>

[33] 2D., F. i, p. 437.   [34] Secs. 101-118.

independent thing, capable of explaining other things on its own account, but is rather "dependent," and itself needs to be explained. Yet all ordinary as well as scientific explanations represent such arbitrary abstractions. Certain "dependent" aspects are taken to be self-subsistent entities in terms of which other phenomena are explained. "Something," atom, electron, etc., is always accepted as ultimate and independent, which, when we come to reflect upon it seriously, is in reality relative and dependent. In the *De Motu*, Berkeley proceeds to show how certain of the most fundamental scientific categories are, in fact, just such hypostatizations, or, as he puts it succinctly, "the abstraction or division of things truly inseparable." [35]

Space, for example, as a thing, something given all at once as "boundless in every direction, immobile, insensible, permeating and including all matter," [36] Berkeley considers to be an illegitimate abstraction which, if consistently thought through, is "nothing." [37] Space without its essential relation to the nonspatial, to time, the perceiving mind, and particular bodies, is "infinite immobile indivisible, insensible without relation and without distinction." [38] The only way in which we can possibly arrive at the conception of absolute space is to think of the annihilation of all the finite relative spaces which we know. But this process of relation or mediation must not be hypostatized into a separate thing, for, if we then attempt to define what we mean by this "thing," it is really nothing (*merum nihil*). Absolute space, to be truly absolute, must include relation in it. Space, as space, requires relative, perceived spaces to be absolute, just as these finite spaces require the absolute, single space to be spaces. Neither can be meaningfully separated as an entity distinct from the other. Without relation and distinction ("sine relatione et sine distinctione"), absolute space becomes nothing. If there is any such thing as absolute space it must not be regarded as a "thing" that is given in its entirety, once and for all, as an independent entity, but as a form or process, constantly in *statu nascenti*, as well as in *statu*

---

[35] "abstractio seu divisio rerum vere inseparabilium." D. M., sec. 47, F. i.

[36] "spatium undequaque immensum, immobile, insensibile, corpora universa permeans et continens." D. M., sec. 52.

[37] D. M., sec. 53.

[38] "Quod reliquum est vocant spatium absolutum, omni relatione quae a situ et distantiis corporum oriebatur, simul cum ipsis corporibus, sublata. Porro spatium illud est infinitum, immobile, indivisibile, insensibile, sine relatione et sine distinctione. Hoc est, omnia eius attributa sunt privativa vel negativa: videtur igitur esse merum nihil." Sec. 53.

quiescenti.[39] Absolute space is a norm or an ideal by means of which we reduce all actually existent spaces to a state of relativity, but this norm or ideal must not be hypostatized or thought of as itself a given or existent "thing," though it has a given or existent aspect, for, as a system of relations, it presupposes something to relate. Thus space is not a concept which can be thought by "pure intellect," for this is "directed towards spiritual and unextended things." [40]

It is, indeed, this incomplete or relative aspect of space that Berkeley stresses against the abstract absolute of Newton, although the conclusion towards which his concrete logic is driving him is quite clear. The abstract relative is equally illegitimate. The only spaces that can ever be given or presented are fragments, relative to "bodies," with an arbitrary up and down, left and right, forward and back.[41] But it is only the unseen, purely conceptual, ideal, absolute aspect of space as space which enables us to arrive at this result. What we call space, that is, is bipolar. On the one hand, there is the finite, "given" aspect, stressed by Berkeley in the *Principles* and the *De Motu*, and, on the other hand, the infinite, absolute, conceptual aspect, stressed by him in the *New Theory of Vision*. What we call space is a constant tension between these two poles, a passage from one to the other, from the whole which is only a whole of parts, back again to the parts which are only parts of a whole,—a passage which, from its very nature, cannot be complete. Abstract logic attempts to fix one or the other of these aspects into a distinct entity existing in its own right, but in doing so either ignores the relative, viewing some arbitrary frame of reference as the absolute (regarding the part as a whole), or ignores the absolute (as Berkeley himself at certain points in the *De Motu*), viewing space as a sum of relations or incomplete spaces (regarding the whole as a part or a sum of parts). What we call space, however, is an endless oscillation between these poles, between the whole and the

---

[39] Hence Berkeley's approval in the *Of Infinites* of Locke's distinction "between the idea of infinity of space and the idea of space infinite," the latter being "an endless growing idea." *Of Inf.*, F. iii, p. 410.

[40] "Extensio autem est qualitas positiva. . . . Fugit insuper *intellectum purum* quum facultas illa versetur tantum circa res spirituales et inextensas, cujusmodi sunt mentes nostrae, earumque habitus, passiones, virtutes, et similia." D. M., sec. 53, F. i.

[41] "Nam sursum deorsum, sinistrorsum, dextrorsum, omnesque plagae et regiones in relatione aliqua fundantur. . . ." Sec. 58.

part, the conceptual and the perceptual, the absolute and the relative.

The concept of time is also infected with the same essential instability. We cannot refer meaningfully to the temporal without contrasting it with the non-temporal or the eternal. That this contrast is essential to what we mean by time is evidenced by the simple and ancient reflection that time itself cannot be thought of as temporal. Hence, even in his first meditations on this subject, Berkeley is forced to introduce the supplementary concept of the τὸ νῦν,[42] the constant present, the unchanging "eye" of time itself, past which flows the endless current of the non-temporal. And again our abstract logic fastens upon either one or the other of these aspects, turning it into a substance, and hence either denying the non-temporal flux as unreal or illusory, or, in a confusion even more deplorable, denying time, or the eternal, in the name of time. But this eternal is also caught in the web of relativity, for it is eternal and unchanging only in the reflected light shed upon it by its image, and thus itself becomes an image, for the changeless requires change as its background.

The treatise is chiefly devoted to an examination of the category of motion, a category obviously of the greatest importance to the reigning mechanical philosophy, and the subject chosen by the French Academy for its prize essay. Here again, as a result of his concrete logic, Berkeley finds that mechanical philosophers have tended to separate things which in reality are inextricably intertwined. "Motion," he states, "is never submitted to our senses without corporeal mass, space and time."[43] It is, of course, possible to coin a word for motion in and for itself, and even to convince ourselves that it stands for something "independently" existing in experience. But reflection upon the *meaning* of the term must convince us that we are none the less falsifying a reality which in itself cannot be so abstracted, for there can be no real motion without a thing moved.[44]

Not only does motion presuppose the category of thing or substance, but also time and space. To talk about "the abstract nature of motion isolated completely from all considera-

<hr/>

[42] C. B. J., 9.

[43] "Motus nunquam in sensus nostros incurrit sine mole corporea, spatio, et tempore." D. M., sec. 43.

[44] Cf. "Motion distinct from ye thing moved is not conceivable." C. B. H., 435; J., 449.

tions of space and time" gives rise to "great difficulties" and "definitions far more obscure than the thing itself." [45] The "abstract quintessence" of motion, isolated from space and time, is only a word.[46] But, if this is correct, motion must share in the relativity essential to all space, and it will be meaningless to speak of a purely absolute motion which is neither up nor down, nor left nor right, nor backwards nor forwards, nor towards anything nor away from anything. Such a motion, since it is no motion in particular, is not motion at all, but, as it can be defined only through negation, is, like absolute space, "nothing," a pure form or norm, an ideal presupposed by the relative or particular motions, but not itself ever present as a given thing. Motion is, then, a tension between its incomplete, relative moments and the absolute which relativizes them, for all motion must be relative. One globe, for example, if all other bodies be annihilated, cannot be supposed to move,[47] for where or in what direction could it move? Nor could we conceive of motion with even two globes, for, without some fixed coordinate system involving other bodies, we cannot even imagine their circular motion about a common center.[48]

Berkeley, however, is not content with a general statement of his views. After examining and criticizing in detail the Newtonian doctrine of absolute space and absolute motion, he proceeds to certain particular Newtonian experiments, testing them in the light of his conclusions. He begins with the famous rotating bucket, in which the water rises along the edges, owing to the relative increase in the "tangential forces." [49] It may be very *useful* to analyze the concrete phenomenon into tangential and centripetal components for purposes of computation. Berkeley compares this with the "useful hypothesis" in geometry which considers a curve as consisting of an infinite number of straight lines, although it really does not consist of them.[50] We must not, however, confuse the products of our

[45] "Sunt tamen qui motum, tanquam ideam quandam simplicem et abstractam, atque ab omnibus aliis rebus sejunctam, contemplari student. . . . Hinc nascuntur magnae difficultates de natura motus, et definitiones, ipsa re quam illustrare debent longe obscuriores." D. M., sec. 43.

[46] "Sed qua ratione abstracta illa motus quintessentia (ut ita dicam) intelligi possit, non video." *Ibid.*

[47] "Adeo ut, si reliquis corporibus in nihilum redactis, globus, exempli gratia, unicus existere supponatur; in illo motus nullus concipi possit: usque adeo necesse est, ut detur aliud corpus, cuius situ motus determinari intelligatur." Sec. 58.

[48] Sec. 59.

[49] Sec. 60.

[50] "Quo modo curva considerari potest tanquam constans ex rectis infinitis, etiamsi revera ex illis non constet, sed quod ea hypothesis ad geometriam utilis

analysis with the concrete phenomenon itself. The equatorial expansion of a body subjected to centrifugal force does not really develop "in an infinite number of rectilineal directions." [50a] These are only pictures in the imagination of the physicist,— products of his *useful* analysis. The fact that actually confronts him is a *circular motion*, the center of gravity of which is not a single point, but a number of points moving in the periphery of a circle.[51]

Berkeley does not allow us to forget that, on the Newtonian presupposition of absolute space, the motion of the water cannot be truly circular at all, since it is "strangely compounded" not only of the motion of the bucket, but of the diurnal motion of the earth around its axis, of the monthly motion of the earth and the moon around their common centers of gravity, and the annual motion of the earth around the sun; nor can we stop even here, for how can we tell whether the whole system of things is at rest or moving in a straight line with a uniform velocity? [52] Thus, when we think our analysis through, we become lost in a maze of abstractions, and the original circular motion with which we started is lost. These abstractions must not be taken with ultimate seriousness. They may be *useful* temporarily for purposes of computation. But they must be transcended, if we wish to get to the real nature of the thing,— the concrete phenomenon which confronts us. Berkeley sums the whole matter up by stating that absolute motion "is utterly useless for the classification of motions," since "determination or direction is essential to motion, and this certainly consists in relation." [53] To understand the true nature of motion, therefore, it is necessary "to guard against abstractions," and "to be content with relative measurements." [54]

sit eodem modo motus circularis spectari potest tanquam a directionibus rectilineis infinitis ortum ducens, quae suppositio utilis est in philosophia mechanica. Non tamen ideo affirmandum, impossibile esse, ut centrum gravitatis corporis cujusvis successive existat in singulis punctis peripheriae circularis, nulla ratione habita directionis ullius rectiliniae, sive in tangente sive in radio." Sec. 61.

[50a] *Ibid.*

[51] Sec. 61.

[52] "Uti vel ex eo patet quod, quum secundum illorum principia qui motum absolutum inducunt, nullo symptomate scire liceat, utrum integra rerum compages quiescat, an moveatur uniformiter in directum, perspicuum sit motum absolutum nullius corporis cognosci posse." Sec. 65.

[53] "Cum ergo spatium absolutum nullo modo in sensus incurrat, necesse est ut inutile prorsus sit ad distinctionem motuum. Praeterea determinatio sive directio motui essentialis est, illa vero in relatione consistit." Sec. 63.

[54] Sec. 66.

Newton's absolutes are justifiable only as *useful* abstractions. If absolutized or turned into self-subsistent entities (absolute spaces and times, etc.) to which other abstractions are *reduced*, they inevitably distort reality, for all given phenomena are only phenomena, and therefore relative or "dependent." There is no frame of reference which may be regarded without qualifiaction as absolute, for it is only by ignoring, forgetting, or distorting that we may regard a given frame *as if* absolute. The true absolute is banished by its nature from the field of existence. It can never be given. It is an even greater mistake to think of it as a given "thing," existing in some mysterious *given* realm beyond all givenness, though it is true that there could be no actual givenness without it. The trouble with Newton's absolutes is that they are not really absolutes at all, but only relative phenomena masquerading as such. They represent an artificial hypostatization of a certain aspect of reality, which, if consciously performed, may be defensible and serviceable with respect to certain *ends*. But these ends are realized only through distortion, for accuracy at a certain point means inaccuracy at another. Berkeley's treatment of the category of causation is of particular interest because of the consistency with which, in contrast to his earlier psychologism, he is now forced to exclude all "action" from the realm of "ideas" or objects, and to identify it finally as "the work of Mind." The "action" which pervades and ultimately "explains" the physical world is not a primitive sort of psychic energy, but a mode of thought, and "Natural Philosophy" is founded *not* on psychology but on logic.

Berkeley discovers a widespread confusion of the pure category of causation with a given, relative phenomenon. As Newton seems to have confused the essence of space itself with the system of the fixed stars, so does abstract or common-sense thinking confuse the category of action or causation with the phenomenon of motion. We often think of force, introspectively or psychologically, as if it were some "creative" source of action "in" bodies, just as the "power" of moving our limbs is "in" us. But if we faithfully examine what we mean by body, we shall find that it "contains" nothing of this sort. Take away all such qualities as extension, impenetrability, and figure, and nothing remains,[55] for this exhausts what is given as body. These qualities are all passive. We can in no manner

---

[55] Sec. 22.

deduce from any of them such a "principle" of motion as gravitation, for example. When we say that a body is heavy, therefore, all we have a right to mean is that it is borne downward, or that it resists us to a certain degree. To say that the body contains any inherent force which makes it do this is to invent a word for the unknown, in the same manner as those who explain heat by a calorific principle. Filling the world with such essences is only developing a misleading vocabulary. Thus, Berkeley maintains that the issue between Newton and Torricelli as to whether the force is aroused only temporarily while the body is changing its state, or whether it remains, as constituting the impetus, is an abstract type of discussion which really has no place in science.[56]

Berkeley also comes into conflict with Leibniz at this point, insisting that he "confounds impetus with motion," [57] and that his "elementary nisus" and "force" are "not to be found in nature, but are arrived at by abstraction." [58] This is also true of the Newtonian "attraction," which is "employed by Newton not as a true and physical quality, but only as a mathematical hypothesis." [59] The task of science is simply to describe the motions given in direct experience, and to state them as simply as possible in "rules" or formulae. It may, indeed, be useful to refer to force or "action" as an element in such a formula or equation, but then "we are not able to distinguish the action of a body from motion." [60] If we attempt to do this, however, and think of force as a moving principle "inherent" in bodies, and as in some way responsible for the motion, we are going beyond the given phenomena, and therefore beyond the proper field of science. Motion is "no action," [61] but a phenomenon presented to us in sensory experience. Science must stick rigidly to this experience, and not trespass in other "higher" fields, which lead beyond "experience" to logic and metaphysics.

The scientist is thus restricted to the description of the succession of phenomena, and he has no right to suppose that "bodies" have real forces or powers, by which they act on each other, to produce these phenomena. Nevertheless, there is a universal tendency of the human mind which leads us inevitably to go beyond the given facts and illegitimately to attribute

---

[56] Sec. 67.
[57] Sec. 16.
[58] Sec. 17.

[59] Ibid.
[60] Sec. 11.
[61] 2D., F. i, p. 431.

causation to ideas, "than which nothing can be more absurd and unintelligible"; [62] for "when we perceive certain ideas of Sense constantly followed by other ideas, and we know this is not of our own doing, we forthwith attribute power and agency to the ideas themselves." This tendency to connect constantly associated ideas together by the relation of cause and effect is later referred to by Berkeley as a "mere custom or habit," [63] for there is no "necessity" in such a connection, the relation being only the arbitrary relation of sign to thing signified.[64] This "custom or habit" has become so ingrained that it has even affected the scientist. "The physicist considers the series or successions of sensible things and the laws by which they are connected and their general order, viewing what precedes as cause and what follows as effect." And it is for this reason that he sometimes tends to say that the moving body is the "active" cause of motion in the other, or that it impresses motion on it, or attracts it, or impels it.[65] All that the physicist has the right to say, however, is that a certain phenomenon in experience has always been observed to precede another. Berkeley is very far from denying causation altogether. What he is denying is causation as an existing object or "idea." What he is asserting is causation as a logic or a way of thought. "Both by rational reflection and experience," he says, "we know that nothing is active except mind," [66] not *my* mind nor *your* mind, but mind, or pure thought. Causation is a category. To reify this category, and to confuse it with the passive "ideas" or objects in such a way that "forces" are attributed to bodies, is like confusing absolute space with the system of the fixed stars. Berkeley shows that the mechanical philosophy itself recognizes this implicitly in the first law of motion. Perseverance in an impressed action can no more be said to be an *action* than existence. When mechanics, therefore, speaks of an "impelling" body it is only in a Pickwickian sense, for "the impelling body is just as much impelled, and the impelled impelling." [67]

The "things" which common sense thinks it observes in the external world are not things at all, nor is the "space" observed by common sense really space, nor the "time" really time, nor

[62] Pr., sec. 32.

[63] N. T. V. V., sec. 28, F. ii, p. 392.

[64] "Ideas which are observed to be connected together are vulgarly considered under the relation of cause and effect, whereas, in strict philosophic truth, they are only related as the sign to the thing signified." N. T. V. V., sec. 13, F. ii, p. 387.

[65] D. M., sec. 71.

[66] D. M., sec. 40.

[67] D. M., sec. 70.

are any of the active causes it so confidently finds itself "intuiting" in nature really causes. Space, time, substance, motion, causation are categories or norms, not observed nor even existent, but underlying or conditioning the whole observed world of nature, phenomenalizing or relativizing it. Nowhere in nature is there an absolute, although as nature it requires such an absolute or norm. But norms are not things or substances, but forms of that universal mind or logic which is thinking the real world. Common-sense reflection and the uncritical metaphysics which attempts to formulate itself on this basis use these categories unconsciously, and hence think of them objectively as "things" existing in the world. But as such existent entities they unfortunately cease to be absolute. We are, therefore, reduced to the position of pure phenomenalism or relativism which only accentuates the dilemma. Everything is relative, fragmentary, or incomplete. But what enables us to make such a judgment? Can it be anything but the absolute itself, for which or to which all appearance must be denominated relative? The importance of the *De Motu* is that it brings us to this standpoint of the pure norm or category. There is no true causation, for example, in nature. Natural events simply occur. They cannot explain one another. The question of causation or explanation is a transcendental question which must take us beyond nature altogether. We can never come to "understand" the world by observation, no matter how accurate. Understanding or explanation is a matter of categories supplied by reason and by reason alone. In place of the metaphysics of common sense, therefore, Berkeley suggests a metaphysics based upon logic. For all explanation is "placed under" or presupposes [67a] certain universal norms or categories, such as substance and causation, which cannot be given or observed at all, but must rather be supplied beforehand by "thought." In so far as this may be said to exist, it is neither a substance nor a cause, but the λόγος itself, the universal mind. "Nothing is active but mind." [68] No ultimate explanation of nature can be given without a critical examination of this mind and its categories, for all explanation must be made in terms of them.

[67a] "supponit." D. M., sec. 34.   [68] "activum nihil praeter mentem." D. M., sec. 40.

The Practical View of Science

But all this, it may be said, is nothing more than what we have already seen to be the result of Berkeley's *Three Dialogues*, in which his realization of the relativity of the "objective" world leads him to a theory of "eternal archetypes." Even the application of this relativity argument to scientific categories is foreshadowed in sections 103 to 118 of the *Principles*, where, after briefly pointing out the relativity of perceived motion, space, and time, he says with respect to the sciences that "they do not ascend into any inquiry concerning those transcendental maxims which influence all the particular sciences."[69] This only verifies the natural conclusion that the *De Motu* is a late elaboration of certain conceptions he had at first intended for Part III of the *Treatise*. The ordinary concepts of science are ultimately unjustified as hypostatizations of "transcendental" categories not properly existent. But why then are such concepts employed at all? It is in answering this natural inquiry that the most striking originality of the *De Motu* appears. The artificial absolutes of science must have some justification, though from the "transcendental" standpoint they are only abstractions. It is in his "practical" justification of common sense, a new note in Berkeley's writings, the careful reader may say, that the real meaning of the *De Motu* lies, not in a covert but inescapable absolutism. It is the relativity of all human knowledge and experience that is here revealed, such a reader may observe, precisely *not* the absolute. What Berkeley is anxious to prove is the relativity of space, the relativity of time, and the relativity of actual motion. Science, it is true, cannot waste itself away in tracing out this infinite regress. It must step in at some point and arbitrarily select a frame of reference, perhaps, or an "atom," which it must consider *as* an absolute. But such absolutes are absolutes only by courtesy. They are absolutes only *as if*. They are essential for the practical purposes of science, for science cannot deal with all things, all at once. It must select, abstract, distort, and approximate, or it cannot "get on" or even exist. It is true that its explanations are not properly explanations at all, that its exactness is only a pseudo-exactness obtained by artificially ignoring or forgetting huge ranges of experience. But all this is justified *practically*,

[69] Pr., sec. 118.

for, in the end, it is *useful*. This "usefulness" is the very meaning of knowledge, in the realm of relativity in which we are placed.

There are traces of this position on almost every page of the *De Motu*, and it is not difficult to see how closely it accorded with the general scepticism in which Berkeley's first experiments with logic ended. If all conceivable positions are abstract or relative, even our scepticism, then must not thought or logic, after finally destroying itself, leave us exactly as we were before? Is not the pragmatic lapse into common sense, in its very illogicality, the only possible "logical" conclusion? Since no theory, however subtle or refined, can be anything more than an abstraction, must we not abandon the search for the absolute (for truth), and simply proceed with any theory that seems plausible and regard it *as if* true? Thought alone is a purely destructive negation that must end by leading us back to that "life" from which it has arisen, and to which it must return. If left to itself, it must discover this, and come "to nothing." But if subordinated to the higher ends of "action" in the first place, realizing its own relativity, it may render important service as an "instrument." Page after page of the *De Motu* testifies to the intensity with which, during this practical phase of his life, Berkeley was embracing such a pragmatic view of science, a natural outcome of the devastating scepticism in which his thought had terminated.

Thus, almost in the very first sections of the treatise, Berkeley speaks of abstract words, through their very inadequacy, as being "useful in argument" [70] and "convenient in the teaching of disciplines." [71] But this "usefulness" amounts to much more than the abbreviation and systematization of unwieldy factual knowledge. "Force, gravity, attraction, and words of this sort," he says, "are useful for the knowledge and computation of motion and moving bodies," not for the understanding of the real nature of motion, since that is concrete, "but only as a mathematical hypothesis." [72] Berkeley offers as an example of what he means the calculation of "the composition and resolution of forces . . . by means of diagonals and the sides

[70] "voces generales et abstractas in disserendo utiles esse videant." D. M., sec. 7.

[71] "idoneae ad tradendas disciplinas." Sec. 7.

[72] "Vis, gravitas, attractio, et huius-modi voces, utiles sunt ad ratiocinia et computationes de motu et corporibus motis; sed non ad intelligendam simplicem ipsius motus naturam . . . sed solummodo ut hypothesin mathematicam." Sec. 17.

of parallelograms. These serve the ends of computation and mathematical demonstration: but it is one thing to serve the ends of computation and mathematical demonstration, and another to exhibit the nature of things." [73]

We have already considered the example of centrifugal and centripetal forces which Berkeley also adduces to illustrate the same point, that obviously artificial devices may often be of "use" in calculation, though, if taken literally, they give rise to a distortion of the truth. Thus, "it may be a useful hypothesis in geometry to consider a curve as if it consisted of an infinite number of straight lines, although really it does not consist of them." [74] We cannot compute with given facts. It is, therefore, necessary to invent certain mathematical figments which can be conveniently manipulated, though "in the true nature of things they are sought in vain." [75] Berkeley later adduces the famous example of the square root of minus one in this same connection. [76] Such concepts may, like the absolute space of Newton, be *useful*. But we become at once entangled in inextricable difficulties if we take them too seriously. [77] It may be "useful" to regard force, action, and attraction as if they really inhered in bodies, though, when we become clear as to what we really mean by "body," it is impossible to regard this supposition as more than a pretence. This is a necessary pretence, however, since, if science cannot discover actual absolutes, it must manufacture artificial ones, fixed spaces, fixed atoms, and fixed forces, in terms of which it can calculate and explain various events, though these fixed "realities" are really not real, and must themselves, in the end, be explained in terms of others, and so on. But the *practical* aims of science brook no such dallying with the inconvenient, concrete truth.

There is one abstraction which underlies all scientific procedure, as it underlies all common-sense reflection. This is the abstraction of an external or objective world from the subjective nexus in which it is embedded. This "world" is reified into an independent substance, and then split up into little,

[73] "aliud est computationi et demonstrationibus mathematicis inservire, aliud rerum naturam exhibere." Sec. 18.

[74] "Quo modo curva considerari potest tanquam constans ex rectis infinitis, etiamsi revera ex illis non constet, sed quod ea hypothesis ad geometriam utilis sit, eodem modo motus circularis spectari potest tanquam a directionibus rectilineis infinitis ortum ducens, quae suppositio utilis est in philosophia mechanica." Sec. 61.

[75] "etiamsi in ipsa rerum veritate et corporibus actu existentibus frustra quaererentur." Sec. 39.

[76] Alc., VII, F. ii, p. 344.

[77] "quod penitus animo infigere oportet." D. M., sec. 40.

separate, independent substances, facts, objects, or events, which are observed just as they are, and to which, having once been thus interpreted, all further interpretation must conform. In fact, all further interpretation is only a matter of convenience, for the center of scientific attention lies in this objective aspect of experience which it has abstracted and reified into a self-subsistent world. Thus, the famous discussion between Newton and Torricelli concerning the force "impressed" on a mobile body by percussion is wholly artificial. Whether we think of a new force being aroused in the impelled body, or with Torricelli maintain that there is a transfer of the same force, although they "seem to contradict each other, none the less so long as each one discovers consistent facts, the thing may be *conveniently* explained by both." [78] No matter what explanation may prove most convenient, "in either case the fact will be identical, the difference lying in words only." [79] The whole procedure of science is dominated by the principle of convenience, with respect to the basic abstraction of the world of "fact," which is crystallized, by an uncritical employment of the category of substance, into fixed "objects" or "events." These are then "observed" and fitted into artificial schemata, classifications, or laws, which do not really explain anything, but which are of *convenience* in predicting "events," though no events do actually happen exactly according to them. Thus, as Berkeley says of physical "explanation," "a physical thing is explained not by assigning it its truly active and incorporeal [logical] cause but by demonstrating its connection with the principles of mechanics." [80] There is no true action, causation, or synthesis in this isolated region, and it is, indeed, easy to see why such causation cannot be tolerated. The whole field of science must be artificially prepared by the abstract logic of common sense with its stabilizing category of substance, so that the natural philosopher may be free to manipulate these dead essences as he pleases to produce the most *convenient* arrangement. It is absurd to speak of an impelling body in physics, for all bodies are equally passive and impelled by the abstract logic which has fixed them into dead facts or sub-

[78] "At vero, tametsi inter se pugnare videantur Newtonus et Torricellius, nihilominus, dum singuli sibi consentanea proferunt, res satis *commode* ab utrisque explicatur." Sec. 67; my italics.

[79] "idem erit quoad rem, differentia existente in nominibus tantum." Sec. 68.

[80] "Physice igitur res explicatur non assignando eius causam vere agentem et incorpoream, sed demonstrando eius connexionem cum principiis mechanicis." Sec. 69.

stances. Thus, "a moving body is impelled against a quiescent body," no matter how manifestly we seem to intuit it as "active." [81]

There can be no true causation or synthesis in such a "convenient" world, but only an endless "succession" of sensible effects, frozen into "things" or substances, which are what they are, because the logic we are using has decided, as a matter of convenience, to regard them as such. Thus, "the physicist considers the series or successions of sensible things and the laws by which they are connected and their general order, viewing what precedes as cause and what follows as effect. And it is for this reason that we say the moving body is the cause of motion in the other, or that it impresses motion on it, or attracts it, or impels it." [82] The task of science is prescribed by a certain logic, of which it is for the most part unconscious. Its task is first to abstract an external "world" from the content of consciousness, to split it up into a number of isolated things, facts, or data, and then to read off these data in various arrangements, according to their utility, a concept which seems at last to have offered Berkeley a means of escape from that concrete scepticism in which his first reflections had entrapped him.

PHILOSOPHIA PRIMA

The theoretical constructions of science and common sense are abstractions, it is true, hypostatized relativities, but these are justified by the ends of practice, by their convenience for the larger ends of life. It may have seemed to Berkeley for a moment as if this were the only way out of the intellectual *cul de sac* into which he had fallen. Reason is by its nature abstract or relative, and cannot justify itself, for the absolute necessarily lies beyond it. But as a tool or "instrument," fulfilling the "practical" ends of life, its abstractions may be justified, not finally, perhaps, but justified at least by something irrational lying beyond them. Hence we at least escape the pathetic *petitio principii* exemplified by a "reason" attempting to justify itself.

[81] "Corpus motum in quiescens impingitur; loquimur tamen active, dicentes illud hoc impellere." Sec. 70.

[82] "Physicus series sive successiones rerum sensibilium contemplatur quibus legibus connectuntur, et quo ordine, quid praecedit tanquam causa, quid sequitur tanquam effectus, animadvertens. Atque hac ratione dicimus corpus motum esse causam motus in altero, vel ei motum imprimere, trahere etiam, aut impellere." Sec. 71.

But there were several reasons which made it impossible for Berkeley to find any permanent philosophical relief from a pragmatic "make-believe," which is capable of deceiving only by being itself undeceived. If all the resting points of reason are only arbitrary and relative, this is all the more true of the "useful," no matter how much irrational content is smuggled into it. If there is any concept which manifestly refers beyond itself and is intrinsically cursed with relativity, that concept is utility. Something, to be useful, must be useful "to" or "for" something. The means require an end. Nothing can be useful by itself. Hence utility cannot be significantly asserted without going beyond itself to what is not merely useful but intrinsically valuable. If taken as the fundamental norm, if absolutized into "pragmatism," utility leads us into a *regressus infinitus* as hopeless as that of "reason" and, indeed, markedly similar to it in that, for example, it leads inevitably to an absolute. The end cannot itself turn out to be another means, and so on, or it must become impossible to assert the means even as means. If everything were only useful, nothing would be useful, since there would be nothing for which or to which they could serve. Just as an absolute norm of truth is implied by any rational assertion, so is an absolute norm of value implied by any assertion of utility. Without such an absolute, utility loses its meaning and dissolves away. This is why the *De Motu* cannot be regarded as a pragmatic tract. It is quite clear in the end that Berkeley is once again in the dilemma of absolute scepticism. The pragmatic solution is only absolutism or scepticism in a thin disguise, for pragmatism is the equivalent, in the realm of value, of scepticism in the realm of reason. And just as in the field of reason the scepticism of all relative truths only makes more evident the oblique reference to an absolute norm, so also, in the field of value, the notion of utility succeeds in relativizing all finite values only from the vantage point of an infinite absolute. How can we assert all human truths to be fictions unless we already know *a priori* what it is to be absolutely true?

It is not surprising, therefore, to find Berkeley, precisely on the basis of his pragmatic relativism, falling into exactly the dilemma of his dialogues, and forced to the assertion of the same sort of absolute. Thus, he is able to take the pragmatic position that scientific concepts are "useful" abstractions only by contrasting them with the absolute, the "concrete particu-

lars" or "things themselves."[83] We cannot refer meaningfully
to the artificial "ends of computation and mathematical demonstration" without referring obliquely to "the nature of
things." [84] His pragmatic scepticism can be asserted only on
the ground of some higher insight into the "true nature of
things." If all were hypothesis, if pragmatism were true, we
should never become aware of the fact, and it would be altogether impossible for us significantly to maintain pragmatism.
The pragmatic or abstract sciences, such as mathematics and
mechanics, which are based on "useful" postulates, require,
therefore, a higher science, something to which Berkeley now
gives the significant Aristotelian name,—*philosophia prima*.[85]
In concluding the essay, he sums up his position in a few pregnant sentences as follows: "In physics and sense-experience,
whatever takes place pertains only to apparent effects. In
mechanics, abstract notions of mathematics are admitted [for
purposes of convenience]. In *philosophia prima*, or metaphysics,
it is a question of incorporeal things, of the causes, truth and
existence of things." [86]

Thus, as we should expect from the critique of phenomenalism contained in the *Three Dialogues*, Berkeley is no longer able
to attach any ultimate finality to sense experience. The Platonism of the dialogues, however, is now deepened by a careful
reading of Aristotle. All experience is relative and contradictory. It both is and is not, and possesses, therefore, only "a
relative or *hypothetical existence*."[87] Sensory things are not
things at all, but "apparent effects" which exist only relatively
or "ectypally," and depend upon an "archetypal" or non-

[83] "Melius itaque foret, si, missa qualitate occulta, homines attenderent solummodo ad effectus sensibiles; vocibusque
abstractis (quantumvis illae ad disserendum utiles sint) in meditatione omissis,
mens in particularibus et concretis, hoc
est in ipsis rebus, defigeretur." Sec. 4.

[84] "Haec mechanicae et computationi
inserviunt: sed aliud est computationi et
demonstrationibus mathematicis inservire, aliud rerum naturam exhibere." Sec.
18. Cf. sec. 39, and especially sec. 66,
where Berkeley warns specifically against
confusing "mathematical hypotheses"
with "the natures of things" ("distin-
guere inter hypotheses mathematicas et
naturas rerum").

[85] πρώτη φιλοσοφία. Cf. *Physics*, A,
192a 36, and B, 194b 14. Berkeley himself cites Book A of the *Physics* in D. M.,
sec. 57. He cites books of the *Physics* in
secs. 48, 32, 26, and 19. Cf. also Aristotle,
Metaphysics, E, 1026a 24, and K, 1061b
19.

[86] "In physica, sensus et experientia,
quae ad effectus apparentes solummodo
pertingunt, locum habent; in mechanica,
notiones abstractae mathematicorum ad-
mittuntur. In philosophia prima, seu
metaphysica, agitur de rebus incorporeis,
de causis, veritate, et existentia rerum."
Sec. 71. Cf. Arist., *Meta.*, 1026a.

[87] 3D., F. i, p. 474.

existential type of reality. By effects, however, Berkeley does not mean the effects of some external action impressed upon us from an outside source, but the effects of a way of thought which is not *my* way of thought nor *your* way, but a universal logic,— *philosophia prima.* "The incorporeal things," which are the object of this science, are no longer spirits, but "causes" in general. *Philosophia prima* is the study of the underlying incorporeal things (*res incorporeae*), such as "cause," "truth," and "existence," on the basis of which we are justified in holding to a pragmatism which asserts all objective or observable causation to be motion, all possible truth to be fiction, and all phenomenal, or given, existence to be "hypothetical." *Philosophia prima* is, therefore, logic, for in studying the true causes of things we are forced back of all presented causes or successions to the "true seat of forces," [88] which is thought itself, or pure form.[89] Back of all causes lies the incorporeal form of "causation" itself, just as back of all truths lies truth, and back of all existing things, the eternal or archetypal form of "existence." [90] But just as all natural knowledge presupposes these absolute forms, so do these absolute forms presuppose the absolute itself. "Thus natural philosophy either presupposes the knowledge of God or it is transformed into a higher science." [91]

The *De Motu*, furthermore, reveals the extent to which Berkeley has now abandoned that spiritism or psychologism of his early thought, which confused the transcendental with the empirical, and the logical with the natural. "Those who seek the principle of motion in spirits must either understand by the word spirit something corporeal or incorporeal. If something corporeal, no matter how tenuous, nevertheless difficulty arises: [since we are then confusing subject with object]: if incorporeal, no matter how true it may be, nevertheless it does not properly pertain to the physical . . . [for] the whole of natural philosophy lies in experiments, the laws of motion, and the principles of mechanics together with what may be deduced from them: but whatever involves other things must be referred

88 "Verae sedis virium." Sec. 71.

89 "πῶς δ'ἔχει τὸ χωριζὸν [εἶδος] καὶ τί ἐστι, φιλοσοφίας τῆς πρώτης διορίσαι ἔργον." Arist., *Physics*, B, 194b 14.

90 Cf. Arist., *Meta.*, K, 1061b 31, 32.

91 "Itaque cognitionem de Deo vel supponit philosophia naturalis, vel mutuatur ab aliqua scientia superiori." Sec. 34. Cf. Arist., *Physics*, A, 192b 3 and 4: "πάλιν δὲ ἄλλην ἀρχὴν ἀρξάμενοι λέγωμεν."

to another higher science." [92] Berkeley here recognizes the full force of the objection, so fatal to his early psychologism, that it considered the psyche, something "tenuously" corporeal, as if it were incorporeal, something objective, as if it were truly the subject. Hence arises the conception of psychology as the basic "science of man" or "human nature," underlying all other sciences, that futile dream of the *Aufklärung* to which he himself had formerly given countenance. Psychology, as such a fundamental science of sciences, ceases to be psychology. It is transformed into "a certain higher science" (*superiori alicui scientiae*), and becomes logic and metaphysics. Psychology, that is, must either be an "objective" science, studying certain phenomena or appearances within the general framework of nature (space and time), or it must become transcendental logic or metaphysics. Any "middle course" is mere confusion. "I have now distinguished," says Berkeley in conclusion, "the question of truly active causes, and drawn them from the shadows in which they can be involved," the shadows of psychology. The "principles" of motion cannot be found here, since psychology itself rests upon such principles. "To deal with them is the business of Metaphysics or *philosophia prima*." [93]

The appeal to the practical, while it enables Berkeley to "explain" and relativize the fundamental concepts of science, and affords him considerable insight into the origins of common sense, leads him in the end to the same predicament as his first experiments with rationalism. He succeeds in comprehending science only by means of the same speculative absolute which had dominated his early writings. Pragmatic scepticism is still scepticism, and leads him to the same relative absolute as rationalistic scepticism. Just as reason at last proves itself irrational, so does pragmatism prove itself impractical. Both rationalism and irrationalism, consequently, end in the same meaningless morass of meaning, for an absolute that is itself a

---

[92] "Qui a spiritibus motus principium petunt, ii vel rem corpoream vel incorpoream voce *spiritus* intelligunt. Si rem corpoream, quantumvis tenuem, tamen redit difficultas: si incorpoream, quantumvis id verum sit, attamen ad physicam non proprie pertinet . . . philosophus naturalis totus sit in experimentis legibusque motuum, et principiis mechanicis, indeque

depromptis ratiociniis; quidquid autem de aliis rebus protulerit, id superiori alicui scientiae acceptum referat." Sec. 42.

[93] "Causae vere activae meditatione tantum et ratiocinio e tenebris erui quibus involvuntur possunt, et aliquatenus cognosci. Spectat autem ad philosophiam primam, seu metaphysicam, de iis agere." Sec. 72.

form of scepticism, and is, in other words, itself relative to the relative, is no absolute. Yet all reason, as well as all unreason, seems to require such a being. Any such being which we conceive, however, seems, through our very conception of it, to be made relative; and, as Berkeley says of those who followed Newton and More in attributing absolute existence to space, we are caught in "the absurdity of attributing necessary existence to anything save God alone," the truly necessary and absolute being.[94]

The attempt to make science and reflection serve the ends of "life" lands us in exactly the same dilemma as the pretensions of reason for reason's sake, and we are either involved in a meaningless regress or referred back to that same absolute which is itself relative, that God who is God only in contrast to man, that same implacable field of relative meaning or significance from which there is seemingly no escape. It is no wonder, therefore, that Berkeley turns in desperation from his scientific and philosophical studies, abandoning for the time being his transcendental science of *philosophia prima* to plunge again, and this time more deeply and irrevocably, into the wilderness of practical action. Perhaps in the practical itself, rather than in the philosophy of the practical, some solution may be found.

[94] "Qua ratione mens humana facillime liberatur a magnis difficultatibus simulque ab ea absurditate tribuendi existentiam necessariam ulli rei praeterquam soli Deo optimo maximo." Sec. 56.

CHAPTER XI

PLANS FOR THE NEW WORLD

BERKELEY arrived in London during the late summer or early fall of 1720. He brought with him books and *objets d'art* for his friends Lord Percival and Lord Pembroke. Through the latter, he became acquainted with the Earl of Burlington, who shared his enthusiasm for architecture and was interested in his accounts of the splendours of the Borghese Palace and the magnificent ruins of Calabria.[1] In a letter written at this time, Pope speaks of a projected dinner with Bishop Atterbury, who was most anxious to see Berkeley. Soon after, he spent a week at Twickenham, for the characteristic letter of invitation has fortunately survived. "I take you to be almost the only friend I have," writes Pope, "that is above the little vanities of the town, I expect you may be able to renounce it for one week, and to make trial how you like my Tusculum, because I assure you, it is no less yours and hope you will use it as your own country villa, the ensuing season."[2] Arbuthnot, who had just finished the elegant scientific skit in the first book of Scriblerus, may at last have come around to Berkeley's view. In any case, he was furnished with further details concerning Vesuvius, and further criticisms of the new mechanical philosophy. But in spite of his delight in conversing with such friends, Berkeley was profoundly depressed by the worldliness of the times.

THE RUIN OF GREAT BRITAIN

The days of the South Sea Bubble had suddenly come to an end. The Sunflower Company, the Human Hair Company, and the Sawdust Company were no longer names to conjure with.

[1] "Berkeley gained the patronage and friendship of Lord Burlington, not only by his true politeness and the peculiar charms of his conversation which was exquisite, but by his profound and perfect skill in Architecture; an art which he had very particularly and accurately studied in Italy, when he went and continued abroad four years with Mr. Ashe, son of the Bishop of Clogher. With an insatiable and philosophic attention Berkeley surveyed and examined every object of curiosity." Warton: *Essay on the Genius and Writings of Pope*, 5th ed., vol. II, pp. 194 ff., London, 1806.

[2] Not published by Fraser; *Pope*, vol. IX, p. 6, Elwin and Courthope, London, 1886. The letter is dated 1722.

The three hundred million pounds that had so rapidly changed hands were now safely in the possession of the more unscrupulous adventurers who had managed to escape the angry public. But though the fever of speculation had passed, the effects of cynicism and moral laxity remained. The cleverness which so easily masqueraded as intellectual penetration and so readily found apologies for atheism and vice seemed in complete ascendancy, and now aroused Berkeley's enmity. Once again, he identifies as his enemies those "free-thinkers" who, in their unrestricted rationalism, have confused "liberty" and "licentiousness" [3] and have made it "fashionable" in the name of religion "to decry religion." But he could no longer express his antipathy to the "new" currents of thought in the light satiric tone of his *Guardian Essays* or in the cool scepticism of the *De Motu*, for the practical aspect of the issue lay too nakedly before his gaze, sharpened as it was by four years of absence from his country and by much disturbing meditation. The bitter tone of the short, "occasional" *Essay* that he published at this time shows, even in its title, the degree to which he is in direct opposition to the rationalistic "spirit of the age" that he had himself done much to propagate in his earlier writings. He was now preparing to combat this spirit not only with his pen but with his life as well. It is not the philosopher, calmly diagnosing his country's ills from a distant, "rational" vantage point, who, in 1721, wrote the *Essay Towards Preventing the Ruin of Great Britain*, but a man, himself caught in the exigencies of existence, and feeling the intimate, practical anxieties of his state.

"The corrupt and degenerate age we live in," he says, "has brought forth new and portentous villainies," [4] the source of which is to be found primarily in those shallow philosophic views which enable us to rationalize our sins, so that "vice and villainy have by degrees grown reputable among us. Other nations," he continues, "have been wicked, but we are the first who have been wicked on principle." [5] This "principle" he now more confidently associates with the "free-thinkers" or rationalists of the day, who center "all our cares upon private interest" and contract "all our hopes within the enjoyment of this present life." [6] Such a "narrow" philosophy must eventually end in the "Epicurean notions, [7] cozenage and stock-

[3] F. iv., p. 321.   [5] *Ibid.*
[4] *Ibid.*, p. 337.   [6] *Ibid.*, p. 331.   [7] *Ibid.*, p. 338.

jobbing" [8] which are so prevalent that Berkeley says, "it is to be feared the final period of our State approaches." [9]

He thinks, however, that the great shock of the South Sea collapse may startle the nation out of its complacency. This encourages him to write his address. Even unpalatable advice may obtain a hearing in painful times. "As a sharp distemper by reclaiming a man from intemperance, may prolong his life, so it is not impossible but this public calamity that lies so heavy on the nation may prevent its ruin." [10] The remedies that Berkeley advocates are, indeed, drastic ones, and they remind us of those which Socrates recommends in the early books of the *Republic* for the "purging" of his state. In the first place, it is extravagant to hope to become rich by piling up counters. "Industry," writes Berkeley, "is the natural sure way to wealth." [11] Money is useful to the nation only "as it promoteth industry." [12] If it circulates through many hands "without producing labour and industry in the inhabitants" it is "direct gaming." [13] This is the beginning of a series of economic speculations which, culminating in the famous *Querist* notes, led him finally beyond the accepted economic doctrines of the day into regions later more fully explored by Adam Smith and Hume.

But labour and industry are only the foundations for a healthy commonwealth. Among the other elements necessary for the completion of the structure, Berkeley lays great stress upon the arts. Fresh from his Italian tour, he deplores the lack of public monuments and national galleries.[14] Like Plato, he sees in art not only a medium for the presentation of purely aesthetic values, but a powerful educational force as well. "Those noble arts of architecture, sculpture and painting do not only adorn the public, but have also an influence on the minds and manners of men, filling them with great ideas, and spiriting them up to an emulation of worthy actions." [15] Like Plato again, with the great educational possibilities of the drama in mind, he defends the institution of censorship. Strongly condemning the corrupt Restoration stage of "these last ninety years," and particularly the institution of the masque, he urges a return to the "noble entertainment" which "gave those fine

[8] *Ibid.*, p. 336.
[9] *Ibid.*, p. 337.
[10] *Ibid.*, p. 336.
[11] *Ibid.*, p. 323.

[12] *Ibid.*
[13] *Ibid.*
[14] *Ibid.*, p. 332.
[15] *Ibid.*, p. 333.

lessons of morality and good sense to the Athenians of old, and to our British gentry above a century ago."[16] It was his new sense of the supremacy of the practical that led him back to a spirit which profoundly transcended the "rationalistic" temper of his own time.

But Berkeley was not satisfied with censorship of drama alone. He strongly opposes Mandeville and the other writers who defended luxury on economic grounds, and goes so far as to advocate the regulation of dress in the direction of simplicity; nor is he even content with this. "Dress," he says, "is not the only thing to be reformed; sumptuary laws are useful in many other points." Only by this means does he think it possible to recover "the natural plainness and good sense of the English,"[17] which has recently "degenerated" to "Epicurean notions" and become "venal" and "corrupt."[18] For the general purification of language and the encouragement of public spirit, he proposes the plan he had developed ten years before, with his brilliant literary friends, for an "Academy of ingenious men"[19] who should encourage the study of national history, which he finds singularly neglected, and foster other public projects. He mentions the French Academy in this connection, but thinks that it "is prostituted to meaner purposes"[20] than those he has in mind, — the fostering of public feeling and religion. His remarks on the political turmoil of the time are even more non-partisan than his previous "Advice to Tories." He now urges both Whigs and Tories to remember that "it is impossible for either party to ruin the other without involving themselves and their posterity in the same ruin,"[21] and advises them that "to get the better of the other," they must "first get the better of themselves."[22]

Berkeley is under no illusions as to the palatability of such advice. "I know," he says, "it is an old folly to make peevish complaints of the times."[23] But the crisis which the nation was passing through, he thought, might give such words a temporary hearing. However this may have been, it is certain that they were of the profoundest importance in his own development, for as his hopes of reform died, his disgust with the moral cynicism and laxity of England led him to stake his hopes on the building of a new and purer civilization across the sea.

[16] *Ibid.*, p. 331.
[17] *Ibid.*, p. 328.
[18] *Ibid.*, p. 338.
[19] *Ibid.*, p. 333; cf. [p. 201], and Qu. 186.
[20] *Ibid.*
[21] *Ibid.*, p. 334.
[22] *Ibid.*
[23] *Ibid.*, p. 337.

BERMUDA

Berkeley took leave of London in the fall of 1721, and returned to Trinity College [24] after an absence of almost ten years. It was time, indeed, for him to look after his own affairs. He was now thirty-six years old, and had as yet no stable position. Shortly after his return he was appointed Hebrew Lecturer. This added a small amount to his stipend, and he was also appointed to the honorary task of devising a Latin inscription for the King's equestrian statue in Dublin, which finally led to a court presentation and a medal.[25] But his total emoluments from the College could not have amounted to more than two hundred pounds per year. Not only was this inadequate as a means of support, but the burden of his academic duties now weighed heavily upon him, and he also missed his friends in England. Never very strong in health, he found that his manifold activities absorbed all of his strength, and left him no time nor energy for study,[26] nor for the prosecution of those larger practical designs which were now fermenting in his mind.

The usual path led from the college to the Church, and it was only natural for Berkeley to expect some such advancement, especially since he had been formerly refused the living of St. Paul's on political grounds, which he must have considered altogether unjust. It was a fortunate coincidence that the Deanery

---

[24] The story told by Warton (vol. II, p. 194) and Stock (*Memoirs*) that Berkeley went to Ireland at this time as chaplain to the Duke of Grafton is definitely false. Berkeley's letters to Percival show clearly that he was connected with the College (see particularly letter of October 12, 1721). The letter which Fraser printed in his *Life and Letters of Berkeley* (1871), and which he maintained was proved by "internal evidence" to be written by Berkeley in 1721, was, as a matter of fact, written by another George Berkeley not later than two years after Berkeley's birth. Cf. Lorenz, *Archiv für Gesch. der Phil.*, vol. XIII, 1900, p. 541; also the review of Stock's *Memoirs* in *Gent. Mag.*, December, 1776.

[25] "Whilst he was among them [the Irish] they chose him to write the inscription which is under the statue of his late Majesty, and afterwards he was desired

to wait upon his present Majesty, when he accepted of being Chancellor of the University of Dublin, and preserves the golden medal given him on that occasion to this day." Baron Wainwright to Mrs. Clayton, February 9, 1731, in the *Memoirs of Viscountess Sundon* by Mrs. Thomson, London, 1847, p. 177. See also Berkeley to Percival, July 29, 1722, and Berkeley, *Poems*, p. ccxxv. Baron Wainwright, a native of Chester, was an Irish Baron who was the friend of many notable people and enjoyed a high repute in Ireland. He thought of accompanying Berkeley to the Indies. He later became a judge, and died during the famine of 1741.

[26] "If I could prosecute my studies in health and tranquillity, that would make me as happy as I expect to be in this life, but in the College I enjoyed neither. . . ." Berkeley to Percival, August 7, 1713, Oxford.

of Dromore then fell vacant. This was a lesser Deanery, being worth only two hundred pounds a year, but the duties were light, and it accorded exactly with Berkeley's needs, — providing a modest means of subsistence and, what was more important, freedom of movement in the prosecution of a certain project. He thus reminded the Duke of Grafton, the Lord Lieutenant, of "his promises,"[27] and wrote to his intimate friend Percival, on whom he knew he could count for assistance.[28]

---

[27] Percival letter, October 12, 1721.

[28] Mr. G. A. Johnston has cast suspicion on Berkeley's personal character in thus seeking advancement (Johnston, *Devel.*, p. 334, note). That Berkeley was eager to gain a position which would provide him with leisure and adequate emolument must, of course, be admitted, and also that he sought his friend's aid, but that, when judged by the standards of the times, he was guilty of selfishness is another matter. Personal charges of this sort must be substantiated by evidence extending over considerable periods of a man's life, and justified in connection with the customs of the age. When read in the light of what is generally known of his character, the Percival letters of this period offer no evidence of a persistent self-seeking which is in any way "remarkable" (*ibid.*, p. 334, note). It must be remembered that the only method for advancement in the Church was through personal influence. It is no sin to have powerful friends. Furthermore, the Deanery Berkeley wanted was a lesser office, which he wished primarily for the sake of study and other projects which his later actions show were far from selfish.

Two of Mr. Johnston's specific charges are peculiarly serious.

1. Mr. Johnston asserts that when the Leslie lawsuit seemed hopeless, Berkeley "devised an ingenious scheme for securing the Deanery without fighting the case to the bitter end. According to this plan, Leslie was to be made a Bishop. If that were done, the Bishop of Dromore would probably not press his right to appoint to the Deanery, and Berkeley's entry would accordingly be unopposed" (*ibid.*, p. 335, note). This hypothesis is presumably based on the following parenthetical remark in a letter to Percival of September 7, 1722: "I flatter myself with hopes of seeing your Lordship in London this winter, if I can steal so much time from my lawsuit; which besides that it gives me but a very discouraging prospect (the only way of getting possession of the Deanery being I am fully persuaded to make Dean Leslie a Bishop) hath this inconvenience, that it keeps me from my friends in England though I have a letter of absence." Such remarks to an intimate friend certainly betray a sense of uneasiness and discouragement on Berkeley's part, concerning his immediate prospects. That they constitute "an ingenious *scheme* for securing the Deanery" is hardly apparent.

2. Mr. Johnston next alleges that "The Dean of Derry was seriously ill, and Berkeley thought that, if the proper means were used, he might obtain that Deanery on the death of the Dean" (*ibid.*, p. 335, note). The evidence for this statement is the following letter to Percival (October, 1722):

"As to my own affair, I could wish it were one brought to any conclusion, being prepared for the issue, be it what it will, and I think as indifferent about it as one can well be supposed to be on a like occasion.

"My Lord Duke hath taken one step of late that pleases everyone, I mean the presenting Dr. Bolton to the Bishopric of Clonfert. He could not possibly have pitched upon a person more universally esteemed and unenvied. There is another of that name, Dean of Derry, who lieth dangerously ill of a palsy, and is indeed past hopes of recovery. My friends think that in case of a vacancy, I may have some pretensions to my Lord Lieutenant's

Grafton seemed cordial, but kept Berkeley waiting several months, asking him to testify concerning his allegiance to the government, in order to prevent a repetition of the unjust politi-

---

favour; especially if his Grace shall not think fit to recommend my adversary to a Bishopric, without which I have little or no prospect of succeeding to the Deanery of Dromore."

I am unable to find anything in these statements to justify Mr. Johnston's insinuations with reference to Berkeley's character. Percival is an intimate friend, and Berkeley certainly wishes to keep him in touch with the situation, which has complicated political aspects.

Even Mr. Johnston cannot find any ulterior motives in the Bermuda project; hence he maintains that Berkeley's character, at this time, underwent an extraordinary revolution in which he ceased to be primarily selfish but made the public welfare his motto. "So far," says Mr. Johnston, "Berkeley seems to have been a decidedly calculating man, with a fixed determination to do the best he could for himself. But suddenly, in 1723, he intimated to Percival his dramatic decision to go as a missionary to the new world. And thenceforth his motto was *non sibi sed toti mundo*" (*ibid.*, p. 335, note). Such a *volte-face* is improbable, but not impossible. If anything like this occurred, however, it is remarkable that his intimate letters to Percival should show no trace of it.

Furthermore, we know from Berkeley himself that he definitely "determined" to spend the rest of his days in Bermuda in May, 1722 (Percival letter, March 4, 1723), precisely in the midst of his "calculating" negotiations for the deaneries, and long before the supposedly incriminating "suggestion" as to the Deanery of Derry which occurred in December, exactly seven months after the admittedly unselfish decision. This decision occurred six months after his application for the Deanery of Dromore, it is true, but we can hardly suppose that such a weighty resolution could occur without much preliminary reflection, so that it is more than probable, particularly when we remember that he had just written the idealistic

Essay Towards Preventing the Ruin of Great Britain, that, when applying for the Deanery of Dromore, he had the Bermuda project vaguely in mind. But even supposing that he did not, there is nothing peculiarly selfish or self-seeking in a man of Berkeley's age and prominence applying for a modest ecclesiastical position which could ensure him adequate leisure to prosecute his studies.

We must conclude that there is not the slightest evidence for any such sudden break in Berkeley's character as Mr. Johnston suggests. The man who penned the intensely idealistic *Essay* on Britain in 1721, the chief burden of which is the necessity for "public spirit" and "religion" to avoid a "final ruin" hanging over the community, is certainly the same man who worked out the Bermuda project in 1722, and it is absurd to speak of any revolutionary breach or disturbance between these two episodes.

We know that Berkeley hated the political calls he was forced to make on Grafton (Philip Percival to Percival, April, 1724), but these things were simply necessary. The eighteenth century was not a sentimental age, and ecclesiastical affairs were conducted in an altogether realistic manner. Berkeley's letters to Percival should be compared with those of the Bishop of Killala to the influential Mrs. Clayton, for example (Sundon, *Memoirs*, pp. 196–203). This type of negotiation is evidently offensive to Mr. Johnston. We know that it was also offensive to Berkeley. He did not desire to remain a college "hack." But the ultimate test of his underlying motives in struggling for advancement is what he did with it once attained. There can be no question as to this. Six months after obtaining the richest deanery in the Kingdom, and only three years after his first negotiations, he was on his way to London for the purpose of sacrificing it for the presidency of an imaginary college at the salary of 100 pounds per year. Such idealism is not born overnight. There is no

cal charges which had proved so disastrous four years before.[29] On January 9, the Deanery of Down became vacant, but he wrote Percival that this was above his wishes. Meanwhile his powerful friends in England, Percival, Pembroke, and Burlington, had certainly recommended him to Grafton. The result was that in January Berkeley was appointed Dean of Dromore by the Lord Lieutenant. Unfortunately, however, the jurisdiction of the Lord Lieutenant over this seat was somewhat vague, and the Bishop of Down insisted on putting his man in the place. The result was that Berkeley was involved in a very tedious lawsuit. His opponent was a wealthy man,[30] so that he was forced to undergo a considerable legal expense for which his slender academic income was altogether inadequate. In order to help defray these costs he wrote Percival to see if Grafton could not be prevailed upon to appoint him to the modest office of Cantor of Christ Church. But this proved impossible. "God preserve your Lordship from law and lawyers," he writes Percival in April. The suit dragged on month after month and Berkeley began to despair. But in the midst of these worries and worldly entanglements, the vague dreams of an ideal community which had stirred in his mind ever since his return from Italy suddenly crystallized in the form of a very concrete and practical project which determined the course of his life for the next ten years.

In a letter to Percival of March 4, 1723, Berkeley writes, "It is now about ten months since I have determined with myself to spend the residue of my days in the Island of Bermuda, where I trust in Providence I may be the mean instrument of doing good to mankind." Berkeley does not himself anywhere state exactly how the idea came to him, but there can be little doubt that it arose out of the same chain of thought and feeling which attended his objective insight into the moral laxity and corruption of England on his return from the Continent, and which gave rise to his reform pamphlet.[31] The material details of this tedious lawsuit and the sordid negotiations attending ecclesiastical preferment must have further convinced him of

---

reason for rejecting the judgments of men like Pope and Swift who knew Berkeley personally for long periods of years both before and after these negotiations, and who unreservedly testify to his unselfishness.

[29] Percival letter, May 26, 1716.
[30] Berkeley to Percival, March 15, 1721-22.
[31] Fraser pointed out this connection in 1901, vol. IV, pp. 320, 342.

the social depravity of the old and, as he believed, sinking civilization. Why not escape with a chosen company to enjoy "peace of mind and health of body" [32] in the blessed calm of the Bermudas? It is easy to understand the shift from disgust and despair to such a project in a mind as active as Berkeley's. The romantic beauties of the Bermudas had been celebrated by a whole century of poets. But with increasingly accurate knowledge, "the vex'd Bermoothes" had now become "the blessed summer isles" of Waller and Marvell, crowned with everlasting peace. The appeal of such descriptions to Berkeley's sensitive feeling for nature certainly provided one of the strongest motives for his choice of this "Hesperian Garden" as the site for his college. He himself, both in poetry and prose, made notable contributions to the widespread celebration of Bermuda, describing "the summers refreshed with constant cool breezes, the winters as mild as our May, the sky as light and blue as a sapphire, the ever green pastures, the earth eternally crowned with fruits and flowers." [33]

It seems to have been the idea of escape to such a primaeval "paradise" from the "artificial" complexities of a worldly civilization that caught the imagination of the "society" of the day, but, for Berkeley himself, Bermuda was not so much a haven of refuge as an opportunity for "restoring the Golden Age." [34] Associated most of his life with a university, he appreciated the essential part which education must play in any effective scheme of reform, and we have already spoken of the poignant impression made on him by his long visit to Oxford eight years before. If a new and purer civilization was really to be built up in America, and this was certainly Berkeley's ultimate objective, the basis must be education, and, therefore, a superior university. He immediately started to interest the most promising men of Trinity College in his plan, and in less than a year's time he had actually obtained the promises of three of the younger tutors [35] to give up their established positions and accompany him on his venture. "You will be surprised," writes Dering to Percival, "when you hear the company he has engaged to go with him. Young and old, learned and rich. . . ." [36] Even the obstinate cynicism of Swift melted before such enthusiasm.

[32] Dering to Percival, March 5, 1723.
[33] Berkeley to Percival, March 4, 1723.
[34] Dering to Percival, March 5, 1723.
[35] Rev. William Tomson, Jonathan Rogers, and James King, all Masters of Arts. They agreed to accompany Berkeley for a salary of 40 pounds per year.
[36] Dering to Percival, March 5, 1723.

It is natural to suppose that this enthusiasm was based upon the widespread sentimental idealization of life in the colonies, which was so prevalent at the time. This, however, was not the case. The prospectus in which Berkeley outlined his scheme [37] shows that he cherished no illusions as to the simplicity or purity of life in America. In the first paragraph he speaks of the "ignorance and barbarism" and "most notorious corruption of manners" prevailing in New England.[38] St. G. Ashe, Berkeley's friend, had been instrumental in establishing a branch of the Society for the Propagation of the Gospel at Dublin during Berkeley's student days, and constant contact with the Society provided him with valuable and accurate information concerning the colonies. He drew out several books on the Indies from the Trinity College Library, and, with his gift for concrete detail, was soon in possession of relevant facts. Berkeley, indeed, owed his original idea of a college in the Indies to a piece of information gained from such research. In 1710 General Codrington, a rich planter, had left his estates and a large sum of money to the Society for the Propagation of the Gospel for the establishment of a college in Barbadoes, but Berkeley felt that the "wealth and luxury" and "dissolute morals" of the rich planters there would make a bad environment for a college devoted to such purely intellectual and unworldly aims as he cherished.[39]

There has been much amusement at Berkeley's expense because of his choice of a poetic though utterly remote and insignificant spot which has hardly been able to support a straw hat industry, to say nothing of a university.[40] But the absence of trade was one of the advantages which Berkeley urged most strenuously in favour of his scheme. In his pamphlet he outlines other reasons which led him to select Bermuda as the most favourable site for this new center of civilization.[41] First of all, Bermuda was centrally located so far as the other colonies were concerned, for it must be remembered that the chief settlements at this time were along the coast and in the islands of the West Indies. Furthermore, it was, according to his information, the only island easily accessible to all the colonies. Then, of course, there was the much celebrated climate, the security of the place, and the general probity of the inhabitants, who, be-

[37] Published in 1725.
[38] F. iv, p. 346.   [39] Ibid., p. 350.
[40] Balfour, biog. int. to Sampson's edition of Berkeley's *Works*, 1895.

[41] These are also more succinctly stated in his letter to Percival of March 4, 1723.

cause of the very poverty of the land, had been unable to develop the decadent symptoms of the richer island cultures, such
as that of Barbadoes.

The primary purpose of the new institution was to act as a
general cultural agency in the training of qualified ministers of
the Gospel to take charge of the colonial churches, which at that
time were notoriously "very ill supplied," [42] and to act as a general "Nursery of learning for the education of the natives." [43]
But, secondarily, the university was to fulfill, in harmony with
the aims of the Society for the Propagation of the Gospel,[44] the
duties of the mother country toward the native Indians, and
also negroes,[45] by taking charge of a select number of them at
early ages and giving them the benefits of an European education. The College was thus to aim at the improvement of both
natives and colonists, in keeping with the ideas of a more enlightened English colonial policy, which, unfortunately, did not
gain the ascendancy until a much later day. By such means,
Berkeley felt that it might be possible for America to avoid
many of Europe's mistakes. As we have shown, he had no illusions as to the then prevailing vice and barbarism in the colonies.
But America was not, like Europe, "old in vice." There was
still hope that, if the best of Europe could be effectively trans-
planted, a new and glorious civilization might dawn in this
"land of the setting sun."

> There shall be sung another Golden Age,
> The rise of Empire and of Arts;
> The good and great inspiring epic rage,
> The wisest heads and noblest hearts.

[42] F. iv, p. 348. The Bishop of London had diocesan rights over the American plantations. In spite of the suggestions of Laud and Clarendon and the recommendations in 1714 of the Commission of the Society for the Propagation of the Gospel no step had been taken to found a bishopric in any of the colonies (Wilberforce, *Prot. Episc. Church in America*, 1856, p. 153). Queen Anne had, in fact, been prevailed upon to establish several American bishoprics, but largely owing to the opposition of the Dissenters in the colonies, the plan fell through. As a result of this, the development of the English Church in America was very slow, and the quality of the missionaries unimpressive. Thus, in North Carolina the S. P. G. mission-

aries behaved "in a most horrid manner," and harmed their own cause (Weeks, *Religious Development in North Carolina*, 1892, p. 35). Cf. G. B. Hertz, *British Imperialism in the Eighteenth Century*, London, 1908, p. 130.

[43] F. iv, p. 348.

[44] The aim of the Society for the Propagation of the Gospel, according to its charter, was to preserve the American Indians and negroes from "Atheism, infidelity, Popish superstition and idolatry." Two missionaries were sent to the Iroquois, and John Eliot was enabled to publish his Indian Bible through funds supplied by the Society.

[45] G. B. Hertz, *British Imperialism in the Eighteenth Century*, p. 130.

Not such as Europe breeds in her decay,
Such as she bred when fresh and young,
When heavenly flame did animate her clay
By future poets shall be sung.[46]

Westward the course of Empire takes its way,
The four first acts already past,
A fifth shall close the drama with the day,
The world's great effort is the last.

VANESSA'S LEGACY

Berkeley now allowed the Dromore lawsuit to drop. As he clearly states in one of his letters, however, he felt that it would greatly help his project if he were known as the occupant of a recognized ecclesiastical position rather than an unknown college tutor.[47] Hence, though he was often so ashamed that "he used to retire to the garden,"[48] he kept his place among the petitioners who crowded the "porch" of the Duke of Grafton. On June 3, 1723, his wearisome efforts were rewarded from a totally unexpected quarter in such a propitious way that he must have felt that Providence now favoured his project. Stella's rival, the lovelorn but materially prosperous Vanessa, had at last escaped from her earthly burdens,[49] and when her will was opened, it was discovered that she had made Berkeley an executor. No one was more astounded by this stroke of fortune than the beneficiary himself, who had seen her only once at a dinner party in London almost ten years before.[50] G. M. Berkeley in his *Literary Relics* suggests romantic revenge as the motive for this surprising bequest, and so it has usually been interpreted. "Her last will," he says, "declared what her feelings were: Her appointing Swift's most intimate friend Bishop Berkeley to be one of the executioners of her vengeance shows the violence of her resentment."[51]

But Berkeley, with his views concerning friendship,[52] was not a fitting tool for the execution of romantic vengeance. He did everything in his power in the administration of the Van Hom-

[46] Berkeley to Percival, Feb. 10, 1725–26; cf. Spence, *Anecdotes*, p. 254.

[47] Percival, September 19, 1723.

[48] Philip Percival to Percival, April 24, 1724.

[49] Delany states in his *Observations*, p. 19, that Vanessa gave herself up to "Bacchus" when deserted.

[50] "The Bishop dined but once at the house of Mrs Vanhomrigh, and that was only by chance. This, too, Mrs Berkeley has often heard him say, was the first and the last time of his life in which he ever saw Vanessa." *Biog. Brit.*, vol. III, Add. and Corr., p. 262.

[51] *Literary Relics,* p. xxix.

[52] "Tis a man's duty, tis the fruit of friendship, to speak well of his friend. Wonder not therefore that I do what I do." C. B. J., 754.

righ estate to protect Swift, bitterly resisting the publication of the Vanessa letters which she herself had demanded on her death-bed. To the author of the *Passive Obedience*, who had insisted so fervently on the passionless adherence to the moral rule, irrespective of all consequence, this must have occasioned some reflection. But by this time, Berkeley had seen the necessity of mitigating the rationalistic rigour of his ethical views, and had come to feel that the Christian virtue of charity in administering the law was at least as important as the law itself.[53] Whatever his reasons, he never hesitated in the duty of protecting his friend, and even went so far as to burn the entire original manuscript of the correspondence.[54] But Marshal, the other executor, possessed a copy which was finally published, in spite of Berkeley's opposition.[55] It was no easy task to defend Swift against the insinuations of his enemies, but Berkeley fought for him with every means at his command, maintaining "frequently"[56] that the letters "contained nothing which would either do honour to her character, or bring the least reflection upon Cadenus — not the least hint of a criminal commerce between them in the Letters of either."[57] Of Orrery, the well-known detractor of Swift, Berkeley remarked: "My Lord Orrery would be a man of genius if he knew how to set about it."[58] The fact that Berkeley strongly defended Swift to the end must stand as a most powerful argument on the side of those who take the "favourable" view of the latter's character, for there is reason, as we have already noted, to believe that he knew much more than he told concerning the life of his friend. It is inconceivable that a man of Berkeley's integrity and moral sensitiveness could have continued to shield one in whom he did not fundamentally believe.

[53] This was probably strengthened by his judgment that Vanessa's passion of vengeance would have cooled had she lived longer. See *Lit. Rel.*, p. xxix, note. "Influenced by this idea," he continues, "Bishop Berkeley withheld from the press a series of letters, the publication of which could only have served to torment one already bending under the iron rod of affliction."

[54] Stock suggests that Berkeley burned letters not included in those accessible to Marshal and later published.

[55] "Dr Berkeley disapproved extremely of the publication of 'Cadenus

and Vanessa'; which step, however, was resolved upon, and executed by Mr Marshall, the other executor" (Mrs. Berkeley in *Biog. Brit.*, vol. III, Add. and Corr., p. 262).

[56] Mrs. Berkeley, for example, states that "All Dr Swift's letters to this lady [Vanessa] tended greatly to do her honour." Marshal also maintained that there was nothing "criminal" in the correspondence (F. E. Ball, *Correspondence of Jonathan Swift*, vol. III, app. iii).

[57] *Gent. Mag.*, vol. XLVII, 1777.

[58] *Lit. Rel.*, pp. 154–155.

Berkeley shows his extreme astonishment at Vanessa's strange act in his letter to Percival of June 4, 1723. "Mrs Hester van Homry, a lady to whom I was a perfect stranger, having never in the whole course of my life to my knowledge, exchanged one single word with her, died on Sunday night. Yesterday her will was opened by which it appears that I am constituted executor, the advantage whereof is computed by those who understand her affairs to be worth three thousand pounds. ...." The administration of this estate proved a far more onerous task than he had at first contemplated, and his long correspondence with Prior, whom he was forced to appoint as his legal agent to attend to his affairs in Dublin, shows the extent to which Berkeley was bothered for the next ten years by the debts and other disagreeable details connected with the estate. The other executor, Marshal, seems to have left little undone that could add to Berkeley's administrative difficulties. They disagreed sharply not only with respect to the publication of the "Vanessa" letters, but on other points, particularly in connection with the payment of creditors,[59] so that the bequest was far from an unadulterated blessing. The value of the estate ultimately turned out to be less than first anticipated, Berkeley's share finally amounting to less than two thousand pounds. But, in spite of all this, the money came at a most fortunate moment, enabling him to proceed at once with his project. He was now able to hold before his younger associates something more than hopeful visions, and started immediately to work out the definite organization of the College, and even to draw up rough plans for the quadrangles and buildings. Finally, he gathered all his thoughts together in a pamphlet on *The Establishment of a College in Bermuda.*

THE DEAN OF DERRY

By far the most effective aid for the project came early in May, 1724, when Berkeley was appointed Dean of Derry. This was the richest Deanery in Ireland, being worth fifteen hun-

[59] "I am exceedingly plagued by these creditors," Berkeley writes to Prior from London, December 30, 1725, "and am quite tired and ashamed of repeating the same answer to them, that I expect every post to hear what Mr. Marshal and you think of their pretensions, and that then they shall be paid. It is now a full twelvemonth that I have been expecting to hear from you on this head, and expecting in vain. I shall, therefore, expect no longer, nor hope, nor desire to know what Mr. Marshal thinks, but only what you think, or what appears to you by Mrs. V. Homrigh's papers and accounts, as stated by Clarke, and compared with the claims of creditors long since transmitted from hence."

dred pounds per year, and was far above his expectations. For the sake of his project, however, he rejoiced in this acquisition, as is shown by the letter of May 5 in which he says: "... I do not consider it with an eye to enriching myself, so I shall be perfectly contented if it facilitates and recommends my scheme of Bermuda, which I am in hopes will meet with a better reception, when it comes from one possessed of so great a Deanery." A scheme which could hardly hope for anything but derision as promulgated by an obscure Fellow of Trinity College might very well receive the attention of the world when it was known that it had the sanction of the Dean of Derry. Berkeley now prepared to interest a larger public in the project, for funds were, of course, necessary. He proceeded at once to Derry in June and farmed out the tithe lands, in order to obtain as much ready cash as possible.[60]

He must have felt very hopeful, for he had certainly succeeded in arousing in Dublin the greatest interest in his scheme. Such a friend as Philip Percival called the project a "grand design," and assured his brother that the Fellows of the College who had "determined to bear him [Berkeley] company in his laudable undertaking" were "none of the least ingenious or learned of our Society."[61] He had attained the support of leading churchmen and of the Society for the Propagation of the Gospel, and, most surprising of all, he had penetrated the cynical armour of Swift, who had done his best to discourage him by undoubtedly first-hand evidence concerning "the coldness of Courts and Ministers," but all in vain. Not only was Swift forced to admit the failure of his irony on "impossible" visions and wild romanticism, but, what is almost incredible, he himself was finally converted by his younger friend's eloquence and sincerity, and lent his invaluable support to the "romantic design" by writing his friend Carteret,[62] the new Lord Lieutenant, concerning "one of the first men in the kingdom for learning and virtue," whose "heart will break if his deanery be not taken from him." Swift also wrote several persons in England in favour of his friend. "I am glad," he says a year later in a letter to the Earl of Oxford,[63] who had subscribed two hundred pounds to the project, that "your Lordship is pleased to countenance the Dean of Derry, Dr. Berkeley. He is a true philosopher and an excellent scholar, but of very visionary virtue,

---

[60] Letter to Percival, June 8, 1724.
[61] Philip Percival to Percival, January 19, 1724-25.
[62] September 3, 1724.
[63] August 14, 1725.

and is endeavouring to quit a thousand pounds a year for a hundred at Bermudas."[64] Berkeley had decided to give up his Deanery as soon as possible, for what could more readily recommend his project than such a proof of his own sincerity? So with Swift's blessing he set off the second time for London with a treatise in his pocket. This time, however, he was not striving for a new philosophy, but for a new civilization.

Berkeley, of course, had immediate entry into society, and Bermuda soon became the topic of the hour. His friend Percival not only gave his entire approval and a contribution of two hundred pounds, but seriously considered taking his family with him to dwell in "the happy climate" of this Hesperian garden, which he thought might some day become "the Athens of the world."[65] Mr. Leslie, another elderly and wealthy friend, planned to spend the remainder of his life in Bermuda, and to donate his fortune to the College.[66] Berkeley, in short, by his earnestness, irresistible enthusiasm, and brilliant style caught the imagination of the day. Subscriptions came pouring in.[67] The Scriblerus Club, full of *jeu d'esprit*, calling a meeting for the special purpose of pillorying the popular hegira, after listening for twenty minutes to the author of the project, voted unanimously to proceed with him to the promised land. The society of England, for the moment, was entranced at the prospect of withdrawing from the cares and turmoil of the world to this remote Arcadia.

[64] *Correspondence of Jonathan Swift*, ed. F. Elrington Ball, London, 1913, vol. III, pp. 261–262.

[65] Percival letter, February 6, 1724–25.

[66] Berkeley to Percival, February 10, 1725.

[67] The following lists in Berkeley's hand are found in the Rose manuscripts, Brit. Mus. 39311:

Subscriptions for Bermuda

Lord Pembroke	300
Lord Peterborough	105
Lord Arran	300
Lord Percivall	200
Archibald Hutcheson, Esqu.	200
John Wolfe, Esqu.	100
Edward Harley, Esqu.	100
Benjamin Hoare, Esqu.	100
Lady Betty Hastings	500
Sr. Robert Walpole	200
Duke of Chandos	200
Thomas Stanhope, Esqu.	100

Mrs. Drelincourt	100
Dr. Pelling	100
Another Clergyman	100
Mrs. Read	100
Lady who desires to be unknown	100
Gentleman who desires to be unknown	100
	3005

The following list is written on the other side of the page on which the above is to be found:

Dean of York & his brother	300
Earl of Oxford	200
Dr Stratford	100
Sr. Matthew Decker	100
Lady who desires to be unknown	500
Lord Bateman	100
—— Archer, Esqu. of Soho Square	500
Dr. Rundle	100
Dr. Grandorge	100

Even Bolingbroke, sick at last of men and their intrigues, dreamed of retiring to the island retreat. In a characteristic letter to Swift, he speaks of his wonder at "knowing a man who can espouse in good earnest the opinion of Malebranche; and who is fond of going a missionary into the West Indies." Indeed, there can be no question that *his* Bermuda dreams arose more from disgust with Europe than any love for America. As he himself continues, "my spleen against Europe has more than once made me think of buying the Dominion of Bermudas and spending the remainder of my days as far as possible from the people with whom I have passed the first and greatest part of my life." [68] That the widespread interest in Bermuda did not wholly spring from such selfish motives is proved by the large sums privately contributed for St. Paul's College and the active cooperation of Berkeley's close friends. Arbuthnot, Benson, Hutchinson, Sherlock, and Stratford organized subscription committees whose activities extended over the whole Kingdom. [69] By December, 1725, a fund of thirty-four hundred pounds [70] had been raised, and Berkeley was taking the initial steps to obtain a royal charter.

He manifested a keen interest in the architectural plans for the College, upon which he brought to bear the considerable technical information he had gained on his Italian tour. He himself drew up the plans for the college buildings and the chief lecture hall, which was to be located in the center of a large "circus" consisting of "the houses of the Fellows," to each of

[68] Butler, *Dublin Univ. Mag.*, vol. VII, April, 1836, p. 457.

[69] The following typical subscription letter (January 18, 1725–26, Portland Manuscripts, VII, 1901, p. 417) was written by Dr. William Stratford, Canon of Christ Church, to Edward Harley, later Lord Harley and second Earl of Oxford, who finally subscribed 100 pounds. It gives a very good idea of the campaign:

"If your Lordship has no thoughts yet of returning to town, I must beg to know whether you will be pleased to give me authority to subscribe any sum for you to Dean Berkeley's design. I have promised him to apply to my friends, but I have deferred doing it because I would willingly have the honour of having your Lordship at the head of my list, if you think fit to be a subscriber. No money will be called for till there is sufficient subscribed to build a College, and maintain the Head, three Fellows and five Scholars at least. That may amount to twenty thousand pounds. There is already subscribed above three thousand pounds. Underneath is the account of some sums subscribed:

Lady Betty Hastings	500
Lord Pembroke	300
Lord Arran	300
The Duke of Chandos	200
Lord Percival	200
Mr Hutcheson	200
Sir R Walpole	200
Auditor Harley	100"

[70] Berkeley to Percival, December, 1725.

which "a spacious garden was allotted." Beyond this "aca-
demical circus" there was to be another, composed of "houses
for gentlemen," many of which had been actually "bespoken,"
and Berkeley was requested to superintend the building of them.
There was still another square, designed for shops and the homes
of artificers, and a "Cypress Walk" to be called "The Walk of
Death," which was "solemnly appropriated to the sole purpose
of interment," since Berkeley profoundly disliked the custom of
burying in churches. Along this walk, monumental urns and
obelisks were to be erected.[71] These few scraps of information
are all that we possess of Berkeley's elaborate plans for St. Paul's
College, to which he devoted all his time and energy for the next
ten years. There were now a large number of applicants for
Fellowships, and Berkeley had to turn many away.[72] Among
others, he added to his staff at this time Thomas Blackwell, a
young Scotchman.[73]

His friend Pope participated, as various of his letters show, in
the popular enthusiasm for the project. Thus he writes Swift [74]
from Twickenham that "Dean Berkeley is well and happy in
the prosecution of his scheme." Berkeley was fond of the imagery of the sixteenth Epode of Horace, and used to quote it in
connection with Bermuda.[75] He finally asked Pope to translate
it for him, and Spence asserts that he actually saw the translation,[76] with a new interpretation, — Rome, which withstood
the Allobroges and Hannibal, destroyed by its own strength
and torn by civil war; the imaginary refuge in the sea, "the
blessed fields and rich islands," unravaged by storm and disease,
safe from the cohorts of Ulysses and Sidonian travellers; a
golden age reserved by Jupiter for the coming of a pious race.
But there was a vast amount of material detail for the *vates
fugae*, before he could hope, like the Phocians, to set sail for
the happy isles. In the first place, there was the business of
getting a charter. With untiring energy Berkeley saw to the
drawing up of the document, interviewed the endless series of

[71] *Biog. Brit.*, vol. III, Add. and Corr.,
p. 262.

[72] "You mentioned a friend of
Synge's," Berkeley writes his friend Prior,
August 4, 1726, from London, "who
was desirous to be one of our Fellows.
Pray let me know who he is, and the particulars of his character. There are many
competitors; more than vacancies; and the

fellowships are likely to be very good
ones: so I would willingly see them well
bestowed."

[73] Thomas Blackwell, *Memoirs of the
Court of Augustus*, Edinborough, 1753,
p. 277.

[74] October 15, 1725.

[75] Spence, *Anecdotes*, London, 1820,
p. 252. [76] *Ibid.*

necessary officials, and paid the endless series of necessary fees from his own pocket.[77] In June, 1725, however, the royal seal of George I was at last affixed to the legal document which brought St. Paul's College, Bermuda, into official existence. This process was probably facilitated by the fact that Berkeley gained access to the King himself, through his friend the Abbé Gualtieri,[78] whom he had met in Italy.[79] The Dean apparently made such an impression on the somewhat sluggish consciousness of the first George that he finally took a favourable, though characteristically ponderous, step in behalf of the project.

The Princess of Wales, to whom he had been introduced in 1716 by Molyneux, was so struck by Berkeley's wit and learning that she invited him to share in her bi-weekly intellectual soirées,[80] in which Clarke, Hoadly, and Sherlock were the chief participants. We are told[81] that Clarke and Berkeley usually occupied the center of the arena. Hoadly, who remained a bitter enemy of Berkeley's throughout his life,[82] and Sherlock, who remained a lifelong friend, supported their respective champions. It would be most interesting to know more of these discussions, but unfortunately none of the disputants seems to have referred to them in more than a casual manner. Clarke was, of course, a firm adherent of the by this time orthodox Newtonian view, and he may have attempted to defend the

---

[77] "The charter hath passed all the seals," writes Berkeley to Prior, June 12, 1725, "and is now in my custody. It hath cost me 130 pounds dry fees, besides expedition money to men in office."

[78] Stock, *Memoirs*.

[79] Cf. Italian diary, January 8, 1717, F. iv, p. 226.

[80] Monck Berkeley, *Poems*, p. ccxxv.

[81] Stock, *Memoirs*.

[82] *Ibid*. His strong statement is substantiated by the letters appended to the *Life* of the Bishop of Winchester, quoted in *Biog. Brit.*, vol. II, p. 259, extracts from which run as follows: "I heartily wish that both he, and his brother (Delany) and his brother Berkeley (who is truly the title of his own book), would keep their *minute philosophy* to themselves; or at least, would let religion alone, and not blend them into one consistent lump. They both seem to me to be well qualified to dress out a romance. Dean Berkeley particularly has beautiful imagery, and fine expression, and fruitful invention. But as to the native simplicity of religion, they are made to hurt it; and if they cannot be said to corrupt it, it is only because it is corrupted already to their hands. They do all they can to keep on the corruption; and I only, own Alcephron the most plain attempt to bring obscurity and darkness into all sciences, as well as to make nonsense essential to religion, that the last age has produced. ... But I see even the best of the two [Berkeley's dialogues] flattered and caressed for those very wounds he has given to all that is most worthy of the study or regard of reasonable creatures, I cannot help make an ejaculation, — To what purpose are all endeavours to make knowledge and religion plain and amiable, when a few pretty words, either without a meaning, or with a very bad one, shall, like a charm, dissolve, and tear to pieces all the labours of the Great."

Newtonian hypostatizations of absolute space and time against such criticisms as Berkeley urged in the *De Motu*. If so, he may have found the logical, and therefore more radically sceptical, objections of his opponent as difficult to cope with as the more "metaphysical" difficulties of his recent and more famous adversary Leibniz. If the argument touched on epistemology, Clarke must have found himself in an even more precarious situation, for his abstract "rationalism" had forced him to a traditional form of "representationalism," and he held that the human soul perceived only the "copies" of "real" objects. Against all such "realisms" Berkeley was, of course, now armed with very powerful logical ammunition.

On the other hand, we know that he was himself prepared to maintain an absolute as against a relative mode of existence. If Clarke directed the discussion toward general metaphysical considerations, he may have had difficulty in explaining what he meant by his "divine archetypes" or pseudo-absolutes, which were absolute, that is, only in relation to "sense," a view from which, as we know, he could see no purely "rational" escape, but which never yielded him any ultimate metaphysical satisfaction. Indeed, it must have been most difficult at this time for him to defend or maintain any "view" at all, and he may well have been content, when pressed, to fall back upon the absolute irrationalism into which his concrete logic was inexorably forcing him. If so, we may well imagine the satisfaction of Dr. Clarke at this *reductio ad absurdum* of one who had dared to oppose the authority of his mathematical master, and the contemptuous smile of his satellite at this "most plain attempt to bring obscurity and darkness into all sciences, as well as to make nonsense essential to religion." [83] It is quite possible, however, in view of the Queen's presence, that the argument had to be kept at too polite and entertaining a level to be interesting. Berkeley, at any rate, certainly viewed the meetings as a "drudgery" which he undertook "from a hope of advancing the interest of his College," [84] rather than from any purely theoretical impulse.

He was certainly too busy for the moment to devote much time to serious reflection. In addition to the burdensome arrangements for the College, he was being incessantly plagued by creditors of the Van Homrigh estate. Marshal still dissented to the payment of the debts, and it was even necessary to caution

[83] *Biog. Brit.*, vol. II, p. 259. [84] *Ibid.*, vol. III, Add. and Corr.

Prior "to secure" the money in such a way that Marshal "may not touch it if he would till the said debts are paid." [85] But Marshal's attitude made it impossible to settle the estate,[86] and the almost constant plague of creditors continued unabated. Berkeley in England had to bear the whole "shock." The thought that his administration was not proceeding justly was a source of ever increasing distress.[87] "It would give me the greatest pain possible," he writes, "to think we did not administer in the justest sense." [88] A year later the situation was unchanged, and Berkeley was almost beside himself with business cares. "For God's sake," he writes his friend and agent in Ireland, "disembrangle these matters, that I may once be at ease to mind my other affairs of the College, which are enough to employ ten persons." [89] He was planning to leave for the New World at any moment, and did not wish to have "things at sixes and sevens" when so far away. He was also expecting to make "a purchase of land in Bermuda (which is very dear)" requiring all the possible funds at his command.[90]

Meanwhile, amid all this confusion in his personal business, Berkeley was bringing the affairs of the College to a brilliant conclusion. The subscription committees headed by his friends had piled up a fund which probably amounted to more than five thousand pounds.[91] Bermuda had become a shibboleth, a fashion. Pope wrote one of his friends who was seeking a domicile that he could now choose an ideal dwelling place "in Wales, Dublin, or Bermuda." [92] Not only had many wealthy persons actually planned to retire with Berkeley to his island

---

[85] Berkeley to Prior, July 20, 1725.

[86] Berkeley's opinion of his associate is indicated in a letter to Prior of September 3, 1726, not printed by Fraser: "As for M. [Marshal]," he says, "I had, from the beginning, no opinion of him, no more than you have; otherwise I should not have troubled any body else."

[87] "I am wearied to death by creditors," he writes Prior from London, January 20, 1725-26, "I see nothing done, neither towards clearing their accounts, nor settling the effects here, nor finishing affairs with Partinton. I am at an end of my patience, and almost of my wits. My conclusion is, not to wait a moment longer for Marshal, nor to have (if possible) any further regard to him, but to settle all things without him, and whether

he will or no. How far this is practicable, you will know by consulting an able lawyer. I have some confused notion that one executor may act by himself: but how far, and in what case, you will thoroughly be informed. It is an infinite shame that the debts here are not cleared up and paid. I have borne the shock and importunity of creditors above a twelvemonth, and am never the nearer; have nothing now to say to them: judge you what I feel."

[88] Letter to Prior, July 20, 1725.

[89] Letter to Prior, November 12, 1726.

[90] Ibid.

[91] According to Hertz, 4000 by February, 1726. G. B. Hertz, Brit. Imperialism in the 18th Century, London, 1908.

[92] September, 1726.

paradise, and projected houses in the ideal community, but the whole affair had the outspoken approval of the Prince and Princess, or rather the Princess, and many prominent social and political leaders were on his subscription lists. Even Sir Robert Walpole felt that a contribution was a social necessity, and, understanding that no subscription need be paid before the fund was large enough to build the College and maintain the staff,[93] promised two hundred pounds.[94] In September, 1725, Berkeley writes triumphantly: "In plain English I have good assurance that our College will be endowed beyond anything expected or desired hitherto."

Courts and Ministers

Flushed by success, Berkeley now resolved upon a step which led him, against the advice of his friend Swift, to place the fate of his scheme in the perilous hands of "courts and ministers." If he had steered clear of Parliament and proceeded with his private campaign, it is probable that he could have achieved enough money by this means to go ahead with his plans, independently of the government.[95] But the approbation with which his enterprise was greeted on all hands emboldened him to appeal to Parliament for aid. Perhaps also he wished to relieve his friends of the burdens which the private campaign entailed. This step, however, turned out to be a mistake of such proportions that it finally wrecked the plan. At first, Berkeley went on winning even more astonishing triumphs. With extraordinary patience and ingenuity he discovered, in going through the colonial records, that a large part of the valuable land of the island of St. Christopher, ceded to England by the Treaty of Utrecht (1713), was as yet unsold. He resolved, therefore, to appeal to Parliament for the use of a part of the funds obtained through the public sale of this land. The King gave his assent and directed Walpole to propose it to Parliament. Berkeley was received "in a very cordial manner" [96] by the minister himself, who genially promised a strict "neutrality," [97] though he must have been utterly astounded at the Parliamentary victory won by what he obviously considered a hare-brained and sentimental escapade. It is reported that after the bill had actually passed

[93] F. iv, p. 364.
[94] Portland Manuscripts, VII, 1901, p. 417.
[95] Cf. Hertz, *Brit. Imp.*, p. 231.
[96] *Biog. Brit.*, vol. III, Add. and Corr., p. 262.   [97] *Ibid.*

Parliament with only one dissenting vote, Lord Townshend expostulated with the great practical politician, who replied "that he really thought the preamble of the bill would have ensured its rejection with the English Commons, and that under the conduct of a less dexterous manager this must have been the case." [98] Berkeley had managed in the preceding weeks to have every member of the Commons interviewed either by himself or by a close friend. His own remarkable devotion and persuasive power were thus ultimately responsible for this surprising victory, which he reports to Prior in a letter of May 12, 1726, as follows: "After six weeks' struggle against an earnest opposition from the different interests and motives, I have yesterday carried my point just as I desired in the House of Commons, by an extraordinary majority, none having the confidence to speak against it, and not above two giving their negative; which was done in so low a voice as if they themselves were ashamed of it." [99]

This "earnest opposition" came from the "governors" and especially the "traders to America," whose "mercantile views" led them to apprehend "this College may produce," as Berkeley reports, "an independency in America, or at least lessen its dependency upon England." [100] Percival later states that "a very good Lord" asked him with reference to St. Paul's "whether I thought the Indians would not be saved as well as we? and if I considered that learning tended to make the Plantations independent of their mother country, adding that the ignorance of the Indians and the variety of sects in our Plantations was England's security." [101] This is a typical statement of the position of the opposition which, though temporarily crushed by Berkeley's energy and dexterity, eventually finding a perfect echo in the untheoretical mind of Sir Robert Walpole and the opposition of the dissenting colonists, discovered unobstrusive methods for circumventing Berkeley's hopeful plans. With such a man as Walpole at the helm there was no danger of any colourful thread of idealism creeping into the intricate commercial web of Anglo-American relations. The American policy was thus kept strictly "practical," and the shrewd and business-like mind of the great minister took proper steps that no mis-

---

[98] Ibid.
[99] Letter to Prior, May 12, 1726. Mrs. Berkeley in Biog. Brit., vol. III, Add. and Corr., p. 262, states that "Admiral Ver-non gave the only dissenting vote in the Lower House upon the occasion."
[100] Letter to Prior, May 12, 1726.
[101] Percival letter, December 23, 1730.

guided idealism should in any way foster colonial independence and thus jeopardize the American trade.

At least one observer, however, has noted the fact that what chiefly separated the plantations from the mother country was, first, the comparative weakness of the Church of England, which, in spite of the earnest though unsupported efforts of the Society for the Propagation of the Gospel, had been allowed to languish and deteriorate,[102] and, secondly, the absence of an English educational system.[103] If a few cultural centers such as St. Paul's had been spreading their influence in the colonies throughout the earlier part of the century it might have been more difficult for the French to stir up the Indians, and later for the hot-headed leaders of 1776 to arouse that resentment which was such a perfect crown to the policies of Walpole and Vernon. At any rate, Bermuda, "the most neglected spot in the Empire," would never have become the hot-bed of sedition it proved to be in Revolutionary days.[104]

The parliamentary victory was the beginning of a long and nerve-wracking struggle, in which Berkeley wrestled with the endlessly complicated machinery of government in vain attempts to obtain some assurance of payment. Thanks to his personal audience, King George I, after six anxious months, finally ordered the twenty thousand pounds to be paid in December, 1726. This order was ignored. After a year of waiting, Berkeley presented a despairing petition in which he prayed the King to direct the passing of a warrant providing for the endowment.[105] This, however, proved fruitless, as the King unfortunately died, leaving Berkeley just where he was two years before. "Yesterday," he writes to Prior, "we had an account of King George's death. This day King George II was proclaimed. All the world here are in a hurry, and I as much as anybody; our grant being defeated by the King's dying before the broad seal was annexed to it in order to which it was passing through the offices. I have *la mer à boire* again. . . . At present I am at a loss what course to take." [106] Undaunted, however, by this disappointment he returned to the task and soon had the cumbersome machinery working again. Thanks to the soirées and his general favour with Queen Caroline,[107]

---

[102] G. B. Hertz, *Brit. Imp.*, p. 130.
[103] *Ibid.*, pp. 233 ff.
[104] Hertz, *Brit. Imp.*, p. 240.
[105] *Calendar Treas. Papers*, 1720–28, ed. 1889, p. 437.

[106] Berkeley to Prior, June 15, 1727.
[107] "Just before his embarkation for America, Queen Caroline endeavoured to stagger his resolution, by the offer of an English Mitre; but, in reply, he assured

George II was prevailed upon to renew his father's assent almost immediately after his succession to the throne in June, 1727. Berkeley now realized that there was nothing more to be done except to await the ponderous turning of the wheels of government. So for the moment he dropped the problems of Bermuda and prepared to visit Ireland.

As early as April, Berkeley had written his friend Prior, asking him to find quarters in Dublin for him, and to keep the matter "secret from every individual creature," as he wished to keep his visit as "concealed as possible" for "several reasons." [108] One of the reasons may have been to consult with some of the prospective Fellows [109] concerning the College. But, as Prior brings up the subject of matrimony in his next letter, we may well suspect that there were other than official motives for this visit. [110] Since Berkeley was now decidedly in the public eye, it is quite understandable that he desired to keep his personal affairs in the background. But official details detained him in London. Clarke, [111] his London lawyer, had accepted a bribe from a dishonest creditor and paid an unjust debt, and the affairs of the estate were again in a tangle. He could not tear himself away until late in the winter, and was then detained by rains. Finally, almost a year later, in April, 1728, he left London to take a much needed vacation, and to occupy the small cottage "in a retired situation" and "with access to fields

---

her Majesty, that he chose rather to be President of St Paul's College, than Primate of all England." Mrs. Berkeley, *Biog. Brit.*, vol. III, Add. and Corr., p. 262.

[108] Berkeley to Prior, April 11, 1727.

[109] Berkeley writes to Prior from London, September 3, 1725: "I wrote long since to Caldwell about his going to Bermudas, but had no answer, which makes me think my letter miscarried. I must now desire you to give my service to him, and know whether he still retains the thoughts he once seemed to have of entering into that design. I know he hath since got an employment, etc; but I have good reason to think he would not suffer in his temporalities by taking one of our Fellowships, though he resigned all that. In plain English, I have good assurance that our College will be endowed beyond anything expected or desired hitherto.

This makes me confident he would lose nothing by the change; and on this condition only I propose it to him. I wish he may judge rightly in this matter, as well for his own sake as for the sake of the College."

[110] Hone and Rossi, *Bishop Berkeley*, p. 139, have suggested that the condemnation of his brother for bigamy at Kilkenny may have led to the desire for secrecy on this visit. Since, however, the condemnation occurred before August, 1726, a year before his projected visit and two years before the actual visit, it seems far more likely that the journey concerned his marriage. Berkeley speaks of his brother Thomas' trial in a letter to Prior of September 3, 1726. Cf. A. A. Luce, *Proc. of R. Irish Acad.*, XLI, Sec. C, no. 4, pp. 144–145.

[111] Letter to Prior, February 27, 1727.

and sweet air " which Prior had rented for him in the suburbs of Dublin.

According to Stock, the wedding took place on the first of April. [112] The bride was Miss Anne Forster, "an agreeable young lady" [113] of good family, the daughter of a Chief Justice of Ireland. Berkeley had "been often married by others," [114] and it is probable that he had formerly considered marriage with Miss Anne Donellan, a friend and correspondent of Swift. [115] This acquaintance, which occurred in Berkeley's early days in London, though "friends were consenting, circumstances equal, and her opinion captivated," apparently faded with time. [116] His letters to Prior show, however, that he was planning his marriage with Miss Forster for at least a year before the event, and their acquaintance probably dated from his Trinity College student days.

The marriage seems to have been a happy one. She was a Quietist, and her "reported" interest in Fénelon and other "mystical" writers may have provided, particularly at this time, a strong intellectual bond. [117] She was eager to join the

[112] According to the account given in the *Hist. Reg.* of 1728, the wedding occurred "six weeks" before the sailing, that is, during the first part of August. But this account is inaccurate in other respects.

[113] Boyer's *Pol. State of Grt. Brit.* for October, 1728, XXXVI, p. 313. Cf. Hertz, *Brit. Imp.*, p. 132.

[114] Prior, September 13, 1726.

[115] The evidence for this is afforded by the following letter of Elizabeth Montague, the cousin of Wortley Montague, written at the time of Berkeley's death in 1753: "... Dr. Berkeley had formerly made his addresses to Mrs Donellan: what were her reasons for refusing him I know not, friends were consenting, circumstances equal, her opinion captivated, but perhaps aversion to the cares of a married life, and apprehensions from some particularities in his temper hinder'd the match; however, their friendship always continued, and I have always heard her give him for virtues and talents the preference to all mankind." *Eliz. Montague*, ed. Climenson, London, 1906, vol. II, pp. 25–26.

Cf. *op. cit.*, vol. II, p. 15: "Archibald Bower" (*Nat. Biog.*, vol. VI, p. 48) "fled

to England, and while there made the acquaintance of Dean Berkeley, the old admirer and friend of Mrs Donellan, who was afterwards Bishop of Cloyne."

Anne Donellan was the daughter of Nehemiah Donellan, Lord Chief Baron of the Exchequer of Ireland and a friend and correspondent of Swift. After the death of her father, her mother married Philip Percival, the brother of Lord Egmont, which probably explains her daughter's acquaintance with Berkeley.

[116] In 1735, when Bishop of Cloyne, Berkeley bestowed upon the Rev. Christopher Donellan, this lady's brother, a living worth 300 pounds. The latter was apparently, like his sister, a friend of Swift, for a letter to Swift dated October, 1735, has survived. "The Bishop of Cloyne," he says, "desires you will accept of his best services." *Corresp. of Jonathan Swift*, ed. F. Elrington Ball, London, 1913, vol. V, p. 256.

[117] According to Fraser, "Report bears that she was herself of the school of the Mystics or Quietists, and that her favourite writers were Fénelon, Madame Guyon, and their English disciple, Hooke. ..." F., *Life*, p. 151. Cf. Percival letter, September 3, 1728.

expedition, and brought important material assistance.[118] The summer was spent largely in quiet retirement, though much of Berkeley's time must have been taken up with final preparations for the journey, the collecting of books, and the chartering of a vessel, since in September, 1728, we find his small party of intimate friends at Gravesend ready to embark. "Tomorrow," Berkeley writes his friend Percival, "we sail down the river. Mr. James and Mr. Dalton go with me. So doth my wife, a daughter of the late Chief Justice Forster, whom I married since I saw your Lordship. I chose her for the qualities of her mind and her unaffected inclination to books. She goes with great cheerfulness to live a plain farmer's life, and wear stuff of her own spinning wheel." [119]

The small party, which slipped away from Gravesend almost secretly in the fall of the year, was very far from the triumphal exodus that the first popular enthusiasm might seem to have warranted. Berkeley had as yet received no definite assurance concerning the money, and the report was beginning to circulate that he had actually dropped the design. Nevertheless, his leaving "before the King's bounty was received" called forth a stream of criticism from another circle of friends. The only way out of the dilemma seemed, therefore, to leave with as little noise as possible to prove to the world that he was in earnest and that the delay was none of his making. Thus, he was obliged "to run the risk of a tedious winter voyage." [120] Berkeley had resolved to stop first at Rhode Island, in order to purchase with his own money pasture for supplying his college with fresh meat, the want of which had been urged by some as a serious objection to the whole project.[121] So the ship's prow was turned toward New England.

The company that Berkeley took with him consisted of his wife and a friend, Miss Handcock,[122] two gentlemen of fortune, Messrs. James and Dalton, who planned to settle in Bermuda,

---

[118] Hertz, *Brit. Imp.*, p. 132.

[119] At the same time, Berkeley writes to Prior: "Tomorrow with God's blessing, I set sail for Rhode Island with my wife and a friend of hers, my Lady Handcock's daughter who bears us company. I am married, since I saw you, to Miss Forster, daughter of the late Chief Justice, whose humour and turn of mind pleases me beyond anything that I know in her whole sex. Mr James, Mr Dalton, and Mr Smibert go with us on this voyage. We are now all together at Gravesend. . . ." Letter to Prior, September 5, 1728.

[120] Berkeley to Percival, June 27, 1729.

[121] Portland Manuscripts, vol. VII, p. 467.

[122] The letter to Prior of September 5, 1728, makes it clear that Mrs. Berkeley was not accompanied by her sister, as Fraser states, following the account in the *Annual Register*.

and probably several tradesmen and artists, among whom was Berkeley's good friend, the artist Smibert, and a musician, Duguize. The Fellows were to follow later. The report of the *Register* of 1728, though not altogether accurate, gives an adequate picture of the expedition as it set sail for the New World, September 11, from Gravesend.

The Rev Dr Berkeley, Dean of Derry, who obtained a Patent of his late Majesty to erect a College in Bermudas, like that in Dublin, for instructing of youth in all manner of liberal sciences and learned arts, sailed about the middle of September last for the West Indies, in a ship of two hundred and fifty tons which he hired. He took several tradesmen and artists with him. Two gentlemen of fortune, James and Dalton are gone with all their effects, to settle in Bermudas, the Dean married an agreeable young lady about six weeks before he set sail; the lady's sister is gone with them; they had 400 pounds each to their fortune which they carried with them. They carried also stores and goods to a great value. The Dean embarked 20,000 books [123] besides what the two gentlemen carried. He sailed hence for Rhode Island where the Dean intends to winter and to purchase an estate, in order to settle a correspondence and trade between that island and Bermudas, particularly for supplying Bermudas with black cattle and sheep. The Dean's grant of 2000 pounds on St Christophers is payable in two years time and the Dean has a year and a half allowed him afterwards to consider whether he will stick to his college in Bermudas or return to his Deanery of Derry.

[123] The printer of the *Annual Register* account turned the 20,000 pounds into books, and vice versa.

CHAPTER XII

THE NEW WORLD

THE passage was a long and stormy one, for they were blown far out of their course. Berkeley says, "we were a long time blundering about the ocean," [1] but the whole company finally landed in Virginia early in November, where they were shown many "unexpected honors" from the "Governor and principal inhabitants." [2] At least one of the latter, Mr. Byrd, who talked with Berkeley, was certainly not in sympathy with the project, as he wrote Percival that it might be necessary for the "College" to send military regiments to Florida to scour the country for prospective Indian converts. [3]

The voyage northward from Virginia to Rhode Island "was as speedy and prosperous as could be wished," [4] and the party reached Newport on the twenty-third of January, four months after their departure from England, although interrupted, of course, by their visit in Virginia. [5] Berkeley was welcomed by Dr. Honyman, the Rector of Trinity Church and a missionary of the Society for the Propagation of the Gospel, at whose house he stayed immediately after arrival, and was at once impressed by the natural beauty of the country and the rich opportunities for missionary and cultural enterprise provided by the inhabitants. He himself had probably been influenced by the comments of his Virginia friends on the bleakness of Bermuda, where there was "no bread" nor anything else fit for the sustenance of man "but onions and cabbages," [6] and he professed to Percival his willingness to establish the College at Newport.

---

[1] Letter to Percival, February 7, 1729.

[2] *Ibid.*

[3] Byrd to Percival, January 10, 1729, though Rand dates this letter *June 10*. *Berkeley and Percival*, p. 243.

[4] Percival letter, February 7, 1729.

[5] The Newport tradition, which is stated in the *Annals of Trinity Church*, p. 46, is romantic, but without foundation: "Dean Berkeley arrived in Newport by a circumstance purely accidental, the Captain of the Ship in which he sailed could not find the Island of Bermuda and having given up the search for it steered North until they discovered land unknown to them and which they supposed to be inhabited by savages." Prof. Fraser's statement that the party was four months *en route* to America is also misleading (*Life and Letters of Berkeley*, p. 154). The voyage lasted about two months. Cf. Byrd to Percival, January 10, 1729.

[6] Byrd to Percival, January 10, 1729.

"Were it in my power," he says, "I should not demur one moment about situating our College here." [7] This opinion grew stronger during the period of Berkeley's stay,[8] and he evidently conveyed it to other friends who were less discreet than Percival, for the latter says in one of his letters that the proposed change of location was "mentioned at Court," [9] thus providing an excuse for the government's "policy" of withholding payment.

Berkeley was, of course, much interested in the natives, and we are told that with Colonel Updike he made "many visits to Narragansett to see the remnant of the Indians [10] and render them such service as he might." [11] On one such occasion, he became acquainted with Dr. S. MacSparran, the Scotch missionary, and according to the MacSparran diary he preached in Narragansett at St. Paul's Church on May 11, 1729. He was most enthusiastic over the view from Hammond Hill, even considering it as a possible location for the College.[12] Smibert, the artist, while in Italy, had painted the portraits, later presented to the Czar, of two or three Siberian Tartars, and we are told that he was at once struck by the oriental cast in the features of the natives. Berkeley was deeply impressed by the hopeless state of these Indians, who by this time had been almost exterminated by the effects of drink, smallpox, and economic exploitation. On his return to England, he did all in his power to acquaint the public with the facts, and to arouse some appreciation of the gross injustices suffered by the natives and the general negligence of the "English," who "have done more to destroy their bodies by the use of strong liquors than by any means to improve their minds or save their souls." [13]

During the succeeding year, Berkeley purchased 96 acres of land, next to the farm of the Rev. James Honyman, in the interior of the island. There was a fine hill on the estate, but Berkeley had the house placed in a more protected location. He was, however, exceedingly fond of this hill, which afforded that wide outlook over the surrounding landscape described at the beginning of the fifth dialogue of the *Alciphron*:

[7] Letter to Percival, February 7, 1729.
[8] Cf. Berkeley to Newman, June 27, 1729.
[9] Percival, June 12, 1729.
[10] According to the sermon which Berkeley preached after his return to England there were less than 1000 Indians in Narragansett at this time. F. iv, p. 403.
[11] R. I. Hist. Coll., vol. VII, p. 234. Cf. Updike, *Hist. of the Episcopal Church in Narragansett*, R. I., p. 176,
[12] McSparran, *Diary*, p. xxix.
[13] *Sermon before the Society for the Propagation of the Gospel*, F. iv, p. 403.

Here we had a prospect on one hand of a narrow bay or creek of the sea, enclosed on either side by a coast beautified by rocks and woods, and green banks, and farm houses. At the end of the bay, was a small town, placed upon the slope of a hill, which, from the advantage of its situation, made a considerable figure. Several fishing-boats and lighters, gliding up and down on a surface as smooth and bright as glass, enlivened the prospect. On the other side, we looked down on green pastures, flocks and herds basking beneath in sunshine, while we, in our superior situation, enjoyed the freshness of air and shade.[14]

The beach, which was about a mile away, was also a great attraction, and on clear days, Berkeley was in the habit of walking through the long grass, crossing the small brook which lay between his house and the ocean, to a huge rock with a cleft in the middle, where he would sit in a chair he had brought for the purpose, spending the morning or afternoon in quiet reflection, protected from the sun and wind, and facing a magnificent expanse of sea and wild shoreland. It was here, according to tradition, that most of the *Alciphron* was first composed. Berkeley spent the fall and winter in his comfortable farmhouse, working with the fine library he had brought over with him, and meditating, as he writes Percival, "in a profound solitude." [15]

But though Berkeley speaks of the "retirement" as being very "agreeable" after his "long fatigue of business," [16] his seclusion must be understood only in a relative sense. He mixed freely in the social life of the town, and felt it his duty "to endeavor to be of some use," [17] while awaiting the payment of the funds which would enable him to proceed with the College. Not only did he frequently preach at Trinity Church but he presided at various gatherings of the missionaries and clergy, counselling especially toleration and mutual understanding, and at the last of these meetings in 1731 he spoke to them for two hours and a half. His influence was, of course, resented by the more fanatical ministers of the dissenting sects,[18] but his close relationship with Samuel Johnson and his friendship with

[14] Alc., F. ii, p. 194.
[15] Percival letter, March 29, 1730.
[16] *Ibid.*
[17] Berkeley to Percival, August 30, 1729.
[18] White quotes the following letter from a New England clergyman, dated July, 1731: "Dean Berkeley preached before the clergy at Newport in Rhode Island, some time in the past month. . . . I heard this discourse kept them two hours and a half, which to me is somewhat strange for such an Hypochondriacal disposition. I hear he returns to England some time before Michaelmas. He seems tired of this country, though he has seen nothing of it." H. Vere White, *Bishop Berkeley as a Missionary*, Dublin, 1900.

clergy of other sects, such as Searing and Condy, show that his influence on American church affairs was not entirely negligible. Many of the leading squires became his friends, and with Colonel Daniel Updike he seems to have been particularly intimate. This lawyer and landowner, who later became Attorney General of the Colony, accompanied him on several of his expeditions to Narragansett, and in 1730 was baptized, owing, perhaps, to Berkeley's personal influence, as he was also a member of the small group that gathered around the Dean for the purpose of discussing religious and philosophical questions. This philosophical society, which met regularly at the houses of the members, and which reminds one of the society of his student days at Dublin, included the Rev. John Callender, the first to write a systematic account of the Colony, Stephen Hopkins, who later became Governor, and other younger men, many of whom became prominent in colonial affairs.[19]

SAMUEL JOHNSON

The most interesting of Berkeley's acquaintances at this time was the Rev. Samuel Johnson, the first President of King's College, who became a lifelong friend and a convert to the "Berkeleyan" philosophy. Johnson was a well-read clergyman with a persevering, if not overly profound, interest in reflection. He had studied the new mathematics and the works of Newton, by which he had been greatly influenced, as well as by those of Norris and Malebranche. His dogged sincerity at least is shown by the fact that he had thought his way out of what seemed to him the "demoralizing" principle of "invincible" Grace, and other unpalatable consequences of "Calvinism." As a result of a profound internal and external struggle, he had left the Reformed Church and had become an Anglican. In 1728 he made a trip to England, where he read the works of the Deists, Wollaston, Tindal, Woolston, Collins, and Chubb.

[19] These included James Searing, Pastor of the Second Congregational Church from 1731-55, Jeremiah Condy, who was graduated from Harvard in 1726 and later became Pastor of the First Congregational Church in Boston, a man of "liberal views, and of an inquisitive and literary taste" (R. I. Hist. Coll., vol. VIII, p. iii), Henry Collins, then a successful merchant, who gave the land on which the Redwood Library was later built, and whose portrait was painted by Smibert (R. I. Hist. Mag. vol. V, p. 81), Edward Scott, who had been for twenty years master of the grammar school and who later became a judge and one of the Commissioners to revise the laws of the Colony, and, of course, Honyman and Johnson.

Although he was a confirmed "rationalist," he was, like Berkeley, bitterly opposed to the secular spirit of these writings, which he felt to be definitely "irreligious and immoral." [20] In his *Autobiography*, he classes Shaftesbury, as well as Mandeville, with that "blight" of secular writers who seemed to be making such "a great noise in the nation" that "it seemed as if Hell itself was broke loose to undermine and demolish Christianity." [21] In England also he had run across Berkeley's *Principles* from which "he had conceived a great opinion" [22] of the author.

He must have been pleased, therefore, when, on his return to America in 1729, his friend Honyman was able to introduce him to the Dean himself. They conversed together on various philosophical questions concerning the soul and other topics, such as the existence of a "principle of perception" in "beasts," [23] upon which the somewhat "objective" mind of Johnson had focussed. Johnson showed such interest in these discussions that Berkeley presented him with the *New Theory of Vision* and the *Dialogues*, [24] requesting that he send in return any objections which might occur to him. The result of this meeting was an exchange of letters that is of some interest in connection with the development of Berkeley's metaphysical views. Johnson was able to offer a fairly intelligent criticism of the early writings, and Berkeley's answers often show the extent to which he had advanced beyond them. Johnson's own philosophical treatise, the *Elementa Philosophica*, which is an altogether uninspired sketch of the "Berkeleyan" philosophy, [25] has the advantage, through its almost mechanical accuracy, of shedding some light on certain phases of Berkeley's

[20] Johnson, *Autobiography*, in *Samuel Johnson*, ed. Schneider, vol. I.
[21] S. Johnson, *Autobiog.*, pp. 23–24.
[22] *Ibid.*, p. 25.
[23] Johnson letter, February 5, 1730.
[24] *Ibid.*
[25] In 1752 Johnson sent this work to Berkeley with a letter, dated August 12, in which he states that the work proceeds from "an earnest desire that I might if possible be some way instrumental in promoting the interest of learning in this uncultivated country, which I have long thought could not be better done so far as these studies are concerned than by endeavouring as much as I could to gain their attention to your Lordship's most excellent writings, and I have thought this would best be done by publishing some small manual for young students exhibiting a short sketch of them with references, which I have here attempted . . . since I could not consult your Lordship before printing this, I thought I would humbly ask the favor of your remarks that whereinsoever I have made any mistakes or misrepresented your sense or injected any wrong notions of others, you would do us the favor to take notice of them to me. . . ." *Samuel Johnson*, vol. II, p. 329.

more mature thought, especially the theory of archetypes, which had been left hitherto undeveloped.

Johnson's first letter of September 10, 1729, enumerates certain objections occurring to him in connection with his reading of the *New Theory of Vision* and the *Dialogues*. He sets them down, numbered as follows:

1. Is not the new theory inconsistent with the position of Newton and the accredited results of scientific research?

2. If all secondary causes are eliminated, does not this contradict a basic empirical intuition? If, for example, I light a fire, and then leave the room, when I return must I not suppose that something has been proceeding independently of me?

3. Would not God be a more perfect craftsman, had He made the world develop by itself, without having constantly to watch over His work?

4. Does not the destruction of matter make an adequate explanation of evil impossible, since God must then be responsible for evil as well as good?

5. Why the complex bodily mechanism, and especially why sense organs, if God impresses sensations on our minds without them?

6. If physical organisms do not exist, then we shall, of course, not have them after death, and there can be no "resurrection of the body."

7. The next few questions deal with the conception of archetypes, and are of peculiar interest, though Berkeley does not deal with them until his second letter. If the whole world exists archetypally and necessarily in God (as in the theory of the third dialogue), asks Johnson, then must there not be an archetype of the candle I now see, in which its visible and tangible qualities are necessarily united? Also, if there are archetypes for the ideas of the trees I see, must there not be an archetype for the idea of the distance between them? Johnson is consequently not prepared to give up the Newtonian conception of an absolute, objective space, and refers several times specifically both to Newton and to Clarke.

Berkeley answers the first six objections in a letter of November 25, 1729,[26] apologizing for his tardiness, which, he says, has been caused by ill health.[27] As to the first point, Berkeley

---

[26] Fraser, ii, p. 14, erroneously gives the date as June 25, 1729. See Schneider, *Johnson*, vol. II, p. 270.

[27] Berkeley refers to his illness as "a gathering or imposthumation in my head which confined me several weeks." Berkeley to Johnson, November 25, 1729.

denies categorically that his system in any way contradicts the empirically verified laws of science. In the end, these laws deal with elements abstracted logically from our concrete experience. We may invent all sorts of complex, symbolic ways of stating them,[28] but the basic "facts" are only "phenomena" which require no separate world of "absolute" or abstract matter. Indeed, we cannot "separate" such a world without joining it not only to that from which it is separated, but to the underlying logic which is "performing" these operations.

As to the second question, Berkeley distinguishes very sharply, as in the *De Motu*, between scientific or "convenient" explanations and those which may be considered "true." There are "true" causes and mere "occasions," preceding phenomena, or signs. Science, he says, and common sense deal with the latter only.[29] The lighting of the fire is, therefore, a sign which we have learned to associate with the other attendant phenomena we call the fire, and is only in this restricted sense a "cause." With respect to the third objection, Berkeley criticizes very sharply the anthropomorphic analogy on which it is based. God is the creator of the world, not its fashioner, so that the analogy between God and a human artisan, who is always limited by some matter, inevitably breaks down. It is, therefore, no sign of imperfection in God, who created the world from nothing, to say that without His constant conserving activity it would shrink again to nothing.[30] Berkeley is now conscious of agreeing to some extent with the "scholastic" tradition, though he does not refer to Malebranche.[31]

The irrational tendencies of Berkeley's thought at this time are further evidenced by his answer to Johnson's next question, concerning "evil." "As to guilt," says Berkeley, "it is the same thing whether I kill a man with my hands or an instrument; whether I do it myself or make use of a ruffian."[32] It does not help to solve the "problem" of evil to introduce intermediate machinery, such as matter, for what is the source of "matter"? Berkeley says that light will be shed on the prob-

---

[28] The example Berkeley uses is the definition of "momentum" as "moles in celeritatem ducta," which, he insists, "convenient" as it may be, "is a mere circle," or tautology, a "trifling proposition" in the language of the *Commonplace Book*, since, in the end, "moles" and "momentum" both mean the same,

i.e. "quantity of matter," and, as in all mathematical propositions, "the conclusion is taken for granted in one of the premises."

[29] Berkeley to Johnson, November 25, 1729.
[30] *Ibid.*
[31] *Ibid.*   [32] *Ibid.*

lem "if we consider that all guilt is in the will, and that our
ideas from whatever cause they are produced are alike inert." [33]
Our *will* has been created free, and only by the manner in
which we employ this free agency can we be morally judged.
Without such a free power of action, we should cease to be
responsible individuals. We cannot, therefore, blame God for
making us free. He is now quite clear that what we call the
"sense organs" are regularly recurring clusters of ideas belonging to the "phenomenal" world of "appearances." The body,
together with the perceived self, is part of the complex and
orderly world of sense-impressions, and thus possesses only a
"relative or hypothetical" existence. Hence, with respect to
the sixth objection, concerning the "resurrection," Berkeley
has an answer, though Johnson noted the marked change in tone
from that of the "proof" for "natural immortality" given in
the *Principles*.[34] "It seems very easy," Berkeley now declares
more guardedly, "to conceive the soul to exist in a separate
state (i.e. divested from those limits and laws of motion and
perception with which she is embarrassed here) and to exercise
herself on new ideas, without the intervention of these tangible
things we call bodies."[35] How easy it still was for Berkeley to
fall into his early spiritism, and to speak of a fixed "soul"
substance again, is shown not only by this passage, but by the
hold which this new abstraction or "matter" took upon the
imagination of his disciple, who lovingly bestowed upon it all
the grandiose epithets the materialist applies to his substance,
and doggedly and convincingly reduces it to the absurd:

Oh happy day! when we shall be delivered from these gross, sickly, and unwieldy bodies, when we shall get at liberty from these prisons of flesh and
blood, and be furnished with pure fine and ethereal bodies and with perfect,
clear, and exquisite senses and understandings, and when without let or hin-
drance with the utmost freedom, vigor, and agility, we shall, in company with
other pure, philosophical and devout spirits, be under advantage at pleasure
to waft ourselves anywhere through the vast fields of ether and more nearly
survey the mighty systems of the works of God.[36]

The next exchange of letters is more important, and gives
further light on the new and non-spiritistic position into which
Berkeley had gropingly thought his way. In his answering

[33] *Ibid.*
[34] Johnson to Berkeley, February 5.
1730.

[35] Berkeley to Johnson, November 25,
1729.
[36] Notes, *Samuel Johnson*, vol. II, p.
260.

letter of February 5, Johnson says that there are still three main objections which trouble him. The first concerns the divine archetypes which Berkeley had not discussed in his previous letter. Johnson asks Berkeley concerning this critical development of his thought, and wonders whether he is right in referring to all ideas as "unum et idem in Archetypo, though multiplex et diversum in Ectypo."[37] In his reply, as we should expect, Berkeley agrees to this general distinction, though he insists that archetypes in "the Divine mind" are quite different from "the absolute rational existence," distinct from "any mind whatsoever,"[38] maintained by Locke, Descartes, the materialists, and apparently by Johnson himself. In his *Elementa*, Johnson, in working out this "doctrine," refers to Plato (*Republic* VI), to Cudworth, Malebranche, and particularly Norris' *Ideal World*. He speaks of "a perpetual communication with the great father of lights," and uses other Augustinian phrases, such as "the Fountain of all light." The eternal truths of morality and logic are in Him "as one Archetypal and Eternal Light of Truth; but as they are from Him reflected on the various objects in our finite minds they appear various and manifold, as sensible light is one in the sun though it becomes various colours and other sensible qualities in different objects."[39] This at least testifies to the fact that Berkeley still held the theory of archetypes, to which, in the *Dialogues*, his concrete logic had forced him, though, as his reply shows, he would doubtless have objected to Johnson's formulation as "absolute," or abstract, "rationalism." Indeed, the many appeals to the principle of "abstraction" and "abstract ideas" contained in Berkeley's two letters show that it is really this fundamental point of method which is at issue between them. At the end of his first letter, he ventures "to recommend" to his friend that he "consider well" whether "any new objection that shall occur doth not suppose the doctrine of *abstract* general ideas." It was not so much that he disagreed with *what* Johnson said, as with the way in which he said it, and, therefore, with everything he said or could ever say.

Hence, with respect to the rugged tenacity with which Johnson clings to space and time as absolute properties "in God" to which "our ideas" are "correspondent," Berkeley

[37] Johnson to Berkeley, February 5, 1730.
[38] Berkeley to Johnson, March 24, 1730.
[39] S. Johnson, *Elementa Philosophica*, *op. cit.*, vol. II, p. 383.

feels it useless to "argue" further, simply referring his Newtonian friend "to what I have published." I make no scruple
"to use the word Space," writes Berkeley, "as well as other
words in common use; but I do not thereby mean a distinct
absolute being," for the absolute cannot be asserted to "exist,"
as other "things." It was rather difficult for Johnson to grasp
such refined distinctions. Thus, with respect to "the punctum
stans" and "the τὸ νῦν of the Platonists," to which Berkeley
had evidently referred in their first conversations, Johnson says,
"I can't tell what to make of these words," and "whatever the
matter is, the longer I think of them the more they disappear and
seem to dwindle away into nothing." That the temporal cannot be conceived, except in relation to the eternal, however, had
now become for Berkeley an almost commonplace application
of his concrete logic, as is indicated by his reply of March 24:
"By the τὸ νῦν," he says, "I suppose to be implied that all
things, past and to come, are actually present to the mind
of God, and that there is in Him no change, variation, or
succession."

Johnson's third objection deals with the *esse percipi* principle.
He wonders if one cannot sleep without dreaming, and if
children and animals cannot also have "souls" which "exist"
without thinking and perceiving. He asks if Locke is not right
in maintaining that there are different degrees of being, and
that we exist more fully in so far as we think more intensely.
Berkeley naturally answers this old and common-sense question
with a decided negative, for here again, the issue is not a
question of "doctrine" but of logic. If we can objectify
"existence" into a "thing" which is "given" to us from some
independent (or abstract) external source, then it will be possible, as Johnson insists, to think of "existence" without
"thought" and "perception." This, as Berkeley admits, "was
a notion that Mr. Locke held," and which, indeed, "runs
through his whole book of Human Understanding." Berkeley,
however, reasserts his agreement rather with the "principles"
of "Des Cartes," that "thought" belongs to the essence of the
mind, but goes much further in asserting that "existence" is
in a similar dependent status. There can be no "existence;
exclusive of perceiving and being perceived," for "I cannot
find I have any such idea," nor is such a thing possible, for how
can I have an idea or object without having it? Existence is
itself a thought or category presupposed by all objects or ideas,

and it is absurd to think of existence itself as existing, like an atom or a tree, for instance. There is no escape (as Johnson suggests) by means of the quantitative notion of degree, for "degree" is also a thought-form. Any existence, no matter of how slight a degree, still "supposes" existence, and hence the mind or λόγος. It is no wonder, therefore, that Johnson's "logical" mind found final refuge in the intellectualistic absolute suggested in the *Dialogues*. Hence, he speaks in his *Elementa* of "eternal truths necessarily existing, independent of any created mind, or anything existing in nature," [40] without appreciating the difficulties which prevented Berkeley from finding any permanent satisfaction in such a rationalism, or in any sort of *ism* whatever.

This scepticism is, indeed, the most noteworthy feature of the letters to Johnson, and the flexibility with which Berkeley seems to take a position only to throw it immediately to one side must have baffled more than once the matter-of-fact mind of his disciple, for whom a thing was either so or not so. "It is a common fault," says Berkeley in his first letter, "to be too much wedded to our own opinions. I am so sensible of this in others that I could not pardon it to myself if I considered mine any further than they *seem* to me to be true." [41] Time and again he casts a certain doubt upon those "opinions" he had, in the more sanguine days of his youth, so confidently presented to "the learned world" as "proofs" and "demonstrations" which he now finds his young follower "embracing" with such real relief. He himself disavows the "system" which Johnson so gratefully discovers in his early writings, and even refers to that work in which fifteen years before he had proposed to "utterly destroy Atheism and Scepticism," [42] "accurately define" the "measures of right and wrong," and "reduce" the "Principles of Natural Religion" into "regular systems," [43] as written "rather" with the view "of giving hints to thinking men." [44] "What you have seen of mine," he adds, "was published when I was very young, and without doubt hath many defects.... I do not, therefore, pretend that my books can teach truth. All I hope for is, that they may be an occasion to inquisitive men of discovering truth."

[40] Johnson, *Elementa*, vol. II, *op. cit.*, p. 464.
[41] Berkeley to Johnson, November 25, 1729.
[42] F. i, p. 376.
[43] *Ibid.*, p. 377.
[44] Berkeley to Johnson, November 25, 1729.

It is quite clear that Berkeley is far closer to that "forlorn scepticism" against which he so majestically warned his readers in the introduction to the *Principles*, [45] than to the mood of dogmatic rationalism in which he undertook that work. Yet he is too much of a sceptic to take his scepticism with any whole-hearted seriousness, though it has required fifteen years of intellectual disillusionment for him to probe far enough into the meaning of scepticism to see that what we usually call by this name is not scepticism at all, but only a convenient means of disregarding other persons' prejudices and substituting others of our own, or at best an abstract or rationalistic irrationalism, falling, by its very opposition, into the same fallacy it opposes. True scepticism is not an *ism* at all, but thought in its intrinsic purity, impelling us through all "positions," goading us on, when it finds us resting in affirmation or denial, by forcing us, instead, to think. Thus, while Berkeley can no longer regard his earlier treatises as of any positive importance, he cannot deny them a certain negative value. By reading them it is not impossible that "prejudices, which have been many years taking root, should be extirpated." [46] Prejudices of thought can be extirpated by thought, and "systems" by counter-systems. Certain "hints" may, perhaps, free the mind from some obsession, and even start it on that restless quest to which there can be no "satisfaction." In the passage from one position to another lies truth. "I could wish," concludes Berkeley in his letter of March 24, though with little hope of being understood by a mind like that of Johnson, "that all things I have published on these philosophical subjects were read in the order wherein I published them."

NEWPORT SERMONS

The secluded life at his farm, which he called Whitehall, enabled Berkeley to think his way through many problems, enjoying the advantage of a leisure he had not possessed since his early Trinity College days. But the affairs of his College gave him much anxiety. There was no sign of any action on the part of the Treasury. In the fall, almost a year after his arrival, he seems to be trying to prop his waning hopes by remembering past assurances and official sanctions. "I doubt not," he writes Percival, "the Treasury is backward in all payments;

---

[45] F. i, p. 237.   [46] Berkeley to Johnson, November 25, 1729.

but I cannot, I will not, understand that they can form any resolve to withhold a grant conveyed in such legal and authentic manner by His Majesty's patent under the broad seal, though it may possibly be postponed for some time."[47] There is no question that Berkeley would have been glad to locate the College in Rhode Island, and he unofficially wrote some of his friends in England to this effect.[48]

But at the end of the winter, he declares that he is "ready to set sail" for Bermuda "as soon as the money is paid." [49] After he received letters speaking of "the universal report" in England that he was settling in Rhode Island,[50] he reaffirms his original intention even more strongly. "Bermuda after all," he says, "is the proper place." [51] He thought of submitting a letter to the Treasurer, and even of a lawsuit, but Percival assured him that such measures would be fruitless.[52] "The design," wrote his friend a few months later, "seems too great and good to be accomplished in an age where men love darkness better than light, and nothing is considered but with a political view." [53]

At home, the wits made open jest of the Bermuda College, and, one by one, even his close friends deserted him. James and Dalton moved away to Boston, and did their best to persuade Berkeley to accompany them, but he would not be moved from his quiet retreat. The constant anxiety had undermined his health,[54] and he gave himself up entirely to that sort of "practical" contemplation in which his concrete logic was more and more deeply involving him. Scepticism cannot rest content with any "position" whatsoever, least of all itself. No proofs nor demonstrations can satisfy it, for what "proof" can be found whose cogency is not destroyed by a reference or relation to premisses? The more "convincing" a "proof," the more unconvincing its result, for a proof becomes convincing only by "dependency," by connection with something else. If the whole world were rational or proved, therefore, everything would then be dependent or connected, and nothing would be proved or rational. Everything would "follow from" something else, and so on. But nothing would then really follow from anything, for

[47] Berkeley to Percival, August 30, 1729.

[48] Berkeley to Newman, June 27, 1729.

[49] Berkeley to Percival, March 29, 1730.

[50] Percival letter, September 20, 1729.

[51] July 20, 1730.

[52] Percival letter, July 9, 1730.

[53] Percival letter, December 23, 1730.

[54] Letter to Percival, July 20, 1730.

there would be no absolute resting point capable of standing alone, and "having" consequences. Neither is it possible to find refuge in the "whole" of such dependent relations, for such a whole is "dependent" on its parts, and any "Absolute" which the human mind can "prove" is relative to the relative, hence dependent upon it, and hence not "Absolute." The absolute, upon which scepticism really rests, or with which it is really identical, is a far different sort of absolute, the absolute itself, which gains its absoluteness not from the fact that it is "proved" or even conceived, but precisely from the fact that it is not "proved or conceived." It is hardly surprising, therefore, to find Berkeley, as we have seen, rejecting those teleological "considerations" that Johnson urges in behalf of the Creator,[55] as well as the "cosmological" and "ontological" arguments that Johnson found "helpful" in conceiving Him. Berkeley's scepticism cannot rest content with such "arguments," for do they not advance only by making their absolutes dependent upon premisses? The failure of such arguments lies in their success. It is no wonder, therefore, that Berkeley does not reply to the question about his previous "argument" for "the natural immortality of the soul," which Johnson raises at the end of his second letter; nor can his scepticism find any rest in "scepticism" as a position; nor, indeed, can it find any rest at all. Scepticism, like other *isms*, is cursed with meaning, or relativity. It also leads beyond itself, or rather leads up to a beyond where all paths end. Scepticism, if truly sceptical, must be absolute. It is not surprising, therefore, to find Berkeley, throughout this period of life, seeking relief from the endless proddings of his concrete logic in the realm of the alogical, turning from reason to faith, from dogmatisms to dogma. The living current of his thought now flows through his sermons, and it is to these that we must turn.

The notes which have survived from this period show that Berkeley often preached at Trinity Church. He was at once impressed by the number of different religious sects, speaking himself of the "strange medley of different persuasions which, nevertheless, all agree in one point, viz. that the church of England is the second best." [56] The bigotry which made sectarian differences a primary topic of polite conversation, and even excluded books by Anglican theologians from the Yale

---

[55] Berkeley to Johnson, November 25, 1729.

[56] Berkeley to Percival, March 28, 1729.

library,[57] seemed to Berkeley to arise from an absurd confusion of the rational with the irrational, and many of his sermons embodied attacks upon "Phariseeism" of various kinds. He was also bored by the slavishness with which the colonials attempted to imitate or even outdo the forms and fashions of the mother country. His daughter-in-law tells an incident of one of his Newport Quaker friends, the proud possessor of a solid gold teapot, who was greatly pleased at learning that even Queen Caroline was not so fortunate.[58] She also relates that all sects agreed at least in following the mode. "In one thing, however," she says, "the different sectarists both men and women agreed, viz. in a rage for finery, to the great amusement of Bishop Berkeley's two learned, elegant friends, Sir John James and Richard Dalton Esqu.: the men in flaming scarlet coats and waistcoats, laced and fringed with the brightest glaring yellow. The sly Quakers not venturing on these charming coats and waistcoats, yet loving finery, figured away with plate at their sideboard or rather beaufait." [59]

There were, at this time, as his daughter-in-law informs us, no less than sixteen different religious groups in the small island less than twenty miles in circumference, and it was apparently customary for strangers to ask their visitors, "Pray, of what religion are you?" and then to discourse with them at tea concerning their respective differences.[60] Berkeley's sermons seem to have been well attended, even the Quakers in their broad-brimmed hats coming in large numbers, and sometimes many were forced to stand in the aisles.[61] Berkeley's long schooling in scepticism, with the tolerance [62] of absolute intolerance which it had forced upon him, evidently afforded a marked contrast to the humanistic rationalism which was already devitalizing the dissenting sects. He did his best to oppose this tendency,[63] and in a letter to Percival describes one Whit-Sunday, "the occasion being so proper," [64] when he "could not omit speaking against that spirit of delusion and enthusiasm which misleads those people: and though I did it in the softest manner and with the greatest caution, yet I found it gave some offence, so bigoted are they to their prejudices." It may have

[57] Letter to Johnson, March 24, 1730, *Johnson*, vol. II, p. 284.
[58] Berkeley, *Poems*, p. liv.
[59] *Ibid.*
[60] *Ibid.*, p. ccccli.

[61] Updike, *op. cit.*, p. 73.
[62] *Ibid.*
[63] Cf. F. iv, p. 376.
[64] Berkeley to Percival, August 30, 1729.

been on this occasion that, in order to lift his criticisms above any partisan level and to recall his listeners to the essential and universal irrationalism upon which their own dissent was founded, he emphatically said, "John Calvin was a great man." [65] Many of his discourses were practical homilies directed against such evils as slander [66] and the mistreatment of slaves resulting from the widespread belief that there was no necessity of baptizing inferior creatures.[67] He even went so far as to take steps, after his return to England, to get a legal opinion that baptism was consistent with slavery, and to have this opinion published and circulated through the colonies.[68]

These sermons embody a further development of the tendencies already observed in his *Guardian* essays and the Italian addresses. There is, in the first place, a sense of futility, arising partly from a realization of the limitations of reason, but made even deeper now by that feeling of despair in which all sincere striving with the world must end. Berkeley has, by this time, experienced not only the dialectic of reason, which ends in scepticism, but also something of the dialectic of life, which ends in death. No scepticism is really complete and final, until it is lived. It is as if Berkeley gains now, almost for the first time, an insight into the pathos of human existence. Just as his concrete logic finally showed him how every human theory carried with it the germs of its own decay, inevitably breaking into contradictions and falling back into that same sea of scepticism from which it took its rise, so now the passage of his own life shows him how all human goals and purposes are also fraught with finiteness and tinged with a certain anxiety which leads them, in the end, to a similar death. What dialectic reveals to our thought, time reveals to *us*, and one is the image of the other. "To consider the ways of men," says Berkeley at the beginning of one of his sermons, "one would think them never to die." [69]

This is the unmistakable undercurrent of the Rhode Island sermons. He speaks, for example, of the "uncertainty of time" and the corresponding certainty of "brevity."[70] A little earlier,

---

[65] Updike, *op. cit.*, p. 73.

[66] F. iv, p. 388.

[67] Berkeley was very careful to have his own slaves baptized. See *Annals of Trinity Church*, p. 51. "On the eleventh of June of this year, Dean Berkeley baptized three of his negroes, Philip, Anthony,

and Agnes Berkeley." Cf. Updike, *op. cit.*, p. 73.

[68] *Sermon preached before the Society for the Propagation of the Gospel*, F. iv, p. 404.

[69] F. iv, p. 386.

[70] *Ibid.*, p. 387.

he connects the "lapsed state" of all mankind with the endless
disagreement, "opposition," and "war," which is as characteristic of the social as of the intellectual world.[71] It is visible, he
says, in one of the sermons which has been preserved intact, to
all who have "any thought or reflection" that "the understanding of man" is "obscure," that "his will" is "perverse," "his
passions irregular," and that "the consequence" is "an unquiet
conscience, an anxious terrour of mind, and a fearful looking for
judgment."[72] We are "sentenced to lead a short and sorrowful
life, a life of pains and trouble, under a perpetual horrour of
death."[73]

To speak of any "salvation" from such a "lapsed state"
shows not only lack of insight, but lack of understanding, since
the more we think, the more we expose ourselves to the relativity
and contradiction to which thought is by its nature condemned,
just as the more we "act," the more irrevocably we become
embedded in the flux of time. There can be no hope save in a
hopelessness which is absolute. Having learned by years of
painful reflection that reason can be justified only by an absolute which is entirely inconceivable and altogether beyond it,
Berkeley can now condone no "plausible" rationalism in his
theology. "Natural religion," while he continues to grant it a
subordinate importance,[74] is identified with the "Decalogue"
and the legalistic attitude of the "Pharisees," who "preferred
rites to weightier matters." The legalistic or rationalistic mind
reduces religion to a mass of formulae, which "vanish like
shadows" with "a clearer [i.e., unclearer] view" of "things."[75]
The attempt to make religion "reasonable" and natural succeeds only in destroying it by anthropomorphism and subjectivism. There can be no salvation, no religion without a
transcendence so absolute as to escape even the concept of transcendence, for what is meant must be more than the sense in
which time transcends the temporal and logic transcends nature.
What is necessary is a concept above and beyond concepts and
the web of relations which our reason weaves. Hence, Berkeley
selects as the text of another sermon which has survived from
this time: "Without controversy great is the mystery of Godliness," I Timothy iii. 16.

[71] Ibid., p. 373.
[72] App., Sermon 2, being the second
version of the sermon on the text "Without controversy great is the mystery of
Godliness." I Timothy iii. 16.
[73] App., Ser. 2.
[74] F. iv, p. 371.　　　[75] Ibid., p. 372.

All traces of Arminianism are now as distasteful to him as to his Calvinistic auditors. "Jewish the religion of legal justice," he jots down in his notes for a sermon preached the first of September, 1729, "Christian of saving grace; grace from the beginning." [76] There can be no question of God's conforming His ways to us and our legalistic reasonings, for then He would not be God, but only the image of man. "The mystery of Godliness is great and wonderful throughout this whole dispensation." [77] The preponderant number of texts and quotations chosen from Paul, "the father of all believers," [78] show, even without the additional testimony of the content, that Berkeley was now turning back more and more to the "primitive Christians, than whom" there are "none wiser or better now." [79] It is, therefore, no wonder that we find him uttering sentiments a little strange to the more "modern" tendencies of his own church. We have already noted his tribute to Calvin, and there are certain features of his doctrine which help us to understand his popularity with the dissenting colonists. Thus, in speaking of "the elect," he says: "the steps or method of his providence in separating and preserving them amidst all the casualties and corruptions, the vicissitudes and changes of this inferior world" are "without doubt great mysteries." [80] There is no further attempt, as in the *Passive Obedience*, to build up an independent "science" of ethics, for what could this be but another man-made theory, and life is too important a matter for such abstractions. The "reasonings of philosophers" cannot "possess men," and "eternal life," not the concept of eternity, is treated no longer as a "thesis" of "natural religion," but as dependent for "its truth and certainty" upon the "full and explicit revelation thereof." [81]

Berkeley's discussions with Clarke had, perhaps, already put him on his guard against the dangers of that Arianism to which an abstract logic leads the unwary rationalist, and several of his sermons defend the category of revelation against the converse fallacy of Sabellianism which was already beginning to sap the vitality of the New England sects. "The divinity of our Saviour," he says in one of his earlier notes, though "denied of late years," is "a fundamental article of the Christian

[76] *Ibid.*, p. 379.
[77] App., Ser. 2.
[78] *Ibid.*
[79] F. iv, p. 386.

[80] App., Ser. 2.
[81] App., Ser. 3. "This is the promise that he hath promised us even eternal life." I John ii. 25.

faith." [82] He naturally recognized, both in the tendency to reify the different hypostases of the Trinity into separate beings, as well as in the "opposed" tendency to reduce them all to emanations or appearances of some one substance lying back of them, examples of the same abstract and rigid mode of thought with which he had contended, without realizing its full implications, throughout the earlier portion of his life. If there is to be such a thing as revelation, it must be God who reveals Himself. It is the fact of revelation which necessarily brings the doctrine of the Trinity in its train. [83] But revelation is neither direct, nor immediate, nor abstract. It is "mystery," or "doctrine," or dogma. [84]

What is revealed is the absolute impossibility of any such revelation, for the God who reveals Himself is a *Deus Absconditus* who reveals Himself only by not revealing Himself, through the "great mystery of the incarnation." [85] Were He anything less than this He could not be God, but only an anthropomorphic image. What is revealed is the absolutely transcendent, something so transcendent as to be immanent, something revealed only in the utter impossibility of its revelation, not an absolute, but *the* absolute, which is beyond all reason and rational relation, and hence truly absolute. What else can such an absolute be but "mystery," or "doctrine," or dogma, the end, as it is the beginning, of all knowledge, and the crisis or negation of finite existence? Hence, Berkeley wastes no more time on naive Deistic "proofs" of God, on a humanistic religion of "value" with a man-made mechanism for the fulfillment of ethical codes, dreams, or wishes. There must be contradiction, mystery, "Grace from the beginning," [86] or we are worshipping a creature of our own construction, a plausible thesis — the conclusion of a syllogism.

It is this phase of his newly-discovered absolute that enables Berkeley to state his faith in universal terms, and to oppose with all the strength at his command the sectarian spirit which was, in the colonies, gradually substituting either external observances or abstract reasoning for the sense of the absolute. It is the "rationalists" who prefer their own logic to the truth, the "Pharisees" who "preferred rites to weightier matters." [87] Revelation is not restricted "to a family," nor "to a nation,"

[82] F. iv, p. 376.
[83] *Ibid.*, p. 377.
[84] *Ibid.*, p. 378.

[85] App., Ser. 2.
[86] F. iv, p. 379; cf. p. 381.
[87] *Ibid.*, p. 372.

but is "to the whole world," [88] for who has not, in some form or other, himself recognized in his existence the absolute transcendence of that which can in no sense be recognized? It is "sad," therefore, "that religion, which requires us to love, should become the cause of our hating one another. But it is not religion . . .," [89] it is the humanism, the Sabellianism, the Arianism, which an all too human logic substitutes for it, that divides us into man-made schools and sects, leading us to "judge," while ignoring the "beam in our own eye." [90] True religion makes us hate not others, but ourselves. Let us "look narrowly into ourselves," says Berkeley to his sectarian audience,[91] " to examine whether we have not the same or as bad or worse," for are we not "all criminals at the same bar "? [92]

Every human code or sect is condemned from the first by its very humanity to error and destruction, as every human theory, no matter how subtle or refined, is doomed to contradiction and decay. We have not even begun to sense the meaning of scepticism, if it is used only as a convenient weapon against other peoples' views, nor have we even begun to grasp the meaning of religion, if it is used merely as a means of destroying Baals and Jupiters. They should all be asserted. Have they not all grasped something of the truth? And is not this their tragedy, for which of them in gaining something of the truth must not disappear before the truth? Sooner or later we must confront the fact that the "understanding," which, through its misguided attempts to unify us, really drives us apart with its abstract codes and statutes, is "ignorant and impotent." [93] There is "a way" that "seemeth right unto man, but the end thereof is . . . death, anguish and remorse." [94] There is no escape, no human means of explaining or defining what is good and what is bad, for "moral good and evil depends on unseen springs." [95] Finally, "who art thou that judgest another?"

Berkeley's studies have taught him too much concerning the meaning of scepticism to enable him to rest here or, indeed, anywhere. Scepticism is not an attitude, nor a belief, but a restless movement, converging on one position, which is beyond all positions, the absolute. There is no peace to be found in any theory, any passion, any instinct, any faith, but only in a final negation of them all, — "bending them to the will of God." [96]

[88] *Ibid.*
[89] *Ibid.*, p. 375.
[90] *Ibid.*, p. 389.

[91] *Ibid.*, p. 390.
[92] *Ibid.*
[93] *Ibid.*, p. 384.

[94] *Ibid.*
[95] *Ibid.*, p. 390.
[96] *Ibid.*, p. 384.

Thus, to the fifteen varieties of self-assured sectarianism confronting him at Newport, Berkeley preached of "the Church invisible." [97] There is "nothing" more evident to "whoever reads the Scriptures with attention," he says,[98] "than that God from the beginning designed to select out of the corrupt mass of mankind a peculiar people to himself sanctifyed and distinguished from the rest of the world by faith and repentance, animated by the spirit of God, supported and enlightened by His Grace, so conducted through this world as not to suffer by the contagion of it." But the "Council of God concerning His elect" is secret and predeterminate," [99] and many of the "visible Church" are "not of the invisible." [100] It is not surprising, therefore, that in turning the attention of their spiritual leaders to the doctrine of Calvin, whom many, at least verbally, acknowledged as a leader, he succeeded only in arousing their resentment, and that the impression he left was that of a disagreeable and "hypochondriacal" disposition. [101]

FAILURE

Berkeley had now given up all hope of carrying out his plans, and was preparing to return home. "I have received such accounts on all hands," he writes to Percival on March 2, 1731, "both from England and from Ireland that I now give up all hopes of executing the design which brought me into these parts. I am fairly given to understand that the money will never be paid." His friends had all left him. The delay has been so long, he continues, "that I am absolutely abandoned by every one of them. This disappointment which long lay heavy on my spirits I endeavor to make myself easy under by considering that we know not what would be eventually good or bad, and that no events are in our power.[102] Upon the whole, my thoughts are now set towards Europe, where I shall endeavor to be useful some other way." One of the "accounts" he speaks of was a letter from Dr. Downs, Bishop of Down, written in an "impertinent" manner to the Dean "requiring him to come home, and calling his scheme idle and simple." [103] Percival had also given him to understand that "the wits"

97 *Ibid.*, p. 380.
98 App., Ser. 2.
99 *Ibid.*
100 F. iv, p. 380.

101 H. V. White, *op. cit.*
102 Cf. Alc., F. ii, p. 32.
103 Percival journal, March 10, 1731.

were having a great deal of fun at his expense.[104] In the autumn
of 1731, Berkeley left Newport for Boston, where he preached
at King's Chapel, designed by an architect he himself had
brought to America. Forced at last to admit failure in the
project to which he had devoted most of his fortune and ten
years of his life, he set sail on the twenty-first of September for
England with his wife and his son Henry.[105]

In spite of his intimate friendship with Johnson, which continued for the rest of his life, and his first enthusiasm for
America, Percival's diary provides conclusive evidence that
Berkeley's impression of the Colony was hardly a favourable
one, and he seems to have been very glad to reach home. Percival writes, November 1, 1731: "Dean Berkeley who arrived
Saturday last from Rhode Island dined with me, and seems
rejoiced that he treads English ground, after three years absence in a country of which he gives a very indifferent account."
He seems to have felt very definitely the lack of culture and
learning in New England. As he says in the *Alciphron*: "the
first care of mankind is to supply the cravings of nature; in the
next place they study the conveniences and comforts of life.
But the subduing prejudices and acquiring true knowledge,
that Herculean labour is the last; being what demands the
most perfect abilities, and to which all other advantages are
preparative."[106]

On the evening of January 12, 1732, he had dinner with
Oglethorpe and Percival at the latter's house, when, according
to the host, "we sat from dinner to ten o'clock discussing of our
Carolina project."[107] Percival was a friend of Oglethorpe's,
and had become one of the sponsors of the Carolina scheme.
Berkeley must have been somewhat cynical about the possibility of getting money from Walpole for any sort of altruistic
enterprise, but he willingly gave his consent to transfer all his
claims on the government to Oglethorpe. The St. Christopher's
money, which had given rise to such far-reaching dreams,
ultimately came to ninety thousand pounds. As a result of
the efforts of Berkeley and Percival, ten thousand went to
Georgia,[108] in a form of altruism which Walpole could understand. After all, it cost money to maintain jails. A verbal

[104] Percival letter, July 20, 1730.
[105] A daughter, Lucia, was buried at
Newport, September 5, 1731.
[106] Alc., I, F. ii, p. 34.

[107] Percival diary, January 12.
[108] *Journal of the House of Commons*,
XXII, p. 203.

concession, at least, was made to religious proprieties, as a warrant was issued on July 30, 1733, directing the money to be appropriated "towards defraying the charges of settling foreign or other Protestants" in Georgia.[109]

On May 8, 1733, the House was asked to grant financial assistance to the King, in connection with the marriage of his daughter to William Charles Henry Frizo, Prince of Orange, which would tend "to the further security of the Protestant succession to the Crown of these realms, and to the Protestant interest in Europe," [110] though the real reason for this unprecedented dowry was that the Prince was as defective in advantages of fortune as in graces of person.[111] On May 10, a Committee of the House advised that the dowry should be raised out of the St. Christopher's funds.[112] On June 13, the King gave his "consent" to the Act, and on March 14, 1734, the payment was made to the royal consort. Thus, Berkeley's dream of a new civilization ended in the establishment of a penal colony and the wedding of a forlorn princess to a dwarf, which Hervey,[113] the Court biographer, assures us was in "extreme good taste."[114]

The political realism of the Townshends and Walpoles, which had defeated him at last, seemed to have its rise in the same "narrowness" he had struggled against in the Newport sectarians, and which he now associated with the naturalistic or rationalistic point of view. During the last days of his residence in America, he had set himself the task of examining again the philosophic presuppositions of his old enemies the free-thinkers, but in a far more thorough-going fashion than before. "What they foolishly call free thinking seems to me the principal root or source not only of opposition to our College but of most other evils in this age, and as long as this frenzy subsists and spreads it is in vain to hope for any good either to the mother country or colonies which always follow the fashions of Old England." [115] The result of this examination was the *Alciphron*, published shortly after his arrival in England, and the most widely read of all of Berkeley's works.

[109] *Cal. of Treas. Papers*, 1731–34, ed. 1898, p. 393, quoted by Hertz, *Brit. Imp.*, chap. VI.
[110] *Jour. of H. of Comm.*, XXII, p. 142.
[111] Hervey, *Memoirs*, p. 235.
[112] *Jour. of H. of Comm.*, XXII, p. 145.
[113] Pope's *Sporus*.
[114] Hervey, *op. cit.*, p. 224.
[115] Letter to Percival, March 2, 1731.

CHAPTER XIII

CONCRETE ETHICS AND RELIGION
(THE ALCIPHRON)

THE *Alciphron* is a polemic treatise directed not so much against a set doctrine as against a social tendency or movement. This is why Berkeley chose the dialogue form, for he realized that he was opposing a way of thought, or state of mind, rather than a definite system. It was, therefore, necessary first to present his characters in the form of concrete individuals, and then to consider them "in the various lights of atheist, libertine, enthusiast, scorner, critic, metaphysician, fatalist and sceptic."[1] Berkeley specifically disclaims any serious attempt at unity of doctrine so far as his opponents are concerned. He has to make Lysicles and Alciphron successively defend the various arguments with which the naturalism of the period attempted to justify its attitude and way of life. These doctrines are, of course, combatted by the acumen of Euphranor, reinforced by the erudition of Crito.

But it is Berkeley himself who performs the far more difficult feat of refuting gibes and sneers. Nothing annoyed him more than the assumption on the part of the latitudinarians that the muses were on their side, that their opponents were nothing but dull pedants, and that virtue and religion were inconsistent with intelligence. But though this contemporary polemic provides the background and plot of the dialogue, Berkeley is led, in the course of its development, to a most significant refinement of his speculative scepticism.

The first dialogue refers at the beginning to the Bermuda disappointment, in a passage describing the uncertainty of events and the necessity of making "good use even of the very worst."[2] The chief characters are then introduced as Lysicles, the smart young man about town, Alciphron, the more thoughtful free-thinker who prides himself on his "rationality," Euphranor, the keen, unprejudiced countryman, and Crito, the clergyman who fortifies Euphranor's arguments with a wider learning. Alciphron starts the discussion by defining free-

---

[1] Alc., advertisement.   [2] Alc., F. ii, p. 32.

thinking as the single-hearted pursuit of truth without reference to the prejudices and superstitions aroused by "the cunning of statesmen" and "the imposture of priests." [3] The truth, he insists, is of a "stable, permanent, and uniform nature." [4] The free-thinker cannot, therefore, rest satisfied with the multitude of utterly diverse opinions which masquerade under the common name of Christianity. He becomes first a latitudinarian, but then, perceiving that there are other religions which agree with Christianity only in professing a single God, he leaves the fold of Christianity for "a more enlarged view of things," [5] and becomes a Deist. Finally, extending his view to other nations of the globe which differ concerning the nature and even the existence of God, he becomes an atheist, free from all contrary opinion and prejudice. This is "the masterpiece and finishing stroke" of free thought. Berkeley, in the person of Euphranor, points out that such a desolating process of abstraction must end by eliminating the views of the free-thinker himself, for he also has opinions which differ from those of others. A truth which is held to consist in abstract identity must end by destroying itself, for such identity removed from all difference is nothing. [6]

Yet "reason" seems to imply just such an impossible or inconceivable norm, for "reason is the same . . . in all times and places." [7] "Reason" is thus guided by an ideal which, if realized, would make itself superfluous and impossible. Reason is necessarily abstract and concrete as well. It stands in its own way. It must consist in an incessant attempt at self-annihilation which can never succeed so long as reason is reason. It is no wonder that such considerations lead Berkeley in the *Alciphron* to a more indirect method of investigation. The effort to discover "truth" in the field of ethics by means of rational argument seems particularly futile, for "the moral actions of men" are not objects that can be studied and reasoned about like ordinary phenomena. When so studied or reasoned about, they cease to be moral actions and become psychology. As a result of his general scepticism, we find Berkeley in the second and fifth dialogues, for example, addressing himself not to the question of "truth" at all, for this is an abstraction, but rather to the question of value, for "is not the general good of mankind to be regarded as a rule and measure of moral truths,

---

[3] *Ibid.*, p. 36.   [5] *Ibid.*   [7] *Ibid.*, p. 62.
[4] *Ibid.*, p. 45.   [6] *Ibid.*, pp. 61, 62.

of all such truths as direct or influence the moral actions of men?" [8] The discussion of this question, indeed, which leads to a collision with Mandeville, occupies the whole of the second dialogue.

In the third dialogue, Berkeley launches a polemic against Cratylus (Shaftesbury) which is unusually savage, even when allowance is made for the stress and bitterness which characterize this period of his life. This polemic continues at intervals throughout the remainder of the work, for at almost every point Berkeley finds perfectly typified in Shaftesbury an abstract mode of thought, the shallowness and triviality of which strike him all the more forcibly in that he himself once traveled the same road. The "chaste unaffected style" [9] of this "divine characterizer of our times," [10] which has been so greatly admired by foreigners imperfectly acquainted with the language, fills Berkeley with a disgust which is surpassed only by his scorn of the content itself, — an aestheticism which places "morals on the same foot with manners" [11] and views life as a pretty play. It is with a sense resembling relief that Berkeley falls back upon that moral "vice" and "wickedness" dismissed by the romantic spectator as only "a little soft shadowing of evil," which "sets off the luminous parts of the creation and so contributes to the beauty of the whole piece." [12] "Vice" at least awakens us from such aesthetic contemplation of external harmony and rudely reminds us that life finally reaches a point where it is to be taken seriously, that there are subjects in the world as well as objects, and that "it is impossible to account" for "blots so large and black" by Shaftesbury's sublime "principle." [13]

In the fourth dialogue, Berkeley discards the Deistic "proofs" for the existence of God as "dry and jejune," and subjects his own rationalistic argument of the third dialogue between Hylas and Philonous to a devastating scrutiny, which clearly reveals that the all-inclusive absolute to which this argument led him does not possess the "attributes" of God at all, [14] since it is nothing but the general field of meaning within which he was operating. The "proof" which Berkeley now offers in *Alciphron IV* indicates the new depths to which his scepticism has taken him, and his general discouragement with all the "results"

---

[8] *Ibid.*, p. 63.
[9] *Ibid.*, p. 222.
[10] *Ibid.*, p. 349.
[11] *Ibid.*, p. 143.
[12] *Ibid.*, p. 189.
[13] *Ibid.*
[14] *Ibid.*, pp. 188–189.

of his past reflections, for it represents a return to the "proof" of the *Principles*, although now stated in such a way as to make manifest its paradoxical character. According to this "proof" we "see" God, just as we "see" a man, i.e., by not seeing Him. Berkeley "proves," in other words, that we "see" God by proving that we do not, as a matter of fact, really "see" anything at all, but that everything "seen" is interpretation, and hence subject to question. The whole solid world we think we see is a construction; seeing itself, for example, is certainly not seen. Our "sense" of reality, therefore, is an "intuition" or, in other words, an act of faith that our interpretations are really correct and that a demon is not perhaps deceiving us. The dogmatic certainty of the *Principles* [15] toward "this great truth" is now missing, for it is only through a realization of the irrationality hovering over every moment of our lives that the existence of God becomes rational, only through a realization of the relativity of all "proof" that God is "proved." If we once gain some understanding of the difficulties involved in "seeing" another self, for example, a "mystery" we accept throughout our waking life, we shall find, by comparison, little difficulty with the mystery of "seeing" God. "If the arguments for a Deity be not conclusive," says Berkeley, summing up his "proof," "then shew me by what better arguments you can prove the existence of that thinking thing" you call yourself.[16]

In the fifth and sixth dialogues Berkeley subjects to a cool examination "the new theories which our acute moderns have endeavored to substitute in place of religion." [17] "Truth," exclaims Alciphron, "is the only divinity that I adore. Wherever truth leads, I shall follow." [18] But this abstract divinity leads him, unfortunately, only to endless pros and cons. There are grounds on the one hand for believing that "natural religion" is able to prove the fundamental tenets of religion, and on the other hand for believing that it is incapable of dealing with "the divine nature," since "God is infinitely above man." [19] We are assured by reason, on the one hand, that God is wise and good, and on the other that His attributes are incomprehensible; on the one hand that the world must be a beautiful and harmonious system, and on the other that it is a dismal dungeon.[20] It is possible to find "grounds" for any-

---

[15] Sec. 149.   [17] *Ibid.*, p. 151.   [19] *Ibid.*, p. 187.
[16] Alc., p. 162.   [18] *Ibid.*.   [20] *Ibid.*, p. 190.

thing, and there is nothing, however unplausible, that cannot be rendered plausible from a certain "point of view." It is with evident relief that Berkeley turns once more from this tangle of reasons and counter-reasons in the fifth dialogue to a discussion of the "usefulness" rather than the abstract truth of certain conceptions. But this category, while it leads us beyond the abstract field of contemplation, can give us no permanent satisfaction, for of what use is it to know that something is useful, unless we know at the same time for what, and to what it is useful, or in other words, unless we possess a whole philosophy of value? The pragmatic note, which runs through the writings of this period, is, therefore, an expression of Berkeley's dissatisfaction with the rational, an aggravation of his scepticism rather than in any sense an "answer." There is no more effective manner of damning a thing to relativity and instability than by calling it "useful."

Pragmatism, relativity, scepticism is a path that leads Berkeley to the practical philosophy which is outlined in the sixth and seventh dialogues, and which forms the climax of the work. The whole rational or theoretical way of examining reality, including pragmatism and scepticism, is an abstraction, which is, therefore, by itself incapable of yielding valid conclusions with respect to the final issues, and Berkeley's scepticism has at last pushed him to such issues. The world of reason is a world of objects contemplated from the outside. Rational religion, therefore, becomes a theory of the universe, and rational ethics an aesthetic theory. But concrete religion and concrete ethics, as they actually are, belong to another realm entirely, for they do not concern objective entities, but *myself*. "Those words which denote an active principle, soul or spirit do not, in a strict and proper sense, stand for ideas. And yet they are not insignificant neither; since I understand what is signified by the term *I*, or *myself*, or know what it means: although it be no idea, or like an idea, but that which thinks and wills, and apprehends ideas, and operates about them." [21] Outside of the "outside" world, back of it, or before it, lies the self with its "thoughts" and "operations," its norms or "rules."

Berkeley had grasped, even in the *Commonplace Book*, something of the significance of this distinction, for he had then maintained that all the categories, even "existence," must be given a different meaning when applied to "spirit," which is no object or "idea." What Berkeley's struggles with the practical have now taught him is that truth itself must be given a different meaning in this connection. Ordinary reflection unconsciously presupposes its own norms and simply applies them to various objects or ideas, as it finds by "observation" that such and such a theory is true, or that such and such an object is beautiful. Such reflection is abstract. When we think concretely we must think the objects together with the norms, and must grasp the whole world of objects as transfused by the mysterious something that is not something, which we call the self. Such thinking cannot be decided by an appeal to the "given," or to any objective reality, since what is at issue is something that can never be turned into an object of any sort. To the categories of existence, therefore, we must add those of value, or validity, as the object must be supplemented by the subject. Berkeley's concrete logic has thus made him sensitive to a new level of existence. The concrete *esse*, the *esse percipi*, is lived existence, the field of "our conduct and actions."[22] So different is this concrete existence which we live from the ordinary world of objects *in* which we live that what is unintelligible or even nonsense from one point of view may be perfectly intelligible from the other. Such normative conceptions as "original sin" and other "mysteries" may have a perfectly definite concrete or practical meaning, though from the abstract objective point of view they are "mysteries," and the attempt of "reason" to explain them in the usual manner is "as fruitless as the pursuit of the philosopher's stone in chemistry,"[23] since we are confusing two entirely distinct and opposed types of thinking and two entirely opposed types of explanation, one abstract the other concrete.

It is this sense of a new field of concrete, lived actuality, or practical existence, that dominates the last pages of the *Alciphron*. What is commonly called reason is incomplete, since it abstracts from the subjective, the superrational, the normative aspects of experience. But in such realms as ethics it is precisely the subjective and normative that is in question. In ethics we cannot employ the usual rational or "natural" methods, because the "objects" of discussion are ourselves, not objects at all. The discovery that such a realm must exist, and the sceptical consequences of this discovery in relation to all "natural" or objective theories of ethics, such as those of the

---

[22] *Ibid.*   [23] *Ibid.*, p. 337.

Deists and Shaftesbury in particular, is the "essence" of Berkeley's *Alciphron*. From this practical vantage point one can understand the ironic rationalism of the first four dialogues and the savage criticism of Shaftesbury's aestheticism, which fails precisely by attempting to build an objective ethics, an aesthetic morality, or an objective theory of the subjective. Even the pragmatic scepticism of the third and fifth dialogues becomes clear. The key to the whole lies in the seventh dialogue, which begins with the seemingly irrelevant discussion of language and abstraction, for here it is shown that the two realms do not stand upon a level of equality, but that the practical is the more concrete and fundamental of the two. Existence itself does not exist. Rather it is a norm, or form of evaluation. Objectivity is a form of subjectivity, and knowledge, in the end, is itself practical, for, after all, knowing is a mode of action. Hence in knowing we are really acting under the guidance of the same ends or norms which govern our "ordinary" practical behaviour, and logic is a branch of ethics. It is not surprising, therefore, that Berkeley is forced to turn once again to the field of moral theory. Perhaps here an answer may be found to the scepticism which has driven him beyond "reason" and its contemplative absolute.

The Critique of Mathematical Ethics

To understand the ethics of the *Alciphron* we must first remind ourselves of the *Passive Obedience* and the attempt of Berkeley's youthful reflections to work out Locke's suggestion of a mathematical or demonstrative system of Ethics. It is quite clear, even from the external form of the *Alciphron*, that Berkeley has altogether abandoned this alluring dream of his youth, and before proceeding to a closer examination of the dialogues we must consider what reasons led him to give up the search for moral principles possessing "the same immutable, universal truth" as "propositions in geometry." [24] These reasons are contained in germ in Berkeley's earlier thought, especially in the *Commonplace Book*, although they are not developed to any sort of systematic coherence until the *Alciphron*.

In the first place, there is Berkeley's discovery of the analytic or "trifling" character of mathematical propositions which

[24] P. O., 53, F. iv, p. 133.

occurred early in the course of his reflections at Trinity College, and which led him to mitigate his early enthusiasm for a subject so "certain" and yet so "trifling" or abstract. Thus, after a careful study of Locke's chapter eight, Book IV, Berkeley comments that "to demonstrate morality it seems one need only make a dictionary of words and see which included which . . .," [25] and then, noting the verbal character of such a procedure, he declares very pointedly: "Locke's instances of demonstration in morality are according to his own rule trifling propositions." [26] Moral propositions are not analytic statements of the meanings already contained in certain concepts. They are, to use Locke's term, instructive. The general form of a moral proposition is *x is right* or *x is valuable*. And the normative predicate contains something that cannot be analyzed out of the subject. The mathematical analytic method, therefore, can be of only secondary importance in the field of ethics. Value judgments involve the attribution of a unique normative predicate to some entity, and are consequently synthetic rather than analytic in character. We have already noticed Berkeley's attempt to substitute a method of concrete "reasoning" which should do justice to the world confronting us for a "demonstration," which, though certain and precise, is empty and, in the end, "only verbal." [27] The evidence of the *Commonplace Book* goes to show that ethical considerations, and particularly his discovery of the analytic character of Locke's ethical demonstrations, played a dominant role in this whole transition. Once we have arrived at the concepts of morality, analysis undoubtedly may bring about clarity, but the fundamental concepts must be synthetic in character, and therefore derived from another source, through another type of logic. Morality may only "be demonstrated as mixt mathematics." [28] The basic propositions which concern the "real truth" are derived from a synthetic mode of thought which is nevertheless rational, for "reasoning and science doth not altogether depend upon words or names." [29] Berkeley's abandonment of the mathematical method in ethics, therefore, is a result of his discovery that this method is verbal or analytic in character, and is really a part of his attempt to work out another method of "reasoning" which should do justice to the concrete reality, to content as well as to form.

[25] C. B. J., 702.   [27] C. B. J., 816.   [29] C. B. J., 895.
[26] C. B. J., 703.   [28] C. B. J., 768.

The *Commonplace Book*, however, also reveals another reason underlying Berkeley's criticism of the purely "demonstrative" method which is further elaborated in the *Alciphron*. This arises from his realization of the unique and ineffable character of the will, which is "*purus actus*, or rather pure spirit not imaginable, not sensible, not intelligible, in no wise the object of the understanding, no wise perceivable." [30] The mathematical method deals only with static concepts and the analytic clarification of such concepts, which are already assumed or "given." It is unable to cope with the dynamic process which passes from one to another, and which is the essence of "activity," whether it be of a moral or an "intellectual" character. In discussing the self or spirit in section 139 of the *Principles*, Berkeley says that it "is neither an idea nor like an idea, but that which perceives ideas, and wills and reasons about them." When we *reason* about ideas we are doing much more than analyzing the implications of an idea, for such a procedure does not advance. It stays altogether within the compass of the given idea. It clarifies but does not progress. It may be certain and precise, but it is sterile. The mathematical system must "assume" itself to begin with, and the resulting process is a mere elaboration of something which was already there. Reflective movement arises only in connection with the selection of the basic postulates and in the application of the system as a whole, which necessarily involve the joining of concepts mathematically unanalyzable from one another. But to the mathematical method, in and for itself, such syntheses remain extralogical and unintelligible. One may become sufficiently obsessed with the advantages of this method even to question the reality of such dynamic movement, in which case all "action" or relation is denied, and the world becomes a set of isolated concepts or ideas, each of which may be analyzed into component units neither derived from nor related one to another. Thus Berkeley says in the *Principles*: "It is even probable that this opinion may have produced a doubt in some whether they had any soul at all distinct from their body; since upon enquiry they could not find they had an idea of it." [31]

The essence of "the soul," as Berkeley has now come to understand it, consists precisely in synthesis or passage from one point to another, and such passage can never itself be transformed into a stable point or concept. We may indeed

---

[30] J., 840. Cf. XXI, 527 and 718.   [31] Sec. 137.

tag it with a word such as "relation," but, as Berkeley says, "the obscure ambiguous term *relation* . . . confounds us, deceives us." [32] It deceives us because by naming it we think we have built a concept or idea of it similar to any other static concept, whereas in truth, in that it represents a passage from one such concept to another, it is essentially distinct from them, and must remain unique and irreducible. This realization of the unique status of the will as passage or relation must have disastrous consequences for any proposed application of the analytic method to morality. "We have no ideas of virtues and vices, no ideas of moral actions. Wherefore it may be questioned whether we are capable of arriving at demonstration about them, the morality consisting in the volition chiefly." [33]

Virtues and vices involve action or passage that cannot be crystallized into a fixed concept or set of concepts from which we proceed to deduce analytic consequences. Such a procedure would miss the very essence of the matter, — the creative will. In order to deal with ethical questions, a synthetic or ethical method of "reasoning" which may do justice to the unconceptualizable features of action or relation is required. In place of the "dogmatic" method, which simply takes for granted a certain postulate from which consequences are then deduced, Berkeley adopts, in the second dialogue of the *Alciphron*, a more fluid method that advances more through contrast and comparison than through abstract consistency. He pauses only momentarily to deduce consequences, but weaves in and through the various systems by means of a method which refuses to identify itself with any such system, though as we shall see, it cannot be called unsystematic. It is with the tools of criticism rather than those of dogmatism that Berkeley begins in the second dialogue to examine the systems of ethics.

ETHICAL SYSTEMS

Berkeley first of all turns to the paradoxical system of Mandeville, who had startled the world in 1702 with his advocacy of the thesis that "private vices" are "public benefits," and who later replied to Berkeley's criticism in his *Letter to Dion*. With much of Mandeville's criticism Berkeley must have sympathized, and the latter, in his reply, at one point

---

[32] C. B. J., 746.   [33] C. B. J., 679.

himself suggests that they are really saying the same thing.[34] The great difference between the two is that Mandeville was content to play the various systems against one another without permitting his scepticism to force him on to the practical level in which Berkeley eventually found himself. With respect, however, to the common eighteenth century tenet, one of the most sensational of Mandeville's bag of tricks, that indiscriminate luxury is, as a matter of fact, an economic benefit, and that individual waste of every sort stimulates trade and "circulation," Berkeley allows himself the indulgence of a certain counter-irony, since this thesis of "minute philosophy" enables him to speak a word in defense of Telesilla, "a woman of quality and spirit" who "made no figure in the world, till she was instructed . . . in the tenets of minute philosophy," but then "took a turn towards expensive diversions, particularly deep play, by which means she soon transferred a considerable share of her husband's fortune to several acute men skilled in that mystery, who wanted it more and circulated it quicker than her husband would have done." [35] He is even able to argue in behalf of that "happy hint of a celebrated minute philosopher, who, by profound thinking, has discovered that burning the city of London would be no such bad action as silly prejudiced people might possibly imagine." [36]

Berkeley sees that Mandeville's destructive paradoxes arise from the essential relativity embedded in the concept of utility, which Mandeville, together with his century, had accepted as a basic standard of reflection. Utility may discredit anything (i.e. justify it), since there is nothing that is not useful for some purpose or other. There is no vice whatsoever that cannot be fitted somewhere into this abstract form, nor any institution that cannot, on the other hand, be damned as useless, for utility is pure category or relativity, — scepticism itself. Thus, as Lysicles says, by a short reflection upon the meaning of this tool "we have cleared the land of all prejudices towards government

[34] *Letter to Dion*, p. 48. Mandeville's latest commentator, Mr. Kaye, has pointed out that Mandeville's paradox rests on a perpetual shift from one standard to another, from worldly to other-worldly values, from common sense to "Rigorism." "Religion is one thing," as he remarks in the *Letter to Dion*, page 68, "and trade is another." But the essential ambiguity in the concept of "utility," which Mandeville accepted, with his age, makes it possible to pass imperceptibly from one set of values to the other. Mandeville simply allows "utility" to work out its destiny, and watches over the confusion with a penetrating irony.

[35] Alc., pp. 75–76.

[36] *Ibid.*, pp. 78–79.

or constitution, and made them fly like other phantasms before the light of reason and good sense." [37] The real danger of utilitarianism, as Berkeley perceives, lies not in the pure scepticism with which it is identical, but rather in the cloaking of this scepticism by the false dogmatism with which it is usually confused. When we say that so and so is useful we do not consider with Mandeville whether we mean useful for the eternal salvation of our souls, or useful for "the Brewing Trade." [38] We assume dogmatically some set of values lying ready at hand, and lump them together into some vague concept such as "survival." Instead of being led with Mandeville to further thought (paradox) we are led to the abandonment of thought, and to a relapse into common sense which is all the more confusing from the fact that it is identified with that "reason" or scepticism which it fears as death. Hence, as Lysicles comes to maintain, virtue is not really the indeterminate "useful," but "a trick of statesmen," [39] under which cloak of rationality he smuggles into the discourse a totally unwarranted type of common-sense dogmatism. The danger of utility philosophy lies always in the ease with which it may be identified with common sense. The pure notion, as Berkeley clearly saw, must necessarily lead to further reflection concerning standards. Useful for whom and for what?

Lysicles, when pressed, makes an "appeal to nature" in behalf of sensual pleasure, which, however, turns out to be a boomerang, since it is absurd to hold that the natural is identical with the infantile. The leaves and blossoms of a tree, for instance, are certainly as "natural" as the roots. If we are going to choose any definition of the natural, we must say that what is natural to man is what distinguishes him from other creatures. The only "natural" life for a man, therefore, will be a rational life. Lysicles is forced to admit that there are qualitative differences in pleasures corresponding to the differences in the acts of which the pleasures are perfective. [40] Sense is only "the lowest part or faculty of a human soul," [41] so that prescribing a life of sensual pleasure to a man is as inappropriate as prescribing the life of a mole to an eagle. [42] The essential ambiguity embedded in the "natural" leads on to a more detailed consideration of hedonism.

[37] *Ibid.*, p. 83.
[38] *Letter to Dion*, p. 29.
[39] Alc., p. 86.
[40] *Ibid.*, p. 92.
[41] *Ibid.*, p. 93.
[42] *Ibid.*

Berkeley's concrete logic makes short shrift of the abstract "pleasure" of the hedonist. Pleasure is too clearly dependent on something else. Euphranor asks if it is "not plain that different animals have different pleasures? Take a hog from his ditch or dunghill, lay him on a rich bed, treat him with sweetmeat and music and perfumes. All these things will be no entertainment to him. Do not a bird, a beast, a fish amuse themselves in various manners inasmuch that what is pleasing to one may be death to another?" [43] Pleasures are not independent "entities" which exist substantially, but abstractions from an essential context. They are "perfective" of "acts" which are "different," [44] and the pleasure cannot be dissociated from the "act." To consider pleasures by themselves and to weigh them against one another is to make an illicit abstraction. Furthermore, the pleasure cannot in actuality be distinguished from the whole state of mind or rational judgment which determines that such and such a feeling is really a pleasure rather than a pain. Berkeley points out that a "notion" or rational judgment "often embitters the most lively sensual pleasures, which at bottom will be found also to depend upon notion more than perhaps you imagine: it being a vulgar remark that those things are more enjoyed by hope and foretaste of the soul than by possession." [45]

Sensualism, therefore, for Berkeley, who has obviously been influenced by Plato in this respect, is a state of mind which is so confused that it regards certain things as pleasures which really are not so.[46] Thus the "rakes" make "wrong judgments about pleasure, on the choice of which their happiness depends." [47] The difference between a pleasure that really is a pleasure and a seeming pleasure cannot lie exclusively in the pleasure. The rational judgment of the mind that this is a pleasure enters into what we mean by pleasure. Without this, pleasure would not be pleasure. Its *esse* is *percipi*. Some judgments are true and others false. This provides Berkeley with a qualitative standard, through which he distinguishes between pleasures. The recognition of such differences, of course, brings him far from the doctrine of hedonism. What makes one pleasure "lower" than another cannot be pleasure. Berkeley identifies

[43] *Ibid.*, pp. 92–93. Butler, in his sermons of 1728, 2nd ed., 1729, makes the same point in Sermon 11. Berkeley could have read this.

[44] *Alc.*, p. 92.
[45] *Ibid.*, p. 96.
[46] Cf. *ibid.*, p. 97.
[47] *Ibid.*, p. 101.

this other all-important factor with the rational judgment or notion which enters into the experience and actually constitutes it a pleasure.

SHAFTESBURY

The standard of nature is too ambiguous and the standard of pleasure too abstract to provide any lasting satisfaction to one impelled, as Mandeville was, by the scepticism of the utility principle. So Berkeley next proceeds to examine the tenets of "Cratylus," a "lover of liberty and of his country," who "had a mind to make men incorrupt and virtuous upon the purest and most disinterested principles." Shaftesbury is thus singled out as the most dangerous, as he is the most polished and plausible, of all the Deists. Perhaps it is useless to look for a moral standard in any abstraction such as nature or pleasure. The standard is an ingrained sense, a faculty like sight, "a certain ardour or enthusiasm that glows in the breast of a gallant man." [48] The gloomy doctrine of future rewards and punishments may be necessary to "tempt or scare men of abject spirit," but it "will never produce a true and genuine virtue," [49] for such virtue cannot be produced by fear. There is, therefore, no possibility of filling men with "fruitless hopes and vain terrors," since they cannot be "preached, or reasoned, or frightened into virtue." Rather, all these only obscure the beauty and harmony inherent in the bosom of every man, for virtue is "natural and congenial to every human soul." [50] Virtue is like aesthetic taste. One either has it or not, and if not, it is no more possible to achieve it through futile attempts at cultivation, than to reason sight back into the blind. Virtue is something "had" rather than developed. It is "felt rather than understood, — a certain *je ne sais quoi*, an object not of the discursive faculty but of a peculiar sense which is properly called the *moral sense*."

Berkeley saw in this plausible and inspiring romanticism the apotheosis and quintessence of all the abstract and superficial rationalisms against which he now perceived that he had been struggling both in himself and in his contemporaries for the whole period of his life. It is, therefore, with real difficulty that he finally brings himself to adopt a tone of calm in referring to the "divine characterizer of our times," [51] in whose eyes "our

---

[48] *Ibid.*, p. 122.   [50] *Ibid.*, p. 127.
[49] *Ibid.*, p. 125.   [51] *Ibid.*, p. 349.

learned professors are but bearded boys, and our most celebrated wits but wretched punsters," [52] and who is evidently serious in attempting to put "morals on the same foot with manners." [53] It is doubtless true that morality is not to be found in the rational. But it is certainly hopeless to search for it in the irrational, which is only the opposed abstraction. Berkeley condemns not so much the identification of the good with the beautiful as the idea that either the one or the other is an "object," simply presented for passive acceptation, as common sense believes that its objects are "presented" to sight. Berkeley had seen in his youth that the *esse* of such objects is not a mere "given" *esse*, but that such givenness is bound up essentially with a *percipi* which is not "given" at all. He now maintains that beauty also is essentially bound up with something not given. Indeed, "givenness" itself is another thought form under which it is possible, as in the case of utility, to cloak almost any sort of prejudice. Its chief use in philosophical discussion lies in the granting of a certain spurious type of semi-philosophical dignity to various dogmatisms of common sense.

Berkeley begins with the most simple sensuous types of beauty and points out that "the proportions of an ox," for example, "would not be beautiful in a horse," and that "proportion" always implies "the relation of one thing to another."[54] Moreover, proportion, relation, reference to a whole "are not strictly speaking perceived by the sense of sight." [55] The very essence of beauty, beauty itself, is precisely what is never presented or given. It is rather an ideal or norm not given "by the sense of sight," nor by any sense at all, "but only by reason," and consequently "beauty" is "an object not of the eye, but of the mind." [56] It is "therefore one thing to *see* an object, and another to *discern* its *beauty*." It does not help us to identify the good with the beautiful or the beautiful with the good, for in either case we are plunged into a flux of relativities, each of which points beyond itself to an ideal or norm that escapes description, since it is in no sense "given" as an object.

But if rationality seems unable to account for the norms which guide its endless criticisms and counter-criticisms, and hence remains incapable of formulating an acceptable ethical system, we are certainly brought no further towards a solution

[52] *Ibid.*, p. 222.
[53] *Ibid.*, p. 143.
[54] *Ibid.*, p. 133.
[55] *Ibid.*
[56] *Ibid.*, p. 134.

of moral issues by falling back upon an "innate" sense. By what criterion are we to distinguish between its testimony and the obviously fallible witness of our instincts and passions? "Should it not therefore seem a very uncertain guide in morals, for a man to follow his passion or inward feeling; and would not this rule infallibly lead men different ways, according to the prevalency of this or that appetite or passion?" [57] Such a system of unreason ends in a confusion of appetites rather than in harmony.

But it matters not how much harmony or sublimity such a "system" may be supposed to possess, it cannot under any circumstances be regarded as a "moral" system, unless it is a harmony in disharmony, a harmony not simply existing, but in *statu nascenti*, realized through the autonomous action of moral agents. Shaftesbury's "sublime system" really destroys morality altogether, and leaves us with a contemplated object, finished and dead. This is the prime error of all aestheticism in ethics. By making virtue the object of a "sense" it is turned into an external abstraction, and virtue slips through our fingers. Morality can never be "considered" as an object, for subjectivity is of its very essence. "What beauty can be found in a moral system, formed, connected, and governed by chance, fate, or any other blind unthinking principle?" [58] It matters not how much "order, and harmony" is "diffused" through such a "world." [59] It can never be a "moral" order unless there is disorder and disharmony, struggle and choice. Morality lies precisely in not fitting into such an objective and sublime system, in not doing what would otherwise be done anyway, in not being an "object," no matter how harmonious and sublime. Morality remains totally inaccessible to such an abstract and objective mode of thought, for morality is autonomy, paradox, the imperceptible, the subjective, the concrete. By harmonizing or aestheticizing morality, by making it "clear" and sensible, Shaftesbury has simply eliminated it from his thought.

But morality cannot be wholly eliminated, and mars the perfection of the sublime system with a restless and disturbing contradiction. Even Shaftesbury is at last forced to recognize that virtue is not the automatic absorption into such a system, but rather the "disinterested" relish of something "for its own sake," something, therefore, conscious, autonomous, and pre-

---

[57] *Ibid.*, p. 129.   [58] *Ibid.*, p. 138.   [59] *Ibid.*

cisely non-natural. Once having confused the external universe with the concrete reality, what is really abstract with the concrete, such consciousness in such a universe becomes a homeless paradox. What place has the freedom of "taste" in a tasteless universe; what place has the choice of such a thing as virtue in an amoral world; what place has the supernatural in the natural? This confusion of the abstract with the concrete turns morality into freakishness, or romanticism, an atom masquerading as a man, quixoticism deluding itself with a false sense of superiority over other things as helpless as itself, — what Berkeley calls Stoic pride. Thus, paradox takes its revenge on those who vainly attempt to escape it, and the "Stoic" succeeds in harmonizing the "world" only by sentimentalizing himself into a "knight errant." [60] It is not possible to *act* upon "virtuous" principles without having some sort of ultimate faith in them, for action is something more than "good writing," something to be taken seriously, at least by him who acts. To pretend that this is not the case and that "virtue is its own reward" is to bestow a false importance upon him who performs it.

Once again we have been betrayed by an abstract logic which leads us to confuse its own objective and sublime constructions with the concrete reality in which we actually live. Thought is a form of action and not vice versa, for the thought which constructs systems and systems of systems cannot be confused with the systems it has itself constructed. To penetrate to this level of thought itself must involve a new mode of thought, which is self-conscious, which is subjective as well as objective, which is able to move from one point *to* another, rather than simply to deduce consequences *from* a point that "has been" accepted or postulated, and which is ethical as well as natural or rational. It is this new, concrete level of ethical existence to which Berkeley refers in his criticism of Shaftesbury. But the *Alciphron* takes us much farther than this.

The ethical level is incomplete or paradoxical from beginning to end. This is why the abstract intellect attempts to thrust it from its sublime pictures and systems. The very essence of virtuous action lies precisely in the fact that it is not done "for its own sake," for as soon as it is done, or as soon as it becomes an "it" that can be considered and discussed, "it" becomes a mere object, and ceases to be moral or virtuous. Moral action

[60] *Ibid.*, p. 139.

is performed for the sake of something else which is non-objective, an ideal or norm which reasserts itself in unqualified perfection after every virtuous action, no matter how virtuous it may be. Such a norm is "not strictly speaking, perceived by the sense of sight, but only by reason through the means of sight." [61] It is seen only by not being seen, or rather its being seen is a means to its not being seen. It is the absolute which stands over all our actions no matter how pure or virtuous and negates them all. It is not the self, though it is impossible to conceive of the self without it, but rather the unavoidable "other" of the self, the completion of the self, the judge, relativizing all action to human action, and all virtue to morality.

But while the ethical norm is assuredly not the subject, neither is it to be thought of as an object. To confuse it with such "things" as "nature," "pleasure," "harmony," "self-expression," and so forth is to become even more banal than to identify it romantically with the moral self. It is anything but the finite self, though it is no object. Indeed, it can be understood objectively only through the negation of all such objects, just as it can be understood subjectively only through the negation of all such subjects. The ideal is revealed in any object only by becoming relativized, imperfect, and non-ideal, that is, by being unrevealed. And yet this norm is presupposed by morality, for morality is striving for the ideal, striving for something that is no thing, that is no thought, but without which there could be neither things nor thoughts. No thought can think it, for all thought concretely is action, and action presupposes it, nor can any act realize it, for what act is destined to perfection? It is as impossible to realize the absolute through action as it is to think the absolute through thought.

This is the meaning of Berkeley's *Alciphron*. It expresses the sense of futility gleaned from twenty years of striving in the world. To the absolute scepticism of the thinker is now added the absolute despair of the man of action, and from the union of the two arises a new absolute, as unapproachable as it is inconceivable, which lifts Berkeley's reflections at last to the level of the concrete itself. This level is neither the level of thought nor the level of action, but that of faith. It is a level which is neither subjective nor objective, neither rational nor irrational, neither natural nor moral, though it expresses itself

[61] *Ibid.*, p. 133.

in all these ways, as it is in the end presupposed by all of them. It is a still more concrete level of existence requiring a still more concrete mode of thought with rules and standards of its own. It is, indeed, as far beyond the moralistic mode of thought as it is beyond the narrow abstractions of objective reason. It is impossible to enter this field without actually going through the other two, as it is also impossible to think through the other two "without admitting any part of what is commonly called Faith, Worship, and Religion," [62] since knowledge, in the end, is reduced to morality, and morality, in the end, to worship.

CONCRETE ETHICS

Concrete ethics is religion. But the religion to which Berkeley's rationalism (i.e. scepticism) now forces him is exceedingly different from the Deistic formulae of his youth, those "great articles of religion" [63] which he had set out so valiantly to "prove" for the edification of "sceptics and atheists." He has concretely realized not only the hopelessness of attempting to "prove" religion, but the deeper absurdity of attempting to "prove" anything whatsoever, that ultimate doubt concerning the very principles of proof which arises when one gains a glimpse of thought in its purity, that unfathomable ocean of scepticism from which all the streams of reflection must take their rise, and to which, in the end, they must return. It is only the absolute sceptic who can really convince himself of anything, — only the absolute atheist who can see God. But this conviction cannot be what is commonly called "rational" conviction, since it arises only from the absolute stultification of "reason." Such reason is sufficient to negate itself, but beyond this it cannot go. "We are rationally led to believe," [64] but having reached this point, something else must lead us beyond all categories, beyond all experience, beyond all humanity, beyond all relativity. What else is capable of accomplishing this but faith? Reason is the road to faith, for through reason we are led to doubt, and "the more doubt the more room there is for faith." [65] Faith is the door to a new realm, a new level of thought with its own rules and problems.

There are many passages in the later dialogues which show how acutely Berkeley was aware of the unique problematic in

[62] *Ibid.*, p. 138.
[63] 3D., F. i, p. 478.
[64] Alc., p. 310.
[65] *Ibid.*, p. 360.

which his concrete logic was now involving him, and of the stupid misunderstandings arising from the common confusion of two things so altogether distinct as the realm of "reason" and the realm of faith, where dogma must take the place of theory and revelation must occupy the throne of "thought." Thus, in the seventh dialogue, Berkeley remarks that "whatever there is of mystery in religion, to endeavor to explain and prove by reason is a vain attempt." [66] As a matter of fact, the very idea of such a thing rests on a confusion far deeper than a confusion of categories. "The explication of mysteries in divinity" is "as fruitless as the pursuit of the philosopher's stone in chemistry, or the perpetual motion in mechanics." [67] Such "mysteries" reveal the relativity of everything connected with "natural reason," a term which he had employed in his youth to convey a note of highest eulogy. Now, however, these mysteries are "too obscure to penetrate, or too sublime to reach, by natural reason." [68] In such matters, "reason" "hath neither means nor *right* to judge." [69] Indeed, the failure to recognize the autonomy of the realm of faith by mistaken attempts, such as Berkeley's own *Principles*, to "prove" religion to sceptics, not only must fail dismally, but utterly frustrate, from the beginning, the goal for which they were constructed. "All attempts of this kind, however well intended, have visibly failed in the event; and instead of reconciling infidels, have, by creating disputes and heats among the professors of Christianity, given no small advantage to its enemies." [70]

The first consequence of a proper understanding of the meaning of "faith" is a comprehension of the notion of transcendence which it necessarily brings with it. Thus, "immortality," the "comfortable expectation" of which he had recommended or "proved" on "natural" grounds in his *Principles*, is now a "mystery," something that is not something, but "what eye hath not seen, nor ear heard, nor hath it entered into the heart of man to conceive," requiring faith or "belief." [71] Faith in any perceivable or rationally conceivable object would not be faith. By its very meaning faith requires an object which is really an object, — something independent and therefore transcendent, — and it is only on the ground of faith, which is no "ground,"

---

[66] *Ibid.*, p. 366.
[67] *Ibid.*, p. 337.
[68] *Ibid.*, p. 283.

[69] *Ibid.*, p. 281; my italics.
[70] F. iv, p. 410 (1732).
[71] Alc., p. 339.

that we may believe in such a "thing." It is only the theologian who has the "right," which is no right, to be a "realist," just as it is only the idealist who can become a realist, since it is only through the conception of absolute immanence that we may attain to the absolute or pure idea of transcendence.

Berkeley is far from the modern psychologistic rationalizing of faith as "a human experience" or something "to be felt or lived." This is precisely what faith is not. In fact, faith is the only means of escape from "the egocentric predicament," when correctly or transcendentally stated. It is only after the scepticism of the *Alciphron* that Berkeley is able to speak as a "realist" in the *Siris*. He advanced, as we have seen, beyond that solipsism with which the transcendental predicament is so often confused, during his early youth. But from the transcendental predicament he had not escaped, for there is no escape from this by reason alone. "That from a cause, effect, operation, sign, or other circumstance," says Philonous in the second dialogue, "there may be reasonably inferred the existence of a thing not immediately perceived; and that it were absurd for any man to argue against the existence of that thing, from *his* having no direct and positive notion of it, I freely own. [Solipsism is thus 'absurd.'] But where there is nothing of all this; where neither reason nor *revelation* induces us to believe the existence of a thing; where we have not even a relative notion of it; where an abstraction is made from perceiving and being perceived, from Spirit and idea: lastly, where there is not so much as the most inadequate or faint idea pretended to—I will not indeed thence conclude against the reality of any notion, or existence of anything; but my inference shall be that you mean nothing at all; that you employ words to no manner of purpose, without any design or signification whatsoever. And I leave it to you to consider how mere jargon should be treated." [72]

In other words, transcendental solipsism, or immanentism is rationally inescapable, for how can I really "talk of *conceiving* a thing which is *unconceived*" [73] or speak meaningfully of anything "existing independent and out of all minds whatsoever"? [74] Such an inconceivable is an inconceivable which is really (or concretely) conceived, and hence not purely or absolutely inconceivable, just as such an independence is really (concretely) a logical form, and hence relative and dependent. Nor may we "endeavor to support our opinion on the bare

[72] 2D., F. i, p. 437.   [73] 1D., F. i, p. 411.   [74] *Ibid.*

possibility of the thing," [75] for how can something beyond all rational conception, and hence beyond possibility itself, be possible? Such a thing is possible only by being at the same time impossible. As long as I reflect in any fashion whatsoever I am thus caught in the web of the λόγος, the relative absolute that can assert itself only by denying itself. Never do I arrive at something really independent. The speculative absolute is a whole relative to its parts, and hence dependent upon them, neither truly transcendent nor truly absolute. Yet the existence of such an absolute, as well as the existence of any relative whatsoever, presupposes the existence of a true absolute beyond absoluteness, for what else could reduce the absolute of reason to relativity? Such an absolute is truly transcendent, truly independent of "all minds whatsoever," truly or concretely inconceivable, not merely a conceived inconceivable, but a true inconceivable. Reason may "lead" us to this absolute by relativizing itself. It may prepare the way, — clear the path. But it may not take us further. At this edge, reason stops at its last limit. It may endlessly transcend limits of its own construction, but it can never reach the *ultimate* goal. This lies beyond, though not in the rational, paradoxical sense of a beyond that is also within, but purely, absolutely beyond all minds and all reason as the ultimate norm.

Berkeley's rationalistic idealism is, therefore, forced to the realism of faith, for the norm or "idea" which forces idealism to the negation of everything including itself is not a relative absolute, but the absolute of faith. Through the avenue of transcendent faith, the only conceivable or rather the only truly inconceivable avenue, Berkeley at last finds a justification for realism and materialism, and abolishes the last remnants of solipsism or subjectivism from his thought. The concrete logic has reached its last extremity. It can no longer accompany him, but may point the way. This way is the way of faith. Reason may "lead" us and chart the course, for, since reason itself presupposes the absolute, "the objections made to faith are by no means an effect of knowledge, but proceed rather from an ignorance of what knowledge is." [76] Reason really points a way, which it alone may never take, for reason is doubt, and "the more doubt the more room there is for faith." [77]

The first consequence of faith is "transcendence" or "realism." The next consequence is the immanence of transcen-

[75] Pr., F. i, p. 299.   [76] Alc., p. 340.   [77] *Ibid.*, p. 360.

dence or "revelation," for "how should it be possible for you to know what, or how far, it may be proper for God to reveal?" [78] Since God is what is absolutely "real," absolutely beyond us, the absolute "other" of everything human and rational and empirical, the *object* of faith rather than faith, and since we can in no manner penetrate to Him, He must penetrate to us. Yet in penetrating to us, He must remain absolutely Himself, or it is not "He" who is revealed. Hence, He must be revealed only as the unrevealed, the *Deus absconditus*, or, as Berkeley asks with a touch of irony, "should it not seem reasonable to suppose that a revelation from God should contain something different in kind or more excellent in degree, than what lay open to the common sense of men, or could even be discovered by the most sagacious philosopher?" [79] The necessity for "the doctrine of the Trinity," [80] or the "idea of the union between the Divine and human nature," [81] hence becomes evident, though the mind can "frame no abstract idea" of such a "union" between principles absolutely diverse, nor is it possible "to clear up the notion of *person* to the contentment of a minute philosopher." [82]

Concrete religion, therefore, as it has *revealed* itself to us in all its wealth of historic and dogmatic detail, is no irrational pandemonium to frighten the masses into "obedience," as Berkeley had maintained in his youth. "There is no need to depart from the received rules of reasoning to justify the belief of Christians," [83] not the few abstract maxims of Deism, but the full, concrete "faith of Christians." Not only is it not necessary to depart from "the rules of reasoning" to justify this faith, but these "rules" themselves, through the pure scepticism they induce, lead indirectly to such faith, though the faith itself, which continues the way, springs from a despair far deeper than any purely rational scepticism. "It denotes an active, vital ruling principle, influencing and operating on the mind of man, distinct from every natural power or motive," [84] as "the covenant or dispensation of grace." [85] It is, therefore, associated with "another use of words besides that of marking and suggesting distinct ideas, to wit, the influencing our conduct and actions." [86] The intellectual approach to faith, therefore, is intellectual only in so far as the intellectual

[78] *Ibid.*, p. 266.
[79] *Ibid.*
[80] *Ibid.*, p. 333.

[81] *Ibid.*, p. 334.
[82] *Ibid.*
[83] *Ibid.*, p. 345.

[84] *Ibid.*, p. 322.
[85] *Ibid.*, p. 321.
[86] *Ibid.*, p. 327.

itself, as a form of action, falls under ethical or "operational" norms or "rules." But its fulfilment lies beyond ethical realization, just as its idea lies beyond any rational idea, for, as the norm or rule by which all ethical actions are judged and negated, it is purely transcendent, that is, not transcendent in any sense comprehensible to either rational or ethical thought, but only to that faith for which they prepare the way by setting the mind in motion and loosening it from its dogmatic chains.

It is not surprising, therefore, that Berkeley, having finally penetrated thus far into the meaning of scepticism, should find the traditional "proofs" for the existence of God "dry and jejune." [87] In so far as they possess any value it is that "they may perhaps puzzle, but never will convince." [88] Just as the "realist" necessarily vitiates his realism by making it "naive," and thus drawing the object within the fatal field of immanence, so does the "religious" mind vitiate the very thing it is attempting to protect by proving it and imprisoning it within the immanent, all too human bounds of "rationality." What sort of God could a human mind succeed in comprehending, to say nothing of proving, save a God of its own making, — a golden calf? The real justification for such "proofs" lies only in a possible refinement of the scepticism which may result from them.

The "proof" for God, therefore, which Berkeley considers in the fourth dialogue is no proof at all. The use of the word "proof" in this connection is blasphemy. Hence he discards the more subtle and even more fallacious proof of "the existence of a God" from the "dependency of all things," [89] which he had finally worked out in the third dialogue. There can be no question that this proof does prove something. The relativity of all things does prove "the being of a God," that is, the "being" of an absolute mind or field of meaning with relation to which the meanings of all concepts whatsoever are determined, but the categories are not God. This absolute, which is at the same time not absolute, can be proved to "be," but it is everything and nothing, for by comprehending all meaning within its scope, it becomes itself meaningless. Such an absolute being may be proved. Thus Berkeley states at the end of the *Alciphron* that "the being of a God is capable of

---

[87] *Ibid.*, p. 155.   [88] *Ibid.*

[89] 3D., F. i, p. 448; cf. p. 478. "The being of a God, and incorruptibility of the soul, those great articles of religion, are they not proved with the clearest and most immediate evidence?"

clear proof," [90] but "the being of *a* God" is not God, and "to endeavor to explain and prove by reason the mysteries of His nature . . . is a vain attempt." [91] The rationalistic absolute, scepticism, the disproof of everything else, is only a pathway, not the goal. It proves, in Berkeley's language, "the being of a God," but not God, and "at bottom the *being* of a God is a point in itself of small consequence, and . . . a man may make this concession without yielding much. The great point is *what sense the word God is to be taken in*." [92] God's existence cannot be separated from His essence. He must be apprehended all at once, or not at all. Without the "attributes," God is only an absolute, not the absolute. But the "Divine Nature" is a "mystery." Unless we can prove the "attributes," as well as the abstract "being," our proof is of no consequence, and what "proof" can bear this strain? Hence "it is evident that every syllogism brought to prove those attributes, or which is the same thing, to prove the being of a God, will be found to consist of four terms, and consequently can conclude nothing." [93]

Berkeley, in his fourth dialogue, no longer speaks seriously of "proving" God. What he there considers is the question whether God is or is not actually "seen" [94] with the physical eye and heard with the physical ear, whether or not "God speaks to man in the same clear and sensible manner as one man doth to another." [95] No "arguments for a Deity" can be "conclusive." [96] Such arguments lead, in the end, to the absolute of reason. The only conceivable proof for the absolute must be a proof which emanates from the absolute itself, and which is, therefore, not a proof at all, but something transcending all conceivable proof. God must Himself speak "in the same clear and sensible manner as one man doth to another." [97] God must be seen as a man is seen, but "in a strict sense, I do not see" the "invisible thinking principle or soul," [98] nor, as Berkeley now adds in the *Alciphron*, "do we see anything at all" with the physical eye, nor do we hear anything with the physical ear, for seeing and hearing are transcendental acts. [99] Thus "we do not see a man, if by *man* is meant that which lives, moves, perceives, and thinks as we do," [100] nor "do we see

[90] Alc., p. 366.
[91] Ibid.
[92] Ibid., p. 178.
[93] Ibid., p. 189.

[94] Ibid., pp. 157 ff.
[95] Ibid., p. 162.
[96] Ibid.
[97] Ibid.

[98] Ibid., p. 161.
[99] Ibid., p. 168.
[100] Pr., sec. 148, F. i, p. 341.

anything at all," [101] nor hear anything at all, for seeing and
hearing are creative acts, and all creative acts are subject to
question. There is nothing received by or "given" to me that is
not equally not received and not given. "After the same manner we see God" [102] by not seeing Him at all, for He is the final
postulate of the rationalist, necessary to justify his reasonings
but Himself unjustified, — the inaccessible "mystery" essential to lend meaning to all that is clear and distinct.

In spite of Berkeley's return to his earlier and more paradoxical "proof," the God of the *Alciphron* is not the Deistic Deity
of the *Principles* and his youthful reflections, one of "the great
articles of religion," the inescapable shadow of the concrete
attending all abstract thought, the "irrational" of the rationalist, the postulate of the logician, a *deus ex machina* by means
of which an "answer" is found to otherwise inevitable difficul-
ities. The *Alciphron* is not relapsing into that "mysticism"
which is the "fate" hovering over all "rationalism." His scepticism has carried him beyond both rationalism and mysticism,
as it has taken him beyond all *isms* whatsoever. The God
of the *Alciphron* is not even mentionable without paradox, the
source of unreason rather than reason, though beyond both,
as the absolute limit or crisis of all striving. As the absolute
itself, which reduces even the speculative absolute of reason
to relativity, as the unattainable, the transcendent, this absolute is not *a* God, nor the abstract "being of a God," but God,
the rock against which explanation as well as action must
finally shatter. He is not so much the source of rationality and
intelligibility as the transcendent norm which transforms all
intelligibility into unintelligibility and all good into evil. He is
as inaccessible to reflection as He is to moral effort. He can be
revealed through nothing except Himself alone, for He is known
only by "*His speaking to me.*" [103] But He may speak to us only
through paradox, as He who also does not speak, just as He is
seen only as He who is not and cannot be seen. God speaks to
us and reveals Himself to us as the unrevealed or hidden God.
It is only by turning the world into a miracle that He ceases to
be mystery, for He is the super-rational confronting both the
rational and the irrational, the *Deus absconditus* who is "actually seen,"— by the eyes of faith, and who "actually speaks,"—
through revelation.

[101] Alc., p. 168.   [102] Pr., sec. 148.   [103] Alc., p. 162.

There are, nevertheless, two paths or ways through which we may be rendered sensitive to this discourse, the path of reason which leads to scepticism, and the wider path of action which leads to despair. The *Alciphron*, in the seventh dialogue, shows how the first, as a matter of fact, leads into the second, because of the practical or normative character of all knowledge, which is not so much passive or contemplative in nature as "something of an active operative nature, tending to a conceived good." [104] Hence, the absolute which negates all ethical striving is also the absolute which finally condemns all thought to "relativity" and "dependency," and true scepticism must end in a despair which is the only unfailing source of hope, just as scepticism is the only rational absolute. Hence the method of the *Alciphron* is indirect, for to assert this absolute directly is to deny it, but even negation and denial can only "lead" us toward the goal. By setting the mind in motion, however, by releasing it from the abstractions in which it becomes fixed and dead, scepticism may convey to it enough momentum to carry it on still further. This is the true meaning of the *Alciphron*. In it, Berkeley's concrete logic becomes a propaedeutic, an initial impulse, which "leads" indirectly or dialectically by negation and denial to the affirmation of the absolute. "The more doubt the more room there is for faith."

There is no cherished dogma, no "obvious" principle of common sense that is left unscathed. The favourite thesis of the dogmatic mind, the cornerstone of common sense, the intuition that "we" stand somehow in the midst of a world of solid, fixed, and "given" objects, becomes a delusion, dictated by the desire for a permanence and stability that is nowhere to be found. The "solid" world of objects is founded upon the thin tissue of thought, for objectivity is assuredly not an object, nor is givenness itself given, nor are any of the things we see really "seen" by us. This whole solid world is built upon the sands of meaning. It is a thin film of fleeting "signs," [105] deriving all their "solidity" and fixity from a beyond to which "we" can never penetrate, an ideal of substance as inescapable as it is unapproachable. There is not a single "firm" object of this sort that is not as much not given as given, that is not just as much as it is. And the faith of "common sense" in the permanence of this "world" can be paralleled only by the naive faith of those who "trust their health to a physician" or "their

[104] *Ibid.*, p. 344.   [105] *Ibid.*, p. 172.

lives to a sailor." [106] Yet it is this very "common sense" which, in the more important "concerns" of religion, "will not stir a step without evidence," and will "at every turn expect demonstration." [107]

The "science" in which common sense also has such "implicit faith" is full of "strange paradoxes." [108] Here Berkeley, speaking in terms of the science of his day and in the light of his *De Motu*, stresses the concept of "force" or action at a distance, the extraordinary notion that "contrary forces may at once subsist in the same quiescent body," or that "the force of percussion in a small particle is infinite," [109] concluding that "we shall find it as difficult to form an idea of *force* as of *grace*." [110] The only possible escape from the jangling discords into which "science" inevitably falls as soon as it attempts to introduce meaning into its formulae, is to avoid meaning altogether, and to fall instead into the eager arms of pragmatism. Force is no concept at all, but only a set of "rules and theorems directing men how to act," and thus "of very extensive *use*." [111] This, at least, cannot be denied, even if we have no "distinct idea" of force.[112]

But, as a matter of fact, nothing is more easily deniable than a judgment of utility. What is our criterion of the useful? There are those who assert an even greater "utility" for grace, and "upon what pretence can we deny concerning grace . . . that which we admit with regard to force?" [113] Pragmatism is unfortunately a game which two can play, and there is no quicker road to endless relativity and scepticism than the systematically ambiguous concept of utility. Nevertheless, "science" has chosen "utility" rather than "intelligibility," and thus, while it serves towards "many inventions" and teaches us "to frame engines," [114] it continues to be a meaningless set of formulae. Berkeley does not hesitate to attack with his scepticism the citadel of rational certainty, for though mathematics itself is indeed certain, Berkeley, making use of his early criticism in the *Commonplace Book*, points out that this certainty is purchased at a price. Mathematics becomes "certain" only by becoming analytic or symbolic, and "in its rise, operations, rules, and theorems, is altogether conversant about the artificial use of signs, names, and characters." [115]

[106] *Ibid.*, p. 314.   [109] *Ibid.*   [112] *Ibid.*   [115] *Ibid.*, p. 341.
[107] *Ibid.*   [110] *Ibid.*, p. 331.   [113] *Ibid.*
[108] *Ibid.*, p. 330.   [111] *Ibid.*   [114] *Ibid.*

Mathematics becomes necessary and convincing only by its meaninglessness. As long as we are content to play with our symbols, as a savage plays with his beads, we may "perform with ease and dispatch several arithmetical operations by the help of general rules. Of all which operations . . . the use in human life is very evident." [116] This is true as long as we proceed with the same implicit "faith" that governs the behaviour of the savage. But the minute we seek "to attain precise ideas"[117] we become involved in "difficulties and disputes." [118]

Once we admit the slightest germ of pragmatism into our structure it spreads like a cancer until it has relativized the whole, and who can deny that the first principles of mathematics are simply accepted with pragmatic faith? Woe to him who seeks what mathematics means! Pragmatism and intelligibility vary inversely. The more we *understand* the less pragmatic we have to be, but as Berkeley sees, mathematics is far from the point at which it may dispense with pragmatism. Hence, it offers but little resistance, and falls at once, together with the other sciences, before his sceptical attack. The mathematical sciences, he concludes, "if they are considered, not as instruments to direct our practice, but as speculations to employ our curiosity, will be found to fall short. . . ." [119] Our attitude toward these "reliable" truths of science, therefore, is really superstitious reverence.

The conquest of scepticism over a common sense which abandons itself to the phantasmagory of "experience" and the "science" and mathematics which damn themselves to an easily won utility is comparatively easy. With respect to the more fundamental issues of philosophy, the answer is perhaps not at once so ready, but, in the end, no less decisive. A judicious pondering of the deeper problems underlying science as well as common sense can hardly be supposed to lead to confidence in any of the answers which both common sense and science give so readily as "solutions" of such questions. What, for example, is "the nature of the soul"? [120] Does not the very existence of such a thing as common sense or "psychology" depend upon some sort of answer to this question? But who can be certain of this answer? Yet it is precisely those who have "reached" an "answer" (which is no answer) who condescend to indicate an equally obvious "answer" to such questions as

[116] *Ibid.*
[117] *Ibid.*, p. 345.
[118] *Ibid.*
[119] *Ibid.*, p. 344.
[120] *Ibid.*, p. 271.

immortality. "But," exclaims Crito in the sixth dialogue, "I appeal to your judgment, if a man who knows not the nature of the soul can be assured, by the light of reason, whether it is mortal or immortal?" [121] If one may admit the "union of soul and body," as common sense and psychology must do, what may not one admit? "I cannot comprehend," says Euphranor, "why anyone who admits the union of the soul and body should pronounce it impossible for the human nature to be united to the Divine, in a manner ineffable and incomprehensible by reason." [122] It is always easy to detect the "mystery" in the theory of another, but to purify our own thought, to maintain the edge of our own scepticism, is another matter. What is ordinarily called scepticism is not scepticism at all, but only a thinly cloaked form of self-assertive dogmatism.

If the so-called "mind-body" problem casts doubt upon the whole realm of common-sense thought, the "mystery" of identity may certainly be supposed to do the same for all knowledge whatsoever. How may one and the same essence of triangularity be "present" in the particulars? "Who shall admit the abstract idea of a triangle, and at the same time ridicule the Holy Trinity?" [123] Who can "untie the knots and answer the objections which may be raised even about human personal identity . . . "? [124] An answer to this question is pre-supposed by all significant assertion of any sort. Yet it is pre-cisely those who have never suspected the existence of such problems who ridicule religious faith and mystery! "There are no greater bigots than infidels." [125] Is it strange that Euphranor smiles at the "free-thinker" who takes such earnest satisfac-tion in "proving man no agent, and yet pleading for free thought and action," [126] while not even understanding what he means by freedom? [127]

Berkeley's method in the *Alciphron* is that of *tu quoque* or defence through attack. No greater mistake could be made than to think of the *Alciphron* as religious "Apologetic," and in this respect Berkeley's enemies have seen more sharply than his friends. Benjamin Hoadly, for example, stung by the thrusts of one who dared question the "certain" principles of his Newtonian science and his Newtonian theology, thought "Alciphron the most plain attempt to bring obscurity and darkness into all science, as well as to make nonsense essential

---

[121] *Ibid.*   [123] *Ibid.*, p. 332.   [125] *Ibid.*, p. 314.   [127] *Ibid.*
[122] *Ibid.*, p. 267.   [124] *Ibid.*, p. 334.   [126] *Ibid.*, p. 354.

to religion, that this last age has produced." [128] Berkeley has come to see clearly that no greater disservice can be rendered religion than to "defend" it, to rationalize or humanize it. This is to destroy it. The only possible rational defence of religion is the defence of attack, the defence of scepticism, not the "hasty" scepticism,[129] which is ordinarily another name for dogmatism, of those who "are too ignorant to be humble," [130] but true scepticism, the endless self-torture of pure thought which can find no resting point, least of all in itself, which is forced from one abstraction to another, until it cannot rest, until it is beaten into submission and despair.

This marks the second turning point in Berkeley's reflections, the point at which his practical scepticism reaches its climax, at which his scepticism becomes sceptical of itself, and at which negation becomes absolute negation or affirmation. Berkeley's philosophy, like all true philosophy, now takes the form of absolute philosophy, containing within itself the full moment of scepticism; and it is from this absolutely negative vantage point, which is now absolutely positive, that Berkeley begins an intelligible reconstruction of the world beyond which his concrete logic has taken him. Berkeley calls this vantage point the field of absolute thought, "transcendental philosophy" or *philosophia prima*. He had already recognized its existence in the *Three Dialogues* and the *De Motu*, but he was now able to found it upon the rock of that absolute scepticism to which his practical philosophy had led him. It is only by being first made entirely unintelligible that the world may be rendered intelligible. Reason without the sceptical or critical moment is dogmatism (not dogma), for rationality or intelligibility is an abstraction which is no more to be absolutized than its opposite pole, the irrational or unintelligible. Hence, it is only on the foundation of an absolute beyond reason that the world may be comprehended, only on the basis of the absolute itself that one may erect a true *philosophia prima*. Berkeley does not pro-

[128] Letter of Hoadly, quoted in *Gent. Mag.*, 1774, vol. XLIV, p. 174. Another rationalistic or "Newtonian" response to Berkeley's paradoxes is given by one of Hoadly's friends, who writes: "When I began this letter, I intended to write to you about nothing but Dean Berkeley's book, but have just found out that I have not said one word about it. I have been in the clouds with him these three last days, and think his reasoning very often literally like being there; it is something very exalted and very unsubstantial; a sort of sublime fog, that looks bright and makes one giddy!" *Gent. Mag.*, vol. XLIV, p. 174. Cf. Pope's comment, Elwin and Courthope, VII, p. 264.

[129] *Alc.*, p. 365. [130] *Ibid.*, p. 366.

ceed directly or dogmatically to this goal, but indirectly or critically by showing once more, as in the *Three Dialogues*, its necessity as a presupposition of all responsible inquiry, though he now chooses mathematics, for purposes of brevity and cogency, as his point of departure. Berkeley's practical scepticism has led him to the absolute foundation required for transcendental philosophy. There is a path to *philosophia prima*, so to speak, from above. But does such an existent science as mathematics, for example, require such a thing? Is there a path from below? Berkeley's *Analyst* is an attempt to show that there is such a path.

CHAPTER XIV

THE CRITIQUE OF MATHEMATICS
(THE ANALYST)

In the *Analyst* Berkeley turns his attention once more to mathematics, the eternal refuge of rationalists, the ideal of his youthful enthusiasm, "the supreme apex of human knowledge," and "the foundation of all the sciences."[1] It is an attention, however, now chastened by the progressive frustration of many such dreams, and disillusioned particularly by the discovery of the *Commonplace Book* that mathematical demonstration is analytic in character, and by the criticisms of the *De Motu* and the *Alciphron* which revealed a disturbing pragmatic element in what is called "science." Is there a "science" which does not accept its fundamental concepts and principles on trust? Is there a "science" which does not depend at least to some degree upon such "concepts" as "the algebraic mark which denotes the root of a negative square,"[2] which are doubtless of great "use," but which "as speculations to employ our curiosity . . . fall short"?[3] The pragmatic "justification" for such concepts is hardly satisfactory for, together with the "induction" to which it is so intimately allied, it refers us to an indefinite future in which nothing can be finally tested, least of all itself. The dogmatic faith in what at present seems useful is not only faith, but it is a faith which is apparently without foundation, since, judging empirically (pragmatically), everything at present regarded as useful is destined eventually to be regarded as not useful. Science and mathematics fall an easy prey to scepticism.

The *Analyst* is usually regarded as a more detailed application of this same criticism to the field of contemporary mathematics, or in Berkeley's own words, an *ad hominem* argument to show that the analytic "naturalists" had best set their own house in order before criticizing others for dogmatism, trust in authority, and blind faith. This is no doubt partially true, and much of the *Analyst* is devoted to the task of showing the extent to which a loose pragmatic procedure did prevail, as indeed it

---

[1] *Misc. Math.*, F. iv, p. 60.   [2] Alc., F. ii, p. 344.   [3] *Ibid.*

must prevail, in the most certain of the sciences. To see in this the burden of the treatise, however, is to miss its real significance. The essential feature of the *Analyst* is not the pragmatic reduction of mathematics, which Berkeley had already carried out in the *Alciphron*, but precisely the criticism of this reduction. Berkeley now turns the full force of his logic against the very pragmatism he had previously used to destroy the dogmatic pretensions of "scientific" metaphysics.

Pragmatism is a sceptical device. It was through pragmatism that Berkeley had shown the relativity of certain fundamental scientific concepts in the *De Motu*, and it was in the reassuring form of pragmatism that his scepticism had spread itself in the *Alciphron* through all the fields of knowledge and endeavour. In the *Analyst*, this mask is torn away, and scepticism emerges in its essential form as pure thought. A self-conscious pragmatism is impossible. It must be either a form of unconscious dogmatism, or scepticism in a thin disguise of sweet words. The pragmatic mathematician, who accepts the "utility" of his concepts as a guide, is compared with the ignorant "sailor" who "may practically apply certain rules derived from astronomy and geometry, the principles whereof he doth not understand . . . without having ever considered or comprehended them," [4] learning them solely "by rote" from the prevailing "vogue." Such pragmatism cannot survive reflection and must collapse, at the first awakening of consciousness, into scepticism. But scepticism is pure thought, which cannot rest with any dogmatism, least of all itself. Scepticism is practical philosophy, faith, and dogma (not dogmatism). In the *Analyst*, the negation of Berkeley's scepticism becomes affirmation, and he turns at last to that intelligible rethinking of the world which is rendered possible only through the discovery of the absolute.

Mathematics cannot rest in pragmatism, for it would then be neither necessary nor intelligible, and hence not mathematics. Berkeley therefore abandons both the alternative theories of mathematics that he had successively developed in the course of his reflections. The more primitive of the two is the theory of the early *Commonplace Book*, according to which mathematics is only an empirical science, the study of certain "things sensible." [5] Berkeley had to abandon this theory, since it removed all certainty and "demonstration" from the subject.[6]

Hence, in the later portions of the *Commonplace Book*, he maintains that mathematics, in so far as it is demonstrable, is a matter of symbols,[7] and works out the elaborate sign theory which appears also in the *Alciphron*. Mathematical demonstration is exclusively concerned with signs and their manipulation according to certain "given" rules. Mathematics itself becomes analytic or symbolic, and its necessity is preserved by making it meaningless. In the *Analyst*, however, Berkeley sees that this second course is even more impossible than the former, for the view cannot be held without unconscious contradiction. A mathematics without meaning would not be mathematics, nor even symbolism. It must be *both* necessary and intelligible. Furthermore, this intelligibility cannot be derived from mathematics itself, but only from "a certain transcendental science" which lies altogether beyond it, and yet upon which it must rest as its necessary foundation. Mathematics is the shortest road to *philosophia prima*, — this is the true meaning of Berkeley's *Analyst*. Before examining this most important treatise in detail, we must trace a little further the process through which he won his reconstructive insight, and return for a moment to that absolute scepticism, which is therefore more than scepticism, in which the *Alciphron* finally culminated, and which must be regarded as prerequisite to the "transcendental" suggestions of the *Analyst*.

THE SERMON PREACHED BEFORE THE SOCIETY FOR THE PROPAGATION OF THE GOSPEL

Berkeley had embarked upon his Bermuda enterprise with the full support of the Society for the Propagation of the Gospel, and shortly after his return, he was asked to preach the Anniversary sermon for the year 1731. In this sermon, Berkeley gives a pessimistic account of religion and civilization in America. After remarking that many seemed to have "worn off a serious sense of all religion," he declares that "as for their morals . . . there is nothing to be found in them that should tempt others to make an experiment of their principles, either in religion or government." [8] He reports, however, that, at his instigation, the Solicitor-General had sent over a signed opinion that baptism was not inconsistent with the state of slavery, and hoped that it might result in some moderation of the uni-

[7] C. B. J., 780.   [8] F. iv, p. 403.

versal mistreatment of slaves. He also suggested that the missionaries of the Society come to England for as much of their education as possible, and that they be paid higher salaries. Aside, however, from this gloomy picture of the American colonists, the sermon contains matter of theoretical interest.

It is clear from the first page, where "natural religion" is distinguished from "the Christian," that Berkeley has at last eliminated all traces of Deistic rationalism from his thought. "By the *knowledge* of God," he says, "is not meant a barren speculation, either of philosophers or scholastic divines, nor any notional tenets fitted to produce disputes and dissensions among men; but on the contrary, a holy practical knowledge." [9] The insight into the "practical" import of concrete religion to which his scepticism has finally led causes him to say that "a man may frame the most accurate notions, and in one sense attain the exactest knowledge of God and Christ that human faculties can reach, and yet, notwithstanding all this, be far from knowing them in that saving sense." [10] This "saving knowledge of God," he continues, "is inseparable from the knowledge and practice of His will." [11] True knowledge is something more than contemplative "seeing" or theory ($\theta\epsilon\omega\rho\iota\alpha$), and there are many passages which reveal a complete disillusionment with respect to the finality of such rationalistic norms as "clarity" and "accuracy," which, if exclusively or abstractly maintained, lead only to endless relativity and dispute.

Abstract reason, by its attempt to "clarify" religion, has not only failed in itself, but has done the most irreparable harm to religion. "From the time that divinity was considered as a science, and human reason enthroned in the sanctuary of God, the hearts of its professors seem to have been less under the influence of grace. From that time have grown many unchristian dissensions and controversies of men 'knowing nothing, but doting about questions and strifes of words, whereof cometh envy, strife, railings, evil surmisings, perverse disputings of men of corrupt minds and destitute of truth.' [I Timothy vi. 4, 5.] Doubtless, the making religion a notional thing hath been of infinite disservice. And whereas its holy mysteries are rather to be received with humility of faith, than defined and measured by the accuracy of human reason; all attempts of this kind, however well intended, have visibly failed in the event;

---

[9] *Ibid.*, p. 397.   [10] *Ibid.*   [11] *Ibid.*

and, instead of reconciling infidels, have, by creating disputes and heats among the professors of Christianity, given no small advantage to its enemies." [12] Thus, Berkeley passes judgment upon his own earlier attempts to rationalize religion before he had learned to distinguish between natural religion and religion, between "rational" faith and "true faith," which is "by no means inconsistent with every error in theory." [13]

Berkeley's scepticism with respect to theoretical argumentation has passed into an irony founded upon something more profound than theoretical scepticism. This irony arises from life itself. He finds no stronger evidence of the depraved state of men than in their failure to appreciate their "lapsed state," [14] which might "reasonably be hoped to find an easy admission" in minds "not hardened by impenitency, nor foreclosed by pride, nor biassed by prejudice." [15] His experiences in the colonies, however, had as effectively undermined these illusions concerning the naive or uneducated mind as his earlier experiences in Europe had disillusioned him with respect to the sophisticated or "educated" mind. His hopes for an America "young in vice," as he now perceives, had been entirely false, since "uneducated men" are only the "more apt to tread in the steps of libertines and men of fashion." [16] Berkeley's practical cynicism is now unrelieved by any trace of sentiment, for it has at last reached that critical point from which it is possible to appreciate that the only conceivable hope lies in hopelessness. "Are we not grown drunk and giddy with vice, and vanity and presumption and free-thinking and extravagance of every kind, to a degree that we may truly be said to be smitten with madness and blindness and astonishment of heart?" [17] In such "madness" and "astonishment of heart" may lie hope, even for the Church, for "who knows but the Christian Church corrupted by prosperity, is to be restored and purified by adversity?" [18]

Such hope, however, is rightly called "madness," since it is the irresistible effect exerted by "a due sense of the Divine perfection and our own defects" [19] upon "the weakness and ignorance of men." Religion, as this "madness," is the last crisis not only of thought, but of practice as well, for it is not only scepticism but the irony into which scepticism passes, "the satiety

[12] *Ibid.*, p. 410.
[13] *Ibid.*
[14] *Ibid.*, p. 405.
[15] *Ibid.*
[16] *Ibid.*, p. 406.
[17] *Ibid.*, p. 408.
[18] *Ibid.*, p. 407.
[19] *Ibid.*, p. 410.

and disrelish attending sensual enjoyments, the relish for things of a more pure and spiritual kind, the restless motion of the mind from one terrene object or pursuit to another," which can find no final rest save in "a flight or endeavor above them all towards something unknown. . . ." [20] There can be no valid thought, as there can be no valid practice, that is not touched by the "madness" of this "something unknown," the *Deus absconditus* who can be "perfective" [21] of our nature only by destroying it.

THE FRUITS OF IDEALISM

The annual sermon of the Society for the Propagation of the Gospel was always printed and usually presented to "the King, the Queen, the Prince, the Duke, the Princesses, and the Ladies of the Bedchamber." [22] The great anxiety and disappointment which Berkeley had suffered had seriously affected his health, and soon after the delivery of the sermon, he became ill. He was, therefore, unable to come to Court in person, and Baron Wainwright, one of the few influential friends who remained loyal to him in this discouraging period of his life, wrote to Mrs. Clayton, the close friend of the Queen, asking her to present the sermon to Her Majesty in his stead. [23]

The disfavour and even disgrace into which he had fallen because of the failure of his enterprise added greatly to his distress. Percival, nevertheless, faithfully continued to exert all possible influence in his behalf. Berkeley also saw something of his old friend Pope, and apparently contributed another and somewhat discordant note to the several extraneous influences that were finally embodied in the *Essay on Man*, upon which the poet was at this time engaged. It has been suggested that it was perhaps due to Berkeley that the *Essay*, which is based on the conversation of Bolingbroke and the writings of Shaftesbury, has nothing but sneers for the "smart free-thinker." [24] Berkeley certainly did everything in his power to counteract the Deism which seems to have crept almost subconsciously into the confused "system" of the poet, for Warton relates that he prevailed upon Pope to omit "an address to Jesus Christ"

[20] *Ibid.*, p. 395.
[21] *Ibid.*
[22] Thomson, *Memoirs of Viscountess Sundon*, pp. 176–177.
[23] *Ibid.*, p. 176. According to Warton,

however, it was Sherlock who actually made the presentation to the Queen. II, p. 198, note.
[24] Cf. Balfour, biog. notice; Sampson, Berkeley's *Works*, 1895.

which he had inserted in the original version, persuading him at last that "the Christian Dispensation did not come within his plan." [25] Some genuine religious feeling is also manifested by the poet, in the letter to Swift written two years before, when he was also in contact with Berkeley. "I am," he says, "of the religion of Erasmus, a Catholic; so I live, so shall I die; and I hope one day to meet you [Swift], Bishop Atterbury, the younger Craggs, Dr. Garth, Dean Berkeley, and Mr Hutchinson, in that place to which God, of his infinite mercy, bring us and everybody." [26] Bermuda, which a few years before had been a popular shibboleth, was now a term of scorn and disparagement. Wainwright, writing to Mrs. Clayton in Berkeley's behalf, finds it necessary to ask her to condone and "forget Bermuda." [27] We are told that "it was the fashion of the day," especially in Ireland, to represent Berkeley as deranged,[28] and it was considered a "waggish" thing, even in 1734, to use the phrase "when the Bishop of Cloyne sets out a second time for Bermuda" as a synonym for *never*.[29]

This general attitude of derision was exploited by Berkeley's powerful, political enemies to block his advancement in the Church. The most active of these was probably Hoadly, now Bishop of Salisbury, who had nourished an intense dislike for Berkeley's ideas and person, ever since the debates with Clarke.[30] But his efforts were most effectively and quietly reinforced by those of his brother, the Archbishop of Dublin,[31] and by Walpole. They prevented Berkeley from obtaining the post in the Irish Church to which he would normally have succeeded, and which he most particularly desired. Had it not been for the continued favour of the Queen,[32] they might have thwarted even the formal preferment he finally did receive. Many of the Bermuda subscribers had offered to turn their contributions over to

[25] Warton, II, p. 120; cf. Spence, p. 142.

[26] Letter of November 28, 1729. Cf. the statement of Pope during his last illness, as recorded by Warton (II, p. 119): "I am so certain of the soul's being immortal, that I seem even to feel it within me, as it were by intuition."

[27] Thomson, *Memoirs*, p. 165.

[28] *Ibid.*, p. 177.

[29] Hertz, *British Imperialism*, chap. VI.

[30] Percival journal, February 27, 1732.

[31] *Ibid.*, February 25, 1732.

[32] "The Queen then sent for Berkeley (after his return from America), often questioned him on subjects connected with America, and derived much pleasure from his interesting conversation." Thomson, *Memoirs*, p. 171.

"The Minute Philosopher, a series of Dialogues, written in 1732, by Dr George Berkeley, with which Queen Caroline was so pleased that she had him promoted to the Bishopric of Cloyne" *Autobiog. and Corresp. of Mary Granville*, Mrs Delany, London, 1861, vol. ii, p. 295.

him for his personal use,[33] but he refused, recommending to them "the letting their subscriptions go to the support of a college in Connecticut erected about thirty years ago. . . ."[34] The money which could not be traced he gave to the Society for the Propagation of the Gospel, suggesting that it be used for the purchase of books to be donated to Harvard and Yale Colleges.[35] The result was that his own private fortune had to bear the whole brunt of the enterprise, including the purchase of the farm in Rhode Island. Berkeley naturally felt, therefore, that he had some material claims on the government, since it was through no fault of his own that the project had miscarried.

The Deanery of Down fell vacant at this time, and, as it was worth two hundred pounds per year more than Derry, it would have enabled him to "repair his private fortune," and at the same time would have provided him with "a mark of his Majesty's good countenance,"[36] to some extent counteracting the popular prejudice which follows in the wake of all failure. But his enemies were too strong. Hoadly, the Archbishop of

---

[33] White says that this sum exceeded 5000 pounds. White, *Bishop Berkeley*, p. 14.

[34] Percival journal, March 14, 1732.

[35] The report of the Society for the Propagation of the Gospel for 1748 reads as follows: "Some time ago the Society, at the request of the Lord Bishop of Cloyne, after his remitting a very considerable benefaction for the good uses of the Society, employed part of it in purchasing the most approved books written by the divines of the Church of England, and they sent them as a present to Harvard College, in Cambridge, near Boston, in this province (New England) for the use of the students of the College."

Further evidence concerning the gift is afforded by the *Colonial Society of Massachusetts Publications*, vol. XVI, pp. 615-616: "At a Meeting of ye President & Fellows of Harvard College at Cambridge. September 3, 1733, it was resolved that: Whereas ye Rev'nd Dean Berkley has lately procured a valuable collection of Books, & sent them to Harvard College, voted, yt ye Thanks of ye Corporation be returned by ye President to ye Dean for the above Donation, procured & sent by him; and yt he be desired to make proper Acknowledgments

in behalf of ye Corporation, to those Gentlemen who have contributed to so liberal a Benefaction."

And at a later meeting of the President and Fellows of Harvard College in Cambridge, December 26, 1748, it was resolved: "That Letters of Thanks be sent to the Society for the Propagation of the Gospel, for the large Present of Books Sent by them to the College, as also to the Bishop of Cloyne in Ireland, by whose Influence they were procured; As also a Letter of Thanks to Dr Mead Fellow of the College of Physicians in London, for a new Edition of his Treatise of Poisons lately sent to Us." *Col. Soc. Mass. Publ.*, vol. XVI, p. 796.

Dr. Alexander Hamilton, who traveled through Boston from Maryland, August 15, 1744, mentions these books in his account of the College. "In the library," he says, "are three or four thousand volumes with some curious editions of the classics, presented to the college by Dean Barklay." *Col. Soc. Mass. Publ.*, vol. XV. The catalogue, and possibly some of the books themselves, were later destroyed by the fire of 1764.

[36] Percival journal, March 15, 1732.

Dublin, and his friends convinced the Duke of Dorset, the Lord Lieutenant of Ireland, that Berkeley was "unbeloved and disagreeable in his own country," [37] and prevailed upon him to write a letter to Lord Wilmington, President of the Council, stating that Berkeley was a "madman," and recommending Dean Daniel to the post. According to Percival, the Duke himself was not primarily responsible, being unacquainted with Berkeley, though he may have been somewhat piqued that the latter did not apply to him directly.[38] The Duke's letter has not survived, but Lord Wilmington's reply has been preserved, and it throws much light on the attitude of Walpole and the other Whig leaders:

I had the honor of yr. Grace's letter of ye 3rd inst. on Wednesday last, and the next morning I went to Sir Robert Walpole; as soon as I mentioned the affair of the Deanery of Down, he told me that an application had been made by two Bishops to the Queen for Dean Berkeley, and that before it was settled, application had come from Ireland for Dean Daniel. Though I mentioned this shortly, it was attended with a great many circumstances, and a long detail quite unnecessary to repeat. When Sir Robert on reading yr. Grace's letter came to the part where yr. Grace says that Dean Berkeley was looked upon as a madman he said he always thought so, and had always said it, where it was proper. He desired me to assure yr. Grace that he had never in any instance interfered with your Grace's administration in Ireland, and had used his best endeavors, that if this Deanery had been disposed of to any other person than Dr. Perry, that the declaration of it might be deferred till your Grace's return to England. Upon my asking him, if the Duke of Newcastle had any part in the recommendation of Dean Berkeley he assured me he had not, but thought he was to blame only in not expediting the affair on his receipt of your letter, and consequently, by his dilatoriness, giving time for other applications to be made.

I went on the same day to St. James' in order to have waited on the Queen, but the King was come upon the Queen's side that I could not see the Queen that day. On Friday the Pension Bill was expected in the House of Lords, which prevented my being at St. James that day. On Saturday I endeavored to see the Queen but was prevented by the same reason I was on Thursday. The Queen spoke to me in the Circle and ordered me to attend her on Monday. Accordingly I waited on her Majesty yesterday who was graciously pleased to tell me that she had, on the application of two Bishops, spoke to the King for Dr. Berkeley, but as the King gave her no answer, she looked upon the matter to be undetermined, and that, though she looked upon herself as being so far preengaged for Dr. Berkeley that she could not appear for any other person, yet she would rest it then and not speak to the King any more about it. I asked her Majesty's leave to lay your Grace's letter before the King and

---

[37] Baron Wainwright to Mrs. Clayton, February 19, 1731. Thomson, *Memoirs*, p. 177.

[38] Percival journal, February 25, 1732.

that I might lay the due stress on that part of it in which your Grace says that Dr. Berkeley is very particularly disliked by all the King's friends in Ireland. Having her Majesty's leave, I immediately went on the King's side, and as soon as I came into the closet, I acquainted his Majesty with the contents of your Grace's letter as aforesaid. The King told me that that affair was now all over, for he had just then had letters laid before him from your Grace with an account of the Bishop of Meath's death and your recommendations for a succession in the bench of Bishops which his Majesty thought to be very reasonable, and though he had not yet absolutely determined, yet he believed he should comply with it. However I thought it not improper to insist on that part of your Grace's letter I mentioned and, at the same time, to enlarge on the hardships Dean Daniel had gone through in the cause between him and Whaley. Thus your Grace sees that, though I can say nothing positive yet it seems as if this affair would end as your Grace could wish. . . . [39]

And so it did. On Tuesday, February 22, 1732, Percival "heard the mortifying news . . . that Dean Berkeley has missed the Deanery of Down." [40] It must have been some consolation to Berkeley, however, to learn about this time that the *Alciphron* was published and receiving wide and favourable comment. A note in Percival's diary of February 27, 1732, runs as follows: "My sister Percival said that the Dean's book against the free thinkers was the discourse of the Court, and that yesterday the Queen publicly commended it at her drawing room." That the Queen's sponsoring of Berkeley was not altogether as passive as Wilmington's letter would lead us to believe is also indicated by further evidence from Percival, who states that she demanded to know from Wilmington why the Dean was disagreeable to Ireland, and that he could only reply "he could not tell, unless that he was very great with Dean Swift." [41] But, for the time being, nothing could be done. Berkeley, in his sick-room, amused himself with "certain mathematical matters" which occupied his leisure for the next few years, and which enabled him at last to work out the technical conceptions and general theory of mathematics he had in the *Commonplace Book* originally planned for the third book of the *Principles* [42] and definitely promised twenty-five years before in its first edition.[43] Berkeley finally embodied these researches in a treatise called the *Analyst* which he published in 1734.

[39] Stopford-Sackville Manuscripts, p. 3, 1884.
[40] Percival journal, February 22, 1732.
[41] Percival journal, March 15, 1732.

[42] Cf. C. B. J., 589.
[43] Pr., sec. 133, F. i, pp. 332–333, and *Analyst*, F. iii, pp. 51–52.

THE EARLY CRITICISM OF THE CONTINENTAL CALCULUS
(DE L'HOSPITAL)

Berkeley's criticisms of the new analysis or calculus were worked out at two distinct stages in the development of his philosophy. They are written in an entirely different spirit,[44] and are directed against entirely different objects: first, De l'Hospital, representing the Continental mathematicians; and second, Newton.[45] His first criticism was developed in the middle portions of the *Commonplace Book*[46] and in the treatise *Of Infinites*, written in 1705 or 1706.[47] A short résumé of this criticism is given in the *Principles*, particularly sections 130 ff., while the second is contained in the *Analyst* of 1734. The first criticism deals particularly with the views of the Continental writers Nieuentiit and Leibniz, and Berkeley's chief source book is the *Analyse des infiniment petits* by the Marquis de l'Hospital, which was, at that time, the only readable textbook of the calculus,[48] though in the *Of Infinites* Berkeley refers to

---

[44] Stammler has clearly noted this difference without attempting fully to grasp its meaning. He says: "So, wie die beiden Werke (*Analyst* und *Treatise*) uns hier vorliegen, scheint zwischen ihnen eine Lücke zu klaffen; es scheint so, als ob der *mathematische* Berkeley ein ganz andere sei in seiner Grundstimmung, wie der *philosophische*. Die Einheit des Charakters scheint zerstört." Stammler, *Berkeleys Philosophie der Mathematik*, p. 8.

[45] The importance of keeping these distinct objects of attack clearly in mind is indicated by Berkeley's comment on Jurin, who confused the two, in the *Defence of Free-Thinking in Mathematics*, F. iii, pp. 86-87. ". . . All which is untruly said by you, who have misapplied to Sir Isaac what was intended for the Marquis de l'Hospital and his followers; for no other end (as I can see) but that you may have an opportunity to draw that ingenious portraiture of Sir Isaac Newton and dame Fortune, as will be manifest to whoever reads the *Analyst*."

[46] C. B. J., 300–500.

[47] In the *Of Infinites* Berkeley refers to Newton's *Quadratura* as a "late treatise" (F. iii, p. 412). This was published in 1704.

[48] The doctrine of the "infinitesimal," stated in its full crudity by De l'Hospital, hardly does justice to the thought of Leibniz, whom he professes to follow. Thus in his *Justification of the Calculus*, Leibniz writes in 1702: "Wenngleich es indessen nicht in aller strenge richtig ist, dass die Ruhe eine Abart der Bewegung, oder die Gleichheit eine Art der Ungleichheit ist, ebensowenig wie der Kreis in Wirklichkeit eine Art reguläres Vieleck ist, so kann man trotzdem sagen, dass die Ruhe, die Gleichheit und der Kreis die Grenzfälle der Bewegungen, der Ungleichheiten und der regulären Vielecke bilden, die durch eine stetige Veränderung im Zustande des Verschwindens schliesslich in jene übergehen. Und obgleich diese Grenzen ausgeschlossen, d.h. streng genommen in der Mannigfaltigkeit, die sie abschliessen, nicht mit einbegriffen sind, besitzen sie dennoch deren eigentümlichkeiten, wie wenn sie darin enthalten wären. Dies steht im Einklang mit der terminologie des unendlichen und Unendlichkleinen, nach der z.B. der Kreis ein Vieleck mit unendlich vielen Seiten ist." De l'Hospital quotes only the last line of this (Preface, p. 2, IV) and thus misses the point. Leibniz, *Werke*, Buchenau Cas-

Wallis' *Arithmetic of Infinites* and Leibniz's treatise in the *Acta Eruditorum* for July, 1695. It is quite clear, from the first, that Berkeley does not take exception to the new calculus itself, "the great improvements" of which he specifically recognizes, but only to the doctrine of "quantitys infinitely small," in terms of which the doctrine was generally stated by Continental writers and particularly by De l'Hospital. Berkeley urged both logical and metaphysical objections against this doctrine.

The logical objections to the theory are first stated in the *Of Infinites*, which represents the crystallization of his early researches. He refers, for example, to Wallis, "an approved mathematician," who implies in the ninety-fifth proposition of his *Arithmetic of Infinites* that a finite line, or unity, divided by zero gives a line infinitely long. But from $\frac{1}{0} = \infty$ it must, therefore, follow that the *pars infinitesima* of a finite line is "just nothing," since the "dividend divided by the quotient gives the divisor," or $\frac{1}{\infty}$ must equal o. The infinitesimal quantities are more than nothing. Yet two quantities "whose difference is incomparably small" really have "no difference at all," [49] for such differences are mere "points." Thus, Leibniz says, "Quemadmodum si lineae punctum alterius lineae addas quantitatem non auges." [49a] But if space is infinitely divisible, how can there be any such thing as a point, in the sense of a last quantity? On the other hand, even if we do think of such a limit or "indivisible point," this is very different from the "differentia" of an ordinate in a parabola which, according to the Continental writers, is a "real quantity." Hence, this, in turn, must possess a derivative or differential, which can itself "be subdivided in infinitum and so on." Berkeley is aware of the conception of a limit, but shows its inconsistency with the Continental view of a differential as an "incomparably small" quantity. There are three inconsistent views of the infinitesimal to be found among the mathematicians. First, it is implied by Wallis to be zero. In this case it cannot, of course, function as a differential. Second, it may be a

---

sirer, Leipzig, 1924, vol. I, p. 104. Cf.   [49] F. iii, p. 411.
Stammler, *Berkeleys Philosophie der Math.*,   [49a] *Ibid.*
p. 39, note.

limit, or indivisible point. Then, however, it cannot be an incomparably small quantity. Third, it may be such a quantity which can be infinitely subdivided, but then it must either be something, in the sense of a finite quantity, or nothing.

Berkeley notices another inconsistency in the prevalent views. De l'Hospital admitted not only differentials of the first order but also *differentiae differentiarum*, and so on.[50] Nieuentiit, however, insisted that "only infinitesimals of the first order" are "real quantities." The following orders he simply eliminated, "making them just so many noughts." [51] Berkeley points out the inconsistency in this position, which "is the same thing as to say the square, cube, or other power of a real positive quantity is equal to nothing." [52] If finding the differential is an operation which gives us a real quantity, as, for example, the cube of an integral number, it is absurd to limit this process only to one step and deny that it is possible to cube the cube. On the other hand, Nieuentiit denies with good reason a conception which must imply that there is a "positive quantity or part of extension which, though multiplied infinitely, can never [53] equal the smallest given extension." [54] Berkeley concludes that "they are both in the wrong."

In the early treatise *Of Infinites*, he restricts himself to the task of pointing out such inconsistencies in the Continental writers. He does not include Newton's theory of fluxions in his attack, since Newton maintains in the *Quadratura* that "his method of fluxions can be made out a priori without the supposition of quantities infinitely small." With such a strict logical demonstration Berkeley has no quarrel. His only aim is to point out the "inextricable difficulties" which arise in connection with the doctrine of an infinitesimal. He never dreamed

---

[50] The exaggerated pretensions of De l'Hospital's widely read work are indicated in the following passage, quoted by Stammler, *Berkeleys Phil. d. Math.*, p. 47. "L'Analyse qu'on explique dans cet ouvrage, suppose la commune; mais elle en est fort différente. L'Analyse ordinaire ne traite que des grandeurs finies; celle-ci penetre jusques dans l'infini même, elle compare les différences infiniment petites des grandeurs finies; elle découvre les rapports de ces différences: et par là elle fait connaître ceux des grandeurs finies qui comparées avec ces infiniment petits sont comme autant d'infini. On peut même dire que cette Analyse s'étend au delà de l'infini, car elle ne se borne pas aux différences infiniment petites; mais elle découvre les rapports des différences de ces différences, ceux encore des différences troisième, quatrième et ainsi de suite, sans de trouver jamais de terme qui la puisse arrêter. De sorte qu'elle n'embrasse seulement l'infini mais l'infini de l'infini ou une infinité d'infinis." De l'Hospital, *Analyse*, Preface.

[51] F. iii, p. 411.

[52] *Ibid.*

[53] Fraser writes "ever."

[54] Pr., sec. 130.

of disputing the efficacy of the calculus itself as a practical discipline. His attack is rather directed at the logical foundations of the theory. He even takes care to remove Leibniz from the range of his adversaries, for he "acknowledges his Calculus differentialis might be demonstrated *reductione ad absurdum* after the manner of the ancients." [55] In so far as the new method may be developed through such a strict method of proof, Berkeley again has no quarrel with it. But he does take exception to Leibniz's statement in *Acta Eruditorum*, July, 1695, that "nimia scrupulositate arti inveniendi obex ponatur." Berkeley maintains in the *Analyst* that it is impossible to be "too scrupulous in Mathematics," and that the "principles" of geometry must be as incontestable as the consequences drawn from them. His attack is made primarily from the logical standpoint.

In addition to these purely technical difficulties, Berkeley also objects to the doctrine of infinitesimals on empirical grounds, though these objections cannot be reduced to the single point that "infinitesimals are impossible because imperceptible." [56] This statement does not quite do justice to Berkeley's position, as a careful reading of the *Of Infinites* and the *Commonplace Book* will show. In the former treatise, which must be taken as the crystallization of this early position, Berkeley uses Locke as a point of departure, and quotes a passage from the *Essay* in which infinity as "an endless growing idea" is distinguished from infinity as a "quantity" which is "terminated," or "the infinity of space" from "space infinite." [57] Berkeley maintains that this distinction will "deliver us from that obscurity and confusion which perplexes otherwise very great improvements of the Modern Analysis," [58] for "we can have an idea of the former, but none at all of the latter," [59] and "'Tis plain to me we ought to use no sign without an idea answering it." Infinity, therefore, as a rule or principle of unterminated growth is justifiable. It is only when we try to

---

[55] F. iii, p. 412.

[56] Johnston, *Devel. of Berkeley's Phil.*, p. 273. The very sentence from the *Analyst* which Johnston quotes to prove this point contains the word "comprehend," and, in the next sentence, Berkeley proceeds to say that second and third degree fluxions, as conceived by Newton, "exceed . . . all human understanding." He concludes his remarks in this paragraph with the statement that "the clear conception" of such entities will "be found impossible." It need not be emphasized that such statements cannot be immediately judged as "sensualism" without further discussion.

[57] *Essay*, Book II, ch. 17, sec. 7.

[58] *Of Infinites*, F. iii, p. 410.

[59] *Ibid.*

sensualize such a rule and present it objectively to ourselves that we find we "have no idea." Of the rule, however, Berkeley states explicitly "we have an idea." It is quite clear that he is here using the term "idea" not in the sense of sense-impression, but in the general Lockian sense, as "the immediate object of thought.[60] His argument does not depend upon the assertion that infinitesimals are unreal because they are not sense-impressions, but upon the fact that they are not real in the sense in which the Continentals take them to be real, as things or perceivable quantities.

It is the reification or sensualization of infinity that Berkeley objects to. It is clear, from the *Commonplace Book*, that he is not disputing the notion or concept of infinity, but only that of infinity as an idea or quantity. He even admits that there is a certain sense in which a sensory idea can be said to be infinite, although not as "an *idea* too great to be comprehended or perceived all at once.[61] Berkeley argues with good reason that "there can be no such *thing* as a line quavis data minor or infinitely small."[62] All empirical "things" must be given, and must be given as finite entities consisting of finite parts, because of the perceptual threshold. It is partly from this fact, Berkeley believes, that the mathematicians have supposed the existence of another extension "without the mind," which may be infinitely divisible, although the extension we perceive is not so. In other words, they have committed "the grand mistake" of supposing that "we have *ideas* of the operations of our minds."[63] Infinity is such an operation. In the notion of the infinitesimal, it has been reified, and then abstracted from experience, and set in an independent realm without the mind. Thus, Berkeley says it is only when infinitesimals "are taken for something" that we fall into contradiction.[64] Since such a reality is not perceived, we then make the mistake of supposing "extension to exist without the mind, or not perceived."[65]

The sensualism of Berkeley's early attack consists not in the fact that he denied any sort of objective reality to "concepts" or "operations of the mind," but in the fact that he tended to keep them in rigid isolation from one another. Hence arose his view that the infinite as an "operation" can have nothing to do with the perceived world of objects, and his attempt to work

[60] J., 424.
[61] J., 475.
[62] F. iii, p. 410; my italics.

[63] J., 179.
[64] J., 349.
[65] J., 355.

out an "empirical" mathematics which should exclude all such pure concepts. The chief importance of the later portions of the *Commonplace Book*, as we have seen, lies precisely in the overcoming of this abstract mode of thought. But his early attack on infinitesimals came before he grasped the concrete unity of spirit, and is, therefore, rightly considered "empirical." Given objects are always finite, because of the sensory threshold. Infinity is, therefore, a rule or operation, which can never be given in this way. It is not and cannot be a thing. In connection with this, Berkeley makes several very pointed criticisms of the stated position of the Continental mathematicians, and shows conclusively that their conceptions of the infinitesimal are confused and contradictory.

The Later Criticism. Newton's Fluxions

Berkeley's first attack on the infinitesimal in the *Of Infinites* and the *Principles* was directed against the Continental mathematicians, particularly De l'Hospital and Nieuentiit. Newton's theory of fluxions is expressly excluded. Accordingly, in the second edition of 1734, Berkeley omits the careless reference to "fluxions" contained in *Principles*, section 132. His first criticism deals only with the Continental conception of an infinitesimal as a quantity infinitely small. In the *Of Infinites*, as we have noted, he expresses his faith in Newton's statement in the *Quadratura* that his doctrine can be worked out "a priori" without any such conception. The second edition of the *Principia*, however, which appeared in 1713, did not justify this assertion, as Berkeley discovered by a most careful examination. Indeed, the Newtonian view of fluxions seemed subject to just as serious criticisms as the Continental analysis. After returning from America in 1729, therefore, Berkeley worked out his objections to both methods, but now particularly to the method of fluxions which he had not before considered, and published them together with a proposed solution of the difficulties, and various suggestions stated in the form of queries as the *Analyst*, which he further elaborated in the *Defence of Free-Thinking in Mathematics*, published in 1735.

Berkeley first considers the proofs which Newton offers for his new method in the *Principia*, and begins with the example of the rectangle changing in area,[66] showing that the Newtonian

---

[66] *Principia*, II, sec. 2, lemma 2, casus 1.

procedure in this instance is "illegitimate and indirect." [67] Suppose the product or rectangle AB is increased by continual motion and that the increments of the sides A and B are a and b. Newton's proof proceeds as follows. When the sides A and B are lesser by one half of their moments, the rectangle was:

$$\left(A - \frac{a}{2}\right)\left(B - \frac{b}{2}\right) = AB - \frac{aB}{2} - \frac{bA}{2} + \frac{ab}{4}.$$

But as soon as the sides A and B are increased by the two halves of their moments the rectangle becomes:

$$\left(A + \frac{a}{2}\right)\left(B + \frac{b}{2}\right) = AB + \frac{aB}{2} + \frac{bA}{2} + \frac{ab}{4}.$$

Subduct the former from the latter and the remaining difference, or increment, will be: $aB + bA$.

It may be shown, however, that this Newtonian increment is not the moment of AB at all, but the moment of an entirely different rectangle, that of

$$\left(A - \frac{a}{2}\right)\left(B - \frac{b}{2}\right)$$

when the moments of the sides of this new rectangle are a and b. Thus, before *this* rectangle suffers any increment its area is:

$$\left(A - \frac{a}{2}\right)\left(B - \frac{b}{2}\right) = AB - \frac{Ab}{2} - \frac{Ba}{2} + \frac{ab}{4}$$

But after the sides have undergone the respective increments a and b, the area is:

$$\left(A - \frac{a}{2} + a\right)\left(B - \frac{b}{2} + b\right) =$$

$$AB - \frac{Ab}{2} + Ab - \frac{aB}{2} + \frac{ab}{4} - \frac{ab}{2} + aB - \frac{ab}{2} + ba.$$

Now subduct the former from the latter, and we have: $Ab + aB$. Berkeley rightly brings the discussion back to the rectangle AB, and shows that if the sides of this rectangle undergo any real increase to $(A+a)$ and $(B+b)$, the product must involve a quantity ab. Whether this be called an infinitesimal, or a fluxion, or an increment, or moment, we cannot escape the difficulty. Either we have a real quantity ab, which cannot be ignored without sophistry, or the expression simply reduces down to a product of the form AB. Never can we reach a logically justifiable means of arriving at the moment aB plus bA. Berkeley's objection against this Newtonian example is justified.

He next considers the proof which Newton offers through his method of infinite series.[68] Here it is a question of the fluxion of X^n. Before giving Newton's proof, Berkeley lays down the following lemma: "If with a view to demonstrate any proposition, a certain point is supposed, by virtue of which certain other points are attained; and such supposed point be itself afterwards destroyed or rejected by a contrary supposition; in that case, all the other points attained thereby, and consequent thereupon, must also be destroyed and rejected, so as from then forward to be no more supposed or applied in the demonstration." Then he proceeds to repeat Newton's proof in exact detail.

Suppose X is "a flowing quantity," and O its increment. When X becomes $X + O$, X^n becomes $(X + O)^n$ or

$$X^n + nO \cdot X^{n-1} + \frac{nn-n}{2} OO \cdot X^{n-2} + \ldots \ldots$$

The increment $O = n \cdot O \cdot X^{n-1} + \frac{nn-n}{2} OO \cdot X^{n-2} + \ldots \ldots$, or after dividing both sides by

$$O: \; 1 = nX^{n-1} + \frac{nn-n}{2} O \cdot X^{n-2} + \ldots \ldots$$

Let the increments now vanish,[69] and their last proportion will be $1 : nX^{n-1}$.

Berkeley now refers to his lemma, and offers the following objection. In the last step, when we say, "let the increments be nothing," the former supposition through which we derive the series is "destroyed," and yet a consequence of that supposition, the expression nX^{n-1}, is retained. If we suppose the increments to vanish completely, then we must also suppose their proportions to vanish. Berkeley now compares the Newtonian procedure with that of De l'Hospital in his *Analyse des*

<hr/>

[68] "per Methodum Serierum infinitarum," Newton, *Intr. ad Quadraturam Curvarum, Opuscula*, III, p. 206, Geneva, 1744.

[69] "Evanescant iam Augmenta illa at eorum ratio ultima erit $1 : : nX^{n-1}$." *Intr. ad Quadraturam Curvarum*, p. 207.

Infiniment Petits, and points out that both are based on the supposition that "a quantity infinitely diminished" can be rejected, or be nothing, though it is at the same time a quantity, and therefore something. Thus, "it is supposed that no quantity is bigger or lesser for the addition or subduction of its infinitesimal, and that consequently no error can arise from such rejection of infinitesimals." [70] Berkeley insists that such loose reasoning is inconsistent with the ἀκρίβεια of geometry, and refers to Newton himself in this regard. [71] It may be replied that the conclusions are accurately true, and hence the principles and methods as well. Berkeley now sharply rejects this pragmatic justification, for "the truth of the conclusion will not prove either the form or the matter of a syllogism to be true." [72] He realizes the methodological character of his criticism, for he says, "I have no controversy about your conclusions, but only about your logic and method," [73] for "I consider the geometrical analyst as a logician."

Berkeley's criticism of Newton culminates in a triple dilemma. There are only three possible ways of viewing the geometrical "momentum," each of which, however, is inconsistent with other elements of the theory. It may either be a finite quantity, or an infinitesimal, or an indivisible point. [74] But the momentum cannot be a finite quantity, for Newton says explicitly: "Cave intelligas quantitates magnitudine determinatas, sed cogita semper diminuendas sine limite." [75] Nor can it be an infinitesimal, for in the introduction to the *Quadratura*, Newton says: "Volui ostendere quod in methodo fluxionum non opus sit figuras infinite parvas in geometriam inducere." [76] Only the third possibility remains. The momentum must be a "mere limit" or point. Berkeley does not, of course, have in mind the modern conception of limit as "boundary value" or bounding relation. What he means is an indivisible point which "may be the limit of a line," as a moment may terminate a period of time. This point is here conceived by Berkeley as something discontinuous with the quantity which it bounds, or as not involving space at all. There is no room in this view for a last space, or a last velocity. There is only the real magnitude, and the terminating point which is no magnitude at all. There

[70] *Analyst*, F. iii, p. 29.
[71] *Ibid.*
[72] *Ibid.*, p. 30.
[73] *Ibid.*

[74] *Def. of Free-Thinking in Math.*, sec. 36, F. iii, p. 84.
[75] *Principia*, I, sec. 1, schol. 2.
[76] P. 207.

can be no question that Berkeley's analysis here failed to do justice to the principle of continuity, which played a crucial rôle at least in certain phases of Newton's thought and an even more crucial rôle in that of Leibniz. Nevertheless, he disposes of the third alternative by referring to *Principia*, II, lemma 2, casus 1, where Newton says that the moments are supposed to be divided "Ubi de lateribus A et B deerant momentorum dimidia, &c." Such a concept is, of course, inconsistent with that of an indivisible point.

There is little question that Newton himself at least vaguely conceived of a fourth possibility, that of a last, or boundary, value, which could be approached by a continuous series, and the failure to recognize this fourth possibility is doubtless the chief weakness in Berkeley's attack. Such a conception, however, was certainly not clearly stated or consistently maintained by Newton throughout the whole period of his reflections, and Berkeley did good service in pointing out inconsistencies which, though they may be excused in a genius attempting to reconcile new thoughts with the accepted forms, and, therefore, "wrestling with false principles," are nevertheless a scandal in mathematics and the sciences. His famous "lemma," though at first rejected by the over-zealous defenders of Newton, played an important part in the later development of the theory of the calculus, and is now universally accepted.

SUGGESTIONS

Although Berkeley insists that the contradictory concept of the "infinitesimal," as well as the confused concept of the "fluxion," must be eliminated, he never questions the results of the new method. He therefore attempts to show how these results may be explained on the "received principles" without resorting to increments or "quantities" of any sort which are something and yet at the same time nothing at all. For example: Suppose $AB=X$, $BC=Y$, $BD=O$, and $X^2 =$ the area ABC: it is proposed to find Y, the fluxion or rate of increase of the area as X increases.

When X increases to $X+O$, X^2 becomes $X^2 + 2XO + O^2$, or ADH. The increment of X^2 will be the area $BDHC$ or $BDFC + CFH$. Now, let CFH be QO^2. Then, $2XO + O^2 = YO + QO^2$, or dividing by O, $2X + O = Y + QO$.[77]

[77] Fraser writes $2XO = Y + QO$, iii, p. 36. The Sampson ed. is correct.

If we follow the Newtonian procedure, and allow O to "vanish," we derive the fluxion $Y = 2X$.

Berkeley admits "that the problem is rightly solved and the conclusion true." [78] It cannot be denied that if the area is changing with respect to X as $A = X^2$, the ordinate Y is changing as $Y = 2X$. But he again denies the validity of the loose conception of "vanishing." It is not legitimate to suppose O to

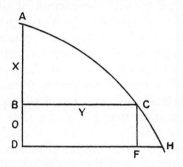

"vanish," unless we reject all the consequences derived from supposing it to be a real increment, and, therefore, the expression $X^2 + 2XO + O^2$ on which the whole procedure depends.

Berkeley now suggests that the conclusion is true not because O "vanishes" but because from the nature of the curve $Q = 1$, so that $QO = O$, and therefore $2X + O - QO = Y$, the desired result. He is correct in dismissing the loose conception of increments which are at the same time no increments, and in searching rather for a more adequate method of expressing the ratio belonging to the decreasing increments. Fluxions are not what is left *after* the increments are destroyed, but something emerging *in* the vanishing of the increments through all values. [79] In attributing the emergence of the new property to the cancellation of expressions on opposite sides of an equation, he is at least right in suggesting that the fluxion results from a ratio or relation holding between the decreasing but always finite increments of X and those of Y, rather than from the mysterious nature of a something which is also nothing. In identifying this relation with that of cancellation he certainly over-simplified the situation, and only vaguely approximated the all-important conception of "limit." Unless we suppose some such cancellation, or ratio between finite quantities, however, Berkeley is

[78] *Analyst*, F. iii, p. 37.   [79] Cf. p. 44: "May we not call them the ghosts of departed quantities?"

clear that we fall into the same underlying contradiction which vitiated the then prevailing accounts of the derivation of fluxions, namely, that of regarding nothing as at the same time something.

For example: Suppose X to be the abscissa of a curve, and Z another and greater abscissa. Suppose furthermore that the respective areas are X^3 and Z^3. $Z-X$ will then be the increment of the abscissa, and Z^3-X^3 the increment of the area. If we now simply divide (Z^3-X^3) by $Z-X$, we obtain the quotient Z^2+ZX+X^2 and if $Z=X$ this quotient reduces to $3X^2$, the derivative of X^3, without introducing any mysterious entities such as fluxions or infinitesimals. Berkeley, however, points out that whatever language we prefer to use, the very same fallacy is nevertheless involved. The first step is achieved only through the supposition that $Z \neq X$, for only then will Z^3-X^3 be a real quantity yielding anything when divided by $Z-X$. The basic supposition is, therefore, inconsistent with the later assumption that $X=Z$, and the result unjustifiable.

Furthermore, what right have we to suppose that the result is a fluxion? Berkeley insists that it is possible to develop signs and symbolic procedures which may have practical efficacy, though "upon a narrow scrutiny" it is "impossible to frame any idea or notion whatsoever" of the actual quantities that must be involved, if our discussions are in any sense applicable to experience.[80] Thus, following the *Quadratura Curvarum*, Berkeley asks us to suppose a line KO described by the motion of a point continually

	a	b	c	d
K	L	M	N	O

accelerated, so that in equal parts of time, unequal parts KL, LM, MN, etc., are generated. Suppose that a, b, c, d, e denote the velocities of the generating point at the several periods of the increments so generated. It is, of course, clear that these increments are proportional to the sum of the velocities with which it is described, and that these sums of velocities generated in equal portions of time are represented by the lines KL, LM, MN, etc. Also the last velocity generated in the first portion of time may be expressed by a, the last in the second by b, etc., so that a is the velocity of LM in *statu nascenti*, etc. These

[80] *Ibid.*, p. 44.

velocities themselves may be considered as flowing quantities, and we may thus conceive of the rate of change or velocity of the velocity, and so forth, which series may be developed as follows:

> a = increment of velocity in first moment.
> $b - a$ will be the increment of this increment in the second moment.
> $(c-d) - (b-a)$ = increment of the increment of the increment in the third moment, etc., in the following series:
> $a : b-a : c-2b+a : d-3c+3b-a : e-4d+6c-4b+a,$ etc.

Berkeley insists that though this procedure is logically (tautologically) justifiable, it does not lead us to any clear conception of what we really mean by the velocities of velocities, etc., "in themselves." [81] On the one hand, we have a symbolic procedure, and on the other the concrete reality. By what right do we join the two? How may we be sure that our mathematics is applicable? Berkeley insists that the pragmatic fact of success in controlling nature is no adequate test. Science cannot rest on mere "working." It cannot prove its principles by its conclusions. The scientist must proceed with absolute logical rigour, "nor can any geometrician have a right to apply the rules of the great author without first considering his metaphysical notions whence they were derived." [82] In the case of fluxions or infinitesimals Berkeley insists that the scientist cannot proceed without a knowledge of "the original real nature of fluxions," [83] which he finds lacking in all the contemporary expositions of the new doctrine, including that of Newton. Not only must the scientist proceed with absolute logical rigour, but he must also have a precise and clear notion of his fundamental concepts, and, furthermore, be certain of their applicability to experience. The achievement of this last requirement must finally involve a theory of experience and a theory of knowledge, or in Berkeley's words "metaphysics." Thus he asks "Whether anything but metaphysics and logic can open the eyes of mathematicians and extricate them out of their difficulties." [84]

When we view Berkeley's polemic against the new analysis as a whole, several weaknesses become apparent. He fails particularly to do full justice in his technical discussions to the con-

[81] *Ibid.*, sec. 37, pp. 45-46.
[82] *Ibid.*, p. 50.
[83] *Ibid.*
[84] *Ibid.*, qu. 51, F. iii, p. 58.

cept of a limiting value, which is at least vaguely discernible in Newton's writings, in spite of the looseness of such expressions as "reduced to nothing," or "vanishing." His attempt to explain the efficacy of the calculus through the cancellation of opposed errors was at least correct in avoiding the assumption of infinitesimal quantities. His query [85] "whether the same things which are now done by infinites may not be done by finite quantities" was a brilliant insight fully verified by the results of later mathematical thought. The theory of cancellation, however, remains in the *Analyst* a pregnant suggestion which he is able to apply only to a few special cases, although such mathematicians as Maclaurin, Lagrange, and Carnot adopted the idea.[86]

Berkeley shows considerable skill in the technical development of his suggestions as well as a very accurate knowledge of the Newtonian classics and the ancient geometers.[87] The criticism summed up in his famous "lemma" uncovered important vaguenesses and inconsistencies not only in the methods of the Continental tradition represented by such a work as that of De l'Hospital, but in those of Newton as well, thus preparing the way for a more exact and adequate logical foundation for the new technique. Berkeley's sharp polemic against the loose pragmatic procedure of the day and his insistence on rigorous as well as intelligible logic in science were certainly not without influence even in his own lifetime.

MATHEMATICS AND MEANING. THE CRITIQUE OF PRAGMATISM

Berkeley succeeded in proving in the *Analyst* that the contemporary presentations of the new analysis were confused and contradictory, and that the writings of Newton were not free from error. He also made certain fruitful technical suggestions concerning the overcoming of these difficulties. It may be asked, however, whether there is no deeper meaning back of this criticism. Is the *Analyst* of exclusively mathematical interest?

[85] Qu. 54, F. iii, p. 59.
[86] Smith, *Source Book of Mathematics*, p. 633.
[87] Berkeley's editors have been so careless with respect to his mathematics, however, that it is difficult to gain any accurate conception of his thought from the current editions; as, for example, the series on page 49, which is misprinted by both Fraser and Sampson. Cf. Newton's *Intr. ad Quadraturam Curvarum*, p. 208.

Is it a purely technical treatise, dealing with irregularities in mathematical procedure, or is there a genuine philosophical content? Berkeley was a philosopher, and even while entering other fields, we must suppose him to be writing and thinking primarily as a philosopher. It is evident throughout the course of his investigations that this is, as a matter of fact, the case.[88] A careful examination of the *Analyst* will show not only that there is a deeper meaning back of the symbols, but that this treatise represents a most vital turning point in the development of Berkeley's philosophical reflections.

In the first place, he makes it clear at several points that the *Analyst* as a whole is an "*argumentum ad hominem* against men who reject that very thing in religion which they admit in human learning."[89] Will it not serve "to abate the pride, and discredit the pretensions of those who insist upon clear ideas in points of faith, if it be shown that they do without them even in science"?[90] The whole *Analyst* must, therefore, be viewed as an application of the *tu quoque* method of the *Alciphron*, which proceeded to justify faith by the judicious employment of scepticism. The pragmatic attack on "mathematical science," the great stronghold of rationalism, had already been begun in the seventh dialogue, where Berkeley points out that the analytic rules or methods of mathematics are "altogether conversant about the artificial use of signs,"[91] and are hence subject to the norms of "operation." The *Analyst* might be viewed, therefore, as only a detailed development of the argument of the *Alciphron* through which mathematical science was reduced to the level of sign manipulation, and logic to the level of symbolic logic. Mathematics and logic, according to this view, would be altogether "conversant about signs upon the skilful use and management whereof they entirely depend."[92] In themselves they are altogether analytic or "trifling" in character, since, in themselves, they are without meaning. In themselves they consist only in the manipulation of symbols, and once we have the signs with which we start, and the rules of "operation," the symbols with which we must end are a foregone conclusion. Hence results the absolute necessity and certainty of mathematical "demonstration."[93] "All sciences, so far as they are

---

[88] Thus he says, p. 30 (F. iii): "I have no controversy about your conclusions, but only about your logic and method." Cf. qu. 51, F. iii, p. 58.

[89] *A Defence of Free-Thinking in Math.*, F. iii, p. 64. [90] *Ibid.*
[91] Alc., F. ii, p. 341.
[92] *Ibid.*, p. 342.
[93] *Ibid.*; cf. C. B. J., 780.

universal and demonstrable by human reason, will be found conversant about *signs*. . . ." [94]

This position, of course, falls an easy prey to Berkeley's scepticism. The wholly artificial and abstract separation of form from content upon which such a theory rests makes the attribution of any content whatsoever a matter of caprice. Mathematics becomes analytic and abstractly consistent only by becoming meaningless, and hence by ceasing to be mathematics, for even the attribution of necessity to such a procedure rests upon an extraneous assumption. To assert that we are dealing with symbols, with quids and quods, requires justification from some other source. The pragmatic justification, which Berkeley recognizes as the only possible refuge for such thinking, is itself a half-hearted form of scepticism, for utility may mean anything or nothing. If all meaning is externally joined to mathematics from the outside, because in someone's opinion such meaning may be useful, then mathematics as mathematics, or as anything at all, rests solely on faith. It is a blind religion which "may be of use, although its object is not distinctly apprehended." [95] Mathematics is entirely subjectivized, and is not a science at all, for it has no object, but is "rather something of an active operative nature" [96] which certain persons may believe in as possessing a mysterious utility, just as the primitive savage believes in the mysterious efficacy of ritual observances. Such a view does not lead to scepticism; it is already scepticism with a cloak of deceptive nomenclature.

What is precisely the essential feature of Berkeley's *Analyst*, however, is not the statement of such a position, but the criticism of it. The *Analyst* is a development beyond the *Alciphron* rather than an extension of it. In the *Analyst* Berkeley becomes at last critical of his own criticism, and sceptical of his scepticism. The symbolic or pragmatic view of mathematics is self-destructive, for it presupposes utility as a fixed axiom, or first principle. But on what ground? Even the absence of a first principle is a first principle. "You will perhaps maintain," says Berkeley in the *Analyst*, "that problems may be solved without those inconceivable suppositions; and that consequently the doctrine of fluxions as to the practical part stands clear of all such difficulties." [97] But such pragmatism, as a matter of fact, falls more hopelessly into just these difficulties.

[94] Alc., p. 342.   [96] *Ibid.*, p. 344.
[95] *Ibid.*, p. 346.   [97] *Analyst*, pp. 40–41.

"I answer that if in the use or application of this method those difficult and obscure points are not attended to, they are nevertheless supposed." [98] We cannot escape our presuppositions by the easy method of ignoring them. They are there all the same. "It is with the method of fluxions as with all other methods, which presuppose their respective principles and are grounded thereon; although the rules may be practised by men who neither attend to, nor perhaps know the principles." [99]

By adopting this latter course, by turning his science into a maze of abstruse formulae with no meaning but pragmatically justified (i.e. unjustified), the mathematician has ceased to be "a man of science," [100] although he "may pass for an artist, computist or analyst." [101] He will, therefore, resent the question of meaning, and will insist that it is "vain," "metaphysical," and unnecessary to an exact scientist. [102] But by ignoring such questions, he has really ceased to be a scientist, for those who "seek truth by rational means . . . are never averse to have their principles looked into, and examined by the test of reason." [103] The exactitude of such a science rests upon inexactitude, and its certainty upon uncertainty. Everything it now considers useful may really not be useful at all; everything certain is certain to "evolve" into uncertainty. The pragmatic scientist, therefore, is "a mere computer" [104] who has learned "by rote" a set of principles and a way of thinking which happens to be "in vogue." [105]

Even if the pragmatic test could succeed in showing in any one case that a theory was really useful in its results (which is inconceivable) the theory could not be regarded as in any sense proved, for what sort of logic justifies you in "demonstrating" your "principles by your conclusions." [106] It is assuredly "peculiar" and "inverted" to suppose that "the truth of the conclusion" will "prove either the form or the matter of a syllogism to be true." [107] But to suppose that by discovering the utility of a theory (even granting that such a thing could be finally determined) we are then entitled to argue back to the truth of the theory, is to give up all pretensions to science. It is to think on a level with the voodoo-man, whose theories are assuredly justified to the extent to which his practice is able to

[98] Ibid., p. 41.   [99] Ibid.   [104] Qu. 44, F. iii, p. 57.
[100] Ibid.   [101] Ibid.   [105] Defence of Free-Thinking in Math.,
[102] Ibid., pp. 50–51.   F. iii, p. 69.
[103] Defence of Free-Thinking in Math.,   [106] Analyst, p. 30.
F. iii, p. 69.   [107] Ibid.

justify them, or "as any ordinary man may solve divers numerical questions, by the vulgar rules and operations of arithmetic, which he performs and applies without knowing the reasons of them." [108] But such pragmatism, or "induction," which must end by giving up reflection altogether and simply relapsing into the dogmas of common sense, is the inevitable consequence of formal logic or logistic. "In every other science," says Berkeley finally to his mathematical opponent, "men prove their conclusions by their principles, and not their principles by their conclusions. But if in yours you should allow yourselves this unnatural way of proceeding, the consequence would be that you must take up with Induction, and bid adieu to Demonstration." [109] The "taking up with induction," or pragmatism, is in reality a confession of defeat. How, except by miracle, is the certain to arise from the uncertain, the universal from the particular, the eternal from the temporal, or value from fact? To suppose or "assume" such things is superstition.

The only means of escape from such superstition is the possession, from the very first, of a clear structure of meaning. No "symbol" or "rule" must be employed for an instant without an insight into its meaning. No one has "a right to apply the rules of the great author without first considering his metaphysical notions whence they were derived" or "without a precise, clear, and accurate conception of the principles." [110] Without this, the mathematician or logician is "a mere computer," utilizing something which must be considered "a knack," rather than in any way "a science." [111] To fall back upon "notes, signs, or symbols" is to be "deluded" [112] by word magic. A symbol without a meaning is not even a symbol, not even a mark, not even a quid. There is no refuge from pragmatism, psychologism, common sense, empiricism, induction, voodooism, save in meaning or intelligibility, which must be followed through to its last absolute and hence metaphysical consequences.

The first result of considering things meaningfully rather than pragmatically or psychologically is that they are considered as objects. We cannot mean without meaning something, and this object or content cannot be identified with the subjective meaning. There can be no signifying without

[108] *Ibid.*, p. 41.   [110] *Ibid.*, p. 50.   [112] *Analyst*, pp. 45–46.
[109] *Ibid.*, p. 30.   [111] Qu. 35, F. iii, p. 56.

significance, no meaning without something meant. Hence, if mathematics is to be meaningful, it must mean an object. In the *Analyst*, therefore, Berkeley constantly attempts to direct the attention of the mathematicians to the *object* signified by such a thing as a "fluxion." If this is anything more than an expression in certain mystic formulae, it must mean something or stand for an "object." Thus, in addition to the formal requirements of geometry, such as "clear definitions" and derivation of properties "by a perpetual well-connected chain of consequences," Berkeley adds the even more essential requirement that "the objects be still kept in view and the attention ever fixed upon them." [113] He complains of the vague "analogies" employed by the modern analysts in explaining their mysterious concepts that "however expedient such analogies or such expressions may be found for facilitating the modern quadratures, yet we shall not find any light given us thereby into *the original real nature of fluxions*; or that we are enabled to frame from thence just ideas of fluxions considered in themselves." [114] The *Analyst* is, therefore, more than a technical correction of certain errors in mathematical procedure. It is an essay in a field unexplored and unexplorable by mathematicians as mathematicians, the field of the philosophy or meaning of the calculus, or the calculus in its "original real nature." Without an understanding of this original real nature the analysis is only a formula, something with which to solve problems, a fashion happening to be "in vogue." "Whether men," queries Berkeley,[115] "may properly be said to proceed in a scientific method without clearly conceiving the object they are conversant about?"

The investigations incorporated in the *Analyst*, therefore, lead Berkeley to abandon his theory of mathematics without meaning, and to return to the earlier theory of the *Commonplace Book*, according to which mathematics was a "science" devoted to the study of certain objects, though his conception of the nature of these objects is now a very different one. He no longer thinks of mathematics as an empirical science studying extended figures by induction, for with induction we "bid adieu to Demonstration." [116] But the necessary or demonstrable character of mathematics does not mean that it is to be regarded as a mere matter of symbols and rules without intelligibility. Mathematics must be necessary and demonstrable,

[113] *Ibid.*, p. 18.
[114] *Ibid.*, pp. 49, 50; my italics.
[115] Qu. 4, F. iii, p. 52.
[116] *Analyst*, p. 30.

and yet possess an object, or meaning. Without both of these seemingly opposed factors mathematics cannot be mathematics, for in the one case, as an empirical or inductive science (the view of the early *Commonplace Book*) it is deprived of all necessity, while in the other it is deprived of all meaning and reduced to the level of a game. Mathematics must be *both* objective, or meaningful, and necessary.

Berkeley no longer confuses the object of mathematics with sense-data or extensions. The object of mathematics is determined by the meaning of the category of "quantity." [117] "Whether the finding out proper expressions or notations of quantity," Berkeley asks, "be not the most general character and tendency of the mathematics?" [118] He is no longer forced to divide mathematics artificially into geometry as an empirical science studying certain sense-data, i.e. extensions, the "mixed mathematics" of the *Commonplace Book*, and algebra, or general mathematics, which involves the basic principles governing the manipulation of signs and is thus allied with logic. Such a view must make the application of the one to the other an incomprehensible mystery. The unity of mathematics lies in the unity of the field of meaning determined by the category of quantity. Wherever there is quantity, whether it be spatial, temporal, or kinematic, there is the possibility of mathematical treatment. Berkeley thus speaks of "geometrical quantity" [119] when considering space relations, since there are still other "sorts" of quantity, as well as the pure category or concept of quantity in itself which yields its mathematical meaning to the other forms of externality.

Berkeley even gives one or two interesting suggestions concerning the nature of this fundamental meaning, though such a discussion hardly falls within the scope of the *Analyst*. Thus he asks in Query 24, "whether a quantity be not properly said to be known, when we know its proportion to given quantities?" A quantity, that is, can be known only through its relation to other "given" quantities, and so forth. Relativity or reference to an other beyond itself is embedded in the very nature of what we mean by quantity, which is the pure form or essence of externality or relativity. Hence, as Berkeley intimates, it is not only "time and motion," temporal and kinematic quantity,

---

[117] Cf. Pr., sec. 118, F. i, p. 324, where Berkeley speaks of mathematics as "limited by the consideration of quantity," though this suggestion is entirely undeveloped until the *Analyst*. [118] Qu. 25, F. iii, p. 55. [119] Qu. 13.

which is relative or regressive, but "all quantity" whatsoever is "in a flux," [120] not a temporal flux, but that more fundamental flux which time presupposes, the logical flux or relativity of pure thought.

Berkeley also suggests, however, that there may be certain critical points at which mathematics must reach the limit of quantity and pass beyond the field determined by this category. Hence, he queries, "whether the bringing nothing under the notion of quantity may not have betrayed men into false reasoning?" [121] He even suggests at one point that this may be at the bottom of the "mystery" of "fluxions," which "are neither finite quantities, nor quantities infinitely small, nor yet nothing," but perhaps "the ghosts of departed quantities." [122] The limit, that is, which a quantitative ratio may approach is beyond any assignable quantity, because it is, in a sense, beyond quantity itself. The limit is not an indefinitely varying quantity, but the stable quality-quantity which emerges as the law or principle of such variation, the permanent essence of "departed quantities." It is such insights as these that constitute the true importance of the *Analyst*, rather than the more sensational achievement of having demonstrated technical inaccuracies in such works as Newton's *Principia*. This is secondary to the general issue of meaning which Berkeley so sharply and pointedly raised. What is the object of mathematics? Admitting the analytic demonstrations and symbol systems, *of what* do we assert them to be true, and by what right? *Quid juris?*

Until we have answered this question, we are playing a symbolic game, which may or may not be important. No form of empiricism or induction can answer this question. Pragmatism is an evasion, not an answer. This question must lead beyond all empiricisms and pragmatisms, beyond all "science," and certainly beyond all mathematics.[123] It can lead those who like Berkeley seriously ask it in only one direction, toward "a certain transcendental science superior to and more extensive than mathematics, which it might behove our modern analysts rather to learn than despise." [124] This "transcendental science" is transcendental because it is presupposed by all sciences, in-

---

120 *Ibid.*
121 Qu. 40.
122 *Analyst*, p. 44.
123 Hence the motto chosen for the *Defence of Free-Thinking in Mathematics*

from Aristotle, *Meta.*, x, 4: Ἐπεὶ δὲ ὁ μαθηματικὸς χρῆται τοῖς κοινοῖς ἰδίως, καὶ τὰς τούτων ἀρχὰς ἂν εἴη θεωρῆσαι τῆς πρώτης φιλοσοφίας.
124 Qu. 49.

cluding mathematics and even itself, for it is the science of *meaning*, logic, or the λόγος. Until we become clear as to what we mean by meaning, nothing else can become clear, for everything whatsoever depends upon meaning, including clarity. Unless such a logic, which must be at the same time a metaphysics, is developed and understood, the clarity of mathematics is only a spurious clarity, resting upon an obscurity that must keep breaking through at every critical point. "Whether anything but metaphysics and logic," queries Berkeley, "can open the eyes of mathematicians and extricate them out of their difficulties?" [125]

Berkeley's commentators have been content to remark upon the technical acumen and mathematical skill which enabled him seriously to annoy several leading mathematicians of the time, — a feat deemed very clever for a Bishop. But few have cared to follow him into the depths of the transcendental philosophy to which these mathematical researches led him, and which, in his own eyes at least, constituted its real importance. From this point on, Berkeley's philosophy is transcendental philosophy, and it is into its profound depths that we must at least attempt to follow him.

[125] Qu. 51.

PART IV

PHILOSOPHIA PRIMA. THE "SYSTEM" OF THE SIRIS

"He that would make a real progress in knowledge must dedicate his age as well as youth, the later as well as first fruits, at the altar of Truth." *Siris*, sec. 368.

PHILOSOPHIA PRIMA. THE "SYSTEM"
OF THE SIRIS

IN THE last few chapters, we have attempted to show how the scepticism engendered by Berkeley's youthful rationalism became so formidable as to lead him beyond the speculative to the practical, and finally to the realm of faith. Experience is even more destructive to practical striving than is the speculative absolute to theory. The absolute to which such "striving" leads is neither a speculative absolute of intelligibility nor an ethical ideal, but "something unknown," the *Deus absconditus*. It was not until he had achieved "faith" that Berkeley could begin to think rationally. Philosophy *then* became necessary, just as faith had become necessary, once he had fallen into the toils of scepticism.

If reason is faith, as Berkeley had at last discovered, it is no less true that faith is reason. The absolute is assuredly not rational. But neither can it be supposed to be irrational. It is impossible to have faith without having faith in *something*, and there is no way of shedding any sort of light upon the object or meaning of faith save through reason. The absolute is certainly not the speculative field of meaning, but neither is it meaningless, for it could not, indeed, be the one without the other. Just as faith is the inescapable "refuge" of reason, so is reason the inescapable "refuge" of faith, and we are forced inevitably from the one to the other. There can be no "blind" faith, for not to see is to see nothing. Before we can reason we must have faith in reason. Whether we think of the larger frame, within which all reasoning takes place, pragmatically, or truly pragmatically, that is practically, or truly practically, that is religiously, we cannot escape the reference to this larger frame. Reason, to be reason, requires the irrational. To begin to reason presupposes faith. But we cannot have faith without having faith in something. A blind faith is not true faith at all, but only the vague beginning of a faith that requires reason for its completion. True faith knows that in which it has faith, though it knows it only through having faith in it. *Credo ut intellegam.* It is the destiny of faith to be "questioned," and to answer this "question" faith must make itself intelligible. In and through his achievement of faith, Berkeley, the Bishop of Cloyne, at last becomes a philosopher.

We have now traced the course of Berkeley's development, first as a youth of vague and disquieting intuitions, then as a young man full of enthusiasm for reason and its mathematical ideal, determined to work out his "position" according to the most rigid laws of logic, and to demonstrate everything, except, of course, demonstration. We have then attempted to trace the development of the scepticism into which this enthusiasm passed through its various stages of scepticism proper, pragmatism, practical philosophy, and finally faith. During this period Berkeley appears successively in the role of "philosophical" sceptic, man of action plunging into the turmoil of the "life" of his day, idealist building a new civilization in a land beyond the sea, practical philosopher, combating the reigning ethos of his "time," and finally, appreciating something of the irony touching each component of this recurring cycle, the man of faith.

Now, at last, he emerges as a philosopher. His past reflections and experiences were not philosophy at all, but propaedeutic. Without intuition, without logic, and particularly without scepticism and the practical philosophy which follows in its train, there can be no true philosophy, for philosophy is more than these, standing as it does between the absolute and the relative, as the mediator, revelation, or λόγος. Finding itself embedded in the temporal, it is not content until it has penetrated to the eternal, when it assumes its proper task of revealing to the temporal that which lies beyond. It is only from such a vantage point that the unending task of philosophy, as it has revealed itself, is even conceivable. There is nothing that does not fall within its province, for the home of philosophy is beyond all horizons. There is no fixed doctrine, system, or absolute that will not yield to a scepticism resting on what lies beyond them all, even beyond scepticism itself. It is for this reason that the greater philosophical systems are at the same time more fragile, and seem to disappear more readily into the flux of historic relativity. This is because they have carried within themselves the germs of dissolution. All true philosophy is relative, because it is founded upon the absolute. This attempt to bring the temporal world into relation with eternal being, to cast a dim but unworldly light upon the world, is philosophy, and it is for this last and most absorbing task that Berkeley, the disappointed rationalist and defeated idealist, has finally qualified himself.

CHAPTER XV

THE BISHOP OF CLOYNE

His great dislike for political intrigue made the idea of returning to Ireland most distasteful to Berkeley, for he was now opposed by most of the influential Irish prelates, particularly by the Bishop of Down, who had written him an "insolent" letter during his stay in America.[1] Furthermore, all his best friends lived in England. He would not, therefore, consider returning to his Deanery, which, under the circumstances, would amount to an admission of failure and disgrace. For a time, the English Deanery of Canterbury was considered, although this was a distinctly subordinate position worth eight hundred pounds per year. Yet even this proved impossible, as none of the English churchmen could be got to "go to an honorable banishment in Ireland."[2] The situation was saved, however, by the continued favour of the Queen and the sudden vacancy of the minor Bishopric of Cloyne in Southern Ireland. As it actually turned out, the acceptance of this Bishopric meant a considerable financial loss,[3] but it meant also that Berkeley could return with the mark of royal approval, rather than under the stigma of defeat. On the evening of January 17, 1734, when Percival returned home from Parliament, he "found Dean Berkeley," who acquainted him that "this morning he kissed the King's and Queen's hands for the Bishopric of Cloyne."

Berkeley planned to return to Ireland, but the illness of his wife forced a delay of several months. In this interval, he occupied himself chiefly with the prosecution of the controversies to which the *Analyst* had given rise, but finally crossed to Ireland in the spring. He was consecrated as Bishop of Cloyne on Sunday, May 17, 1734, in St. Paul's Church, Dublin, and almost immediately afterwards made the rough and difficult journey of one hundred and fifty miles to his small Diocese, which, at that time, included forty-four churches and fourteen thousand Protestants. This secluded corner of the Kingdom proved an ideal spot for quiet meditation. His health was now

---

[1] Cf. Percival, *Journal*, February 27, 1732.

[2] *Ibid.*, March 15, 1732.

[3] Letter to Prior, March 2, 1734, F. *Life*, p. 215.

too delicate for violent effort, and grew increasingly worse. He was ill a great part of the time. Four years later he complains of an "habitual colic."[4] Shortly after, he writes that only the constant care of his wife makes his life, "embittered by sickness," tolerable.[5] For the time being, however, he was able to carry on his mathematical discussions with Jurin and Walton. But, as it became evident that they had altogether failed to grasp his meaning and that there was no advantage in further repetition, he let the matter rest and turned his attention to subjects of more interest to those about him. He was appalled at the squalid misery which prevailed among the inhabitants of his remote Diocese, and his observations gave rise to a chain of practical reflections concerning social and economic questions, the first part of which emerged in 1735 as the *Querist*, not finally completed until 1737.

THE QUERIST

The scepticism which had become an essential element in all of his reflections now led him, as in the *Analyst*, to state his thoughts indirectly in the form of queries, rather than directly as assertions. His diagnosis of the distresses of the unfortunate country in which he was born was probably the fairest and one of the most original that had yet appeared. While the 595 queries of which this work consists are somewhat fragmentary and inchoate, if considered as a whole, they are, nevertheless, in themselves brief, to the point, and suffused with a very delicate and delectable irony. Berkeley, in general, agreed with Swift that the ultimate source of distress lay in the idleness, squalor, and poverty of the "native Irish."[6] But while Swift's inflammatory pamphlets spring from a hatred of Whig government, and while he strove primarily to avenge his adopted country, Berkeley's queries are written in a spirit of cool sympathy.

In the process of considering practical remedies for the widespread misery in Ireland, Berkeley is led into an examination of the ultimate basis of wealth and a consequent criticism of the prevailing mercantilist theory, which suggests in certain respects, although only in a fragmentary manner, the later theories of Hume and Adam Smith. The ultimate sources of

---

[4] Letter to Johnson, May, 1738, F. *Life*, p. 258.

[5] Letter, fragment probably, to James sometime in 1741, F. *Life*, p. 268.

[6] F. iv, p. 454, Qu. 357.

wealth, Berkeley thinks, are "the four elements and man's labour therein." [7] The drift and aim of every wise state should be "to encourage industry in its members," [8] rather than to accumulate land or material wealth of any sort, for "the true idea of money is that of a ticket or counter." Indiscriminate luxury for the few, he believes, unlike Mandeville, to be an unimportant factor in the stimulation of trade, [9] and he is ready to root it out by sumptuary laws if necessary. With Plato, he held that too great wealth was as evil as too great poverty, and he asks "whether a woman of fashion ought not to be declared a public enemy?" [10] and whether "the fine gentlemen whose enjoyment is only to dress, drink, and play, be not a public nuisance?" [11]

He looked upon idleness as a betrayal of trust, and wonders "whether a door ought not to be shut against all other methods of growing rich, save only by industry and merit? And whether wealth got otherwise would not be ruinous to the public?" [12] He thinks it absurd that "the wealth and prosperity of our country" should "hang by a hair; the probity of one banker, the caution of another." [13] Accordingly he suggests in several concrete instances the extension of governmental activity in the building of canals, the control of fashions, [14] the formation of a "mart of literature" for the encouragement of the arts, [15] and particularly the formation of a public or national bank, which he thought would greatly facilitate exchange and stabilize credit. Finally, he compares the community to an organism, circulation of money to the circulation of the blood, and legislature to the mind or soul. [16] While, like Plato, he is even passionately "democratic" in asserting that any "scheme for the welfare of this nation" must take in "the whole inhabitants," [17] and in expressing his confidence that "all men" have "faculties of mind or body which may be employed for the public benefit," [18] he is very far from any sentiment concerning the masses, and appreciates clearly that true "democracy" presupposes a "brain" in the social organism.

The many pregnant queries concerning education show the extent to which his mind is now becoming saturated with the

[7] *Ibid.*, p. 422.
[8] *Ibid.*, Qu. 3.
[9] Qu. 167, 175, 339, 374.
[10] Qu. 141.
[11] F. iv, p. 568, Qu. 62.
[12] Qu. 218.

[13] Qu. 275.
[14] Qu. 13, 422.
[15] Qu. 186. Cf. pp. 201, 283.
[16] Qu. 579–593.
[17] Qu. 255.
[18] Qu. 351.

writings and spirit of Plato. He asks, for example, "whether an early habit of reflection, although obtained by speculative sciences, may not have its use in practical affairs." [19] He believes that the establishment of another college in the country would greatly foster the interests of learning, both by a "useful emulation" [20] and by added material facilities. He is the first to suggest that Catholics be allowed to enter Trinity College. [21] He is appalled by the ignorance of the law-makers of his day and the prevailing system which secures material rather than educational advantages for the eldest son. Berkeley first queries, "whether our peers and gentlemen are born legislators? Or, whether that faculty be acquired by study and reflection?" [22] And finally he wonders, "What right an eldest son hath to the worst education." [23]

His daughter-in-law informs us that he used to say, "If I had the voice of Stentor, I would become hoarse in calling on all, *Take care of the education of your children.*" [24] He himself supervised the classical training of his own children, being unwilling to entrust these all-important studies to a tutor, though "for several years he paid four hundred pounds per annum to different masters to instruct his children in Music, Painting, Fencing, Riding and French." [25] One of the music teachers was an Italian master, Pasquilino, who was even given a chaise and a pair of horses for his private use. [26] Berkeley invited the seven children of his brother Robert, [27] who had settled in the vicinity, to share in the lessons, and the episcopal palace must at times have resembled an academy of the arts. In writing to his friend Gervais, [28] who was delegated to purchase a bass viol in France, Berkeley says, "we are musically mad." [29] Mrs. Berkeley was devoted to music, his son George played the viol, and William the violin. The parental supervision, indeed, seems at certain points almost too diligent, for we are told that "his sons were never suffered either to ride or walk out unattended by a careful servant," [30] but the state of the countryside may have justified such precautions.

[19] Qu. 197.
[20] Qu. 188.
[21] Qu. 191.
[22] Qu. 182.
[23] Qu. 330.
[24] Berkeley, *Poems*, p. cccclxxix.
[25] *Ibid.*, p. ccxliv.
[26] Eliza Berkeley tells an anecdote concerning one of his unfortunate experiments in the English language. Berkeley, *Poems*, p. ccccxi n.
[27] Scholar of Trinity College 1719, and later Rector of Middleton, about three miles from Cloyne.
[28] Isaac Gervais, later a Dean, but at this time Rector in Younghall, Waterford.
[29] September 6, 1743.
[30] Berkeley, *Poems*, p. ccxliv.

Free-Thinking and the Plague

In the year 1735 a good deal of excitement was awakened in Ireland by the discovery of an atheistical society, led by a certain Peter Lens, who called himself a "blaster" and presided at meetings devoted to various blasphemous purposes, including the drinking of a toast to the Devil. Berkeley became considerably aroused over this new, practical manifestation of "free-thinking," and in 1736 published *A Discourse Addressed to Magistrates and Men in Authority occasioned by the Enormous License of the Times.*

This pamphlet considers religion not in itself "as a system of saving truths" with a non-human "sanction," but only with respect to its influence upon "the civil constitution" and "society." [31] There is never any question of attempting to justify religion by its secondary social effects in the Deistic manner. "Men groping out their way by the dim twilight of nature, did only approach, some nearer some farther off;" but "all were short of the truth." [32] As for the rationalistic hue and cry against "prejudice" and "faith," Berkeley makes the reply of the *Alciphron*. To destroy all "prejudice" in the Deistic sense is to destroy reason as well, for what "argument" do the free-thinkers adduce for "argument" itself, — what "stands under" the understanding? The attempt of "rational" minds, therefore, to "extirpate" prejudices [33] is only "in order to introduce prejudices of another kind," [34] and "while they rail at prejudice, they are undoing themselves." [35]

The deep sense of practical pessimism into which his theoretical scepticism has passed, and which now characterizes all his reflections, appears on every page of this address. There are many references to the "wicked times," and "these giddy times." [36] He now felt himself completely at odds with the thought and feeling of his generation. "Our prospect is very terrible," he concludes, "and the symptoms grow stronger every day." [37] In such a setting, the Deistic demand for "freedom" naturally appears to him as in reality a demand for the greatest tyranny, the covert tyranny of "passions" which urge "to great evils," what is called "reason" only "furnishing means to achieve them." [38] Such "freedom," while often

---

[31] F. iv, p. 503.
[32] *Ibid.*, p. 497.
[33] *Ibid.*, p. 499.
[34] *Ibid.*
[35] *Ibid.*, p. 500.
[36] *Ibid.*, p. 489.
[37] *Ibid.*, p. 505.
[38] *Ibid.*, p. 484.

thoughtlessly confused with the demands of the Reformation, as "the setting up of private judgment, or an inward light in opposition to human and divine laws," is in reality a "present impending danger," capable not only of destroying the work of the Reformation, but "sufficient to dissolve any human fabric of polity or civil government." [39]

Human judgment is fallacious, and human nature imperfect. It is not from any sense of the righteousness of existing institutions that Berkeley resists radicalism of every kind, for "Divine authority is superior to all human prejudices, institutions and regards whatsoever. And it is wise, although at the risk of liberty or life, to obey God rather than man." [40] It is not, therefore, that the authority of the state is worthy of our trust, but that the authority of the revolutionist is much less so. By refraining from every sort of violence, by "submission for conscience," [41] rather than for any external power, we may indicate or demonstrate that sense of the transience and relativity of all human authority and power, in which the only true freedom lies. Those who imagine that they may "remedy" whatever is "amiss, and render a people great and happy, merely by a new plan or form of government" [42] are following a great delusion. There is no revolution, no "reform," no abstract freedom that must not end in tyranny, for freedom without authority is no longer "freedom." Concrete freedom, or genuine freedom, like genuine morality, must be based upon authority, but where is a human or "rational" authority to be found which is capable of demanding perfect submission? What authority can be found which is strong enough to free us from the slavery of passion, and thus to afford a trustworthy foundation for morality? Neither "moral sense" nor "rational principle" is sufficient, for neither is really free from passion. "As for a moral sense, and moral fitness, or eternal relations, how insufficient those things are for establishing general and just notions of morality, ... is ... evident." [43] The only authority capable of demanding absolute or free submission is an authority which is at the same time no authority, or a reason which is at the same time no reason, "the first link of authority being fixed at the throne of God." [44] If this link is weakened all links are weakened. If this authority is jeopardized, all authority is jeopardized, and freedom is lost at the same time. The respect for the norm which

[39] *Ibid.*, p. 501.   [41] *Ibid.*, p. 491.   [43] *Ibid.*
[40] *Ibid.*, p. 490.   [42] *Ibid.*, p. 492.   [44] *Ibid.*, p. 491.

lies at the basis of morality can be justified only by the abso-lute, and the separation of morality from religion means im-morality. "The modern schemes of our free-thinkers who pre-tend to separate morality from religion, how rational soever they may seem to their admirers, are, in truth and effect, most irrational and pernicious . . . ." [45] Concrete morality is absolute morality. In the autumn Bishop Berkeley attended the Irish House of Lords in Dublin, and delivered an address on the topic of "blasters" and free-thinkers in general, which, we are told, was received with great applause.

In accordance with the recommendations of the *Querist*, Berkeley had attempted to do all in his power to encourage native industry by the establishment of a spinning school for the children of Cloyne, a workhouse for vagrants, and he em-ployed regularly more than one hundred men in agricultural work on the episcopal estate.[46] He also refused to inclose the great common where the poor came to cut their peat, and which they used as a pasture for their cows, pigs, and poultry, and further instances of his charity are recorded. These philan-thropic endeavours, however, were interrupted by the great frost in 1739,[47] which caused a scarcity of wheat with resultant famine and plague. Great numbers of the poor perished in 1740 and 1741, and Berkeley shared in the common suffering through the loss of his daughter Sarah on March 6, 1740.[48] "The dis-tresses of the sick and poor," he writes his friend Prior, "are endless." The following incident related by his daughter-in-law, which must have occurred during the frost, shows how keenly he felt the burdens of those about him, and how strin-gently he bound himself by the principles of the *Querist*.

On the commencement of the hard frost in 1739–40, the Bishop went down to breakfast the first Sunday without a grain of powder in his wig; Mrs. Berkeley, the Chaplain, and some company staying in the house on visit, all called out at once to enquire "what ailed his Lordship?" Bishop Berkeley replied "a great deal ails me; for our poor are all about to be starved. We shall have a famine. We shall have a very long frost; and I am sure it has already killed all the potatoes in this kingdom; therefore the poor must de-pend upon flour; so no powder will I, or shall any individual of my family wear until next harvest." They assured him that it disfigured him exceed-ingly, and that the men would look dirty. All persuasion was vain. He,

---

[45] *Ibid.*, p. 489.
[46] *Ibid.*, p. 534 (JJ).
[47] Cf. Berkeley, *Poems*, p. ccccxiii.

[48] His third son, John, born in April, 1735, died in October of the same year.

during the frost, and until the summer, gave either in gold or in bank note every Monday morning, twenty pounds to proper persons to distribute among the poor of the little town of Cloyne, besides what they received daily, hourly, out of his kitchen, and housekeeper's room.[49]

In the small-pox epidemic which followed the famine, Berkeley was temperamentally unable to stand idle and watch the people die. Since there were few qualified physicians in his remote part of the country, the family was largely dependent on him for medical assistance, and the people of the surrounding country also began to come to him for similar advice. He never turned anyone away, no matter how hopeless or loathsome the disease.[50] Never of robust health himself, he had always taken a certain interest in medicine, and now, though well along in years and even declining in health, he threw himself into the task of curing the sick with the same characteristic energy which had almost converted London to immaterialism, and had overwhelmed it with Bermuda. There can be no question as to the sincerity with which he brought the whole force of his learning and persuasive power to bear on this new task, and the personal sacrifices he made in advising and treating every variety of applicant and defending his characteristically original views.

It is difficult for a modern reader to avoid judging the result of Berkeley's therapeutic experiments in the light of more recent knowledge. But when the primitive state of medicine is remembered, and it is borne in mind that the practice of bleeding, for example, was used as a standard remedy for almost all diseases, and that a leading physician of the time actively maintained that wine in large quantities [51] was the chief means of immunity to the plague, Berkeley's famous panacea is seen in a more proper perspective. During his visit to America, he had observed the use of tar-water as a preventive against the small-pox,[52] and had discovered that this remedy originated with the Indians. During the epidemic of 1740–41, nothing better being at hand, he used tar-water as a remedy, in the case of his own family and others who applied to him, with what he considered good results.[53]

He then began to read medical and chemical works, and learned that tar-water was generally known even by the an-

[49] Berkeley, *Poems, loc. cit.*
[50] Cf. *Further Thoughts on Tar Water,* especially F. iii, pp. 344–345, 351.
[51] Willis, F. iii, p. 327.

[52] *Siris,* F. iii, pp. 142, 148.
[53] Prior, February 8, 1741, F. *Life.* p. 263.

cients as a mild antiseptic. He delved into botany and glimpsed a connection between the life-giving principle or essence embodied in the juice or sap of coniferous trees and the universal source of life and motion, light or fire, from which it must have been derived. This essence, if it could be separated from the gross covering in which it was embodied, ought to prove, as it seemed to him, a stimulating tonic, and generally aid the vital forces of the body to repair all sorts of damage. In addition to this, Berkeley thought that he had discovered by experiment that tar-water, in the fine, soluble form which he prescribed, penetrated to the remotest capillaries of the body, clearing them of obstructions of all kinds. This was the theoretical foundation of the many treatises with which he and his friend Prior bombarded the plague-stricken country, and which made tar-water for several years a fashion throughout Europe. Tar-water factories sprang into existence. There was a large warehouse in London, and the new remedy was shipped to all parts of the civilized world. The apothecaries met in protest against this new and simple remedy which was depriving them of lucrative business. The medical profession, while it did not seriously question the restricted therapeutic value of the new medicine,[54] attacked it as a supposed panacea, and a pamphlet war began.

Berkeley himself never dogmatically claimed that his remedy was a panacea, though he "suspected" its general "tonic" quality.[55] "Tar water" was a mild antiseptic, and in the form which Berkeley recommended, it was probably harmless unless taken in huge quantities, and even then probably less harmful than many other standard remedies of the day. His philosophy of medicine, fantastic as it now sounds, was at least a wholesome reaction against the various mechanical systems then in vogue, and may have helped to spread the discontent which ended the popularity of such Newtonian treatises as that of Mead on "The Power of the Sun and Moon over Human Bodies" (1704), and finally terminated the whole "mathematical" era in medicine. In any case, much of Berkeley's practical effort, as well as his philosophical speculation during the last years of his life, revolved around the new health-giving remedy.

[54] Cf. Diederick Wessel Linden, M.D., *A Treatise on the Origin, Nature, and Virtues of Chalybeat Waters and Natural Hot Baths. To which is added an Appendix on the Selter Water, 1752.* In the appendix he refers with approval to the medical use of tar-water. See also *Siris*, F. iii, p. 184, — Sir John Floyer, etc.

[55] First letter to Prior, F. iii, p. 312.

The Meaning of the Reformation (Letter to Sir John James)

An exception to this absorbing interest, however, is provided by a long letter which he wrote in 1741 to his old friend Sir John James, who was apparently on the verge of becoming a Catholic.[56] This letter, while it contains many indications of the general pessimism and despair which was the natural culmination of his practical philosophy, such as the reference to "the cold and dry writings of our modern divines," [57] nevertheless constitutes the first specific evidence of that reconstructive effort which occupies the later years of the Bishop's life. This latest creative phase is characterized by a faith that is more than faith, and a rationalism that is more than rationalism. It is perhaps best understood as an attempt to chart a certain middle course, avoiding all such "positions" or extremes, including the extreme of mediocrity or eclecticism. The "light of nature" is relegated by a devastating "even" [58] to the level of a subordinate abstraction, and reminded of its "beginning" in the "Father of Lights." [59]

But if the letter is free from the blind "reason" of which these "modern" times so "smell," [60] neither can it be confused with the pragmatism or blind faith with which it is so intimately associated, and which Berkeley had himself employed as a counterpoise to the dogmatism of its opposite pole. "It is dangerous," says Berkeley, now enlightened by the critical researches of the *Analyst*, "arguing from our notion of the expediency of a thing to the reality of the thing itself." [61] The letter to Sir John James thus avoids the pretensions of the Deist as well as those of the "enthusiast," of free thought as of the abstract authoritarianism which is its antithesis. This middle road which is as dangerous as it is difficult to follow, Berkeley finds embodied in the ideals of the Protestant Reformation.

This Reformation, as Berkeley understands it, is nourished by a scepticism so deep as to lie beyond the reach of any purely

[56] James died a few months after this letter was written. According to Eliza Berkeley, he had at one time bequeathed most of his large estate to "his dear friend Bishop Berkeley," who, however, hearing of the matter indirectly through Benson, wrote "a thundering letter to the latter saying, "Do you tell James that I will not have his fortune. Bid him leave it to his relations. I won't have it." Monck Berkeley, *Poems*, p. ccclx n.

[57] F. iv, p. 521.

[58] "even to the light of nature." *Ibid.*, p. 532.

[59] *Ibid.*, p. 526.

[60] *Ibid.*, p. 522.   [61] *Ibid.*, p. 523.

rational irony. "We hold all mankind to be peccable and errable . . ." for "we are like men in a cave, in this present life, seeing by a dim light," [62] and "we *dare not* talk in the high, unerring, positive style." There is no system of thought, however profound and subtle, that does not at last betray its source in the wavering understanding of the human creature. "Man is fallible," [63] and the essential weakness of the source extends through the whole expanse of human endeavour. There is no institution, least of all the Church, no matter how powerful or impressive it may be, that can permanently conceal its lowly origin. All churches are in a "most corrupt and erroneous state," and "the particular churches of Jerusalem, Antioch, Alexandria, Rome, &c. have all fallen into error." [64] Every human thought ends, as it begins, in confusion, and every human feeling is cursed with instability. "The security and repose of souls is pretended or promised," [65] but where is it to be found? Who or what is capable of quieting the ultimate doubts of a genuine sceptic? Who or what is capable of pacifying real despair, save the despair itself? This is the sense of the Reformation. It is only through scepticism that one may discover the speculative absolute, and similarly it is only through despair that one may arrive at that practical absolute, which appears precisely not to the "enthusiast" nor to the mystic hero, but to the sceptic and the atheist, for "God knows how to extract good from evil." [66]

There can be no other authority but this, and no other revelation but the revelation which He Himself makes of Himself through "the outward light of His written word" [67] and the inward light of the λόγος.[68] To grasp or apprehend something perfectly non-human, beyond rational as well as emotional comprehension, "we have need . . . of aid and light from above," [69] for "there is no judge of spiritual things but the Spirit of God." [70] Any confusion of this authority with that of a human construction, no matter how vast or powerful, is superstition and "bias." "An affection conceived towards a particular church . . . is, I apprehend, to be suspected. Most men act with bias. . . . It is our duty to try and divest ourselves of all bias whatsoever," [71] for it is not until our minds are divested of the last

[62] *Ibid.*, p. 525.
[63] *Ibid.*, p. 527.
[64] *Ibid.*, p. 526.
[65] *Ibid.*, p. 527.

[66] *Ibid.*, p. 530.
[67] *Ibid.*, p. 524.
[68] Cf. *Ibid.*, p. 523.

[69] *Ibid.*, p. 522.
[70] *Ibid.*
[71] *Ibid.*, p. 525.

trace of human faith and certainty, not until they have probed the last depths of scepticism and atheism that they become fit receptacles for the "inward light." [72] The "Universal Church" is not to be confused with any visible "political or national Churches" whatsoever,[73] and "the members of this Universal Church are not visible by outward marks, but certainly known only to God, whose Spirit will sanctify and maintain it to the end of time." [74]

Salvation is an absolute mystery. "Many are called, but few are chosen. Therefore there is no reckoning the elect by the number of visible members. There must be the invisible grace. . . ." [75] This Grace, or "inward light," [76] never works directly or mystically. It is a light which is at the same time darkness, an authority which is at the same time freedom. The abstract authoritarianism, which demands "submission," forgets that all submission is really free, and hence degenerates into mere force and ceases to be authority. "Not seeing at all, how can we choose . . .?" Each must choose, and "see" with "his own private eyes," or he "will not see at all.[77] Every power of rational judgment must be utilized to the utmost pitch of intensity. "There must be a proper disposition of the organ." [78] But there must be something more as well. There must be a real, external, transcendent, independent object and a real, external, independent light, or there will be nothing to see. Freedom without authority, reason without faith, end in the darkness of subjectivism and caprice. There must also be "a degree of daylight to make us see," [79] or we shall see nothing. It is true that each must see "with his own private eyes," but he must see *something*, and "by a common light." [80] Can we expect the eye to be its own sunshine?

Such is Berkeley's interpretation of the Protestant Reformation, which he took to be the assertion of a concrete reason, conscious of its "realistic" basis in a transcendent norm extending beyond itself, and a concrete faith, conscious of its obligation to explain itself or, in Berkeley's own words, its "duty to try and divest [itself] of all bias whatsoever." [81] He was aware of the extreme difficulty of maintaining the delicate equilibrium between the two, the danger, which must always attend the

[72] *Ibid.*, p. 522.　　[76] *Ibid.*, p. 522.　　[79] *Ibid.*
[73] *Ibid.*, p. 525.　　[77] *Ibid.*, p. 524.　　[80] *Ibid.*, p. 524.
[74] *Ibid.*, pp. 525, 526.　[78] *Ibid.*, p. 522.　　[81] *Ibid.*, p. 525.
[75] *Ibid.*, p. 526.

Reformation, of falling into blind faith, or more especially of falling into its opposite, blind reason. He saw that the absolute faith to which his scepticism had led him could become a truly rational or Protestant faith only by becoming intelligible or philosophical, and it was to this attempt that he devoted the last years of his reflective life.

There was all the more need of haste in this undertaking, as he knew that he had not long to live. "The years I have lived," he writes, "the pains I have taken, and the distempers I labour under, make me suspect I have not long to live." [82] The intensity with which he devoted himself to philosophical studies did not, however, prevent him from taking the keenest joy in his family. In a letter to his friend Johnson, he speaks of the "star-like beauty" of his daughter Julia, and he was especially fond of his son William, who had "a particularly uncommon affection" for his father. He also entertained many friends of the family at Cloyne. Isaac Gervais, the good-humoured Huguenot divine, who had settled in Waterford, seems to have been a frequent visitor. In spite of these domestic affairs, and his philanthropic medical work among the poor, he had much leisure for those "transcendental" speculations which finally found their embodiment in the Siris, the last, as it is the most difficult, though at the same time the most decisive statement of Berkeley's philosophy.

THE BACKGROUND OF THE SIRIS. CREDO UT INTELLEGAM

The Siris, through its breadth of scope and its chronological position, is the only one of Berkeley's works which may even pretend to be a statement of that first philosophy towards which his thought and life were carrying him. But so vast is the scene of these speculations, and so dim the light through which our earthly vision is asked at many points to penetrate, that the Siris itself, as Berkeley constantly reminds us, cannot be considered anything more than a series of "hints to awaken and exercise the inquisitive reader." [83] Such is the vagueness of Berkeley's method and the obscurity of its object that many of his modern commentators have dismissed the Siris altogether as a senile aberration. It must be granted that this easy course is preferable to an over-simple and over-confident interpretation. Nevertheless the Siris, as the last published statement

[82] J. J., F. iv, p. 533.　　　　[83] Siris, sec. 350.

of Berkeley's maturity, cannot be passed over without at least a struggle to wring meaning from the apparent confusion of its sentences. Before passing directly to this task, however, it will be advisable to review briefly the course taken by Berkeley's reflections up to this critical point, in order to focus all available light upon what must be viewed as the climax of his speculative endeavours. There can be no better commentator upon an obscure work than the author himself, and the *Siris*, if it is to be understood at all, can be understood only in the light of the earlier writings and the course of development which is embodied in them.

"I could wish," wrote Berkeley to his disciple, "that all the things I have published on these philosophical subjects were read in the order wherein I published them." [84] A comprehension of the development here indicated is peculiarly necessary for the understanding of the *Siris*. This development, as we have attempted to show, was dictated by the underlying purpose of grasping things as they really are in themselves, or concretely. This purpose led Berkeley at first through sensualism and the various phases of abstract rationalism which are to be found in the writings of his early Trinity College days. They culminate in the discovery of a speculative absolute, in the third dialogue between Hylas and Philonous, which is the foundation for a scepticism that leads him beyond the theoretical realm altogether to pragmatism, practical philosophy, and finally the faith into which such practical philosophy must resolve itself. All truly practical philosophy is founded upon scepticism, and it is Berkeley's various attempts to discover the real or concrete meaning of scepticism with which we have been concerned in the last few chapters. Berkeley's conclusion is, as we have seen, that the true meaning of scepticism is to be found only in the absolute. Practical philosophy ends, as it begins, in faith.

Perhaps the most obvious feature of Berkeley's *Siris* is that it is a return to reason and metaphysics on a grand scale. Does this, then, represent an abandonment of practical philosophy, and a relapse into the eighteenth century dogmatism of the *Principles?* It is equally apparent, once this question is asked, that it cannot be answered in the affirmative. The "reason" to which Berkeley is now once more trusting himself is very different from the "reason" of the *Principles*. It is a reason

[84] Letter to Johnson, March 24, 1730.

chastened by the scepticism of Rhode Island and the *Alciphron*, and humbled not so much by its failure as by the success which lies in its transformation into practical philosophy. The reality to which it now directs itself is no longer the "given" reality of common sense, which may be proved, and used, and passed aside, but transcendent norms, or "Divine Ideas," of which "the most refined human intellect, exerted to its utmost reach, can only seize some imperfect glimpses." [85]

There is not a word of the *Siris* that does not breathe the spirit of scepticism, and it is, indeed, only by embodying this scepticism in itself as one of its moments that Berkeley's thought is able to rise to speculative heights untouched by his earlier dogmatic treatises. His concrete logic has at last become conscious of itself as practical activity, guided by norms or ideals neither given nor existent, but transcendent or absolute in character. The apprehension of such norms can come only through practice. This is the final result of Berkeley's experiments with sceptical or practical philosophy. He has now become conscious of the normative character of reflection, as well as of all action, since reflection itself is "active" or normative in character. What else is capable of negating every theoretic "position" or "result," save the speculative absolute or norm? What else is capable of negating every practical achievement, every finite character, save the norm or absolute of practice? It is the absolute faith engendered by such scepticism that lies at the basis of the rationalism of the *Siris*. Rational self-consciousness has a dual aspect. The first and more obvious aspect is negation, but this is justified or completed only by the correlative affirmation that lies at the basis of the *Siris*.

This affirmation, however, is quite opposed to the dogmatic assertion of first principles from which "theorems" are "deduced." Such a method is impossible for philosophy, as Berkeley's criticism of "mathematical science" has enabled him to see. The more certain such demonstrations become, the more uncertain become the first premises upon which they rest; the more analytic the deduction, the more synthetic the "inductive" or dogmatic content required to give it meaning. Induction is the inevitable curse that follows in the train of deduction, making both an easy prey to scepticism. To abstract or separate analysis from synthesis in this fashion is to reduce the former to tautology and the latter to caprice. Unless the premisses can be absorbed into the argument, so that the deduction may be said to provide itself with its own premisses as it proceeds, there can be no such thing as "certainty," for scepticism may always be trusted to show that abstract deduction is a meaningless game, and that induction or synthesis without the analytic moment is arbitrary dogmatism. Unless we come to terms with such scepticism before we begin, unless we incorporate it in our thought as an essential element, it will revenge itself upon us from outside. There is not a single assertion in Berkeley's *Siris* which is not rendered undogmatic through the consciousness of its dogmatism, or which is not absolutized through the consciousness of its relativity, not an assertion which is not at once corrected by becoming more than what it first purported to be, or which is not forced by its latent scepticism to something else.

The method of the *Siris*, therefore, is no longer the direct affirmative method of mathematics, but the indirect method of assertion through negation. It proceeds not by unconsciously asserting something and then, when it is too late, attempting, by a deduction, to discover what has already been asserted. It stands still at no point. It advances, not by making a series of gratuitous leaps, but "by insensible transitions," [86] by "transitions," that is, which are at the same time not transitions at all, since the end is already present at the beginning, and the analysis develops through synthesis. A principle is asserted only to be negated, for truth lies rather in the passage or "transition" from one such arbitrary and therefore erroneous starting point to another. It is only *through* "the veils of prejudice and error" which are "singly taken off one by one" [87] that we may "glimpse" the truth, only *through* abstract affirmation, corrected by sceptical negation, that we may advance in understanding. It is "through erroneous principles, and long ambages of words and notions" that we may "struggle upwards into the light." [88]

What, then, is to be our guide in this "struggle"; what is to be the motive spring of that scepticism which negates all notions, as "long ambages of words," and leads us "by insensible transitions" beyond all "erroneous principles"? What is its norm? What else can this be save something beyond all theoretical principles whatsoever, something beyond any conceivable sort of beyondness? What else can this be save the

---

[86] *Ibid.*, sec. 297.   [87] *Ibid.*, sec. 296.   [88] *Ibid.*

absolute itself, and how may the absolute be humanly approached save through faith? The scepticism which guides the transitions of the *Siris* is, therefore, the absolute scepticism of faith, and he avoids the rationalistic dilemma of the premiss by starting with the absolute as his premiss. He avoids the rationalistic necessity of starting with an illegitimate assumption by starting with an absolutely illegitimate assumption, so illegitimate as to be beyond the scope of reason altogether, and therefore neither legitimate nor illegitimate. He presupposes nothing because he presupposes everything. Philosophers complain that a treatise on metaphysics should begin with a discussion of the laws of logic, or the limits of human knowledge, or at least something universal and profound. Berkeley begins his metaphysics with a discussion of tar-water.

"Profundity" and "rigour" he now gladly leaves to him "who professedly delivers the elements of a science" and who is, therefore, "more obliged to method and system, and tied down to more rigorous laws, than a mere essay writer." [89] He asks, therefore, to "be pardoned if this rude Essay may draw the reader into remote inquiries and speculations that were not perhaps thought of either by him or by the author at first setting out." [90] He would gladly join those who have smiled at the attempt to introduce a metaphysical tract with oil and turpentine. What beginning could be more ridiculous, — and what less? Is there any beginning that is not arbitrary and hence illegitimate? Berkeley's answer to this predicament of the *raisonneur* is to begin with what is before all beginnings and beyond all reasoning, that which can be grasped only with the aid of faith, though more than faith is required for its comprehension. It is the taking up of faith into itself as one of its own moments which distinguishes the *Siris* from all his earlier works, as well as most of the works of the eighteenth century. It is not that these works did not also require faith, for how else does one acquire first premisses or beginnings? Faith cannot be attacked save through a counter-faith. How can one "argue" at all save upon premisses? The difference is that Berkeley has taken his premisses into his argument, that he has absorbed faith or scepticism into his reasoning, every step of which moves, so to speak, between the affirmative pole of faith and the negative pole of scepticism. The faith of the *Siris* is a self-conscious faith that is at last aware of itself and its furthest im-

[89] *Ibid.*, sec. 297.   [90] *Ibid.*

plications, and is, therefore, something more than faith, while the faith of the rationalist, the faith of the *Principles*, is something hidden behind an array of arguments, something existing in isolation, and hence not truly faith, but only an assumption, a postulate, a presupposition, or induction. It is this self-conscious presence of the absolute element in Berkeley's *Siris* that lends it its peculiar irony, and which is responsible for certain doctrinal features that seem to be in the most direct contradiction to the very spirit of his earlier writings, and which we must now briefly note.

The first and most important result of the actual incorporation of faith or scepticism into his method of thought is a complete change in Berkeley's attitude to history. He starts out in the *Commonplace Book* as an innovator, an "upstart," not pinning his "faith on the sleeve of any great man," [91] and full of cynical scorn for the "absurdities" of "the several sects of philosophy." [92] "I am inclined to think," says the young author of the *Principles*, "that the far greater part, if not all, of those difficulties which have hitherto amused philosophers, and blocked up the way to knowledge, are entirely owing to ourselves. We have first raised a dust, and then complain we cannot see." [93] All that is necessary is solid reflection upon new principles, and the house will be set in order. "My purpose, therefore, is to try if I can discover what those Principles are which have introduced all that doubtfulness and uncertainty, those absurdities and contradictions into the several sects of philosophy." [94]

The light of reason is like a fire that destroys everything it approaches, until, having burned away all obscurities, it consumes itself. Berkeley, having lived through this consummation of reason, and having realized concretely its meaning, is no longer able to abandon himself to it with the enthusiasm of his youth. His reason, having been humbled before its norm, is now capable of humbling itself still further before the past. It acquires, through the absolute faith that has been forced upon it, that derivative faith in the relative which is the prerequisite to all genuine historical study. "The successful curiosity of the present age," says the author of the *Siris*, "in arts, and experiments, and new systems, is apt to elate men, and make them overlook the Ancients . . . yet it must be owned that the an-

[91] C. B. J., 464.
[92] Pr. Int., sec. 4.
[93] *Ibid.*, sec. 3.
[94] *Ibid.*, sec. 4.

cients too were not ignorant of many things as well in physics as metaphysics, which perhaps are more generally, though not first, known in these modern times." [95]

Berkeley, indeed, goes even farther, for there is an actual superiority to be found in ancient thought, which was "not overlaid with languages and literature . . . more exercised and less burdened than in later ages." [96] Historic study is a leap into the unknown, and more perhaps, than any other discipline, requires that sort of creative imagination which arises only from the implicit faith of self-abnegation. The realism of pure transcendence is the gateway to history, for as long as one is committed to the rigid structure of his own dogmatic thought-scheme, one can gain no real appreciation for the past. Confirmed scepticism is the absolute prerequisite for any historian of philosophy. This prerequisite Berkeley now possessed, and he was enabled thereby enormously to widen the panorama of his reflections, and to enrich them through a vital contact with the thought of the past. No longer does the history of philosophy appear to him, as it must to any rationalist, as a strange series of "absurdities and contradictions," but as a living, growing tradition, the truth and profundity of which lies precisely in its transcendence of any fixed formulation. The truth of the history of philosophy lies not in any one of the "systems" in which it has at certain times expressed itself, but precisely in its passage or "transition" from one such crystallization to another. A "final" crystallization or "agreement" of thought would be its death. Berkeley is thus able, at last, to read the history of thought with intelligence, not as a set of abstract fragments, but as a single growth, or "divine tradition, θεοπαράδοτος φιλοσοφία." [97] The consequences of this faith in the past are of the highest importance in understanding Berkeley's later reflections.

The absolute *credo* of the *Siris* is like a lantern which he holds before himself, and in the light of which his reason is then able to make out the contours of many dim regions hitherto unexplored. If this light first enables his thought to penetrate into the obscurer depths of the history of philosophy, and thus leads him to reverse his earlier rationalistic attitude to the difficulties and "contradictions" of the ancients, it has a no less striking effect upon his attitude towards the world of nature. This world had been, for his earlier speculations, nothing but a thin

<hr>

[95] *Siris*, sec. 265.   [96] *Ibid.*, sec. 298.   [97] *Ibid.*, sec. 301.

veil separating him from the reality lying beyond it, a web of symbolic shadows with no inherent meaning of their own. It is even a question whether, in view of his earlier phenomenalism, Berkeley could speak meaningfully of "nature" at all. In the *Siris*, however, we find him referring with perfect confidence to a realm of nature, and elaborating a philosophy of nature which has impressed almost all commentators as a glaring "contradiction" to the subjectivism of the earlier works.[98]

Of Berkeley's spiritism there are, indeed, in the *Siris* only a few vestigial traces. As we have attempted to show, this "contradiction" dissolves into intelligibility once we have penetrated through the various rigid positions or disguises assumed by Berkeley's method at different stages in his thought to the dynamic logic or method itself. This logic not only forced him to reduce matter to appearance, but, as we have noted, forced him to the next step, the reduction of appearance itself to appearance, of phenomenalism itself to phenomenality.[99] Spiritism was destined to go the way of matter, as was thought or rationality itself, and even the practical irrationality lying beyond it. Independent substantiality is to be discovered neither in rational philosophy nor in practical philosophy, but beyond them both in an absolute apprehended by faith alone. It is only through the negation of everything else that this absolute may be glimpsed with the eyes of faith. But once glimpsed, the previous negations become affirmations. The world of nature is an appearance lacking substantiality. But, as an appearance *of* the absolute it no less certainly possesses it. The approach to the absolute is possible only through negation, but recession from the absolute is positive through its source.

With the absolute justification of faith, one may dare to be a realist, and it is as a realist, even as a materialist, that Berkeley speaks in the *Siris*. It is only because of his idealism, however, that he dares to be a realist, only because of his absolute idealism that he dares at last to be a materialist. As the pure potentiality *of* actuality, even matter, the "something I know not what," the bare "quiddity" of the earlier writings, receives a perfectly justifiable minimum of meaning. The symbolism of sense, even as such, is not a curtain of shadows, but a rational discourse, the last components of which are saturated with in-

---

[98] Cf. especially *ibid.*, sec. 190, where he refers to "this whole natural world *in which we subsist*" (my italics).

[99] Cf. chap. VI.

telligibility, for even the meaningless bears meaning. Thus, while it is absurd to think of natural philosophy as philosophy, naturalism is as legitimate a construction as spiritism, and one has as much right to speculate concerning nature as concerning spirit. It is not surprising, therefore, that most of the *Siris* is taken up with the construction of a natural philosophy in its own right as the necessary complement to the spiritism of his early works. This construction is natural philosophy, not merely an accurate picture of the world, but an examination into the *meaning* underlying nature, a study of "the whole series of things in this visible world," [100] in an attempt to distil out of it the "rules" or "structure" that is "necessary to make the world intelligible." [101]

This is what distinguishes the natural philosopher from the naturalist, or philosophic scientist, who is content with the establishment of sequences, who is content, in Berkeley's language, with the "grammar" [102] of nature, without reading between the lines, or in any way discovering their meaningful content. The philosophic naturalist, like the philosophic historian, can never be content with sequences. He must struggle farther in the attempt to discover the meaning inherent in all nature as in all history. He must, therefore, when studying history, study much more than history, and when studying nature, study much more than nature, for meaning always extends beyond itself. Meaning can never be confined, but slips through all definitions. It is to be apprehended only through comparison and contrast, never through direct assertion. It asserts only indirectly by denial, and negates by assertion. It can never be given through any external inlet, nor can it be "given" at all, for its source is the infinite completion of itself, or the λόγος, which is self-contemplation or act. There is no means of comprehending or understanding save through intelligibility itself, which is active thought or "notion." It matters not how clearly or succinctly or cogently a thing may be presented, or given, or defined. It will nevertheless be misunderstood if there be no active key to unlock its meaning. This meaning can never be exclusively a passive content. It is always more than whatever is or can be given. Meaning can never be exhausted. It is infinite, and yet self-contained.

The first result of Berkeley's discovery of the meaning of scepticism is the attempt of the *Siris* to penetrate, by means of

[100] *Siris*, sec. 255.   [101] *Ibid.*, sec. 256.   [102] *Ibid.*, sec. 252.

faith, to the meaning of history, to think through history not unintelligibly, as a mere sequence, but intelligibly as a judge (ἵστωρ). The second result is his attempt to build a philosophy of nature, not a given structure of law, for even should all natural laws be at last fitted into one such orderly, given structure, the question of its meaning would still remain unanswered. Underlying both the philosophy of history, as well as the philosophy of nature, there is something more fundamental, philosophy in itself, or first philosophy. The *Siris* is, above all, an attempt to explore the field of *philosophia prima*, and "when we enter the field of *philosophia prima* we discover another order of beings — mind and its acts; permanent being; not dependent on corporeal things; nor resulting, nor connected, nor contained, but containing, connecting, enlivening the whole frame. . . ." [103] The last and most essential achievement of Berkeley's experiments with scepticism is the justification of reason itself, or the speculative absolute which is presupposed by everything whatsoever, which permeates all reality, including reality itself, with its invisible, incorruptible threads of meaning, "nor resulting, nor connected, nor contained, but containing, connecting, enlivening the whole frame."

It is the return to this standpoint, which is no standpoint, the speculative absolute of the *Three Dialogues*, "the infinite Mind of God,"[104] that, above all else, distinguishes the philosophy of Berkeley's *Siris*, though there is now no danger of his confusing this with the absolute itself. In addition to "an universal Mind, enlightening and ordering all things . . . there is also τὸ Ἕν or τ'Ἀγαθόν . . . the *Fons Deitatis*. . . ."[105] Prior to the speculative absolute of reason there is the absolute; prior to the second hypostasis there is the first; above the λόγος τὸ Ἕν. It is only because it is founded upon that which is beyond all reason, as it is beyond all unreason, that the *Siris* is enabled to manifest itself as philosophy. Berkeley's thought, having penetrated to what must be finally referred to as ἄνους and ἄλογος,[106] is able to read and interpret with the eye of faith the revelation of the λόγος, which does not result, since it is the source of all resulting, which is not connected, because it is connection itself, and which is not contained, for no matter how vast a system may be supposed, it cannot be supposed to contain its meaning. No matter how far forward we travel, meaning will still be before

[103] *Ibid.*, sec. 293.   [105] *Siris*, sec. 341.
[104] F. i, p. 452.   [106] *Ibid.*, sec. 352.

us; no matter how far back we travel, meaning will still be back of us. Hovering over all real things as the essence of reality, underlying all questions, lies meaning itself, or the λόγος.

It is the light of the λόγος which Berkeley attempts in the *Siris* to focus upon the fleeting sequences of history and nature. Having destroyed the world by scepticism, he is able to reconstruct it by faith. That which in abstraction or isolation is the death of negation becomes in the hands of the absolute, as the *second* hypostasis, the "cause," or the life of creation. Having negated all reality in his early works, having discovered the absolute power of reflection, he is now able to use this negative power to affirm reality. Logic, which, if left to itself, consumes all things in the fire of scepticism, as the λόγος, meaning, or revelation, becomes the source of all creation and affirmation.

CHAPTER XVI

THE SIRIS

THE *Siris* is neither the statement of a "position" nor a "view of the world" nor even a "philosophy" in the ordinary sense of this word, but the record of a struggle. Indeed, to anyone who has followed with any care the process of Berkeley's progressive disillusionment with respect to his early psychologism, it is quite evident why he should prefer to cloak the "results" of his life of reflection in the form of a few pages of comment upon several ancient authors, appended to a treatise concerned primarily with the cathartic virtues of tar-water. To anyone, therefore, expecting a "system," or at least a few definite "points" summing up Berkeley's conclusions, his final philosophic treatise must prove a disappointment. The aphorisms of the *Siris* embody, it is true, all the results of his earlier reflections, but they complete and fulfill these earlier thoughts in the same manner in which the outermost circle of a panorama completes what lies within. In this sense, the *Siris* was always present to Berkeley's reflection, from the rude intuitions of the *Commonplace Book* to the strict methodological queries of the *Analyst*. Berkeley's last work carries within itself all the stages we have attempted to trace, but it has to be understood, if at all, not so much as a single, inclusive system, as the transition from one such system to another, not so much contemplation or theory as that struggle through theory in which Berkeley's reflective life essentially expressed itself.

We find in the *Siris* not so much a new stage or "conclusion" as a correction of past stages brought about by this struggle, not so much a different philosophy as the philosophy of these philosophies. "Truth," says Berkeley, "is the cry of all, but the game of a few. Certainly where it is the chief passion, it doth not give way to vulgar cares and views; nor is it contented with a little ardour in the early time of life; active, perhaps, to pursue, but not so fit to weigh and revise." [1] The *Siris* is the weighing and revision lying implicit all the while in the more reckless intuitions of his youth. His thought, which began with the inchoate perceptions of the *Commonplace Book*, lying on the

---

[1] *Siris*, sec. 368.

border-line between sensation and reflection, now ends with an intuition which is also inchoate, though for a very different reason. He now recognizes the intermediate realm which he himself has traversed as the field of reason or the λόγος, an actuality still cursed with potentiality, a dualism inveterately haunted by the ideal One which alone makes it possible. This mediate character of reflection is referred to again and again. Thought, he says, must begin in a "low situation," peering vaguely "through the dusk of a gross atmosphere, gathered from wrong judgments daily passed, false opinions daily learned, and early habits of an older date than either judgment or opinion," [2] a "dusky region" of "darkness and dreams." [3] Nevertheless it is possible for the mind, "reaching on and struggling," to gain some foothold in an "upper region." [4] Here the mind shakes off its "slumber" and emancipates itself "from those prejudices and false opinions that so straitly beset and cling" to it and regains a sense of "truth and intellectual ideas." [5]

It is not difficult to recognize in this description the advance which is so pregnantly suggested in the *Commonplace Book* and so definitely made actual in the early writings, from a rationalism obscured by sensualism, subjectivism, and spiritism, to the pure rationalism of the third dialogue between Hylas and Philonous. It is not difficult to recognize in the further struggle upwards towards that which "is not the light that enlightens, but the source of that light," since "even truth and knowledge are not the good itself," [6] the traces of that ripening scepticism which led him beyond the speculative totality of the intelligible world to the Absolute itself. It is only "then" that we "perceive the true principle of unity, identity, and existence." [7]

To one who has made such an ascent, says Berkeley, "those things that before seemed to constitute the whole of Being . . . prove to be but fleeting phantoms." [8] Such a one "beholds things in a new light and in a new order," and will "change his system and perceive that what he took for substances and causes are but fleeting shadows." [9] The *Siris* incorporates this dual "change" of "system," which is not only a passage from one system to another, but a passage beyond all systems to that which makes them possible, and for which they become only

[2] *Ibid.*, sec. 340.   [5] *Ibid.*, sec. 314.   [8] *Ibid.*
[3] *Ibid.*   [6] *Ibid.*, sec. 343.   [9] *Ibid.*, sec. 295.
[4] *Ibid.*, sec. 341.   [7] *Ibid.*, sec. 294.

"fleeting phantoms." But though they are bound together by a certain "Chain" (σειρά) which welds them into absolute unity, they remain, nevertheless, distinct. "There runs a Chain throughout the whole system of beings. In this Chain one link drags another. The meanest things are connected with the highest." [10] As "air becomes igneous, so the purest fire becomes animal, and the animal soul becomes intellectual: which is to be understood not of the change of one nature into another but of the connection of different natures." [11]

It is not difficult to see that what thus comes to such explicit formulation is nothing but Berkeley's "concrete" logic, the "mental mode of reasoning" of which he spoke in the *Commonplace Book* and which finally led him away from his spiritism as inexorably as it had earlier led him into it. The Chain which gathers the disparate elements into a single unity, and binds the lowest together with the highest, is the *Siris*, concrete logic, or pure thought. Emerging from the chaos of potentiality, it passes through all systems, and finally beyond itself.

The Sources of the Siris

We have already noted the world-weariness which emerges from the later criticisms of rationalism, in which Berkeley came to terms with the thought of his own time not only in the realms of mathematics and natural science, but also in the speculative fields of moral and religious philosophy. He continued to speak of the enemy opposing him in all these fields as "the mechanical philosophy," [12] though he no longer thought of substituting any other dogmatic system, such as the spiritism of the *Principles*, in its place. He now realizes that what he was opposing was no particular system, nor moral code, but a logic, a state of mind, the spirit of the age which, "by engrossing men's thoughts and fixing their minds on corporeal objects, and the laws of motion," had at last fundamentally "indisposed them for spiritual, moral, and intellectual matters." [13] He now conceives the dogmatic rationalism of the free-thinkers as a fixation of spirit which, if carried far enough, might make it impossible for a truly "modern" mind to find any refuge from itself. He refers to this sterilization of imagination as "Fatalism and Sadducism," [14] and identifies it as that same paralysis of spirit which

---

[10] *Ibid.*, sec. 303.　　　　[12] *Ibid.*, sec. 331.　　　　[14] *Ibid.*

[11] *Ibid.*, sec. 274.　　　　[13] *Ibid.*

leads modern men to "think themselves too wise" to learn [15] from any extraneous source, and leads them finally to a spiritual narcissism in comparison with which conscious dogmatism is a form of insight.

Berkeley, therefore, makes no claim to a systematic discussion which would inevitably move in the atmosphere he is combating. It is not the modern arguments which he is now opposing so much as the sense of self-sufficiency lying back of them, and in the attempt to find some method of suggesting an antithesis profound enough to stir the modern spirit to self-consciousness and imaginative life, he takes the only possible course of falling back upon the past. The extent of his dissatisfaction with the whole tone of the Enlightenment, in which his own reflections had taken root, is indicated by the fact that it is not the immediate past nor even the mediaeval past to which he turns in his despair, but to the very earliest thought of the western world, for "in these days the depths of that old learning are rarely fathomed." [16] Perhaps in this old learning may be found sparks of wisdom struck from an altogether different source, and therefore possibly capable of furnishing the antithesis he sought. The *Siris* is hence a running exposition and commentary to "the notions of the great men of antiquity." [17]

For the last twenty years of his life, Berkeley steeped himself in Greek philosophy, and the results of his study show the intensity of his concentration, and in many particular respects, a depth of insight which is quite remarkable when contrasted with the then prevailing superficiality of historical study in philosophy. An adequate understanding of the *Siris* is rendered difficult not only by the unique character of the work, and the absence of any philosophic exegesis with which it may be compared, but by the general lack of interest in the treatise itself since Berkeley's time. Aside from the preliminary researches of Campbell Fraser,[18] and the notes contained in the German edition of the *Siris*,[19] there are practically no textual studies to

[15] *Ibid.*
[16] *Ibid.*, sec. 332.
[17] *Ibid.*
[18] Fraser is the only one of Berkeley's English commentators who has recognized the importance of the *Siris* as a metaphysical work. His textual notes in volume three of Berkeley's works are often of great aid in tracking down Berkeley's sources. In many cases, however, he neglects to mention the specific editions of the ancient authors to whom he refers, and many of the texts which he cites have been superseded since his time. There are, furthermore, many source problems with which he does not attempt to deal.

[19] *Siris übersetzt und herausgegeben von Luise Raab und Dr. Friedrich Raab*, Meiner, 1913, pp. 121 ff. These notes generally follow Fraser.

which an interpreter may refer. The result is that one wishing to gain a grasp of the meaning of the work must possess not only some first-hand knowledge of the ancient texts but also some knowledge of the texts available in the eighteenth century. It has been necessary, therefore, to burden the following discussion with an unwieldy mass of source material not hitherto made readily available for students of Berkeley. It is quite essential to have the original passages cited by him and their ultimate sources in mind, in order to comprehend the delicate and detailed criticism to which he subjects this material, and which he often embodied in his paraphrase or translation of the text.

As his studies proceeded, it seemed to him that he discerned in the history of Greek reflection a development at least vaguely resembling that of his own youth, from a sensuous to a more purely rational way of thought, from idea to "notion," from cosmology to epistemology. He even saw a parallel between the period of the Greek Enlightenment and the Enlightenment of his own day, which he had combated all his life, but which had also determined the form of his opposition. Most eagerly of all, therefore, he studied the later phases of Greek speculation wherein he seemed to recognize not only a fulfilment and transcendence of the Enlightenment, but also many of the answers he had himself more dimly intuited, to the sceptical questions which had carried his own speculations beyond the limits of any abstract rationalism. We must now undertake a more detailed examination of these stages of Greek speculation, in the hope of understanding more clearly the manner in which Berkeley was able to project his own thought into them, and theirs into his, until the historical judgment ($\ddot{\iota}\sigma\tau\omega\rho$) led him, in the final phases of the *Siris*, enormously to broaden and deepen the channels of his own philosophy.

THE PRE-SOCRATICS

Berkeley's knowledge of the Pre-Socratic philosophers was gained chiefly from the *De Placitis Philosophorum* ($\pi\epsilon\rho\grave{\iota}\ \tau\hat{\omega}\nu$ $\dot{\alpha}\rho\epsilon\sigma\kappa\acute{o}\nu\tau\omega\nu\ \phi\iota\lambda o\sigma\acute{o}\phi o\iota s\ \phi\nu\sigma\iota\kappa\hat{\omega}\nu\ \delta o\gamma\mu\acute{\alpha}\tau\omega\nu$), which was at that time attributed to Plutarch, and the philosophical biographies of Diogenes Laertius ($\pi\epsilon\rho\grave{\iota}\ \beta\acute{\iota}\omega\nu\ \delta o\gamma\mu\acute{\alpha}\tau\omega\nu\ \kappa\alpha\grave{\iota}\ \dot{\alpha}\pi o\phi\theta\epsilon\gamma\mu\acute{\alpha}\tau\omega\nu\ \tau\hat{\omega}\nu\ \dot{\epsilon}\nu\ \phi\iota\lambda o$-$\sigma o\phi\acute{\iota}\alpha\ \epsilon\dot{\nu}\delta o\kappa\iota\mu\eta\sigma\acute{\alpha}\nu\tau\omega\nu\ \beta\iota\beta\lambda\acute{\iota}\alpha\ \delta\acute{\epsilon}\kappa\alpha$).[20] Berkeley knew both of these

[20] Cf. Leigh and Sotheby cat.

works with considerable accuracy, and cites them frequently.[21]
He was also, of course, acquainted with Book A of Aristotle's
Metaphysics and with the compilations of Stobaeus.[22] He refers
to the latter, however, only in connection with later Pythagorean philosophy.[23] Berkeley was aware of the relative inaccuracy of these sources [24] and of the necessity for critical interpretation. On the whole, when allowance is made for the condition
of historical study in his day, the picture of Pre-Socratic philosophy which he was finally able to construct was remarkably
accurate.

Greek philosophy, as Berkeley interpreted it, began with reflection upon "things sensible and natural." [25] The mind, insufficiently conscious of itself and its logic, tended to hypostatize everything, including itself and its own concepts, into
natural entities of some sort. Thus, while "Thales held the
mind of the world to be God," [26] he did not sharply distinguish
mind from the world, or rather he thought of mind as a material
substance. Berkeley hence classifies this view with the tenet of
Democritus, who is reputed to have "held the soul of the world
to be an igniform deity," [27] and saw in the advance of Greek
speculation the gradual separation of the two factors from the
original amalgam in which they were intermixed. The natural
or sensible aspect finally crystallized into the purely mechanical
"Democritic hypothesis," [28] and the mental or logical aspect
was at least isolated from its earlier spatial associations in the
concepts of φιλία and νεῖκος as maintained by Empedocles in
contradistinction to the στοιχεῖα,[29] and even from its psychological context in the concept of νοῦς distinguished from ὕλη, as
maintained by Anaxagoras. Berkeley insists that the φιλία of
Empedocles "is no blind principle but acts with intellect," [30]
and that "Anaxagoras ascribed the motive faculty to mind." [31]

[21] Diogenes Laertius in secs. 166, 211.
Plutarch in secs. 168, 268, 272, 273.
[22] L. and S. cat., no. 225.
[23] The reference to Ocellus Lucanus in sec. 279 is *ultimately* derived from Stobaeus, *Eclogae*, as Fraser states (iii, p. 258 n.), but from *Ecl.*, I, 13, 2, *not* I, 16. Berkeley, however, may have gained this information from some modern compen-dium such as the *Opuscula Mythologica*, Amstelaedami, 1688, which contained a large number of Ocellus fragments, includ-ing that from the *Laws* (p. 537).

[24] Cf. *Siris*, secs. 168, 211, 268.
[25] *Ibid.*, sec. 348.
[26] *Ibid.*, sec. 322; cf. *De Placitis Phil.*, I, 7, and Diels, *Vorsokratiker*, 4th ed., I, p. 12, fr. 23.
[27] *Ibid.*, sec. 322; *Plac.*, I, 7; cf. Diels, *Vors.*, II, p. 29, fr. 74.
[28] *Ibid.*, sec. 251; cf. 273.
[29] *Ibid.*, sec. 259; cf. *Plac.*, I, 3.
[30] *Ibid.*
[31] *Ibid.*, sec. 320; cf. *Plac.*, I, 3, and Diog. Laert., II, 6.

Berkeley realizes, however, that the distinction was still imperfect, for Empedocles views his φιλία as a "natural" or "sensible" force,[32] and Anaxagoras' νοῦς is, in the end, confused with a mechanical principle. The general tendency to select fire as a divine principle in nature deeply impressed the author of the *Siris*. Berkeley cites in this connection Democritus,[33] Heraclitus,[34] Empedocles,[35] Hippasos,[36] and the "Pythagorean philosophers," [37] and traces the theory back from Heraclitus to Hippasos,[38] and from Hippasos to Pythagoras, and from Pythagoras to Egypt, where he "had travelled." [39] Berkeley also remarked upon the tendency to identify fire with air (αἰθήρ).[40] These doctrines, especially as interpreted by the Neo-Pythagorean and Neo-Platonic writers, influenced Berkeley in the formulation of his own philosophy of nature, although he was careful not to confuse the original moving principle with its fiery vehicle or instrument.[41] While this very confusion of nature and logic, of matter and mind, led to the identification of Providence with blind fate, as in Empedocles,[42] it tended, on the other hand, towards the purification of the original conception of matter. Hence Berkeley is able to discover in the ἄπειρον of Anaximander the forerunner of Aristotle's materia prima, a "*pura potentia*, a mere possibility," [43] not what the moderns call matter, neither qualitative nor quantitative but "no more than infinite or indefinite." [44] The unconscious mixture of physics with logic which characterized the Pre-Socratics, while it had a most wholesome effect upon their natural philosophy, corrupted their metaphysics and logic.

Berkeley viewed Parmenides, however, as an important exception to this tendency, and, following Plotinus [45] and Plato himself,[46] identified the great Eleatic as the forerunner of a new

[32] *Ibid.*, sec. 348.

[33] *Ibid.*, sec. 322; cf. *Plac.*, I, 7.

[34] *Ibid.*, sec. 177; cf. *Plac.*, I, 3.

[35] "If we may credit Plutarch, Empedocles thought aether or heat to be Jupiter." *Ibid.*, sec. 168; cf. *Plac.*, I, 3.

[36] *Ibid.*, sec. 177; cf. *Plac.*, I, 3.

[37] *Ibid.*, sec. 211.

[38] Heraclitus and Hippasos are mentioned together by Aristotle, *Meta.*, A, 984a. Cf., however, *Plac.*, I, 3, and Diels, *Vors.*, I, p. 36, fr. 1a (Suidas).

[39] *Ibid.*, sec. 177. Cf. Isocr., *Bus.*, 28; Diels, *Vors.*, I, p. 28, fr. 4.

[40] *Ibid.*, sec. 168. For Empedocles cf.

Plac., I, 3 (Diels, *Vors.*, I, p. 205, no. 33), and for Anaxagoras cf. Xenophon, *Mem.* (Diels, *Vors.*, I, p. 392, no. 73).

[41] *Ibid.*, sec. 280 *et passim*.

[42] *Ibid.*, sec. 271.

[43] *Ibid.*, sec. 318.

[44] *Ibid.*

[45] *Enneades*, 5, 1, 8, ed. Creuzer, 489c: " Ἥπτετο μὲν οὖν καὶ Παρμενίδης πρότερον τῆς τοιαύτης δόξης, καθ' ὅσον εἰς ταὐτὸ συνῆγεν ὂν καὶ νοῦν, καὶ τὸ ὂν οὐκ ἐν τοῖς αἰσθητοῖς ἐτίθετο. τὸ γὰρ αὐτὸ νοεῖν ἐστι τε καὶ εἶναι λέγων. . . . "

[46] *Parm.*, 135. 136.

logical era in philosophy. "Heraclitus, Protagoras, Empedocles," he says, "considered things sensible and natural; whereas
Parmenides and his party considered τὸ πᾶν not as the sensible
but as the intelligible world, abstracted from all sensible
things." [47] Berkeley sees in Parmenides [48] not the representative of a corporeal monism, nor of any sort of pantheism, but
first and foremost the discoverer of the "intelligible" or "intellectual world." [49] Parmenides, with the aid of Pythagoreanism,
first [50] freed thought from the trammels of sensualism. What we
commonly call things are not really things at all, "being in a
constant change, ever perishing and producing." [51] Reflecting
upon the inner meaning of Parmenides' doctrine, he came to see
in it the same sort of criticism of the concept of substance which
he had himself worked out in his early writings.

Parmenides' "οὐσία," writes Berkeley, "is generally translated substance but more properly essence." [52] "Οὐσία" is not a
substance, but the essence of substantiality, the thought-form
necessarily presupposed by any corporeal or incorporeal thing.
Parmenides is thus the discoverer of the realm of essences
"which never changing are still the same, and may therefore
be said truly to exist." [53] When Parmenides, therefore, speaks
of the "One" or the "Whole," he is not using these words naively in the sense of what is ordinarily considered to be a thing,
but as "the Whole of real beings, . . . the intellectual world, not
allowing reality of being to things not permanent." [54] When it
came to the development of his great discovery, however, Parmenides, like all the Pre-Socratics, tended to fix his concepts
into static or abstract things; hence the tendency of the Eleatic
intelligible world to collapse into a fixed substance, conceived

[47] *Siris*, sec. 348.
[48] Berkeley's sources for Parmenides
were probably Arist., *Meta.*, A 986b, Diog.
Laert., and especially the Platonic *Parmenides* (cf. sec. 351), which in its entirety he seems to have regarded as of the
utmost importance not only for the understanding of Plato, but also indirectly for
the understanding of Parmenides. The
comment which Fraser finds it necessary
to make (iii, p. 291, n. 2), while it reflects
a popular view, is the direct antithesis of
what was obviously Berkeley's opinion.
Cf. sec. 348. In sec. 351 Berkeley definitely attributes to "Zeno and Parmenides" the first chain of abstract conse-

quences derived from the hypothesis of
the One in Plato's *Parmenides* (*Parm.*,
137–142), while the *concrete* discussion of
the categories (142–152) he refers simply
to the dialogue ("in the same Parmenides"). This clearly indicates the
sense in which Berkeley understood Plato
to have advanced beyond the Eleatic
dialectic of abstraction.
[49] *Siris*, sec. 349.
[50] *Ibid.*, sec. 336.
[51] *Ibid.*
[52] *Ibid.*, sec. 336. Cf. Augustine, *Civ.
Dei*, XII, 2. Berkeley knew the *Civ. Dei*
well. Cf. Alc., V, F. ii, p. 203.
[53] *Ibid.*   [54] *Ibid.*, sec. 349.

in such a way as to be analogous to a material sphere. It was in freeing the Eleatic dialectic from this tendency to fixation or abstraction that Berkeley saw (in sec. 351) the most important achievement of the Platonic *Parmenides*.

It is not that Parmenides himself applied the category of *being* dogmatically to a new set of objects, but that, by penetrating back to the pure concept, he discovered their significance. Substantiality itself is not a substance, though it is prior to the latter. Being itself cannot be supposed to exist in the ordinary sense, although what, one may ask, can be supposed to exist more truly than being itself? But being itself is grasped only in thought. Hence Parmenides' basic principle that "to understand and to be are . . . the same thing." [55] As Berkeley so acutely perceived, this is not to say that thought is the only thing that exists, in the ordinary sense of existence, as Parmenides is sometimes interpreted, i.e. idealistically, but that existence, in the true or pure sense, is to be found only in the field of meaning or intelligibility. True existence may be meant, indeed it must be meant, but it cannot be sensorially experienced, since all objects of sense are "*in fieri*" and "have no stability." [56]

This is why Berkeley is now able to set forth far more clearly and profoundly the conclusion which he had vaguely stated in the third dialogue that "God," who must be supposed to know things as they really are, "knoweth all things, as pure mind or intellect; but nothing by sense. . . ." [57] What he had dimly glimpsed as a result of his own early struggles with the concept of substance he now grasps as the ultimate and necessary presupposition of all thought. Knowledge, if it is to be truly knowledge, cannot be natural or objective in character, since any such natural explanation would already presuppose the existence of pure knowledge or intelligibility. The discovery of this field of pure meaning was first made by "that subtle metaphysician Parmenides," who thereby really inaugurated a new critical or epistemological stage in the development of Greek philosophy.

PLATO AND ARISTOTLE

Berkeley views Plato and Aristotle as the heirs of Parmenides and his discovery of the intelligible world. There are, he says, only "two sorts of philosopher," those who allow themselves

[55] *Ibid.*, sec. 309.   [56] *Ibid.*, sec. 336.   [57] *Ibid.*, sec. 289.

to be beguiled by the external surface of reality, "the flowing philosophers," and those who penetrate through the show of sense to the intelligible world and that which is "fixed and immovable." [58] He is quite aware, however, of the inaccuracy of such a metaphor as that of penetration through a veil, or any sensuous metaphor whatsoever. Such metaphors accept dogmatically the vague and incoherent concept of being which common sense attaches indiscriminately to whatever seems to confront it, whether it truly exists or not. They imply, therefore, that the sensuous veil or curtain in some sense or other exists, whereas, as Berkeley so acutely perceived, the whole meaning of Parmenides' discovery lies in the insight that "things sensible and perishing ... do not in strict truth exist at all, being always generating or *in fieri* ... without anything stable or permanent in them to constitute an object of real science." [59] The question raised by Parmenides and pursued by Plato is not the question whether we are to apply the concept of existence here or there, to this realm or that realm, but a prior question, the question of intelligibility. What does the concept itself mean? This is not to be decided by any amount of exploration or penetration in the ordinary sense. Meaning cannot be given or presented except by the λόγος itself. "Science consists not in the passive perceptions, but in the reasoning upon them, — τῷ περὶ ἐκείνων συλλογισμῷ." [60]

This insight into the nature of the world of meaning enables Berkeley at last to view his early spiritism in its proper perspective. The relativity of sense objects to a percipient is simply one example of the instability or unreality permeating all objects or "things." Hence, in commenting upon the *Theaetetus*, he says "if anyone saith a thing is, or is made, he must withal say, for what, or of what, or in respect of what, it is or is made. ... Agreeable to which doctrine it is also further affirmed by Plato, that it is impossible a thing should be sweet and sweet to nobody." [61] Subjectivity is one form of dependence or relativity. But to set up the finite self as a substantial thing is to commit the same fallacy as the materialist, "for, that *anything* should exist in itself or absolutely, is absurd." [62] No specific sort of being can be real or self-existent, since prior to it is being itself. Real being, if it is to be found at all, is not to be

[58] *Ibid.*, sec. 348.
[59] *Ibid.*, sec. 304.
[60] *Ibid.*, sec. 305: *Theaetetus*, 186d.

[61] *Ibid.*, sec. 311: *Theaet.*, 160.
[62] *Ibid.*, sec. 311; my italics.

found in the flux of sense, but only in the λόγος, or realm of meaning, which exists prior to what we call reality. Being, as it truly is, may be meant but not perceived.

What impressed Berkeley as the essential feature of Plato's doctrine was his tireless search for the pure concept, for that which requires no assumption or presupposition but which exists in its own right and thus may be said purely and truly to be. He refers several times in this connection to a passage of Socrates' second speech in the *Phaedrus*.[63] In this passage, which seems to have exerted a singularly powerful effect upon Berkeley's mind, Socrates, referring to the immortals (ἀθάνατοι) who stand upon the "outer surface of the sky" (ἐπὶ τῷ τοῦ οὐρανοῦ νώτῳ), speaks of their vision as follows:

None of the poets of this world has ever sung of this super-celestial place appropriately, nor will any poet ever sing of it appropriately. Nevertheless, it must be described in some such way as this, since we must dare to speak the truth itself especially when speaking of truth. There abides that which is colourless and formless and intangible, actually existing essence (οὐσία ὄντως οὖσα) which is seen only by reason, the pilot of the soul, and in which all true knowledge has its center. As the divine understanding is nourished upon reason and unmixed knowledge, so the understanding of each soul which is concerned to absorb proper sustenance, beholding being through the succession of time, is content, and, contemplating truth, is nourished and rejoices until once more the revolution of the heavens shall bring it back to the same point in the circuit. In this circuit, the soul beholds justice itself (αὐτὴν δικαιοσύνην), temperance, and knowledge, not that which is brought forth in time, nor that which is relative, being one thing for one, and something else for another, as directed only towards those things which we are now in the habit of calling existent, but actual knowledge in that which is actually existent (ὅ ἐστιν ὄν ὄντως). And having glimpsed in this way such things as actually exist (τὰ ὄντα ὄντως), and having feasted itself upon them, it sinks back again into the heavenly sphere, and returns home.

It is to this passage that Berkeley refers when he speaks of "the first and most simple Being, free from all matter and composition. This is that οὐσία ὄντως οὖσα of Plato, which employeth mind alone; which alone governs the world." [64] It is to this passage again that he refers when, in following the lead of Augustine,[65] he compares the Platonic conception of being with Exodus iii. 14.[66] "According to both," says Berkeley, "God is He who truly is, ὁ ὄντως ὤν." What is only dependent or relative to something else cannot itself be said truly to be, since we can never be sure what we mean by the dependent until we have

[63] *Phaedrus*, 247c–e.   [65] *Civ. Dei*, VIII, 11.
[64] *Ibid.*, sec. 268.   [66] Sec. 342.

understood that upon which it depends. It is, indeed, meaning-less to speak of the dependent as *itself* at all, for its essence lies beyond it. But the meaningless cannot be, for being is assuredly a form of meaning. True being "employeth mind alone" (μόνῳ θεατὴ νῷ) because what is in itself pure being can only be thought or meant, never objectively perceived. It "governs the world" (κυβερνήτης), because "governing," or prior to, the world of existence is existence itself, the things which actually are (τὰ ὄντα ὄντως), or essential meaning itself (οὐσία ὄντως οὖσα).

Berkeley cites another specific example of the same sort from the *First Alcibiades*.[67] Here again, in discussing the question of self-improvement, Socrates refers to the existence of a prior question, — what do we *mean* by the self? "In what manner," asks Socrates, "is the essence of the self (αὐτὸ τὸ αὐτό) to be found? For, knowing this, we should then easily discover what we ourselves are (τί ποτ' ἐσμὲν αὐτοί), but being in ignorance of the former, we shall never discover the latter." The definition of the self as the soul is discarded as only approximate (μὴ ἀκρι-βῶς ἀλλὰ καὶ μετρίως), for before we can determine the nature of the soul, which is a particular existent in time, we must first discover what is meant by the self itself. "First the self itself (αὐτὸ τὸ αὐτό) must be understood. But instead of *the* self (ἀντὶ τοῦ αὐτοῦ) we have considered the nature of each particular self (αὐτὸ ἕκαστον) and what it may be." [68]

Berkeley comments on this passage as follows: "In man the monad or indivisible is the αὐτὸ τὸ αὐτό the self-same self, or very self; a thing in the opinion of Socrates, much and narrowly to be inquired into and discussed, to the end that, knowing our-selves, we may know what belongs to ourselves (ἡμῶν αὐτῶν) and to our happiness." [69] Berkeley was thus at last able to perceive the meaning of his early struggles with the categories of sub-stance, existence, and the self, which he concluded in the *Com-monplace Book* to be neither knowable nor existent in the ordinary sense. What he had been seeking for were the pure con-cepts or meanings, freed from all admixture of accidental appli-cation, though in his inability to discover them in objective ex-perience he had at first grouped them together with abstract ideas and denied their existence. In the *Siris*, however, he finally appreciates the full significance of his discovery, in the third dialogue, of the realm of ideas. Presupposed by the

[67] 129b and 130d; *Siris*, sec. 346.   [69] *Siris*, sec. 346.
[68] Alc., I, 130d.

"concrete" world of experience, rendering it concrete, permeating it with meaning, making it possible, and hence actual, lies the realm of pure essences. Without these, no reality of any sort can *be*, for reality itself is an essence (οὐσία ὄντως οὖσα).[70]

It may be supposed that Berkeley's late adherence to the Platonic theory of ideas is tantamount to a complete abandonment of his early polemic against abstract ideas. There is, indeed, one passage [71] where he speaks of "the Mind her acts and faculties" as "being *abstract* from sensible matters." But shortly afterwards [72] he speaks of the χωριστὸν εἶδος as "not an abstract idea compounded of inconsistencies and prescinded from all real things, as some moderns understand abstraction; but . . . distinct or separate from all sensible and corporeal beings." That is, the Platonic idea is in no sense derived from a prior particular reality through a certain disintegration, but the opposite is rather the case. The idea is prior to the particular limited existences we call real, and the world of ordinary experience is rather to be viewed as a mutilation of the ideal. We have already pointed out that Berkeley's polemic was in no sense a denial of universals, but rather an assertion of their autonomous rights. Once we understand what we mean by a universal we cannot conceive of it as something pieced together from the fragments of preexistent particulars. The universal is something *sui generis*, though bound up with particulars. Not only is the Platonism of the third dialogue and of the *Siris* not inconsistent with the denial of abstraction, but it is a necessary consequence from it. Since the universal cannot be derived from the particular, it must exist eternally and *per se*, nor does Berkeley, at least, interpret Plato as meaning that the ideas exist apart from reality in an abstract realm of subsistence.

Not only do the ideas not subsist, but it may be truly said that they alone exist, for existence itself is an idea. "According to that philosopher, goodness, beauty, virtue, and such like, are not figments of the mind, nor mere mixed modes [73] nor yet abstract ideas in the modern sense, but the most real beings,

[70] While Cassirer's discussion of Berkeley's development in his *Erkenntnisproblem*, II, pp. 275 ff., is written with great insight as well as accuracy, I cannot agree with his conclusion that "die rationale Erhöhung der Erkenntnis [in the *Siris*] lässt das Erfahrungswissen unberührt" (p. 323). To say that experience without intelligibility is actually nonexistent is hardly to leave it "unberührt."

[71] *Siris*, sec. 297.

[72] *Ibid.*, sec. 323.

[73] Note the reference to Berkeley's early Lockianism. Cf. Locke, *Essay*, ii, XXII, 4, 5.

intellectual and unchangeable." [74] Particulars cannot exist abstractly in isolation from them, for, in so far as the particulars are real, the ideas are bound up with them as intimately as it is possible to conceive, namely as constituting their very essences. "In Plato's style, the term *idea* doth not merely signify an inert, inactive object of the understanding, but is used as synonymous with αἴτιον and ἀρχή cause and principle." [75] The ideas do not exist apart from the sense reality, for there is only one reality and that is ideal; reality is meaning. The great discovery of Greek thought, as Berkeley at last came to perceive, was the determination of the logical character of reality. This discovery, first glimpsed by Parmenides, was fully grasped in the writings of Plato and Aristotle.

The defect in the Eleatic dialectic, as Berkeley saw it, lay in its tendency to fix the ideas, to think of them as things, or even to hypostatize them into one single being analogous to a material sphere. There are many passages in the *Siris* which repeat Berkeley's earlier warnings [76] against the tendency to reify or hypostatize ideas. This essential feature of his early doctrine of abstraction is now of the utmost importance to him in understanding the later thought of Plato and Aristotle. Thus, in referring to Aristotle's definition of Theology,[77] he says "by abstracted, χωριστόν, he understands separable from corporeal beings and sensible qualities," [78] not abstract, that is, in the sense of independence from other ideas or meanings, for such separation would be meaningless.[79]

Berkeley found in Plato's *Parmenides* the most instructive example in ancient thought of his own concrete logic, and the clearest evidence of Plato's transcendence of the Parmenidean tendency towards reification of thought, a tendency which led to unfortunate misunderstandings of his true teaching. Berkeley refers [80] definitely to this dialogue, summarizing first the argument which shows abstractly that "τὸ Ἕν" doth not exist" in any sense, so that it cannot be said to "exist in time." [81] He then comments upon the opposed proposition from the second contrary, or concretely thought hypothesis:[82] "nevertheless it is admitted in the same Parmenides that τὸ νῦν is everywhere

[74] *Siris*, sec. 335.
[75] *Ibid.*, sec. 335.
[76] Cf. chap. V.
[77] *Meta.*, E 1026a 11.
[78] *Siris*, sec. 307.
[79] Cf. *ibid.*, secs. 297, 323, 335.
[80] *Ibid.*, sec. 351.
[81] *Parm.*, 137–142.
[82] *Ibid.*, 142–156.

present to τὸ "Εν." [83] In other words, the unity of thought itself (τὸ "Εν) is present in all diversity (everywhere), not, however, as a succession of instants, but as an eternal now, within which differences are mediated. "Instead of a temporary succession of moments," says Berkeley, "there is one eternal Now or *punctum stans*, as it is termed by the schoolmen." [84] This was doubtless suggested to Berkeley by the important interlude in which the concept of the timeless point (ἐξαίφνης) *between* the instants of time is developed, as that "out of which change takes place," [85] or that movement of thought which is prior to the movement of time.

It is the apprehension of this concrete movement of thought which constitutes the real advance of the Platonic *Parmenides* beyond the abstract dialectic of the Eleatics, and which affords Berkeley, as it afforded Plato, a means of reconciling the abstract with the concrete. "The One," remarks Berkeley, "or τὸ "Εν may be conceived either by composition or division. As, on the one hand, we may say the world or universe is One Whole . . . so we may, on the other hand, consider τὸ "Εν by division or abstraction, as somewhat in the order of things prior to mind." [86] But in neither case, he adds, is there any genuine abstraction "so long as the *unum*, or τὸ "Εν is supposed not to exist without mind." Abstraction itself, in other words, is a form of togetherness; separateness a relation. Even when we think of the One as prior to mind and separate from it, we are thinking the two together. This, Berkeley sees as the basic lesson of the *Parmenides*. There is an instability or motion in thought itself which cannot be hypostatized as a set of fixed entities, but must be viewed as an eternal moment (ἐξαίφνης) between the moments of time, out of which develops the meaningful diversity of pure thought. This diversity constitutes the core of reality lying within all that is real. That such a view was also the inevitable culmination of his own earlier reflections is apparent in the most mature of these writings, the *Three Dialogues*. But in the *Siris* this doctrine is stated with perfect consciousness of its relation to Greek thought.

There is, therefore, no question that Plato's development of the discovery of Parmenides seemed to him the true culmina-

---

[83] *Ibid.*, 152e: "τό γε μὴν νῦν ἀεὶ πάρεστι τῷ ἑνὶ διὰ παντὸς τοῦ εἶναι."

[84] *Siris*, sec. 351.

[85] *Parm.*, sec. 156d: "τὸ γὰρ ἐξαίφνης

τοιόνδε τι ἔοικε σημαίνειν, ὡς ἐξ ἐκείνου μεταβάλλον εἰς ἑκάτερον."

[86] *Siris*, sec. 354.

tion of classical Greek philosophy. "Aristotle and his followers," he says, "have made a monstrous representation of the Platonic ideas," [87] but in spite of misunderstandings and minor divergences he realizes that, so far as the essential matter is concerned, the identification of reality with meaning, Aristotle is in agreement with his master.[88] Thus, after citing Parmenides' definition of knowing as being,[89] he mentions the *Seventh Epistle* [90] as indicating that Plato also was of this opinion. He proceeds [91] with citations from the *De Anima* to show that for Aristotle also "actual knowledge and the thing known are all one." [92] Berkeley quotes the *De Anima* to show that Aristotle held the soul "to be the proper place of forms . . . which doctrine, first maintained by others,[93] he admits under this restriction, that it is not to be understood of the whole soul, but only of the νοητική, as is to be seen in his third book De Anima." [94] He interprets the doctrine of the *De Anima* as implying that "the forms are the beings," since "by the form everything is what it is." [95] He first follows Themistius' statement that the identity of thought and being is to be understood in a subjective sense, or that "the things are where the knowledge is, that is to say, in the mind," but at once withdraws this phraseology, coinciding as it does with his early spiritism, and corrects himself in the next sentence by stating the doctrine "as it is otherwise expressed, that the soul is all things." [96]

The Greek view, with which he now identifies his own, is not that the forms reside in the individual soul, hence making knowledge possible, but that the individual soul is to some extent able to grasp the forms. In this way, Berkeley eradicates the last traces of psychologism from his epistemology. Knowledge is possible not by placing the world in a "soul" dogmatically accepted as a fixed "entity," but by placing the soul in the world,[97] that is, the intelligible world. Berkeley now realizes

[87] *Ibid.*, sec. 338.
[88] Cf. *ibid.*, sec. 315.
[89] *Ibid.*, sec. 309.
[90] Cf. *Epist.* VII, 342d.
[91] *Siris*, sec. 310.
[92] *De An.*, III, ch. 7, 431, 1.
[93] Berkeley discovered this doctrine in the Pseudo-Aristotelian *Theologia*, and hence held it to be of Egyptian origin. Cf. sec. 269. This Arabian version of selections from Plotinus was translated into Latin in 1519 as *Sapientissimi philoso-*

phi Aristotelis Stagiritae Theologia sive Mystica philosophia secundum Aegyptios. It was printed in Du Val's edition of Aristotle's Works, Paris, 1619.
[94] Fraser erroneously refers to chap. VIII. Berkeley, however, is clearly referring to chap. IV, 429, 27: "καὶ εὖ δὴ οἱ λέγοντες τὴν ψυχὴν εἶναι τόπον εἰδῶν, πλὴν ὅτι οὔτε ὅλη ἀλλ' ἡ νοητική, οὔτε ἐντελεχείᾳ ἀλλὰ δυνάμει τὰ εἴδη."
[95] *Siris*, sec. 310.   [96] *Ibid.*
[97] Cf. *ibid.*, sec. 190.

that the whole of his early thought was only a gradual appreciation of the unique and prior status of the intelligible as against what was commonly confused with reality. Reality presupposes absolute reality, and knowledge presupposes absolute knowledge, such as can be explained through itself alone. "God," as Berkeley had maintained in the third dialogue,[98] "knows or understands all things. . . . But God is a pure spirit, disengaged from all . . . natural ties. . . . God knows or hath ideas; but His ideas are not conveyed to Him by sense, as ours are." He now restates this culminating intuition of his early thought in a sharp and almost plastic form.[99] "God," he says, "knoweth all things, as pure mind or intellect; but nothing by sense, nor in nor through a sensory." There is no possible way of explaining intelligibility, save through intelligibility itself. No "natural" or "sensory" explanation of knowledge is possible, for it would presuppose what it was attempting to explain. Meaning, essence, or form lies at the root of reality. This doctrine, culminating in the non-naturalistic metaphysics of Aristotle, Berkeley now recognizes as the fundamental insight underlying all true philosophy, though he himself was able to win it only by passing through the phenomenalism and spiritism of his early works.

Having discovered the nature of being, Berkeley is now in a position to appreciate the significance of non-being. Having penetrated to the pure form or concept, he is able to appreciate the significance of that matter through which his thought has passed. Since what exists is pure form or being itself, what is non-formal or material is non-existent. It is not that pure matter exists in some vague and inchoate form, but that it does not exist at all, since it is formless. This is the true meaning of Parmenides' famous proposition. Matter is the meaningless, — the non-existent. It signifies "no positive actual being"; [100] it means the meaningless. Matter is the absence of form, "a mere privation, as silence or darkness." [101] But if the meaningless is the absence of meaning, it is, therefore, dependent upon meaning, or itself a form of meaning, just as seeing nothing is after all seeing. It is senseless to speak of blindness except in connection with one who could see. The meaningless presupposes meaning, and matter presupposes form. Unless there were being, there could be no non-being. The meaningless it-

[98] 3D., pp. 458–459.
[99] Siris, sec. 289.
[100] Ibid., sec. 317.
[101] Ibid., sec. 306.

self derives a minimum of meaning by reflection, so to speak, from that which has meaning. What is not, in so far as it comes within the scope of reason at all, is. It is at this point that Berkeley finds himself able to draw most heavily upon the thought of Aristotle. What remained for Plato a dim half-spatial intuition was realized by Aristotle in the articulated form of thought. "It must be observed," says Berkeley,[102] "that Aristotle distinguished a twofold existence — potential and actual. It will not, therefore, follow that, according to Aristotle, because a thing is it must actually exist." [103] What is not, may nevertheless be. Matter is not, in the sense that it is potentially, for the potential is what is not, and yet what nevertheless is. What we call absolute non-being, or nothing, is in reality, or concretely, the non-being of being, the negation of what is. Matter is potentiality. As we have already pointed out, Berkeley identifies Anaximander as the discoverer of matter in this sense. His τὸ ἄπειρον, says Berkeley, "means no more than infinite or indefinite," [104] indefinite, that is, in the sense of being *not* this or that, and hence, in a certain sense, both. What is neither *x* nor *y* is potentially either or. This infinite receptacle from which infinite worlds emerge and to which they return, contains so much that it contains nothing. It is "a *pura potentia* a mere possibility," [105] a nothing which nevertheless is. The determination of "a twofold existence — potential and actual" [106] or δύναμις and "ἐνέργεια or act" [107] — is singled out by Berkeley as an essential philosophic contribution of Aristotle, something dimly intuited by Plato, lying latent in the ἄπειρον of Anaximander, but never profoundly and distinctly apprehended until the writing of the *Metaphysics*.

For the conception of potentiality Berkeley has Aristotle to thank. But in the metaphysical development of this idea he again finds it necessary to return to Plato. "That matter is actually nothing but potentially all things is the doctrine of Aristotle." [108] When it is recognized, however, that the soul knows all things under the form of potentiality, and that we also "believe it necessary that whatever exists should exist in

[102] *Ibid.*, sec. 312.
[103] Berkeley refers here specifically to *Meta.*, Θ, 3, and doubtless had the following sentence in mind: " ὥστ' ἐνδέχεται δυνατὸν μέν τι εἶναι μὴ εἶναι δέ, καὶ δυνατὸν μὴ εἶναι εἶναι δέ, ὁμοίως δὲ καὶ ἐπὶ τῶν ἄλλων κατηγοριῶν δυνατὸν βαδίζειν ὂν μὴ βαδίζειν,

καὶ μὴ βαδίζον δυνατὸν εἶναι βαδίζειν." 1047a 20.
[104] *Siris*, sec. 318.
[105] *Ibid.*
[106] *Ibid.*, sec. 312.
[107] *Ibid.*, sec. 250.
[108] *Ibid.*, sec. 317.

some place," [109] we are led further, with Plato, to identify matter or potentiality with "place or space." [110] The potential in relation to us, or as known by us, is "place." [111] But "to understand and to be are . . . the same thing." [112] Hence matter or potentiality is "place." Does it not contain all things, while in itself remaining nothing? Is it not "made up of negatives," [113] or, in the language of the *De Motu*, "infinite, immobile, indivisible, insensible, without relation, and without distinction," so that "all its attributes are privative or negative," being "really nothing." [114] But this nothing nevertheless is, and Berkeley's mature thought, fructified by his reading of Aristotle and impelled, as always, by his concrete logic, finally asserts it to be "potentially all things." [115] It is "neither an object of understanding nor of sense," [116] and is, following the *Timaeus*, only "made out by a certain, spurious way of reasoning — λογισμῷ τινι νόθῳ μόγις πιστόν." [117] Nevertheless it is known, though only "μετ' ἀναισθησίας ἁπτόν, that is, to be felt as darkness is seen or silence heard, being a mere privation," [118] the form of potentiality, the otherness brooding over everything we call the world, the form of sense, which is, therefore, neither sense nor thought.

But if space is potentiality, that which remains always "there," the positive or objective aspect of matter, the container or receptacle (χώρα), the negative aspect, matter as not containing this or that or anything at all, the infinity or indeterminateness of space is time. Matter, as that from which all things come and to which they return, is the receptacle, but matter as the negation of all determination, the fluidity of what "is ever fluent and ever changing," is time. Together they constitute the endless otherness or infinite potentiality which is the framework in which "generating and perishing" take place,[119] or rather the form of generation and decay, neither that which is nor that which is not, but that which may be. This negation or potency hovering over the realm of becoming is what we mean by fate or necessity, which resists the infusion of intelligible form. "Blind fate and blind chance are at bottom much the same thing, and one no more intelligible than the

[109] *Ibid.*, sec. 318.
[110] *Ibid.*
[111] τόπος, *Timaeus*, 52b.
[112] *Siris*, sec. 309.
[113] *Ibid.*, sec. 317.
[114] *De Mot.*, sec. 53.

[115] *Siris*, sec. 317.
[116] *Ibid.*, sec. 306.
[117] *Tim.*, 52b.
[118] *Siris*, sec. 318.
[119] *Ibid.*, sec. 306.

other." [120] Possibility is the locus of necessity, for necessity is the determination of the indeterminate, — chance or caprice.

The objects of the world arise from the mixture of form or meaning with potentiality or matter. Such objects do not exist merely by not existing. They are not only held *in potentia*, but they are. In so far as they exist, potentiality is for the moment at least excluded from them. It is, however, never completely excluded. It hovers over them as their fate or destiny, which finally absorbs them into itself. Form or meaning never completely enters into matter. There is always a resistance which ends in the fluency of time. Thus, there is a second sort of object which may be said to exist under limitation, being "ever fluent and changing, generating and perishing, appearing and vanishing." [121] On the other hand, in order to exist at all, such objects presuppose the pure "form or species that is neither generated nor destroyed, unchangeable, invisible, and altogether imperceptible to sense," [122] for in order to be said to exist at all in act as distinct from in *potentia*, objects must at least participate in that which truly is. Indeed, as has already been pointed out, it is only from the standpoint of the intelligible that we can appreciate the meaning of the unintelligible. It was only after Plato that Aristotle was able to apprehend the full significance of *materia prima*. Matter, the meaningless, is the privation of meaning. But have we not also maintained that actuality is the exclusion of potentiality? Things become actual only by the elimination of possibility. The meaningless cannot be understood without form or meaning, but is it not equally true that form or meaning cannot be understood without matter? It is Berkeley's denial of this apparent consequence of his revived Platonic intellectualism that is really the key to the understanding of the *Siris*, as it is really the key to the understanding of Berkeley's development as a whole.

We have already noted that it was this consequence of his early rationalistic position, which culminated in the *Three Dialogues*, that led him to abandon theoretical philosophy as a hopeless because endless regress of mediation. There is a world of insensible ideas. But in the only matter in which they are accessible to us they are infected with the same sort of infinity and impurity which subjects the world of space and time to the fate of becoming. There is an intelligible matter which seems to relativize ideas, just as "sensory" matter relativizes the

---

[120] *Ibid.*, sec. 273.   [121] *Ibid.*, sec. 306.   [122] *Ibid.*

objects of place. In speaking of an ordinary object we cannot say simply that it is, but we "must withal say for what, or of what, or in respect of what it is." [123] Is not the same, however, also true of the intelligible realm? What form or category seems capable of standing alone in relationless autonomy, or intrinsic being? Can form itself, or pure being, be given any significance save in relation to matter? To ask such questions is to answer them. The essence of meaning is context, and without its context of non-being, even being itself, at least as we know it, loses its significance. This is what led Berkeley away from his early Platonism, to turn in despair to the practical. The intelligible world seemed cursed with the same blind or infinite necessity that reduces the sensory world to an indefinite flux of becoming. Being itself, in the purest form in which it is known to us, is made relative by the infinite potency of non-being, and hence is subject to an intelligible destiny. The intelligible world, therefore, offers no escape from the flux of relativity, for meaning itself is in flux, and thought is wafted to and fro from one idea to another by a dialectic as infinite as that which finally negates all finite things. Berkeley's reassertion of the theory of ideas in the *Siris* indicates that he at least felt he had found a solution. What was this solution? To anyone who has followed the stages of Berkeley's practical development and who has studied with any attention the later pages of the *Siris* the answer will not be uncertain. This answer, as Berkeley came to understand it, in the light of his reading of Greek philosophy, centers about the concept of transcendence.

He doubtless found the solution of the difficulty at least indicated in the Aristotelian doctrine of the priority of actuality. Thus, he states it as the Peripatetic doctrine that it is actuality which is "positive," matter being "mere privation." [124] After all, no matter how tenuous a being we ascribe to potentiality, it must nevertheless be. But then non-being will be excluded from it, and it will become dualized or relative. Where are we to find a being, and hence a derived non-being, that is not dependent, but which purely and absolutely is, or which actually contains its other in itself? Unless there exists such an absolute being, even the intelligible realm flows away in an endless and therefore meaningless chain of vicious circles. Non-being is indeed the absence of being. But then is not being the absence

---

[123] *Ibid.*, sec. 311. [124] *Ibid.*, sec. 306.

of non-being? What gives us the right to assert priority, — to give our dialectic a direction? If there is no such right, meaning dissipates itself in the indefinite, since every concept which has meaning refers beyond itself to another, and is hence overcome by the same fate which eventually negates all finite existence. Is there no concept which, so to speak, contains its own meaning in itself, and, therefore, may be truly said to be?

Aristotle's assertion of the priority of the actual, culminating in the concept of pure form or actuality, undoubtedly influenced Berkeley. This is perhaps why he took the position that Aristotle is really in agreement with the doctrine of ideas. But for an even deeper appreciation of the meaning of the self-complete or self-enclosed form, the truly actual meaning (οὐσία ὄντως οὖσα), Berkeley unquestionably turned again to Plato. Here he found as "sublime hints" and "flashes of light" those very insights in which the last practical phase of his own development had culminated. A self-enclosed or autonomous meaning is no longer a meaning, for context is the essence of meaning. If there is to be an intelligible world, therefore, it can be justified only by something beyond intelligibility, for only such a being can be truly intelligible or existent. Being, in the purest form rationally accessible to us, is infected with the matter of non-being, like everything else we see, touch, or think. That which truly is, must be beyond being, as it is beyond meaning. Just as the realm of sense presupposes intelligibility, so does the intelligible world presuppose what is beyond intelligibility. If the indefinite dialectic of thought is ever to find an end, if it is to be given a direction, this direction cannot be found in thought alone. Thought cannot end in the contemplation of itself, for such a process is infinite and indeterminate. The direction of the intelligible dialectic must come from that which *yields* intelligence, while remaining itself beyond it. Only in Value can thought come to rest. Berkeley quotes the sixth book of the *Republic* to illustrate his meaning.[125] "Light and sight," he says, "are not the sun: even so truth and knowledge are not the good itself, although they approach thereunto." In this respect, much as he was influenced by Aristotle, Berkeley found that he was forced more and more to follow in the path of Plato, who "describes God, as Moses, from His being" as "He who truly is, ὁ ὄντως ὤν," [126] as "author of all good, author of no evil, and un-

---

[125] *Ibid.*, sec. 343.　　　　[126] *Ibid.*, sec. 342.

changeable," [127] and who, in his "*Letter to Hermias*, speaks of God, the ruler and cause of all things as having a Father." [128] The final realization of this essential movement of thought, however, Berkeley found in the eclectic and Neo-Platonic writers of the second and third centuries A.D. whom he viewed together as constituting the culminating phase of Greek philosophy.

NEO-PLATONISM. THE PHASE OF TRANSCENDENCE

Berkeley looked upon Hellenistic philosophy not as the decay, but as the final culmination of Greek speculation. If he learned the meaning of the philosophy of nature from the Pre-Socratics and Aristotle, and if it was primarily through Plato that he appreciated the significance of the intelligible world, it was especially through the Neo-Platonists that he was led to apprehend the meaning of his own struggles with the problem of the practical. From the Neo-Platonists he learned not only the meaning of transcendence but, as a result of this, the meaning of philosophy itself as a revelation of the system or structure of the whole of being, the λόγος. It was only through the intelligible world that Berkeley was able to grasp something of the significance of the world of becoming; it was only through his discovery of the principle of transcendence that he was able to shed some light on the meaning of meaning.

This concept of transcendence lies at the basis of the *Siris*, and it is only upon this basis that Berkeley at last dares to construct a system of philosophy in the strict sense of the word. All his other works are fragmentary discussions of isolated problems or equally restricted polemics. Only in the *Siris* does he at last dare to outline a system embracing in its scope not only detailed phenomena in the realm of nature but the intelligible itself. The title of the work is taken from the Greek word σειρά, a term used constantly by Proclus in the sense of a logical system or chain in which the species of each successive level are bound together by their common participation in a higher genus. Berkeley's view of nature is organic or pantheistic in character, for the world is "a Chain or Scale of beings, rising by gentle, uninterrupted gradations from the lowest to the highest, each nature being informed and perfected by the participation

---

[127] *Ibid.*, sec. 320. Cf. *Rep.*, II, 381, and *Tim.*, 29–30.

[128] *Ibid.*, sec. 359: "καὶ τὸν τῶν πάντων

θεὸν ἡγεμόνα τῶν τε ὄντων καὶ τῶν μελλόντων, τοῦ τε ἡγεμόνος καὶ αἰτίου πατέρα κύριον ἐπομνύντας. . . ." *Epist.* VI, 323d.

of a higher." [129] He defends the "tenet of the Stoics that the world was an animal," [130] and takes over in his own philosophy of nature the Stoic and Pre-Socratic conception of a πνεῦμα νοερόν, or fiery energy, binding the various parts of the physical universe together in a single whole, and containing the distinct, rational seeds, λόγους σπερματικούς,' [131] of "all natural things."

But while there is truth in the natural philosophy of the Stoics, they are insufficiently conscious of the transcendental basis upon which their pantheism really rests. Thus, they are forced to qualify their materialism. The energy or fire, to which they allot such an important role, is "not simply fire" but τὸ ἡγεμονικόν, the ruling force or "governing principle of the world." [132] The Stoic pantheism, like the early cosmological thinking upon which it is founded, while it is illuminating as natural philosophy, is most inadequate as Theology. Pantheism is able to shed a certain dim light upon the lower by crudely mixing it with the higher, but all insight into the relation between the two is lacking. The immanence of pantheism is rendered conceivable through the idea of transcendence. It is only God who is capable of being omnipresent, but He is capable of being everywhere only because He is nowhere. [133]

While the philosophy of the Stoics, like that of the Egyptians, when properly understood, "doth not . . . lead to atheism," there is much that is "wrong in their way of thinking." [134] Stoicism remains dogmatic metaphysics, because it represents a return to the Pre-Socratic reification of concepts, without any prior examination of their meanings, and hence falls an easy prey to the sceptical attack of the middle and newer Academy. Pure or critical dogmatism is attainable only by way of scepticism, and Berkeley must have noted the similarity between the passage of Platonism through scepticism and practical eclecticism to the transcendentalism of the later Neo-Platonists, and the later practical stages of his own development. In the Neo-Pythagorean and Neo-Platonic writings of the first cen-

[129] *Siris*, sec. 274.
[130] *Ibid.*, sec. 172.
[131] *Ibid.*, sec. 229. This Stoic conception was also adopted by Plotinus, who speaks of the ideas present to the soul as λόγοι σπερματικοί or γεννητικοί (2, 3, 16), sometimes referring to them collectively as the λόγος (3, 2, 16, *et passim*). Berkeley was also familiar with Philo (cf. sec. 284), for whom the mediating action or causal efficacy of the intelligible forms, or collectively the λόγος, was, of course, a central conception. Berkeley probably possessed a Greek edition of Philo in his library. Cf. L. and S. cat., no. 467. The same conception also plays an important role in the thought of Augustine.
[132] *Ibid.*, sec. 172.
[133] *Ibid.*, sec. 358.
[134] *Ibid.*, sec. 300; cf. 288.

turies after Christ Berkeley found in the doctrine of transcendence the key not only to the past history of Greek speculation, but to his own intellectual development as well. The *Siris* is an attempt to think the world through as an intelligible system or chain, or, in other words, to construct a philosophy. Such an attempt, as Berkeley perceives, is possible only through the notion of transcendence, for to state the matter crudely, the lower can be explained only by the higher, and hence to explain everything it is necessary to refer to what transcends everything.

The universe can be thought as a whole, or a chain, or in other words rendered intelligible, only through its relation to something absolutely beyond it, for if that which binds the species or elements of the universe together is itself present in each of them, another entity is required to unify these parts.[135] The supreme entity, through which all entities are explained, cannot itself be an entity. The meaning of the world cannot be in the world of which it is the ultimate sense or λόγος.[136] The final phase of Greek reflection, as Berkeley came to understand it, was the phase of transcendence, approached, as in his own development, by the pathway of practical philosophy. The first philosophy, or *philosophia prima* of the *Siris*,[137] is developed in the form of a running commentary upon the transcendental and hence practical literature of this last phase of Greek reflection, a commentary to which we must now turn our attention.

The De Mundo

When allowances are made for the state of classical studies in his time, Berkeley's scholarly judgment, as we have already noted, was remarkably sound. In the case of the Pseudo-Aristotelian *De Mundo*, however, which he regarded as authentic,[138] he went astray. The "difference of style," he thought, could be explained by the fact that it was "a letter to a king." [139] Berkeley's error becomes more excusable, however, when it is remembered that responsible scholars argued for the authen-

[135] Cf. Proclus, *In Platonis Theologiam*, Book II. Berkeley constantly refers to this work in the *Siris*, and the Hamburg edition of 1618 is listed in the L. and S. cat., no. 756.

[136] Hence Proclus calls it πάσης σιγῆς ἀρρητότερον καὶ πάσης ὑπάρξεως ἀγνωστό-τερον. *In Plat. Theol.*, II, 11, p. 110, cited by Zeller, *Phil. d. Griechen*, 3rd ed. III, 2, p. 792.

[137] Secs. 285, 293.

[138] *Ibid.*, sec. 328.

[139] *Ibid.*

ticity of this work as late as 1829, and that it was not until Zeller's analysis [140] that the question was definitely settled. [141]

The early part of the treatise is Stoic in tone, and is probably deeply influenced by the thought of Posidonius, though the author here and there adds a Peripatetic touch. [142] The early chapters betray a distinctively Stoic enthusiasm for the cosmos, and for the single force which binds the parts together into a whole, and brings unity out of opposition and even catastrophe. The author follows Aristotle in supposing the universe to consist of five concentric spheres with the earth at the center, then water, air, and fire in the order named. The outermost sphere of the heavenly bodies consists of "a certain fifth essence, an aethereal nature unchangeable and impassive." [143] The subtlest of the changing earthy elements constitutes the next ring which is "lighted up or set on fire by the aethereal and Divine nature." [144]

Berkeley was influenced by these ideas in his own cosmology. But what interested him in this treatise even more was the subtle modification, particularly in chapter six, of the pantheism of the earlier chapters. In this chapter, God is conceived not as Himself immanent in the universe in the orthodox Stoic fashion, but as ruling the universe indirectly as a First Cause. After this first impulse each thing moves according to its special nature. God remains to direct the course of events, but He is seated on high, beyond the heavens, and pervades the universe through various mediating agencies, as a Great King rules His Kingdoms. This further development of Stoicism accorded precisely with the direction of his own thought, and he states the doctrine as follows: "God, indeed, is in His Heaven but . . . His power, or

[140] *Phil. d. Griechen*, 3rd ed., vol. III, pp. 631 ff.

[141] The *De Mundo* was contained in Erasmus' edition of Aristotle (1531, Lib. I, p. 161) as well as in the edition of Sylburgius (1587, vol. III), both of which were probably in Berkeley's library. Cf. L. and S. cat., nos. 244, 1434.

[142] Cf. W. Capelle, "Die Schrift von der Welt," *Neue Jahrb. f. Klass. Alt.*, XV, 1905, p. 529.

[143] *Siris*, sec. 167. This idea of aether as a fifth element is non-Aristotelian, though not, of course, the general distinction between the heavenly and earthly spheres. "Caeli autem et astrorum sub-

stantiam quidem aethera nuncupamus, non, ut quidam quod cum ignea sint, urantur, peccantes in nimium alteratam ab igne virtutem, sed quia semper currant circumlata, elementum entem aliud a quattuor incorruptibile ac divinum." Lorimer, *The Text Tradition of Ps. Aristotle "De Mundo,"* Oxford, 1924, versio Siculi 392a.

[144] *Ibid.* Cf. Lorimer, vers. Sic. 392a: "Sed huius ipsius (partis corruptibilis) prima quidem est subtilium partium et flammea substantia ignita ab aetheria ob eius magnitudinem et motus velocitatem."

a force derived from Him doth actuate and pervade the universe." [145] He also gives a paraphrase in English of the similes in which the author of the treatise expresses his thought. He declares, says Berkeley, "that the Divine force or influence permeates the entire universe, and that what the pilot is in a ship, the driver in a chariot, the precentor in a choir, the law in a city, the general in an army, the same God is in the world." [146]

OCELLUS LUCANUS

This same combination of dynamic pantheism with transcendence Berkeley found in the more ancient tract attributed to the "Pythagorean," Ocellus Lucanus.[147] The treatise of Ocellus, which is more Peripatetic than Pythagorean in tone,[148] was probably written in the second century B.C. It is primarily a defence of the doctrine of the eternity of the world, which was, at the time of its composition, one of the more important points maintained by the Peripatetics against the Stoic school.

What particularly impressed Berkeley in the treatise, however, was its conception of cosmic harmony as founded upon the universal influence of a super-cosmic being. The two elements are no doubt confused, and the comparison of the universe with an organism involves "mistake or impropriety." [149] But Ocellus' recognition of the transcendence of the supreme being, as in the case of the De Mundo, represents an advance beyond the crude pantheism of the Stoics. Hence, "it should seem reasonable to say, with Ocellus Lucanus the Pythagorean, that, as life holds together the bodies of animals, the cause whereof is the soul; and as a city is held together by concord, the cause whereof is law, even so the world is held together by harmony, the cause whereof is God. And *in this sense* the world, or Universe, may be considered either as one Animal or one city." [150]

[145] *Ibid.* Cf. Lorimer, vers. Sic. 398b: "Honestius autem atque convenientius ipsum quidem residere in suprema regione, vim vero per universum orbem progressam solem et lunam movere et totum caelum volvere necnon terrenis fieri causam salutis."

[146] *Ibid.*, sec. 328. Cf. Lorimer, vers. Sic. 400b: "Universaliter autem quod in navi quidem nauta, in curru vero auriga, in choreis autem choraula, in civitate vero lex, in agmine vero dux, hoc deus in mundo. . . ."

[147] This tract would have been available to Berkeley in several forms, among which is the *Opuscula Mythologica. Physica et Ethica. Graece et Latine.* Amstelaedami Apud Henricum Wetstenium, 1688. This work includes the fragment from Stobaeus (referred to by Berkeley), but is not listed in the L. and S. cat.

[148] Cf. Harder, Ocellus Lucanus. Text u. Kommentar. Berlin, 1926.

[149] *Siris*, sec. 279.

[150] *Ibid.*, sec. 279 (my italics). This is a loose translation of the first part

TIMAEUS OF LOCRUS

Berkeley also cites "Timaeus Locrensis, that ancient Pythagorean, author of the book concerning the Soul of the World." [151] This treatise [152] is a summary of certain portions of Plato's *Timaeus*, interpreted on the basis of what is, on the whole, a Stoic point of view, although the author is an eclectic, probably of the first century A.D., [153] and may have had access to an ancient Pythagorean tradition or sources since lost. Berkeley notes the astrological doctrine contained in the treatise, according to which "souls excepting only the rational or intellectual part" are "derived from the celestial luminaries." [154] This doctrine accords with his own consciously Stoic conception of a primal fire containing the active principles of things.

He was also probably influenced by the attempt of the author to reconcile Plato with Aristotle, and more particularly by his assertion of the equivalence between Aristotle's πρώτη ὕλη and the χώρα of the *Timaeus*. [155] Even more striking, however, is the conception developed by Timaeus "of a most ancient philosophy, even in his time, ἀ πρεσβύστα φιλοσοφία stirring up and recovering the soul from a state of ignorance to the con-

---

of the fragment from the *Laws* quoted by Stobaeus I, 13, 2 (not I, 16, as stated by Fraser iii, p. 258, n. 2). Berkeley doubtless possessed a copy of Stobaeus in his library. Cf. L. and S. cat., no. 225. But he could have gained his information from the *Opuscula Mythologica*, p. 537, which is certainly the source of the error in Fraser's reference to Stobaeus. The text which Berkeley uses, as corrected by Harder, runs as follows: Ὄκελλος ἔφησεν εἶναι αἴτιον δι' ὅ γίνεταί τι. λέγει γὰρ ἐν τῷ Περὶ νόμου οὕτως. Συνέχει γὰρ τὰ μὲν σκάνεα τῶν ζῴων ζωά, ταύτας δ' αἴτιον ψυχά. τὸν δὲ κόσμον ἁρμονία, ταύτας δ' αἴτιος ὁ θεός· τὼς δ' οἴκως καὶ τὰς πόλιας ὁμόνοια, ταύτας δ' αἴτιος νόμος. τίς ὢν αἰτία καὶ φύσις τὸν μὲν κόσμον ἁρμόχθαι διὰ παντὸς καὶ μηδέποτ' ἐς ἀκοσμίαν ἐκβαίνειν, τὰς δὲ πόλιας καὶ τὼς οἴκως ὀλιγοχρονίως ἦμεν; The rest of the fragment may have influenced Berkeley in his own interpretation of Aristotle. Thus, ordinary things

bear within themselves, as the matter of which they are composed, the essential cause of their dissolution (ἐξ ἃς συνέστακεν ὕλας, τὰν αὐτὰν αἰτίαν ἔχει τᾶς διαλύσιος). But that which is ever passive (ἀειπαθὲς) requires or is governed (κυβερνῆται) by that which is ever active (ἀεικίνατον) and therefore prior in capacity (τὸ πρῶτον τᾷ δυνάμει). The note of transcendence is especially clear in the contrast with which the last sentence ends: ". . . τὸ δὲ ὕστερον, καὶ τὸ μὲν θεῖον καὶ λόγον ἔχον καὶ ἔμφρον, τὸ δὲ γενατὸν καὶ ἄλογον[τὸ μεταβάλλον]."

[151] *Siris*, sec. 298.
[152] περὶ ψυχᾶς κόσμω; available in the *Opusc. Myth.*
[153] Cf. Taylor, *Comm. on Plat. Tim.*, Oxford, 1928, pp. 655 ff.
[154] *Siris*, sec. 282. Cf. *Opusc. Myth.*, p. 556, although Berkeley *could* have gained this information from Stobaeus I, 41, 39.
[155] Cf. pp. 439 ff.

templation of Divine things." [156] If one is to take the conception of transcendence seriously, it is a necessary consequence
that the knowledge of transcendence must itself have a transcendent source. Hence arises the notion of a divine tradition in
philosophy, θεοπαράδοτος φιλοσοφία,[157] which began to play such
an important role in the speculations of the Hellenistic period,
and to assume an ever increasing signifcance in Berkeley's own
thought.[158]

THE CHALDEAN ORACLES

The idea of a most ancient philosophy of transcendental
origin was even more closely connected with the philosophical
poem quoted so frequently by the Neo-Platonists as the *Chaldean Oracle*, or simply the *Oracle*.[159] For Proclus, its authority
ranked with that of Homer and Orpheus. The Stoic fire cosmology is placed by the author of this work in a most distinctively transcendental setting which leads to a sharp contrast
between the sensible and the intelligible worlds. Beyond the latter is the fatherly νούς itself, the holy fire from which all reason
is derived, though He is even farther removed from sense, to
which He penetrates only through the mediation of the second
νούς, with whom He is generally confused. This Highest God is
shrined in silence. He is the Source of Sources in which everything comes to rest, and from which even matter springs. What
comes from Him most directly is the fiery lightning, and what
holds all things together is ἔρως, of which, as in Plato, there is a
heavenly and earthly form. Man has a bit of the divine reason
in him, and the soul itself is constituted of divine fire.

The poem is, therefore, like the works we have just considered, a mixture of Stoic immanence with Platonic transcendence, although the fire worship in which it culminates may
indicate, as Berkeley supposes, a direct oriental influence. It is
deemed possible, through magical rites and formulae, to induce
the divine essence to appear in a fiery form. Berkeley, who fol-

[156] *Siris*, sec. 298. The archaic text, to
which Berkeley probably refers, runs as
follows: " καί σύνεσις, καί ά πρεσβύστα
φιλοσοφία, ἀποκαθάραμεναι ψεύδεα (ψευδέας
δόξας) ἐνέθηκαν τὰν ἐπιστήμαν, ἀνακαλεσά-
μεναι τὸν νόον ἐκ μεγάλας τᾶς ἀγνοίας, χα-
λάσασαι ἐς ὄψιν τῶν θείων." *Opusc. Myth.*,
p. 565. He could not have discovered
this in Stobaeus.

[157] *Ibid.*, sec. 301.
[158] Cf. App., Ser. 3.
[159] The poem was probably an eclectic
product of the latter part of the second
century A.D., though Zeller considers it to
be of late Neo-Platonic origin. Porphyry
was, however, acquainted with the work.
Cf. Kroll, *Die Chaldaischen Orakel*, Rhein.
Mus. L, 1895, pp. 636 ff.

lowed Proclus in accepting the fragments as expressing an ancient, oriental tradition, notes the correspondence of this theory with the Stoic πῦρ νοερόν.[160] He also comments upon the phrase ἐσσάμενος πυρὶ πῦρ,[161] and compares it with certain expressions in the Psalms.[162]

THE HERMETIC WRITINGS

A similar oriental influence is discernible in another group of Hellenistic documents to which Berkeley often refers. In the Hermetic literature he again found that modification of Stoic immanence through a Platonic feeling for transcendence which was more and more becoming the dominant element in his own practical philosophy. On the one hand, God is viewed as the soul or mind of the world, using fire as His instrument in the making of all things,[163] and yet, on the other hand, He cannot be viewed as a maker, since this involves change and imperfection,[164] but must be conceived rather as an utterly transcendent and ineffable being, to be understood only as beyond all understanding.[165] The *Corpus Hermeticum* is a collection of seventeen documents, the first of which is entitled Ἑρμοῦ Τρισμεγίστου Ποιμάνδρες. Ficinus published a Latin translation of the first fourteen documents in 1471, in which he made the mistake of supposing that this heading stood for the whole collection. The blunder was corrected by Patrizzi, who printed the *Hermetica*, together with other matter, in 1591.[165a] Certain parts of this, including the *Hermetica*, were republished in London in 1611.[166] This may have been Berkeley's source for the "Hermetic Writings," although the fact that he also speaks of the *Pimander*[167] shows that he was familiar with some version of the trans-

---

[160] *Siris*, sec. 182; cf. 179.
[161] *Ibid.*, sec. 179. This phrase is quoted by Proclus, *In Parm.*, 769, 7: "δεσμῷ Ἔρωτος ἀγητοῦ, ὃς ἐκ νόου ἔκθορε πρῶτος ἐσσάμενος πυρὶ πῦρ συνδέσμιον, ὄφρα κεράσσῃ πηγαίους κρατῆρας ἑοῦ πυρὸς ἄνθος ἐπισχών." Kroll writes περὶ for πυρὶ (*De Oraculis Chaldaicis*, Bresl. Philol. Abh. 7, 1894, p. 25). Berkeley never refers directly to the *In Parm.*, and whether he had access to this work is a matter of conjecture. The phrase does not occur in the Chaldean fragments collected by Psellus (Migne, *Patrologia*, 122, pp. 1115 ff.).

[162] *Ibid.* He refers to Ps. 104, 2 and 4.
[163] Cf. Scott, *Hermetica*, Oxford, 1924, I, p. 198: "νοῦς δέ, ὀξύτατος ὢν πάντων τῶν νοηματῶν, καὶ τὸ ὀξύτατον πάντων τῶν στοιχείων ἔχει σῶμα, τὸ πῦρ. δημιουργὸς γὰρ ὢν ὁ νοῦς ὀργάνῳ τῷ πυρὶ πρὸς τὴν δημιουργίαν χρῆται." Lib. X, 18.
[164] Scott, *Herm.*, I, p. 188, Lib. X, 3.
[165] *Ibid.*, p. 191: "τότε γὰρ αὐτὸ ὄψει, ὅταν μηδὲν περὶ αὐτοῦ ἔχῃς εἰπεῖν." Lib. X, 5.
[165a] 2nd ed., Venice, 1593.
[166] Cf. Scott, *Herm.*, Bibl. Int.
[167] *Siris*, sec. 178.

lation of Ficinus.[168] Berkeley was quite aware of the fact
that the attribution of these writings to the god Hermes, or
to the mysterious personage Mercurius Trismegistus, was a
mere device,[169] though he did, however, believe, as is indeed
probable, that they contained elements derived from an ancient
Egyptian tradition. "Though the books attributed to Mercurius Trismegistus," he says, "were none of them wrote by him,
and are allowed to contain some manifest forgeries, yet it is also
allowed that they contain tenets of the ancient Egyptian philosophy though dressed, perhaps, in a more modern garb." [170]
Berkeley cites many specific passages from the Hermetic
writings, which he appears to have read very thoroughly. Thus,
he refers to them in order to show that a pantheistic view of
nature, "whatever misconceptions there may be," can be held
without "Atheism," so long as "Mind or Intellect is understood to preside over, govern, and conduct the whole frame of
things." [171] For example, in the Hermetic writings, though God
is clearly a transcendent being, He is nevertheless "all things,
not only actual but possible. . . . And therein it is said, Shall I
praise Thee for those things Thou hast made manifest, or for
the things Thou hast hidden? Therefore in their [the Egyptians'] sense, to manifest was to create; the things created having been before hidden in God." [172]
Berkeley was deeply influenced by the vitalistic form of the
Hermetic pantheism. "If we may trust the Hermaic Writings,"
he says, "the Egyptians thought all things did partake of
life,"[173] and he constantly speaks of all nature "as alive and in
motion." [174] These concepts are also often juxtaposed in the
Hermetic literature.[175] He also remarks upon the "doctrine of
Trismegistus in the *Pimander* that mind is clothed by soul, and
soul by spirit." [176]

---

[168] The Divine Pymander was translated into English by Dr. Everard and
printed by R. White for T. Brewster and
G. Moule at London in 1650.
[169] Cf. Siris, sec. 298, which makes
Fraser's many warnings superfluous.
[170] Ibid.
[171] Ibid., sec. 326; cf. 287.
[172] Ibid., sec. 325. Cf. Scott, Lib. V,
9: "οὐδὲν γάρ ἐστιν ἐν παντὶ ἐκείνῳ ὃ οὐκ
ἔστιν αὐτός. ἔστιν αὐτὸς καὶ τὰ ὄντα καὶ τὰ
μὴ ὄντα. (Note how Berkeley translates
τὰ μὴ ὄντα as *the possible*.) τὰ μὲν γὰρ
ὄντα ἐφανέρωσε, τὰ δὲ μὴ ὄντα ἔχει ἐν

ἑαυτῷ." Also: "διὰ τίνος δὲ καὶ ὑμνήσω σε;
ὑπὲρ ὧν ἐποίησας, ἢ ὑπὲρ ὧν οὐκ ἐποίησας;
ὑπὲρ ὧν ἐφανέρωσας, ἢ ὑπὲρ ὧν ἔκρυψας;"
Lib. V, 11.　　　[173] Ibid., sec. 273.
[174] Ibid., secs. 267, 291, etc.
[175] Cf. for example, Scott, I, p. 234,
Lib. XII: "πᾶν τοίνυν ἴσθι καθολικῶς, ὦ
τέκνον, τὸ ὂν ἐν κόσμῳ κινούμενον. τὸ δὲ κινούμενον καὶ ζῇ:" cf. Lib. XI, 8a.
[176] Ibid., sec. 178. Cf. Scott, I, p. 194:
"ψυχὴ δὲ ἀνθρώπου ὀχεῖται τὸν τρόπον
τοῦτον, ὁ νοῦς ἐν τῇ ψυχῇ, ἡ δὲ ψυχὴ ἐν τῷ
πνεύματι." Lib. X, 13. Cf. Lib. XII, 13b,
14a, p. 230.

In addition to the "Pimander," Berkeley cites the *Asclepian Dialogue*, a Latin translation of one of the original Hermetic Libelli entitled Ἑρμοῦ τρισμεγίστου βίβλος ἱερὰ πρὸς Ἀσκλη-πιὸν προσφωνηθεῖσα and sometimes called the Λόγος Τέλειος, or Crowning Discourse of Hermes Trismegistus. Berkeley discovers in this discourse his own view of abstract space or matter as non-being or the meaningless. "With regard to absolute space," he says, "it is observed in the Asclepian Dialogue, that the word *space* or *place* hath by itself no meaning; and again, that it is impossible to understand what space alone or pure space is." [177] Berkeley was finally impressed by the clear manner in which Trismegistus, in his discussion of fate, expresses the subordination of non-being to being, of the necessity of matter to the freedom of God, of immanence to transcendence. "In the Asclepian Dialogue," he observes, "it is expressly said that fate follows the decrees of God." [178]

The Neo-Platonic System

Berkeley learned the elements of his philosophy of nature from the Pre-Socratics and their Stoic followers, his epistemology from Plato and Aristotle, and in the Neo-Pythagorean and eclectic writers of the early Roman Empire he discerned fragmentary insights into the nature of the transcendent being which alone renders such a thing as significance and hence philosophy possible. But it is only with the Neo-Platonists that all of the elements are woven into a systematic or philosophic whole. In Neo-Platonism Berkeley saw, as we have noted, the crowning synthesis in which the development of Greek philosophy culminates, and it is, of course, in the light of this synthesis that he interprets the nature of antecedent thought.

---

[177] *Ibid.*, sec. 270. Cf. Scott, I, p. 320: "Similiter vero de loco dicendum est; quod vocabulum solum, intellectu caret. Locus enim ex eo cuius est quid sit apparet: principali enim dempto, nominis significatio mutilatur. Quare aquae locus, ignis locus, aut his similium, recte dicemus. Sicuti enim inane esse aliquid impossibile est, sic et locus solus quid sit dinosci non potest. Nam si posueris locum sine eo cuius est, inanis videbitur locus; quem in mundo esse non credo. Quod si inane nihil est, nec per se quid sit locus apparet." Lib. III, 34a.

[178] *Ibid.*, sec. 272. Cf. Scott, I, p. 362: "Ascl. Quam ergo rationis partem εἱμαρμένη vel fata incolunt O Trismegiste? Tris. Quam εἱμαρμένην nuncupamus, O Asclepi, ea est effectrix rerum omnium quae geruntur semper sibi catenatis necessitatis nexibus vinctae. Haec itaque est aut Deus summus, aut ab ipso deo qui secundus effectus est, et omnium caelestium terrenarumque rerum firmata divinis legibus disciplina." *Ascl.*, III, 39.

Just as the early sections of the *Siris* can be understood only by means of the later, which consist almost exclusively of comments upon Plotinus and his followers, so, for Berkeley, the early history of Greek philosophy is to be understood only as a propaedeutic or introduction to the *Enneades*. It is clear that, more than in the case of any other strictly philosophical system, he recognizes the inner agreement of his own thought with that of the school of Plotinus.

Berkeley refers several times to Iamblichus, and was clearly familiar with the *De Mysteriis Aegyptiorum*.[179] While "the supreme Divinity" must be regarded as "the most holy and venerable Being," transcendent and "at rest, reposing within himself," [180] yet, in spite of this, "Jamblichus . . . taught that there was an intellect that proceeded to generation, drawing forth the latent powers into light in the formation of things." There is, therefore, in Iamblichus the same combination of dynamic immanence with transcendence already noted in the Hermetic writings. On the one hand, "the world" is "one Animal," [181] but, on the other hand, "there is a principle of the soul higher than nature, whereby we may be raised to a union with the gods, and exempt ourselves from fate." [182] Communication with the gods is something unique and super-rational; yet the religious view of the world is the only entirely rational one. The transcendent is, nevertheless, immanent, and what is diverse is nevertheless identical.

In the identity of diversity, the immanence of transcendence, Berkeley saw the methodological essence of the great logical system of Proclus. Of the works of this philosopher, Berkeley himself cites only the *In Platonis Theologiam*,[183] but he was probably familiar with several of the other great Platonic commentaries.[184] We have already mentioned the fact that the

---

[179] *Siris*, secs. 269 and 274. Jamblichus, *De Mysteriis*, Ap. Ald. 1497, is listed in the L. and S. cat.

[180] *Ibid.*, sec. 269.

[181] *Ibid.*, sec. 274.

[182] *Ibid.*, sec. 272.

[183] L. and S. cat., no. 756. Procl., *In Platonis Theologiam*, Hamburg, 1618.

[184] Berkeley's edition of the *In Platonis Theologiam* contained also the *Institutes of Theology*. Besides this, Berkeley undoubtedly knew the Latin translation of excerpts from the *In Alcibiadem Priorem Platonis* published by Ficinus under the title of *Procli de Anima ac Daemone, de sacrificio & Magia* at Venice, 1497, and contained in all the standard editions of his works. Furthermore, Berkeley could have known something of Proclus' commentary *In Timaeum Platonis*, through the Latin version of Thomaeus, published at Venice in 1525, though he does not specifically cite it. The whole of this commentary appeared in an edition of Plato by Joh. Valderum at Basel, 1534. Cf. also Fabricius, *Bibl. Gr.*, VIII, 1717, p. 524.

title of the *Siris*, as well as its basic form, is derived from the word σειρά, which occurs constantly in Proclus.[185] That this choice of a title carries a deeper significance is indicated by the passages in the work where Berkeley specifically refers to his conception of reality as that of a "Chain or Scale of beings, rising by gentle, uninterrupted gradations from the lowest to the highest."[186] In one essential passage, he makes clear that he does not mean "the change of one nature into another,"[187] or abstract otherness, but "the connection of different natures,"[188] an otherness which yet preserves a connection or strand of identity, and thus remains actually or concretely the same.[189] There are no differences which are not mediated and finally absorbed, no gaps between which infinite gradations cannot be discovered, nothing so transcendent that it is not immanent.

This analysis in synthesis Berkeley recognized as the logical core of the Neo-Platonic teaching, as of his own. Was not the impulse that had guided him from his earliest reflections upon the nature of sense-objects to his later struggles with the problem of the transcendent the constant effort to avoid abstraction? To avoid abstraction is to mediate otherness, not to destroy it, but to reveal the concrete system within which it is other. Must not his own thought, therefore, be viewed as an emanation in which one central logical core becomes aware of itself as an abstraction, and therefore unfolds itself into something further, which nevertheless remains the same? There are no separate (abstract) elements in the Chain of the world, but always mediating, intervening links. It is the very essence of thought to distinguish by uniting, and to unite by distinguishing. Berkeley now consciously presents his thought in this form, the form of Proclus, as of his own concrete logic. The universe is a chain of separate links holding themselves together in a single series or σειρά.

Many detailed aspects of the thought of the *Siris* owe their origin to Berkeley's reading of Proclus. There is, for example, his reference to Proclus' version of the theory of recollection. "Proclus," he says, "compares the soul, in her descent, invested with growing prejudices, to Glaucus diving to the bottom of the sea, and there contracting divers coats of sea-weed, coral and

---

[185] The genitive form σειρᾶς obviously suggests the English equivalent selected by Berkeley. Cf., for example, *In Tim.*, ed. Diehl, I, p. 454, l. 30; II, p. 24, l. 25; III, p. 229, l. 12, *et passim*.

[186] *Siris*, sec. 274; cf. 284, 303.
[187] *Ibid.*, sec. 274.
[188] *Ibid.*
[189] Cf. Proclus, *In Tim.*, 19c; Diehl, I, p. 63, l. 5.

shells, which stick close to him and conceal his true shape."[190]
Of particular importance, however, is the psychology of personality and its participation in "the first One" through its "τὸ ἕν
or unit."[191] Knowledge of the first Essence is possible only by
transcending the duality of knowing, and sinking into the absolute of thought itself, which is before all thoughts, a oneness
with the unity of self-consciousness, and, therefore, through
this, a oneness with God.[192]

The necessity of mediation between soul and body leads
Berkeley also to speak approvingly of Proclus' doctrine of "a
luciform aethereal vehicle" of the soul (τὸ αὐγοειδὲς [τῆς ψυχῆς]
ὄχημα),[193] also uncreated and unchangeable but hovering between material and non-material.[194] Although it is doubtless
true that Berkeley saw in the logical chains of Proclus the most
adequate development of his own conception of a concrete logic,
and while the form as well as the title of his final work may thus
be regarded as derived from the thought of the great Successor,
it is nevertheless true that, in content, his philosophical system
shows more clearly the influence of Plotinus himself. While the
author of the *Enneades* was not so conscious of the logical
groundwork of his thinking as Proclus, it is nevertheless clear
from the number and nature of the citations that Berkeley regarded him as the great original genius among the Neo-Platonic
writers, perhaps more in sympathy with the essential movement
of his own reflections than any other philosophical writer, including even Plato.

PLOTINUS

The *Siris* shows that Berkeley possessed an intimate knowledge of the *Enneades*.[195] He also cites the pseudo-Aristotelian
Theology, *De Secretiore Parte Divinae Sapientiae secundum*

---

[190] *Siris*, sec. 313. Cf. *In Alc. Pr.*
Creuzer, vol. I, p. 224: "Δεῖ τοίνυν τὴν
ἐντεῦθεν μέλλουσαν ὀρθῶς ἐπ' ἐκείνην τὴν
ἄγρυπνον περιάγεσθαι φύσιν, κοσμῆσαι μὲν
τὰς δευτέρας καὶ τρίτας δυνάμεις καὶ συνηρ-
τημένας αὐτῇ, καθάπερ τῷ θαλαττίῳ γλαύχῳ
τὰ φύκια καὶ τὰ ὄστρεα. κωλῦσαι δὲ τὰς ἔξω
προϊούσας αὐτῆς ὁρμὰς, ἀναμνησθῆναι δὲ
τῶν ὄντως ὄντων καὶ τῆς θείας οὐσίας, ἀφ'
ἧς ἡ κάθοδος καὶ πρὸς ἣν σπεύδειν προσήκει
τὴν σύμπασαν ἡμῶν ζωήν." Cf. *Rep.*, X,
611 sq.
[191] *Siris*, sec. 345; cf. 333, 356.

[192] Cf. *In Platonis Theologiam*, Book I.
[193] *In Tim.*, 348b; cf. 164b, 165b.
[194] *Siris*, sec. 171. Cf. Zeller, *Phil. d.
Griechen*, 4th ed., III, 2, 876. We have
already noted the occurrence of this doctrine in the Hermetic literature. Berkeley
may also have run across a similar view
in Porphyry, or Plutarch, *Moralia*, 626c.
[195] *Plotini Opera Philosophica*, Basel,
1580, are listed in the L. and S. cat., no.
242. This edition contained both the
Greek text and the Latin translation of
Ficinus, to which Berkeley often refers.

Aegyptios,[196] which, though he was unaware of the fact, was really, as is now known, a paraphrase of selections from the later *Enneades*. The influence of Plotinus pervades the whole of the *Siris*, and many of his citations of the older Greek thinkers concern passages commented upon in the *Enneades*. There can be no question that it was really through the eyes of Plotinus that Berkeley tended to interpret Plato, as well as the whole history of Greek speculation.

Berkeley, of course, has no difficulty in discovering in Plotinus the conception of non-being as potentiality.[197] "It is impossible to understand," says Berkeley, "what space alone [pure non-being] is." [198] He then cites Plotinus [199] with respect to the dependency of space or non-being. Pure negative otherness, or "non-ness," he then asserts to be the ultimate source of "the notions of external existence, independence, necessity, and fate." [200] Abstract otherness is not even meaningless, for the meaningless requires meaning to be significant. Otherness is not an independent thing or stuff, but a relation which remains identical in its opposition. Negation is always the negation of something. Non-being presupposes being, difference presupposes identity, matter presupposes form, potentiality presupposes actuality, or, in the words of Plotinus, "the world is in the soul." [201]

The being of non-being, the actualization of potentiality, is what we mean by the existence of the world of nature, an existence that is not pure, but something involving otherness or potentiality in its nature, and thus made to exist here rather than there, and now rather than then. The eliminated potentialities, however, are not absolutely eliminated. They hover

---

[196] *Siris*, secs. 269, 321, 359. This work was not included in the editions of Aristotle listed by Leigh and Sotheby, no. 1434, *Aristotelis Opera*, Gk. et Lat. a Sylburgio Francof., 1587, and no. 244, Arist., *Opera ab Erasmo*, Basel, 1531. Berkeley must, therefore, have had access either to the edition of Carpentarius (1573), or more probably the Arist., *Opera*, ed. Du Val, Paris, 1619. In this edition the Aristotelian *Theology* is printed in Latin (following the translation of Carpentarius) under the title: *Aristotelis Libri XIV de Secretiore Parte Divinae Sapientiae secundum Aegyptios*, Tomus II, p. 1035. This work was first translated into Latin in 1519, though it was preserved by the Arabs throughout the period of the Middle Ages. Carpentarius' translation, which was Berkeley's only source of reference, is quite inaccurate. Cf. Dieterici, *Die Sogenannte Theologie des Aristotelis*, Leipzig, 1883.

[197] Plotinus, however, asserted that place is posterior to matter (2, 4, 12) and would, therefore, not fully agree with Berkeley's tendency to follow the *Timaeus* in identifying the two.

[198] *Siris*, sec. 270.

[199] Cf. 5, 5, 9. Fraser's text reads 5, 5, 3.

[200] *Siris*, sec. 271.

[201] *Ibid*., sec. 270.

over the thing as its fate or necessity and finally destroy it, absorbing it again into the matter of which it was formed. But since matter is itself form, since the otherness which relativizes and destroys every natural object is an identity, the course of nature, or necessity, expresses an "order" or system. This presence of being in non-being, this identity in diversity, is "the beauty and harmony of the world" as understood by reason. Berkeley thus approvingly cites Plotinus' explanation of evil as order,[202] and his assertion that "even . . . excesses, defects, and contrary qualities conspire to the beauty and harmony of the world."[203] When it is realized that perishing is the same as creation, that independence is a form of dependence, and that diversity is itself identity, necessity becomes purpose, and fate is seen to be Providence. As "that same philosopher [Plotinus] observes," it is a "governing Reason produceth and ordaineth all those things."[204]

But "Plotinus indeed saith, that which acts naturally is not intellection, but a certain power of moving matter, which doth not know but only do."[205] There is something which actualizes potentiality, which mediates between being and non-being, bringing the former out of the latter. This is "Will," or that which acts. It is absurd to speak of *the* soul as being in the world, since the world as a system or identity of diverse elements already presupposes an actualizing force to bind them together. Hence, Plotinus "expressly" affirms "that the soul is not in the world, but the world in the soul."[206] That which knows or realizes order, and is hence prior to it, is soul, though not *my* soul. The world, to be a world, must know or see itself.

---

[202] *Ibid.*, sec. 262. Cf. Plot., *Enn.*, 3, 2, 18.

[203] *Ibid.*, sec. 262; cf. sec. 334: "Plotinus represents God as order"; also sec. 252, where Berkeley probably refers to *Enn.*, 3, 3, 6.

[204] *Ibid.*

[205] *Ibid.*, sec. 254. Fraser's conjecture of *Enn.*, 4, 4, 13, is erroneous. The reference is to 2, 3, 17: "ὁ γὰρ λόγος ἐν ὕλῃ ποιεῖ, καὶ τὸ ποιοῦν φυσικῶς, οὐ νόησις, οὐδὲ ὅρασις, ἀλλὰ δύναμις τρεπτικὴ τῆς ὕλης, οὐκ εἰδυῖα, ἀλλὰ δρῶσα μόνον, οἷον τύπον καὶ σχῆμα ἐν ὕδατι, ὥσπερ κύκλος, ἄλλου ἐνδόντος εἰς τοῦτο τῆς φυσικῆς δυνάμεως, καὶ γεννητικῆς λεγομένης τὸ ποιεῖν, εἰ τοῦτο ποιήσει τὸ ἡγούμενον τῆς ψυχῆς, τῷ τρέφειν τὴν ἔνυλον καὶ γεννητικὴν ψυχήν." Creuzer, 147 c and d. This passage is quoted by Cudworth in connection with his doctrine of "plastic nature." Cf. *Intell. System*, I, 3, 37. Berkeley, however, does not interpret it as implying an independent "matter."

[206] *Ibid.*, sec. 270. This reference is not to 5, 5, 3, as stated in Fraser's text, but to 5, 5, 9: "Ὅρα δὲ καὶ τὸν κόσμον, ὅτι ἐπεὶ εἰ μηδεὶς κόσμος πρὸ αὐτοῦ, οὐκ ἐν κόσμῳ αὐτὸς, οὐδ' αὖ ἐν τόπῳ. Τίς γὰρ τόπος πρὶν κόσμον εἶναι; τὰ δὲ μέρη, ἀνηρτημένα εἰς αὐτόν, καὶ ἐν ἐκείνῳ, ψυχὴ δὲ οὐκ ἐν ἐκείνῳ, ἀλλ' ἐκεῖνος ἐν αὐτῇ. οὐδὲ γὰρ τόπος τὸ σῶμα τῇ ψυχῇ, ἀλλὰ ψυχὴ μὲν ἐν νῷ. σῶμα δὲ ἐν ψυχῇ. νοῦς δὲ ἐν ἄλλῳ. ἐκεῖνο δὲ οὐκ ἐν ἄλλῳ." Creuzer 528d.

Hence "Plotinus in his Fourth Ennead showeth it to be his opinion that the world seeth itself and all its parts." [207]

But if the process of actualization requires an infinite potentiality to be actualized, and an actualizer to select and realize this potentiality, it is even more essential that there be something to actualize. Soul occupies its middle station between the infinite diversity of potentiality or non-being and the unity of being only by grace of the latter. Purpose or realization requires an end or goal to be realized. The act of knowing requires an object. No psychological theory of meaning, no matter how refined, can by its nature be adequate, since such a theory of meaning must first require meaning in order to begin. Hence Berkeley now altogether abandons his psychological theory of universals as relations, acts, or "notions," [208] and follows rather "Plotinus," who "supposeth that the Soul of the universe is not the original cause or author of the species, but receives them from Intellect, the true principle of order and distinction, the source and giver of forms." [209] With this acceptance of the Neo-Platonic conception of the active reasons, or λόγοι, disappear the last traces of Berkeley's psychologism. Meanings cannot be identified with the psychological acts through which they are meant, a view which is only slightly more adequate than the theory which would identify meaning with sensible things. Meanings are, as a matter of fact, presupposed by both physical and psychical reality. Prior to both nature and soul lies the intelligible world, which, if properly understood, as by Plotinus, is constituted by "real things . . . independent of the soul . . ." but "neither sensible nor clothed with sensible qualities." [210]

In this discovery of the priority of logic or intelligibility, first made by Parmenides, Berkeley saw the foundation stone upon which the whole course of Greek speculation is based, and in the *Siris* he at last realizes that it is the foundation stone upon

---

[207] *Ibid.*, sec. 210. The reference may be, as Fraser suggests, to 4, 5, 8.

[208] Cf. particularly the second edition of the *Principles*, secs. 27, 142 (1734); and also Alc., VII. It must be remembered, however, that the doctrine of universals as acts has its roots in the distinction of will vs. idea in the *Commonplace Book* (cf. chap. II) and that even the use of the word "notion" for noetic *acts* occurs as early as 1713 in the third dialogue, F. i, p. 448.

[209] *Siris*, sec. 262. Cf. "τοῦτο γὰρ καὶ δυνατώτερον, καὶ ποιεῖν ἐν ψυχῇ δυνάμενον. κατ' εἴδη ἄρα ποιεῖ. Δεῖ τοίνυν καὶ αὐτὴν παρὰ νοῦ ἔχουσαν διδόναι. νοῦς δὴ ψυχῇ δίδωσι τῇ τοῦ παντός. ψυχὴ δὲ παρ' αὐτῆς ἡ μετὰ νοῦν τῇ μετ' αὐτὴν ἐλλάμπουσα καὶ τυποῦσα. ἡ δὲ, ὥσπερ ἐπιταχθεῖσα ἤδη ποιεῖ." II, 3, 17. Creuzer, 147e.

[210] *Ibid.*, sec. 316. Berkeley refers in the previous passage, from which this conclusion is drawn, to *Enn.*, 2, 6, 3, as Fraser states.

which rested not only his own earlier speculations, but all pure speculation. Prior to real things is reality, which is no "thing," but rather logic, or the intelligible core of the world. It is this core of meaning that yields explanatory power to all explanation, though it can itself never be explained in this sense, since any such explanation would already presuppose it. Through this logical pattern, the objects of space and time are actualized by soul. It is this reason which lends meaning to all things, constituting their essences, or making them what they *are*. "All created beings," says Berkeley, "were made by the Word; which is accordingly styled the Cause of all causes." [211] It is the Cause of causes, since it is the logical essence of causation itself, which is presupposed by all causes as their intelligible meaning. Prior to any question concerning the existence of anything here and now is the question concerning the nature of the thing itself, or that which it *is*. Prior to the potential is the actual; prior to the world of becoming the world of being; and prior to existence, essence. [212]

Meaning cannot be derived from existence, since existence, to be existence, already has meaning. Hence the Cause of causes, the pattern according to which the world was fashioned, is to be found in the intelligible world. It is only by reference to such forms that the δημιουργός carves out a world from the infinite stuff of potentiality, and it is only by reference to such a stable and unified structure of meaning that we are able to recognize what appears, before it is once more consumed by that non-being which constitutes its destiny. Without this stable core, everything would be consumed in a chaos that would not even be meaningless, for to be possible is to be non-contradictory; but if x is possible, non-x is equally possible, so that nothing is possible which is not equally impossible. Even

---

[211] *Ibid.*, sec. 359. Cf. *de Secr. Par. Div. Sap.*, to which Berkeley here refers: "Deus igitur summus, ut antea dictum est, nullius rei procreatae causa est, sed ipsius causae opifex: haec vero illius opus. Quoniam nullam communionem habet cum ipsis rebus procreatis.

Verbum quod primo procreatum, ab opifice primario constitutum est, ut causa omnium entium quae ab eodem originem habent." Lib. X, caps. xvii and xviii, ed. Du Val, p. 1070.

The phrase "causa causarum" is used frequently in connection with the Word, or λόγος, or *intellectus agens*, as thus conceived. In Lib. X, cap. xvii, p. 1069, for example, it is said that the "Verbum expressum, causa causarum omnium appellatur. . . ." Cf. also Lib. X, cap. xix, p. 1072: "Ideoque inter omnia quae sunt, extrema, sicut dictum est, connectuntur ea communione quae inter causam & effectum intercedit. In qua suprema est, causa prima verbo divino proxima, in qua consistit causa causarum omnium."

[212] The three Neo-Platonic hypostases are, of course, the four causes of Aristotle with the exception of matter.

that anything should be definitely possible, it must be what it is, existent in its own right, permanent and self-identical. To find this, we must pass through the realm of becoming, which is relativized by potentiality, to the field of forms. Such logical forms do not exist here rather than there, nor now rather than then, but simply exist. The intelligible essence of being does not exist now nor there. It simply is, and rests with itself in eternal self-sufficiency. The forms, furthermore, do not exist spatially, even in the process of being mixed with potentiality or matter, since this process occurs through the mediation of Soul, and "it was a doctrine of those ancient sages, that Soul was the place of forms, as may be seen in the twelfth book of the *Arcane Part of Divine Wisdom according to the Egyptians*." [213]

But the existence of plural forms means diversity, and diversity is otherness, potentiality, or abstraction. Does this not mean that there is an intelligible matter or destiny that rules the realm of actuality, as temporal things are ruled by fate? Berkeley is at last fully able to appreciate the answer which Plotinus gives to this question. The forms are not distinguished by the otherness of space and time. But they are distinct, for, "as Plotinus remarks, incorporeal things are distant from each other not by place, but (to use his expression) by *alterity*." [214] There is a divine or intelligible matter corresponding to its spatio-temporal image in the field of sense. There is pure or essential potentiality which hovers over actuality, in the form of that *alterity* or non-being without which even being itself, in its most intelligible form, would have no significance.

---

[213] *Siris*, sec. 269. Berkeley refers here to *de Secr. Par. Div. Sap.*, Lib. XII, cap. iii, ed. Du Val, p. 1075, where it is argued that only the faculty or potentiality of receiving forms is inherent ("ingenitam") in the soul, not the forms themselves.

"Quare cum animus paratissimus sit ad recipiendas per abstractionem formas omnes rerum sensilium, nullam earum profecto insitam habet. Ex eoque formarum locus dicitur."

This implies, of course, as Berkeley doubtless noted, in accordance with his own view, that space is itself a form of potentiality or faculty ("facultas").

[214] *Ibid.*, sec. 329. Fraser's conjecture of 3, 6, 15 is possible, but Berkeley is more probably referring to 6, 4, 4: "Οὐδὲν οὖν ἡμῖν παρὰ τοῦ πλήθους οὕτω προϊόντος, ἐξεύ-

ρηται εἰς εὐπορίαν, ἐπεὶ καὶ τὸ ὂν πολλὰ συγ-χωροῦμεν εἶναι ἑτερότητι, οὐ τόπῳ. Ὁμοῦ γὰρ πᾶν τὸ ὂν, κᾂν πολὺ οὕτως ᾖ, ἑὸν γὰρ ἑόντι πελάζει, καὶ πᾶν ὁμοῦ, καὶ νοῦς πολὺς, ἑτερότητι οὐ τόπῳ, ὁμοῦ δὲ πᾶς." Creuzer 648 A and B. Cf. 5, 9, 6.

Ficinus' free translation runs as follows: "nihil itaque nobis ex multitudine sic profluente perspicue compertum est ad dubitationem conferens explicandam. Quando quidem et ipsum ens esse multa concedimus alteritate quadam, sed non loco. Simul enim est ens universum, quamvis ita sit multiplex: nempe, ut Parmenides ait, ens enti propinquat, ac simul est universum. Quin etiam intellectus est multiplex alteritate, non loco, sed simul est omnis."

There is an eternal passage or negation in the realm of forms, of which time is the sensuous image, just as space is the sensuous equivalent of the inclusiveness of concepts. Forms cannot be included without excluding others. Hence, there is an endless dependency or relativity in the intelligible world, an eternal dialectic passing through the realm of forms, just as fate passes through the realm of space as time, which is the "soul" or actualization of the potentiality of space. In the same way, dialectic, or negation, or synthesis is the "soul" or actualization of the identities and differences lying statically or potentially in formal logic. Even the logical essence of being requires a logical matter or non-being,[215] which hovers over all meaning as its potential, meaningless fringe, for meaning is achieved only by paying the price of the meaningless. The unity of intelligibility is rendered possible only by an intelligible diversity that is equally essential. Logical completeness is gained only by recognizing the incomplete, and logical absoluteness only by recognizing the finite. It is true that, as Plotinus maintained, everything is present in the λόγος, or absolute whole of reason. This is, indeed, its fatal imperfection, for it is so complete that even the incomplete is to be found there, and is itself so perfect as to be imperfect.

The realm of meaning is a microcosm in which universality, individuality, perfection, and imperfection are all alike present, mutually negating and conditioning one another, and making up one all-inclusive system of systems. It is absurd to assert

---

[215] This is why the Word, or λόγος, cannot be supposed to be the first and true cause of things, but only the mediating cause, since it only attaches preexistent forms to preexistent matter, and hence "acts" only occasionally or instrumentally. God is "the source and original of all things; which He produceth, not occasionally or instrumentally, but with actual and real efficacy. Thus the treatise *de Secretiore Parte Divinae Sapientiae* in the tenth book saith of God, that He is not only the first agent but also that he it is who truly acts or creates, *qui vere efficit.*" Sec. 321.

This citation proves definitely that Berkeley used the translation of Carpentarius probably in the ed. of Du Val. Cf. Lib. X, cap. iv, p. 1065: "Intellectus enim animum eiusmodi vere non efficit.

Quoniam omne quod vere efficit idem quoque procreat elementum rei, substantiam scilicet formae subiectam, & formam conservatricem elementi. Intellectus autem neque animi elementum, neque eius formam efficit. Quare neque ipsius animum vere dicetur efficere: etiam si medium quiddam sit inter causam huius efficientem primam: rationemque habeat efficientis ultimi, quod idem est proximum. Primum enim agens Deus est, qui vere efficit."

Berkeley doubtless saw in this Neo-Platonic conception of pure or absolute creation the confirmation of his earlier and more confused criticism of Malebranche's occasionalism or instrumentalism in the second dialogue between Hylas and Philonous.

that this absolute is nevertheless thought, and hence not absolute, since it is the very essence of what is meant by thought to penetrate to what is other than itself and to absorb this other into a unity, which nevertheless exists only by virtue of the diversity which it absorbs. Its absoluteness, that is, lies precisely in its not being truly absolute. The λόγος is, therefore, a mediating chain (σειρά) of diverse links uniting what lies beyond itself. Thought must have an object which it knows and understands and assimilates into a system. But the assimilation is never pure. The system remains a system of objects, a unity in diversity, a subject unable to know itself save as object, an infinite regress of potential assimilation never perfectly achieved, for that perfect, systematic unity towards which all knowing advances, if ever achieved, would have no meaning. Without the meaningless, without otherness, or potentiality, there could be no meaning.

A meaning finally absorbing this otherness into itself would be beyond meaning, and yet all meaning presupposes such a transcendent source as its final cause or end. How can thought strive for a unity, if no such unity exists? And yet such unity cannot exist actually or intelligibly, since existence requires non-existence. Beyond existence, beyond eternity, beyond all meaning whatsoever, therefore, lies meaning itself, as pure, unknowable, non-existent oneness, necessarily presupposed by all duality, but only approached by the infinite and self-stultifying dialectic of the λόγος, which *yields* this meaning and reality to all that is. Lying beyond being, in the same way in which being lies beyond becoming, is the transcendent One, or source of meaning. Between this absolute being beyond being (οὐσία ὄντως οὖσα) and absolute non-being, endlessly expressing the inexpressible, and thereby yielding moments of actuality to the non-existent, never resting, never failing, never succeeding, moves the mediator or λόγος. Eternity, which is the atmosphere in which it moves, is the pattern of time, but this eternity is itself only the image of that truth which it can never express, though by this very failure of expression it expresses it, and thus, through its endless contradiction, bestows a meaning upon all things.

The dualism or potentiality that permeates the field of reflection reduces it to the level of a totality or whole which is "dependent" upon its parts. The unity which it achieves is at best a spurious or partial unity, although without perfect unity the duality of reflection would be impossible. Species may be distinguished only within a genus. The basic species of the λόγος, therefore, being and non-being, actuality and potentiality, require a *summum genus*, inaccessible to either. Just as the chaos of potentiality presupposes actuality, so does actuality itself presuppose the one, which is beyond being. Berkeley's own dissatisfaction with the speculative absolute at which he had arrived in the *Three Dialogues*, and his transcendence of rationalism in the final, practical period of his intellectual development, enabled him to appreciate the logical necessity underlying the mystical apex of Greek reflection, Plotinus' conception of the One.

Beyond the absolute whole of reflection, which binds every phase of reality together into a contradictory unity of parts, lies the Absolute, or the One itself, that which purely and actually exists with no admixture of negation, — or that which has *all* otherness or potentiality within itself, not external to it as a repelling pole which would reduce it to dependence and duality. All such duality and dependence must be within itself, or it cannot be truly one and actually existent (τὸ ὄντως ὄν). Only by thus including diversity may it really exclude it, since if diversity is still external, the One will not be one, but one *of* many. It must not include diversity, however, as a reflective whole includes its parts, by weaving them into a system which is more than themselves, so that the mind is forced from one to the other, until it gains a sense of a third and higher unity which is capable of binding this whole, or one, to the parts which are other than itself. The One must be one with its parts, and thus ever alike one. "The Supreme Being, saith Plotinus, as he excludes all diversity, is ever alike present." [216] Just as meaning itself is everywhere in space and time, since they themselves are forms of intelligibility or being, and therefore nowhere, so is the One everywhere present in meaning, since being in itself, as meaning, must be one.

With the aid of Plotinus, Berkeley is thus able to eradicate from his thought the last traces of that abstract rationalism with which he had struggled ever since the intriguing mathematical ideal of the Enlightenment had taken possession of his youthful mind and had led it on step by step to the all-inclusive, speculative absolute of the third dialogue. This reason,

[216] *Siris*, sec. 358. Fraser's conjecture of 5, 5, 9 is possible. Cf., however, 3, 8, 9; 6, 8, 16; *et passim*.

however, as Berkeley now sees, manages to include everything within its scope only by remaining itself outside them as the ineffable irrational one, or subject, for which they are objects. The system of systems, the One, into which thought binds its objects, is never present, but rather presupposed by all reflection. To arrive at this transcendent one, this meaningless source of meaning, the mind must flee all objects, all duality, and sink into itself. Here, in mystic rapture, it may commune with the Most Supreme Being. "Therefore the flight of the mind towards God is called by the Platonics φυγὴ μόνου πρὸς μόνον." [217]

Here, the pure soul meets that which is the guide and source of reason itself, the final inexpressible source of meaning, that towards which reason strives but which it never attains. This ineffable communion with the One Berkeley finds most perfectly stated in a passage of Proclus [218] which he quotes near the end of the *Siris*.[219] "Proclus observes . . . that, as in the mysteries, those who are initiated at first meet with manifold and multiform Gods, but, being entered and thoroughly initiated, they receive the Divine illumination and participate the very Deity: in like manner, if the soul look abroad, she beholds the shadows and images of things; but returning into herself she unravels and beholds her own essence: at first she seemeth only to behold herself; but having penetrated farther she discovers the mind. And again still farther advancing into the innermost sanctuary of the soul, she contemplates the θεῶν γένος. And this, he saith, is the most excellent of all human acts, in the silence and repose of the faculties of the soul to tend upwards to the very Divinity; to approach and be closely joined with that which is ineffable and superior to all beings. When she comes so high as the first principle, she ends her journey and rests. Such is the doctrine of Proclus." [220] Such is, therefore, the doctrine which Berkeley recognized as the culminating phase of Greek reflection, and in which he found the closest approximation to the conception which he was coming more and more clearly to appreciate as the guiding principle of his own life of reflection.

[217] Sec. 358. Cf. *Enn.*, 6, 9, 11.
[218] *In Plat. Theol.*, Book I.
[219] Sec. 333.

[220] *In Plat. Theol.*, I, 3, p. 7 (Hamb., 1618).

The Philosophy of the Transcendent

While Berkeley undoubtedly learned more from the Neo-Platonists than from any other school of philosophy, and while his philosophy of nature and his epistemology may be regarded as essentially Neo-Platonic, it is nevertheless clear to anyone making a careful study of the latter portions of the *Siris* that he cannot finally and fundamentally agree with them. He takes exception, for example, to "the doctrine of Proclus" in the next paragraph. It is not true that the soul is the proper means for knowing the deity. This humanistic and spiritistic theory which Berkeley had himself maintained in his early writings [221] is precisely contrary to the fact. It is not that the soul knows God through herself "but . . . on the other hand, that the contemplation of God is the proper means to know or understand our own soul." [222] The ancient doctrine that knowledge is rendered possible only by oneness with the known object is untrue. Knowledge is always of an other, or object, and the oneness is rather conditioned by the otherness than the otherness by the oneness.

It is the great delusion of the rationalist that he actually *is* the objects he knows, and that through thought alone, therefore, he may attain the goal for which thought strives. To the Greeks, for whom man was a rational animal, this dogma seemed to result in the view that the world was meaning or idea. To the moderns, for whom man is subject or soul, it seems to result in that subjectivism or psychologism of which perhaps the clearest example is to be found in the early spiritism of Berkeley himself. What Berkeley now sees is that if it were really true that like knows like, or if, as Descartes stated it, we must know ourselves better than anything else, because we *are* ourselves, there could be no such thing as knowledge, for the known object must be other than the knowledge through which it is known. It is, therefore, not through ourselves that we know ourselves but precisely through that which is absolutely other than ourselves. Knowledge requires an object. To know ourselves there must be an other, not an other which is at the same time an identity, but the absolute other, which is presupposed

[221] Cf. especially 3 D., F. i, p. 448: "For, all the notion I have of God is obtained by reflecting on my own soul, heightening its powers and removing its imperfections. I have therefore, . . . in myself some sort of an active thinking image of the Deity."

[222] *Siris*, sec. 334. Berkeley here refers to *Alcibiades*, I, pp. 132–133.

by any such relative otherness. An otherness, which is other
only within an all-embracing identity, is not a pure other.
Furthermore, unless the otherness or objectivity upon which
knowledge is dependent is justifiable, or truly objective,
knowledge itself is not justifiable. To know truly means to
know what is other than our knowing. The object must be
prior to our knowing of it. But this absolute object is not identical with the known object, since the known object is merely the
other *of* the knowing subject, and thus relative or subjective.
The absolute other, presupposed by the relative otherness of
knowledge, cannot be known, or in other words, it must be
known otherwise than through knowledge. This other way is
faith, for only through faith may the absolutely independent or
objective be known. Yet knowledge, to be knowledge, or knowledge of something, requires something prior to it, and hence
may be legitimized only through faith in the transcendent or
independent ($\tau\grave{o}$ $\check{o}\nu\tau\omega\varsigma$ $\check{o}\nu$). This transcendent is not what is
known as transcendent, for the object of knowledge is tran-
scendent in this sense. Such objects are transcendent only by
being non-transcendent, — that is by being known.

To legitimize our knowledge, we must assert that what we
know is not identical with our knowing of it, or else we know
nothing. Knowing is itself both realistic and idealistic, since,
as the mediator or $\lambda\acute{o}\gamma o\varsigma$, it involves both an identity and a diversity. Remove either pole and knowledge is destroyed. There
is no being without non-being; no knowing without that which
is unknown. But the unknown is prior to the known, for it is
possible to conceive (through faith) of an absolute or unknown
object, but it is impossible to conceive of knowledge without
something to know. In this respect, Proclus' understanding of
the true meaning of transcendence must have seemed more adequate to Berkeley than Plotinus', for while the former does describe the final union in which philosophy culminates as a mystic
enthusiasm, he does, nevertheless, introduce for the first time
the conception of faith, the highest faculty of the human soul,
transcending the lower faculties, love and truth.[223] Love leads
us through beauty to truth; truth reveals to us the intelligible
world, but only faith reveals to us what is absolutely other than
ourselves, and hence the Absolute itself, the unknowable.[224]

[223] Cf. *In Plat. Theol.*, II, 11. Also *In Tim.*, I, p. 212.
[224] Cf. *In Plat. Theol.*, IV, 10, p. 194, and I, 24, pp. 61 ff. Also Zeller, *Phil. der Griechen*, 4th ed., III, 2, 883 and 885.

The Neo-Platonists approached the conception of pure transcendence, but vitiated it by their theory of mystic participation. The transcendent being of Neo-Platonism is still opposed to a transcendent non-being or matter. But neither the one nor the other is truly what it purports to be, for the non-being nevertheless is, and the being gains its absolute significance only by an opposition to the nothingness of matter. Such transcendence is spurious and illegitimate, for it is an otherness marred by the identity of relation. Being, no matter how absolute or pure, is as dependent upon non-being as non-being upon being, and the supreme oneness which reason finally seeks as a refuge from this circle of mediation is nothing but mediation itself, the identity which requires a prior diversity to absorb. The Supreme Being of the Platonists, therefore, is not the Supreme Being at all, but only the rational and hence contradictory reflection of this supremacy in the λόγος. The escape from all objectivity and otherness to the One is itself dictated by reason, and is hence no escape at all, but a return of the λόγος into itself. Its other is only itself, as is shown by the cancellation of otherness in the mystic ecstasy.

Reason cannot escape itself by reasoning about the irrational. To grasp this, something absolutely and ultimately other than reason is required. The One, into which the mystic is absorbed, is nothing but the spurious absolute of reason, — the complete whole of reality, the speculative absolute which conditions all reflection and mediation. Mysticism is itself the pure, intrinsic essence of rationalism, and the Neo-Platonist is merely developing the intellectualism of his predecessors to its logical culmination. The mystic escape of reason from itself is nothing but a return of reason into itself, or another circular oscillation in that perpetual round of mediation in which reflection consists. Neo-Platonism is once more λόγος philosophy. This is why Berkeley prefaces his criticism of the Neo-Platonic Trinity with a reference to "St. Augustine in his Commentary on the beginning of St. John's Gospel, who, having declared that Christ is the Wisdom of God by which all things were made, observes that this doctrine was also found in the writings of philosophers, who taught that God had an only begotten son, by whom are all things." [225] Berkeley discerns, however, in the *Enneades*, and

---

[225] *Siris*, sec. 359. The words of St. Augustine to which Berkeley here refers help us to understand his dissatisfaction (expressed in the following sections) with the philosophic or Platonic Trinity as a partial or inadequate reflection or media-

particularly in Plato himself, traces of an irrationalism more profound than the spurious unreason of the rationalist. In speaking of the Sixth Book of the *Republic* he says "truth and knowledge are not the good itself, although they approach thereunto," [226] and a little farther [227] "Plato teacheth that the doctrine concerning the One or Unit is a *means* to lead and raise the mind to the knowledge of Him who truly is." [228] That which is truly transcendent, and hence beyond even the rationalistic irrational or One, can be apprehended practically only through the Good, which is more than a concept. It is only through the principle of Value that the various levels of the Neo-Platonic absolute can be arranged in a hierarchy. Without such a principle the field of meaning becomes a self-enclosed or meaningless circle, in which being is dependent upon non-being and non-being upon being, and in which it is purely arbitrary to consider one as prior to the other. The prior, to be prior, requires the posterior in the same manner in which the posterior requires the prior. So far as meaning or intelligibility is concerned, neither is really prior to the other. Purely *logical* priority is impossible, since degrees of priority depend upon absolute priority, and that which is absolutely prior must be autonomous or self-sufficient. But logic or meaning can never be autonomous, since meaning essentially refers beyond itself, and is hence imperfect or intrinsically posterior. Priority is a principle of Value. Only in the perfection of the Good may we discover that which is truly self-sufficient, but such perfection, while it involves completeness, is a whole not of parts but a whole of Value. It

---

tion of the truly transcendent, which is to be approached (pervenirent) only *practically*. What the Neo-Platonists failed to see is that *mare transeundum est*.

"Nam inveniuntur et ista in libris philosophorum: et quia unigenitum Filium habet Deus, per quem sunt omnia. Illud potuerunt videre quod est, sed viderunt de longe: noluerunt tenere humilitatem Christi, in qua navi securi pervenirent ad id quod longe videre potuerunt; et sorduit eis crux Christi. Mare transeundum est, et lignum contemnis? O sapientia superba! irrides crucifixum Christum; ipse est quem longe vidisti: *In principio erat Verbum, et Verbum erat apud Deum.* Sed quare crucifixus est? Quia lignum tibi humilitatis eius necessarium erat. Superbia enim tumueras, et longe ab illa patria

projectus eras; et fluctibus huius saeculi interrupta est via, et qua transeatur ad patriam non est, nisi ligno porteris. Ingrate, irrides eum qui ad te venit ut redeas! Ipse factus est via, et hoc per mare: inde in mare ambulavit, ut ostenderet esse in mari viam. . . . Propter te crucifixus est, ut humilitatem doceret; et quia si sic veniret ut Deus, non agnosceretur. Si enim sic veniret ut Deus, non veniret eis qui videre Deum non poterant. Non enim secundum id quod Deus est, aut venit, aut discedit; cum sit ubique praesens, et nullo loco contineatur. Sed secundum quid venit? Quod apparuit homo." *In Joannis Evangelium,* Tractatus II, 4. [226] *Siris,* sec. 343.

[227] *Ibid.,* sec. 355.
[228] My italics.

may, therefore, be said to be truly prior, since that which is perfect in this sense does not require the imperfect, though the imperfect does require it. Only through such perfection can the universe be ordered in a scale or hierarchy or σειρά, and the logical dialectic of meaning itself given a meaning or direction.

But that which is self-sufficient or perfect in itself is beyond meaning, and can be reflected or understood only *through* the λόγος. In itself it can be grasped by faith alone, as that which is utterly and absolutely prior to all absolutes. Perfection may not be understood theoretically but only practically, though all understanding, if it is to *have* anything to understand, presupposes it. Prior to philosophy, or the study of intelligibility, therefore, is Theology, the study of Value, or what is good in itself. The speculative whole, or absolute, which is necessarily presupposed by the rationalist, as the ideal synthesis in which all contradictions find their ultimate meaning and sink into a harmony, is itself a contradiction, or a harmony of disharmonies. If it should really and truly dissolve all contradictions, it would cease to be a harmony, and would, indeed, lose all significance, since without contradictions other than itself to be resolved, it would cease to be what it is, — *their* resolution.

The absolute of reason must be apprehended finally as a norm. But this ideal of reason presupposes priority or ideality, which is in no sense a totality. Hence, as Berkeley says, "if we should say that all things make one God, this would, indeed, be an erroneous notion of God," [229] for though the forms are prior to everything which exists, priority itself is prior to them. "*Philosophia prima*," therefore, which is the study of intelligibility, or "the real and true causes" of things, necessarily transforms itself into "metaphysics" or "theology," — the study of the intrinsic good.[230] Intelligibility itself can be understood only practically, or through the principle of Value. "Theology and philosophy," says Berkeley, "gently unbind the ligaments that chain the soul down to the earth, and assist her flight towards the sovereign Good." [231] The *Siris* is not only an expression of philosophy but of that in which philosophy must end, theology. It is, therefore, not only an expression of reason, but of that in which reason begins, faith.

But is this not mysticism? Call it faith, theology, or what we will, does not knowledge of God imply oneness with Him, and, therefore, in some sense the self-exaltation of the mystic hero

[229] *Siris*, sec. 288.   [230] *Ibid.*, sec. 285.   [231] *Ibid.*, sec. 302.

who has seen the Good? Such knowledge of the Good can never be, if the perfect is to be kept pure from relation and imperfection, and thus truly prior. Mysticism is blasphemy. How then can the perfect be apprehended without soiling it? To such a question there can be only one conceivable answer — which is strictly inconceivable. We cannot know or apprehend the Good. The pure soul, or mystic, like the absolutist is deluding himself. The divine whole, in which he thinks he is absorbed, is nothing but himself, and the divine trance is nothing but the delusion of an intellectual narcissism. He is caught in the web of an inextricable solipsism, since the other he knows so ecstatically is nothing but himself and the oscillations of his own noetic mechanism.

There is no apprehension of the Good. But it may apprehend us. Identity may never bring forth diversity nor immanence become transcendence, but the transcendent may become immanent, and out of that which is absolutely diverse, identity may emerge. Prior to affirmation is negation; prior to idealism, realism; prior to the subject, the absolute object. Since we can never approach that which is perfect or which truly is ($\tau\grave{o}$ $\ddot{o}\nu\tau\omega\varsigma$ $\ddot{o}\nu$), it must approach us, if there is to be any contact. Since affirmation can never become negation, negation must become affirmation. Since we cannot apprehend the transcendent, it must apprehend us, though not in a fashion which can be understood, since were this the case, *we* should be grasping *it*, and knowledge would be a solipsistic delusion. This is the meaning of faith.

Since knowledge cannot create its object, the object must first exist, and then create knowledge, or send it to us as the mediator or the Word.[232] We cannot escape solipsism or humanism if we suppose that such knowledge was "originally struck from the hard rock of human reason."[233] It must rather be "derived ... by a Divine tradition from the Author of all things."[234] We have already observed how Berkeley discovered cases of the doctrine of a Divine tradition in Timaeus Locrus and the Hermetic writings. He found it, however, even more clearly stated in the *Enneades*,[235] although still mixed with the mysticism which

[232] *Ibid.*, sec. 359.
[233] *Ibid.*, sec. 360.
[234] *Ibid.*
[235] "It seems a remarkable confirmation of this, what Plotinus observed in his fifth Ennead, that this doctrine of the Trinity — Father, Mind, and Soul — was no late invention, but an ancient tenet." (Sec. 360.)

This reference is to *Enn.* 5, 1, 8, not 5, 1, 5, as Fraser suggests. After citing the Second Epistle (312e) and comment-

transforms so much of the Neo-Platonic theology into a demon-
ology. But the purest form of the doctrine Berkeley found, as
we have already noted, in the ultimate source of Neo-Platonism,
and he himself quotes the *Second Epistle* at length,[236] remarking
upon Plato's caution in enjoining Dionysius "over and over,
with great earnestness, not to suffer what he communicates
concerning the mysteries of the Divine nature to fall into
illiterate or vulgar hands," since "nothing would seem more
ridiculous or absurd to the common run of mankind." [237]

Divine knowledge, gained through a faith or "tradition"
having its origin in the Good itself, is something very different
from the mystic ecstasy of the rationalist, since through faith
there is no question of oneness with God. "Pure souls" [238] require no faith, for they already see God. Faith is the possession
of man alone, and the object of faith is an absolute object, or
that which is entirely other than man, though it is only through
this absolute other that we are what we are. Through the
passage of reason into faith and the apprehension of that which
is (τὸ ὄντως ὄν), everything else also sinks back into what it is.
Through the absolute unreason of faith, reason once more becomes possible. The struggle of thought to overcome itself,
which leads it into the practical, and from the practical to that
faith which is the presupposition of the practical, at last ceases,
and reason, resting from its endless endeavors to become unreason, is once again content to be reason, or the λόγος, transmitting its message of meaning across the gulf from being to
non-being, but never giving itself up wholly to the one or to the
other. Even matter, or non-being, being the absolute negation
of that which absolutely is, or rather *not* being this, content to
occupy its lowest but necessary position in the chain or hierarchy of value, ceases to be the spurious non-being which *is*, and
sinks back into that utter nothingness which is *not*.

The *Siris*, therefore, ends on a note of sober irony. Purified
by dialectic, reason gladly yields up its demonic pretensions
and resumes its more modest role of mediation or relation.

---

ing upon the phrase τοῦ αἰτίου πατέρα
of the Sixth Epistle (323d) Plotinus remarks that the Trinitarian conception
(ἀγαθός, νοῦς, ψυχή, or, as Ficinus translates, bonum, idea, anima) is no recent
doctrine but: "καὶ εἶναι τοὺς λόγους τούσδε
μὴ καινούς, μηδὲ νῦν, ἀλλὰ πάλαι μὲν εἰρῆσ-
θαι μὴ ἀναπεπταμένως, τοὺς δὲ νῦν λόγους

ἐξηγητὰς ἐκείνων γεγονέναι μαρτυρίοις πι-
στωσαμένοις τὰς δόξας ταύτας παλαιὰς εἶναι
τοῖς αὐτοῦ τοῦ Πλάτωνος γράμμασιν."
Creuzer, 489b, cf. *ibid.*, sec. 365.

[236] *Siris*, sec. 365.

[237] Berkeley also refers in sec. 366 to
Phaedrus, 246, in the same connection.

[238] *Ibid.*, sec. 367.

Man, the rational animal, abandoning his attempts to become something other than what he is, to mystics, intellectuals, and "pure souls," accepts his lot. "As for the perfect intuition of Divine things," says Berkeley, "that he supposeth to be the lot of pure souls, beholding by a pure light, initiated, happy, free and unstained."[239] As for himself, however, realizing at last that he is neither pure, nor free, nor unstained, he becomes content with "those glimpses" [240] vouchsafed him by a higher source, and which are hence "within" his "reach." Like one who, in awakening from a terrible dream, finds himself taking an extraordinary satisfaction in the most commonplace and ordinary objects, he rediscovers the true value of reason or understanding as his own true and proper essence. Secure in the certainty that the transcendent absolute, which is the source of meaning, is beyond reason, he becomes aware, with an equal certainty, that it is likewise beyond unreason, and understands at last that the only method of achieving true and essential irrationality is to follow reason itself, the intrinsic paradox. Following this to the essential source (οὐσία ὄντως οὖσα) which it mediates, reason may then return, carrying some of its radiance to spread through the world as intelligibility. Hence, carried by paradox beyond paradox, faith, embodying itself in the Word, becomes reason, and expounds its mystery as Theology.

The Trinity

The supreme mystery which the λόγος reveals, that which lies beyond meaning as its own proper essence, is not the abstract One, the τὸ Ἕν of the Neo-Platonists, which becomes one only by excluding the many and thus relativizing itself, but that which is essentially or concretely one, — the Trinity. While "it is certain that men of greatest fame and learning among the ancient philosophers held a Trinity in the Godhead," such doctrines are nevertheless only "hints," and the rationalist, pursuing them "with too much curiosity," succeeds only in becoming bewildered.[241] Hence, "it is not to be supposed that either he [Plato] or any other philosophers of Greece or the East had by the light of nature obtained an adequate notion of the holy Trinity; nor even that their imperfect notion, so far as it went, was exactly just." [242] Yet "though it may be well presumed there is

239 *Ibid.*
240 *Ibid.*

241 Sec. 364.
242 *Ibid.*, sec. 360. Berkeley here refers

nothing to be found on that sublime subject in human writings which doth not bear the sure signatures of humanity," Berkeley himself, through his enforced practical recognition of transcendence, and exactly because of this, dares to write of it, and confesses that he has learned much from "eminent heathens" who were "no strangers to that mystery." [243]

Through a knowledge (which is not knowledge) that the otherness, reducing all reason to abstraction, is no mere potentiality, no non-being which nevertheless is, but an absolute otherness or transcendence, reason gives up the attempt to be what it is not and becomes once more reason, or the λόγος, — revelation. Philosophy, having transformed itself into Theology, is once more able to exist as philosophy, and reason, having passed into practical philosophy and discovered its basis in faith, once more dares to fulfill its rational function of relation. But unless that which it reveals be absolutely other than itself, it can reveal nothing. What it reveals, therefore, is the absolutely transcendent, that which is not only beyond reason, but beyond unreason as well, that which is beyond all conceivable or inconceivable formulations, that which is beyond even beyondness, and other than otherness, an object which is at the same time not an object at all, but the object of faith. It is not only beyond consistent formulation, but beyond contradiction, not only beyond contemplation but beyond paradox, not only beyond the dialectic of meaning which proceeds through ever-widening synthesis to the speculative absolute of reflection, but beyond the practical dialectic of concrete existence, which proceeds through unmediated oppositions to the absolute transcendence of value.

It is his realization that the synthetic dialectic of reason is really or concretely a practical dialectic which led Berkeley to appreciate the true distinction between the dogma of the Trinity and the various rationalistic or Platonic approximations he had discovered in his study of Greek philosophy. It is not the

---

particularly to Plato's *Second Epistle*, 312d, a passage emphasized by Plotinus, 5, 1, 8, and quoted by Berkeley (sec. 365): "Περὶ τὸν πάντων βασιλέα πάντ' ἐστὶ, καὶ ἐκείνου ἔνεκα πάντα, καὶ ἐκεῖνο αἴτιον ἁπάντων τῶν καλῶν. δεύτερον δὲ, πέρι τὰ δεύτερα, καὶ τρίτον πέρι τὰ τρίτα." He follows Plotinus in interpreting this cryptic passage to refer to the Neo-Platonic trinity of

ἀγαθός, νοῦς, ψυχή, or bonum, idea, anima. Cudworth, with whom Berkeley was familiar takes the same view. *Intell. System*, I, iv, 36.

[243] *Siris*, sec. 363. Berkeley refers to the Renaissance Platonists Bessarion and Eugubinus at this point, in addition to Cudworth.

infinite, rational self, or ψυχή of Platonism, which is capable of acting and thinking practically, but only the concrete or finite self. The mystic, who participates in the absolute, is no more truly a subject than the absolute in which he participates is truly an absolute. Nothing could more strikingly indicate the typically rationalistic character of this situation than the "synthesis" in which each factor mixes with something already mixed with itself. The purification of the moment of transcendence involves a corresponding purification of the moment of non-transcendence, which must be concretely or practically apprehended as something more than conceptual negation. This practical self is not the abstract "I" of the rationalist, into which may be read the whole eternal content of thought, but the individual self in its concrete finiteness. "*We*," says Berkeley, "are sprung from the Father, irradiated or enlightened by the Son, and moved by the Spirit." [244] It is only the individual, in his naked singularity, who is capable of being practically apprehended by a perfection truly absolute.

This absolute other is first of all that which truly is (τὸ ὄντως ὄν). As approached by the synthetic dialectic of reason, it is the final unity, or τὸ Ἕν of the Neo-Platonists,[245] though to be truly or concretely One it must contain its other in itself, and thus lie beyond reason as the single source of its essential duality. As approached by the unmediated dialectic of practical existence it is the "Good," [246] or the source of perfection. But the One, which is the source of knowledge, and the Good, which is the source of perfection, to be what they are, must first be. Such absolute being cannot derive its existence from something external, like finite things, nor can it, like the concept of being, derive its meaning from something beyond it, for in either case it would not purely and essentially be (οὐσία ὄντως οὖσα). First of all, therefore, the transcendent must be the source of itself, and hence the source of both knowledge and goodness, or, as Berkeley says, "the source of all perfection, or *Fons Deitatis*." [247] Lying beyond both reason and perfection, it is apprehended only practically, or through faith, as the "Principle" or "Father." [248]

<hr>

[244] *Ibid.*, sec. 362.
[245] *Ibid.*
[246] *Ibid.* "Good, Word, and Love," F. iii, p. 297, by which Berkeley indicates the consubstantiality of the First and Third Persons of the Trinity. That which

truly is, with no admixture of non-being (τὸ ὄντως ὄν), must be *perfectly*, or is itself the "Good."
[247] *Ibid.* An Augustinian phrase.
[248] *Ibid.*

But, as pure transcendence, the First Person of the Trinity is an abstraction. Unrevealed being would not perfectly be. "How could power or authority avail or subsist without knowledge ?"[249] The transcendent must become immanent, the absolute revealed. "There never was a time supposed wherein τὸ Ἕν subsisted without intellect; the priority having been understood only as a priority of order or conception, but not a priority of age."[250] As the other, which bears or expresses meaning or being, it is the "Word" or λόγος[251] that yields meaning or essence to what is not, making it what it is, mediating between what truly is and what is not as relation or "Mind."[252] But, as that which is more than any such objective or rational expression can indicate, as not only reason but as revelation not to abstract mind or life (ψυχή), but to concrete individuals, it is the "Son." By the "Son," says Berkeley, "we are irradiated or enlightened."

It is, however, with the Third Person of the Trinity that the meaning of the transformation of the synthetic dialectic of reason into a practical dialectic becomes most clearly apparent. The objective concept (ψυχή) of the Neo-Platonic Trinity becomes "Spirit." It is "by the Spirit," says Berkeley, that "we are moved."[253] The still abstract concepts of "Life," "Soul," and even "Love," by means of which Platonism attempted to apprehend itself, are now seen by Berkeley only to "bear analogy"[254] to that "Spirit" by which we are concretely or practically "moved." It is only Spirit which "moves" between the infinite chasm separating Absolute Value from the absolutely valueless, and thus bearing the actual content of Revelation concretely as faith. It is, therefore, only spirit which apprehends this absolute opposition, and thus makes the mediating activity of reason possible.

Taken rationally, Spirit itself is a synthesis or inseparable wholeness of being and knowing, not the relative wholeness of mediation, but the absolute holiness which passes *entirely* into whatever it touches. As the realization or completion of Being, it is that which passes out of itself and knows itself as "Soul."[255] As the return of Soul into its source, or the completion of Wisdom, it is "Love."[256] Taken as the *essential* completion of being and knowing, it is that without which they cannot be what they

---

[249] *Ibid.*, sec. 361.

[250] *Ibid.*, sec. 352.

[251] *Ibid.*, sec. 362.

[252] *Ibid.*

[253] *Ibid.*

[254] *Ibid.*

[255] *Ibid.*

[256] *Ibid.*

are, and therefore, the absolutely prior, or the source. But, taken in and through itself practically, it is the perfection of Value, what is absolutely or intrinsically Good. Thus no Person of the Trinity can be thought without the others. "How could power or authority avail or subsist without knowledge ? or either without life and action?" [257] Being is prior to perfection, but perfection is also prior to being. Without the Holiness of Spirit, being would not absolutely and perfectly be, nor would knowing truly and perfectly know. It is equally true, however, that perfection requires being and knowledge truly to be (τὸ ὄντως ὄν). The Absolute Value must truly or absolutely exist as *causa sui*; it must absolutely know, though the otherness through which it knows or reveals itself is only itself. This Trinity of Absolute Being, Absolute Knowledge, and Absolute Perfection reflects itself in the three aspects belonging to the nature of any finite thing, its efficient cause, its formal cause, and its final cause. Such a thing, therefore, does vaguely constitute an image of the Trinity, though only in a confused and indeterminate manner. In so far as it is understood, however, it must be understood either through the source of its being, ontologically, through its essence, epistemologically, or through its value, practically or axiologically. It is, therefore, true to say that all things are understood through the Trinity, which is itself beyond understanding. This does not mean, however, that it is the irrational of the mystic. As Absolute Value it is rather the source of rationality as well as of irrationality.

Having reached this goal, which is so paradoxical as not to be even altogether paradoxical, Berkeley's concrete logic at last comes to rest. Without such a transcendent object, the world dissolves into a chaos not even intelligible enough to be meaningless, for there can be no meaninglessness without meaning. In the light of that essential being which is beyond reason and intelligibility, the world becomes intelligible. The "venerable mystery" of the Trinity is that supreme and central link binding the various levels of reality together into a single chain, the *Siris*. It is the central link, uniting being with non-being, actuality with potentiality, since it stands beyond them both as the eternal center about which they revolve in the orbits of intelligibility, but without which they resolve into a meaningless regress. Through this core of perfection, reason is able to understand the links of successive chains joined together in a meaningful whole. In the innermost orbit, closest to the Divine and immediately touched by the outpouring of its Holy Spirit, is the sphere of faith, upon which is based all practical aspiration and the thought of Value. Beyond this innermost sphere lie the realms of generation and decay, moving in perpetual oscillations about their timeless center and fading off into the exterior darkness of an absolute Non-being. But between them, relating that which is to what is not and thus transforming the former into actuality and the latter into potentiality, catching inadequate "glimpses" of everything but actually grasping none, always seeking, never finding, granting meaning to the meaningless but thereby corrupting the meaning it seeks to grant, always confused and never content, in itself only when it is out of itself, understanding something other than itself and thus not understanding it, the essence of connection, identity, or otherness, — lies the λόγος. Confusing the pale reflection of all things which it mirrors upon its surface with actuality, it pieces these reflected fragments together into an absolute whole, a synthesis which it mistakes for the world, but which at once turns into nothing at all, since the λόγος cannot forsake its own nature. Its synthesis of syntheses becomes itself pure antithesis, its whole sinks to the level of a part, and the spurious certainty, momentarily generated by this perfect harmony, becomes absolute scepticism, not the absolute itself, but only a pathway to the practical. Comprehending its own nature, however, in passing through the practical and in glimpsing that which is truly beyond itself, the absoluteness of its synthesis is maintained, — and as relation, mediation, or the reflection of an absolute antithesis, it sinks into its proper place as the middle link in the universal chain.

Thus, while Berkeley's concrete logic led him finally beyond all logic to the sphere of the practical and beyond this to the transcendent, here, strangely enough, he discovered its justification, in apprehending the significance of faith. Berkeley's method of abstraction, the chain uniting the various strands of his thought into a whole, the *Siris*, does not fail him even at the last transcendent link. Reason is at least indispensible in warding off error and purifying faith. Hence, he easily detects the kernel of abstraction lying at the core of the latitudinarianism of the Cambridge Platonists, and the abstract attempts of "the learned Doctor Cudworth" [258] to arithmeticize the Trinity. Concrete logic is not the concrete itself. But in its subordinate, intermediate station, as the mediator, the critic, the purifier, the λόγος, it performs an essential function in pursuing its abstract and intermediate absolute, the ideal of truth. What is deepest and most important lies utterly beyond it as "venerable mystery," [259] and truth itself, when thus approached, becomes finally inaccessible; but nevertheless "we may discern some glimpse of truth by long poring on it," [260] since Truth or meaning leads us inevitably beyond itself to that perfection of which it is the λόγος or expression.

[258] *Ibid.*, sec. 352.   [259] *Ibid.*, sec. 365.   [260] *Ibid.*, sec. 368.

CHAPTER XVII

THE MEANING OF BERKELEY

BERKELEY completed the *Siris*, his last and definitive philosophical work, in 1744. His health, already failing, was further impaired by the exhausting study and meditation which had been necessary for its composition. He himself declared, according to his first biographer Stock, "that this work cost him more time and pains than any other he had ever been engaged in." He was able, however, to carry on his episcopal duties with unabated zeal, and several more or less occasional writings of this period have survived.

Among these is a "Letter to the Roman Catholics of The Diocese of Cloyne," which he wrote in 1745 in a remarkably sympathetic tone, advising them against siding with the Pretender, whose conquest, he maintained, would be a disaster to them as well as to the representatives of the Irish Protestant Church, whom he similarly advised in "A Letter to his Clergy by the Bishop of Cloyne on the Occasion of the Rebellion in 1745." The friendly recognition of Catholics by a Protestant Bishop was an unprecedented step in the history of the Irish Church.

The See of Cloyne had never been congenial,[1] and the Earl of Chesterfield, who had come to admire Berkeley's character,[2] and who was appointed Lord Lieutenant of Ireland in 1745, offered to translate him to the far more pleasant and lucrative Bishopric of Clogher.[3] Berkeley, however, "did not love epis-

[1] "Bishop Berkeley never had any idea of Cloyne as a beautiful situation." Mrs. Berkeley in *Biog. Brit.*, Corr. and Add., III, p. 258.

[2] "Soon after Lord Chesterfield's return from his first Embassy in Holland, Dr. Berkeley presented him with his Minute Philosopher which was just then published, and met with uncommon approbation. His Lordship esteemed the author still more than the book; but no intimacy subsisted between them. When he came to Dublin, with the power as well as desire of rewarding merit, he embraced the first opportunity of showing his regard for so respectable a character, and accordingly made an offer to the Doctor of changing his Bishopric of Cloyne for that of Clogher, which was of a much greater value." Dr. Maty's *Memoirs of Lord Chesterfield*, vol. I, p. 163, *Misc. Works of Lord Chesterfield*, Dublin, 1777.

[3] "... That nobleman [Chesterfield] offered to him the See of Clogher where he was told he might immediately receive fines to the amount of ten thousand pounds, he consulted Mrs. Berkeley as having a family, and with her full appro-

copal translations," [4] and in spite of the entreaties of his intimate friends refused the offer.[5] In 1746 he was mentioned in connection with the Primacy.[6] His indifference to this suggestion, however, is indicated in a letter to Prior written in 1747.[7] "As to what you say," writes Berkeley, "that the Primacy would have been a glorious thing, for my part I could not see, all things considered, the glory of wearing the name of Primate in these days, or of getting so much money, a thing every tradesman in London may get if he pleases . . . and for doing good to the world, I imagine I may, upon the whole, do as much in a lower station." The extent to which he loathed the whole machinery of self-promotion involved in ecclesiastical preferment is also revealed in the following ironical letter which he addressed at this time to Dr. Clarke, the Vice Provost of Trinity College, who had solicited his recommendation. Berkeley writes: [8]

I would not suppose your affairs are at all the worse for my not being in towne; for, to speak the truth, I would have been of no use with my Lord Lieutenant unless he had given me a decent opportunity of speaking to the point by consulting or advising with me about it, a thing which I had no right to expect. I have been told His Excellency expressed a particular esteem for you publickly at the Castle, on occasion of the compliment you made him on his first arrival. This personal prepossession in your favour, grounded on his sense of your merit, is, in my opinion, worth twenty recommendations, even of those great men in power, who alone have a right to make them. To conclude, I wish you all success in your undertakings, being with sincere regard &.

That the remoteness of the realm, into which his practical speculation had led him tended to make him even somewhat oblivious to ecclesiastical as distinguished from theological issues is indicated by the essay addressed to the Irish Catholics in 1749, entitled *A Word to the Wise or an Exhortation to the R. C. Clergy of Ireland*, in which he pleads for tolerance and cooperation to achieve the welfare of "Our Country." He comments particularly upon the poverty and sloth of the "native

bation not only declined the Bishopric of Clogher, but the offer which accompanied that proposal of any other translation which might become feasible during Lord Chesterfield's administration. The Primacy was vacated before the expiration of that period." *Biog. Brit.*, Corr. and Add., p. 258.

[4] *Biog. Brit.*, *loc. cit.*
[5] *Ibid.*
[6] *Ibid.*; cf. Fraser, *Life and Letters*, p. 302.
[7] March 22, 1747; Fraser, *op. cit.*, p. 315.
[8] Bernard, *Peplographia Dublinensis*, III, p. 77; not published by Fraser.

Irish" as a disgrace to the land and to the Church. He says
that the prevailing conditions lead one to suspect that the Irish
are the only nation which is "wedded to dirt on principle," but
he, for his part, refuses to believe that there is any necessary
connection between indolence and Catholicism.[9] He exhorts
the Catholic clergy "to act with vigour in this cause"[10] of
awakening their fellow "wretched countrymen from their
sweet dream of sloth." In some cases, he concludes, it is wise
even "ab hoste doceri," but qualifies this remark almost immediately by a final paragraph which is as characteristic for
its tact as for its spirit of tolerance. "In truth," he says, "I
am no enemy to your persons, whatever I may think of your
tenets. On the contrary, I am your sincere well-wisher. I consider you as my countrymen, as fellow-subjects, as professing
belief in the same Christ. And I do most sincerely wish, there
was no other contest between us but — who shall most completely practice the precepts of Him by whose name we are
called, and whose disciples we all profess to be."[10a] A very civil
reply, signed by the Roman Catholic clergy of the Diocese of
Dublin, was printed soon after in the *Dublin Journal*.

Berkeley saw clearly that he was fighting a losing battle
against Deism and "free-thinking," and that his contemporaries
were being carried in a direction diametrically opposed to that
of his own conviction and life. The "impiety" and "indifference" within as well as without the Church continuously op-
pressed his thought. In a letter to his friend Gervais,[11] he
speaks of the "wretched and unhappy times," and concludes
with the melancholy words of Horace:

> Aetas Parentum, pejor avis, tulit
> Nos nequiores, mox daturos
> Progeniem vitiosiorem.

The extent to which his hard-headed countrymen had misread
the clear and simple treatises of his youth leads him to see the
hopelessness of expecting them to follow him into the transcendental regions where his later speculations had taken him.
The thought takes ever firmer possession of his mind that he is
now a stranger to the time. In a short letter concerning earth-
quakes,[12] he concludes that there seems nothing in the physical
situation of London which should render it immune to such a

<hr>

[9] F. iv, p. 556.
[10] *Ibid.*, p. 555.
[10a] F. iv., p. 557.

[11] February 24, 1746.
[12] *Gent. Mag.*, XX, p. 166, 1750. Cf.
pp. 161, 162.

catastrophe, and "whether," he remarks, "there be anything
in the moral state thereof that should exempt it from that fear,
I leave others to judge."

His health was becoming too precarious for the performance
of anything more than his necessary ecclesiastical duties. In
1750, however, a short collection of conversational aphorisms
preserved by his wife was published under the title *Maxims
Concerning Patriotism*.[13] According to the twentieth maxim,
"He who saith there is no such thing as an honest man, you
may be sure is himself a knave," and the incident of which this
statement is perhaps the conclusion is recorded in full by his
daughter-in-law:

> His predecessor once on a visit at Cloyne to Bishop Berkeley asserted
> (a vast circle at the table) that "all mankind were either knaves or fools."
> Bishop Berkeley instantly said, "Pray my good Lord, to which class does
> your Lordship belong?" He hummed a little while, then replied "Why, I
> believe to both." Bishop Berkeley made a graceful assenting bow; and, when
> relating the anecdote, used to say "There never was a truer character given
> by man of any man."[14]

In 1751 his son William died, and the letter which he wrote his
friend Benson, Bishop of Gloucester, shows how deeply he was
affected. "I had set mine heart too much upon him," he writes,
"more perhaps than I ought to have done upon anything in this
world." The final paragraph reveals clearly the sense of
spiritual isolation that increasingly marked his later years.
"Thus much suffer me," he concludes, "in the overflowing of
my soul to say to your Lordship, who, though distant in place,
are much nearer to my heart than any of my neighbors."[15] His
daughter-in-law states that, after this time, he seemed to see
William "incessantly" before his eyes.[16] But though ill and
feeble, he continued to supervise the education of his surviving
children and to carry on his ecclesiastical duties.

In the spring of 1751 he published, on Whitsunday, a sermon
on the text: "Thy will be done in earth as it is in Heaven,"
which was probably his farewell to the pulpit, and which constitutes the last surviving record of his speculative life. His
thought has now reached a stage impossible to express in an

---

[13] F. iv, p. 561.
[14] Berkeley, *Poems*, p. ccclix n.
[15] March 8, 1751, F. *Life*, p. 325, — a
statement hard to reconcile with the view
of Berkeley as the national philosopher of
Ireland.

[16] "The Bishop used frequently to say
to Dr. Berkeley [George Jr.], I see him
incessantly before my eyes." *Ibid.*, p.
ccccxxxviii.

abstractly philosophical form, though he is equally far from an abstract anti-rationalism. There is now no trace of the juvenile enthusiasm for reason which had led him previously to hope great things from the "new philosophy," to place the human mind at the heart of reality, and to subordinate even God, as in the *Passive Obedience*, to the eternal laws of nature. This sermon is saturated with the thought of transcendence. "Religion," he says, "is nothing else but the conforming our faith and practice to the will of God. To this single point," he adds, "may be reduced all religion, all moral vertue, all human happiness." [17] The infinite difference between this God and the rational postulate of the early works is indicated by Berkeley's statement that "our understanding is in its own nature not only very weak and imperfect, but much obscured by passion and prejudice." [18] There are, he says, "many unsearchable perfections in the Deity, whose nature is infinitely above our knowledge. . . ." [19]

Yet Berkeley's scepticism is far too radical to enable him to find refuge in irrationalism. If the natural light of reason is an untrustworthy guide, as it most evidently is, then it is even more absurd to trust any other human faculty, such as will. "It will be very evident," says Berkeley, "that we are too imperfect creatures to be governed by our own wills," [20] and again, "our power is at least as imperfect as our knowledge." [21] The weakness and fallibility of reason are, indeed, discovered by reason itself, not by any other "higher sense." Reason is man's "distinguishing character," [22] and "whatsoever is most reasonable is most natural to him." [23] It is not, therefore, necessary to rely upon any mystic intuition to "shew how reasonable it is, that the will of God should be done upon earth." [24] It is reason itself which appreciates that "there is no reason so right, no rule so just as the will of God," [25] and hence passes beyond itself to revelation. Indeed, what we call reason is only the beginning of this passage beyond itself, and reason, taken concretely in its entirety, is precisely the revelation of that which is transcendent. It is only in this "subordinate" position, as dependent on a perfection which is higher than itself, that reason ceases to be

---

[17] A. A. Luce, *Hermathena*, vol. XXII, 1932, p. 38.
[18] *Ibid.*, p. 36.
[19] *Ibid.*, p. 32.
[20] *Ibid.*, p. 31.

[21] *Ibid.*, p. 36.
[22] *Ibid.*, p. 39.
[23] *Ibid.*
[24] *Ibid.*, p. 31.
[25] *Ibid.*, p. 38.

dependent upon something lower than itself, and thus becomes what it truly is, the mediator or λόγος.

We now find hardly a trace of the subjectivism and psychologism of his youth. *Percipi*, far from contributing to the objectivity of *esse*, is rather a relativizing and distorting factor. What is true in our perceptions is derived from an *esse* existing in its own right, and hence lying beyond them. Reason itself cannot achieve true being, though it may lead us away from the flux of mere perception, and thus point the way. There is no *esse cognoscere*, however, for "our understanding is in its own nature . . . weak and imperfect."[26] The more we think, the more we are led away from thought to that which lies essentially beyond it as its source, the principle of value (ὃ ὂν ὄντως). It is with respect to this underlying principle that the dialectical contrast between the objective and the subjective, what truly is and what seems to be, the truly transcendent and the spuriously transcendent, becomes most sharply defined. Hence, Berkeley now abandons the identification of the good with the dogmatic concept of interest, uncritically accepted in the *Commonplace Book*[27] as that which men desire. Solipsism in ethics can no more withstand scepticism than solipsism in epistemology. It is, says Berkeley, "no sure sign that a thing is good, because we desire, or evil because we are displeased with it."[28]

This fundamental antithesis between practical action and the transcendental norm conditioning it is the final "result," if it may be so called, of Berkeley's concrete logic, since the synthesis of reason is only the mediation of this polarity. Reason itself, in its entirety, is practical in character, and hence, like every other form of action, reduced to relativity and subordination by its norm. The last "result" of Berkeley's concrete logic is an antithesis rather than a synthesis. Beyond the speculative absolute of reason is the absolute itself and the "creatures."[29] "Life" is neither an idealistic absorption in the divine whole nor a naturalistic process, but a voyage or "pilgrimage"[30] in which "we" are brought into relation with that which we are not. Neither as "organisms" nor as phases of the absolute would we be what we really are, "creatures" acting from choice. Prior to "the infinite mind of all things" is man the creature; prior to synthesis is antithesis. But practical or axiological choice is confronted not by a being which at the same

[26] *Ibid.*, p. 36.
[27] *Commonplace Book*, J., 547.
[28] Luce, *op. cit.*, p. 35.
[29] *Ibid.*, p. 31.   [30] *Ibid.*, p. 39.

time is not, and a non-being which nevertheless is, but by an absolute antithesis, the either/or. This absolute antithesis, between a being which truly is and a non-being which is *not*, is prior to the mediating antitheses of reason which are at the same time syntheses. Prior to theory is practice.

The final human virtue is "resignation," [31] in which "the inferior faculties remain subordinate," [32] and man sinks to the level of a "creature." The "will or mind of man, in this subordinate, regular situation, may be said to act in its proper sphere, and answer the ends for which it was created." [33] This is the positive side of virtue. But, since virtue can never be complete, this aspect alone is an abstraction. Resignation is primarily antithesis. The will of man cannot be "thus subordinate," [34] and hence must remain "dislocated" and "be restless and uneasy." [35] We are to live our lives neither with the easy confidence of the pagan nor with the fanatical confidence of the mystic but with "care." [36] Virtue itself is beyond our reach. We may hope only for "zeal." [37]

It is obviously impossible to reconcile Berkeley's last sermon with the mystical dream-idealism of his early writings, which historical tradition has permanently attached to his name. In this last surviving fragment, he does not speak as one whose philosophy has united him permanently with the universe, nor as one who has been able to quiet his doubts by pleasant dreams, either rational or emotional. What seems rather to dominate these pages is that "distrust" of which he spoke in the *Commonplace Book* [38] as having "disposed" him even in childhood for "new doctrines." The concrete level of existence to which this "distrust" has finally forced him is dominated by antithesis rather than synthesis, by anxiety rather than confidence. Berkeley speaks in his last address not as the mouthpiece of the λόγος, but as a man. The nothingness which he had so vainly endeavored to grasp in his reflections assumes in this context the more concrete shape of death, and the restless scepticism which had led him "through all the sciences" [39] now takes the more concrete form of an "anxiety" or "care," appropriate not so much for a disembodied spirit as for a man about to die.

---

[31] *Ibid.*, pp. 34 ff.
[32] *Ibid.*, p. 38.
[33] *Ibid.*, p. 39.
[34] The earlier Trinity College Ms. writes "coincident with."
[35] Luce, *op. cit.*, p. 40.
[36] *Ibid.*
[37] *Ibid.* Cf. early sermon, "Let your zeal be according to knowledge."
[38] J., 275.   [39] F. i, p. 92.

His Will, drawn in July 1752, contains an item which seems astonishingly inconsistent to those who accept the common view of Berkeley as a romantic subjectivist or "immaterialist," but which loses something of its strangeness when read in the light of his later reflections. The document reads as follows: [40]

In the name of God Amen. I, George Berkeley, Bishop of Cloyne, being sound of mind and memory, do make this my last Will and Testament.

First, I do humbly recommend my Soul into the hands of my blessed Redeemer by whose merits and intercession I hope for Mercy.

As to my Body and Effects, I dispose of them in the following manner: —

It is my will that my Body be buried in the Churchyard of the parish in which I die:

Item, that the expense of my funeral do not exceed twenty pounds, and that as much more be given to the poor of the parish where I die:

Item, that my Body, before it is buried, be kept five days above ground or longer, even till it grow offensive by the cadaverous smell, and that during the said time it lye unwashed, undisturbed, and covered by the same bed-clothes in the same bed the head being raised upon pillows.

Item, that my dear wife Anne be sole executrix of this my Will, and guardian of my children — to which said wife Anne I leave and bequeathe all my worldly goods and substance, to be disposed of as to her shall seem good:

Item, it is my will that in case my said wife should die intestate, all my worldly goods, substance and possessions of what kind soever, shall be equally divided among my children:

In witness whereof I have herewith put my hand and seal this thirty-first day of July Anno Domini, One thousand seven hundred and fifty-two.

GEORGE CLOYNE.

It is apparent that the curious item concerning the "body" is not written from the standpoint of "immaterialism." Berkeley's concrete logic has, indeed, carried him beyond all *isms*. He speaks now not as a "spirit" but as a "man," confronting the nothingness which hovers over all concrete existence. The item undoubtedly expresses a certain lack of confidence in medical science, which is not surprising in the author of the *Siris*. Berkeley wishes to die, as he had come to live, remote from the thoughts and attentions of his contemporaries, in peace and "undisturbed."

The deaths of his old friends Prior and Benson intensified his sense of loneliness. In a letter written in the previous spring [41] to the active Gervais he had expressed his intention of finding a retreat where he could die in peace, as far as possible from that modern spirit which he could now no longer share.

[40] F. *Life*, p. 345.   [41] April 6, 1752, F. *Life*, pp. 333-334.

For my own part I submit to years and infirmities. My views in this world are mean and narrow: it is a thing in which I have small share, and which ought to give me small concern. I abhor business, and especially to have to do with great persons and great affairs, which I leave to such as you who delight in them and are fit for them. The evening of life I choose to pass in a quiet retreat. Ambitious projects, intrigues and quarrels of states-men, are things I have formerly been amused with; but they now seem to be a vain, fugitive dream.

In 1752, Berkeley took active steps to realize this dream of retiring even further from the world to "that city of eternal evening" where he had first sensed the futility of worldly affairs, and where "a number of gentlemen living independ-ently" make "divine things their study." [42] Accordingly, he attempted to resign his Bishopric, but George II, curious as to the origin of this strange application, upon discovering the identity of the applicant, swore that Berkeley should die a Bishop, though he might live where he pleased. In August, 1752, he set out for Oxford with his wife, daughter, and son. He was so ill that for the last part of the journey he had to be carried on a litter, but he survived the change of domicile, and settled down in a small house on Broad Street near Christ Church. For the next months he lived the life for which he had so long hoped, revising and editing several of his works, but spending most of his days in quiet meditation. On the four-teenth of January, at tea, while his wife was reading to him from the fifteenth chapter of the *First Epistle to the Corinthians*,[43] his daughter, offering him another cup, observed that he did not reach out his hand, and it was discovered that he was dead.

BERKELEY'S PHILOSOPHICAL DEVELOPMENT

To one first becoming acquainted with Berkeley's philosophy as a whole, it appears more as a chaos of conflicting theories and opinions than as a consistent "system." In the early writings he is an empiricist, denying the pure concept as an ab-straction, or even a word, and appealing to direct sensory ex-perience and the psychical "action" of the will as the only concrete realities. In the *Siris*, sense experience and will sink to the level of "fleeting shadows," possessing no intrinsic reality, since they are always *in fieri*, and reality itself is held to

---

[42] Letter to Sir John James, F. iv, p. 530.   [43] *Biog. Brit.*, III, 258.

be apprehended only through the pure concept. In the early writings, the realm of nature is no more than appearance for the individual self, and the view of matter, even as an instrument in the hands of God, is dismissed as too extravagant for serious discussion. In the *Siris*, Berkeley takes great pains to outline a philosophy of nature based upon just such an "imperceptible," material instrument. It is not difficult to recognize Locke, even where disagreement with him is expressed, as the great inspirer of the *Commonplace Book*, whereas in the *Siris* he is not even mentioned.

The difference between the youthful and the mature Berkeley is perhaps most clearly understood when we realize the extent to which all the early positions revolve about man as psychologically conceived. Reality is what man perceives or wills. The good is what man psychologically desires. Even God is a necessary rational postulate constructed after the analogy of the human soul. In the later writings, man sinks to a "subordinate" position, and humanism is replaced by transcendentalism. Being is no longer being because we take it to be so, nor is anything true because we believe it, nor anything really good because we desire it. Truth, being, and value, as humanly conceived, are seen to be possible only through a transcendental perfection. Man himself can be what he is only through his relation to that which lies beyond himself essentially. This is without doubt the chief contrast dominating Berkeley's works as a whole, and dividing them into an earlier and later group. But many other differences, often occurring in successive works, strike the eye of even the superficial reader. There is, for example, the sharp antithesis between the loose pragmatic procedure advocated in the *Alciphron* and the rigid rationalism of the *Analyst*, and there are many other "contradictions" no less evident. If Berkeley's thought as a whole is to be comprehended it must be conceived as a development. Without a sense of the direction of his reflections, they dissolve into a chaos of separate "positions." When understood chronologically, however, these isolated points become significant.

The key to this development, as we have attempted to show, is Berkeley's theory of abstraction, or what we have called his "concrete logic." This is the constant method which, expressing itself in the various positions through which Berkeley successively passed, holds them together as an unified structure, finally philosophically realized in the *Siris*. Various and even essentially opposed as are the points of view and "theories" maintained in his published writings, there is, nevertheless, not one of these which does not embody a polemic against abstract ideas. The "new principle" of the *Commonplace Book*, as we have seen, is itself an application of the concrete or "mental" mode of reasoning. The doctrine of abstraction, says Berkeley in the *New Theory of Vision* of 1709, "is the prolific womb which has brought forth innumerable errors and difficulties, in all parts of philosophy and in all the sciences." [44]

It is unnecessary to comment upon the vital role played by the doctrine of abstraction in the *Principles*, since this is made sufficiently clear by the author himself in the methodological introduction with which he found it necessary to preface the work. The *Dialogues*, written in 1713, make use of the principle of abstraction not only to show the relativity of all objects or ideas but also "the dependency I find in myself. . . ." [45] Berkeley's logic leads him here to the conception of the speculative absolute, or as he phrases it, "the infinite mind of God, in whom we live and move and have our being." [46] "How doth it follow," he asks, "that because I can pronounce the word *motion* by itself, I can form the idea of it in my mind exclusive of body? or, because theorems may be made of extension and figures without any mention of *great* or *small*, or any other sensible mode or quality, that therefore it is possible such an abstract idea of extension should be . . . apprehended by the mind?" [47]

The essential importance of Berkeley's concrete logic in the argument of the *De Motu*, written in 1720, is equally apparent. "Melius itaque foret," he says, "si, missa qualitate occulta, homines attenderent solummodo ad effectus sensibiles; vocibusque abstractis (quantumvis illae ad disserendum utiles sint) in meditatione omissis, mens in particularibus et concretis, hoc est in ipsis rebus, defigeretur." [48] That the important development of Berkeley's thought during the ten succeeding years did not at any rate change his attitude towards abstraction but is rather to be viewed as a result of his concrete method is indicated by the letter to Johnson of November 25, 1729, in which he cautions his ambitious disciple "to consider whether any new objection that shall occur doth not suppose the doc-

44 Sec. 125.   46 *Ibid.*, p. 453.   48 Sec. 4.
45 F. i, p. 448.   47 *Ibid.*, pp. 403–404.

THE MEANING OF BERKELEY 491

trine of *abstract* general ideas." [49] The concrete method is emphasized in unmistakable language in the *Alciphron* of 1732. "I do not deny," says Berkeley, almost repeating the words of the *Principles* and the earlier letter to Leclerc, "it [the mind] may abstract in a certain sense: inasmuch as those things that can really exist or be really perceived asunder, may be conceived asunder, or abstracted one from the other; for instance a man's head from his body, colour from motion, figure from weight. But it will not thence follow that the mind can frame abstract general ideas, which appear to be impossible." [50]

Finally, we have seen, at the end of his life Berkeley rediscovered his concrete method in the dialectic of Proclus and Plotinus, and incorporated it in the thought transitions of the *Siris*. What is most truly real or "in itself" is no longer apprehended in the fleeting show of sense but rather in the χωριστὸν εἶδος. This, however, is "not an abstract idea compounded of inconsistencies, and prescinded from all real things, as some moderns understand abstraction." [51] Reality (ὅ ὂν ὄντως) is not to be gained through any intellectualistic dismemberment of what is "given" to us, for everything that is "given," including the self to which it is "given," is dependent or relative, and therefore already abstract and unreal. Actually existing reality (οὐσία ὄντως οὖσα), therefore, is to be found only in the transcendent.

While it cannot be denied, therefore, that Berkeley's conception of the truly real underwent the most revolutionary changes during the course of his reflections, it must, on the other hand, be granted that the goal towards which he was striving remained essentially the same. The guiding motive of Berkeley's thought, from its earliest inceptions to the last pages of the *Siris*, is the attempt to understand reality concretely, or to think things together as they really are. Stated negatively, this means the avoidance of verbalism, partiality, or abstraction in general, and it is in this form that Berkeley tended to think of his aim in the early writings. During this period of his life, it seemed to him that his goal might be achieved solely through the rejection of certain more or less obvious forms of abstraction, such as the stubborn verbalism lying at the root of such a theory as materialism. A concrete or synthetic logic must be

[49] Schneider, *Samuel Johnson*, vol. II, p. 274.

[50] Alc., VII, F. ii, p. 328.
[51] Sec. 323.

substituted for the "symbolic" logic of ordinary discourse. Instead of verbalizing certain phases of reality, and hence granting them a spurious substantiality, it is necessary to think the aspects together synthetically, or concretely, as they actually are. This at first seemed to him a very simple matter, and he often appeals, as in the *New Theory of Vision*, to "any man's experience." [52]

It did not take him long to discover, however, that common sense is a tissue of artificial verbalisms, and that the problem he had set for himself was something far more difficult than he had, in the first enthusiasm of youth, supposed. Concrete thought can be achieved by nothing short of a revolutionary development not only in the logic of philosophy but in that of ordinary thought as well. There is not only a veil of language, separating us from things as they are in themselves, but a veil of sense, and finally, and most difficult of all, a veil of thought, for thought, even at its most concrete level, is still only thought, and hence abstraction. Concrete thought, therefore, must be something more than thought. This is why Berkeley, at the end of his life, ceased to state his goal negatively in terms of the avoidance of abstraction, as though reality could be thought adequately by the mere adherence to a few easily remembered rules. In the *Siris*, the goal is stated positively as the thought of τὰ ὄντα ὄντως, though it is not difficult to recognize in this more mature statement the *res ipsae* of the *De Motu* [53] and the early writings.

But whether stated negatively as the avoidance of abstraction, or positively as concrete or absolute thought, the aim of all of Berkeley's philosophical endeavours from first to last was not to think reality conveniently, neatly, beautifully, morally, or even convincingly, but to think reality concretely as it is. His reflection began with a distrust of the artificial hypostatizations of language. It ended with a far deeper distrust of the artificial hypostatizations of thought itself, which, if employed uncritically, raise an insurmountable barrier between ourselves and truth. But whatever the specific form assumed by Berkeley's scepticism, it was always directed against whatever exaggerations, preconceptions, or peculiarities seemed most obstinately to obstruct our apprehension of things as they really are. To achieve this goal, Berkeley was willing to pay any price, in youth the price of absurdity and paradox in the eyes of his hard-

[52] Sec. 43.   [53] Sec. 4.

headed contemporaries, in maturity the price of that complete neglect which is the natural reward of one for whom the very spirit and content of the age in which he lives has become incredible and strange. The key to the understanding of Berkeley, not as the inventor of paradoxical phrases, not as the builder of another system of philosophy, but as a thinker, lies in his uninterrupted effort to think reality neither cleverly, nor economically, nor rationally, nor irrationally, but rather as it *is*.

This effort led to the almost always original and sometimes devious course of reflections we have attempted to follow in these chapters. First of all, filling him with discontent at the mathematical ideal which, in the manner of Descartes and Locke, he had himself enthusiastically brandished before the world in his earliest publications, it led him, in the *Commonplace Book*, to abandon mathematical proof as analytic or symbolic in character. Mathematical thought, in spite of its deceptive "certainty," is not adequate for the purposes of philosophy, because of its abstractness and artificiality. Leaving the mathematical method, therefore, to those who prefer tautology to truth, Berkeley proceeded to develop his concrete or "mental" mode of reasoning as a means of thinking things together, or as they really are, rather than clearly and distinctly. Reality in the concrete is not mathematical, and it is more important in philosophy at least to adapt one's thought to the outlines of reality itself, even when vague or confused, than to a certain set of convenient but arbitrary rules.

Reality, furthermore, is far from being the set of isolated terms which the intellectualist moves about, or "relates" at will. [53a] In reality, the terms are already related, and without their essential contexts would not be what they are. Ordinary thought is abstract in that it beholds things now from one point of view, now from another, always attempting to dignify and perpetuate its perspectives through the categories of reality and substance, but thereby closing its mind to the fringe of context or relation really essential to these hypostatizations. The deep-seated distrust which Berkeley found opposing him at every point is in truth the confusion we feel when customary abstractions, or so-called "real things," dissolve in the acid of reflection and leave us confronting — reality. Berkeley's concrete logic is the attempt to remain conscious of the relative whole or universe of discourse within which anal-

[53a] Cf. C. B. J., 746.

ysis proceeds. When this all-important context is kept in mind, the analytic components cease to be isolated "things" or substances, and sink to the level of phases or, as Berkeley calls them, "considerations" of a larger whole, which is far more difficult to grasp. When one's attention, however, is concentrated upon this whole, he may become thoroughly aware of the artificiality of the analytic technique, and may utilize this technique, subordinating it, that is, to the ends of truth, rather than truth to "considerations."

The fringe of meaning, in which truth lies, constantly eludes the grasp of the intellectualist as long as he takes his analysis too seriously. There is not one of Berkeley's early discoveries which does not rest upon insight into an essential synthetic connection between aspects eluding the grasp of an abstract logic which would regard them as independent things or entities. Thus, colour and extension, which are conceived analytically as discrete entities, are in reality "concreted" together in such a way that colour is impossible without the latter, and universals, which abstract logic considers to be independent, subsistent entities, are bound up with what it calls *particulars* in such a way that it is impossible to conceive of the one without the other. But the most important and dangerous instance of such abstraction Berkeley discovered in what is generally called the external or material world. Such a world, as it is ordinarily conceived, in abstraction from the internal or psychical, is meaningless. A material object without a mind to perceive it is an artificial construction without actual or concrete existence.

Berkeley at first confused concrete reality with the "given" world of "experience," and it was not until the end of his early reflections that he succeeded in purifying his thought from the consequences of this unfortunate error. Experience, he first maintained, consists of two elements, a world of passive objects or ideas and an active self or will. The *esse* of the one is *percipi;* the *esse* of the other *percipere*.[54] His concrete logic soon led him to see, however, that there was an essential connection between the two such that the former is inconceivable *in the concrete* without the latter. This truth he incorporated in the formula *esse est percipi*, which is by no means an analytic tautology, but the indication of a necessary, synthetic relation. At the very climax of the *Commonplace Book*, Berkeley perceives that

[54] C. B. J., 426.

the relation is one of mutual interdependence such that the act of perception, as it is in reality, is also inconceivable without an object to perceive. The phrase *esse est percipi* was probably the result of this important movement of thought, since both the active and passive sides of perception are telescoped together in the concrete word *percipi*. Berkeley nevertheless still clung to his original notion of an independent, truncated will or soul substance "given" in experience, or, in his own words, something of which we have a direct intuition by a certain reflexive act of mind. It was not until the third of the *Dialogues between Hylas and Philonous* that Berkeley fully appreciated the significance of the dialectic of the *Commonplace Book*, and explicitly recognized the relativity of all meaning, the artificiality of all abstraction, and hence the "dependency" in the self or will. It is the persistence of the early soul substance or "intuitive" view, however, in the *Principles* and the first two dialogues, which is responsible for the subjectivism of these early writings, as well as for the consequent confusion of idealism with psychologism in the later English tradition.

Criticism of Berkeley has ignored the concrete logic underlying his thought which, as is indicated by the dialectical discussions of the *Commonplace Book*, leads to an entirely different sort of idealism. History, however, has "frozen" Berkeley, so to speak, at the point in his development at which his synthetic logic had destroyed all fixed substances or abstractions save the empirical self or psyche. The result of thus relativizing everything with respect to an artificially stabilized or "intuited" self is the solipsism or psychologism so perfectly analogous to the "materialism" which had easily fallen before the attack of his "mental" logic in the *Principles*. But once this logic had started its destructive course, there was no stopping it by any fixed abstraction, or by the "intuition" and "self-evidence" with which such an abstract logic seeks in vain to ward off the pricks of scepticism. In the third of the *Dialogues*, the self is explicitly recognized as being in a state of "dependency" exactly analogous to that of all intuited objects whatsoever. Never again does the uncritical "we" or "I" creep into Berkeley's thought, nor is the absolute ever again confused with the finite subject. All such finite objects are relative or dependent, — one upon the other. He sees that such a universal relativity is impossible without some transcendental basis, and hence explicitly introduces into the argument the Platonic theory of ideas which had previously been obscured by his spiritism and the "causal" theory of perception to which it inevitably led. The differences between our finite perceptions require a transcendental or ideal identity, as their discontinuity and incompleteness require that which is continuous and complete. Berkeley's concrete logic thus brings him to that speculative absolute which is the final conclusion of his early reflections, and to which he refers as the "infinite Mind in whom we live and move and have our being."

The most obvious consequence of Berkeley's discussion of the absolute of reason is scepticism, and all of Berkeley's speculations after this critical period contain a sceptical moment. None of the abstract things or entities of common sense is really a substance at all, nor is even what we call by the name "I" or "we" a fixed entity capable of existing in isolation from external things. Such "things" are rather phases of something lying beyond. When we come to the pure "ideas" presupposed by such empirical objects, it seems at first as though here at least we were confronted with something self-existent. But the very priority of such forms is a relation which reduces them to dependency. The dialectic of reason cannot rest either with the immediate or the mediate, with object or idea. It reaches its goal only in that infinite mind or absolute within which all that is real finds a place. But this absolute is nothing but scepticism, or the pure form of reason itself, which thinks all things, passes through them, and rests with none. It does in a sense include its objects, and is hence the synthesis or absolute whole of reality, but it includes them only by relativizing or transcending them. As the absolute whole, it is relative to its parts, or dependent upon them, and is hence not the end or goal of reason at all.

The speculative absolute is not really the absolute, but only reason itself. Nevertheless, while it does not transcend the form of reason, it does transcend all specific rationality, and hence contains a moment of absoluteness. It is at least sufficient for the purposes of scepticism, and capable of negating, or setting in flux, any theoretical formulation. After the third dialogue, therefore, Berkeley's rationalism divides itself into the aspect of scepticism on the one hand and absolutism on the other, though, at first, this absolute moment consists only of a vague fermentation arising from the insight that reason is in no form, not even the most transcendental form which is thinkable, the absolute itself. "God is a Being of transcendent and unlimited perfections." [55]

This dissatisfaction with reason and the Deistic presuppositions of his early writings, while it may be discerned as a vague undercurrent in the third dialogue, did not actually take possession of Berkeley's consciousness until his sudden plunge into contemporary life in 1713. In London, he was able to observe the broad, cultural results of the "scientific philosophy" he had himself been propagating. Greeted upon his arrival by the *Discourse* of Anthony Collins, he made an extended first-hand study of the free-thinkers and their clubs. The mass of dull and badly reasoned tracts and arguments disgusted him almost as intensely as the moral torpor of the Deists themselves, and he was glad to make use of the opportunity afforded him by Steele of opposing as bitterly as he could the very rationalism he had so ingeniously defended in his earlier writings. Turning to his friends among the great wits of the day, all of whom affected scorn for the smart free-thinker, he found them, nevertheless, Deists at heart. Indeed, the verbal wit and external gracefulness with which men like Pope and Addison attempted to counterbalance the vacuum they had created to replace their souls, only intensified his disgust.

Retiring to the quiet atmosphere of Oxford, and there meditating alone in the country, he realized that his enemy was nothing less than the age itself. Free-thinking was not an ephemeral social phenomenon, confined to a few Collins' and Chubbs', but the modern spirit itself. Wearing the disarming guise of the "light" of reason it is welcomed by the aspiring mind, which is then seared and blinded to such a degree that it is finally willing to part with every birthright, even its innate freedom and very rationality, in return for plausible argument. Having attempted to convey something of this revised conception of Deism to the general public in his *Guardian* essays, Berkeley, abandoning altogether his life of contemplation, plunged, as a practical idealist, into the stream of contemporary "life," resolved upon the hopeless task of combating the spirit of the age. Such writings as have survived from this practical stage of his life are all critical or polemic in tone. Contemplation is not carried on for its own sake. The center of his spiritual axis has shifted from the contemplative to the active, from the theoretical to the practical.

First of all, in the *De Motu*, he employs his scepticism to attack the dogmas of Newtonian science by laying bare the essential relativity in the spatial and temporal absolutes upon which the whole mechanical edifice was founded. What finally confirmed his scientific scepticism was the "pragmatic" argument which was the sole justification for its loose and uncritical procedure. It is, therefore, in the vague and inarticulate form of "utility" that the principle of value, closely associated with his scepticism, really enters Berkeley's thought as an active principle. Later, it was to become a fully developed and articulate theory purged of its humanistic implications. In the *De Motu*, however, as undeveloped pragmatism, it is only an ally to scepticism, helping it to break down scientific dogmatism by revealing the extent to which its "advance" is based not upon what is true, but rather upon what seems to be "useful."

In the *Alciphron*, Berkeley turns his sceptical weapons upon the moral philosophy and theology of Deism, as embodied particularly in Shaftesbury's system of "sweetness and light." The *Alciphron* is governed by the same alliance of scepticism with practical philosophy which dominated the *De Motu*, but the essential relation between the two is far more profoundly grasped, and the conception of value, which is now the determining force in Berkeley's thought, is no longer left at the incoherent level of "pragmatism," but is deepened into practical philosophy. In the seventh dialogue, Berkeley fully works out his conception of practical knowledge, and grasps the significance of that faith in which it culminates, though the latter is perhaps even more distinctly apprehended in the sermon preached by Berkeley after his return from America.

The absolute, approached at last through this culmination of his practical philosophy, enables him in the *Analyst* to see the possibility of a permanently stable basis for rationality, which he now realizes is to be identified with neither the superficial plausibility of the Deist nor the equally superficial irrationality of the pragmatist, but only with the intrinsic intelligibility of mediation. Resting upon the foundation of a philosophy of value, reason may dare at last to be intelligible. Berkeley, therefore, revives the Platonic theory of ideas, to which his earliest speculations had finally forced him in the third dialogue, and to which he had given the name of *philosophia prima* in the *De Motu*. It is only upon the critical foundation of such a "transcendental science" of meaningful logic or intelligibility that any science, including that of mathematics, may securely rest. Otherwise, proceeding "pragmatically," the "scientist" will be, like "the ignorant sailor," mechanically following a routine the meaning of which he does not understand.

Just as the meaning which is granted to existent facts by science arises from a field of pure significance lying beyond existence, so does the field of significance itself have its origin in a further transcendental source. This final absolute is the absolute of value. Berkeley's concrete logic, having passed into a scepticism capable of setting all concepts in flux, could clearly have no further end. Having passed through the theoretical dialectic of synthesis, and the practical dialectic of antithesis, it rests, if this may be said to be rest, with that which is neither the absolute whole of reason nor the absolutization of any human ideal, but the absolute itself, the transcendent. The first philosophy, or as Berkeley calls it, the transcendental philosophy of meaning, resting on this basis, and the interpretation, or meaning, which this in turn was able to bestow upon the world of existence, he outlined in the *Siris*, with the assistance of the Greek writers who, as he increasingly realized, were the discoverers of the field of true significance. In the *Siris*, reason sinks into its proper, mediate station as the λόγος, moving between the non-being which is commonly called "existence" and that which truly is. In this intermediate position, it affords, to one caught in the toils of time and change, a way to the eternal, as well as a means of expression to the philosopher, firmly established in absolute scepticism, who wishes to transmit something of the *value* of significance to the world.

Both of these movements are apparent in the *Siris*. It is, on the one hand, the most philosophical of all of Berkeley's works, being written like all true philosophy, from the absolute point of view. It is not forgotten, however, that such a point of view (which is no point of view) is possible, humanly speaking, only on the ground (which is no ground) of paradox or faith.

The *Siris*, therefore, is even more than *first philosophy*. It is the record of a struggle. It is only through the endless contradictions of the λόγος that being touches us. It is only after all ends have been condemned and all concepts set in motion by the goad of negation that the transcendent may be apprehended. God speaks only to the sceptic, and often not to him.

It is for this reason that after his last excursion into transcendental philosophy Berkeley returns soberly to "this mortal state." [56] It is not an organism which is *transcended*, nor a psychological being, nor a logical being, nor an alogical soul, for experience itself transcends these, but all of them, in their entirety, taken together concretely as man himself, "the creature." The final position, therefore, to which Berkeley is led by his concrete logic is the position (which is also no position) of concrete existence, or practical philosophy. It is this "position" which is actually the farthest from the abstract psychologism with which he started, though at first the two seem identical. Fortunately, however, man is not psychology, nor is he biology nor logic nor philosophy, nor a substance, nor the categories, nor the absolute, but a "creature" passing through all of these.

Such was, in brief, the strange and tortuous course of reflection through which Berkeley was driven by his pertinacious attempt to think concretely. Many aspects of this development, particularly in its final stages, remain obscure. Berkeley's later writings are generally philosophical rather than psychological in character, and offer almost insuperable difficulties to the modern reader. The thought is critical, and therefore unclear. The ideas are also not *distinct*, but merge in a most confusing manner. The *Siris*, furthermore, is so full of ancient lore that it is difficult to discern how much is Berkeley and how much is Plato or Plotinus. These reasons are sufficient to explain why Berkeley remains, and must remain for us, who have followed a very different course, the youthful genius who completed the work of Descartes in establishing psychological subjectivism on its apparently impregnable throne.

There is no more typically modern picture than that of the young Berkeley throwing away his mediaeval textbooks and, together with a few chosen spirits of Trinity College, plunging with iconoclastic enthusiasm into the study of the "new philosophy." Except for a tinge of deep religious feeling, which he could not altogether conceal, his early writings breathe the very breath of modernism on every page. His subjectivism is clearly an outgrowth of the Lockianism with which he was saturated at an early age, merely Locke, in fact, made partially consistent with himself. He speaks of Newton with genuine admiration, and, indeed, made such a profound study of the

[56] *Siris*, sec. 367.

works of this great writer that he was able to detect several very minor fallacies therein, — thus contributing to future mathematical research. Experimental science is the one field he properly excepts in the *Commonplace Book* from the general devastation he glories in accomplishing. His *New Theory of Vision* is a brilliant contribution to the budding science of psychology, and his concept of the sensory minimum or threshold has played an important role in the history of that peculiarly modern subject.

The picture of the older Berkeley, however, poring over Ocellus Lucanus and other obscure and ancient writers, having failed to convert himself to his subjectivism, is anything but persuasive. His writings are no longer self-assured. The *Siris* is written in a style so restrained as to be almost hesitant. If many aspects of Berkeley's later system are plunged in obscurity, one fact stands out with perfect clearness. Wherever his concrete logic has led him, it has certainly taken him extremely far from anything that has any right to be called modern. The *Siris* is not only obscure but obscurantist.

The disrelish Berkeley now affects for the Deistic shibboleths of his youth often approaches something not far removed from a contempt which is rendered even more disconcerting by the fact that, in this case at least, his opinion cannot be totally disregarded as that of a tyro. There is no phase of the modern spirit which he did not actually live through with burning ardour in the time of his youth. The respect he evinced for "reason" and the mathematical method had been worthy of the most impeccable *Aufklärer*. Now, however, he treats Newton with scant respect and, on the whole, prefers to fall back on the Stoics for his natural philosophy. The unmitigated psychologism of his youth, which had led him to confuse reality with what we perceive and truth with what we think, is completely abandoned for a Platonism which, whatever else may be urged against it, may at least be maintained without *implicit* contradiction. The self-assured humanism which had led him to identify the good with the useful and to think of God as an exaggerated man now gives way to a transcendentalism so thoroughgoing that it transforms the apprehension of truth into paradox. Indeed, it is the growing weight of transcendentalism in his thinking that led him to that disillusionment with modernism which is the dominant feature of his later life. Whether we view him as one of the first of those atavistic minds which have sought solace in the past from the burden of modern progress, or whether we think of him as one whose life is in a sense prophetic of some far distant disillusionment of the modern spirit with itself, the facts are sufficiently inescapable.

Berkeley's philosophy is, like his life, a process in which he passes from mathematical rationalism to practical philosophy, and from practical philosophy to the absolute. His concrete logic led him finally from humanism to religion, from Locke to Plato, from psychologism to transcendentalism. During this transition, the science to which he had made such original contributions becomes in his eyes a system of unintelligible incantations; the humanistic ethics which he had embraced so eagerly, a superficial rationalization of selfishness, and the Deistic religion he had himself defended, a form of sacrilege too trivial to be considered blasphemy. In this he may have been mistaken. The historian, however, cannot but record the fact that so brilliant and influential a genius, after contributing to many sciences, and by his acumen and wit startling his shrewd contemporaries, retired to a distant corner of the world to bury himself in the writings of a bygone day, and withdrew at last to what he considered a haven even more remote, to die.

APPENDIX

THREE UNPUBLISHED SERMONS

APPENDIX

THE following three unpublished sermons were found among the Chapman Mss. in the British Museum, Add. Ms. 39306. They are undated, and Berkeley's habit of "developing" a sermon gradually on a certain text makes the problem of determining even an approximate date most difficult. Sermon I and Sermon II possess a common introduction, the former being probably an earlier version of the latter. Sermons on this text: "Without controversy great is the mystery of godliness": I Timothy iii, 16 were preached at Newport, August 3, 1729,[1] and at King's Chapel, Boston, September 12, 1731.[1a] The notes of this sermon contain citations identical with certain of those in the Ms. (for example, "the seed of the woman shall break the serpent's head," and the "paschal lamb"), and there are also other similarities. I suggest, therefore, that Sermons I and II are both versions of the sermon first preached in 1729. This hypothesis is further corroborated by the fact that the notes for another sermon preached at Newport on the subject of immortality[2] reveal marked similarities with Sermon III.

It is, at any rate, clear from internal evidence that these sermons, even if they were not actually preached at Newport, date from what we have called the third or "practical" period in Berkeley's reflections. During this period he abandoned his earlier rationalistic theories of religion, and these sermons indicate the degree in which his understanding of the significance of Christianity was consequently deepened and intensified. Sermon III, in particular, should be compared with *The Revelation of Immortality*, II Timothy i, 10, preached in 1708 during Berkeley's Deistic youth.[3] Why Fraser should have chosen this youthful discourse and omitted the more mature and interesting work is not clear. The only reason suggesting itself is a desire to portray Berkeley in rationalistic terms as a "philosopher" rather than as a theologian. That Berkeley himself transcended the motive lying back of such a distinction, as well as the distinction itself, is proved by his later writings. A complete and critical edition of his sermons would doubtless shed much light on this phase of his development.

[1] Notes of sermons, F. iv, p. 376.
[1a] Cf. Rand, *Berkeley's American Sojourn*, p. 45.
[2] Undated, F. iv, p. 386.
[3] *Ibid.*, p. 87.

SERMON I

I Timothy: iii, 16

Without controversy great
is the mystery of Godliness.

The creation of this visible world for the use and comfort of man, our very life and being which, as it was originally bestowed, so it is daily preserved by the divine providence, every good thing we enjoy and all the evils we escape, are so many blessings that call for our attention and gratitude.[1]

But the most adorable instance of the Divine Goodness and that which claims our utmost love and reverence is the deep and mysterious counsel of God for our redemption, without which all our other advantages must have soon ended in death and misery. What could it avail us if, while our temporal concerns were provided for, our eternal welfare had been neglected: if while our bodies were cherished with the good things of this life, our souls had been left a prey to our passions and vices, and the necessary woes entailed upon them?

The depraved condition of humane nature ever since the fall of our first parents is no secret, it being evident by the light of reason in all times and places, that the understanding of man did then become obscure, his will perverse, and his passions irregular; in a word, that our nature was debased and corrupted, having lost that rectitude and perfection which it must be supposed to have had coming new-made out of the hands of its Creator. Inasmuch as the good which we approve we do not, and the evil which we disapprove, that we do.

The consequence of all which must be an unquiet conscience, an anxious terrour of mind, and a fearful looking for of judgment. This much was visible by the light of nature to all mankind, as many I mean, as had any thought and reflection. But they knew not by what means mankind came into this wretched state, or how they were to be delivered from it. They knew not by what light the darkness of the world could be dispelled, by what grace or Spiritual aid the body of sin could be subdued, or by what atonement the guilt thereof was to be expiated and the punishment avoided.

But of all these things we find a full and adequate, yet a clear and positive account in the holy Scriptures: We find there that our first parents were, indeed, created spotless and innocent, and placed in a state of happiness suitable thereunto. But that through the insinuation of Satan they transgressed the command of God, and so fell from that happy and innocent state: That as heirs incur a forfeiture by the treason of the father, so the whole race of mankind were involved in the guilt, and obnoxious to the penalty incurred by their first parents.

That by these means the posterity of Adam were in him doomed to dye, banished from the lightsome mansions of Paradise into a vale of tears, sentenced to lead a short and sorrowful life, a life of pains and trouble, under a

---

[1] The following invocation appears as a marginal note to the first page of the manuscript: "Prevent us, O Lord, in all our doings with thy most gracious favour and further us with thy continual help that in all our works begun continued and ended in thee we may glorify thy holy name and by thy mercy attain everlasting life through Jesus Christ."

perpetual horrour of death and, what was infinitely worse than temporal death, an eternal estrangement from the living God whose grace and favour they had forfeited.

In this comfortless estate, with every remove the darkness still became grosser, and the love of sensuality became stronger in the sons of men till by degrees they forgot the God who made them, and were insensibly drawn to worship the creatures, sun, moon and stars, idols of their own making, dead men and devils, even the most contemptible and odious of plants and animals. Conformable to such absurd worship was their practice, they knew no bounds but their appetites, they were at no pains to subdue their passions, but on the contrary, sought only how to gratify and enflame them. In consequence whereof the world was filled with acts of violence and injustice, and one scene of vice and wickedness overspread the whole earth.

And as we find this sad account of the degeneracy and corruption of mankind in holy Scripture, so we find in the same a constant, uninterrupted scheme of providence for redeeming them out of it so clearly marked out yt he who runneth may read. An early ray of this broke out and shew'd itself just after the original disobedience of our first parents in that promise of God that the seed of the woman should bruise the serpent's head, which feeble and obscure light did gradually clear up by the subsequent dispensations of providence.

Nothing is more evident to whoever reads the Scriptures with attention than that God from the beginning designed to select out of the corrupt mass of mankind a peculiar people to himself, sanctifyed and distinguished from the rest of the world by faith and repentance, animated by the Spirit of God, supported and enlightened by his grace, so conducted through this world as not to suffer by the contagion of it, a people whose hope is in the heavens, whose ultimate aim and end is an eternal state of happiness and glory.

This society of peculiar persons who in all ages preserved a knowledge of the true God, and endeavoured to conform their lives and actions to his will, looking beyond this present world and aspiring to things above, this society, I say, of peculiar persons is called the church, whereof Jesus Christ is the Redeemer, the life which actuates, the center which unites, and the head which governs and conducts the whole.

The secret and predeterminate Counsel of God concerning his elect, those whom he hath conditionally elected according to his true knowledge, and the steps or method of his providence in separating and preserving them amidst all the casualties and corruptions, the vicissitudes and changes of this inferior world are without doubt great mysteries.

But above all other things the relation of Jesus Christ to his Church, his union with it and conduct towards it, his coming down from heaven, taking our nature upon him, preaching to sinful men, submitting for their sakes to dye upon the cross, then rising again and ascending into glory (and after all, sending his Spirit to abide with us to enlighten and sanctify the hearts of his elect) [2] — this, above all other things, seemeth to be without controversy the great mystery of Godliness, which is plain from the context or words foregoing and following those of my text — *These things write I unto thee hoping to come unto thee shortly. But if I tarry long that thou mightest know how to behave thyself in the house of God which is the Church of the living God, the pillar and*

[2] Added later.

ground of truth. And without controversy great is the mystery of Godliness: God was manifest in the flesh, justify'd in the Spirit, seen of angels, preached unto the Gentiles, believed on in the world, received up into glory. And it may well be said that the mystery of Godliness is great and wonderful throughout this whole dispensation [3] of the Messiah, the Author and finisher of our faith. Nor is it less excellent than wonderful, being full of grace and goodness to the Sons of men, as will be manifest if we take an extensive view of things and trace them from their origins.

It is evident there are two parts in the composition of man: The mind which is pure and spiritual, which is made in the image of God, and which we have in common with angels: and the corporeal part, containing the senses and passions which we have in common with brute beasts. The former tends to the knowledge and love of God as its true center, to vertue, piety and holiness, to all things excellent and praise-worthy: the latter inclines to the world, to sensible objects, to carnal things such as may gratify our grosser affections and appetites. The former of celestial origin, and inspired by the breath of God, would lift us up to heaven; the latter of terrene extraction and derived from the dust would sink and depress us down to the earth. The former is an intellectual principle that knows its true good, that leads to order and decency, to temperance, moderation, and justice. The latter is a blind and brutish principle that drives us on to satisfy our passions without rule or limit and without discerning our true happiness.

It is evident that in a regular situation of things the former divine principle should be uppermost, should rule and govern in our nature. This constitutes the divine life, or the spiritual man. Whereas if the carnal earthy part prevail and contrary to order become the upper and ruling principle, there ensues a life of blindness and misrule, of vice and woe. And this constitutes what is called in Scripture the carnal man: in whom the image of God is blurred and defaced and the divine life extinguished, he being alive unto sin and dead unto righteousness.

Such was the condition of mankind corrupted and estranged from God, at what time our blessed Saviour came down upon earth to inform and instruct us by his doctrine, to raise and animate us by his example, and by the sacrifice of himself to reconcile us to his father: in one word to save sinners.

I do not say all sinners, but such as being sensible of their estate desire and long for a better, such whose endeavours cooperate with the grace of God, such as by performing the conditions of the new covenant are entitled to its promises. To these Christ is a redeemer and mediator. Their repentance is not vain: their sincere though imperfect endeavours are accepted, what was amiss being pardoned, and what was defective being supplied through his merits and interception, and their future conduct directed by the light and grace of his holy Spirit.

As many as have repentance towards God and faith in Jesus Christ reap the benefit of his coming. They form a peculiar people who are styled the church. These are said to become new creatures, to be renewed in their minds, to be regenerate or born again, having a new life unto righteousness; which inward regeneration of the Spirit is set forth and signified unto us by the outward rite of baptism or ablution by water.

---

[3] Berkeley appears to have used the above as an introduction to two different   sermons. That which follows was omitted on Whitsunday.

This society of regenerate persons into whom new life is put by the Spirit of Christ residing and dwelling in them, who are living temples of the holy Ghost, is linked together by the internal bond of charity (an outward sign or badge whereof is the holy communion of the lord's supper), and they being animated by one Spirit drawing grace and life from the same fountain, become members of one body of which Christ is the head, drawing grace and life from the same fountain.

I say the regenerate and elect of God, though living in different ages and different parts of the world, are yet joined and knit together by professing the same faith, by submitting to the same laws, by entertaining the same hope, by being inwardly moved by the same spirit of love and holiness and reliance on Christ Jesus.

Which society of Christian men in holy Scripture goeth by various denominations, and is put in several lights. It is said to be a chosen generation, a royal priesthood, an holy nation, a peculiar people: it is spoken of sometimes as a kingdom whereof Christ is king: sometimes as a building aptly fitted together whereof Christ is the foundation or corner stone: at other times as a body whereof he is the head.

All which emblemes and allusions agree in this, that they set forth the Messiah as a Prince and ruler of a great people: a people holy and chosen, which from sinners he has made pure, from slaves he has made free, from dead he has made alive: whose hearts and affections he hath renewed, which he hath reconciled and dedicated, a living temple to God. A people to whom he gives laws, whom he instructs and governs, and will finally lead to a state of glory and happiness.

It is true no man hath seen this spirit of Christ which incorporates and unites, which moves, sanctifys, and governs the members of his church. But neither is the soul of man any more than the spirit of Christ visible to eyes of flesh and blood; they are, nevertheless, both of them plainly to be seen in their effects.

From the speech and motion of a man we evidently infer the soul or spirit within him, and are in no danger of confounding a dead carcase with a living man. After the same manner the workings of the Spirit of Christ do sufficiently declare and shew themselves in their outward effects, that light and knowledge of divine things, that love and unanimity, that piety and vertue, that peace and comfort which so plainly distinguish true Christians from ungodly and carnal men.

You see by what marks and tokens the flock of Christ are known, and these marks do declare what obligations you have entered into by professing yourselves members of his church. Let us not flatter ourselves, as too many are apt to do, that an outward respect to rites and ceremonies, to sacraments, to hearing and reading the Scripture and frequenting the public worship of God will alone be able to avail us, obtaining the ends for which those means were appointed, without the practice of an inward and sincere piety, without cutting off the right hand and plucking out the right eye, that is without mortifying every lust and cultivating every vertue. A practice no less salutary to the soul than disagreeable to flesh and blood.

Everyone knows the prevailing principle in humane nature is self-love. This under the direction of well-informed reason should lead us into the true methods of obtaining happiness; but it is a blind principle that takes part with our passions and flatters us in the enjoyment of ease and pleasure: It is too apt upon slight grounds to raise our hopes and lessen our fears, to interpret everything too much in our own favour, making our own obligations more easy and less binding, and straining the promises and engagements of others to our own views beyond their true sense and intention. Hence it is that in all ages men have been prone to mistake the gracious promises, covenants, and dispensations of God towards mankind however clearly and explicitly revealed.

Thus in the early times of Christianity there were found those who understood the liberty of the gospel to absolve them from all obedience to moral laws and the civil institutions of their country, though in truth it means no more than an exemption from observing Jewish rites and ceremonies. Thus also in our own daies we see one set of men, instead of leading a vertuous godly life in order to be saved, propose to themselves the attaining of that end by the practice of wild austerities and superstitions.

While another kind of Fanatics, possessed with Spiritual pride, a fond conceit of themselves, and high scorn of their neighbours, flatter themselves that they alone are the elect and predestinate of God, though in their lives and actions they shew a very small degree either of piety toward God or charity toward man.

Lastly it is to be feared there are men of all professions that, without repenting of any one sin, without improving any one vertue or mortifying any one desire, in short without giving themselves any the least trouble either in thought, word, or deed, imagine themselves entitled to the benefits of Christ's passion merely because they have been baptized and are called Christians. So miserably do men impose upon themselves in that one thing necessary, the great article of salvation.

To state the matter truly it cannot, indeed, be denied that the methods of divine providence in dealing with the sons of men are full of mercy and indulgence even towards the most notorious sinners. But at the same time it must be acknowledged inconsistent with the other attributes of God, his wisdom and justice, to save a careless and unrepenting sinner.

There is some analogy between the methods of grace and the ordinary course of nature. Providence hath made provision for our welbeing both in this life and in that which is to come: but a supine indolence and neglect on our part will equally deprive us of both these advantages.

As in the one case, if we neglect to sow the corn, and to spin the flax and wooll, we are left to perish with cold and hunger: so in the other if we neglect to perform our part by faith and good works, notwithstanding all the schemes of providence to save us we shall be irrecoverably lost.

God in the language of Isaiah hath planted his vinyard in a very fruitful hill, he hath fenced it and gathered out the stones thereof, and planted it with the choicest vine, and built a tower in the midst of it, and also made a winepress therein. The good and gracious God hath furnished us with faculties to perform our duty: he hath given us the light of nature and reason to discern it; he hath farther explained and promulgated his will by the mouth of prophets and apostles; he hath sent his well-beloved son into the world to instruct and exhort us, and to lay down his life, a sacrifice for our sins; he strengthens and assists our weak endeavours with his grace;[4] and hath planted a con-

---

[4] (*Holy Spirit*) correction.

science in the breast of every man which never fails to check and admonish him. What more could be done to his vinyard that he hath not done unto it?

And what more doth God require at our hands than to make the proper use of these advantages and not to grieve his holy Spirit but to cooperate with his gracious intentions to sanctify a peculiar people to himself and to rescue us from the slavery of Sin and Death.

Now that all here present may partake of this redemption and at the last day be numbered among this peculiar people, God of his infinite mercy grant, to whom, the father, son, and holy ghost be ascribed, as is most due, all honour, praise, might, majesty, and dominion now and evermore.

SERMON II

There are copies of this sermon, one in the hand of George Berkeley, Jr., and another in that of H. J. Rose, made in 1855. I think there is little question, however, that the original copy is in Berkeley's own hand. The later pages of the Ms. are watermarked and torn across one corner.

It is possible that this is the text of the sermon preached by Berkeley at King's Chapel, Boston, just before his departure for England in 1731. Rand (Berkeley's American Sojourn, p. 45) quotes the following note from the diary of Benjamin Walker: "On Lord's Day 12 [September, 1731] in ye morn Dean George Berkeley preacht. in ye [King's] Chapel from ye 1st Epistle to Timothy ye 3rd Chap., Verse 16, and a fine sermon; according to my opinion I never heard such a one. A very great auditory."

I Timothy: iii, 16
Without controversy great is
the mystery of Godliness.[1]

The creation of this visible world for the use and comfort of man, our very life and being which as it was originally bestowed so it is daily preserved by the divine providence, every good thing we enjoy, and all the evils we escape, are so many blessings that call for our attention and gratitude.

But the most adorable instance of the Divine Goodness and that which claims our utmost love and reverence is the deep and mysterious counsel of God for the salvation of mankind, without which all our other advantages must have soon ended in death and misery. What would it avail us if, while our temporal concerns were provided for, our eternal welfare had been neglected: if while our bodies were cherished with the good things of this life, our souls had been left a prey to our own passions and vices and the necessary woes entailed upon them?

The depraved condition of humane nature ever since the fall of our first parents is no secret to many heathen, upon whom the ends of the world are come — to us who are taught in Divine Authority that the understanding of man was obscure, his will perverse and his passions irregular; in a word that our nature was debased and corrupted as having lost that rectitude and perfection, that purity and spotless innocence which it may be supposed to have had upon its coming new-made from the hands of its Creator. Inasmuch as the good which we approve we do not, and the evil which we disapprove, that we do.

The consequence of all which was an unquiet conscience, an anxious terrour of mind, and a fearful looking for of judgment. This much was visible by the light of nature to all mankind, as many I mean, as had any thought or reflection.

But of all these things we find if not a full and adequate, yet a clear and satisfactory account in the holy Scriptures: We find there that our first parents were, indeed, created spotless and innocent and placed in a state of happiness suitable thereunto. But that through the insinuation of Satan they transgressed the command of God, and so fell from that happy and innocent

---

[1] The first five pages of introduction are a later, slightly altered version of the introduction to Sermon 1.

state: That as heirs incur a forfeiture by the treason of the father, so the whole race of mankind were involved in the guilt and liable to the penalty of their first parents.

That by these means the posterity of Adam were in him doomed to dye, banished from the lightsome mansions of Paradise into a vale of tears, sentenced to lead a short and sorrowful life, a life of pains and trouble, under a perpetual horrour of death, and they forgot the God who made them, and were insensibly drawn to worship the creatures, sun, moon and stars, idols of their own making, dead men and devils, even the most contemptible and odious of plants and animals. Conformable to such absurd worship was their practice, they knew no bounds but their appetites, they were at no pains to govern their passions by reason but sought only how to satisfy and enflame them. In consequence whereof the world was filled with acts of violence and iniquity and one scene of vice and folly overspread the whole earth.

And as we find this sad account of the degeneracy and corruption of mankind in the holy Scripture, so we may discover in the same divine oracles a constant, uninterrupted scheme of providence for redeeming them out of it so clearly marked out yt he who runneth may read. An early ray of this broke out and shew'd itself just after the original disobedience of our first parents in that promise of God that the seed of the woman should bruise the serpent's head, which feeble [2] light did gradually clear up by the subsequent dispensations of providence.

Nothing is more evident to whoever reads the Scriptures with attention than that God from the beginning designed to select out of the corrupt mass of mankind a peculiar people to himself sanctifyed and distinguished from the rest of the world by faith and repentance, animated by the Spirit of God, supported and enlightened by his grace, so conducted through this world as not to suffer from the contagion of it, a people whose hope is in the heavens, whose ultimate aim and end is an eternal state of happiness and glory.

This society of peculiar persons who in all ages preserved a knowledge of the true God, and endeavoured to conform their lives and actions to his will, relishing things spiritual and looking beyond this present world and aiming to things above, this society, I say, of peculiar persons, is called the church, whereof Jesus Christ is the Redeemer, the life which actuates, the center which unites, and the head which governs and conducts the whole.

The secret and predeterminate Counsel of God concerning his elect, those whom he hath conditionally elected according to his true knowledge, and the steps or method of his providence in separating and preserving them amidst all the casualties and corruptions, the vicissitudes and changes of this inferior world are without doubt great mysteries.

But above all other things the relation of Jesus Christ to his Church, his union with it, and behavior towards it, his coming down upon earth, taking our nature upon him, preaching to sons of men, submitting to die on the cross, then rising again and ascending into glory. This I say above all other things seemeth to be without controversy the great mystery of Godliness, which is plain from the context or words foregoing and following the words of my text — *These things write I unto thee hoping to come unto thee shortly. But if I tarry long that thou mightest know how thou oughtest to behave thyself in the house of*

***

[2] *and obscure* crossed out.

*God which is the Church of the living God, the pillar and ground of truth. And
without controversy great is the mystery of Godliness: God was manifest in the
flesh, justify'd in the Spirit, seen of angels, preached unto the Gentiles, believed on
in the world, received up into glory.* And it may well be said that the mystery
of Godliness is great and wonderful throughout this whole dispensation of the
Messiah, the Author and finisher of our faith.

But to make you more sensible of this I shall consider the Messiah under
three distinct articles as head of the church, as prefigured by the law, and as
foretold by the prophets. On all which you will perceive a most amazing mystery of Divine goodness towards the sons of men gradually disclosing itself
through the several periods of time, and shining forth more and more unto a
perfect day.

"I know that Messias cometh which is called Christ." (John 4, 25, Samaritan). "Art thou he that should come or do we look for another." (Matt.
11, 3, John's disciples).

Among all the instances of God's goodness to mankind [3] there is none either
in its nature more wonderful or in its effects more beneficial or in its influence
more extensive than sending the Messiah upon earth for our redemption to
destroy Satan's kingdom and redeem the world. A glympse of this intended
blessing was hinted immediately after the fall in that prediction that the seed
of the woman should bruise the serpent's head. Hence an opinion prevailed
of some great person to come who was to be prophet, prince, and deliverer
of mankind. Nor was this belief peculiar to the Jews, for we see by what the
Samaritan woman saith in the words of my text — *I know that Messias cometh,*
that the same expectation was commonly entertained by the Samaritans also.
But in a peculiar manner it possessed the nation of the Jews in general, and
more particularly at or about the time of our Saviour's birth. Hence it was
that the disciples of John the Baptist put the question to our Saviour: Art
thou he that should come or do we look for another? The dispensation
of . . . [4] of the law and the prophets having . . . in a long series of ages during
the . . . amazing mystery of divine . . . of time and shining forth . . . of the
truth . . . of the types and figures . . . prophets.

Now to take things from the original, it . . . is evident there are two parts
in the composition of man: The mind which is pure and spiritual, which contains the image of God, and which we have in common with angels: and the
corporeal part, containing the senses and passions which we have in common
with brute beasts. The former tends to the knowledge and love of God as its
true end and center to vertue, piety and holiness, to all things excellent and
praiseworthy: the latter inclines to the world, to sensible objects, to carnal
things such as may gratify our grosser affections and appetites. The former
of celestial origine and inspired by the breath of God would lift us up to
heaven; the latter of terrene extraction and derived from the dust would sink
and depress us down to the earth. The former is an intellectual principle that
knows its true good, that leads to order and decency, to temperance, moderation and justice: The latter is a blind and brutish principle that urgeth us on
to gratify our passions without rule or limit and without discerning our true
happiness.

It is evident that in a regular situation of things the former or divine principle should be strongest in our nature. This constitutes the divine life, the

[3] *the sons of men* corrected.   [4] Ms. torn.

life of God, or the spiritual man. Whereas if the carnal earthy part prevail, and contrary to the order of things become the upper and ruling principle, there ensues a life of blindness and disorder, of vice and woe. And this constitutes what is called in Scripture the carnal man: in whom the image of God is blurred or defaced and the divine life extinguished, he being alive unto sin and dead unto righteousness.

Such was the condition of mankind corrupted and estranged from God, at what time our blessed Saviour came down upon earth to inform and instruct us by his doctrine, to raise and animate us by his example, and by the sacrifice of himself to reconcile us to his father: in one word to save sinners.

I do not say all sinners, but such as being sensible of their estate desired and longed for a better, such whose endeavours cooperated with the grace of God manifested in Christ Jesus such as by performing the conditions of the new covenant are entitled to its promises. To these, Christ is a redeemer and mediator. Their repentance is not vain: their sincere though imperfect endeavours are accepted, what was amiss being pardoned, and what was defective being supplied through his merits and interception.

As many, I say, as have repentance towards God and faith in Jesus Christ reap the benefit of his coming. They are separated from the common mass of mankind and form a peculiar people which is called the Church of Christ. These are said to become new creatures, to be renewed, to be regenerate or born again, having a new life unto righteousness; which inward regeneration of the Spirit is set forth and signified unto us by the outward rite of baptism or ablution by water.

This society of regenerate persons into whom new life is put by the Spirit of Christ residing and dwelling in them, who are living temples of the holy Ghost, is linked together by the internal bond of charity (an outward sign or badge whereof is the holy communion), and they, being animated by one and the same Spirit, become members of one body of which Christ is the head.

I say the regenerate and elect of God, though living in different ages and distant parts of the world, are yet joined together and united by holding . . . the same faith, by submitting to the same laws, by entertaining the same hope, by being inwardly moved by the same spirit of love and trust in Christ Jesus.

Which society of Christian men in holy Scripture goeth by various denominations and is put in several lights.[5] It is spoken of sometimes as a kingdom whereof Christ is king; sometimes as a building aptly fitted together whereof Christ is the foundation or corner stone: at other times as a body whereof he is the head.

All which emblemes and allusions agree in this, that they set forth the Messiah as the prince and ruler of a great people: a people holy and chosen, which from sinners he has made pure, from slaves he has made free, from dead he has made alive: whose hearts and affections he hath renewed, which he hath reconciled and dedicated a living temple to God. A people to whom he gives laws, whom he instructs and governs, and will finally lead to a state of glory, happiness and repose. If anyone should ask who hath seen this spirit of Christ, which incorporates and unites, which renews, sanctifys, and governs the members of his church, I answer that in like manner as the soul of man is

---

[5] *It is said to be a chosen generation, a royal priesthood, an holy nation, a peculiar people*: Notation.

invisible even so the Spirit of Christ is not visible to flesh and blood; they are nevertheless both of them plainly to be seen in their effects.

From the speech and motion of a man we evidently infer the soul or spirit within him, and are in no danger of confounding a dead carcase with a living man. After the same manner the workings of the Spirit of Christ do sufficiently declare and manifest themselves in their outward effects, that light and knowledge of divine things, that love and unanimity, that piety and vertue, that peace and comfort which so plainly distinguish true Christians from ungodly and carnal men.[6]

Now this spiritual Society which derives life and union from its head Christ Jesus, together with the various offices and relations which Christ was to bear with regard to his church, have been plainly prefigured in the Old Testament, which is the second point that I proposed to speak of. I say the predeterminate purpose and scheme of God for the salvation of men. First then this great mystery [7] was in the law and history of the Old Testament (early dawned forth and [8] in some sort) hinted or shadowed under several natural and sensible representations, that so the carnal minds and grosser apprehensions of mankind might be gradually formed and prepared by outward ordinances and figures [9] for the spirit and truth which was couch'd [10] beneath. In which sense, the Law also was a Schoolmaster to lead the Jews unto Christ.

Thus the ark of Noah built by the command . . . a select number of persons . . . the general inundation . . . . . represents the . . . within its enclosure . . . God, and reserved by his gracious care out of that general inundation of wickedness and vice of blindness and idolatry which overspread the whole face of the earth. Another plain figure of the same thing was the conduct of God toward the Israelites. For as that nation were by his particular favor rescued from a state of servitude in Egypt; and through many perils and difficulties preserved and brought safe unto the land of Promise; even so the Church of Christ, that spiritual Israel, hath been freed from the slavery of Sin, a bondage worse than that of Egypt, and put into a state of grace and Christian liberty, and is by the Spirit of God in Christ separated from the rest of the world, and in spite of all the powers of darkness, all the snares and obstacles of this life, safely conducted into the Heavenly Canaan, that happy region of life and . . . which God hath prepared . . . which the Israelites . . . a type of figure of that celestial head, the word of God, which nourisheth the souls of his elect under the dispensation of the Gospel. The blood of the Paschal lamb which was a protection to the children of Israel from the destroying angel plainly represents the Church's being redeemed by the blood of Christ, the lamb slain from the foundation of the world. And the Scape-goat on whom the sins of the people were laid did manifestly indicate and set forth the Messiah who was to bear the guilt of all mankind. The external washings and purifications of the Jews, their sacrifices and atonements, were so many signs and presages of that inward purging of the soul from Sin by the final atonement of that great sacrifice Christ Jesus, who offered himself a ransom for the sins of the whole world. The very promise of a Messiah that should be

---

[6] What follows is completely independent of Sermon 1.

[7] of Godliness crossed out.

[8] was crossed out.

[9] of the Jewish Law of things to come crossed out.

[10] concealed crossed out.

victorious over his enemies . . . kingdom hath received a sign . . . blessed Saviour who hath tri- . . . . subdued the enemies of . . . of the earth to a holy obedience to the meek reception of his law, and erected a spiritual kingdom in the hearts and affections of men.

Sensible and corporeal objects are fitly used as figures of Spiritual things. And though carnal-minded men might stick in the letter without looking any further, yet there have not been wanting in all ages of the church pious and devout men who looked behind the vail, who endeavoured to recommend themselves to God, by an inward purity of heart, who raised their hopes above the perishing things of this world, and comforted themselves in the prospect of a Spiritual Redeemer. But when the fulness of time was come, Christ and his apostles took away the vail and opened the seals. They have clearly explained to us that those things which the Jews understood carnally had a spiritual meaning: that the Kingdom of God was not flesh but Spirit. That the promise was of a spiritual Messiah that . . . people and which it most con- . . . were not the Gentiles but . . . that it is not the out . . . in word circumcision of the heart which renders us truly acceptable to God. They have made us sensible what it is to be a true Israelite, what is the true fast, the true Sacrifice, and the true bread of heaven.

And indeed that the Jewish law, their rites and ceremonies and the whole dealings of God with that people were all figurative things and relative to higher and more important concerns seems reasonable to conclude from hence, that considered in themselves they seem unworthy of the notion we have of God. It is, I say, unsuitable to the holiness, the purity and perfection of the divine being, to think he could ultimately propose any other worship than that which should be in Spirit and truth. Nor doth it suit with his wisdom power and goodness to suppose he would predestinate and lead men into temporal enjoyments, things so unsatisfactory in their nature, and so . . . ishing in their duration as to their last hope and end. Nor is it to be imagined that the favor of God the . . . all the nations upon earth, . . . the Jews. . . . now said St. Paul, plainly . . . accounted the father of all believers, that there is no difference between the Jew and the Greek: that the Jewish Law was only a shadow of good things to come. Hence also it is that we find the prophets saying in sundry places that their speeches are obscure and not to be understood till the end, that the covenant and law should be renewed, that the commandments given to the Jews were not good, that their sacrifices were abominable, which is to be understood of the letter without the Spirit: of the outward ritual performances abstracted from inward sanctity of heart and soul (which alone can render us acceptable to God).

And as the Messiah was typified and prefigured by the law of the Jews, so was he plainly foretold by their prophets, which was the third point I proposed to speak of. That God would send a Redeemer was intimated from the beginning, immediately after the fall of man, as hath been before observed; and this same event hath from that time downwards been repeated . . . a succession of Holy and inspir- . . . . successively attested to by . . . the rest of the prophets . . . the Messiah, the whole East, if we may believe Heathen writers, was big with the same expectation, nor can there be opigned any age or period of time in which Christ was not either adored or expected. In this great point both Jews and Gentiles, old and new Testament center and unite. This is the seed of Abraham in which all the nations of the earth were to be blessed: This is the star of Jacob, the Scepter, that was to rise out of Israel: This is the root of Jesse that was to be an ensign to the people. Particularly to recount the prophecies that relate to him would be an endless work, the old testament throughout being full of allusions and predictions concerning the Messiah.

He was not only prophesied of in gross, but the minutest parts and circumstances of his character were distinctly pointed at and foretold. That he should have a forerunner; that he should be an infant born in Bethlehem of the tribe of Judai of the house of David; that he should heal . . . blind and feet to the lame; . . . lighten the Gentiles, and a . . . whole world; that he should . . . many ways; that he should be a stumbling block and stone of offence, to be rejected by the builders, but that God should make this stone the chief stone of the corner; that it should grow into a great mountain and fill the whole earth; that he should be put to death, have gall for his drink, have his hands and feet pierced, have lots cast for his cloaths; that he should rise the third day, ascend into heaven, sit on the right hand of God, be victorious over his enemies and be adored by the Kings and nations of the earth.

And as these circumstances and characters of the Messiah are plainly and distinctly foretold, so also is the time of his coming. The prophecies are very clear that before the scepter should depart from Judah, under the fourth monarchy, or in the time of the Roman empire, before the destruction of the second temple, and in the seventieth week of Daniel, that is 490 years after the edict for rebuilding of Jerusalem, Christ should come, that a reconciliation should then be made for ini(quity),[11] that everlasting righteousness should be brought in, . . . prophecy should be sealed up, and the . . . accordingly it came to pass that . . . established, while the second tem- . . . still subsisted, at the expira- . . . that the son of God made his appearance in the world, was born at the very place and time predicted, wrought all those miracles and did and suffered all those things spoken of him in the old Testament, reconciled mankind to God, introduced everlasting righteousness, and sealed up what is accomplished, the visions and prophecies. As the prophet Haggai foretold, God did shake or move all nations, and the desire of all nations came.

Such were the prophecies concerning the Messiah, and such was their completion. But I have mentioned only a few out of some hundreds, the old Testament being full of allusions to the new. And though the bare comparing the prophecies with the events might to a reasonable mind yield sufficient proof of the coming of the Messiah in the person of our Lord Christ Jesus, yet the evidence will be still stronger if we consider that those prophecies were not uttered by one person or in one and the same age; but that there was from the beginning a succession of different persons who in various and distant countries of the world all conspired to foretell the same (events, and that those . . .) [12] prophecies that contain (such clear and undoubted proof of the) [13] Christian religion are (acknowledged to be true and) [14] divine by the most inveterate enemies of Christianity. The whole nation of the Jews, under the curse of God and bearing evident marks of his vengeance, cast out from their own country and dispersed throughout the world without prince, prophet, temple, altar or sacrifice, without one jot of authority or one foot of land that they can call their own, do nevertheless unaccountably subsist a distinct people to this day; a spectacle to all nations, a living monument and proof of

---

[11] H. J. R. (Henry John Rose), interpolation.

[12] *Ibid.*
[13] *Ibid.*

[14] *Ibid.*

that Messiah whom they crucified, (and of that very religion which they continue to blaspheme.)

The accomplishment of the Jewish prophecies in our blessed Saviour is, I say, a plain proof of our Religion. And (it hath pleased God to confirm) this proof by a perpetual miracle, in as much as the Jews, against all example, under the hatred and scorn of all mankind still subsist, preserving their ancient language and the writings of the prophets: by which means they become unsuspected guardians and witnesses to those very Scriptures which contain their own condem(nation by setting forth a number) [15] of plain and precise praedic(tions of the nature and office of) [16] Christ, and so evidently de(scribing that person as the) [17] Messiah whom their fathers cru(cified, and thus brought ruin) [18] upon them and their posterity.

If it be asked how comes it to pass that the Jews themselves do not submit to the clear evidence of their own antient prophecy and acknowledge Christ for the Messiah, I answer that this blindness and obstinacy of theirs is a further confirmation of the truth of those sacred oracles: it is itself an accomplishment of what was foretold by the prophets. That the vinyard of God, when he looked that it should bring forth grapes brought forth wild grapes; that he should stretch out his hands all the day long to a rebellious people; that they should be stricken with darkness and blindness and astonishment of heart. The truth is, they were a people, whose hearts and hopes were set upon the good things of this world, who took all according to the letter, and in their Messiah expected a temporal victorious Prince that should conquer their enemies by the sword, and erect a Jewish empire over the nations of the earth. And not finding these things in Jesus Christ, they at first rejected him, and have ever since continued to disown him.

And yet to minds less gross and carnal, such as have just notions of a right way of thinking, it will appear that Christ (came in truth in) [19] great lustre and dignity, (that he cured all) [20] manner of diseases, that he performed so (many miracles, that wind) [21] and sea, that death and (life and every creature) [22] obey'd his voice, — what were all these things, but so many glorious testimonys to the son of God? What is it that the Devils were dispossessed and their oracles everywhere silenced, that the ceremonies of the Jews and the idolatry of the Gentiles were at once abolished, that the true God who for so many ages had been unknown to the Heathen world was publickly owned and worshiped by men of all nations, that thousands of wicked persons who had lived without God in the world should at once be converted from the grossest immoralities and vices to a life of vertue and holiness, what is all this, I say, but that the day spring from on high had visited the Gentiles, that a light had shone upon those who sate in darkness and the shadow of death? Is it not a literal accomplishment of what had been foretold by the prophet Joel that God would pour out his spirit upon all flesh? Lastly, what is it that the same person who, when living, had not where to lay his head, who was even betray'd, denied, and forsaken by his own disciples, that this same Jesus, after being put (to a shameful and cruel) death,[23] without any human (assistance but the ministry) [24] of a few illiterate fisher (men should conquer the) [25] learning and wisdom (of philosophers the p)ride [26] of princes, the blindness and ob-

[15] *Ibid.*	[18] *Ibid.*	[21] *Ibid.*	[24] *Ibid.*
[16] *Ibid.*	[19] *Ibid.*	[22] *Ibid.*	[25] *Ibid.*
[17] *Ibid.*	[20] *Ibid.*	[23] *Ibid.*	[26] *Ibid.*

stinacy of mankind, and be adored and preached throughout the world, that at the name of Jesus every knee should bow, that we should all acknowledge him for our Lord, follow him as our Leader, trust on him for our Deliverer. Is not this a conquest in the noblest sense, wherein the powers of darkness are subdued and a new kingdom of light and righteousness established by the Messiah ?

(Having therefore my Brethren explained to you, so far as I was able wherein consists that great mystery of Godliness, the Church of Christ, and kingdom of God), it remains that I exhort you so to behave yourselves as becometh dutiful subjects of this kingdom, and worthy members of this Church.[27] Let me entreat you to put a just value on the high privileges you are entitled to as Christians to consider that you are (in the words of the Apostle) come unto Mount Sion, unto the city of the living God, the heavenly Jerusalem, and to an innumerable company of angels, to the . . . eral assembly and church of the first born, which are written (in Heaven and to Christ) [28] the Judge of all, and to the Spirits of (just men made perfect),[29] and to Jesus the mediator of the (New Covenant),[30] that we may be touched . . . [and] that we may be so deeply affected with a just (full) sense of those blessings, and express the same in our lives and conversations. God & . . . . . . let us on this solemn festival . . . In a deep sense of all whi . . . opportunity of this solemn feast . . . birth of our blessed Saviour . . . re(flect on the inest-(imable benefits)) . . . great mystery of the incarnation and na(ture of our Lord and the e)stimable [31] benefits that unless we are . . . may receive thereby.

[27] (Insert a piece from the 4th (4to) on Xt came to save sinners.)

[28] H. J. R., interpolation.

[29] *Ibid.*

[30] *Ibid.*

[31] *Ibid.*

SERMON III

This Easter sermon, the most interesting of the three, is preceded by Berkeley's own signature, and is written in his hand. It bears marked similarities to the notes of a sermon on a text taken from I Cor. xv, preached at Newport.[1] The new anti-Deistic movement in Berkeley's thought is made clearly manifest. His constant omission of the Deistic phrases "natural light" and "natural religion" is particularly significant.

I John: ii, 25.

This is the promise that he hath promised
us even eternal life.

Christ came from heaven on this very message from God to man, to bring life and immortality to light, and to assure us that whoever believeth in him shall not perish but have everlasting life. He takes away all ambiguity as to the sense by the clearness and plainness of his declaration. He proves its truth by his own resurrection. And not by this alone but also by every other miracle in the Gospel. The principal drift and aim, the scope and summary whereof was the inculcating this great point of salvation through the obedience and satisfaction of God the Son; and surely of all the doctrines that ever were promulgated this was at once the most cheering, the most amazing, and the most consoling. This is the promise that he hath promised us even eternal life.

This is that peculiar faith and hope which hath wrought such a wonderful change in the world, destroyed so many impious schemes of idolatry, abolished or reduced so many vices. This is the inheritance of Saints, the encouragement and support of martyrs, and the general joy of all true believers.

Eternal life is the ultimate end of all a Christian's views. It is for this he denies his appetites, subdues his passions, and foregoes the interests of a perishable world. Nor is this at all inconsistent with the glory of God being the last end of our actions, forasmuch as this very glory constitutes our heaven or felicity in the other world.

We are wonderfully strengthened in this hope of eternal life, when we consider the resurrection of our blessed Saviour, than which nothing could be more apt to produce in us a strong persuasion that we our selves also shall rise from the dead. Since he, whose promise we depend upon, is himself become the first-born from the dead, confirming his promise by a full and adequate instance, a matter of fact which our Lord takes care to attest in the clearest manner: he appears often and to many in open day-light, he submits to trials of sense, walks, talks, eats and drinks, ascends publicly into heaven before several hundred eye-witnesses, and thereupon many thousands are converted. The expectation of so many ages, such mighty miracles, the concurring testimony of so many wise and good men confirm us in the belief that Jesus Christ rose from the dead, and became the first fruits of them that slept. Especially when we consider how the benedictions of patriarchs, the oracles of prophets, the types of antiquity are at once compleated, explained, illustrated in that marvellous event. An event which, as it proves and exemplifies

[1] F. iv, pp. 386 ff.

a life to come, offers to your meditation an article of faith not less interesting and important than singular and amazing. And indeed there is no such anti-dote to vice, no such guard of virtue, no such comfort in affliction as a right belief and thorough persuasion of a future state.

Now to make my following discourse more useful and methodical I shall in the first place endeavor to prove that our expectation of a future state is sup-ported by good reasons drawn from the nature of things,[2] and secondly that it is supported by the prevailing consent and general authority of all mankind.

First then I am to show that the belief in a future state is collaterally supported by good reasons from the nature of things. It is a natural way of proceeding to argue from things past to things future, from things known to things unknown, from visible things to invisible. Let us then look abroad into this world which was at first created and is still preserved and governed by God. Let us try whether we can discern therein any marks and tokens, foot-steps or traces, parallels or examples whereby to illustrate and infer a resur-rection. And indeed it is hardly possible to open our eyes and not see some-thing that puts us in mind thereof. All the parts of this corporeal world are in a flux and revolution, decaying and renewing, perishing and rising up again. The various successions and returns of light and darkness, winter and summer, spring and autumn, the generation of plants and fruits of the earth, are all in some sort so many instances of this truth.

Resurrection, I say, how strange so ever at first sight will be found natural, that is conformable, to the course of nature in her ordinary productions, which nature is the work of God. In the common course of things, that which was dead reviveth, that which was sown in the earth riseth again out of the earth. The winter is a kind of death to most things. The plants and herbs of the field decay and disappear. Fruits and seeds fall to the ground and therein moulder and rot. The trees are disrobed of their beauty and look like dead and dry timber. In the spring all nature revives. New plants, new blossoms, new leaves. That which was sown being older, and after sowing corrupted in the ground, now riseth again, fresh and young.[3]

For so much as we can gather from this visible frame of things there is a similitude in the operations of Providence. The God of nature acts by general and uniform laws.[4] The burial of Humane bodies is then to be regarded as the sowing of seed in the earth.[5] Other things that are sown rise again at the end of the year, and after the season of corruption is expired, at the end of the great year, the consummation of all things, our bodies shall rise again accord-ing to the express word of God.

Surely there is nothing incongruous in supposing that the same omnip-otence which before our eyes raiseth so many fair plants and flowers and fruits out of the dust of the earth, should from the same dust in due time raise up humane bodies.

Nor are there wanting in the natural course of things instances of the Resurrection even of animals. Thus the silkworm lies without sense or motion, is dead and actually buried in a tomb of her own spinning. But after some

[2] *light of nature* crossed out.
[3] *And may we not hope the good and gracious God will do as much for Man whom he hath made after his own image as we see him do every year to the meanest vegetables of the field.* Crossed out.
[4] *And if so may we not in reason think with St. Paul that* crossed out.
[5] *And if* crossed out.

daies, her head, limbs, and former shape being perished and thrown by like old clothes, she revives in a new form, and that which in its former state crawled on the ground, is now become a quite different animal and flies abroad with wings.[6]

But farther the spiritual nature is not capable of being consumed by fire or dissolved by water or broken by any accident. Moreover the justice of God which is concerned to punish or reward in another life those good and evil actions which meet with no retribution in this; also our own fears and hopes, these natural presages which spring up in the minds of men, are so many probable arguments to dispose and lead us to the belief of a future state; even although Divine Revelation had been silent on this head.

We may add as a farther proof on this point, that natural appetite of immortality, which is so generally and deeply rooted in mankind, and which we cannot suppose implanted in us by the author of our being, merely to be frustrated. This would not be of a piece with the other dealings of God towards man.

It will be hard to produce any parallel to this in any part of the creation, or to assign a single instance wherein God hath given appetite without a possibility of satisfying it, or on purpose to teaze and disappoint his creatures. Nor is there any reason for believing this in the present case more than in any other.

It cannot be said, that God who gave us this life wants power to give us another after this, if he will.[7]

Seeing therefore that God hath implanted in us a strong desire of immortality we have just grounds to think there is a probability of having this as well as all other natural desires contented. And thus the nature of things [8] would have afforded rational hopes of a future state to all mankind, even had no express declaration of it been ever made on Divine Authority.

In the next place I come to consider how far Authority contributes to the establishing of this point, and shall endeavor to show that Gentiles, Jews, and Christians, although their persuasions be not equally pure, nor their notions equally just concerning this matter, do yet all concur in the same general belief of another life after this.

The Gentiles had not only a notion of a future state, but also in some sort, an idea of a resurrection. Their wise men imagined that after a certain period the world was to be renewed, the same scenes to be passed through again, the same men and actions to return. Such was anciently the doctrine of many who passed for sages especially in the East. And this was in all probability the effect of tradition, altered and defaced in a long tract of time. The same tradition improved by the fancies of men appears to have given birth to a great variety of notions.

[6] *This same resurrection is also observed in other insects and caterpillars. And although these instances are no direct proof of our resurrection, yet they shew that there is no absurdity or incongruity with the nature of things in that supposition* crossed out.

But there are other, and those direct proofs of a life to come discoverable by reason, inasmuch as crossed out.

[7] *Neither can it be said, that he will not do a thing so agreeable to all notions of reason and justice, as to reward and punish those actions in a future state, which met with no retribution in the present* crossed out.

[8] *very light of nature affords* crossed out.

Some devised Elysian Fields under ground, others imagined islands of the blessed in the ocean: some conceived a future state of heroes and good men in an upper region among the stars and planets, others that dead men would revive and live a second life in human bodies upon earth. Some again held a transmigration of souls into the bodies of beasts, birds, and insects, suitable to the brutal and degenerate lives they led in a former state.

But however men may differ in their particular conceptions of a future state, the general notion was still the same. It was, and is the prevailing opinion throughout the world, that a life of virtue and goodness will raise, ennoble, and beautify mankind hereafter. And, on the contrary, that a life of vice and wickedness, will depress and degrade them after this life, into a low and wretched state of being.

This hath been the universal persuasion in the remotest ages and the most distant countries. You will find it obtain in the East and West, in the North and South, in times ancient and modern, among Mahometans and other idolaters, for such they are in truth with all their abhorrence of images; whether knowing or ignorant, civil or barbarous, they all agree in this general sentiment, which hath always been strongest in the most wise and virtuous, the most reasonable and intelligent of mankind.

This matter of fact will be most evident to whoever is at pains to consult the histories and accounts of the several parts of this habitable world. I say it will upon the whole appear, that the doctrine of a future state is attested to and confirmed by the general consent of nations, as well as by the especial suffrage of the wisest men in all ages.[9]

And as the belief of a future state is supported by the authority of the Gentile world in general, so neither is that of the Jewish Nation in particular wanting. And here it must be owned that Moses the Law-giver of the Jews doth not teach or insist upon the immortality of the soul and the hopes of another life as the *great* motive to obedience.[10] Peace and plenty, prosperity and success in their undertakings, victories over their enemies, a land flowing with milk and honey, these and such like temporal blessings, were the particular rewards, which the Jews were given to expect for their observance of the Mosaic Law.[11]

Moses is to be considered as a lawgiver under God to the nation of the Jews. He enjoyns them national statutes, and assigns them national rewards and punishments. His precepts are calculated for men, considered rather as members of society than as single individuals, as inhabitants of the world — rather than as candidates for a better. The main end, I say, of his laws is to promote the well-being of the Jewish society, to keep it united within it self, and separate from all others, and especially to preserve and perpetuate the worship of Jehovah, Father, Son, and Holy Spirit, the true God [12] distinct from that of Idols of Imagination. This view, however, doth not hinder but

[9] *And, although there might have been some doubt and obscurity, in the minds of even those wise men, with regard to the certainty of this their opinion, yet what their opinion was cannot be doubted* crossed out.

[10] Marginal notation: *But observe this (?) was considered as subjects of a Theo-* cratical govern. — *And of the body politic there is no resurrection.*

[11] *Those statutes which God vouchsafed to give you as their temporal king* (notation).

[12] *is a God existing in one person (?) whom the Mohamedans worship as well distinct from all idols made by man and . . .* (marginal notation).

that some doctrines or truths of [13] religion, universally known [14] and handed down by [15] immemorial tradition, might have been supposed, rather than taught as peculiar doctrines of the Jews. The Patriarchal Faith in a Promised Messiah was the Consolation of Israel extracted from the Precepts of Mosaic Polity.

It must nevertheless be granted that the Jews had the notion of a future state, not only from [16] tradition,[17] common to them with the rest of mankind, but also from the Promises of the Patriarchs, and those peculiar instances of Enoch and Elias being translated into heaven, and moreover from the general promises of God, that he would be their God, that he would bless them and reward them, which promises, that they were understood to imply something higher than the things of this life,[18] is plain from the epistle to the Hebrews, wherein it is expressly said of them, that they sought and desired a better country, that they confessed themselves strangers and pilgrims upon earth, that they looked for a city which hath foundations, whose founder and builder is God.[19]

But however silent Moses may have been on that head it cannot be denied that subsequent inspired witnesses among the Jews do give the plainest [20] intimations thereof. Job indeed was not a Jew by birth, but his history is written in the language of the Jews and received by them as an [21] authentic part of Scripture. Now *his* testimony for a resurrection and future state is very full and explicit. *I know*, saith he, *that my redeemer liveth, and that he shall stand at the last day upon the earth, and though after my skin worms destroy this my body, yet in my flesh shall I see God.* [22] Nothing can be plainer than this. The holy psalmist also is is very clear in the following words — *therefore my heart is glad and my glory rejoiceth, my flesh also shall rest in hope, for thou wilt not leave my soul in Hell, nor suffer thy holy one to see corruption.* And in the hundred and fourth psalm there is something that hints at a future state or general resurrection. *Then hidest thy face*, saith the psalmist, Ps. 104, 29, 30, *they are troubled: Then taketh away their breath, they dye and return to the dust: then sendest forth thy spirit, they are created, and thou renewest the face of the earth.*

Solmoon expressly saith — *the dust shall return to the earth* (Eccles. 12, 7) *and the spirit to God who gave it.*[23] Isaiah foretells that the Lord God will swallow up death in victory, and will wipe away tears from all faces; and again — *thy dead men shall live* (Is. 25, 8 and 26, 19), *together with my dead body shall they arise: awake and sing ye that dwell in the dust* — the same prophet at the

---

[13] *natural* crossed out.
[14] *by the light of reason* crossed out.
[15] *universal and* crossed out.
[16] *natural reason and* crossed out.
[17] *things* crossed out.
[18] *at least by the patriarchs* crossed out.
[19] *Notwithstanding all which it must be owned that throughout the old testament, the special and express promise relates to the present life, and only the general and obscure one to a future. The direct contrary of which we observe in the New Testament, where on all occasions the promise of a future state is clearly proposed as the great motive to a Christian life, whereas temporal advantages are but slightly and rarely intimated* crossed out, showing Berkeley formerly *denied* Moses' eschatology.
[20] *the plainest* crossed out. A correction made later by someone other than Berkeley.
[21] *however rejected by some as an*, an external correction.
[22] Cited also in Newport notes, F. iv, p. 387.
[23] Also cited in Newport notes, *loc. cit.*

close of his prophecies maketh express mention of new heavens and a new earth.

Can there be conceived an apter image of the resurrection, than Ezekiel's vision of the valley filled with dry bones — *Thus saith the Lord unto these bones.* (Ezek. 37) *Behold I will cause breath to enter into you and ye shall live. And I will lay sinews upon you, and bring up flesh upon you, and cover you with skin and put breath in you.* — *And when he had thus prophecied to the dry bones, there was a noise and, behold! a shaking, and the bones came together, bone to his bone, and when I beheld lo! the sinews and flesh came upon them,* — which with what follows contains a compleat and lively description of men rising from the dead.[24] Again, can anything be plainer and fuller to the purpose than what is said by the prophet Daniel. *Many of them* (Dan. 12:2) [25] *which sleep in the dust of the earth shall awake, some to everlasting life, and some to everlasting contempt.*

And if from all these passages it be evident that a future state was alluded to, and foretold by the Jewish Prophets: so it is no less evident, that it was the received opinion among their best men, as appears from the second book of the Maccabees, which, though it is an Apocryphal piece, may nevertheless be allowed to shew what the opinion of the Jews was, at the time wherein it was written. It is there recorded that one of the seven brethren cruelly put to death by King Antiochus, when he was at the last gasp cried out — *Thou like a fury takest me out of this present life: but the King of the world shall raise us up, who have died for his lambs, unto everlasting life.* Others of them spake to the same effect. But the youngest expressly declared when he came to die, that his brethren were dead under God's covenant of everlasting life.

And indeed, what but this hope could inspire men with courage to undergo the most cruel torments, and lay down their lives, rather than transgress the laws of God? And thus much may suffice to shew the opinion of those, who lived under the Jewish dispensation concerning a future state.

But although neither Jew nor Gentile were altogether strangers to the doctrine of life and immortality, yet the revelation of the Jews was not so clear, nor the reasonings of philosophers so plain and demonstrative, as to possess men with a general and strong hope of another life. The full explicit revelation thereof, and the universal persuasion of its truth and certainty, was reserved to the gospel. These are the glad tidings that occur in almost every page of the new testament.

This is what constitutes the tenor or burthen, if I may so say, both of gospels and epistles. This was the main end of our saviour's preaching: this sure hope is the anchor of the soul, grounded on faith in Christ; this is the promise that he promised us even eternal life, saith the apostle in the words of my text. I shall not therefore hold a candle to the sun or spend more words to prove a fact so plain and evident, which is also exemplified in the resurrection of our blessed Saviour which we commemorate this day.

Upon the whole it is manifest, the belief of a future state is not only conformable to right reason, but also confirmed by the concurring assent of Gentiles, Jews and Christians. This doctrine, I say, is equally supported by reason and authority; which are the two points I proposed to prove.

To conclude I shall only observe as in all other things we see a gradual progress to perfection, even so in the economy of Religion, the first dawning

---

[24] Cf. Newport notes, *loc. cit.*   [25] Also cited in Newport notes, *loc. cit.*

thereof in the Jewish nation was like the infancy of a child, weak and sensual, taken up with rites and ceremonies, and types of things to come. But the Christian religion enlargeth our view and extends our prospects. It raiseth our hopes from sensible things to things spiritual, from this life to that which is to come, from earth to heaven. That light which in its original was glimmering and obscure still shineth forth more and more unto perfect day.[26]

Happy for us, if we guide our steps by this light, in the waies of Virtue and Piety. Happy, if the Sun of righteousness rising upon our Minds, discover the true worth and value of things. Thrice happy for us, if it warm our affections at the same time that it enlightens our understandings; if, overlooking the little accidents, the transient pleasures and distresses of this present life, we fix our hopes on that eternal state, where the worm dieth not, and whose pleasures never fade away. An immortality of woe or of happiness! Sufficient to engross all our attention, to alarm all our fears, and feed all our hopes.

God grant the apprehension of these things may so thoroughly affect your minds, and sink so deep into your hearts as to produce those virtuous habits, those Christian graces, which may conduct you through all the temptations and hazards, the turns and changes of this mortal state, and finally fit you for those happy mansions that God hath prepared for [27] those who love him.

[26] *God grant this doctrine we have preached unto you may so thoroughly affect your minds and sink so deep in your hearts as to produce those vertuous habits and Christian graces which may finally make* you partakers of eternal life. Now to God *etc.* (marginal note).

[27] *such as are his faithful servants here on earth* crossed out.

BIBLIOGRAPHY

BIBLIOGRAPHY

NOTE: The following list does not include the titles of *all* works cited in the text and notes. It *does* include the titles of most of the important works *directly concerning Berkeley* which have been published in Europe or America, together with *all* titles of such works abbreviated in the footnotes. The names of *all* authors cited are contained in the Name Index. For a more exhaustive Berkeley bibliography, together with useful information concerning manuscript remains, the reader should refer to T. E. Jessop's *Bibliography of George Berkeley*, Oxford, 1934.

Aaron, R. I. A Catalogue of Berkeley's Library, *Mind*, N. S., vol. XLI, 1932, pp. 465–475.
—— Locke and Berkeley's Commonplace Book, *Mind*, N. S., vol. XL, 1931, pp. 439–459.
Abbott, T. K. Bishop Berkeley and Professor Fraser, *Hermathena*, Dublin, vol. III, 1877, pp. 1–39.
—— Sight and Touch, An Attempt to Disprove the Received (Berkeleian) Theory of Vision, London, 1884.
Adamson, R. "Berkeley," Encyclopedia Britannica, 9th ed., Edinburgh, 1875.
Alexander, A. Idealism of Bishop Berkeley, *Presbyterian Review*, New York, vol. VI, 1885, pp. 301–314.
Allen, W. O. B., and McClure, Edmund. History of the Society for Promoting Christian Knowledge, 1698–1898, London, 1898.
Anderson, Rev. J. S. M. The History of the Church of England in the Colonies and Foreign Dependencies of the British Empire, London, 1856. Ch. 28 on Berkeley's efforts in behalf of the Colonial Church. See also under Berkeley.
Annual Register, London.
—— Memoirs of the late Dr. Berkeley, Bishop of Cloyne, vol. VI, 1763, part 2, pp. 2–5.
Anonymous. Answer, (An) to a Letter to the Right Rev., the Bishop of Cloyne, occasioned by his treatise of tar-water, London, 1744.
—— Anti-Siris: or, English wisdom exemplified by various examples, but particularly the present demand for tar-water, on so unexceptionable authority as that of a r(ight) r(everend) itinerant schemist (Bishop Berkeley). In a letter from a foreign gentleman at London to his friend abroad, London, 1744.
—— Berkeley and his Time, *Saturday Review*, London, vol. XXXI, 1871, pp. 525–526.
—— Berkeley and Idealism, *Blackwood's Magazine*, Edinburgh, vol. LI, 1742, pp. 812–830. A review of Bailey's work on Berkeley's N. T. V. by J. F. Ferrier.
—— Berkeley's Metaphysical Works, *Saturday Review*, London, vol. XXIV, 1867, pp. 317–319. Unsigned but reprinted in Stephen's *Horae Sabbaticae*, London, 1892. Cf. *Sat. Rev.*, vol. XXIV, pp. 408–410, and 470–472.

Anonymous. Bishop Berkeley, *British Quarterly Review,* London, vol. XXVI, 1857, pp. 75–118.

—— Bishop Berkeley's Philosophy vindicated from injurious imputation by K. H., *Gentleman's Magazine,* vol. LVIII, 1788, pp. 955–956.

—— Bishop Berkeley's Siris, *Retrospective Review,* London, vol. XI, 1825, pp. 239–252.

—— Fraser's edition of Berkeley, *British Quarterly Review,* London, vol. LIII, 1871, pp. 482–515.

—— George Berkeley, The Georgian Era, London, vol. I, 1832, pp. 219–220.

—— Letter, (A) to the Bishop of Cloyne occasioned by his Lordship's treatise on the virtues of tar-water, London, 1744.

—— Letter, (A) to the . . . Lord Bishop of Cloyne. By a gentleman in the army in the year 1739, Harleian Miscellany, London, 1809, vol. III, pp. 177–183.

—— London Daily Post Boy, An anonymous critical letter concerning the fourth dialogue of the Alciphron, September 9, 1732.

—— Memoirs of the late Dr. Berkeley, Bishop of Cloyne. See Annual Register.

—— Mr. Bailey's reply to an article in Blackwood's Magazine, *Blackwood's Magazine,* vol. LIII, 1843, pp. 762–770. Unsigned but written by J. F. Ferrier.

—— Passive Obedience. Review, *Gentleman's Magazine,* vol. LV, 1785, p. 805.

—— The Life and Works of Bishop Berkeley, *Nation,* New York, vol. XIII, 1871, pp. 59 ff.

—— The Idealism of Berkeley and Collier, *North British Review,* London, vol. LIII, pp. 368–377. Signed H. W. C.

—— Vindication (A) of the Reverend D(octor) B(erkeley) from the scandalous imputation of being the author of a late book, entitled *Alciphron; or the Minute Philosopher.* To which is subjoined the predictions of the late Earl of Shaftesbury concerning that book, Edinburgh and London, 1734.

Armstrong, A. C. Berkeley, Bergson, and Philosophical Intuition, *Philosophical Review,* New York, vol. XXIII, 1914, pp. 430–438.

—— The Development of Berkeley's Theism, *Archiv für Geschichte der Philosophie,* Berlin, vol. XXV, 1920, pp. 150 ff.

Aster, E. von. Geschichte der neueren Erkenntnistheorie, Berlin, 1921.

Auschütz, O. Die Berkeleysche Erkenntnistheorie in ihrer Entwicklung, Dissertation, Halle, 1913.

Bailey, Samuel. Letter to a philosopher in reply to some recent attempts to vindicate Berkeley's theory of vision, and in further elucidation of its unsoundness, London, 1842.

—— Review of Berkeley's Theory of Vision, designed to show the unsoundness of that celebrated speculation, London, 1842.

Baker, John Tull. An Historical and Critical Examination of English Space and Time theories from Henry More to Bishop Berkeley, Bronxville, 1930.

Balfour, A. J. Bishop Berkeley's Life and Letters, *National Review,* London, vol. I, 1883, pp. 85–100. Reprinted in *Essays and Addresses,* 2 ed., London, 1893, and as introduction to Sampson ed. of Berkeley's Works, London, 1898.

Baumann, Julius. Die Lehren von Raum, Zeit und Mathematik in der neueren Philosophie, 1869, 2v.

Baxter, Andrew. Dean Berkeley's scheme against the existence of matter and
a material world examined and shown inconclusive. In *An enquiry into the
nature of the human soul*, London, 1733. The first elaborate philosophical
criticism of Berkeley. Cf. also ed. 2, vol. 2, London, 1737, pp. 256–344.

Bayes, Rev. Thomas. Introduction to the doctrine of fluxions, and defence of
the mathematicians against the objections of the author of the Analyst, so
far as they are designed to affect the general methods of reasoning, London, 1736.

Bergson, H. L'intuition philosophique, *Revue de métaphysique et de morale*,
Paris, vol. XIX, 1911, pp. 809 ff.

Berkeley, George. Address on confirmation. First published in Fraser ed. of
Works, London, 1871.

—— Advice to the Tories who have taken the oaths. London, 1715. First
recognized and published by Lorenz in *Archiv für Geschichte der Philosophie*,
vol. XIV, 1901, pp. 293–318.

—— Alciphron: or, the minute philosopher. In seven dialogues containing an
apology for the Christian religion, against those who are called free-
thinkers, Dublin and London, 1732.

—— Analyst, The: or, a discourse addressed to an infidel mathematician.
Wherein it is examined whether the object, principles, and inferences of
the modern analysis are more distinctly conceived, or more evidently deduced, than religious mysteries and points of faith, Dublin and London,
1734.

—— Arithmetica absque algebra aut Euclide demonstrata. Cui accesserunt,
cogitata nonnulla de radicibus surdis, de aestu aeris, de ludo algebraico,
&c., London, 1707.

—— Commonplace Book. First published in Fraser ed. of Works, Oxford,
1871. Also ed. of A. Hecht, Leipzig, 1926, and G. A. Johnston, London,
1930.

—— Defence, (A) of free-thinking in mathematics. In answer to a pamphlet
of Philalethes Cantabrigiensis, intituled, *Geometry no friend to infidelity,
or a defence of Sir Isaac Newton, and the British mathematicians*. Also an
appendix concerning Mr. Walton's *Vindication of the principle of fluxions
against the objections contained in the Analyst*. Wherein it is attempted to
put this controversy in such light as that every reader may be able to judge
thereof, Dublin and London, 1735. Both Philalethes and Walton replied.

—— De Motu; sive, de motus principio & natura, et de causa communica-
tionis motuum, London, 1721.

—— Description of the Cave of Dunmore. First published in Fraser ed. of
Works, Oxford, 1871.

—— Discourse (A) addressed to magistrates and men in authority. Occasioned by the enormous licence, and irreligion of the times, Dublin, 1738.

—— Essay (An) towards a new theory of vision, Dublin, 1709.

—— Essay (An) towards preventing the ruine of Great Britain, London, 1721.

—— Essays in the *Guardian*, 1713. Numbers 3, 14, 27, 35, 39, 49, 55, 62, 69,
70, 77, 83, 89, and 126 are traditionally ascribed to Berkeley.

—— Infinites, (Of). First published by S. P. Johnston, in *Hermathena*, Dublin, vol. XI, 1901, pp. 180–185.

Berkeley, George. Irish patriot (The) or queries upon queries. First published by J. M. Hone in *Times Literary Supplement*, March 13, 1930.

—— Journal of a tour in Italy, 1717–1718. First published in Fraser ed. of Works, Oxford, 1871.

—— Letters.

    Bishop Berkeley on the Roman Catholic Controversy. A Letter to Sir John James, Bart. written in 1741 . . . now for the first time extracted from the imperfect remains of the Bishop's MSS., and edited by J. S. M. Anderson, London, 1850.

    Letter (A) to T(homas) P(rior), Esq; from the author of Siris. Containing some farther remarks on the virtues of tar-water, and the methods for preparing and using it, Dublin, 1744.

    Letter (A second) to Thomas Prior, Esq. on the virtues of tar-water, Dublin, 1746.

    Letter (A) . . . to Thomas Prior, Esq; on the usefulness of tar-water in the plague, Dublin, 1747.

    Letter (A) to Thomas Prior on the petrifactions of Lough-Neagh in Ireland. In *Philosophical Transactions of the Royal Society*, London, no. 481, 1746, pp. 325–328.

    Letter concerning Earthquakes, *Gentleman's Magazine*, vol. XX, 1750, p. 166. Cf. pp. 161–162.

    Letters to Prior. In George Monck Berkeley's *Literary Relics*, London, 1789. Most of these were later printed in Fraser's *Life and Letters*, Oxford, 1871.

    Letters of George Berkeley to Sir John Percival. Seventh Report of the Royal Commission on Historical Manuscripts, Part I, 1879. This correspondence is printed with a few omissions in Rand's *Correspondence of Berkeley and Percival*, Cambridge, Massachusetts, 1914.

    More unpublished Berkeley letters and Berkeleiana. A. A. Luce, *Hermathena*, Dublin, vol. XXIII, 1933.

    Some Unpublished Berkeley Letters. *Proceedings of the Royal Irish Academy*, Dublin, vol. XLI, 1933.

    The Bishop of Cloyne's letter to his clergy. In *Dublin Journal*, October 15–19, 1745. Occasioned by the Stuart Rebellion.

    Two letters from the Right Reverend Dr. George Berkeley . . . the one to Thomas Prior Esq; concerning the usefulness of tar-water in the plague . . . the other to the Rev. Dr. Hales, on the benefit of tar-water in fevers . . ., Dublin, 1747.

—— Miscellany (A), containing several tracts on various subjects. Dublin, 1752. Includes the *De Motu* as well as *Maxims concerning patriotism*, *Farther thoughts on tar-water*, and *Verses on the prospect of planting arts and learning in America* printed for the first time.

—— Observations and remarks on the eruptions of fire and smoak from Mount Vesuvio. In *Philosophical Transactions of the Royal Society*, London, vol. XXX, 1717, pp. 708–713.

—— Passive Obedience, or the Christian doctrine of not resisting the supreme power, proved and vindicated upon the principles of the law of nature, Dublin, 1712.

—— Proposal (A) for the better supplying of churches in our foreign plantations, and for converting the savage Americans to Christianity, London,
1724.

—— Querist (The), containing several queries, proposed to the consideration
of the public, Dublin, 1735–1737.

—— Reasons for not replying to Mr. Walton's *Full Answer* . . ., Dublin,
1735.

—— Sermons.

A sermon preached before the Incorporated Society for the Propagation of the Gospel in Foreign Parts; at their anniversary meeting
in the parish-church of St. Mary-le-Bow, on Friday, February 18,
1731, London, 1732.

Notes for sermons preached at Newport. First published in Fraser ed.
of Works, Oxford, 1871.

On *Let your zeal be according to knowledge*. First published by Luce,
Hermathena, Dublin, vol. XXII, 1931, pp. 16–28.

On *Thy Will be done*. First published by John Wild, *Philosophical
Review*, vol. XL, 1931, pp. 526–536. Cf. A. A. Luce, *Herm.*,
vol. XXII, 1931, pp. 1–41.

The revelation of life and immortality. First published in Fraser ed.
of Works, Oxford, 1871.

Two sermons, on I Tim. i. 2, and on John xiii. 35. Preached at Leghorn. First published in Fraser ed., Oxford, 1871.

—— Siris: a chain of philosophical reflexions and inquiries concerning the
virtues of tar-water, and divers other subjects connected together and
arising from one another, ed. 3, London, 1744. The word *Siris* was
omitted from the first two editions of the same year.

—— Siris and its enemies. In *Gentleman's Magazine*, vol. XIV, 1744, p. 559.

—— Theory (The) of Vision, or visual language, showing the immediate
presence and providence of a deity, vindicated and explained, London,
1733.

—— Three dialogues between Hylas and Philonous. The design of which is
plainly to demonstrate the reality and perfection of humane knowledge,
the incorporeal nature of the soul, and the immediate providence of a deity:
in opposition to sceptics and atheists. Also, to open a method for rendering the sciences more easy, useful, and compendious, London, 1713.

—— Treatise (A) concerning the principles of human knowledge. Part I.
Wherein the chief causes of error and difficulty in the sciences, with the
grounds of scepticism, atheism, and irreligion, are inquired into, Dublin,
1710.

—— Visitation charge. First published in Fraser ed. of Works, Oxford, 1871.

—— Word (A) to the wise: or, an exhortation to the Roman Catholic clergy
of Ireland, Dublin, 1749.

—— Works.

The Works of George Berkeley to which is added an account of his life
and several of his letters to T. Prior, Dean Gervais, and Mr. Pope,
etc., Dublin, 1784, 2v. Contains Stock's biography. Reissued
1820 and 1837.

The Works of George Berkeley. Annotated by the Rev. G. N. Wright
(and the Latin essays rendered into English), London, 1843, 2v.

The Works of George Berkeley, ed. A. C. Fraser, Oxford, 1871, 4v., including Fraser's *Life and Letters*.

The Works of George Berkeley, ed. G. Sampson, London, 1897–98, 3v.

The Works of George Berkeley. . . . Including his posthumous works. With prefaces, annotations, appendices, and an account of his life, ed. A. C. Fraser, Oxford, 1901.

Berkeley, George Monck. Literary Relics, London, 1789.

—— Poems by the late George Monck Berkeley, Esq, LLB, FSSA. With a preface by the editor, consisting of some anecdotes of Mr. Monck Berkeley, and several of his friends, London, 1797. Cf. *Gent. Mag.*, vol. LXVII, 1797, pp. 403 and 455; vol. LXIX, 1799, p. 565. Also J. Nichols, *Literary Anecdotes of the Eighteenth Century*, London, 1815, vol. IX, pp. 733–735.

Bernard, J. H. Bishop Berkeley, in *Peplographia Dublinensis*, London, 1902.

Biographia Britannica. Berkeley, vol. 2, London, 1780. Written by Stock, but notes by Kippis. Also vol. 3, corrections and addenda.

Blackwell, Thomas. Memoirs of the Court of Augustus (continued and completed from the original papers of T. B. by J. Mills), Edinburgh, 1758–63, 3v.

Blackwood's Magazine, London. See Anonymous.

Böhme, Richard. Die Grundlagen des Berkeleyschen Immaterialismus. Dissertation, Erlangen, Berlin, 1892.

Bouillier, Francisque. Histoire de la philosophie cartésienne, ed. 3, Paris, 1868, 2v.

Bourne, H. R. Fox. Life of John Locke, New York, 1876, 2v.

Bowen, Francis. Berkeley and his Philosophy, *Christian Examiner*, Boston, vol. XXIV, 1842, pp. 310–345.

Bradley, C. W. Berkeley's Idealism, *Journal of Speculative Philosophy*, New York, vol. XV, 1881, pp. 67–75.

British Quarterly Review, See Anonymous, London.

Brown, Thomas. Lectures on the philosophy of the human mind, Andover, 1822, 3v.

Browne, Peter. Things divine and supernatural, conceived by analogy with things natural and human, London, 1733.

Bruce, Henry. Life of General Oglethorpe, New York, 1890.

Bruce, J. D. Campailla, Berkeley, and Milton, *Nation*, New York, vol. XCVII, 1913, pp. 32 ff.

Burdeau, Auguste. L'évêque Berkeley, *Revue des deux mondes*, vol. CIII, 1873, pp. 731–736.

Butler, W. A. Gallery of Illustrious Irishmen, *Dublin University Magazine*, vol. VII, 1836, pp. 437–468 and 534–558.

C., H. W. See under Anonymous.

Cahn, Leo. Darstellung und Kritik von Berkeleys 3 Dialogen zwischen Hylas und Philonous, Diss., Giessen, Marburg, 1915.

Carrau, L. La philosophie réligieuse de Berkeley, *Revue philosophique*, Paris, vol. XXII, 1886, pp. 376–399.

Carus, P. Positivism of Bishop Berkeley, *Open Court*, Chicago, vol. VIII, 1894, pp. 4042–4044.

Cassirer, Erich. Berkeleys System, *Philosophische Arbeiten*, Giessen, vol. VIII, 1914, pp. 328–333.

Cassirer, Ernst. Das Erkenntnisproblem in der Philosophie und Wissenschaft der neueren Zeit, ed. 3, Berlin, 1922, 2v.

Claussen, F. Kritische Darstellung der Lehren Berkeleys ueber Mathematik und Naturwissenschaft, Diss., Halle, 1889.

Colborn, George. Berkeley's Philosophie, Diss., Munich, 1873.

Collections of the Rhode Island Historical Society, Providence. Information concerning Berkeley's visit to Newport, vol. VII, 1885, and vol. VIII, 1893.

Collins, Anthony. A Discourse of Free-thinking, occasion'd by the Rise and Growth of a Sect call'd Free-thinkers, London, 1713.

Condillac, Étienne B. de. Essai sur l'origine des connaissances humaines, Paris, 1746.

Cook, A. Ueber die Berkeleysche Philosophie, Diss., Halle, 1886.

Cudworth, Ralph. A treatise concerning eternal and immutable morality, London, 1731.

—— The true intellectual system of the universe, London, 1678. Latin ed. London, 1773.

David, Maxime. Berkeley, in Les grands philosophes français et étrangers, Paris, vol. XVII, 1912.

Delany, Mrs. See Granville, Mary.

Delany, Patrick. Observations upon Lord Orrery's Remarks on the Life and Writings of Dr. Jonathan Swift, London, 1754.

Dennis, John. George Berkeley, in the Age of Pope, London, 1896.

Dick, S. The Principle of Synthetic Unity in Berkeley and Kant, Lowell, 1898.

Didier, J. Berkeley, in Philosophes et penseurs, Paris, 1911.

Diekert, G. Ueber das Verhältnis des Berkeleyschen Idealismus zur Kantischen Vernunftkritik, Konitz, 1888.

Doubleday, Thomas. Matter for materialists; a series of letters in vindication and extension of the principles regarding the nature of existence of . . . Dr. Berkeley, etc., London, 1870.

Douglass, William. Note on Berkeley, in A summary, historical and political of the . . . British settlements in North America, London, 1760, vol. I, pp. 149–150.

Dowding, W. C. Africa in the West: its state, prospects, and educational needs; with reference to Bishop Berkeley's Bermuda College, Oxford and London, 1852.

—— The Revival of Bishop Berkeley's Bermuda College: a letter to the Right Hon. H. Gaulburn, etc., Oxford, 1852.

Erdmann, Benno. Berkeleys Philosophie im Lichte seines wissenschaftlichen Tagebuchs, Abhandlung der Preussischen Akademie der Wissenschaften, Berlin, Phil.-Hist. Klasse, 8, 1919.

Erdmann, J. E. Versuch einer wissenschaftlichen Darstellung der Geschichte der neueren Philosophie, Leipzig, 1842.

Espinas, Alfred. La troisième phase et la dissolution du mercantilisme. (Mandeville, Law, Melon, Voltaire, Berkeley), Paris, 1902.

Fawcett, Edward D. From Berkeley to Hegel, Monist, Chicago, vol. VII, 1896, pp. 4181 ff.

Fénart, M. La dernière philosophie de Berkeley, Annales de philosophie chrétienne, Paris, vol. LXVII, 1897, pp. 198–213.

Ferrier, J. F. Lectures on Greek Philosophy and Other Philosophical Remains, Edinburgh, 1866.
—— See also under Anonymous.
Fischer, Kuno. Geschichte der neueren Philosophie, vol. X, Bacon und seine Schule, Heidelberg, 1897–1904, 10v.
Flemyng, Malcolm. A Proposal for the Improvement of the Practice of Medicine . . . with . . . some remarks on a book entitled Siris (By G. Berkeley, Bishop of Cloyne); and the properties of tar-water, Hull, 1748.
Fowler, R. An attempt to solve some of the difficulties of the Berkeleyan Controversy, Salisbury, 1859.
—— A second physiological attempt to unravel some of the perplexities of the Berkeleyan hypothesis, Salisbury, 1859.
Fraser, A. C. Berkeley, London, 1881.
—— Berkeley and Spiritual Realism, London, 1909.
—— Life and Letters of George Berkeley, Oxford, 1871.
—— See also under Berkeley.
Frederichs, F. Der Idealismus Berkeleys, *Jahresbericht der Dorotheenstädtischen Realschule*, Berlin, 1870.
—— Der phaenomenale Idealismus Berkeleys und Kants, the *same*, 1871.
Freedman, Louis. Substanz und Kausalität bei Berkeley, Diss., Strassburg, 1902.
Fullerton, G. S. Berkeley's Time; Berkeley's Space, *Philosophical Review*, vol. X, 1901, pp. 375–385.
Gentleman's Magazine. See Anonymous.
Georgian Era (The). See Anonymous.
Gerard, J. L'idéalisme de Berkeley, Paris, 1876.
Gibson, James. Locke's Theory of Knowledge and its Historical Relations, Cambridge, 1917.
Gosse, Edmund. A Short History of Modern English Literature (1660–1780), London, 1906.
Gourg, Raymond. Le journal philosophique de Berkeley. Étude et traduction, Thèse de doctorat, Paris, 1908.
Granville, Mary. The autobiography and correspondence of Mary Granville, Mrs. Delany: with interesting reminiscences of King George the Third and Queen Charlotte, ed. the Right Honourable Lady Llanover, London, 1861, 3v.
Grau, K. J. Die Entwicklung des Bewusstseinsbegriffs im 17. und 18. Jahrhundert, Diss., Berlin, 1916.
Green, T. H. Introduction to the Works of David Hume, ed. Green and Grose, Oxford, 1874.
Greenwood, G. G. Professor Huxley on Hume and Berkeley, *Westminster Review*, London, vol. CXLIV, 1895, pp. 1–10.
Grimm, E. Zur Geschichte der Erkenntnisproblems von Bacon zu Hume, ed. 2, Leipzig, 1890.
Grote, John. Exploratio Philosophica, ed. J. B. Mayor, Cambridge, 1866.
Grube, Karl. Ueber den Nominalismus in der neueren englischen und französischen Philosophie, Halle, 1889.
H., K. See Anonymous.

Hales, Stephen. An account of some experiments and observations on tar-water; wherein is shown the quantity of tar that is therein. Which was read before the Royal Society, London, 1745.

Hamilton, Sir William. Discussions in philosophy and literature, education and university reform, ed. 2, London, 1853.

—— Lectures on Metaphysics and Logic, ed. H. L. Mansel and J. Veitch, Edinburgh, 1860–70, 4v.

Hecht, Andreas. Berkeleys Lehre von der Abstraktion, Diss., Leipzig, 1926.

—— Berkeley. Philosophisches Tagebuch, übersetzt, eingeleitet und mit Anmerkungen und Registern versehen von Andreas Hecht, Leipzig, 1926.

Hegel, G. W. F. Sämtliche Werke, XIX, Geschichte der Philosophie, vol. III, Stuttgart, 1928.

Helmholtz, Hermann von. Handbuch der physiologischen Optik, ed. 2, Hamburg, 1896.

Hersey, Marguerite. New Light on the Evidence for Swift's Marriage, *Publications of the Modern Language Association of America*, vol. XLII, 1927, pp. 157–161.

Hertling, J. L. von. John Locke und die Schule von Cambridge, Freiburg i.B., 1892.

Hertz, Gerald B. British Imperialism in the Eighteenth Century, London, 1908.

Hervey, John, Lord. Memoirs of the Reign of George the Second, London, 1848.

—— Some remarks on the Minute Philosopher. Letter from a Country Gentleman to his Friend in London, London, 1732. Ascribed to Hervey in Biographia Britannica, vol. III, p. 252.

Hicks, G. Dawes. Berkeley, London, 1932.

Hoernle, R. F. Alfred. Idealism as a Philosophy, New York, 1927.

Hone, J. M. and M. M. Rossi. Bishop Berkeley; His Life, Writings, and Philosophy. With an introduction by W. B. Yeats, New York, 1931.

Hook, W. Ecclesiastical Biography, London, 1845.

Hughes, Thomas, of Market Rosen. The ideal theory of Berkeley and the real world, London, 1865.

Husserl, Edmund. Ideen zu einer reinen Phänomenologie und phänomenologischen Philosophie, Halle, 1928.

—— Logische Untersuchungen, ed. 4, Halle, 1928.

Huxley, T. H. Bishop Berkeley on the Metaphysics of Sensation, *Macmillan Magazine*, London and Cambridge, vol. XXIV, 1871, pp. 147–160.

—— Collected Essays, New York, 1896.

—— Critiques and Addresses, New York, 1873.

Jackson, Henry. Reflections concerning the virtues of tar-water, London, 1744.

Jaffé, Georg. Ueber die räumliche Anschauungsform. Vierter Dialog zu Berkeleys drei Dialogen zwischen Hylas und Philonous, *Vierteljahrschrift für wissenschaftliche Philosophie und Soziologie*, vol. XXXIII, 1904, pp. 31–65.

James, Henry. Berkeley and his Critics. In *Lectures and Miscellanies*, Redfield, 1852.

Janitsch, J. Kants Urteile ueber Berkeley, Diss., Strassburg, 1879.

Jessop, T. E. A Bibliography of George Berkeley, Oxford, 1934.

Johnson, Samuel.   See under Schneider.
Johnston, G. A.   Review of Rand's *Berkeley and Percival, Mind*, N. S., vol. XXIV, 1915, pp. 266 ff.
—— The Development of Berkeley's Ethical Theory, *Phil. Rev.*, vol. XXIV, 1915, pp. 419–430.
—— The Development of Berkeley's Philosophy, London, 1923.
—— The Influence of Mathematical Conceptions on Berkeley's Philosophy, *Mind*, N. S., vol. XXV, 1916, pp. 177–192.
—— The Relation between Collier and Berkeley. *Archiv f. Gesch. der Phil.*, vol. XXXII, 1920, pp. 162–175.
—— See also under Berkeley.
Johnston, S. P.   Supposed Autograph Letter of Bishop Berkeley. *Proceedings of Royal Irish Academy*, vol. VI, 1901, pp. 272–278.
—— Unpublished (An) essay by Berkeley, *Hermathena*, Dublin, vol. XI, 1901, pp. 180–185.
Joseph, H. W. B.   Berkeley and Kant. Hertz Master Mind Lecture, London, 1930.
Joussain, André.   Exposé critique de la philosophie de Berkeley, Paris, 1921.
Jurin, James.   Geometry no friend to infidelity; or, a defence of Sir Isaac Newton and the British Mathematicians, in a letter to the author of the *Analyst* . . . by Philalethes Cantabrigiensis, London, 1734.
—— The Minute Mathematician; or The free-thinker no just thinker. By Philalethes Cantabrigiensis, London, 1735.
Kaye, F. B.   See under Mandeville.
Klein, T.   Die Fehler Berkeleys und Kants in der Wahrnehmungslehre. *Philos. Jahrbuch der Görresgesellschaft*, vol. XXVII, 1914, pp. 355–367.
Knight, Thomas.   Reflections upon Catholicons or Universal Medicine, London, 1749.
Laird, J.   Berkeley's Realism, *Mind*, N. S., vol. XXV, 1916, pp. 308 ff.
Lechler, G. V.   Geschichte des englischen Deismus, Stuttgart, 1841.
Leclair, A. von.   Der Realismus der modernen Naturwissenschaft im Lichte der von Berkeley und Kant angebahnten Erkenntniskritik, Prague, 1879. Reviewed by Vaihinger in *Vierteljahrschr. f. wissensch. Philos.*, vol. IV, 1880, pp. 391–395.
Leigh and Sotheby.   A Catalogue of the Valuable Library of the Late Rt. Rev. Dr. Berkeley, Lord Bishop of Cloyne. Together with the libraries of son and grandson. Auction, June 6, 1796.   (British Museum.)
Leland, John.   View of the principal Deistical Writers that have appeared in England in the last and present century, ed. 3, London, 1754–56, 3v.
Levi, Adolfo.   La filosofia di Giorgio Berkeley: metafisica e gnoseologia, Turin, 1922.
Lewes, G. H.   Berkeley. In *Biographical History of Philosophy*, New York, 1857.
Loewy, Theodor.   Common Sensibles. Die Gemein-Ideen des Gesichts und Tastsinns nach Locke und Berkeley, und Experimenten an operierten Blindgeborenen, Leipzig, 1884.
—— Der Idealismus Berkeleys in den Grundlagen untersucht. *Sitzungsb. der philos.-histor, Kl. der kaiserl. Akad. der Wissensch.*, Vienna, vol. V, 1891, pp. 1–141.

Lorenz, Theodor. Ein Beitrag zur Lebensgeschichte George Berkeleys, *Archiv f. Gesch. der Phil.*, Berlin, vol. XIII, 1900, pp. 541–549.
—— Weitere Beiträge zur Lebensgeschichte George Berkeleys, the *same*, vol. XIV, 1901, pp. 293–318.
—— Zwei Briefe Berkeleys an Jean Leclerc, the *same*, vol. XVII, 1904, pp. 159–170.
—— Berkeleys Commonplace Book, the *same*, vol. XVIII, 1905, pp. 551–556.
—— Cf. also reviews of editions of Berkeley's Works in *Deutsche Literaturzeitung*, vol. XXIII, 1902, pp. 200–203; *Mind*, N. S., vol. XI, 1902, pp. 249–253; and *Mind*, N. S., vol. XIII, 1904, pp. 304 ff.
Loveday, John (?). Strictures on the life of Bishop Berkeley, by Academicus, *Gent. Mag.*, vol. XLVII, 1777, p. 13.
Luce, A. A. Berkeley and Malebranche, London, 1934.
—— Berkeley's Commonplace Book, *Hermathena*, Dublin, vol. XXII, 1932, pp. 99–131.
—— See also under Berkeley.
Lyon, Georges. L'idéalisme en Angleterre au XVIII siècle, Paris, 1888.
Mabbott, J. D. The Place of God in Berkeley's Philosophy, *Journal of Philosophical Studies*, London, vol. VI, 1931, pp. 18–29.
MacSparran, J. M. A Letter Book and Abstract of Services, Boston, 1899.
Mahaffy, J. P. Descartes, Edinburgh, 1881.
Malan, Daniel François. Het idealisme van Berkeley, Utrecht, 1905.
Malebranche, N. Oeuvres, ed. Simon, Paris, 1859.
Mandeville, Bernard de. Letter to Dion (Berkeley) occasioned by his book called Alciphron, or the Minute Philosopher. By the author of the Fable of the Bees, London, 1732.
—— The fable of the bees: or, Private vices, publick benefits. By Bernard Mandeville. With a commentary critical, historical, and explanatory by F. B. Kaye, Oxford, 1924.
Mansel, Henry L. On the Idealism of Berkeley. In *Letters, Lectures, and Reviews*, ed. H. W. Chandler, London, 1873.
Maty, M. Memoirs of Lord Chesterfield. In *Miscellaneous works of the late Philip Dormer Stanhope, Earl of Chesterfield*, ed. 2, London, 1779.
McCosh, James. Locke's theory of knowledge, with a notice of Berkeley, New York, 1884.
McFee, Donalda. Berkeleys neue Theorie des Sehens und ihre Weiterentwicklung in der englischen Associationsschule und in der modernen empiristischen Schule in Deutschland, Diss., Zurich, 1895.
McLachlan, D. B. Reformed Logic: a system based on Berkeley's philosophy with an entirely new method of dialectic, London, 1892.
Mead, H. R. A Bibliography of George Berkeley, University of California Library Bulletin, Berkeley, no. 17, 1910.
Meinong, A. Hume-Studien I. Zur Geschichte und Kritik des modernen Nominalismus, *Sitzungsber. der kaiserl. Akad. der Wissensch.*, Vienna, Phil.-hist. Kl. vol. LXXXVII, 1877, pp. 185–217.
Metz, R. George Berkeley: Leben und Lehre, Stuttgart, 1925.
Meyer, Eugen. Humes und Berkeleys Philosophie der Mathematik, *Abh. zur Phil. u. ihrer Geschichte*, Halle, vol. III, 1894.
Mill, J. S. Dissertations and Discussions, London, 1859. See also ed. 1875.

Mill, J. S. Examination of Sir W. Hamilton's Philosophy, London, 1865.

Moffett, B. The Life and Thoughts of Bishop Berkeley, *University Magazine*, London, vol. XCIV, 1879, pp. 129–147.

Monck, W. H. S. Space and Vision: an attempt to deduce all our knowledge of space from the sense of sight, Dublin, 1873.

Montague, Elizabeth. Elizabeth Montague, the queen of the bluestockings, her correspondence 1720–61, ed. Climenson, London, 1906, 2v.

Moore, G. E. Refutation of Idealism. In *Philosophical Studies*, London, 1922.

Morgan, C. L. Notes on Berkeley's Doctrine of Esse, *Proceedings of the Aristotelian Society*, London, vol. XV, 1914–15, pp. 100–139.

Morris, C. R. Locke, Berkeley, Hume, Oxford, 1931.

New England Magazine. See under Thurston.

Nichols, J. Literary Anecdotes of the Eighteenth Century, vol. IX, pp. 733–735, London, 1815.

Noel, Roden. The Philosophy of Perception: Berkeley and Kant, *Contemporary Review*, London, vol. XX, 1872, pp. 72–103.

Norton, J. N. The Life of Bishop Berkeley, New York, 1861.

Notes and Queries, London. Note on the Authorship of the Memoirs of Signor Gaudentio di Lucca, vol. II, 1850, pp. 298 ff., and 327 ff.

Oertel, H. J. George Berkeley und die englische Literatur, Halle, 1934.

Olgiati, F. L'idealismo di Giorgio Berkeley, Milan, 1926.

Oliphant, Mrs. M. O. Bishop Berkeley: the Philosopher. In *Historical Sketches of the Reign of George II*, Boston, 1869.

Orange, Hugh W. Berkeley as a Moral Philosopher, *Mind*, vol. XV, 1890, pp. 514–523.

Orrery, Lord. Remarks on the Life and Writings of Dr. Jonathan Swift, ed. 2, London, 1752.

Paget, Stephen. Influence of Berkeley, *Nineteenth Century*, London, vol. LVIII, 1905, pp. 252–258.

Papini, Giovanni. Giorgio Berkeley, Milan, 1908.

Peirce, Charles S. Berkeley's Works, *Nation*, New York, vol. LXXIII, 1901, pp. 95–96.

—— Fraser's Works of Bishop Berkeley, *North American Review*, Boston, vol. CXIII, 1871, pp. 449–472.

Penjon, A. Étude sur la vie et les oeuvres philosophiques de Georges Berkeley, évêque de Cloyne, Thèse de doctorat, Paris, 1878.

Peplographia Dublinensis. Vol. III. Bishop Berkeley, by J. H. Bernard, London, 1902.

Pericker, J. G. De argumentis indirectis pro veritate idealismi critici, Diss., Halle, 1790.

Pfannenberg, I. Berkeley und die englische Romantik, Diss., Freiburg, Berlin, 1930.

Philanthropos. The Bishop of Cloyne defended; or tar-water proved useful, by theory and experiments, in answer to T. R., London, 1744.

Pope, Alexander. Letters between Pope and Dean Berkeley from 1714–22. In Alexander Pope, *Works*, new ed., Elwin and Courthope, vol. IX, pp. 1–6, London, 1886.

Porterfield, William. Treatise on the Eye; or, the manner and phenomena of vision, London and Edinburgh, 1759.

Powicke, F. J.   The Cambridge Platonists, Cambridge, Massachusetts, 1926.
Prior, Thomas.   An Authentic Narrative of the success of tar-water, in curing a great number and variety of distempers, London, 1746.
Publications of the Colonial Society of Massachusetts, Boston.
—— Harvard College Records, vols. XV and XVI, 1925.
Raffel, F. A.   Ist Berkeley ein Freihändler?   Diss., Kiel, 1904.
Raffel, J.   Empirismus Lockes, Berkeleys, und Humes, Berlin, 1887.
Rand, Benjamin.   Berkeley's American Sojourn, Cambridge, Massachusetts, 1932.
—— The Correspondence of George Berkeley and Sir John Percival, Cambridge, Massachusetts, 1914.   Also contains letters from Newman to Percival, and Percival's Journal.
R(eeve), T(homas), M.D.   A cure for the epidemical madness of drinking tar-water, lately imported from Ireland by a certain R(ight) R(everend) Doctor, (G. Berkeley) Bishop of Cloyne.   In a letter to his L(ordshi)p.   By T. R., M.D., London, 1744.
Reid, A.   A letter to the Rev. Dr. Hales, concerning the nature of tar, and a method of obtaining its medical virtue, free from its hurtful oils . . ., London, 1747.
Reininger, Robert.   Locke, Berkeley, Hume, Geschichte der Philosophie in Einzeldarstellungen, Munich, vols. XXII and XXIII, 1922.
—— Philosophie des Erkennens, Leipzig, 1911.   Especially pp. 228–250.
Retrospective Review, London.
—— The Memoirs of Signor Gaudentio di Lucca, vol. IV, 1820, pp. 317 ff.   See also under Anonymous.
Rhode Island Historical Magazine, Newport.
—— Henry Collins, vol. V, 1884.
Ribbing, Sigurd.   Expositio cum crisi idealismi Berkeleyi, Upsala, 1842.
Richter, Raoul.   Der Skeptizismus und seine Ueberwindung, Leipzig, 1908.
Riehl, Alois.   Der philosophische Kritizismus, Geschichte und System.   Vol. I, Geschichte des philosophischen Kritizismus, ed. 3, Leipzig, 1924, 3v.
Risorius, M. A.   Remarks on the Bishop of Cloyne's Siris, London, 1744.
Robertson, G. C.   A. C. Fraser on Berkeley, Mind, vol. VI, 1881, pp. 421–424.
Robins, Benjamin.   A discourse concerning the nature and certainty of Sir Isaac Newton's methods of fluxions, and of prime and ultimate ratios, London, 1735.
—— Controversy with Philalethes Cantabrigiensis in The present state of the republick of letters, London, 1735–36.   Continued in The history of the works of the learned, London, 1737.
Rogers, R. A. P.   Berkeley and Kant, Hermathena, Dublin, vol. XIII, 1904, pp. 232–246.
Rossi, M. M.   Il viaggio di Berkeley in Sicilia ed i suoi rapporti con un filosofo poeta, Archiv f. Gesch. der Phil., vol. XXXIII, 1921, pp. 156–164.
Russel.   An essay on the nature and existence of the material world, London, 1781.
Sampson, George.   See under Berkeley.
Saturday Review, London.   See Anonymous.
Schäfer, Paula.   Die Philosophie Berkeleys und die Entwicklung des Kausalproblems, Diss., Erlangen, 1915.

Schneider, Herbert and Carol. Samuel Johnson, President of King's College; His Career and Writings, ed. H. and C. Schneider, New York, 1929, 2v. Vol. 2 contains the *Elementa Philosophica*.

Schwab, Hans. Der Utilitarismus Berkeleys, Diss., Bonn, 1908.

Selz, Otto. Die psychologische Erkenntnistheorie und das Transzendenzproblem, *Archiv für die gesamte Psychologie*, Leipzig, vol. XVI, 1910, pp. 1–110.

Sergeant, John. Solid Philosophy, asserted against the Fancies of the Ideists; or, the Method to Science Farther Illustrated. With Reflexions on Mr. Locke's Essay Concerning Human Understanding, London, 1697.

—— The Method to Science, London, 1696.

—— Transnatural Philosophy or Metaphysics. Demonstrating the Essences and Operations of all Beings whatever, which gives the Principles to all other Sciences. And shewing the perfect Conformity of Christian Faith to Right Reason, and the Unreasonableness of Atheists, Deists, Antitrinitarians and other Sectaries, London, 1700.

Shargha, Ikbal K. A critical essay on Berkeley's theory of perception, Allahabad, 1900.

Simon, Thomas Collyns. Berkeley's Doctrine on the Nature of Matter, *Journal of Speculative Philosophy*, St. Louis, vol. III, 1869, pp. 336–344.

—— Berkeley, the new materialism and the diminution of light by distance, *Journal of Speculative Philosophy*, New York, vol. XV, 1881, pp. 77–84.

—— Hegel and his connection with British thought, *Contemporary Review*, London, vol. XIII, 1870, pp. 47–49 and 398–421.

—— Introduction to *Treatise concerning the Principles of Human Knowledge*, ed. Simon, London, 1878.

—— Is Thought the Thinker? *Journal of Speculative Philosophy*, St. Louis, vol. III, 1869, pp. 375 ff.

—— Of Hume's supposed inferences from Berkeley and Kant's supposed refutation of them. Appendix to *Principles of Human Knowledge*, ed. Simon, London, 1878.

—— The nature and elements of the external world; or universal immaterialism demonstrated, London, 1847.

Smirnow, A. Berkeley's Philosophy, Warsaw, 1873. (In Russian.)

Smith, John. Select Discourses, ed. Patrick, Cambridge, 1673. (Discourse 7: of the Difference between Legal and the Evangelical Righteousness.)

Sorley, W. R. History of English Philosophy, Cambridge, 1920.

Spence, Joseph. Anecdotes, London, 1820. (Berkeley's Bermuda Project, pp. 190–192.)

Spicker, Gideon. Kant, Hume und Berkeley. Eine Kritik der Erkenntnistheorie, Berlin, 1875. Reviewed by A. Meinong in *Philosophische Monatshefte*, vol. XII, 1876, pp. 337–347.

Sporbert, Richard. Der Gottesbegriff Lockes und Berkeleys, Diss., Leipzig, 1910.

Stammler, Gerhard. Berkeleys Philosophie der Mathematik, Diss., Berlin, 1922. Also *Kant-Studien*, Ergänzungsheft, no. 55, 1922.

Stephen, Sir James F. Berkeley. In *Horae Sabbaticae*, Series 3, London and New York, 1892.

Stephen, Sir Leslie. Berkeley, *Dictionary of National Biography*, vol. 2, 1885.

—— History of English Thought in the Eighteenth Century, ed. 3, London, 1902, 2v.

Stewart, Dugald. Collected Works, ed. Hamilton, Edinburgh, 1854–58, 10v. See especially vol. V, pp. 87–119 (on Berkeley).

Stier, P. T. Analyse und Kritik der Berkeleyschen Erkenntnistheorie und Metaphysik, Diss., Leipzig, 1893.

Stirling, J. H. Professor Fraser's Berkeley, *Journal of Speculative Philosophy*, St. Louis, vol. VII, 1873, pp. 1–17.

—— Was Sir William Hamilton a Berkeleian? *Fortnightly Review*, London, vol. VI, 1866, pp. 218–228.

Stock, J., Bishop of Killala. An Account of the Life of George Berkeley. . . . With notes, containing strictures upon his works, London, 1776. Ed. 2, entitled Memoirs of George Berkeley, D.D., London, 1784.

Stout, G. F. Studies in Philosophy and Psychology, London, 1930.

Sumner, William Graham. Bishop Berkeley and his writings, *Nation*, New York, vol. XIII, 1871, pp. 59–60.

Sundon. See under Thomson, K. B.

Taylor, Alfred E. Mind and Nature, *International Journal of Ethics*, Chicago, vol. XIII, 1902, pp. 55–86.

Teape, Charles R. Berkeleian Philosophy, Edinburgh and London, 1870.

Thomson, Katherine Byerly. Memoirs of Viscountess Sundon, London, 1847, 2v.

Thormeyer, Paul. Die grossen englischen Philosophen Locke, Berkeley, Hume, Leipzig, 1915.

Thurston, C. R. Bishop Berkeley in New England, *New England Mag.*, N. S., vol. XXI, 1899, pp. 65–82.

Tischendorf, Käte. Berkeley als Ethiker, Diss., Jena, 1913.

Torrey, N. L. Voltaire and the English Deists, New Haven, 1929.

Tower, C. V. The Relation of Berkeley's Earlier to his Later Philosophy, Cornell Thesis, Ann Arbor, 1899.

Tracy, A. L. C. D. de. Dissertation sur l'existence, et sur les hypothèses de Malebranche et de Berkeley à ce sujet. *Memoires de l'institut national des sciences*, classe des sciences morales et politiques, vol. III, 1801, pp. 615–634.

Trinity Church, Newport. Annals of Trinity Church, series 1, Newport, 1890.

Tuckerman, H. T. Berkeley, the Christian Philosopher. In *Essays*, Boston, 1857.

Turgot, A. R. J. de. Refutation du système de Berkeley, Oeuvres complètes, vol. 3, Paris, 1808.

Tyler, M. C. Three Men of Letters, New York, 1895.

Ueberweg, Friedrich. Abhandlung ueber die Principien der menschlichen Erkenntnis (translation of the *Principles of Human Knowledge* with notes), Berlin, 1869.

—— Grundriss der Geschichte der Philosophie. 3 Teil, Die Philosophie der Neuzeit, pp. 691 ff., ed. 12, Berlin, 1924.

—— See also controversy between Ueberweg, Simon, Hoppe, and Ulrici in *Zeitschrift für Philosophie und philosophische Kritik*, vols. LV, LVII, LVIII, LIX.

—— Ueberweg's Kritik der Berkeleyschen Lehre. Symposium by Simon, Hoppe, and Schuppe, *Philosophische Monatshefte*, vol. V, 1870, pp. 142–185.

Updike, Wilkins. The History of the Episcopal Church in Narragansett, Rhode Island, New York, 1847.

Veitch, John. Hamilton (Berkeley, pp. 176–191), Edinburgh, 1882.

Wallace, W. B. George Berkeley, *Gentleman's Magazine*, N. S., vol. LXI, 1898, pp. 334 ff.

Walton, J. Catechism of the author of the Minute Philosopher fully answered, Dublin, 1735.

—— Vindication of Sir Isaac Newton's Fluxions against the objections contained in the Analyst, Dublin and London, 1735.

Wartenburg, M. Das idealistische Argument in der Kritik des Materialismus, Leipzig, 1904.

Warton, Joseph. Essay on the genius and writings of Pope, London, 1782, 2v.

Webb, Thomas E. Theistic Idealism: or Berkeley. In *Veil of Isis*, Dublin, 1885.

Weeks, S. B. The religious development in the province of North Carolina, Baltimore, 1892.

Wenley, R. M. British Thought and Modern Speculation, *Scottish Review*, London, vol. XIX, 1892, pp. 141–161.

Whichcote, Benjamin. Aphorisms Moral and Religious, ed. Salter, London, 1753.

White, H. Vere. Bishop Berkeley as a Missionary. Office of the Irish Auxiliary of the Society for the Propagation of the Gospel in Foreign Parts, Dublin, 1900.

Wilberforce, S. The Protestant Episcopal Church in America, New York, 1849. (Cf. also ed. 2, 1856.)

Wild, J. D. An Unpublished Sermon of Bishop Berkeley. With a Foreword, *Philosophical Review*, vol. XL, 1931, pp. 526–536.
    See also under Berkeley.

Willman, Otto. Geschichte des Idealismus, Braunschweig, 1894–97, 3v.

Wills, James. Lives of Illustrious and Distinguished Irishmen, Berkeley, vol. 5, pp. 1–27, Dublin, 1847.

Wills, James and Freeman Wills. The Irish Nation: its history and biography, Edinburgh, 1871–75.

Woodbridge, F. J. E. Berkeley's Realism, Columbia University *Studies in the history of ideas*, pp. 188 ff., New York, 1918.

Wrangham, Francis. British Plutarch, London, 1816.

Wright, G. N. See under Berkeley.

Wyck, van der. Een Monument voor Berkeley, Groeningen, 1873.

Wyld, Robert S. The physics and philosophy of the senses, London, 1875.

Yeats, W. B. Hone and Rossi, *Bishop Berkeley*, Introduction by W. B. Yeats, London, 1931.

Zimmerman, R. Ueber Kants Widerlegung des Idealismus von Berkeley. *Sitzungsber. der kaiserl. Akad. der Wissensch.*, Vienna, philos.-hist. Kl., vol. LXVIII, 1871.

—— Ueber Humes Stellung zu Berkeley und Kant, *ibid.*, vol. CIII, 1883.

Zurkuhlen, H. Berkeleys und Humes Stellung zur Analysis des Unendlichen, Diss., Berlin, 1915.

INDEX

INDEX

The more important references are italicized.